Introduction to Microprocessors

Herbert Brunner
Engineering Manager
Fairchild Semiconductor

Reston Publishing Company, Inc.
A Prentice-Hall Company
Reston, Virginia

This book is dedicated to my wife, Maggie, and our children, Alison and David.

Library of Congress Cataloging in Publication Data
Brunner, Herbert

Introduction to microprocessors

Includes index.
1. Microprocessors. I. Title.
QA76.5.B786 001.64'04 81-13930
ISBN 0-8359-3247-8 AACR2

10 9 8 7 6 5 4 3 2 1

Printed in the United States of America

CONTENTS

PREFACE

A system approach to microcomputers incorporates all the aspects of the system and how the various parts are integrated for the solution of a total problem. System problems utilize all the resources of the microcomputer: inputting, processing, formatting, and outputting the data. The system approach ties many small examples together with the advantages of (1) understanding the example, and (2) appreciating how it relates to the total system.

Another aspect of the microcomputer system is the hardware/software interface. The hardware portion consists of the integrated circuit chips; the microprocessor, memory, and interface devices. The microcomputer is connected to I/O devices and circuitry: switches, LEDs, drivers, keyboards, 7-segment displays, terminals, printers, monitors, and other computers or computer-type equipment. The software is the program that controls the hardware and executes the system function. This book is amply illustrated with program listings and examples relating the software to the hardware.

Reflecting the fast-changing field of microcomputers, the objectives of this book are gaining a comprehensive approach to microprocessor systems, understanding the software/hardware interface, and acquiring a general appreciation of all microprocessors existing today and available in the near future.

This book should prove useful and interesting for students, engineers, programmers, engineering managers, technicians, college instructors, teachers, senior high school students, hobbyists, and others who need a self-study or reference book on microprocessor systems. The book is structured to take the reader from a general introduction to a comprehensive understanding of the microcomputer field.

The two 8-bit microprocessors discussed in this book are the multichip 6800 family and the single-chip 3870 microcomputer. The 6800 family has evolved, in part, into the minimum 1-chip 6801, the minimum 2-chip 6802/6846, the 6809, and the 16-bit 68000; and the family keeps growing. All these microprocessor chips share and are supported by an assortment of peripheral interface devices, four of which are discussed in detail, with examples that illustrate how they are used in a system problem.

The Peripheral Interface Adapter (PIA-6821) is a general purpose parallel I/O device, with two 8-bit ports and four interrupt control lines. It is used to interface switches, keyboards, and 7-segment displays, and has a built-in feature of a pulse and hand-shake mode for parallel communication with printers and other microcomputer-type devices. The Asynchronous Communication Interface Adapter (ACIA-6850) is used to interface the microprocessor to terminal and teletype machines. They are often referred to as UARTS. The Synchronous Protocol Communication Controller (SPCC-6856) is used for synchronous data communications. The 6840 Timer is used as a baud rate generator.

The 6810 is a 1 K bit or 128-byte RAM. The ROM-Timer-PIA (6840) merges the features of three peripheral devices into 1 chip. This is a packaging variation which the reader should learn to distinguish from a functional difference.

The last two chapters discuss advances in the 8-bit and 16-bit families, the 6809 and 68000, respectively. With the basic approach in this book to fundamental concepts, the reader should not feel intimidated when considering these advanced systems. Although the 6809 and 68000 have advanced instruction sets and additional capabilities, they are only incremental modifications of the 6800 family. Generally, many of the additional capabilities can be related to basic concepts, making the 6800 family a good starting point for understanding microcomputers.

ACKNOWLEDGMENTS

My gratitude goes to Dr. Richard V. Tsina of the University of California at Berkeley Extension, for his support in developing the curriculum for classes at the extension, and later with the manuscript. His sense of humor has been a great help.

My thanks to Bob Bobrink for his encouragement. I would like to acknowledge the help of Liz Morse, Irwin Maltz, Jonathon Kagan, Craig O'Sullivan, my students, and colleagues too numerous to mention, who have read and offered suggestions on various portions of the manuscript.

My special thanks go to Kay Grant for typing and proofreading the manuscript, and to Ellen Cherry of the Reston Publishing Company for what seems to be a tireless effort in preparing the book for publication.

My thanks and appreciation to my wife, Maggie, for all her support, from reading and editing a technical manuscript, to the help and understanding necessary to complete this book.

In addition, I would like to extend my appreciation to Fairchild Semiconductor, where I have worked for the past eight years. Fairchild has offered me the opportunity to learn and develop with the new and exciting field of microprocessors. All Fairchild references in this text are to the semiconductor divisions of the Fairchild Camera & Instrument Corporation, a Schlumberger Company.

Motorola, Inc. is the primary source and Fairchild Camera & Instrument Corporation and Mostek Corporation are the second sources for various parts of the 6800/68000 microprocessor families. Similarly, Mostek Corporation is the primary source for the 3870 and Fairchild Camera & Instrument and Motorola, Inc. are both second-sources.

In this book I have used information, tables, and diagrams from Fairchild documents and data sheets. The documentation originates from Motorola and Mostek and is part of the respective second-source agreements. In the bibliography, where applicable, two sources are referenced, the original and the Fairchild document.

Second-source agreements are legal agreements between companies to purchase and/or exchange technical and manufacturing information about a product. Both manufacturers then sell the product under their own labels. This is not the same as companies that independently develop and manufacture an equivalent product, as with many of the 64K RAM and some microprocessor chips.

I should also like to extend my appreciation to Motorola and Mostek for developing a family of microcomputer chips that I have learned to work with and respect. Without their microprocessor development and permission to reprint, this book could not have been written.

Herb Brunner
San Jose, California

1 Elements of a Microprocessor

1-1 WHAT IS A COMPUTER?

There is no universal agreement on how to define a computer. Turing defined it as a sequential machine that, given enough time and a large enough memory, can compute any computable function.

Expanding this definition, a computer is a machine with the ability to input, modify, store, and output data determined by a sequence of instructions contained in a memory. Within its decision-making capability the computer can modify the sequence in which the instructions are executed according to the data tested. In other words, a computer is a device that is programmable, and that can output data that are a function of both its program and its previous inputs. A microcomputer is essentially a small computer, and the preceding definitions are equally valid for small as well as larger computers.

These definitions, however adequate, do not offer the person unfamiliar with computers any intuitive feel for them. Another way of viewing a computer, therefore, is a *general-purpose* machine, in contrast to a special-purpose machine. A pencil, an ashtray, and a chair are examples of special-purpose machines; they all have one primary function in that they are recognized and defined by virtue of their configuration.

A general-purpose machine, on the other hand, can perform a variety of functions without being reconfigured or changed in appearance. The human being is a good model of a general-purpose or multifunction machine. People can type, drive cars, fly airplanes, swim, cook, and perform any number of tasks without altering their appearance. Computers, like people, are general-purpose machines in that they perform a variety of tasks and are not defined by a particular function or configuration.

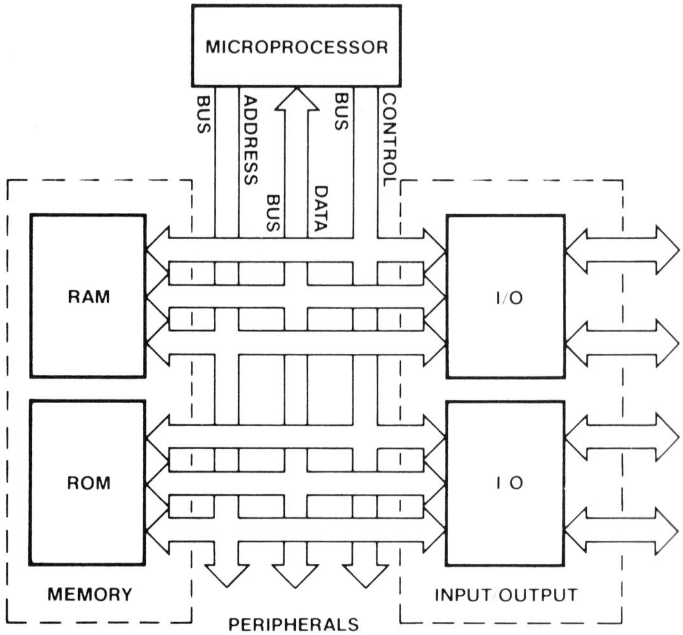

Figure 1-1. Block diagram of microcomputer.

This discussion is equally valid when related to other electronic machines. The computer is different from special-purpose electronic machines, such as radios or televisions, whose schematics are unique and easily recognizable. Computer schematics, although recognizable as computers, are multifunctional, and it is important for the reader to understand that a computer's function is not defined by its schematic or configuration. Figure 1-1 is a block diagram representing a schematic of a computer that can function as a calculator, a video game, or as an industrial controller for ovens, stoves, or washing machines.

A program is a sequence of instructions that describes, in computer terminology, how to perform a required function or task. It is not unlike an instruction manual on how to type, drive a car, swim, or cook. The instruction words, therefore, are analogous to a person's vocabulary. Someone with a 2000-word vocabulary can describe a function with fewer words than a person with a 200-word vocabulary. This does not imply that both people cannot describe the task equally well. Dictionaries should define complex words in terms of basic vocabulary. For example, an algorithm is defined as *a prescribed sequence of well-defined rules or operations for the solution of a problem in a specified number of steps and executed in a finite time.* People with limited vocabularies would have to restate the definition, which in the example is 24 words, with many more words.

This also applies when comparing instruction sets of different computers. All computers, minicomputers, and microcomputers can perform the same functions. Computers with smaller, more basic instruction sets, however, generally require more time and more instructions to execute comparable programs written with a larger, more sophisticated instruction set.

A description of the basic organization of a computer is that a program or several programs are often stored in the computer memory. The computer user must know how to access the appropriate program (i.e., type, drive, or cook). When executing a typing program, for example, the user must first address the typing program stored in memory and, second, access the data, which are the words to be typed. There are two sources of data, memory and input data. If a letter being typed is copied, then the source data are input data to the computer. However, if the letter being typed is from the original thoughts of the typist, then the data are accessed from memory. Therefore, a program from one place in memory is accessed to act on data from either another part of memory or an input source.

While executing the typing program, the typist can be interrupted by a phone call. The typist accesses the "phone answering program" and in taking a message handles data. If the message is written, it is output data, but if the message is remembered, then it is data stored in memory.

The computer has the same capability of interrupting a primary program (typing) to respond temporarily to a secondary program (phone). This capability is described under interrupt routine.

1-2 PARTS OF A MICROCOMPUTER

There are three parts to a microcomputer, as shown in Fig. 1-1: the microprocessor, the memory, and the input/output, along with the buses that connect them.

Microprocessor

The "head," or more properly the reasoning ability and controller of the microcomputer system, is the microprocessor, sometimes termed the *central processor unit* (CPU) or *microprocessor unit* (MPU), and often referred to as the *processor.* This is where the program is executed, through which all data are routed and modified, and where the program execution sequence is determined.

Memory

Almost all present-day computers use the same memory to store both instructions and data. All computer memories are random-access memories, which means equal access to each memory location. Temporary data, which are easily changed, are stored in a *read/write*-type memory, which also has the random-access capability. This type of read/write, random-access memory is referred to as RAM. The reader, however, should more accurately think of this type of memory as a read/write memory.

Permanent memory is nonvolatile so that the program or data are not lost when power is disconnected from the computer system. This offers the user the option of turning power off when the system is not in use and, in addition, permits a portable computer system. RAMs, however, are volatile and do not retain data when power is disconnected.

Programs are often but not necessarily stored in permanent memory. In one type of permanent memory, called *read-only memory* (ROM), the data or program is stored by the semiconductor manufacturer. These ROMs also have random-access capability.

The programmable read/write memory (PROM) is also a permanent memory that is programmed by the user rather than by the manufacturer.

The erasable programmable read/only memory (EPROM) is similar to the PROM in that it is programmed by the user. The EPROMs, however, are reusable. The data stored can be erased by exposing it to ultraviolet light.

All the memories described are random-access memories.

Memory Types—Applications

In developing microcomputer products, there is a need for each memory type. When writing programs the programmer must continuously modify the program. In these cases the program being written is stored in RAM where it is easily changed. As the program nears completion, it may be stored in PROMs or EPROMs, which are more permanent and portable forms. During this debugging phase, others verify and buy off the programmer's work. If system problems are detected, the program in PROM or EPROM is still easily modified. When the system is finalized, the user purchases coded ROMs from the semiconductor manufacturer.

In large volume, ROMs are the least expensive form of permanent memory, and generally PROMs have a faster access time than EPROMs.

Input/output (I/O)

The third part of a computer is the input/output, universally referred to as I/O. These devices are comparable to the five senses. For example, the eyes, ears, and nose are input-only devices, whereas the hands and the mouth are sometimes inputs and sometimes output devices. The mouth is an input for food and taste as well as the output for speech, so it can be considered both an input and output function. The 8-bit microcomputer has 8-bit parallel I/O devices comparable to 8-fingered hands. Fingers can be considered outputs when holding a pencil, typing, or ringing a doorbell, but they are also input devices when feeling a temperature or sensing a texture. In the same way that only one finger need carry this information, there are techniques with the microcomputer for masking or blocking out the information from the other inputs.

Buses

All the components of the 8-bit microcomputer system are wired together with three buses: the 16-bit address bus, the 8-bit data bus, which defines the size of the microprocessor, and the control bus. In a microcomputer system only two components communicate with each other at any one time: the processor and another memory or peripheral device. The address bus is outputted from the processor to all the other components and selects the one device being addressed. The data bus is bidirectional, and data move either to or from the processor and the selected device only. All the other components not selected have the data output pins disabled (high impedance state of three-state device) or electrically disconnected from the data bus. The control bus synchronizes all the peripheral devices to the processor, aids in selecting the device that is addressed, and indicates the direction of data flow—read or write.

Any device tied to the buses is defined as part of the microcomputer system. All other devices communicate with the processor through the I/O port of the peripheral devices.

1-3 NUMERIC NOTATION

The width of the data bus defines the size of the microcomputer, and an 8-bit data bus defines an 8-bit microcomputer. The *byte* is the generally accepted computer word for 8 binary bits. There are 256 combinations in a byte:

$$2^8 = 2^4 \times 2^4 = 256$$

There are many number bases, among them the binary, decimal, and hexidecimal number systems. The most universally used number base is the decimal number, base 10. All digital computers use the binary number, base 2. The hexidecimal (hex) number is base 16. One hex character is equivalent to and can represent 4 binary bits, and because of this convenient notation, it will be used extensively throughout the book. See Table 1-1 for hexidecimal numbers. A number may be expressed as a decimal number, 2-hex characters, or 8-binary bit. The decimal number 90 is equal to the hex number 5A, and they are equal to the binary number 0101 1010. The % symbol indicates a binary notation.

$$90_{10} = 5A_{16} = \%\ 0101\ 1010_2$$

There are three acceptable notations for the hex number in the 6800 system: the base 16 ($5A_{16}$), or an H after the number (5AH), or a $ before the number ($5A).

$$5A_{16} = 5AH = \$5A$$

The number 1024 is a binary thousand and often is rounded out and referred to as a K for kilo. Throughout this book 2^{16} is referred to as 64K, the size of the memory to be addressed.

$$2^{16} = 2^6 \times 2^{10} = 64 \times 1024 \approx 64K$$

A 2-byte number can be expressed with 4-hex characters or as a 16-bit binary number. See Table 1-2 for some often-used hex numbers.

The reader should be aware that, although the hex notation is used, the computer manipulates binary numbers. As such, the hex numbers should be converted into binary numbers when performing binary arithmetic or logic operations, and then the result is converted back to hex notation.

1-4 PROGRAMMING MODEL

The programming model for the 6800 consists of the processor's registers and 64K of memory shown in Fig. 1-2. To program in machine language, the user must know the registers, how they function, and the memory organization. This book is an introduction to assembly language programming of the 6800, and a general approach for assembly language programming of any machine. Assembly language is a set of computer-abbreviated mnemonic instruction symbols that are easily converted to machine code. In addition to understanding the registers, the student must know the instruction set and the addressing modes.

Table 1-1. Hexadecimal Numbers

Decimal	Hex	Binary
0	0	0000
1	1	0001
2	2	0010
3	3	0011
4	4	0100
5	5	0101
6	6	0110
7	7	0111
8	8	1000
9	9	1001
10	A	1010
11	B	1011
12	C	1100
13	D	1101
14	E	1110
15	F	1111

Table 1-2. Commonly Used Numbers*

	127	= 007FH	= %0000 0000 0111 1111
	128	= 0080H	= %0000 0000 1000 0000
	255	= 00FFH	= %0000 0000 1111 1111
	256	= 0100H	= %0000 0001 0000 0000
½K	≈ 512	= 0200H	= %0000 0010 0000 0000
1K − 1	≈ 1023	= 03FFH	= %0000 0011 1111 1111
4K − 1	≈ 4095	= 0FFFH	= %0000 1111 1111 1111
4K	≈ 4096	= 1000H	= %0001 0000 0000 0000
32K	≈ 32,768	= 8000H	= %1000 0000 0000 0000
64K − 1	≈ 65,535	= FFFFH	= %1111 1111 1111 1111

*% indicates a binary number.

A programmer must be able to predict, as he moves, by single-cycling through the program, what is happening to the data in each of the registers and at every memory location, thus putting the programmer in charge of the machine. This capability is necessary for debugging and checking programs. When debugging, the programmer examines the data in each register and memory location. If the predicted data do not agree with the examined data, there is an obvious error.

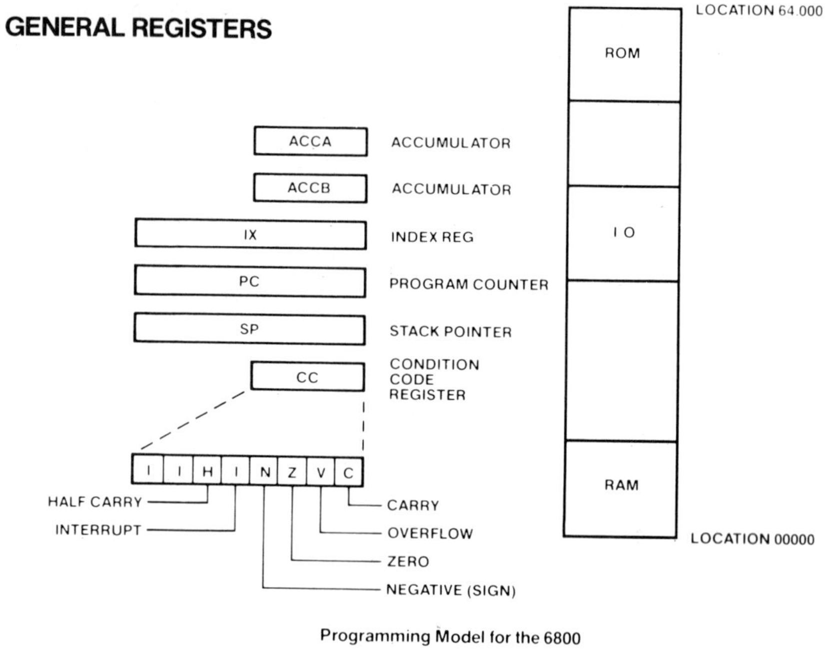

Figure 1-2. Programming model for the 6800.

General Registers

This section describes each register and its functions (see Fig. 1-2). The general registers consist of the two accumulators, a program counter, a stack pointer, an index register, and the condition code register. The accumulators and the condition code register are 8-bits long, and the other three registers used to address 64K of memory are 16-bits long. Only six of the least significant bits (LSBs) of the condition code register are used.

Accumulators There are two accumulators, A and B (Acc A and Acc B). When the discussion refers to either accumulator they will be referred to as accumulator X (Acc X). Accumulators have two primary functions. The first is that they are the crossroads and main intersection through which all data are routed into and out from the microprocessor and to and from memory. The second function is that most of the data to be modified pass through them. These features are generally true of all computers.

Program Counter (PC) The program counter is a 16-bit register and as such can point to the full 64K memory field. The counter might better be labeled the program counter. It points to the instruction, in fact the byte, of the program being executed.

Conversely, to find the instruction being executed the programmer may examine the program counter. Normally, the program counter automatically increments (autoincrements) through the program, which is why it is called a counter. The program flow may be altered by stuffing a new address into, or modifying, the present address in the program counter. This description is generally true for all program counters.

Stack Pointer (SP) The stack pointer specifies an area of RAM memory known as the stack. The stack is a last in, first out (LIFO) memory, and for the 6800 it is generally, but not necessarily, located in high RAM. As data are loaded into the stack, it is transferred from an accumulator into the next empty contiguous stack location. The main function of the stack is to store the return address of a subroutine or an interrupt. Additionally, during interrupts the data of the accumulators, condition code register, and index register are also stored in the stack until the return from an interrupt.

Two instructions, PUSH and PULL, are quick and efficient 1-byte instructions associated with the stack. The PUSH instruction will both load data into the stack and autodecrement the SP. The SP will then be pointing to the next empty location. Conversely, the PULL instruction will both autoincrement the SP and transfer the data from the stack back to an accumulator. The symbol for a PUSH is ↓ and for PULL it is ↑. When empty, the SP points to the top of the stack.

Index Register (IX) Primarily, the index register is used for the indirect addressing of data in memory. Perhaps a more appropriate name might be "data pointer," because the index register points to a location in memory where data are to be accessed. The accessing of data with the index register always requires two steps. The first is to ensure that the index register is pointing to the proper location, and the second that the data may be accessed.

In the minicomputer field the index register is generally referred to as a "single-level register indirect addressing." In other microprocessors it is called the "data counter."

To access blocks of data the index register is initialized at the beginning of the block; then it sequences or counts through the block, which may account for calling it a data counter.

An additional capability of the 6800 index register, and the reason for its name, is that an effective (E) address may be obtained by adding an offset to the contents of the index register.

$$E = (IX) + \text{offset}$$

Condition Code Register (CC) The 8-bit CC register consists of 6 bits: the carry, overflow, zero, negative (sign), interrupt, and half-carry; and the two unused most significant bits (MSBs) are latched at ones. Certain CC bits change as data are modified by the processor. The change indicates the status of the new data as a result of the operation. Branch instructions are used to alter the program flow, changing the sequence of instructions that are being executed, according to the contents of the condition code register. Since the CC bits indicate the status of the data, a branch operation will result as a consequence of testing one or more of the CC bits.

Memory

The microprocessor has the capability of addressing a 64K memory space in which each memory location stores a byte of data in each unique address or memory space. The memory address in itself does not indicate how data stored in that space are to be used; rather, the usage is indicated on the device level. It could represent a number, a letter, an address, or another value.

An analogy might be that of a 64K shelving capacity in a department store stocking a variety of items, such as shirts, towels, and sweaters. Although most shelves are backed by a wall, some are like post office boxes where the mailman can put data in each box from one side, while the renter can extract it from the other side. RAMs can be compared to the shelf with the wall behind it, while I/O ports are comparable to the post office box. Random access memory refers to each shelf or memory location being equally accessible to the processor.

Memory has three unique sections: RAM, ROM and I/O for memory mapped I/O. In the 6800 system, RAM is generally allocated to low memory. ROM, PROM, and EPROM are located in high memory where the interrupt vectors are stored. The middle portion of memory is reserved for the peripheral I/O devices.

A typical distribution of memory is shown in Fig. 1-3 with four 128-byte RAM devices, for a total of ½K of RAM, two 1K ROM devices, two peripheral interface devices (PIA), and an asynchronous communication interface adapter (ACIA); each device is indicated by the lowest address of memory that device occupies. For example, the first RAM's starting address is Loc 0000 and it occupies the 128 contiguous memory locations through Loc 007FH and is referred to as RAM zero. The second RAM is referred to as RAM 80H, the third as 100H, and the fourth as RAM 180H. The two ROMs occupy the top 2K of memory space. The first is referred to as ROM F800H and the second as FC00H. There are two PIAs, each occupying four contiguous memory locations. The first starts at, and is referred to as, PIA 8002H and also

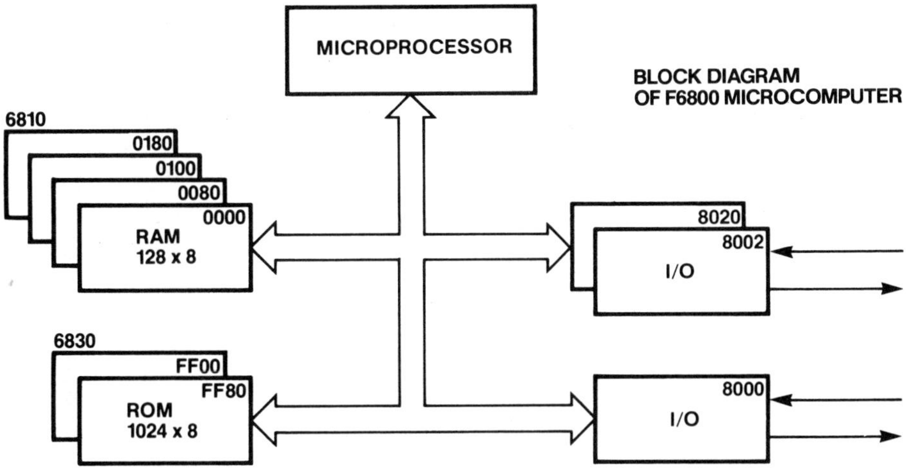

Figure 1-3. Typical microcomputer and memory assignments.

occupies Loc 8003, 8004 and 8005H. The second is referred to as PIA 8020H, and occupies its own four memory locations. The ACIA occupies Loc 8000 and 8001H.

1-5 ARITHMETIC AND LOGICAL OPERATIONS

The reader must understand how the arithmetic and logical operations of the microprocessor modify the data to be able to predict the result of these operations. There are five basic operations: two arithmetic operations, addition and subtraction; and three logical operations, AND, OR-inclusive, and Exclusive-OR. Three additional operations are derived from the subtract operation: complement, negate, and compare. The notation for these operations are

$+$	Addition
$-$	Subtraction
$\cdot$	Boolean AND
$\odot$	Boolean (inclusive) OR
$\oplus$	Boolean Exclusive-OR
$\approx$	COMPLEMENT or Boolean NOT
	NEGATE is the 2's complement of a number

The symbol ( ) is defined as "the contents of" whichever register or memory location is named within the parentheses.

Each of the five basic operations has two inputs and a result. An example of the notation for the ADD operation, where one of the inputs is from accumulator A and the second input is from a memory location M, is

$$R = (\text{Acc A}) + (\text{M})$$

which would read "that the contents of accumulator A are added to the contents of memory location M to form a result R." For convenience, however, it will be written as

$$R = A + M$$

and the parentheses that indicate "the contents of" will be dropped.

Likewise, when a reference is made to the contents of accumulator B, then only B will be the symbol, and when an accumulator is referred to without specifying which (A or B), then X will be the symbol.

Bit Notation

A byte is made of 8 bits.

bits	7 6 5 4 3 2 1 0
	$b_7b_6b_5b_4b_3b_2b_1b_0$

These are referred to as bits 0 to 7, where bit 7 is the MSB and bit 0 is the LSB (least significant bit).

When reference is made to an accumulator, a memory location M, or a result R, then

Register Memory or Result	Notation
Acc A	$A_7\ A_6\ A_5\ A_4\ A_3\ A_2\ A_1\ A_0$
Acc B	$B_7\ B_6\ B_5\ B_4\ B_3\ B_2\ B_1\ B_0$
Acc X	$X_7\ X_6\ X_5\ X_4\ X_3\ X_2\ X_1\ X_0$
Memory	$M_7M_6M_5M_4M_3M_2M_1M_0$
Result	$R_7\ R_6\ R_5\ R_4\ R_3\ R_2\ R_1\ R_0$

Addition

The notation for the ADD operation is R = A + M, which reads "the contents of Acc A are added to the contents of memory M forming a result R."

$$\begin{array}{rr} A & A_7\ A_6\ A_5\ A_4\ A_3\ A_2\ A_1\ A_0 \\ +M & +M_7M_6M_5M_4M_3M_2M_1M_0 \\ \hline R\ \boxed{C} & R_7\ R_6\ R_5\ R_4\ R_3\ R_2\ R_1\ R_0 \end{array}$$

A numeric example of addition is

$$\begin{array}{rr} X & 1001\ 1010 \\ +M & +1100\ 1001 \\ \hline R\ \boxed{1} & 0110\ 0011 \end{array}$$

where the carry is placed in a square to the left to distinguish it from the result.

Subtraction

The notation for the SUBTRACT operation is R = X − M, where the contents of a memory location are subtracted from the contents of an accumulator, and the result represents the difference.

$$\begin{array}{rl} A & A_7\ A_6\ A_5\ A_4\ A_3\ A_2\ A_1\ A_0 \\ -M & -M_7M_6M_5M_4M_3M_2M_1M_0 \\ \hline R\ \boxed{C} & R_7\ R_6\ R_5\ R_4\ R_3\ R_2\ R_1\ R_0 \end{array}$$

There are two ways to perform a subtraction: (1) by the rules for binary subtraction and (2) by adding the 2's complement of the minuend. The difference will be the same with either procedure, but the borrow bit will be complemented from each other. The 6800 has a subtract instruction and the result is indicated:

	6800 result		2's comp result	
Minuend	1100 1010	1's comp	1010 0110	1's complement of subtrahend
Subtrahend	−0101 1001	Plus one	+1	
Difference	[0] 0111 0001	2's comp	1010 0111	2's complement of subtrahend
			+1100 1010	minuend
	Borrow	[1]	0111 0001	difference

The 6800 sets the borrow bit according to the rules of a binary subtraction. The carry bit is called the borrow bit when referring to a substract operation. They are the same bit.

Boolean AND

The notation for the Boolean AND or the logical AND operation is R = X · M, where each bit of an accumulator is ANDed with the corresponding bit of a memory location M to form a result R.

$$
\begin{aligned}
R_0 &= X_0 \cdot M_0 \\
R_1 &= X_1 \cdot M_1 \\
R_2 &= X_2 \cdot M_2 \\
R_3 &= X_3 \cdot M_3 \\
R_4 &= X_4 \cdot M_4 \\
R_5 &= X_5 \cdot M_5 \\
R_6 &= X_6 \cdot M_6 \\
R_7 &= X_7 \cdot M_7
\end{aligned}
$$

X	1010 1100
AND	· · · · · · · ·
M	1100 1001
R	1000 1000

An AND operation is used to mask or block out bits by ANDing them with 0's. Conversely, selected bits may be passed for further examination by ANDing them with 1's.

Boolean OR

The notation for the Boolean OR or the logical inclusive-OR operation is $R = X \odot M$, where each bit of an accumulator is ORed with the corresponding bit of a memory location M to form a result R.

$$
\begin{aligned}
R_0 &= X_0 \odot M_0 \\
R_1 &= X_1 \odot M_1 \\
R_2 &= X_2 \odot M_2 \\
R_3 &= X_3 \odot M_3 \\
R_4 &= X_4 \odot M_4 \\
R_5 &= X_5 \odot M_5 \\
R_6 &= X_6 \odot M_6 \\
R_7 &= X_7 \odot M_7
\end{aligned}
$$

X	1 0 1 0 1 1 0 0
OR	⊙⊙⊙⊙ ⊙⊙⊙⊙
M	1 1 0 0 1 0 0 1
R	1 1 1 0 1 1 0 1

When there is a 1 in any of the corresponding bits of either an accumulator or a memory location, then the 1 will be passed to the result bit.

Exclusive-OR

The notation for the exclusive-OR operation is $R = X \oplus M$, where each bit of the accumulator is exclusive-ORed with the corresponding bit of a memory location M to form a result R.

$$
\begin{aligned}
R_0 &= X_0 \oplus M_0 \\
R_1 &= X_1 \oplus M_1 \\
R_2 &= X_2 \oplus M_2 \\
R_3 &= X_3 \oplus M_3 \\
R_4 &= X_4 \oplus M_4 \\
R_5 &= X_5 \oplus M_5 \\
R_6 &= X_6 \oplus M_6 \\
R_7 &= X_7 \oplus M_7
\end{aligned}
$$

X	1 0 1 0	1 1 0 0
Exclusive-OR	⊕⊕⊕⊕	⊕⊕⊕⊕
M	1 1 0 0	1 0 0 1
R	0 1 1 0	0 1 0 1

The exclusive-OR is, in effect, a logical comparison of corresponding bits. When the corresponding input bits are the same, the result bit is a 0, but when the result bit is a 1 the corresponding input bits are different.

Complement

The COMPLEMENT operation, sometimes called the 1's complement, executes a logical NOT and has one input and a result. The result replaces the contents of either an accumulator or a memory location with its complement, where each bit is replaced by the complement of that bit. The COMPLEMENT operation always returns the result to whichever accumulator or memory location it originated from. A line above the number is referred to as the bar and is the notation for the complement of the number.

$$
\begin{array}{r}
1\ 1\ 1\ 1\quad 1\ 1\ 1\ 1 \\
-\ \overline{X}_7\overline{X}_6\overline{X}_5\overline{X}_4\ \overline{X}_3\overline{X}_2\overline{X}_1\overline{X}_0 \\
\hline
X_7X_6X_5X_4\ X_3X_2X_1X_0
\end{array}
\quad \text{or} \quad
\begin{array}{r}
1\ 1\ 1\ 1\quad 1\ 1\ 1\ 1 \\
-\ \overline{M}_7\overline{M}_6\overline{M}_5\overline{M}_4\ \overline{M}_3\overline{M}_2\overline{M}_1\overline{M}_0 \\
\hline
M_7M_6M_5M_4\ M_3M_2M_1M_0
\end{array}
$$

$$
\begin{array}{r}
FF \\
-\overline{X} \\
\hline
X
\end{array}
\qquad
\begin{array}{r}
1\ 1\ 1\ 1\quad 1\ 1\ 1\ 1 \\
-\ 1\ 0\ 1\ 0\quad 0\ 0\ 1\ 1 \\
\hline
0\ 1\ 0\ 1\quad 1\ 1\ 0\ 0
\end{array}
$$

Negate

The NEGATE operation has one input and the result is the 2's complement of the input. The 2's complement of a positive number is a negative number, and the 2's complement of a negative number is a positive number. For example, the negate (or the 2's complement) of +4 (0100) is −4 (1100), and the negate (or 2's complement) of −4 (1100) is +4 (0100). The 2's complement result is returned to whichever accumulator or memory location it originated from. It is not a basic machine operation, but is derived by subtracting the number from 0 to form the 2's complement.

$$R = 0 - X$$

$$R = 0 - M$$

	0 0 0 0 0 0 0 0		0 0 0 0 0 0 0 0
	$- X_7X_6X_5X_4\ X_3X_2X_1X_0$		$- M_7M_6M_5M_4\ M_3M_2M_1M_0$
	$R_7R_6R_5R_4\ R_3R_2R_1R_0$		$R_7R_6R_5R_4\ R_3R_2R_1R_0$
0's	0 0 0 0 0 0 0 0	or	0 0 0 0 0 0 0 0
−X	− 0 0 1 1 1 1 0 0		− 1 1 0 0 0 1 0 0
2's comp X	1 1 0 0 0 1 0 0		0 0 1 1 1 1 0 0

1-6 INSTRUCTION SET AND ADDRESSING MODES

The 6800 has 72 instructions and 6 addressing modes. This section is an introduction to the instruction set listed in Appendix A and will show the student how to interpret an instruction listing.

An instruction can have either one, two, or three bytes which will be stored in contiguous memory locations. The first byte is always the *operation code* (opcode), and the second or third bytes, if any, are the *operands* (see Fig. 1-4).

Instruction Definitions

The primary definition of an instruction is given in the Boolean/Arithmetic Operation column of the data sheet. Typical examples are

$A \leftarrow A + M$	add memory to accumulator A
$A \leftarrow \overline{A}$	complement accumulator A
$M \leftarrow \overline{M}$	complement memory

IX ← IX + 1	increment index register
A ← M	load (transfer) accumulator A from memory

A ← A + M Add accumulator A Describing the add accumulator instruction, it reads "the contents of memory location M is added to the contents of accumulator A, and the result replaces the contents of accumulator A."

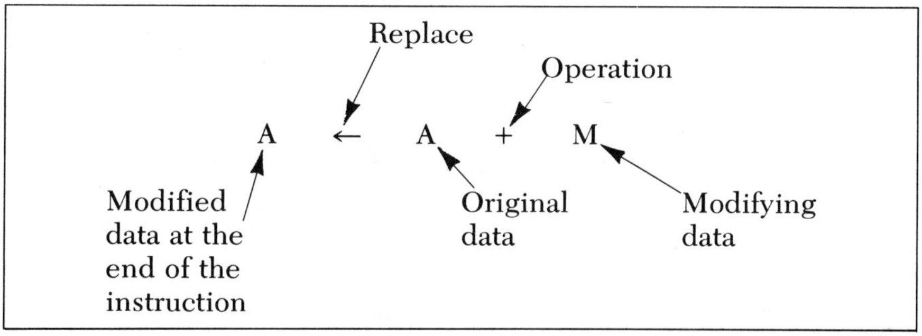

The contents of accumulator A are modified by the operation and the modifying data. The result replaces the data in accumulator A at the end of the execution phase. Instructions without reference to a memory location are 1-byte instructions with opcode only, where the operand is implied. While an instruction with reference to a memory location has two parts, opcode and operand, the operand specifies one of 64K memory locations.

A ← $\overline{\mathbf{A}}$ Complement accumulator A This is a 1-byte opcode instruction because there is no reference to a memory location.

M ← $\overline{\mathbf{M}}$ Complement memory This is a multibyte instruction where the opcode portion of the instruction specifies the operation (complement) and the memory location is specified by the operand. The contents of the memory location (M) are complemented and returned to that location.

IX ← IX + 1 Increment index register This is a 1-byte instruction with opcode only, with the opcode implying the register (index) and the operation (increment).

A ← M Load (transfer) accumulator A from memory This is a multibyte instruction where the opcode specifies the register (A) and the operation (load). The operand portion specifies the memory location from where the data will be transferred.

Therefore, instructions generally have three types of information:

- The name of the general register, which contains one of the data sources and to where the result will be returned.
- How the data contained in the general register are to be modified or to or from where they are to be transferred.
- The memory location (M) of the modifying data, or the memory location to or from where the register data are to be transferred.

The instructions listed in Appendix IA are

Table 1	Accumulator and Memory Instructions
Table 2	Index Register and Stack Manipulation Instructions
Table 3	Jump and Branch Instructions
Table 4	Condition Code Register Manipulation Instructions

The Accumulator and Memory Instructions are generally used to modify data in, or transfer data to or from, one of the accumulators. The Index Register and Stack Manipulation Instructions are used to modify and manipulate one of the pointer registers. The Jump and Branch instructions modify the program counter either conditionally or unconditionally. The branch instructions conditionally modify the program flow according to the data tested and reported by the condition codes. The Condition Code Register Manipulation Instructions set or reset one of the condition codes and transfer data between the accumulator and the condition code register.

Interpreting the Instruction Table

Scanning across the top of Table 1-3, the first column is the operation performed by the instruction. The next column lists the mnemonic (Mnem), the symbolic name of the instruction. A mnemonic gives a recognizable name that hints at the function of the instruction. ADDA is the mnemonic for "add to the contents of accumulator A,"

Table 1-3. Accumulator and Memory Instructions

Operations	Mnemonic	Addressing Modes					Boolean/Arithmetic Operation	Cond. Code Reg					
		Immed	Direct	Index	Extnd	Implied	(All register labels refer to contents)	5	4	3	2	1	0
		OP ~ =	OP ~ =	OP ~ =	OP ~ =	OP ~ =		H	I	N	Z	V	C
Add	ADDA	8B 2 2	9B 3 2	AB 5 2	BB 4 3		A + M → A	↕	•	↕	↕	↕	↕
	ADDB	CB 2 2	DB 3 2	EB 5 2	FB 4 3		B + M → B	↕	•	↕	↕	↕	↕
Add Acmltrs	ABA					1B 2 1	A + B → A	↕	•	↕	↕	↕	↕
Add with carry	ADCA	89 2 2	99 3 2	A9 5 2	B9 4 3		A + M + C → A	↕	•	↕	↕	↕	↕
	ADCB	C9 2 2	D9 3 2	E9 5 2	F9 4 3		B + M + C → B	↕	•	↕	↕	↕	↕
And	ANDA	84 2 2	94 3 2	A4 5 2	B4 4 3		A · M → A	•	•	↕	↕	R	•
	ANDB	C4 2 2	D4 3 2	E4 5 2	F4 4 3		B · M → B	•	•	↕	↕	R	•

and ADDB stands for "add to the contents of accumulator B."

The next column heading has the five addressing modes (immediate, direct, index, extended and implied) associated with the accumulator and memory instructions. The mnemonics are listed in the vertical column and the addressing modes are listed in the rows across the page. Notations at an intersection mean that an addressing mode is available for that instruction. If it is blank, there is no addressing mode, and therefore no instruction. There are three symbols under each addressing mode columns: OP ~ ≈

OP is the OPERATION CODE (opcode), and the hex number in the column is the machine code for the first byte of the instruction.

~ is the symbol for the number of MPU cycles it takes to execute the instruction. The total time taken to execute the instruction is the number of cycles (~) times the clock period. For a 1 megahertz (MHz) clock the period is 1 microsecond (μs); therefore, it takes 2 μs to execute a 2-cycle instruction.

≈ is the number of program bytes in the instruction.

Scanning the top row of Table 1-3, the first mnemonic is ADDA. This operation has instructions for each of the four addressing modes: immediate, direct, indexed, and extended. Each addressing mode gives the operand a different method for specifying the effective address to the memory location that contains M. The 6800 microprocessor refers to the four instructions as one instruction with four addressing modes. Other microprocessors, however, treat these as four separate instructions. The advantage of the 6800 notation is that the user is required to memorize fewer mnemonics.

The next column is the Boolean/Arithmetic Operation, which gives a mathematical notation for the mnemonic operation in the first column.

The last column is the Condition Code Register; it indicates which condition code bits are affected by each instruction. There are four general cases:

Definitions	Symbols
The bit is unaffected by the instruction	•
The bit is forced to 1	S
The bit is forced to 0	R
The bit reflects the status of the modified data	↕

Program Format

Programs are written in a well-defined format. The examples used to illustrate the function of an instruction are written according to the prescribed format. A program has six fields (sections): location, machine code, label, mnemonic, operand, and comment fields, separated by at least one space.

Machine Generated		Programmer Generated			
Loc	Machine Code	Label	Mnem	Operand	Comment
0020	4F	COUNT	CLR A		
0021	B7 8004	LOOP	STA A	OTPORT	Port initialized
0024	BD 0090		JSR	TIME	Time delay
0027	4C		INC A		
0028	81 0B		CMP A	#OBH	
002A	26 F5		BNE	LOOP	
002C	20 D5		BRA	TILOOP	

Location The location is a hex address where the first byte of the instruction is located. For a multibyte instruction, the second and third bytes are stored in the next higher memory locations.

Machine code The machine code is the hex notation for the instruction and is translated (decoded) by the computer. For multibyte instructions the first byte is called the opcode, and second and third bytes, if any, are called the operand.

Label The label is a symbolic notation for an instruction location and is used to indicate a place where the program can "go to." Labels are necessary when preparing programs to allow convenient notations, and before an instruction has been assigned a permanent location in memory.

Labels are generally written with six or fewer uppercase letters and numbers with no spaces allowed, and they must start with a letter character. They are usually written as abbreviations for a place in the program to branch or go to. For example:

Label	Place in the Program
START	Start of the program
COUNT	Place to count
CNT	Place to count

NEWKEY	Place where a new keyboard enters into the program
LOOP	Place to return to in a loop
LOOP2	Another place to loop back to
BBALL	Bouncing ball routine

Mnemonics The mnemonic is the symbolic notation for the first byte of an instruction, and for a one-byte instruction it is the instruction itself. The opcode is the machine code for the mnemonic and the operand.

Operand The operand indicates how to calculate the effective memory location for multibyte instructions. It is at times referred to as the *symbolic operand* to distinguish it from the machine-code operand.

Comment The comment field is used in whatever way the programmer finds helpful. Most often the comments are functional descriptions of the operation performed by the instruction. However, in this chapter it is most often used to list, in hex, the relevant data at the end of each instruction.

The information in the three right-hand columns, mnemonics, operand, and comment fields, is generated by the programmer and called the *assembly language source code.* This is the notation used throughout the book.

The information in the two left-hand columns, memory location and machine code, is called the machine language or object code. It is the program format used by the machine. The information in the memory location field indicates where the first byte in machine code of each instruction is stored.

Illustrates the program as it is stored in memory

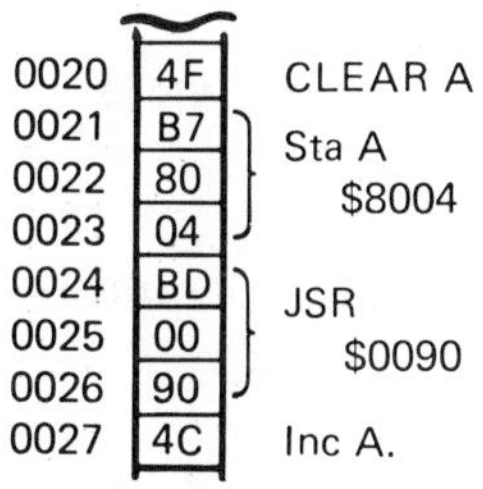

The process of translating the program from assembly language to machine code is to *assemble* the program. This assembler process is a mechanical procedure that can be performed by a machine called an assembler, or manually by a user. The sequence of events in getting a program to work is first to write the program with mnemonics, then assemble it, and finally lead the program into memory. To start the program running, point the program counter by loading it with the address where the program begins.

Addressing Modes

The addressing modes are summarized in Fig. 1-4. Figure 1-5 shows where the different addressing modes are used in a program. For

1-Byte: OPCODE

- Implied Addressing: Performs operations on the general registers.

2-Byte: OPCODE | OPERAND

The operand for

- *Immediate Addressing*
  Places a constant (data) into ACC A or B
- *Direct Addressing*
  Is used to directly address the 1st 256 addresses of memory
- *Index Addressing*
  Adds an offset from 0 to 255 to the IX register which is then used to address the data in memory
- *Relative Addressing*
  Used for branching. Adds an offset from −128 to +127 to the PC

3-Byte: OPCODE-OPERAND

The operand for

- *Immediate Addressing*
  Places a constant (address) into the IX or SP registers.
- *Extended Addressing*
  Used for the absolute addressing of 64k of memory.

Figure 1-4. Instruction word format.

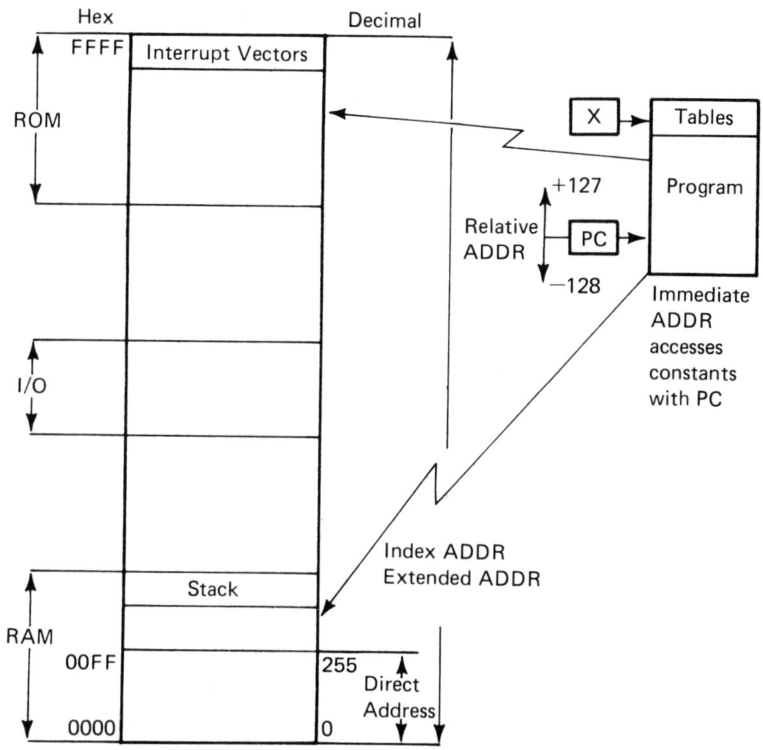

Figure 1-5. Addressing modes, where they apply.

example, the 2- and 3-byte instructions all affect memory, and the operand specifies a memory location. A typical memory map, otherwise called memory organization, for the 6800 microprocessor is shown in Fig. 1-5. The 2-byte direct addressing mode instructions are used for the quick storage and retrieval of the most active data in low memory, base page zero. This implies that low memory is reserved for RAM-type memory devices. High memory, with the interrupt and reset vectors, is reserved from ROM-type memory devices. With an I/O memory-mapped organization, the I/O peripheral devices are tied to middle-memory addresses.

Programs are stored in either RAM or ROM memories. While developing and debugging a program, it is stored in RAM where it can easily be modified. When the program is complete, it is often stored permanently in ROM at high memory. The program, wherever it is stored, is selected by pointing the program counter to the starting address of that location. The program flow is modified by the branch instructions that are used in the decision-making process. Programs often use tables and constants, and they are often stored adjacent to or as part of the program.

The program uses a stack to save the return addresses from subroutines, and it often uses high RAM locations. The stack fills from the top down.

The indexed and extended addressing modes can access any part of the 64K of memory. The extended addressing mode is used to access a single memory location, while the index addressing mode is used to access blocks of data and to search tables.

Implied Addressing Mode

The implied instructions are always 1-byte instructions, opcode only. The accumulator and memory instructions in Table 1, Appendix 1A, are all executed in 2-cycle times.

			← Comment Field →			
Machine Code	Opcode	Operand	Acc A	Acc B	Index	Mem Loc
4F	CLR A		00	—	—	—

The CLEAR A instruction is defined in the Boolean/arithmetic operation column as 00 → A. It is a 1-byte instruction, and its machine code is 4F; after the instruction is executed, the contents of accumulator A will be zero.

5F	CLR B		00	00	—	—

After the CLEAR B instruction is executed, the contents of accumulator B will be zero.

4C	INC A		01	00	—	—

The INCREMENT A instruction is defined by A + 1 → A, and in this case will add 1 to the 0 from the previous clear instruction. After the instruction is executed the contents of accumulator A will be 01.

43	COM A		FE	00	—	—

The COMPLEMENT A instruction is defined by $\overline{A} \rightarrow A$, and in this case will complement the contents of Acc A from hex 01 to hex FE.

The implied instructions in Table 2, Appendix IA modify the index register and stack pointer and are 4-cycle times long. Assume that the index register contains hex 1234 and the stack pointer contains hex

89AB. The decrement index register instruction is defined by IX − 1 → IX. If at the beginning of this instruction the contents of the index register were hex 1234, then after the instruction is executed the contents of the index register would be hex 1233.

Machine Code	Opcode	Operand	← Comment Field →			
			Acc A	Acc B	Index	SP
09	DEX		FE	00	1233	89AB

The increment stack pointer instruction is defined by SP + 1 → SP; in this case, 1 will be added to hex 89AB to form hex 89AC.

31	INS		FE	00	1233	89AC

$$
\begin{array}{lcl}
\text{Hex 89AB} & = & \%1000\ \ 1001\ \ 1010\ \ 1011 \\
+1 & & +1 \\
\hline
\text{Hex 89AC} & = & \%1000\ \ 1001\ \ 1010\ \ 1100
\end{array}
$$

In Table 3, Appendix IA, the implied instructions are the return from a subroutine or interrupt and set software interrupts SWI. In Table 4, Appendix IA, the implied instructions are used to set or reset a condition code bit or transfer data to or from the CC register.

Two-Byte Immediate Addressing Instruction

The 2-byte immediate instructions apply to the accumulator only. They are used to introduce a constant into the program via the accumulators. Data may be variable or constant. For example, today's date is a variable, but a birthdate is a constant.

In writing a program where the constants are specified, they must be part of the program. In the 2-byte immediate instruction, the first byte is the opcode, and the second byte, which is the constant, is the operand. The definition of immediate addressing used to calculate the effective address of the memory location (M) and to satisfy the statement A + M → A is that the constant is contained in the second byte of the instruction immediately behind the opcode. Although this is a clumsy way of defining immediate addressing, it is the one most widely used. In this case, a more exact interpretation of A + M → A is that the data themselves are the operand.

The immediate addressing mode is indicated by #, and a hex number is indicated by $ at the beginning of the operand. If the programmer wants to add immediate a constant hex 34 to accumulator A, it is written

ADD A #$34

and the machine code has two contiguous bytes, 8B 34.

PC	8B
PC + 1	34

The program counter first points to the opcode (8B) and then is auto-incremented, after which it is pointing to the data (34) in the memory location (M) immediately behind the opcode.

The definition of load accumulator immediate addressing is defined by M → A, where the constant data are the operand. When the instruction is executed, accumulator A contains the constant hex 34.

Machine Code	Opcode	Operand	← Comment Field → Acc A	Acc B	Index	Mem Loc
86 34	LDA A	#34H	34	01	1233	

The definition of add immediate A is A + M → A, where the constant data are the operand. The addition of hex 34 plus hex 5A is hex 8E, which are the data remaining in accumulator A after the instruction has been executed.

8B 5A	ADD A	#5AH	8E	01	1233	

	hex 34	=	%0011 0100
plus	hex 5A	=	%0101 1010
is	hex 8E		%1000 1110

The definition of OR immediate B is to take the contents of accumulator B and OR it, with the constant data in the second byte of the instruction: B ⊙ M → B.

Machine Code	Opcode	Operand	Acc A	Acc B	Index	Mem Loc
C4 56	ORAB	#56H	8E	57	1233	

hex 01 = 0 0 0 0 0 0 0 1

ORed = ⊙⊙⊙⊙ ⊙⊙⊙⊙

with hex 56 = 0 1 0 1 0 1 1 0

is hex 57 = 0 1 0 1 0 1 1 1

The definition of the exclusive-OR immediate is $B \oplus M \rightarrow B$. Take the exclusive OR of the contents of accumulator B and constant data in the second byte of the instruction and put the result back into accumulator B.

Hex 57 is equal to binary 0 1 0 1 0 1 1 1

Exclusive-OR ⊕⊕⊕⊕ ⊕⊕⊕⊕

Hex 33 0 0 1 1 0 0 1 1

is Hex 64 0 1 1 0 0 1 0 0

C8 33	EOR B	#33H	8E	64	1233	

Three-Byte Immediate Addressing Instruction

The 3-byte immediate mode instruction always contains a constant, and perhaps it might better be described as a known address capable of addressing 64K of memory. The 3-byte immediate instructions are all listed in Table 2, Appendix IA, under the index register and the stack pointer. Two of the instructions load a constant or known address into the registers, and the third compares for a constant address. An example of the use of these instructions is a mail man delivering mail for the 2000 to the 2100 block. He must know the starting address, the increment to the next address, and the last address. The 3-byte immediate instruction is used for the starting and last addresses.

The load index register immediate instruction is defined by the operation $(M) \rightarrow IX_H$, $(M + 1) \rightarrow IX_L$. The contents of the 2-byte operand referred to as M and M + 1 are loaded in the high and low portions of the index register, respectively. As in all immediate addressing the constants, the known address, are contained immediately behind the opcode for that instruction.

Machine Code	Mnem	Operand	Acc A	Acc B	Index	SP	Mem Loc
CE 12 34	LDX	#1234 H	—	—	1234	—	—

The load, the stack pointer immediate instruction, puts the operand part of the instruction into the high and low parts of the stack pointer, (M) → SP_H, (M + 1) → SP_L, respectively.

Machine Code	Mnem	Operand	Acc A	Acc B	Index	SP	Mem Loc
8E 89AB	LDS	#89ABH	—	—	1234	89AB	—

Direct and Extended Addressing Modes

There are two uses of the word direct. One applies to microcomputers generally and the second refers specifically to the 6800 addressing mode. In direct address, as generally defined, the address of the memory location (M) to be accessed is contained in the operand portion of the instruction.

Direct and Extended Addressing Modes of the 6800

The direct addressing mode of the 6800 is a special case of the extended addressing modes. The 2-byte direct address mode has a 1-byte operand and is therefore limited to accessing data from the first 256 memory locations. The 3-byte extended addressing mode instruction with a 2-byte operand can access the full 64K of memory.

The reason for putting RAM in low memory is to take advantage of the direct addressing mode, which is more efficient for requiring fewer bytes and a shorter execution time. The extended addressing mode is sometimes referred to as absolute addressing.

When writing an instruction in either the direct or extended addressing modes, a 1-byte operand implies the direct and a 2-byte operand implies the extended addressing mode. For example, to AND the contents of Acc A with the data in location hex 3C, the direct addressing instruction is written ANDA 3CH. However, to AND the data in location hex 45C6, the extended addressing instruction is written ANDA 45C6H. There is no restriction, however inefficient, in using an extended addressing instruction for low memory: ANDA 003CH.

Index Addressing Mode

Index addressing and indirect addressing are two terms used throughout the mini- and microcomputer fields. Care must be exercised in defining their meaning with respect to the 6800. In the index addressing mode, the effective (E) address to be accessed is the addition of the contents of the index register (IX) plus an offset, which is the operand portion of the index addressing mode instruction: E = (I) + offset.

Indirect Addressing

When the offset is zero, the effective address is contained in the index register.

$$E = (I) + \text{zero}$$

$$E = (I)$$

This is a special case and is referred to as indirect addressing. In other microprocessors, the register that functions as the indirect addressing mode is referred to as the data counter. In the minicomputer world this would be referred to as single-level register indirect addressing. Indirect addressing is useful for block transfer or block modification of data.

When writing an instruction, the symbol X indicates the indexed addressing mode. Before an indexed instruction is used the index register must be loaded with an address. For example, the load immediate instruction will put a known address (e.g., hex 0123) into the index register: LDX #0123H.

The complement indexed instruction with zero offset is written

COM 0,X

Mnem — offset — Indexed addressing

The definition of the complement instruction is $\overline{M} \rightarrow M$. The complemented data is in location (M), which is computed by the addition of the address in the index register (IX) plus the offset. The contents of the index register are not affected.

Machine Code	Mnem	Operand	Comment Field E = (IX) offset	
63 00	COM	0,X	0123=0123+0	data in loc 0123 is complement
63 01	COM	1,X	0124=0123+1	data in loc 0124 is complement
63 20	COM	20H,X	0143=0123+20	data in loc 0143 is complement
63 FF	COM	FFH,X	0232=0123+FF	data in loc 0222 is complement

1-7 NUMBER SYSTEMS

The three most popular systems used by computers are binary (unsigned), 2's complement binary, and binary coded decimal (BCD)—packed or unpacked. Packed BCD code stores 2 digits per byte; the unpacked stores 1 BCD digit per byte.

Multibyte binary numbers are analogous to multidigit decimal numbers.

Decimal digits		Binary bytes	
	Range		Range
1-Digit	0 to 9	1-Byte	0 to 256
2-Digit	0 to 99	2-Byte	0 to 65535
Multidigit (*N*)	0 to $(10^n - 1)$	Multibyte (*N*)	0 to $(256^n - 1)$

A 1-digit decimal number has a range from 0 through 9. A 2-digit decimal number has a range from 0 through 99 or $10^2 - 1$. For a multidigit number, the range is from 0 through $10^n - 1$, where n is the number of digits. The multibyte number is comparable to the multidigit number where a 1-byte number with 8 bits has a range from 0 through 255. A 2-byte number has a range from 0 through 65,535 or $256^2 - 1$. The multibyte number has a range from 0 through $256^n - 1$, where n is the number of bytes. See Fig. 1-6.

Carry

For a multidigit number, the carry between digits indicates that the limit has been exceeded for that digit. A carry out of the most significant digit (MSD) indicates that the total number exceeds the system capability. For example, when two multidigit numbers are added, and the sum from the unit's digits exceeds 9, a carry is generated and propagated to the ten's digit. Likewise a carry from the ten's sum indicates that the sum exceeds 99. If the computer has limited the number to 6 digits, then a carry out of the MSD indicates that the machine limit has been exceeded.

The carry performs the same function for multibyte numbers. A carry out of the MSByte indicates that the number exceeds the machine limit. Programs are written to test whether the sum has exceeded the machine limit or not, and if so, the program branches to an ERROR routine.

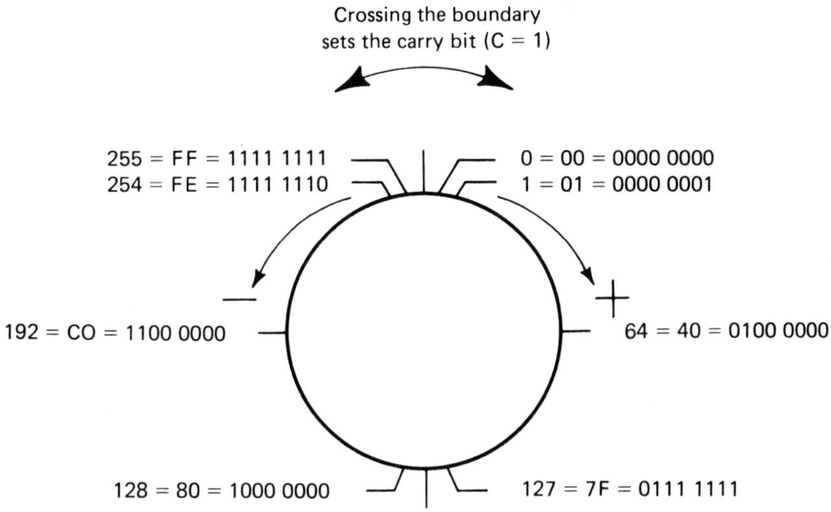

*All numbers have 3 notations: decimal, Hex, and binary

If the result of an arithmetic operation crosses the $FF to $00 boundary, which indicates that the number for that byte has exceeded its range, then the carry bit is set. In an Add operation, the boundary is always crossed going from $FF to 00 direction, and in the Subtraction operation the boundary is crossed going from 00 to the $FF direction.

HINT: For those who have difficulty with the concept, substitute decimal for byte and 9 for $FF, and then make the comparison between multidigit and multibyte arithmetic.

Figure 1-6. Unsigned binary numbers.

Two's Complement Numbers

An 8-bit 2's complement (2's comp) number is a signed binary number that has a range from −128 through 0 to +127. The MSB is the sign bit leaving 7 bits for magnitude: $2^7 = 128$. A 0 in the sign bit indicates a positive number and a 1 indicates a negative number.

Bit Position	76543210	
	00000111	= 2's complement number +7
	11111001	= 2's complement number −7

In Figure 1-7 there are three forms of the numbers from −128 to +127. They are decimal, 2's complement, and hexadecimal. Starting with the number 0, if 1 is added to 0 the results are

Decimal	the result is	+1
2's comp.	the result is	0000 0001
Hex	the result is	01

If the progression is repeated such that 1 is added to +1, for

Decimal	the result is	+2
2's comp.	the result is	0000 0010
Hex	the result is	02

The result is +2 in all three number systems.

This progression will continue until the binary 0111 1111, the most positive 8-bit number, is reached. That is equal to decimal +127, which is the sum of

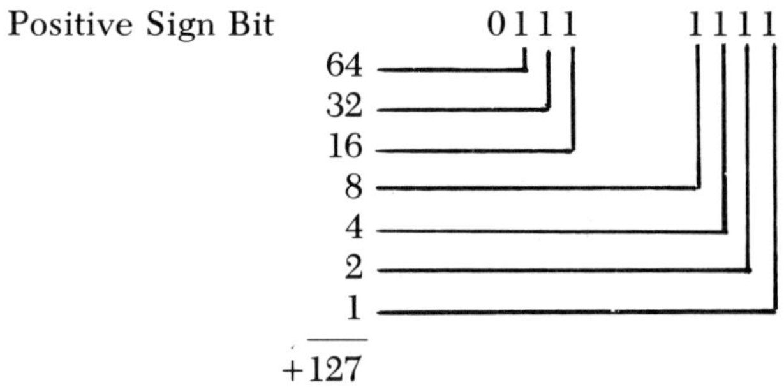

Starting with 0 and going in a negative direction, or subtracting 1 from 0, the results are

Decimal	the result is	−1
2's comp.	the result is	1111 1111
Hex	the result is	FF

The result of 0 − 1 = −1 in the three-number systems.

If 1 is subtracted from −1, the results are

Decimal	the result is	−2
2's comp.	the result is	1111 1110
Hex	the result is	FE

Reversing the process, and adding 1 to −2, the results are

Decimal	the result is	−1
2's comp.	the result is	1111 1111
Hex	the result is	FF

Decimal	Binary	Hexadecimal
+127	0111 1111	7F
⋮	⋮	⋮
+64	0100 0000	40
⋮	⋮	⋮
+2	0000 0010	02
+1	0000 0001	01
0	0000 0000	00
−1	1111 1111	FF
−2	1111 1110	FE
⋮	⋮	⋮
−64	1100 0000	CO
⋮	⋮	⋮
−127	1000 0001	81
−128	1000 0000	80

Figure 1-7. 8-bit's complement numbers.

which restores the number −1.

Continuing the progression, adding 1 to −1, the results are

Decimal	the result is	0
2's comp.	the result is	0000 0000
Hex	the result is	00

Another definition of the 2's complement number is that, to obtain the negative of the number, take the 2's complement, which is the 1's complement plus 1. For example, take the 2's complement of +5 (0000 0101):

+5	0000 0101
1's comp.	1111 1010
+1	+1
	1111 1011 = −5

Now take the 2's complement of −5:

−5	1111 1011
1's comp.	0000 0100
+1	+1
	0000 0101 = +5

The reason that the 2's complement number system is popular with computers is that the same rule converts a positive to a negative number and back again.

Multibyte 2's Complement Number

To obtain a number beyond the range of the 8-bit number (−128 to +127), a multibyte number is used where the sign is the most significant bit (MSB) of the most significant byte. As in any number system, it is necessary to know when the number is "out of range" or has exceeded the machine limit. For the 2's complement binary number, the rules that apply to binary numbers in propagating the carry bit through the bytes of the number apply until the sign bit.

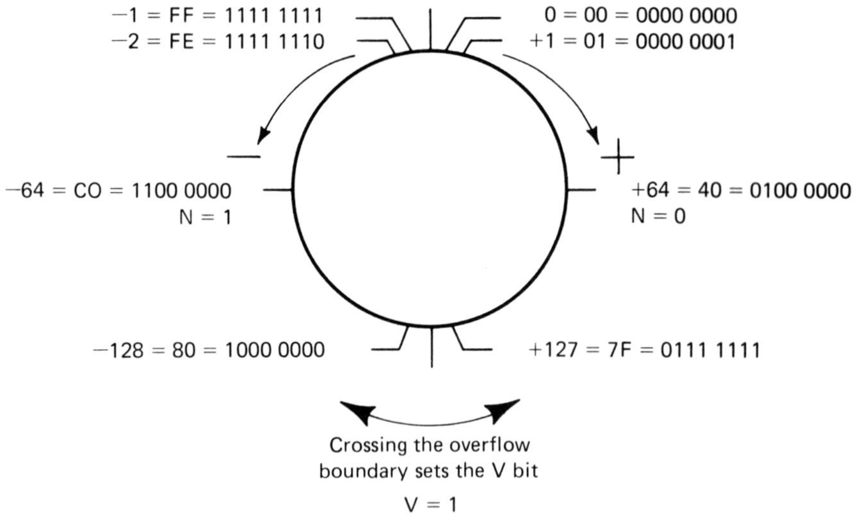

*All numbers have 3 notations: decimal, Hex, and binary

HINT: Setting the overflow bit for 2's complement numbers is comparable to setting the carry bit for unsigned binary numbers, and applies to the most significant bit of the most significant byte.

Figure 1-8. 2's complement numbers.

Overflow Bit for Indicating When 2's Complement Numbers Are Out of Range

When two positive numbers are added together, the result (sum) must be a larger positive number. If the sum is smaller, and in fact negative, then the number has exceeded its range.

$$
\begin{array}{r l}
0111\ 1111 = & \text{2's comp.} + 127 \\
+1 = & +1 \\
\hline
1000\ 0000 = & -128\text{, the number has exceeded its range}
\end{array}
$$

This is an erroneous result and the 6800 microprocessor sets an overflow bit (see Fig. 1-8). At the end of the arithmetic operation, the program should test the overflow bit, and, if it is set, the program branches to an error routine.

The overflow bit is defined as the exclusive-OR of the carryout of the sixth and seventh bits. Since the carryout of the sixth bit is inaccessible to the user, the overflow bit is set by the hardware, which is built into the machine.

1-8 CONDITION CODE REGISTER

A partial definition of a computer is a machine that could test its data and modify or alter the sequence of instructions executed, according to the data tested. The function of the condition code (CC) bits is to report the most current status of the data, so that the appropriate branch instruction may be used to alter the program sequence. The conditional branch instructions test one or more of the condition codes and either take the branch or drop-through, meaning they default and continue with the instruction sequence.

There are six condition codes:

- Carry
- Overflow
- Zero
- Negative (sign)
- Interrupt
- Half-carry (from bit 3)

Carry The carry bit, when set (C = 1), indicates that an unsigned binary number exceeded its range. It will also be applicable to binary coded decimal (BCD) numbers. The range applies to the most positive as well as the most negative boundary.

Overflow The overflow bit, when set (V = 1), indicates that the result of an arithmetic operation has exceeded the 2's complement number system. The processor performs an exclusive-OR between the carry from bits 6 and 7. It applies to the most positive and negative boundary.

Zero The zero bit, when set (Z = 1), indicates that the result of the data is equal to zero. The corollary is when the result is a nonzero number; then the Z bit is reset (Z = 0).

Negative The seventh data bit, the negative bit, is stored in the CC register where it may be tested by the branch instruction. It is often called the sign bit, which indicates a negative number when set (N = 1).

Interrupt bit The interrupt bit, when set (I = 1), masks or inhibits the interrupt request from occurring.

Half-carry bit The half-carry bit, when set (H = 1), indicates that there is a carry out of bit 3. It is used in BCD arithmetic.

A characteristic of the processor that troubles beginners is how the processor can respond to or know which number system the processor is presently handling. The processor of course does not not know. It is the programmer who is keeping track of the number system. The processor tests the data and reports their status according to fixed rules. See the columns for the condition code in Tables 1 through 4 of Appendix IA.

Setting the Condition Code Bits

The rightmost column of the instruction listing (Table 1, Appendix IA) indicates how the condition code bits respond to the instruction. For example, for the ADD ACCUMULATOR instruction,

	1	1	H	I	N	Z	V	C	condition code
Add			↕	•	↕	↕	↕	↕	

There are four options (see Fig. 1-9):

- R The bit is always reset.
- S The bit is always set.
- • The bit is not affected.
- ↕ Test the result of instruction and set if true; clear otherwise.

The first three symbols, R, S, •, are obvious, but beginners have difficulty with the ↕ symbol when handling different number systems. The CC bits respond according to fixed rules, and it is the programmer who is cognizant of the number system.

The carry bit when set (C = 1) indicates that the result of an arithmetic operation for an unsigned binary number from 0 to 255 exceeds

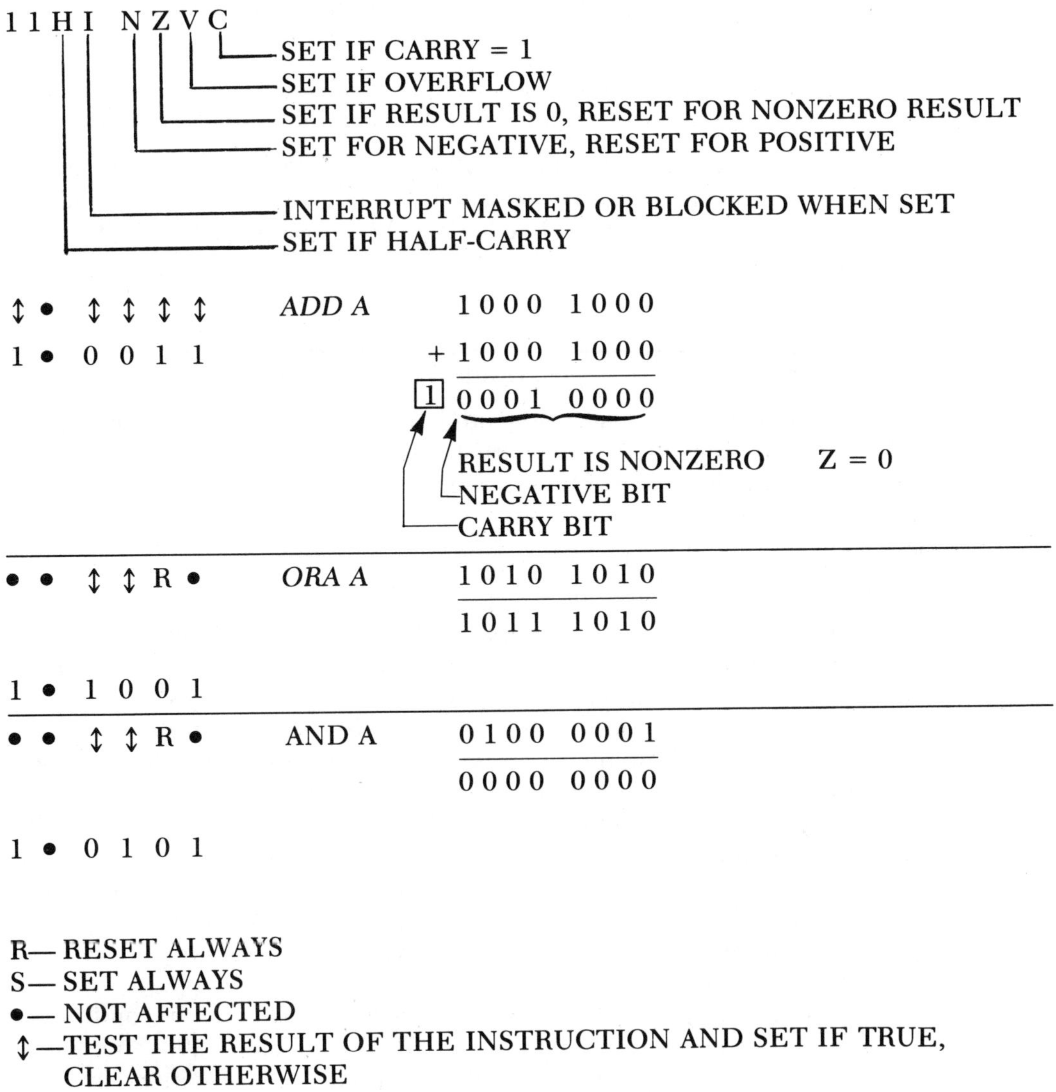

Figure 1-9. Condition codes.

the range, and it is either less than 0 or greater than 255. For the addition instructions the carry bit is set according to the rules of binary addition. For instructions that use the subtract operation, the carry bit (borrow) is set according to the rules of binary subtraction.

The overflow bit when set (V = 1) indicates that the result of a 2's complement addition for numbers between −128 to +127 has exceeded the number range, and it is either less than −128 or greater than +127. The logical check for setting the V bit for an addition is

$$V = \underbrace{X_7 \cdot M_7 \cdot \overline{R}_7}_{\text{sum of 2 negative numbers}} + \underbrace{\overline{X}_7 \cdot \overline{M}_7 \cdot R_7}_{\text{sum of 2 positive numbers}}$$

which reads that the V bit is set when two positive numbers are added and the result is negative or when two negative numbers are added and the result is positive. The logical check for setting the V bit for the subtraction is

$$V = \underbrace{X_7 \cdot \overline{M}_7 \cdot \overline{R}_7}_{\text{neg. no. } - \text{ pos. no. } = \text{ pos. result}} + \underbrace{\overline{X}_7 \cdot M_7 \cdot R_7}_{\text{pos. no. } - \text{ neg. no. } = \text{ neg. result}}$$

which reads that if a negative number minus a positive number equals a positive result, or if a positive number minus a negative number equals a negative result, then the V bit is set (see Fig. 1-8).

1-9 JUMP AND BRANCH INSTRUCTIONS

The program counter keeps track of the instructions being executed, mostly in sequence. However, a jump or branch instruction is used to alter the program flow by modifying the address in the program counter. The jump instruction is a 3-byte instruction and alters the program flow by *stuffing* a new address into the program counter. Branch instructions are 2-byte instructions that alter the program flow by adding the relative address to the program counter. The relative address mode instructions are 2-byte instructions where the operand, the relative address, is a 2's complement number. When the relative address is added to the program counter, the program flow ranges from −128 to +127 bytes relative to where the program counter is presently located.

There are 14 conditional branch instructions and an unconditional branch instruction, branch always (BRA) (see Fig. 1-10). The conditional branch instructions are decision-making instructions and are used to alter the program flow by examining or testing one or more of the condition code bits. This examination is called the *branch test*. If the conditions are not met, the appropriate CC bits are not set or reset accordingly, letting the program counter sequence to the next instruction. Conversely, when the *conditions* listed in Fig. 1-10 are met, the program will take the branch.

A branch instruction is defined by

$$PC \leftarrow (PC) + 2 + REL \qquad \text{if the condition is met}$$

$$\text{or else} \qquad PC \leftarrow (PC) + 2$$

FUNCTION	MNEMONIC	BRANCH TEST
BRANCH ALWAYS	BRA	NONE
BRANCH IF CARRY CLEAR	BCC	$C = 0$
BRANCH IF CARRY SET	BCS	$C = 1$
BRANCH IF = ZERO	BEQ	$Z = 1$
BRANCH IF ≥ ZERO	BGE	$N \oplus V = 0$
BRANCH IF > ZERO	BGT	$Z + (N \oplus V) = 0$
BRANCH IF HIGHER	BHI	$C + Z = 0$
BRANCH IF ≤ ZERO	BLE	$Z + (N \oplus V) = 1$
BRANCH IF LOWER OR SAME	BLS	$C + Z = 1$
BRANCH IF < ZERO	BLT	$N \oplus V = 1$
BRANCH IF MINUS	BMI	$N = 1$
BRANCH IF NOT EQUAL ZERO	BNE	$Z = 0$
BRANCH IF PLUS	BPL	$N = 0$
BRANCH IF OVERFLOW CLEAR	BVC	$V = 0$
BRANCH IF OVERFLOW SET	BVS	$V = 1$

Figure 1-10. Branch instructions.

The first line reads that the program takes the branch and adds 2 plus the relative address to the program counter if the appropriate branch test is valid. The second line reads, or else the program will default or drop through to execute the next instruction by adding 2 to the program counter.

In symbolic programming, labels such as BACK and JMMP are used to indicate where the program will jump or branch to. Labels are a convenient reference for a memory location and during the development of a program when a specific memory location has not yet been assigned.

The following is an example of an endless loop illustrating a forward and backward branch instruction.

PC	Machine Code	Label	Mnem	Operand	Comments
1003	4F		CLR A		N Z V C 0 1 0 0
1004	27 30	Back	BEQ	Jmmp	Z = 1, take the branch
1036	24 CC	Jmmp	BCC	Back	C = 0, take the branch

After the CLEAR A instruction is executed in location 1003, the condition codes are then set as indicated and the program counter is advanced to 1004. The instruction in locations 1004/5 reads, "take the branch if the result is zero ($Z = 1$) to a location labeled JMMP." The opcode for branch if equal (BEQ) is 27, and the relative address is calculated by

$$\begin{aligned} PC &\leftarrow (PC) + 2 + REL \\ 1036 &= 1004 + 2 + REL \\ 1036 &= 1006 + REL \\ 1036 - 1006 &= REL \\ 30 &= REL \end{aligned}$$

an equation is formed when numbers are substituted for the symbols

Since hex subtraction is not intuitive, the numbers may be converted to binary numbers for the subtraction.

Hex 1036	is equal to binary	0001 0000 0011 0110
− Hex 1006		− 0001 0000 0000 0110
30		0000 0000 0011 0000

The relative address in this case is hex 30 and forms the second byte of the instruction.

The program counter is now pointing to location 1036, and therefore the next instruction in the program to be executed is at location 1036/7. Since the branch instruction did not modify the condition codes, they remain unchanged. The opcode for the "branch if carry clear" (BCC) is 24, and the relative address is calculated by

$$\begin{aligned} PC &\leftarrow (PC) + 2 + REL \\ 1004 &= 1036 + 2 + REL \end{aligned}$$

When a number replaces the symbol PC

Then the numbers form an equation:

$$\begin{aligned} 1004 &= 1036 + 2 + REL \\ 1004 - 1036 - 2 &= REL = 1004 - 1038 \\ CC &= REL \end{aligned}$$

Again, since hex subtraction is not intuitive, the numbers may be converted to binary numbers.

Hex 1004	is equal to binary	0001 0000 0000 0100
− Hex 1038		− 0001 0000 0011 1000
CC		1111 1111 1100 1100

The relative address in this case is hex CC and is the 2's complement of −34, to form the second byte of the instruction.

Two's Complement Branch Instruction

There are two categories of branch instructions. The first applies to the 2's complement number system and is identified by testing the V bit as part of the branch test. The second category applies to all other number systems. In the following example it has been assumed that the subtract instruction $A - M \rightarrow A$ has been executed. If the program has to take a branch listed in the table following, a programmer working with either 2's complement or binary numbers has to use the branch instruction from the relevant column.

		2's Complement	Unsigned Branch Instruction
A > M	use	B G T	B H I
A ≥ M		B G E	B C C
A = M		B E Q	B E Q
A < M		B L T	B C S
A ≤ M		B L E	B L S
A ≠ M		B N E	B N E

1-10 CYCLE-BY-CYCLE OPERATION

This section may be skipped by readers not interested in how a microprocessor functions. The emphasis of this book is how to use and apply microprocessors and therefore predict what is happening to the accessible registers. However, readers with an engineering or hardware background may appreciate knowing how two inaccessible portions, the instruction register and the arithmetic/logic unit (ALU), function.

The (ALU) is the place where the arithmetic and logical operations are executed. It is generally represented by a slotted trapezoid, which has two 8-bit inputs and an 8-bit output where the condition codes are set as the data pass through. The instruction register is where the opcode, the first byte of the instruction, is decoded.

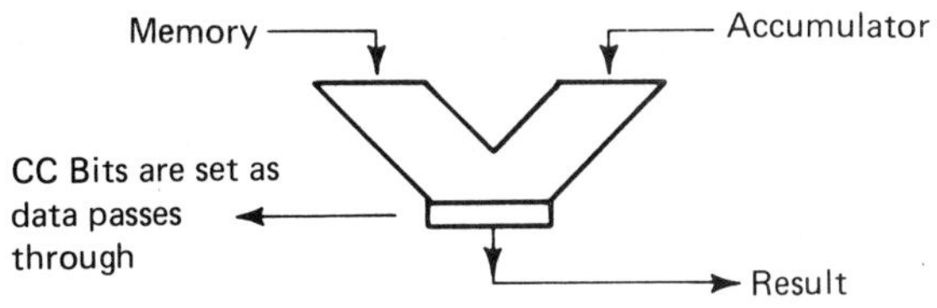

Decoding is the technique by which the microprocessor executes the instruction. The 6800 has 139 different instructions, each opening

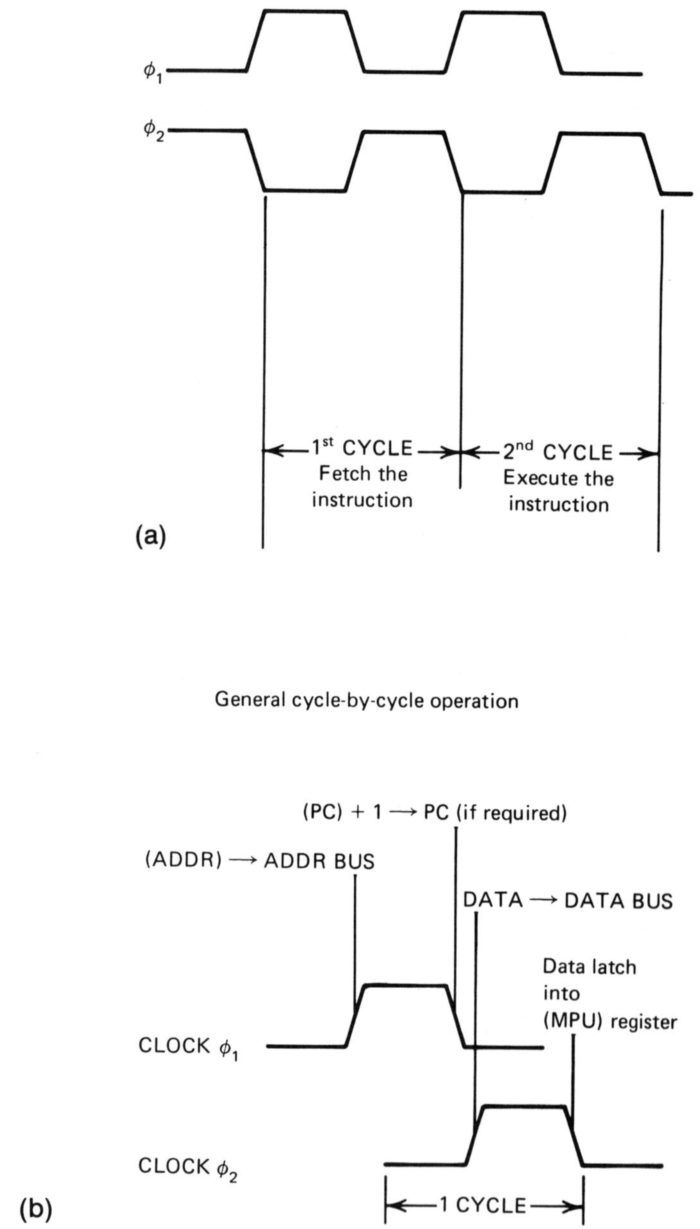

Figure 1-11. The two basic cycles to execute a 2-cycle instruction.

a unique path for data flow through the processor. This is comparable to a machine with a vocabulary of 139 different words. The combinations of programs that can be written with this instruction set are unlimited, which offers the user a machine with tremendously powerful capabilities. In this section the paths opened by two instructions, the load immediate and the add direct, are described in detail (see Figs. 1-11 and 1-12).

There are two levels of program debugging: one is software, and the second is hardware debugging, where an oscilloscope or logic analyzer is required. For hardware debugging it is necessary to have a cycle-by-cycle understanding of a microprocessor operation. The data sheet in Appendix IB has an operation summary for each instruction.

Basic Processor Cycle

The shortest instruction requires two cycles to execute, but there may be as many as 11 cycles. The first cycle always *fetches* the opcode and puts it in the instruction register where it is decoded. The instruction is executed during the second or additional cycles (see Fig. 1-11).

There are 139 opcodes in the 6800 microprocessor, which implies that there are 139 different combinations or ways to modify data. The instruction register decodes, opens the appropriate paths, and selects the required operation of the ALU. The various addressing modes refer to the different paths the data from memory take, and the instruction often indicates the operation to be performed for executing the instruction.

The 6800 requires a nonoverlapping two-phase clock, ϕ_1 and ϕ_2, per cycle. On the rise of ϕ_1 the address of the instruction is put on the address bus, and during ϕ_1 the address propagates from the processor to the memory device. On the fall of ϕ_1, the program counter is incremented if required. On the rise of ϕ_2 the data contained in that memory location, which in this case is the opcode, are placed on the data bus. They propagate down the data bus while ϕ_2 is high, and on the fall of ϕ_2 are latched into the instruction or any other relevant processor register. With multibyte instructions the operand or operands are fetched to form the address of the data in memory location M, which is placed on the address bus. The data in location M can then be modified according to the specified instruction.

Immediate Instruction Cycle by Cycle

To execute a load immediate instruction (see Figs. 1-12, and 1-13), the contents

PC	Machine Code	Mnem	Operand
0000	86 01	LDA A	#01

of the program counter addressing memory location 0000 are put on the address bus during the rise of ϕ_1, and they propagate to the memory device while ϕ_1 is high. On the fall of ϕ_1 the program counter is incremented to 0001, and on the rise of ϕ_2 data (in this case the opcode) start to propagate down the data bus while ϕ_2 is high, and on the fall of ϕ_2 they are latched into the instruction register. This com-

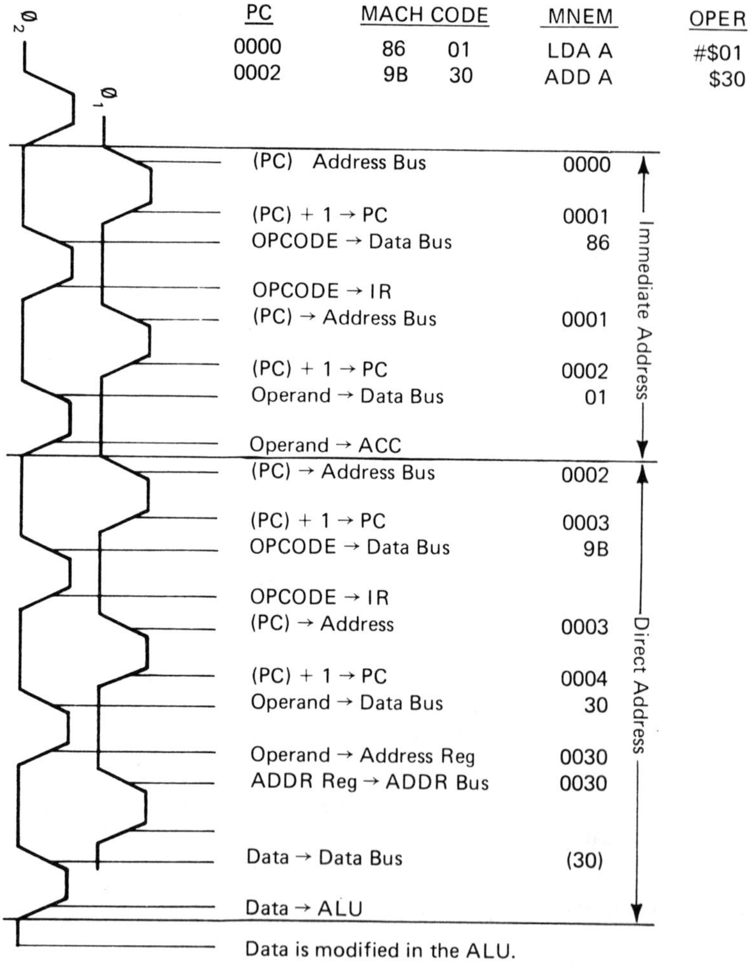

Figure 1-12. Cycle-by-cycle description.

pletes the first cycle. The rise of ϕ_1 is the start of the second cycle, and the program counter puts the address 0001 on the address bus.

On the fall of ϕ_1 the program counter is incremented. On the rise of ϕ_2 the operand, the immediate data, is placed on the data bus. The load

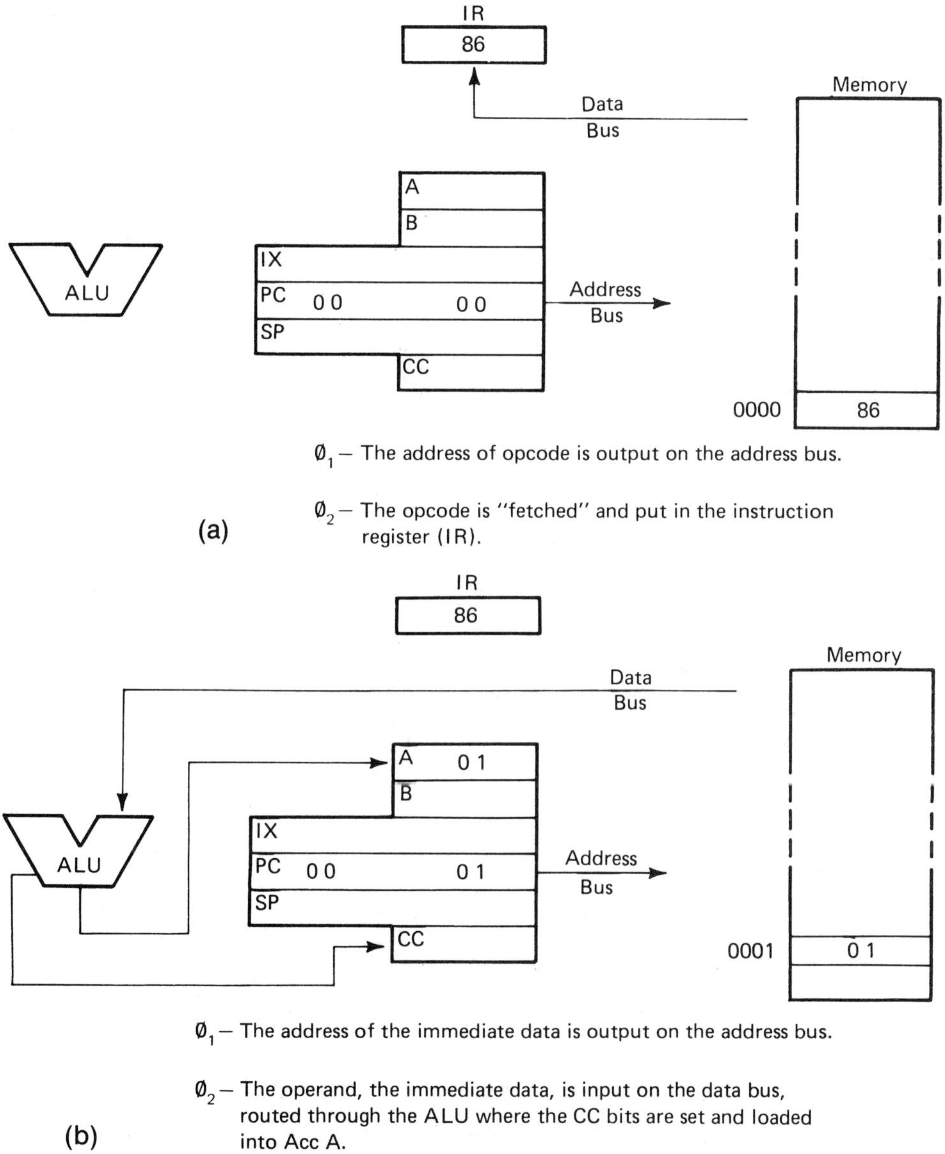

Figure 1-13. (a) First cycle of load immediate instruction. (b) Second cycle of load immediate instruction.

immediate instruction puts the second byte of the instruction into accumulator A via the ALU. During the second cycle the opcode was decoded by the processor and the appropriate paths on the processor were opened, enabling the data to propagate onto the processor and be routed through the ALU, where the condition codes are set, and then passed into accumulator A.

During the execution of this instruction, three registers are affected, the program counter, accumulator A, and the condition code register. The program counter was incremented by 2, once for each byte, the accmulator was loaded with the operand, and the condition code register reported the status of the data that passed through the ALU, in this case 01.

Direct Addressing Cycle by Cycle

The direct addressing instruction is a 2-byte instruction that takes 3 cycles to execute. It takes the data out of one of the low-order 256 bytes of memory and performs the appropriate arithmetic/logic operation, in this case an ADD operation (Figs. 1-12 and 1-14).

PC	Machine Code	Mnem	Opcode
0002	9B 30	ADD A	30H

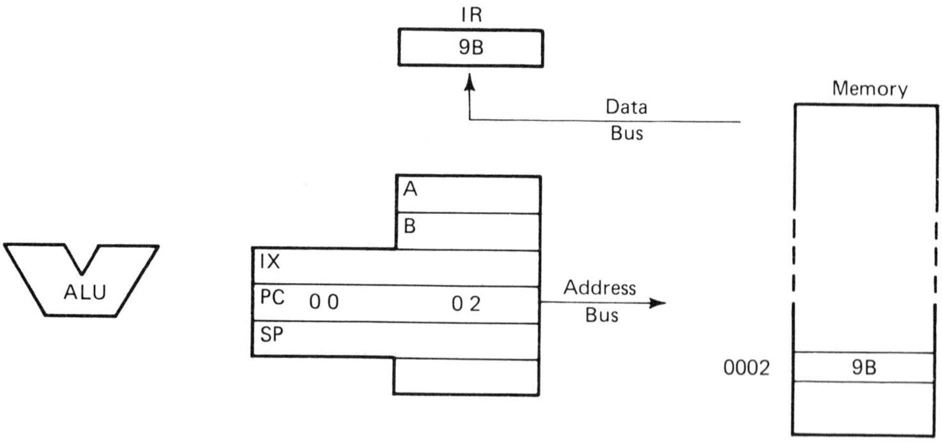

(a)

Ø₁ – The address of the opcode is output on the address bus.

Ø₂ – The opcode is "fetched" and input to the IR register for decoding.

Figure 1-14. The 3-cycle direct addressing instruction. (a) First cycle, (b) second cycle, (c) third cycle.

At the start of the execution, the rise of ϕ_1, the opcode is fetched by placing the address of the instruction from the program counter onto the address bus. On the fall of ϕ_1 the program counter is incremented,

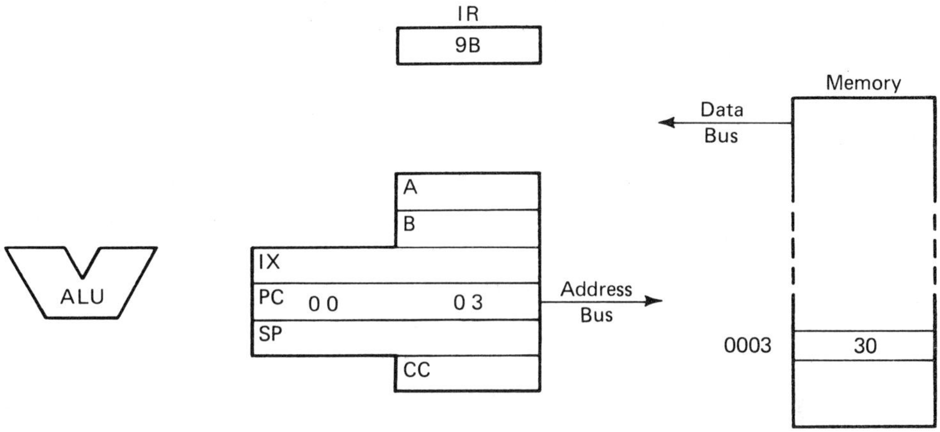

(b) $\emptyset_1$ – The address of the operand is output on the address bus.

$\emptyset_2$ – The operand is input on the data bus.

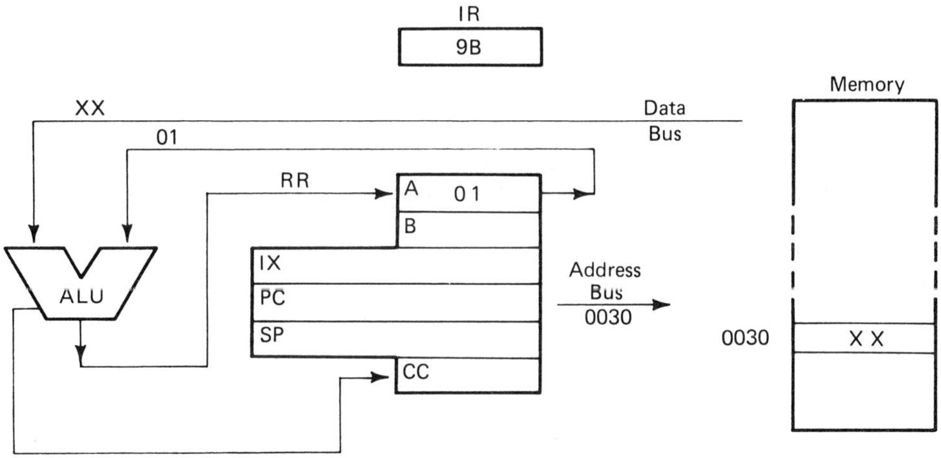

(c) $\emptyset_1$ – The address of the data (derived from the operand) is output on the address bus.

$\emptyset_2$ – The data (XX) from memory and the data from Acc A are routed through the ALU and, in this case, added together. The result is returned to Acc A and the CC bits are set according to the status of the result (RR).

Figure 1-14 continued.

and on the rise of ϕ_2 the opcode is placed on the data bus. On the fall of ϕ_2 the opcode is latched into the instruction register. On the rise of ϕ_1 the address on the data is placed on the address bus, and it propagates to a RAM where the variable data are stored. On the fall of ϕ_1, the program counter is *not* incremented, but the data from memory location 30 are placed on the data bus. On the fall of ϕ_2, the data from accumulator A and the data from location 30 are routed through the ALU, where a result is generated and the condition codes are set accordingly to report the status of the new data. The two sets of input data propagate through the ALU during the cycle, while the contents of the program counter are placed on the address bus. The result of the ALU is complete on the fall of ϕ_1.

1-11 COMPARE AND TEST INSTRUCTIONS

The compare and test instructions all have the same form. They test data in one of the accumulators, for example, compare A − M and set the condition codes accordingly, without modifying the data. They are usually followed by a branch instruction. The compare instruction is an arithmetic compare, performed by subtracting the data in memory location 'M' from one of the accumulators, leaving the data in the accumulator unchanged. In comparing data, it is necessary to examine the data without destroying them. The definition of the compare instruction is A − M, without an arrow (→), indicating that the data in the accumulator are not replaced.

The bit test instructions perform a logical AND function, again setting the condition codes without destroying the data in the accumulator.

1-12 SUMMARY

This section is a summary of some instructions and the registers they modify. Generally, as each instruction is executed, three registers are affected: the program counter by the number of bytes in the instruction, the register or memory location where the data are transferred to or (→) replaced, and the condition code register.

Assume that the program counter is at location 0020, and an ADD IMMEDIATE B instruction is executed.

Loc	Machine Code	Mnem	Operand	Acc A	Acc B	Index	CC NZVC	Mem loc
0020	CB 34	ADD B	#34H	—	34	—	0000	—

PC: the PC is incremented by 2 (contents of register); the contents of Acc B are replaced by 34 CC bits; the bits are set to 0000.

Clear A.

0022	4F	CLR A		00	34	—	0100	—

PC: the PC is incremented by 1; the contents of Acc A are replaced by 00; the CC bits are set to 0100.

Load index register immediate.

0023	CE 0123	LDX	#0123H	00	34	0123	0000	—

PC: the PC is incremented by 3; the contents of index register are replaced by 0123; the CC bits are set to 0000.

Store direct to memory location 0030 from Acc. B.

0026	D7 30	STA B	30H	00	34	0123	0000	0030:34

PC: the PC is incremented by 2; the contents of memory location are replaced by 34; the CC bits are set to 0000.

Store, [indexed], from Acc B.

0028	E7 00	STA B	0,X	00	34	0123	0000	0123:34

PC: the PC is incremented by 2; the contents of memory location are replaced by 34; the CC bits are set to 0000.

Complement Acc B.

002A	53	COM B		00	CB	0123	1001	—

PC: the PC is incremented by 1; the contents of Acc B are replaced by CB; the CC bits are set to 1001.

Decrement Acc A.

002B	4A	DEC A		FF	CB	0123	1001	—

PC: the PC is incremented by 1; the contents of Acc A are replaced by FF; the CC bits are set to 1001.

Compare Acc A to location 0030 direct.

002C	91 30	CMP A	30H	FF	CB	0123	1000	—

PC: the PC is incremented by 2; the CC bits are set to 1000; only two registers, the PC and CC code, are affected.

Branch if the carry is set.

002E	25 57	BCS	moor	FF	CB	0123	1000	—

PC: the PC is incremented by 2; only one register, the PC, is affected.

---

2 Basic Program Organization

Programs are written to solve problems. The initial approach to the problem must view and define the total system, which is the strategic approach. This approach states the problem and results in a specification that includes a system flow chart. The system problem is then broken down into manageable parts, such as routines, subroutines, memory organization, and I/O definition, that can be analyzed separately.

Once this overall strategy is established, the problem-solving procedure moves into the tactical phase. This focuses on how to write the program and implement the associated hardware required for the individual parts.

The separate routines are sometimes referred to as modules. Modular programming is a technique for breaking large system problems into smaller manageable sections, which is the approach used in this chapter. Each section of Chapter 2 discusses an individual routine with its separate specifications: flow chart, memory organization, I/O interface, and program listing.

The system program has four "stand alone" routines, and the program flow is linked by an *input control* routine allowing the user to select any of the four routines to be executed. The four routines share a common subroutine, and a detailed explanation of how microprocessors handle subroutines is given in Sec. 2-2. Section 2-6 gives a discussion of a routine to input data to the microcomputer. All these routines are tied together into a total system problem and form the model for the typical basic program organization.

A *port* is a group of eight input pins, output pins, or any combination of eight I/O pins. The data moves through a port, along the data bus, to or from an accumulator. Routines with only outputs are easier to write than a combination of input and output data routines. We will write three predetermined output light pattern routines: count (Sec. 2-1), bouncing ball (Sec. 2-3), bouncing dark spot (Sec. 2-4).

There are two types of input data routines: those that input data and those that input control information used to control the data flow. Before executing the variable count routine (Sec. 2-6), the start count, end count, and interval count are loaded through the input data port.

A subroutine shared by these four routines generates a half-second delay (Sec. 2-2).

The input control routine samples a set of eight switches from an input port (Sec. 2-5) that selects one of the four routines: count, bouncing ball, bouncing dark spot, or variable counter.

The program and flow chart (Fig. 2-9) that tie all of these routines together are listed at the end of this chapter.

2-1 COUNTER

The first example writes a program that counts from 0 to 10 by 1's and continues repeating this process. There are three constants in this program, the *start count*, the *increment count*, and the *end count*, which in this example are 0, 1, and 10, respectively. The variable, the value of the count, will be stored in Acc A. Figure 2-1 gives the flow chart for this program. The flow chart and its symbols are interpreted as follows:

- The first flow chart symbol indicates that the counter is initialized to the starting count of 0. It is labeled count to mark its place in the program.

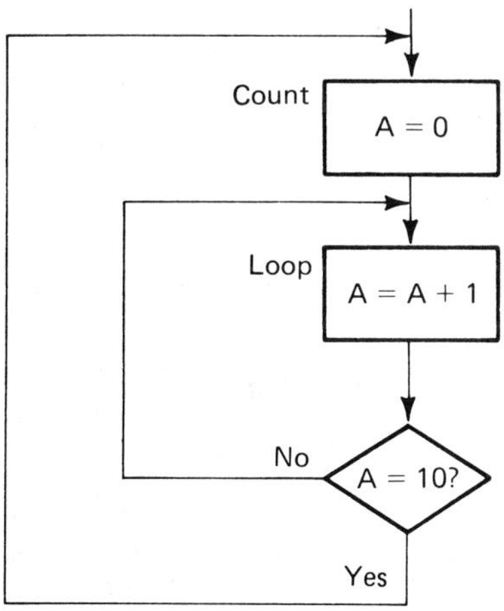

Figure 2-1. Counter flow diagram.

• The second flow chart symbol, labeled loop, indicates that the counter is incremented. In this example it is incremented by 1.

• The third symbol is the decision diamond, in which the condition "does the count equal the end count 10?" is stated. If the decision is no, then the program must return to a place labeled loop, where the variable count is again incremented. If the decision is yes, then the program will return to a place labeled count, and continue repeating the process.

Loops

Computers by their nature are good at executing loops, of which the counter is a prime example. There are three basic parts of a loop:

- Initialize the loop.
- Loop—execute the task specified for the loop.
- Test to exit from the loop and indicate the reentry point.

Coding

After the flow chart is drawn, the strategic part is complete. The programmer can focus on the tactical part, the writing of the code required to perform the function specified by each box. The programmer must select the appropriate 6800 instruction or instructions to execute each function. When more than one instruction can perform equivalent functions, the determining factor will be the instruction with the fewest number of bytes.

A = 0

Loading a zero into Acc A can be implemented with two different instructions, load immediate A or clear A. The 1-byte clear A instruction will be used: CLR A.

A = A + 1

Adding a constant 1 to Acc A can be implemented with different instructions, add immediate A or increment A. The 1-byte increment A instruction will be used: INC A.

A = 0?

Two instructions are necessary to make a decision. The first instruction sets the CC bits to be examined by the second, the branch instruction, which executes the branch. The first part of the decision diamond is the compare immediate instruction, which compares the contents of the accumulator, the count, to a constant, being the end count. The compare immediate A instruction, CMPA #$0A, is a 2-byte instruction which compares by subtracting a constant stored in memory (in this case 10 or hex 0A) from the contents of Acc A (A − M). The difference, the result of the subtraction, is recorded by the condition code bits to be examined by the branch instructions.

Example: If the contents of Acc A are 01 and the constant is 10 or hex 0A, then the condition bits are set accordingly.

A	01	0000	0001
−M	−0A	−0000	1010
R	F7 [1]	1111	0111

C bit = 1	Indicates that M > A
Z bit = 0	Indicates that M ≠ A
N bit = 1	Indicates that the result is negative

Table 2-1 lists the states of the relevant condition code bits (N, Z, C) for the count value from 1 to 11 (hex B). Initially, the number in the accumulator is less than the constant, and the CC bits are N = 1, Z = 0, C = 1. When the value of the accumulator and the constant are equal, the states of the CC bits are N = 0, Z = 1, C = 0.

To complete the decision, a branch instruction must return the program to either the place labeled count or start. If the contents of Acc A do not equal the end count, the branch if not equal (BNE) instruction will return the program to the place labeled count:

```
BNE   COUNT
```

On reaching the end count, the program will drop through or default to the next instruction. In this example either branch always (BRA) or branch if equal (BEQ) will suffice.

```
BRA   START

     OR

BEQ   START
```

The *source count program* is

```
COUNT   CLR A
LOOP    INC A                  INCREMENT COUNT
        CMP A    #$0A          COMPARE TO END COUNT
        BNE      LOOP          IF NO KEEP COUNTING
        BRA      COUNT         ELSE EXIT FROM ROUTINE
```

This program is called the source program. Before it can be loaded into

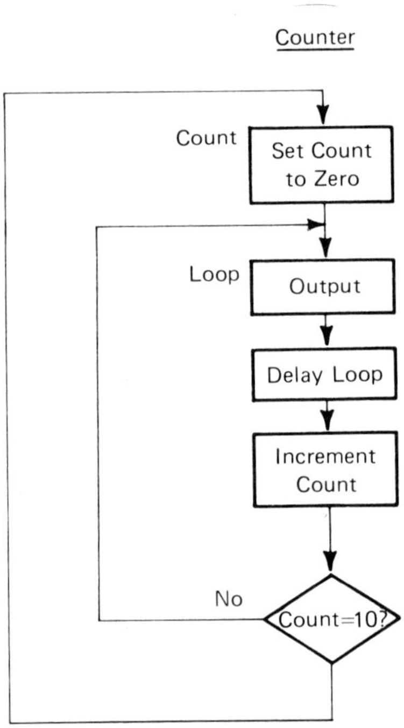

Figure 2-2. Modified flow chart: counter with delay loop flow diagram.

the microprocessor it must be assembled and converted into machine language. An object program is obtained from one source program and a memory location where the program is to be stored. In this example the program is to be loaded into location $0054.

The *assembled code* is:

```
0054 4F        COUNT  CLR A
0055 4C        LOOP   INC A                INCREMENT COUNT
0056 81 0A            CMP A   #$0A         COMPARE TO END COUNT
0058 26 FB            BNE     LOOP         IF NO KEEP COUNTING
005A 20 F8            BRA     COUNT        ELSE EXIT FROM ROUTINE
```

There are two shortcomings to this program:

- There is no output; therefore, the count is not displayed.
- Even with the output to the eight light emitting diodes (LEDs), the microprocessor will execute the program so quickly that the display will not be discernible.

To correct for having no output, the program is modified to output to a port that drives eight LEDs. The "fix" for the nondiscernible display is to keep each count displayed for between 0.5 and 1 s per display. This is achieved by generating a delay loop for between 0.5 and 1 s. The count program is modified by adding the output instruction and a delay routine. The consequence is that the "when to exit from the loop" test has also to be modified by comparing for the end count plus 1 (see Fig. 2-2).

Output

To output data with the 6800 microprocessor, the data must be transferred or stored in a 6820 (PIA) device at memory location 8006 (see Chapter 3 for detailed description of the PIA). It has to be assumed that the I/O port at location 8006 has been initialized as an output port driving eight LEDs through eight inverters.

Port B at location 8006 has been initialized to be an output port. The

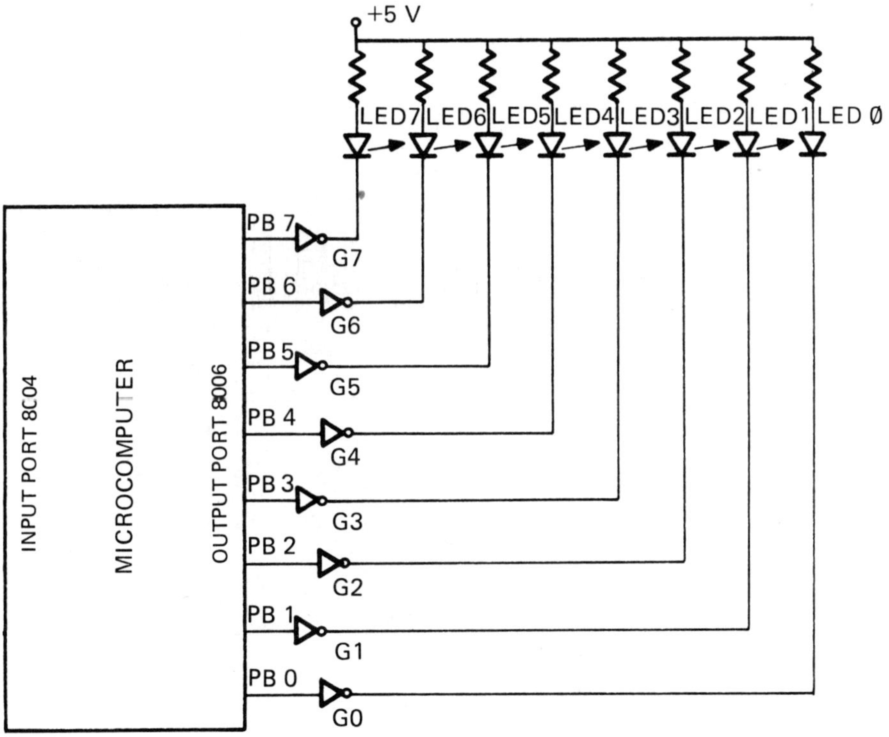

Figure 2-3. Hardware configuration for output Port B at Location $8006 driving 8-LEDs.

eight pins (PB_0, PB_1, . . . PB_7) drive LED_0, LED_1, . . . LED_7, respectively, through inverters. When a logical 1 is output at PB_0 the LED_0 will be turned on, while a 0 at PB_0 will turn LED_0 off. To output from Acc A to port B at location 8006, the programmer can use a "stored extended" instruction: STA A $8006.

Output Display Pattern

The counter counts and displays the numbers from zero to hex A or binary 10, as illustrated at the different time intervals (T) in Fig. 2-4.

- T1 is the initial pattern to be displayed.
- T2 to T11 are the patterns that are displayed as the counter keeps incrementing.
- After displaying the end count at T11, the contents of the accumulator will be incremented to end count + 1. At this time the program will branch back to the start of the program.

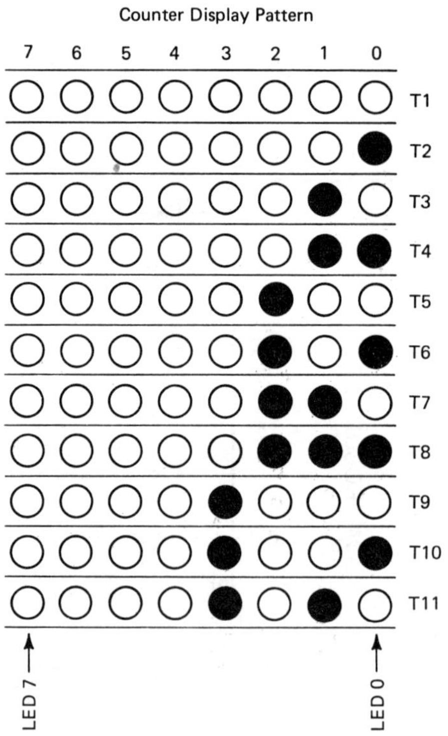

Figure 2-4. Sequence of light pattern display by count routine.

Delay

To generate a 0.5 to 1s delay, a routine has to be written to count through a number that takes 0.5 to 1 s to execute. These routines are called delay loops and are examples of real-time problems. The size of the delay number is calculated in multibyte numbers that can be stored in contiguous memory locations. Eight-bit, 16-bit, and 24-bit numbers are equivalent to 1 byte, 2 bytes, and 3 bytes. Before determining the multibyte number required, it is necessary to compute the time generated by a 1-byte number. In this example, the multibyte number will be stored in location 00, 01, 02, and so on.

0002	0001	0000

One-Byte Delay Loop

			Time
	CLR	$0000	
Delay	INC	$0000	6 cycles
	BNE	Delay	4 cycles
			10 cycles

The "clear extended" instruction puts all 0's into location 00. It takes 6 cycles to execute the increment extended and 4 cycles to execute the branch instruction, for a total of 10 cycles. Assuming that the microprocessor clock is running at 1 MHz, it takes 10 uses to execute one cycle. The routine will stay in the 1-byte delay loop for 256 cycles for a total of 256 × 10 μsec, or 2560 μs or 2.56 ms.

Two-Byte Delay Loop

The 2-byte delay loop will use locations 00 and 01.

```
        CLR    $0000    DELAY LOOP
        CLR    $0001
DELAY   INC    $0000    INC LOC '0'
        BNE    DELAY    BR TO DELAY FOR 256 TIMES
        INC    $0001    INC LOC '1'
        BNE    DELAY    BR TO DELAY FOR 256 TIMES
```

The program counts through memory location 00, and the time generated by the 1-byte example is 2.56 ms. Then the program will drop through and increment location 01 to generate a nonzero number. The branch not equal instruction will route the program back to the instruction labeled DELAY as long as location 01 has a nonzero number. Location 00 will generate a 2.56-ms delay for as many times as it takes the number in location 01 to count up to (in this case) 256, for a total delay of 256 × 256 μsec or 0.65536 s.

```
                  * COUNT WITH DELAY LOOP
                  *
0054 4F           COUNT   CLR A
0055 B7 8006 LOOP    STA A   $8006    OUTPUT COUNT
0058 7F 0000 TIME    CLR     $0000    DELAY LOOP PART OF SUB
005B 7F 0001         CLR     $0001
005E 7C 0000 DELAY   INC     $0000    INC LOC '0'
0061 26 FB           BNE     DELAY    BR TO DELAY FOR 256 TIMES
0063 7C 0001         INC     $0001    INC LOC '1'
0066 26 F6           BNE     DELAY    BR TO DELAY FOR 256 TIMES
0068 4C              INC A            INCREMENT COUNT
0069 81 0B           CMP A   #$0B     COMPARE TO ENDCOUNT +1
006B 26 E8           BNE     LOOP     IF NO KEEP COUNTING
006D 20 E5           BRA     COUNT    ELSE EXIT FROM ROUTINE
```

Predicting the Status of the CC Bits

It is helpful to know the status of the CC bits with each progression of the counter (see Table 2-1). The reader should become proficient at this type of calculation to compute the branch instructions of microprocessors.

Problem 2-1(a) Write the delay routine to generate a 0.5 s ± 10 ms delay using locations 0000 and 0001. Assume a 1-MHz clock. **(b)** Write the delay routine to generate a 1.0 s ± 1 ms delay using locations 0000, 0001, and 0002. Assume a 1-MHz clock.

Problem 2-2(a) Write a delay routine to generate a 0.5 s ± 10 ms delay using locations 0000 and 0001. Assume an 800-kHz clock. **(b)** Write a delay routine to generate a 1.0 s ± 10 ms delay using locations 0000, 0001, and 0002. Assume an 800-kHz clock.

Problem 2-3(a) Write a count program to count from 0 to $68. **(b)** Write a count program to count down from $0A to 0.

Table 2-1 Calculation of the CC Bits

Count	Variable	Constant	Difference Discarded	CC NZVC
T_1	0000 0001	0000 1011	1 1111 0110	1001
T_2	0000 0010		1 1111 0111	1001
T_3	0000 0011		1 1111 1000	1001
T_4	0000 0100		1 1111 1001	1001
T_5	0000 0101		1 1111 1010	1001
T_6	0000 0110		1 1111 1011	1001
T_7	0000 0111		1 1111 1100	1001
T_8	0000 1000		1 1111 1101	1001
T_9	0000 1001		1 1111 1110	1001
T_A	0000 1010		1 1111 1111	1001
B not displayed	0000 1011	0000 1011	0 0000 0000	0100

2-2 SUBROUTINES

Subroutines are a string of instructions that are shared by different routines to conserve memory, rather than having to duplicate the same set of instructions in several places in the program.

The counter program has a routine called a *delay loop* that will be shared with the next program, the bouncing ball. The counter program, therefore, has to be rewritten putting the delay loop routine into subroutine form so that it can be shared with other routines.

Three conditions must be satisfied for subroutines to be implemented:

- "Stack" to save the return address in the main program.
- Location in memory where the subroutine is stored.
- Instruction to "return from the subroutine."

A program with subroutines will jump to different places in memory; therefore, a suggested memory organization with five areas is recommended and will be used for the remainder of the chapter (see Table 2-2). They are

- Variables, starting in location 0000.
- Routines, starting in location 0020.
- Subroutines, starting in location 00B0.
- The stack, at location 00FF filling from the top down.
- I/0 ports, at location starting 8000 to 8022.

Table 2-2. Memory Map

Address	
8000	I/0
00FF	Stack
00B0	Subroutines
0020	Routines
0000	Variables

Table 2-2 is a memory map with suggested locations for the various routines, subroutines, and the stack.

- The count program starts in location 0054.
- The BB program starts in location 0062.
- The delay loop subroutine starts in location 00B0.
- The top of the stack starts in high RAM, 00FF.

If a program is to use a stack, it is recommended that the stack be set up early in the program. This is accomplished by a "load stack pointer immediate" instruction: LDS #$00FF. The stack pointer now points to location 00FF and defines the stack area.

In this case, the delay loop subroutine starts in location 00B0. The last instruction is a "return from subroutine" (RTS). The modified program is listed where the delay loop subroutine has been moved to location 00B0. This program is different from the previous counter program in three ways:

1. The delay subroutine has been moved to location 00B0.
2. It has been replaced by a "jump to subroutine" (JSR) extended instruction.
3. At the end of the delay loop subroutine, a return from subroutine (RTS) instruction has been added to the end of the subroutine.

The flow chart for the count routine is no different whether or not a subroutine is used. The listing is as shown on the following page.

JSR Instruction

Before discussing the jump instruction, it is necessary to understand the ↓ and ↑ symbols. The symbol ↓ means "push," indicating that the data in the relevant register (the PC in this case) are stored on the

```
                 * COUNT PROGRAM
                 *
0054 4F          COUNT   CLR A                  
0055 B7 8006 LOOP    STA A   $8006      OUTPUT COUNT
0058 BD 00B3             JSR     TIME       JMP TO DELAY SUB 'TIME'
005B 4C                  INC A              INCREMENT COUNT
005C 81 0B               CMP A   #$0B       COMPARE TO ENDCOUNT +1
005E 26 F5               BNE     LOOP       IF NO KEEP COUNTING
0060 20 F2               BRA     COUNT      ELSE EXIT FROM ROUTINE
                 *
                 *
                 *DELAY LOOP SUBROUTINE
00B0                     ORG     $00B0
                 *
00B0 B7 8006 DTIME   STA A   $8006      OUTPUT IS PART OF SUB
00B3 7F 0000 TIME    CLR     $0000      DELAY LOOP PART OF SUB
00B6 7F 0001             CLR     $0001
00B9 7C 0000 DELAY   INC     $0000      INC LOC '0'
00BC 26 FB               BNE     DELAY      BR TO DELAY FOR 256 TIMES
00BE 7C 0001             INC     $0001      INC LOC '1'
00C1 26 F6               BNE     DELAY      BR TO DELAY FOR 256 TIMES
00C3 39                  RTS
```

stack and the SP is autodecremented accordingly. Conversely, the ↑ means "pull" and reverses the process performed by the push. The data are loaded back from the stack into the relevant register (the PC) and the SP is autoincremented.

JSR

Jump to Subroutine

Operation:

Either: PC ← (PC) + 0003 (for EXTended addressing)

or: PC ← (PC) + 0002 (for INDexed addressing)

Then: ↓ (PCL)

SP ← (SP) − 0001

↓ (PCH)

SP ← (SP) − 0001

PC ← numerical address

Description: The program counter is incremented by 3 or by 2, depending on the addressing mode, and is then pushed onto the stack, eight bits at a time. The stack pointer points to the next empty location in the stack. A jump occurs to the instruction stored at the numerical address. The numerical address is obtained according to the rules for EXTended or INDexed addressing.

As this instruction is executed, there are six different operations for the JSR extended version of this 3-byte instruction.

PC ← (PC) + 0003 If the jump instruction starts in location $0058 and it is a 3-byte instruction, then the next instruction starts in location $005B.

005B ← 0058 + 0003; first the microprocessor calculates the address of the next instruction.

↓ **(PCL)** **Reads** Push the program counter lower byte onto the stack. In this case, put 5B into stack location $00FF.

SP ← SP − 0001 Decrement the SP to $00FE, which is the next empty stack location.

↓ **(PCH)** **Reads** Push the program counter upper byte onto the stack. In this case, put 00 into stack location $00FE.

SP ← SP − 0001 Decrement the SP to $00FD, which is the next empty stack location.

PC ← numerical address Is the address of where the subroutine is located, and by virtue of stuffing that address into the program counter it will be the next instruction executed by the program.

The time delay of 0.5 or 1 s is generated just as it was in the previous routine. One last instruction is added, which will return the program back to the main routine.

The return from subroutine returns the program to the location in the stack.

Return from Subroutine — RTS

Operation:

SP ← (SP) + 0001
↑ PCH
SP ← (SP) + 0001
↑ PCL

Description:

The stack pointer is incremented (by 1). The contents of the byte of memory, at the address now contained in the stack pointer, are loaded into the 8 bits of highest significance in the program counter. The stack pointer is again incremented (by 1). The contents of the byte of memory, at the address now contained in the stack pointer, are loaded into the 8 bits of lowest significiance in the program counter.

As the return from subroutine instruction is executed, four different operations occur:

SP ← SP + 0001 The SP is incremented and is now pointing to where the PCH is stored in the stack.

↑ **(PCH)** **Reads** Pull the contents of stack location 00FE and store it in an internal auxiliary register.

SP ← SP + 0001 The SP is incremented and is now pointing to where the PCL is stored in the stack.

↑ **(PCL)** **Reads** Pull the contents of stack location 00FF, and together with PCH stuff the return address of the subroutine back into the program counter. By virtue of this the next instruction to be executed is the return address of the subroutine, in this case $005B.

When the return from subroutine is executed, the PC is at 005B and continues with the count routine.

The jump to subroutine (JSR) and return from subroutine (RTS) work together and are called from either the main program or from a higher-level subroutine. The stack is the place where the return address is stored. The sequence of steps and the positions and contents of the program counter and the stack pointer are indicated in Fig. 2-5 a to d.

2-3 BOUNCING BALL

Write a program to turn on one of eight LEDs at a time. Start with LED 1 and move the light until the leftmost LED is turned on. The light then bounces off the leftmost position and starts to move back across until the rightmost LED is on, and then repeat the pattern continuously. Figure 2-6b shows the light pattern as it progresses from

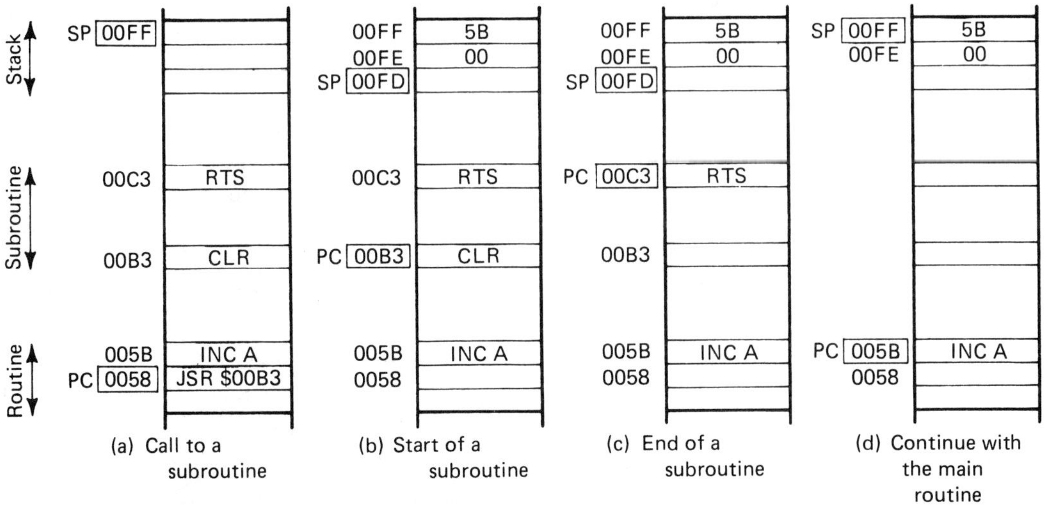

Figure 2-5. Tracing the program counter (PC) and the stack pointer (SP) through a subroutine and back.

T1 to T14. The rules are to have one and only one light on at a time, and that each light must be on for the same amount of time.

The flow chart (Fig. 2-6b) shows a program with two separate loops. The first loop moves the light to the left starting at the location labeled LEFT (loop left), and the second moves the light to the right starting at the location labeled RITE (loop right). One critical part of the program is to select the shift instructions that shift 0's into the accumulator while shifting a single 1 right or left. Another critical part is knowing when and how to exit from each of the loops.

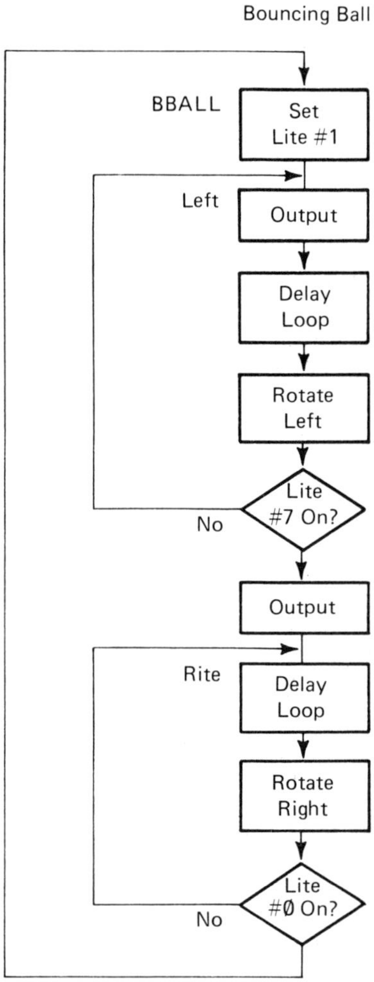

(a) The Bouncing Ball flow diagram.

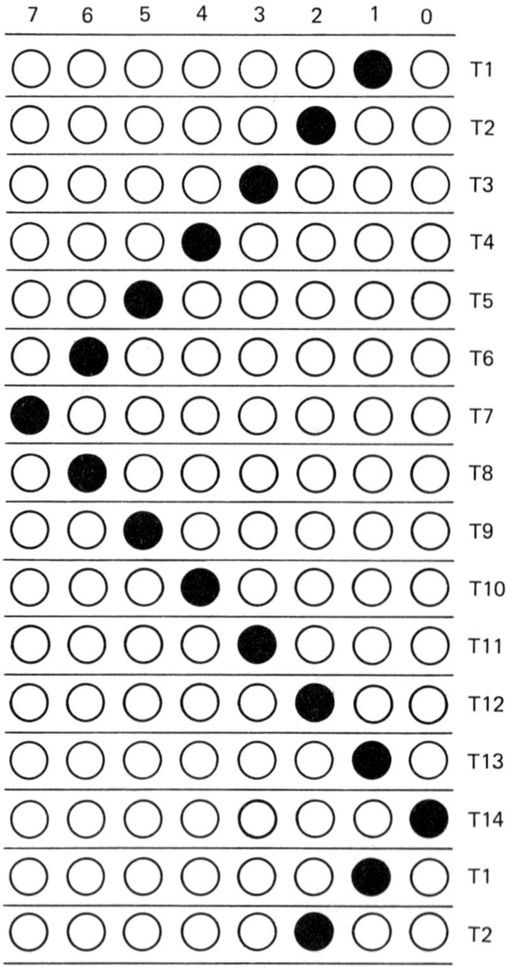

(b) The Bouncing Ball sequence of light patterns from T1 through T14.

Figure 2-6. The bouncing ball.

The branch instruction is used to keep the program in the left loop by testing the status of the sign bit, branch on positive (BPL). When a 1 is finally shifted into the sign bit and indicates a negative signed number, the branch instruction defaults and drops through to continue the program by starting into the right loop. The program will stay in the right loop as long as there is a 1 or nonzero number in the accumulator. When the 1 is finally shifted out, the branch not equal (BNE) instruction defaults and drops through to the next instruction, which routes the program back to repeat continuously the sequence.

Problem 2-4(a) Modify the program using another branch instruction in place of the BPL and BNE to exit from the left and right loops,

```
                   *
                   *BOUNCING BALL
                   *
0062 86 02         BBALL  LDA A  #2       INIT LITE ON AT LED '1'
0064 B7 8006       LEFT   STA A  $8006    OUTPUT POSITION OF BALL
0067 BD 0078              JSR    TIME     JMP TO DELAY SUB
006A 48                   ASL A           SHIFT LITE LEFT
006B 2A F7                BPL    LEFT     KEEP SHIFTING LEFT
006D B7 8006       RITE   STA A  $8006    LEFTMOST LITE ON SHIFT RT
0070 BD 0078              JSR    TIME     JMP TO DELAY SUB
0073 44                   LSR A           SHIFT LIGHT RT
0074 26 F7                BNE    RITE     KEEP SHIFTING RT
0076 20 EA                BRA    BBALL    EXIT FROM ROUTINE
```

(c) Bouncing Ball listing.

```
                   *
                   *DARK SPOT
                   *
0078 86 FD         DSPOT  LDA A  #$FD     INIT DSPOT AT LED '1'
007A BD 008A       LFLOOP JSR    DTIME    JMP SUB FOR DELAY & OUTPUT
007D 0D                   SEC             SET CARRY BIT
007E 49                   ROL A           SHIFT DSPOT RT
007F 2B F9                BMI    LFLOOP   KEEP SHIFTING LEFT
0081 BD 008A       RTLOOP JSR    DTIME    LEFTMOST LITE OFF SHIFT RT
0084 0D                   SEC             SET CARRY BIT
0085 46                   ROR A           SHIFT DSPOT RT
0086 24 F9                BCC    RTLOOP   KEEP SHIFTING RT
0088 20 EE                BRA    DSPOT    EXIT FROM ROUTINE
                   *
                   *
```

(d) Listing for Dark Spot.

Figure 2-6 continued.

respectively. **(b)** Write a bouncing ball problem where the light moves from LED1 to LED6 and back.

2-4 BOUNCING DARK SPOT

Write a program to invert the light pattern of the bouncing ball as shown in Fig. 2.6b by having 1 of 8 unlit LEDs move back and forth. The critical parts of the program are to shift 1's into the accumulator as a 0 shifts down the accumulator, and to select the appropriate branch instruction to exit from the loop. The carry bit must be set to 1 (C = 1) before the rotate right (ROR) and rotate left (ROL) instructions that shift 1's into the accumulator are executed. The condition code bits are set by one of the instructions from Table 4, Appendix IA.

The listing for the program that starts in location $0078 is given in Fig. 2-6d. The set carry instruction (SEC) assures that 1's will be shifted into the accumulator. It is one of the condition code register manipulation instructions. The branch if minus instruction (BMI) will keep the program in the left loop (LFLOOP) until a 0 is shifted into the bit 7 location. Then the branch instruction will default and the program will drop through and continue with the right loop (RTLOOP).

The Dark Spot program shares the same time-delay subroutine with the previous programs.

Problem 2-5(a) Write a program where the dark spot moves from bit 1 to bit 6 and back.

2-5 BASIC PROGRAM ORGANIZATION

The basic computer program (that is not interrupt driven) will have several modes or routines to manipulate data and an input control data routine to control or route the program to the appropriate routine. An input control routine ties several routines (e.g., the counter, bouncing ball, and dark spot) together into one larger program. In addition, the input control routine can discern or select which of the routines is to be executed, and then routes the program to that routine. The most typical example is a calculator that uses a variety of routines, such as add, subtract, multiply, and divide. The input control routine detects and then examines the input to route the program to the appropriate routine. On completion of the function routine, the program returns to the input control routine, which continuously samples the input control data. Where there is no input control data, the program stays in a "holding pattern" or loops to continuously sample the input control data for the next input.

System Problem Configuration and Definition

The *basic program* illustrates how input control data route the program to one of the three previous examples, the counter, bouncing ball, and dark spot routines (Fig. 2-7a). This type of organization can handle many more routines than are illustrated. The reader should be aware that, in this example, the input data are to be examined, but not manipulated or destroyed, and as such they are referred to as input control data.

Programs are written in response to specifications, which might be listed as:

- Input Port 8004 has eight switches.
- A closed switch will input a high voltage, or logic 1, and an open switch will input a logic 0.
- Output Port 8006 drives eight LEDs. A logic 1 output will turn on the appropriate LED, and a logic 0 will keep the LED off.
- When all the switches are open, branch back to the beginning of the input control routine, labelled INCONT.
- When switch 7 is closed, the count routine will be executed, regardless of the state of the other switches.
- When switch 6 is closed, the BBall routine will be executed, regardless of the state of switches 0 to 5.
- When switch 5 is closed, the DSPOT routine will be executed, regardless of the state of switches 0 to 4.

Listing of the Basic Program

The labels on the flow chart of Fig. 2-7b correlate with the labels in the program listing of Fig. 2-7c. For example, INIT is the label for the part of the program where the I/O ports are initialized.

INCONT	Input control routine
COUNT	Counter routine
BBALL	Bouncing ball routine
DSPOT	Dark spot routine

This chapter does not discuss the requirements for initializing the I/O ports. The I/O ports are part of the peripheral interface adaptor (PIA),

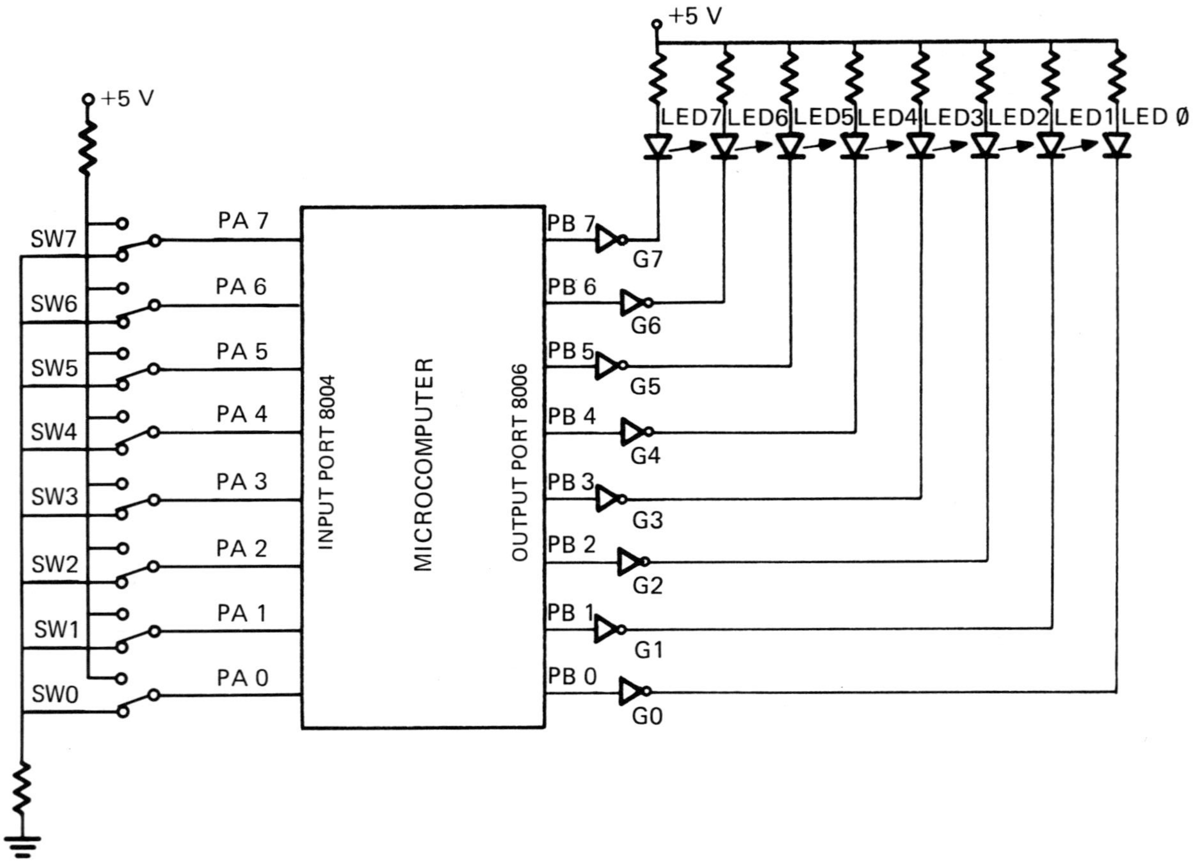

Figure 2-7A. Hardware configuration for basic program flow: Port A @ location 8004 input from 8 switches; Port B @ location 8006 output to 8 LEDs.

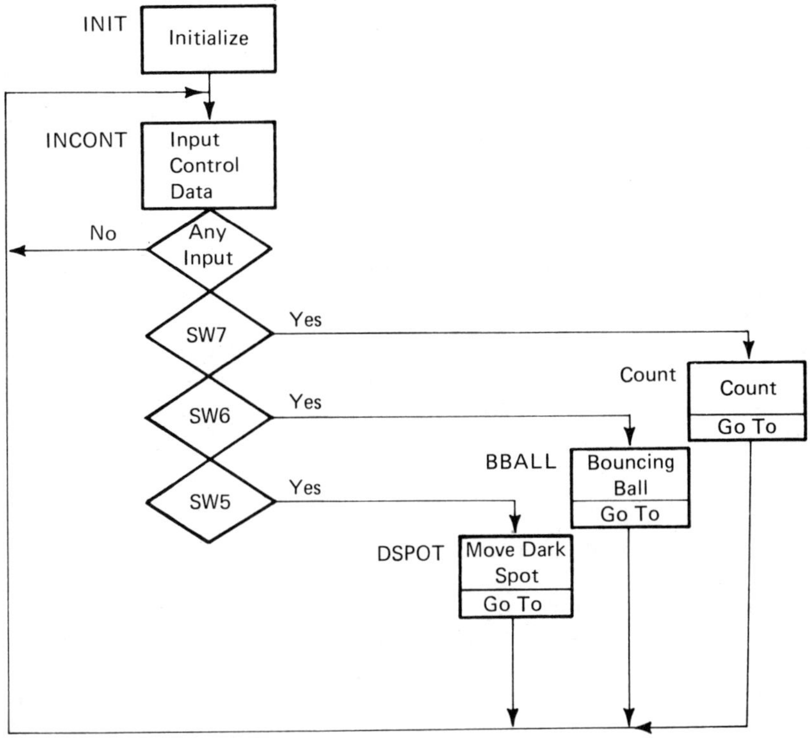

(b)

Figure 2-7B. "Basic Program" flow diagram.

and techniques for controlling the PIA are discussed in Chapter 7.

The reader must accept the initialization procedure as listed in Fig. 2-7c, and these instructions must be included to execute the program.

The Input Control Routine starts at the location labeled INCONT and inputs data from Port A at location \$8004 with a "load extended" (LDA A) instruction. As the input data is transferred to accumulator A the condition code bits are set, reporting the status of the input word. The next instruction, branch if equal (BEQ), will route the program back to INCONT if none of the input switches are closed and a zero is transferred into the accumulator A.

When one of the switches is closed and a non-zero number is transferred into delete accumulator A, the program will default to the next instruction which tests for a closed 7. If it is closed then a branch if minus (BMI) instruction will branch to the location labeled COUNT.

The BIT A Immediate \$40 and BIT A Immediate \$20 instructions test switch 6 and switch 5 for a 1 by ANDing bits 6 and 5 with 1 respectively, without destroying the input data. If the result of the

```
                    * INIT PORT 8006:OUTPUT, 8004,8020:INPUT
0020 86 FF    INIT   LDA A  #$FF
0022 B7 8006         STA A  $8006     INIT PORT 8006 TO OUTPUT
0025 86 02           LDA A  #$02
0027 B7 8005         STA A  $8005     SET UP CONTROL PORTS
002A B7 8007         STA A  $8007
002D B7 8021         STA A  $8021
                    * INPUT CONTROL DATA
                     LDS    #$00FF
0030 B6 8004  INCONT LDA A  $8004     INPUT 'CONTROL' DATA
0033 27 FB           BEQ    INCONT    IF NO SW CLOSED, RTN INCONT
0035 2B 1D           BMI    COUNT     IF SW 7 CLOSED, BR TO COUNT
0037 85 40           BIT A  #$40      EXAMINE SW6 (BBALL)
0039 26 27           BNE    BBALL     IF SW6 CLOSED BR TO BBALL
003B 85 20           BIT A  #$20      EXAMINE STATUS OF SW 5
003D 26 39           BNE    DSPOT     IF SW 5 CLOSED BR TO DSPOT
                    *
0054                 ORG    $0054
                    *
                    * COUNT PROGRAM
                    *
0054 4F       COUNT  CLR A
0055 B7 8006  LOOP   STA A  $8006     OUTPUT COUNT
0058 BD 00B3         JSR    TIME      JMP TO DELAY SUB 'TIME'
005B 4C              INC A            INCREMENT COUNT
005C 81 0B           CMP A  #$0B      COMPARE TO ENDCOUNT +1
005E 26 F5           BNE    LOOP      IF NO KEEP COUNTING
0060 20 CE           BRA    INCONT    ELSE EXIT FROM ROUTINE
                    *
                    *BOUNCING BALL
                    *
0062 86 02    BBALL  LDA A  #2        INIT LITE ON AT LED '1'
0064 B7 8006  LEFT   STA A  $8006     OUTPUT POSITION OF BALL
0067 BD 00B3         JSR    TIME      JMP TO DELAY SUB
006A 48              ASL A            SHIFT LITE LEFT
006B 2A F7           BPL    LEFT      KEEP SHIFTING LEFT
006D B7 8006  RITE   STA A  $8006     LEFTMOST LITE ON SHIFT RT
0070 BD 00B3         JSR    TIME      JMP TO DELAY SUB
0073 47              ASR A            SHIFT LIGHT RT
0074 26 F7           BNE    RITE      KEEP SHIFTING RT
0076 20 B8           BRA    INCONT    EXIT FROM ROUTINE
                    *
                    *DARK SPOT
                    *
0078 86 FD    DSPOT  LDA A  #$FD      INIT DSPOT AT LED '1'
007A BD 00B0  LFLOOP JSR    DTIME     JMP SUB FOR DELAY & OUTPUT
007D 0D              SEC              SET CARRY BIT
```

Figure 2-7C. Listing for Basic Program.

```
007E 49                ROL A            SHIFT DSPOT RT
007F 2B F9             BMI    LFLOOP    KEEP SHIFTING LEFT
0081 BD 00B0 RTLOOP    JSR    DTIME     LEFTMOST LITE OFF SHIFT RT
0084 0E                SEC              SET CARRY BIT
0085 46                ROR A            SHIFT DSPOT RT
0086 24 F9             BCC    RTLOOP    KEEP SHIFTING RT
0088 20 A6             BRA    INCONT    EXIT FROM ROUTINE
00B0 B7 8006 DTIME     STA A  $8006     OUTPUT IS PART OF SUB
00B3 7F 0000 TIME      CLR    $0000     DELAY LOOP PART OF SUB
00B6 7F 0001           CLR    $0001
00B9 7C 0000 DELAY     INC    $0000     INC LOC '0'
00BC 26 FB             BNE    DELAY     BR TO DELAY FOR 256 TIMES
00BE 7C 0001           INC    $0001     INC LOC '1'
00C1 26 F6             BNE    DELAY     BR TO DELAY FOR 256 TIMES
00C3 39                RTS
```

ANDing is a non-zero number that indicates that the switch was closed, and a branch if not equal (BNE) will route the program to the appropriate routine BBALL or DSPOT.

It is important to note that large problems and programs are an amalgamation of smaller problems and programs. The Counter, Bouncing Ball, and Dark Spot routines are small programs that can stand alone. This technique of segmenting a program into stand-alone modules that can later be incorporated into a total program is called modular programming and will be used throughout the book.

2-6 VARIABLE COUNTER INPUT DATA ROUTINES

A variable counter (V-counter) is a counter for which the three parameters, the start count, increment count, and end count, are determined by the user and input to the microcomputer prior to executing the V-counter routine that uses the data.

The counter discussed in Sec. 2-1 counts in a fixed or preprogrammed mode from 0 to $10 by 1's. The variable counter can count from $50 to $90 by 2's, $30 to $60 by 3's or from any start count to any end count by any increment count, where the numbers are 1-byte numbers. This implies that the basic program must be augmented to input data that will be operated on and modified by the V-counter routine.

Another input port with eight switches is added to the microprocessor system to input the count data. The system specification calls for the input data, start, end, and increment count, to be stored in memory locations 03, 04, and 05 respectively.

The hardware is expanded to include an input data port at location

$8020, which consists of eight switches. In this example the port assignments are

Location $8006	Ouput display port
Location $8004	Input control data port
Location $8020	Input data port

See Fig. 2-8. The programmer must know these port assignments to coordinate the hardware and software aspects of the system problem.

In the organization of this program each I/0 port is assigned a separate, distinct function. In fact, the port assignments are arbitrary, and systems may be built where some pins of a particular port may be input pins and others output pins. A specific pin assignment may be changed during the course of a program from an input to an output pin.

In this example the control data word indicates the significance of the input data word when

Start count if	SW 0 is closed and SW 7, 6, 5, 4 are opened
Increment count if	SW 1 is closed and SW 7, 6, 5, 4, 0 are opened
End count if	SW 2 is closed and SW 7, 6, 5, 4, 0, 1 are opened

For the user to input data to the system, the input data must first be entered onto the switch and then the appropriate input control word.

An input routine has two parts, the input data and an input control word to indicate the significance of the input data. Implied in the input control word, as agreed to in the system specifications, is information on what to do with the input data. See Fig. 2-8 for the hardware configuration and Fig. 2-9 a and b for the program listing.

The program for the variable counter is found in the Basic System with Input Data program; then it is selected when control switch 4 is closed. The label for the routine is VCNT. It starts at location $008A. This V-count program is similar to the count program except that the inputs are variables and not constants. The program starts with a load direct instruction that transfers the start count from location 03 to the accumulator. Then the program jumps to the subroutine DTIME, which outputs the data and generates the delay time.

The subroutine has two entry points; D time is the full subroutine and time is an entrance to a subset of the subroutine that generates only the time delay.

The count in Acc A is incremented by the add direct instruction, which adds the input increment stored in location 04 to the contents of the accumulator. The compare direct instruction compares the contents of the accumulator with the end count stored in location 05, and the condition code bits are set accordingly.

In this case, there may be no clear indication that the end count will always equal the count. For example, to count from zero to 100 by 3's, the count will be 99 and then 102, but never equal to 100, the end count. The branch if less or equal (BLS) applies to unsigned binary numbers and takes the branch if either the carry or zero bits are equal to 1: C = 1 or Z = 1. In examining the state of the condition codes in Table 2-1, the BLS instruction will keep the program in the VLOOP until the end count is greater then the count at which time the program defaults to the BRA INCONT instruction and returns the program to sample the state of the input control switches.

Input Data Routine

The selection of the input data, as with all the routines, is controlled by the input control routine. This program, as in most programs, examines the input control word and branches to execute the selected routine. The program then returns to the input control routine. The priority for executing the various routines is established by virtue of

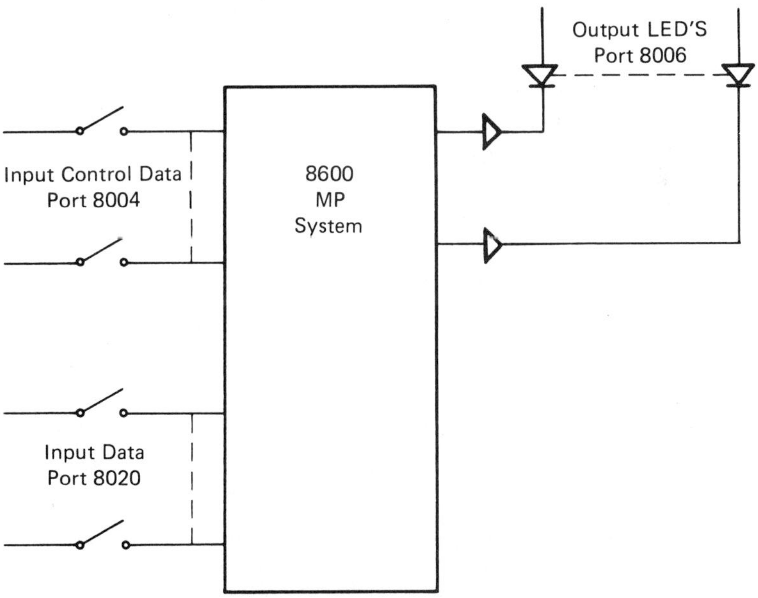

Figure 2-8. Hardware configuration of basic program flow with input data port.

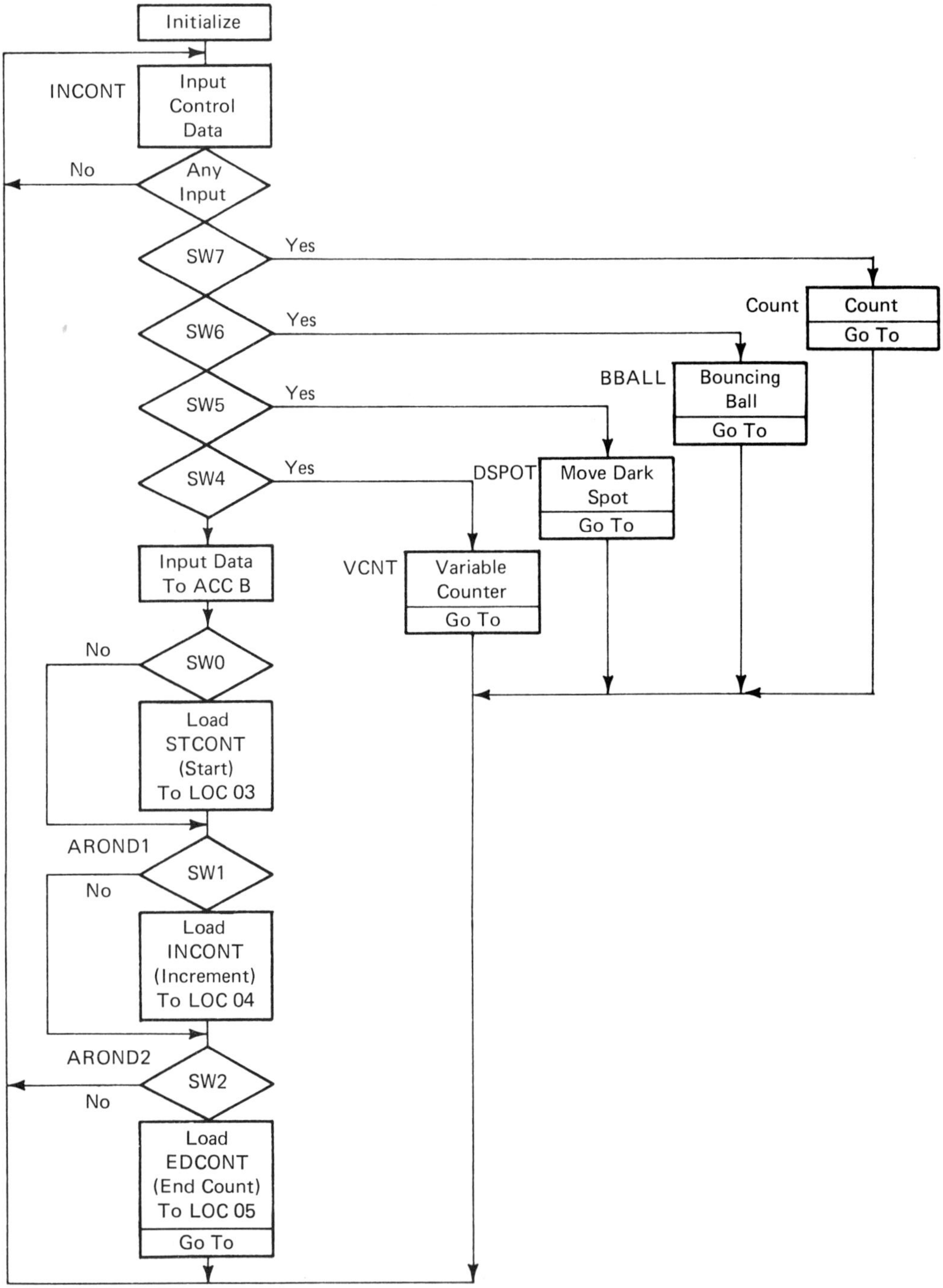

Figure 2-9A. Flow chart for basic program.

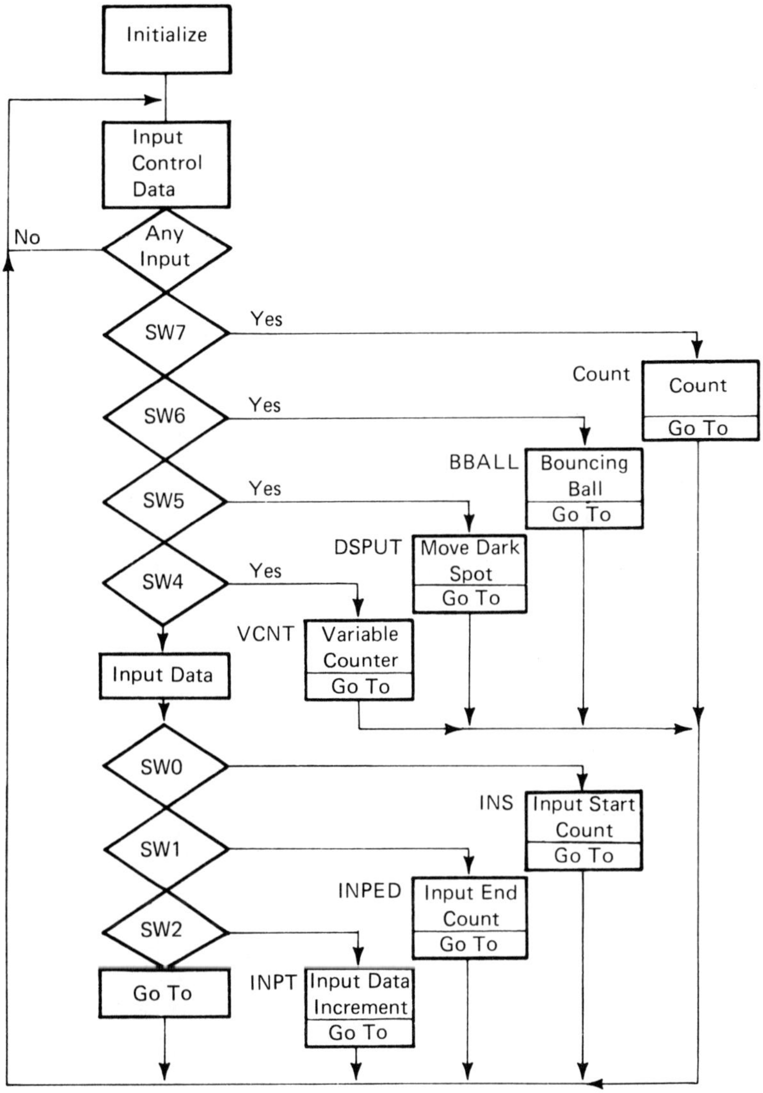

Figure 2-9B. Flow chart for basic program with variable input data.

which bit of the control word is examined first. In this example the sequence for testing is bits 7, 6, 5, 4, 0, 1, 2, where bits 0, 1, and 2 are input data routines. Just prior to testing these bits the input data are loaded into accumulator B, and they are transferred to the appropriate location by testing bits 0, 1, and 2 with the bit test instruction.

Programmers are often required to modify their programs. Good documentation, with a well-organized program with comments and a flow chart if required, permits the programmer to locate each routine with ease. With modular programming, each module can be discussed and modified and easily added to the main program.

Problem 2-6(a) Use the input control switch 3 to display the input control data with a time-delay loop. **(b)** Use the input control switch 3 to display the input control data without a time-delay loop. How does the display vary between parts (a) and (b)? **(c)** Use the input control switch 3 to display the input data word.

2-7 GUIDE TO READING A LISTING

Two types of notations are used in writing a program; symbolic notation and specific address. A label, for example, INCONT, COUNT, and TIME, are symbolic notations for memory locations. When labels are used, the actual address may be determined by examining the machine code for that instruction.

Example 1

```
0030  B6 8004 INCONT LDA A   $8004
0033  27 FB                 BEQ     INCONT
```

The instruction in location 33 is to branch to the location labeled INCONT which is in location 30. The rules for the branch instruction are:

PC ← (PC) + 0002 + REL
PC = 0033 + 0002 + FB   since each address has 4 hex characters
PC = 0035 + FFFB   which in binary is

$$\begin{array}{r} 0000\ 0000\ 0011\ 0101 \\ +\ 1111\ 1111\ 1111\ 1011 \\ \hline 0000\ 0000\ 0011\ 0000 \end{array}$$

PC = 0030

Example 2

```
0035  2B 1D                BMI     COUNT
                *
                *
00054 4F        COUNT   CLR A
```

The instruction in location 35 is to branch to the location labeled COUNT which is in location 54. The rules for the branch instruction are:

PC ← (PC) + 0002 + REL
PC = 0035 + 0002 + 1D   But an address has 4 hex characters
PC = 0037 + 001D   which in binary is

```
      0000 0000 0011 0111
    + 0000 0000 0001 1101
    ---------------------
      0000 0000 0101 0100
```

PC = 0054

Example 3

```
005B BD 00B3         JSR     TIME
00B3 7F 0000 TIME    CLR     $0000
```

The jump to subroutine instruction in location 58 indicates that the subroutine starts in location 00B3 and location 00B3 is labeled TIME.

```
          *VARIABLE COUNTER
          *
96 03     VCNT    LDA A   STCONT
BD 00B0   VLOOP   JSR     DTIME
9B 04             ADD A   INCCNT
91 05             CMP A   EDCONT
23 F7             BLS     VLOOP
20 99             BRA     INCONT
          *
```

Example 4

The machine code indicates that the symbol STCONT is stored in location 03. The machine code for the symbols INCCNT and EDCONT are in locations 04 and 05 respectively.

```
0003                 ORG     0003
0003 0001    STCONT  RMB     1           START COUNT
0004 0001    INCCNT  RMB     1           INCREMENT COUNT
0005 0001    EDCONT  RMB     1           END COUNT
0020                 ORG     $0020
             * INIT PORT 8006:OUTPUT, 8004,8020:INPUT
0020 86 FF   INIT    LDA A   #$FF
0022 B7 8006         STA A   $8006       INIT PORT 8006 TO OUTPUT
0025 86 02           LDA A   #$02
0027 B7 8005         STA A   $8005       SET UP CONTROL PORTS
002A B7 8007         STA A   $8007
002D B7 8021         STA A   $8021
0030 8E 00FF         LDS     #$00FF      LOAD SP
             * INPUT CONTROL DATA
0033 B6 8004 INCONT  LDA A   $8004       INPUT 'CONTROL' DATA
```

```
0036 27 FB              BEQ     INCONT    IF NO SW CLOSED, RTN INCONT
0038 2B 1D              BMI     COUNT     IF SW 7 CLOSED, BR TO COUNT
003A 85 40              BIT A   #$40      EXAMINE SW6 (BBALL)
003C 26 27              BNE     BBALL     IF SW6 CLOSED BR TO BBALL
003E 85 20              BIT A   #$20      EXAMINE STATUS OF SW 5
0040 26 39              BNE     DSPOT     IF SW 5 CLOSED BR TO DSPOT
0042 85 10              BIT A   #$10      EXAMINE SW 4
0044 26 47              BNE     VCNT      IF SW 4 CLOSED BR TO VCNT
0046 F6 8020 INDATA     LDA B   $8020     INPUT 'DATA' FROM PORT 8020
0049 85 01              BIT A   #$01      EXAMINE SW 0
004B D7 03              STA B   STCONT    IF SW 0 CLOSED, STORE STCONT
             *                           (STCONT) IN LOC 0003
004D 85 02              BIT A   #$02      EXAMINE SW 1
004F D7 05              STA B   EDCONT    IF SW 1 CLOSED STORE ENCONT
             *                           (EDCONT) IN LOC 0005
0051 85 04              BIT A   #$04      EXAMINE SW 2
0053 D7 04              STA B   INCCNT    IF SW 2 CLOSED STORE INCCNT
             *                           (INCCNT) IN LOC 0004
0055 20 DC              BRA     INCONT
             *
             * COUNT PROGRAM
             *
0057 4F      COUNT      CLR A
0058 B7 8006 LOOP       STA A   $8006     OUTPUT COUNT
005B BD 00B3            JSR     TIME      JMP TO DELAY SUB 'TIME'
005E 4C                 INC A             INCREMENT COUNT
005F 81 0B              CMP A   #$0B      COMPARE TO ENDCOUNT +1
0061 26 F5              BNE     LOOP      IF NO KEEP COUNTING
0063 20 CE              BRA     INCONT    ELSE EXIT FROM ROUTINE
             *
             *BOUNCING BALL
             *
0065 86 02   BBALL      LDA A   #2        INIT LITE ON AT LED '1'
0067 B7 8006 LEFT       STA A   $8006     OUTPUT POSITION OF BALL
006A BD 00B3            JSR     TIME      JMP TO DELAY SUB
006D 48                 ASL A             SHIFT LITE LEFT
006E 2A F7              BPL     LEFT      KEEP SHIFTING LEFT
0070 B7 8006 RITE       STA A   $8006     LEFTMOST LITE ON SHIFT RT
0073 BD 00B3            JSR     TIME      JMP TO DELAY SUB
0076 47                 ASR A             SHIFT LIGHT RT
```

```
0077 26 F7              BNE     RITE      KEEP SHIFTING RT
0079 20 B8              BRA     INCONT    EXIT FROM ROUTINE
             *
             *DARK SPOT
             *
007B 86 FD   DSPOT      LDA A   #$FD      INIT DSPOT AT LED '1'
007D BD 00B0 LFLOOP     JSR     DTIME     JMP SUB FOR DELAY & OUTPUT
0080 0D                 SEC               SET CARRY BIT
0081 49                 ROL A             SHIFT DSPOT RT
0082 2B F9              BMI     LFLOOP    KEEP SHIFTING LEFT
0084 BD 00B0 RTLOOP     JSR     DTIME     LEFTMOST LITE OFF SHIFT RT
0087 0D                 SEC               SET CARRY BIT
0088 46                 ROR A             SHIFT DSPOT RT
```

```
0089 24 F9              BCC     RTLOOP    KEEP SHIFTING RT
008B 20 A6              BRA     INCONT    EXIT FROM ROUTINE
                *
                *VARIABLE COUNTER
                *
008D 96 03      VCNT    LDA A   STCONT    START CNT TO A
008F BD 00B0    VLOOP   JSR     DTIME     SUB FOR DELAY &OUTPUT
0092 9B 04              ADD A   INCCNT    ADD INCREMENT CNT
0094 91 05              CMP A   EDCONT    COMPARE TO ENDCOUNT
0096 23 F7              BLS     VLOOP     STAY IN VLOOP IF LESS OR EQ
0098 20 99              BRA     INCONT    EXIT FROM ROUTINE
                *
                *DELAY LOOP SUBROUTINE
00B0                    ORG     $00B0
                *
00B0 B7 8006    DTIME   STA A   $8006     OUTPUT IS PART OF SUB
00B3 7F 0000    TIME    CLR     $0000     DELAY LOOP PART OF SUB
00B6 7F 0001            CLR     $0001
00B9 7C 0000    DELAY   INC     $0000     INC LOC '0'
00BC 26 FB              BNE     DELAY     BR TO DELAY FOR 256 TIMES
00BE 7C 0001            INC     $0001     INC LOC '1'
00C1 26 F6              BNE     DELAY     BR TO DELAY FOR 256 TIMES
00C3 39                 RTS

TOTAL ERRORS 00000
```

3 The Peripheral Interface Adapter:

A Programmable Peripheral Device with Interrupt

This chapter is an introduction to programmable peripheral devices (PPD) with interrupt-handling capabilities. The peripheral interface adapter (PIA) is described not only for understanding it specifically, but to offer an approach for understanding and controlling PPDs generally. This chapter also discusses the interrupt-handling capabilities of the PIA and follows the interrupt signal from an input pin on to the microprocessor. The description of how the 6800 microprocessor handles and responds to the various interrupts continues and is illustrated by a typical response.

Associated with each microprocessor are at least a half-dozen PPDs, which represent the third group of devices that make a microcomputer system: the microprocessor, the memory, and the I/O interface devices. See Fig. 1-1. A microcomputer, or any machine, is quite useless unless it performs some meaningful task, which requires the sensing or inputting of data, and responds with an appropriate output, logic, or number data. The need for the variety of I/O interface devices is dependent on the type of I/O application; for example,

- The I/O might be from input switches to controlling output switches, valves, and motors.
- The I/O might be from a terminal.
- The I/O might be from another computer.

The reader might intuitively appreciate that a different type of I/O interface device would be preferred for each I/O function.

In addition to requiring a different I/O interface device for the various applications, each of the various devices should have some built-in flexibility. Flexibility offers a cost advantage to both the semiconductor manufacturer and the user. The cost of most semiconductor devices is a function of the use of that device. The cost of high-volume devices is lower than that of the low-volume devices, and if the volume is too low, a device cannot be supported by the marketplace and will not be manufactured. Flexibility refers to building a device with several modes of operations, which consequently finds a larger market.

Historically, as integrated circuits became more complex, devices were designed with more than one mode of operation. For example, a digital clock chip was designed with two modes of operation, a 12-hour and a 24-hour clock. There is a mode-select pin which, when tied to either ground or +5 V, selects the mode or configures the device to behave as either a 12- or 24-h clock. The ability to select a mode of operation offered the semiconductor manufacturer a design that required the making and stocking of fewer parts, while offering the customer a larger variety of devices, thus benefiting both. The mode-select capability could, by using two mode select pins, be extended to a four-mode clock, 12 hours, 24 hours, 2 days, or 4 days, which is used by TV recorders. The disadvantage of this approach was that, once the device was soldered into the circuit and the mode was selected, it could not be altered. The ability to program the devices allows the selection of the mode of operation through programming, and this has been formalized with the microprocessor peripheral devices. These programmable peripheral devices exist by virtue of the economic advantage they afford for connecting the external I/O devices to the system.

General Characteristics of Programmable Peripheral Devices

All programmable peripheral devices have four types of registers: data input, data output, control, and status registers. Some devices have more than one control and status register. While in some devices these features are merged into one register, the data input and data output may share the same register and the control and status functions may share the same register. However, most PPDs have these characteristic registers and they are each addressable. It should be appreciated that each of the registers on the device has its unique address in the 64K memory space. The registers have contiguous register numbers that start from zero (i.e., 00, 01, 02, 03, etc.). The address of each register is obtained by adding the register number to the memory location of the device. For example, if the PPD is plugged into location \$7000, then the addresses of each of the four registers are \$7000, \$7001, \$7002, and \$7003. If a second PPD is plugged into location

$7004, then the addresses of each of the four registers are $7004, $7005, $7006, and $7007.

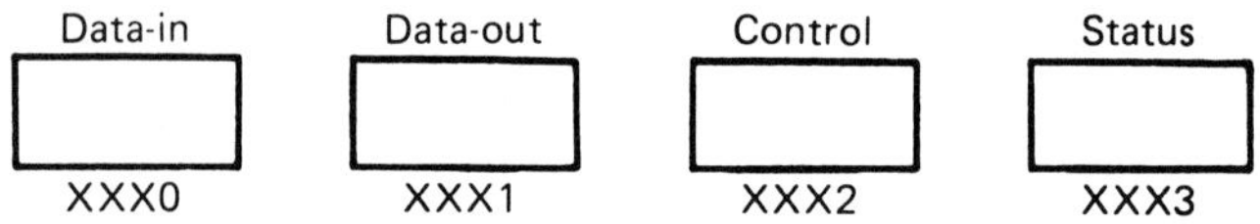

I/O Data Registers.

The programmer must know which registers are input, output, or combined I/O data registers. The programmer, by storing the data in the output register, is effectively outputing data, and refers to it as the output port. Likewise, the program, by loading data from an input register to the accumulator, is effectively inputing data to the microcomputer. The advantage of I/O registers of a PPD is that, when interfacing the microcomputer to a terminal, the programmer, by storing data in the output register, effectively outputs the data to the terminal. The programmer does not have to be cognizant of formating and serializing the data.

Control Register

The control register programs or configures the PPD devices. One of the several operating modes is selected or programmed by loading the control register with the appropriate word. Usually, the control register is loaded once during the initializing phase of the program, much as the 12/24 hour clock chip. The control register, however, may be reloaded or reprogrammed at any place in the program.

PDDs may have one or more control registers, and if they require fewer than 8-bits the control register may be shared with or store some status bits.

Status Register

To know the status of the data on the PPD, the program examines the status register. Some examples are as follows:

- Are there valid data in the input register or new data?
- Is the output register empty or, restated, have the data been

accepted or taken from the output?
- Has an interrupt occurred on this specific device?

The status register indicates:

- If valid or new data have been received by the input register.
- If the output register is empty or, restated, have the output data been transferred?
- If an interrupt has occurred on this device.

The program must then examine the status register to determine the status of a sequence of data before continuing to transmit or receive the next bytes of data.

Polling Versus Interrupts

Polling and interrupts are two techniques by which data flow into and out from the microprocessor through a peripheral device. Polling is the technique by which the data I/O flow is completely controlled by the program, and it is illustrated by the input control routine in Chapter 2. At a convenient place and time in the program, the program polls or interrogates an input port or control line to determine if data are to be input or output. A convenient place in the program is when each task is completed and the results neatly stored away before proceeding on to the next task.

The interrupt, on the other hand, is a means by which an external signal forces the microprocessor to suspend whatever task it is performing and immediately respond to that external signal, the interrupt. The advantage of the interrupt is the quick response of the microcomputer to the interrupt and its function. The disadvantage is that it can occur any time in the program and not at a moment convenient to the programmer.

The manner in which the microcomputer responds to an interrupt is similar to a response to a subroutine. A subroutine is a string of instructions that performs a task, and it can be called from any place in the program. When the subroutine is completed, the program continues on from that point in the program.

An interrupt is similar to a subroutine in that it can occur anywhere in the program, and when the interrupt routine is complete the program again returns to the main routine. Because an interrupt can occur anywhere in the program, care must be exercised to preserve the data in the accumulators, status register, and index register during the interrupt routine. To protect these data, when the 6800 microprocessor responds to an interrupt it automatically stores the data in all of the general registers, except the stack pointer, onto the stack. The return from interrupt (RTI) instruction restores the data from the stack back to the general registers, and the occurrence of the interrupt is transparent to the main program.

Initializing the Microprocessor and Its Programmable Peripheral Devices

Microcomputers, when turned on, go through an initializing procedure, or program, much as people do each day. There are two separate aspects to initializing: ourselves and the people we interact with. The microprocessor is analogous to ourselves and the PPDs are analogous to other people. In the morning, on rising, people go through an initializing procedure by washing, brushing their teeth, bathing or showering, and getting dressed. They have their breakfast and coffee, and do not want to meet or be interrupted by anyone until they have initialized or prepared themselves to interact with others. So the initializing routine must initialize or set the appropriate registers within the microprocessor before initializing the PPDs.

The two basic functions for initializing the PPDs are (1) to configure it to respond appropriately to that particular application, and (2) to permit or block the PPD from responding to an interrupt. Those PPDs that are not programmed to interrupt the microprocessor must, of course, be polled for inputs or outputs. There are two levels of interrupts, the local, or the interrupt from each PPD, and the master interrupt, or the microprocessor response to each of the local interrupts. It makes sense that, when too many PPDs need to be serviced simultaneously, it is the prerogative of the microprocessor to decide whether to respond or to temporarily ignore the local interrupts. The master interrupt response is controlled by the interrupt mask bit (I) in the condition code register. This chapter discusses all the interrupt responses of the 6800 microprocessor and the PPDs.

Referring to our analogy between the initializing process and people's behavior (how they initilize themselves), consider this possibility: a person might wake in the morning and, before he has completely "initialized" himself, the house might be on fire and he might have to run from the house. For such an interruption to the initializing process in the microprocessor there is a nonmaskable interrupt (NMI).

Suggested Approach to All Programmable Peripheral Devices

There are two approaches to learning about a semiconductor device: reading about it in the data sheet or using it in some fictitious example. Because the data sheets are written by experts to sell other experts, it is the author's suggestion that the beginner start to learn each PPD by using some fictitious example. He or she must learn the primary function of the device by reading the data sheet. After that the approach should be as indicated in Chapter 1, that is, to learn

- The function of each register.
- The address of each register.
- To predict the data in each register while single cycling through the program (this is meaningful in the output and control registers but not with the input or status registers).
- The pins of the PPDs.

3-1 PERIPHERAL INTERFACE ADAPTER 6821

The peripheral interface adapter (PIA) provides a universal means for interfacing the microcomputer system to I/O devices such as keyboards, printers, displays, and A/D converters. It has two 8-bit I/O ports, Port A and Port B, where each port and each of the 16 I/O pins are independently programmed as either input or output pins (see Fig. 3-1). Two control/interrupt lines associated with each port are used to facilitate the convenient transfer of data to and from the PIA, often with no external logic.

The control/interrupt lines are used to sense or initiate an interrupt response when data are either available at an input port or when a device at an output port is ready to accept data. Each control/interrupt line can be programmed to respond as either a control or interrupt line. In either case, when the appropriate signal appears at the control/interrupt pin, the event is also recorded in one of the status bits.

The control/interrupt lines have three special functions that can be programmed to send and receive a pulse in conjunction with data transmitted or received through the ports:

- Pulse mode
- Handshake mode
- Follower mode

PIA Pin Assignments

The PIA 6821 is in a 40-pin package with 20 I/O pins, 16 for the two I/O ports and 4 for the control/interrupt lines (Fig. 3-2). Of the 20 remaining pins, 2 are for power, +5 and 0 volts, and 1 is a reset pin that clears or resets all the registers of the PIA. The 17 remaining pins attach the PIA to the microprocessor's busses, 8 of which are connected to the bidirectional data bus. Four are attached to the control bus:

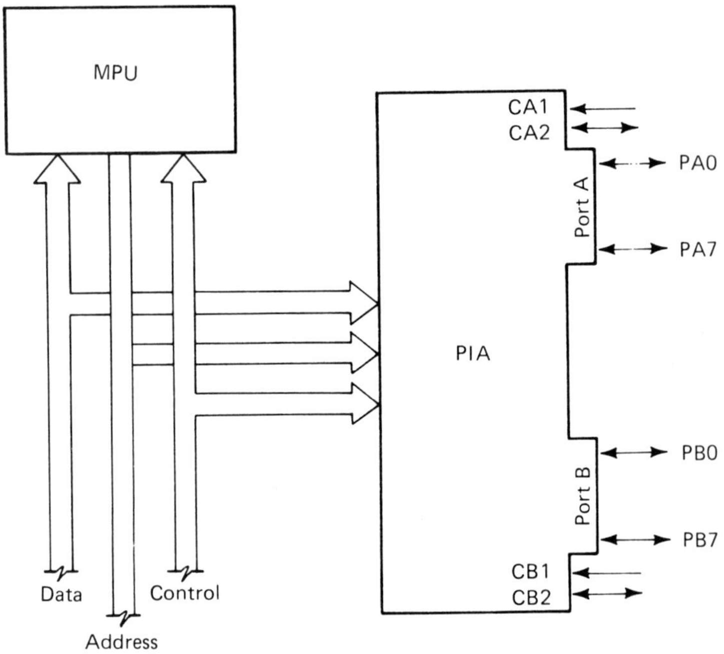

Figure 3-1. PIA I/O and bus connect pins.

- R/W, the read/write pin, which indicates the direction of the data flow.
- Enable or ∅2 pin, which keeps the peripheral devices in synchronization with the processor chip.
- Two interrupt lines, $\overline{IRQA}$ and $\overline{IRQB}$, to pass the interrupt signals from the A and B control/interrupt through to the processor, respectively, that are open-sourced lines.

Five pins are attached to the address bus:

- RSO and RSI, register select pins 0 and 1, attached to address pins A∅ and A1, respectively. They are used to select or address each register on the peripheral device.
- CSO, CSI, $\overline{CS2}$, chip select pins, attach the device into the memory space determined by the user. See Chapter 4.

The two register select pins indicate that each PIA occupies four of the total 64K memory space. The chip select pins indicate where the device fits into the total space. For example, a PIA could be located in spaces (hex)

8000, 8001, 8002, 8003
8021, 8022, 8023, 8024
9000, 9001, 9002, 9003

PIA Registers

The PIA has two symmetrical sections, A and B, but these are not completely identical in function. Each section has three registers, for a total of six registers:

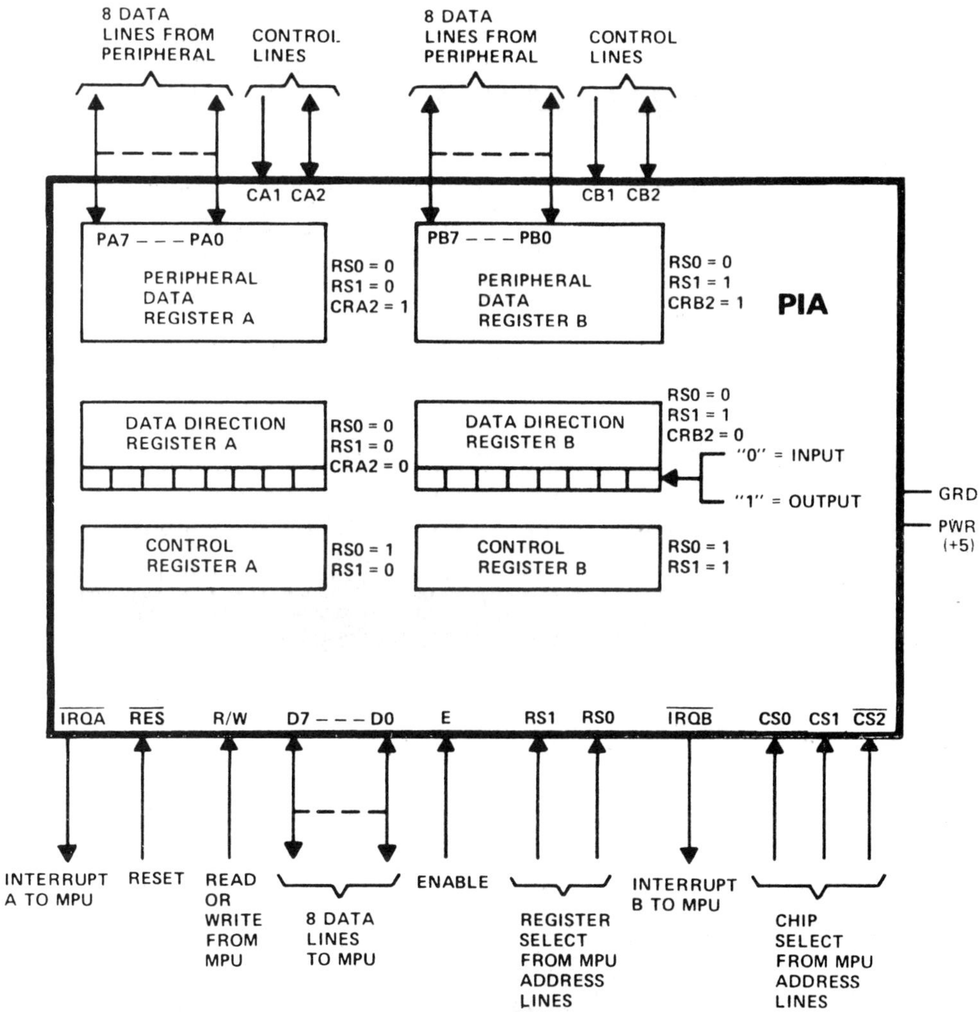

Figure 3-2. PIA block diagram.

- Peripheral data registers A and B are the I/O ports that latch or hold data for output.
- Data direction registers A and B determine which pins are programmed as output pins by putting a 1 into the corresponding register position. It should be noted that the reset pin resets the contents of all the registers to 0's which programs the I/O pins as inputs.
- Control registers A and B are used to program each half of the PIA.

Addressing the PIA Registers

The PIA has six registers and only two register select pins, RS0 and RS1, with which to select them (Fig. 3-3). This is an apparent contradiction since two pins can select only four, not six, registers.

The peripheral data (I/O) register and the data direction register share the same memory space. I/O port and data direction registers on the A side share register space 0, and the I/O port and data direction registers on the B side share register space 2. For example, if the PIA is in memory location $8000 then address

$8000	is	I/O Port A and data direction register A
$8001	is	Control register A
$8002	is	I/O Port B and data direction register B
$8003	is	Control register B

The contradiction of having two registers that share the same memory space is resolved with bit 2 of the control register:

If bit 2 = 0 then the data direction register is addressed
If bit 2 = 1 then the I/O port is addressed

There is no great disadvantage in having both the I/O port and the data direction register share the same memory space. In most applications the states of the I/O pins are initially set by loading the data direction register, which is often not modified during the program.

PIA Control Register

The two halves of the PIA behave nearly identically, the exception being that during the pulse and handshake modes of operation the B side prefers to be programmed as an output port and the A side prefers to be programmed as an input port for data transfers. The two PIA control registers, A and B, program each half of the PIA independently

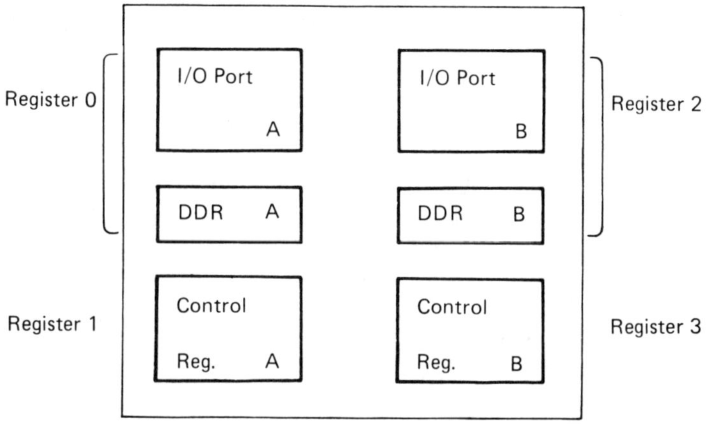

Figure 3-3. PIA register selection—addresses.

Control Register A (CRA)

7	6	5	4	3	2	1	Ø
IRQA1	IRQA2	CA2 Control			DDRA	CA1 Control	

← Status Bits → | ← Control Bits →

Control Register B (CRB)

7	6	5	4	3	2	1	Ø
IRQB1	IRQB2	CB2 Control			DDRB	CB1 Control	

Figure 3-4. Control register format.

and merge the characteristics of the control and status registers. There are four fields of the control register (see Fig. 3-4):

Bits	Control Reg. A		Control Reg. B
0, 1	CAI control		CBI control
2	Register Select	between	I/O port and DDR
3, 4, 5	CA2 control		CB2 control
6, 7	A status bits		B status bits

Addressing and Programming the Data Direction Registers (DDR)

The two DDRs, A and B, are selected by the register select pins RS0 and RS1, in conjunction with control bit 2 (CR-2) of the respective control registers (Fig. 3-5). DDR A is at register location 0 when CRA-2 is 0. DDR B is at register location 2 when CRB-2 is 0.

The reset pulse sets all the registers of the PIA to 0's, which offers the user two advantages. First, by initially loading the DDRs with 0's, it programs each I/O as an input pin. This avoids the problem of inadvertently turning on motors and displays during the power-up sequence, rather than under program control. Second, since control bit 2 (CR-2) is also initially set to zero, the programmer can select and program the I/O pins before proceeding with the program.

		CONTROL REGISTER BIT		
RS_1	RS_0	CRA-2	CRB-2	LOCATION SELECTED
0	0	1	X	Peripheral Register A
0	0	0	X	Data Direction Register A
0	1	X	X	Control Register A
1	0	X	1	Peripheral Register B
1	0	X	0	Data Direction Register B
1	1	X	X	Control Register B

X = Don't Care

Figure 3-5. Internal register addressing.

Examples for Setting I/O Pin Assignment

Assume that two PIAs are in the system at locations \$8000 and \$8020. This furnishes the user with four I/O ports at locations \$8000, \$8002, \$8020, and \$8022 and their respective control registers at locations \$8002, \$8003, \$8021, and \$8023. Assume a reset pulse has just initiated the PIA, and then

- Set Port \$8000 as an input port.
- Set Port \$8002 as an output port.
- Set Port \$8020—bits 0 to 3 as inputs, and bits 4 to 7 as outputs.
- Set Port \$8022—the odd bits as inputs, and the even bits as outputs.
- Set the control bit 2 at all control registers.

The initializing routine:

- Port $8000 is programmed as an input port.

LDA A #$FF	Put all 1's into Acc A
STA A $8002	Move to DDR 8002 and set port 8002 to all outputs
LDA A #$F0	
STA A $8020	Set port 8020 bits 0 to 3 as input; bits 4 to 7 as output
LDA A #$55	
STA A $8022	Set port 8022: odd bits as inputs and even bits as output

- Now set each control bit 2 and enable the programmer to address the I/O port.

```
LDA A #$04
STA A $8000
STA A $8002
STA A $8020
STA A $8022
```

Problem 3-1 Write the same routine using the index addressing mode.

3-2 PROGRAMMING INTERRUPTS

There are four aspects to the interrupt response at the PIA:

- At the input pin of the control/interrupt line, to decide if the input is an interrupt or to be polled, and whether that should be a positive- or negative-going pulse.
- When the interrupt occurs, to store that event in one of the status bits, which on this device are bits 6 and 7 of the control registers.
- If an interrupt is programmed, to pass the signal from an interrupt request pin of the PIA to the interrupt request signal of the microprocessor.
- To reset the interrupt status bits after the interrupt is serviced.

Control/Interrupt Lines CA1, CA2, CB1, CB2

Interrupts originate at one of the four control/interrupt lines CA1, CA2, CB1, and CB2, and they are used to control the flow of data through the I/O ports. They indicate whether there are input data at a port or that an output device outside the microcomputer is ready to accept data. Two critical factors determine each control/interrupt input:

- Whether the response time to an input or output is critical. When a quick I/O reaction is required, the PPD is programmed to respond to an interrupt. When the PPD is to be polled for an I/O, then block or inhibit the interrupt response.
- Whether the PIA is to respond to a positive- or negative-going pulse.

The four variations for programming the way that the PIA responds to an input at either CA1 or CB1 are controlled by bits 0 and 1 of the respective control registers, and are listed in Table 3-1. Control bit 1 (CR-1) determines if the PIA responds to a positive or negative pulse. If CR-1 = 0, then the PIA responds to a negative transition; if CR-1 = 1, then it responds to a positive transition. The status bit referred to as the interrupt flag (IRQ1) in control register bit 7 (CR-7) is set to a 1 when the appropriate transition occurs at the CA1 or CB1 inputs, respectively. This effectively remembers that the event occurred, and it is stored in bit CR-7.

It is worth making a comment on the preference of the PIA to respond to a pulse transition, rather than a logical voltage level, either +5 or 0 Vs. Take the case when a printer, a slow electromechanical device, requests the next byte of data from the microcomputer by putting a high signal on the CA1 pin. The microcomputer can respond so much more quickly than the printer and output the data. If, however, the printer does not respond quickly enough and pulls the signal at CA1 low, then the microcomputer might interpret the high signal at CA1 as a request for the next byte of data. This problem is resolved by having the PIA respond to a pulse transition, rather than a voltage level.

Control bit 0 (CR-0) determines if the PIA responds to an interrupt or not. If bit CR-0 = 1, an interrupt is programmed, and the interrupt signal from either CA1 or CB1 will set the respective IRQA1 or IRQB1 status bit, and the output interrupt request signal at $\overline{\text{IRQA}}$ or $\overline{\text{IRQB}}$, respectively, goes low.

If bit CR-0 = 0, the appropriate input transition at either CA1 or CB1 will set the respective IRQA1 or IRQB1 status bit, but the output interrupt request signals at $\overline{\text{IRQA}}$ and $\overline{\text{IRQB}}$, respectively, remain high, blocking the interrupt signal. It is worth noting that, whether or not an interrupt is programmed, the appropriate transition at the CA1 or the CB1 pins sets the IRQ status bit (CR-7). Polling then is a routine that examines the respective IRQ status bit for an input, and may also

Table 3-1

CONTROL OF INTERRUPT INPUTS CA_1 AND CB_1

CRA-1 (CRB-1)	CRA-0 (CRB-0)	INTERRUPT INPUT CA_1 (CB_1)	INTERRUPT FLAG CRA-7 (CRB-7)	MPU INTERRUPT REQUEST $\overline{IRQA}$ ($\overline{IRQB}$)
0	0	↓ Active	Set HIGH on ↓ of CA_1 (CB_1)	Disabled – $\overline{IRQ}$ remains HIGH
0	1	↓ Active	Set HIGH on ↓ of CA_1 (CB_1)	Goes LOW when the interrupt flag bit CRA-7 (CRB-7) goes HIGH
1	0	↑ Active	Set HIGH on ↑ of CA_1 (CB_1)	Disabled – $\overline{IRQ}$ remains HIGH
1	1	↑ Active	Set HIGH on ↑ of CA_1 (CB_1)	Goes LOW when the interrupt flag bit CRA-7 (CRB-7) goes HIGH

Notes:
1. ↑ indicates positive transition (LOW-to-HIGH)
2. ↓ indicates negative transition (HIGH-to-LOW)
3. The Interrupt flag bit CRA-7 is cleared by an MPU Read of the A Data Register, and CRB-7 is cleared by an MPU Read of the B Data Register.
4. If CRA-0 (CRB-0) is LOW when an interrupt occurs (Interrupt disabled) and is later brought HIGH, $\overline{IRQA}$ ($\overline{IRQB}$) occurs after CRA-0 (CRB-0) is written to a "1".

Table 3-2

CONTROL OF CA_2 AND CB_2 AS INTERRUPT INPUTS
CRA-5 (CRB-5) is LOW

CRA-5 (CRB-5)	CRA-4 (CRB-4)	CRA-3 (CRB-3)	INTERRUPT INPUT CA_2 (CB_2)	INTERRUPT FLAG CRA-6 (CRB-6)	MPU INTERRUPT REQUEST $\overline{IRQA}$ ($\overline{IRQB}$)
0	0	0	↓ Active	Set HIGH on ↓ of CA_2 (CB_2)	Disabled – $\overline{IRQ}$ remains HIGH
0	0	1	↓ Active	Set HIGH on ↓ of CA_2 (CB_2)	Goes LOW when the interrupt flag bit CRA-6 (CRB-6) goes HIGH
0	1	0	↑ Active	Set HIGH on ↑ of CA_2 (CB_2)	Disabled – $\overline{IRQ}$ remains HIGH
0	1	1	↑ Active	Set HIGH on ↑ of CA_2 (CB_2)	Goes LOW when the interrupt flag bit CRA-6 (CRB-6) goes HIGH

Notes:
1. ↑ indicates positive transition (LOW-to-HIGH)
2. ↓ indicates negative transition (HIGH-to-LOW)
3. The Interrupt flag bit CRA-6 is cleared by an MPU Read of the A Data Register and CRB-6 is cleared by an MPU Read of the B Data Register.
4. If CRA-3 (CRB-3) is LOW when an interrupt occurs (Interrupt disabled) and is later brought HIGH, $\overline{IRQA}$ ($\overline{IRQB}$) occurs after CRA-3 (CRB-3) is written to a "1".

be necessary when two or more inputs have been programmed for interrupts, and the program must decide where the interrupt originated.

Control/Interrupt Pins CA2 and CB2

The CA2 and CB2 control/interrupt lines have two degrees of freedom (see Table 3-2). They may be input or output control lines, and are programmed by bits 3, 4, and 5 of the respective control registers. This section discusses the input characteristics when CR-5 = 0; Sec. 3-4 discusses the output characteristics when CR-5 = 1. When CA2 and CB2 are programmed as inputs, bits 4 and 3 are used much like bits 1 and 0 are used to control the CA1 and CB1 lines.

	CA1/CB1	CA2/CB2
Interrupt bit	CR-0	CR-3
Transition bit	CR-1	CR-4
Status bit	CR-7	CR-6

During interrupts, the CA1 and CA2 lines share the $\overline{\text{IRQA}}$ and the CB1 and CB2 lines share the $\overline{\text{IRQB}}$ output pins.

Tracking the Interrupt Signal through the PIA

Tracking the input signals through the PIA is illustrated in Fig. 3-6, where the interrupt is inhibited in Fig. 3-6a and masked or allowed in Fig. 3-6b. Both illustrations apply to the CA1 and CA2 lines. The status bits are READ ONLY bits, which means that they cannot be affected when transferring data from the accumulator to the control register. They are set by an input signal at CA1 or CA2, and they are reset by reading data (LDA) at Port A.

Example: Assume that control register A is loaded with \$04 (Fig. 3-6a), where both CA1 and CA2 are programmed to respond to a negative transistor and inhibit an interrupt.

1. A negative transition at CA1 (pin 40) sets status bit IRQA1 at (CRA-7) high and implies that there is input data at Port A. The program then polls IRQA1 and senses that there is input data at Part A.
2. The IRQA1 status bit is reset by a READ or by having the

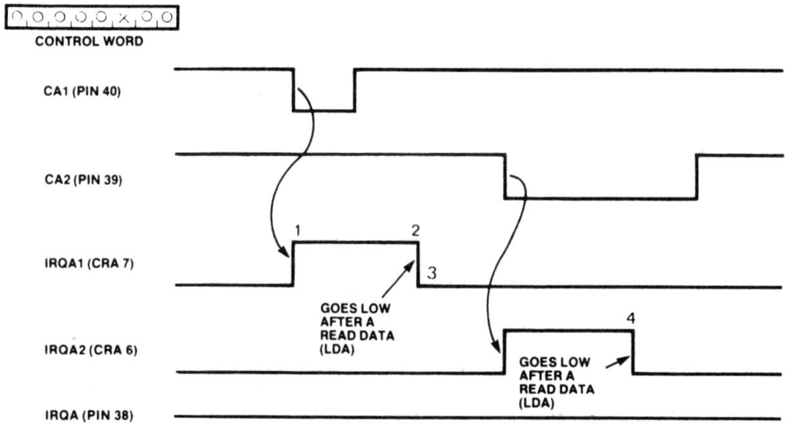

(a) ↓ CA1 and ↓ CA2 (input) control to inhibit interrupt.

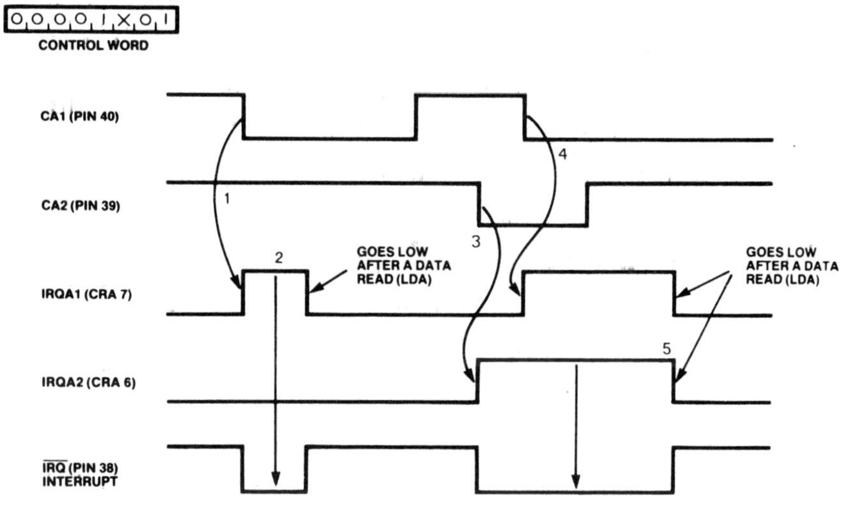

(b) ↓ CA1 and ↓ CA2 (input) control to allow interrupt.

Figure 3-6. Control/interrupt signals.

microprocessor execute a LOAD from Port A instruction.

3. A negative transition at CA2 (pin 39) sets status bit IRQA2 at (CRA-6) high. The program then polls, and if IRQA2 is high, then data have been transferred through to Port B.
4. The IRQA2 status bit is reset by having the microprocessor execute a LOAD from Port A instruction.

Note: The response of the microcomputer system is independent of the CA1 and CA2 pulse widths.

Example: In Fig. 3-6b, assume that an interrupt is enabled by a negative transition loading the control register with $0D.

1. In this example a negative transition at CA1 (pin 40) both sets status bit IRQA1 and outputs interrupt request signal $\overline{\text{IRQA}}$ (pin 38), which is connected to the $\overline{\text{IRQ}}$ pin of the microprocessor.
2. Because of the interrupt, it is assumed that the response of the microprocessor is much faster than without the interrupt. However, the status bit IRQA1 and the output signal $\overline{\text{IRQA}}$ (pin 38) are reset by a READ or LOAD instruction from the microprocessor.
3. A negative transition at CA2 (pin 39) sets status bit IRQA2 and outputs a signal at IRQA (pin 38).
4. If a negative transition occurs at CA2 (pin 39), then status bit IRQA2 is set and the output signal $\overline{\text{IRQA}}$ is already low.
5. A READ or LOAD Port A instruction resets both status bits IRQA1 and IRQA2 and the output signal $\overline{\text{IRQA}}$.

3-3 HOW THE 6800 MICROPROCESSOR RESPONDS TO AN INTERRUPT

The 6800 has four different interrupts, three hardware and one software, whose vectors are stored in the eight highest memory locations, $FFF8 to $FFFF (Table 3-3). The interrupt vector is the starting address of each of the interrupt routines. There are four parts to an interrupt response. The first is to store the return address from the interrupt onto the stack, the same as when calling a subroutine. The second is to store the data in the general registers, except the address in the stack pointer, onto the stack. This action is necessary because the programmer cannot predict when the interrupt will occur, and to assure that the data from the main routine is not inadvertently destroyed, it is advisable to store away the data on the stack. The third part sets the interrupt mask bit, which inhibits the microprocessor from responding to an IRQ signal ($I \leftarrow 1$). Resetting the interrupt mask to zero enables an interrupt request signal from a PPD to pass or to be masked onto the microprocessor. Although all the interrupts set the interrupt mask bit, only the IRQ is inhibited, giving it the lowest interrupt response priority. Having the IRQ set the interrupt mask bit implies that the microprocessor responds to only one interrupt request at a time. The programmer can override this limitation by clearing the interrupt masks.

When returning from an interrupt request (IRQ), the interrupt mask bit is cleared by reloading the condition code register from the stack.

Table 3-3. Memory Map for Interrupt Vectors

Vector MS	Vector LS	Description
FFFE	FFFF	Restart
FFFC	FFFD	Nonmaskable interrupt
FFFA	FFFB	Software interrupt
FFF8	FFF9	Interrupt request

The state of the I-bit had to have been cleared or the IRQ would not have occurred. The fourth part of the interrupt is to vector or jump to the interrupt routine by transferring the vector address to the program counter (Table 3-3).

The three hardware interrupts are each initiated by a pulse at their respective pins: reset, nonmaskable interrupt (NMI), and interrupt request (IRQ). They are listed in their order of priority.

The software interrupt (SWI) is an instruction and is initiated as all other instructions. The four parts of the interrupt,

- Store the program counter
- Store the general registers, except stack pointer
- Set the interrupt mask (I ← 1)
- Vector to address listed in Table 3-3

are listed in Table 3-4. The difference between the software and the three hardware interrupts is that the hardware interrupts are initiated by a pulse at the respective input pin and not by an instruction.

Software Interrupt Instruction (SWI)

The software interrupt instruction (SWI, Table 3-4) was included in the instruction set to be used by a monitor-type program in anticipation of debugging a program. When debugging, a programmer puts a breakpoint at a strategic address location, and when a program passes that point, it breaks or stops the program. This peripheral device converts the interrupt input signal from the transition pulse to a level pulse, which is input to the $\overline{\text{IRQ}}$ pin. The processor fetches the IRQ vectored interrupt address from locations $FFF8 and $FFF9 and then starts the interrupt sequence.

Return from Interrupt

The 6800 has separate return from interrupt and return from subrou-

PROGRAM TITLE: PROGRAMMING I/O PORTS (SEC 3.3)

PAGE OF		PROGRAMMER:							
PC	MACHINE CODE	LABEL	MNEM	OPERAND	COMMENTS	N	Z	V	C
		* LOAD STACK POINTER							
			LDS	#$00FF					
		* LOAD INDEX REGISTER & INITIALIZE I/O PORTS BY							
		* LOADING THE DATA DIRECTION REGISTER							
			LDX	#$8000					
			LDAA	#$55	INITIALIZE PORT A				
			STAA	4,X	AT $8004				
			LDAB	#$0F	INITIALIZE PORT B				
			STAA	6,X	AT $8006				
			LDAA	#$80	INITIALIZE PORT A				
			STAA	$20,X	AT $8020				
			LDAA	#$FF	INITIALIZE PORT B				
			STAA	$22,X	AT $8022				
		* LOAD CONTROL REGISTERS & INITIALIZE CONTROL LINES							
		* SET BIT 2 & SELECT THE I/O PORTS.							
			LDAA	#$15	SET CONTROL A (0001 0101)				
			STAA	5,X	AT $8005				
			LDAA	#$06	SET CONTROL B				
			STAA	7,X	AT $8007				
			LDAA	#$04	SET DATA DIRECTION BIT				
			STAA	$21,X	AT $8021				
			STAA	$23,X	AT $8023				

Table 3-4. Software Interrupt

SWI

Software Interrupt

Operation:

PC ← (PC) + 0001
↓ (PCL) , SP ← (SP)-0001
↓ (PCH) , SP ← (SP)-0001
↓ (IXL) , SP ← (SP)-0001
↓ (IXH) , SP ← (SP)-0001
↓ (ACCA) , SP ← (SP)-0001
↓ (ACCB) , SP ← (SP)-0001
↓ (CC) , SP ← (SP)-0001
I ← 1
PCH ← (n-0005)
PCL ← (n-0004)

Description: The program counter is incremented (by 1). The program counter, index register, and accumulator A and B, are pushed into the stack. The condition codes register is then pushed into the stack, with condition codes H, I, N, Z, V, C going respectively into bit positions 5 thru 0, and the top two bits (in bit positions 7 and 6) are set (to the 1 state). The stack pointer is decremented (by 1) after each byte of data is stored in the stack.

The interrupt mask bit is then set. The program counter is then loaded with the address stored in the software interrupt pointer at memory locations (n-5) and (n-4), where n is the address corresponding to a high state on all lines of the address bus.

Condition Codes:

H: Not affected.
I: Set.
N: Not affected.
Z: Not affected.
V: Not affected.
C: Not affected.

Boolean Formula for Condition Codes:

I = 1

Addressing Modes, Execution Time, and Machine Code (hexadecimal/octal/decimal):

Addressing Modes	Execution Time (No. of cycles)	Number of bytes of machine code	Coding of First (or only) byte of machine code		
			HEX.	OCT.	DEC.
INHERENT	12	1	3F	077	063

tine (RTS) instructions. The difference is that in the return from subroutine the index register, accumulators A and B, and the condition codes are returned from the stack, in addition to the program counter. In other microprocessors there is just one POP or RETURN instruction, which applies to both the return from interrupt and subroutine, the reason being that in these microprocessors the general registers are pushed onto the stack as part of the interrupt routine.

Programming the I/O Ports and the Control/Interrupt Lines

Assume that there are two PIAs, at locations $8004 and $8020, and that for the PIA at location $8004 the following applies:

- Port A at location $8004 has 4 inputs and 4 outputs, alternately starting at PA7 (0101 0101).
- CA1 responds to a negative-going pulse and initiates an interrupt (01).
- CA2 responds to a positive-going pulse and no interrupt (010).
- Port B at location $8006 has four inputs, bits 4 to 7, and four outputs, bits 0 to 3 (0000 1111).
- CBI responds to a positive pulse and no interrupt (10).
- CB2 is not used (000).

The PIA at location $8020 has the keyboard and seven-segment display from Chapter 6:

- Port A at location $8020 has six inputs and an output at PA7 (1000 0000).
- CA1 and CA2 are not used: (00) and (000).
- Port B at location $8022 has all outputs (1111 1111).
- CB1 and CB2 are not used: (00) and (000).

See Fig. 3-7.

3-4 PARALLEL COMMUNICATION

The PIA has features that facilitate the convenient transfer of parallel data to and from printers, instruments, and other computers. Because of the large number of wires, parallel communication is generally used between devices that have close proximity. These features are activated through the control/interrupt line and are controlled by bits 3, 4, and 5 of the respective control registers. The three modes of operations and their CR5, CR4, and CR3 bit codes are as follows:

- Pulse mode (101)
- Handshake mode (100)
- Following mode (110 or 111)

The parallel communication modes are initiated by setting control bit 5 to a 1, which also makes the CA2 and CB2 lines output control lines. The two sections of the PIA, A and B, are different in these communication modes. The B side is always the output or transmitter of data, and the A side is always the input or receiver of data.

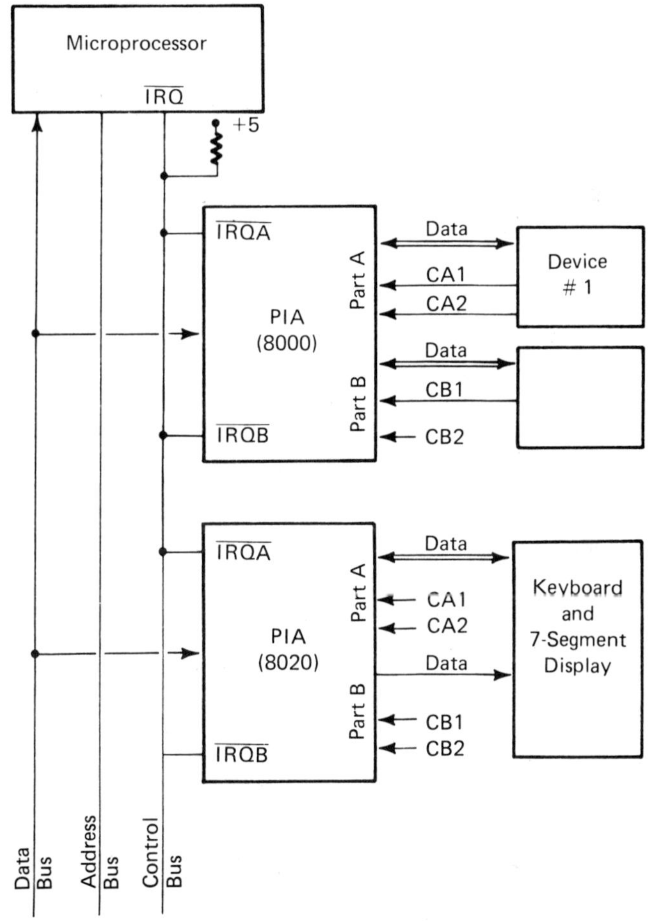

Figure 3-7. Connecting the interrupt request signals between the PIAs and the microprocessor.

General Nature of Control Signals

Before discussing the control signals of the PIA, it is worth discussing the general nature of control signals when transferring data between a transmitting and a receiving device (Fig. 3-8). When transferring data between two devices, the device that initiates the transfer is referred to as the controlling device, while the other is the responding device. The microcomputer could be used in all four positions:

- As the controlling device and receiving data
- As the controlling device and transmitting data
- As the responding device and receiving data
- As the responding device and transmitting data

However, in the examples to follow, the microcomputer will be the responding device. The output control signals at CA2 and CB2 may be either a pulse or a logic level, depending on whether the programmer selects the pulse or handshake modes of operation.

Pulse Mode at Port A

In the pulse mode at Port A (Fig. 3-9), by virtue of executing the load instruction (LDA), the data are transferred to the accumulator, and an output control pulse is automatically placed at the CA2 pin. The control pulse indicates to the transmitting device that the data have been accepted.

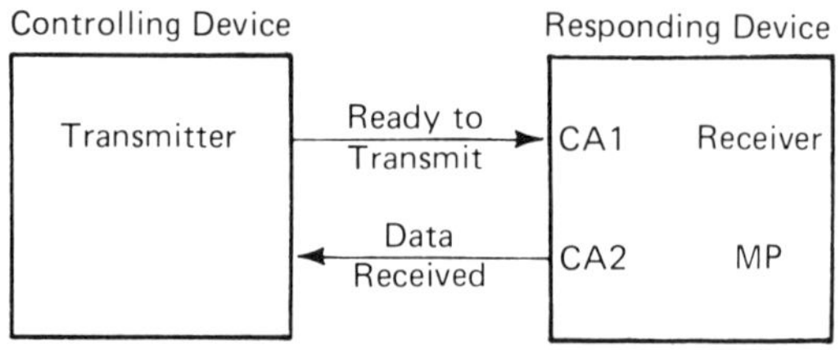

(a) The Transmitter controls the data transfer

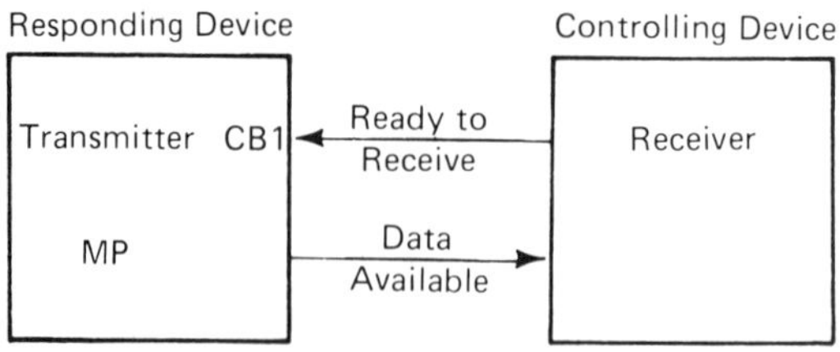

(b) The Receiver controls the data transfer

Figure 3-8. Control pulses for data transfer.

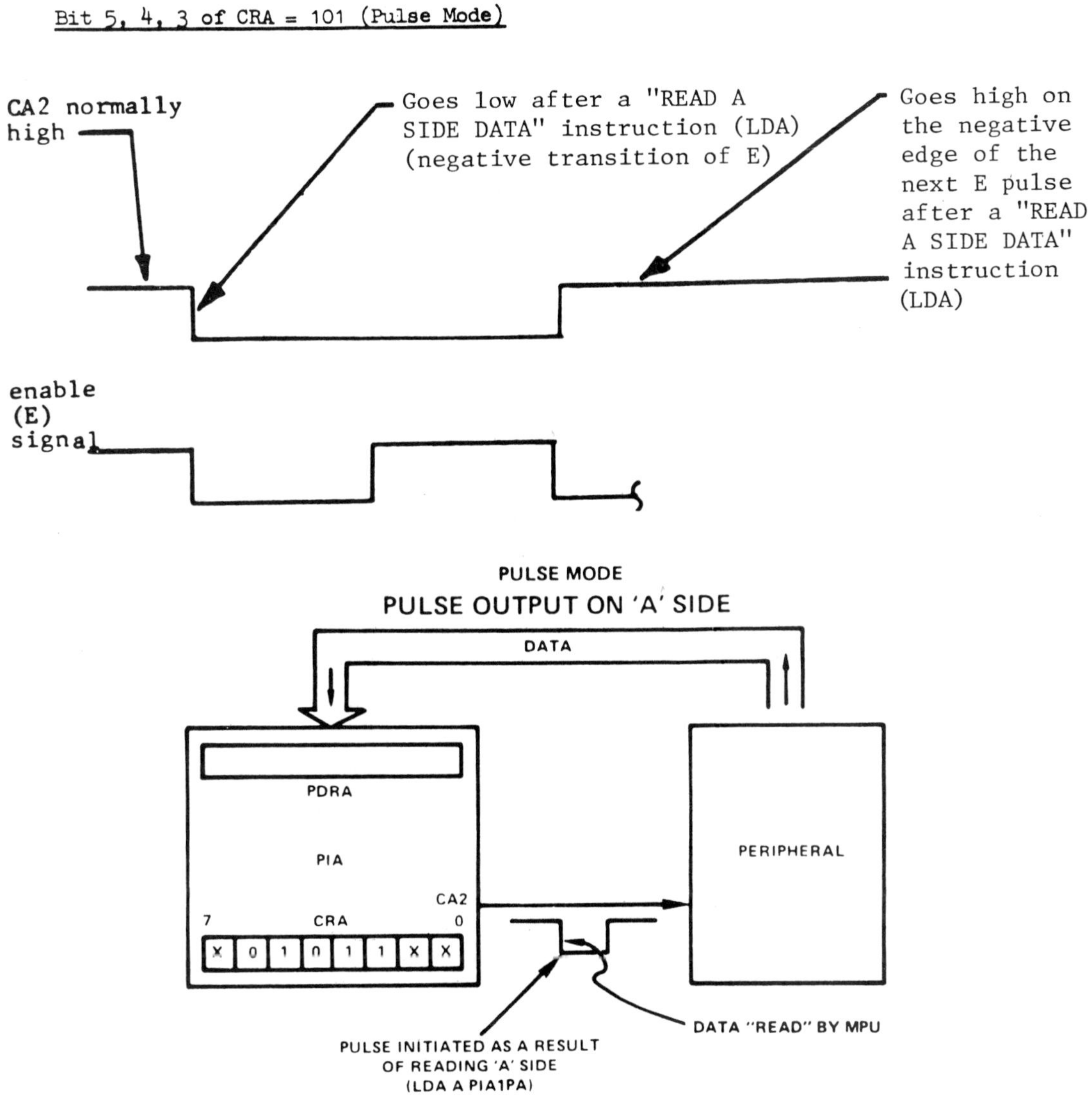

Figure 3-9. Pulse output on "A" side.

In speculating on when the pulse mode, as described, may be used, it seems that the receiver is in control and accepts data whenever it is ready. This implies that the transmitter transmits data at a faster rate than the receiver can accept it. An alternate application of the pulse mode is when the microcomputer responds to an interrupt from the transmitter (Fig. 3-8a). The interrupt may be initiated by a positive or

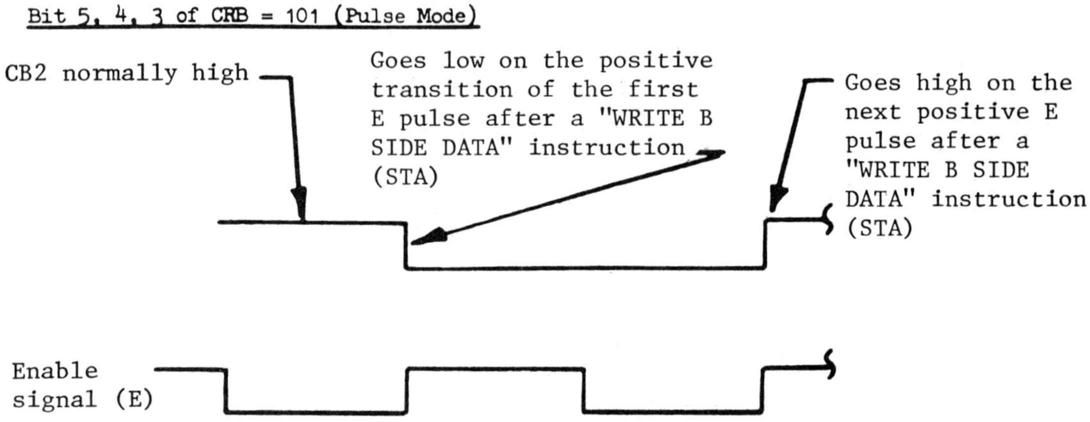

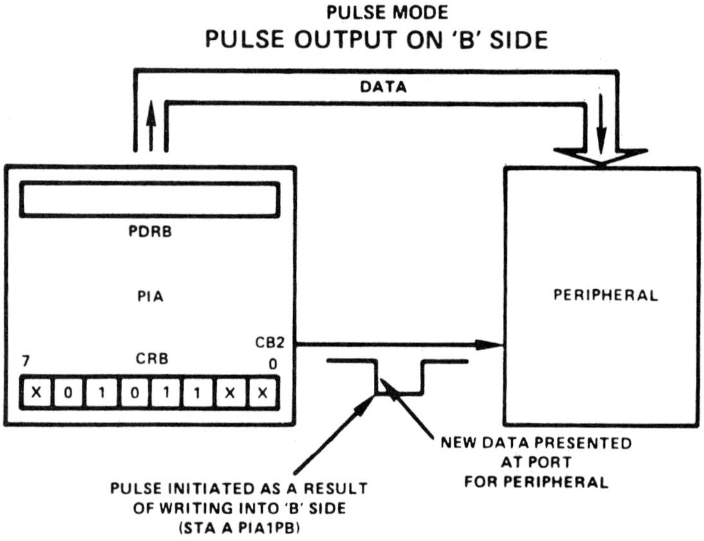

Figure 3-10. Pulse output on "B" side.

negative transition as programmed control bits 0 and 1, CRA-0 and CRA-1, and sets the IRQA1 status bit. Again, by virtue of executing the LOAD instruction (LDA), three events occur:

- The data are input to the accumulator.
- An output control pulse is placed at the CA2 pin.
- The IRQA1 status bit is reset.

The duration of the negative output pulse is one cycle of the ∅ clock.

Pulse Mode at Port B

In the pulse mode at Port B (Fig. 3-10), by virtue of executing the STORE instruction (STA), the output data are transferred to Port B, and a control pulse is placed at the CB2 pin.

Again, the pulse mode at Port B may or may not be used in conjunction with an interrupt from the receiving device. If it is used in response to an interrupt, programmed by control bits CRB-0 and CRB-1, then the STORE instruction outputs the data and transmits the control pulse at CB2. A LOAD from Port B instruction must be executed to clear the IRQB-1 status bit.

Handshake at Port A

Handshaking is a more positive technique for controlling the transfer of data and requires two control lines, one from the transmitter and one from the receiver. Handshaking at Port A (Fig. 3-11) indicates that the microcomputer receives the data. The transmitter sends the initial signal to pin CA1, indicating that the data are available. The PIA is programmed by control bits CRA-0 and CRA-1 to respond to either a positive or negative transition, and to cause an interrupt or not. The programmer must know the nature of the signal from the transmitter to the CA1 pin. If the PIA is programmed to respond to an interrupt, then the appropriate transition on CA1 causes

- An interrupt and sets the IRQA1 status bit.
- Puts a positive transition on the CA2 and output control line.

This positive logic-level signal at the CA2 pin indicates to the transmitting device that the interrupt has started, but that the data have not yet been accepted. The data are accepted by virtue of executing the LOAD instruction (LDA), which

- Transfers the data from Port A to the accumulator.
- Pulls the CA2 control line low.
- Resets the IRQA1 status bit.

The transmitting device, by sampling the state of the CA2 line, can determine when the byte of data was accepted by the microcomputer, and when it is ready to receive the next byte of data.

Handshake at Port B

Handshaking at Port B (Fig. 3-12) is used when data are requested by a receiving device by sending a signal to control pin CB1. Again, CB1 is programmed to respond to a positive or negative transition

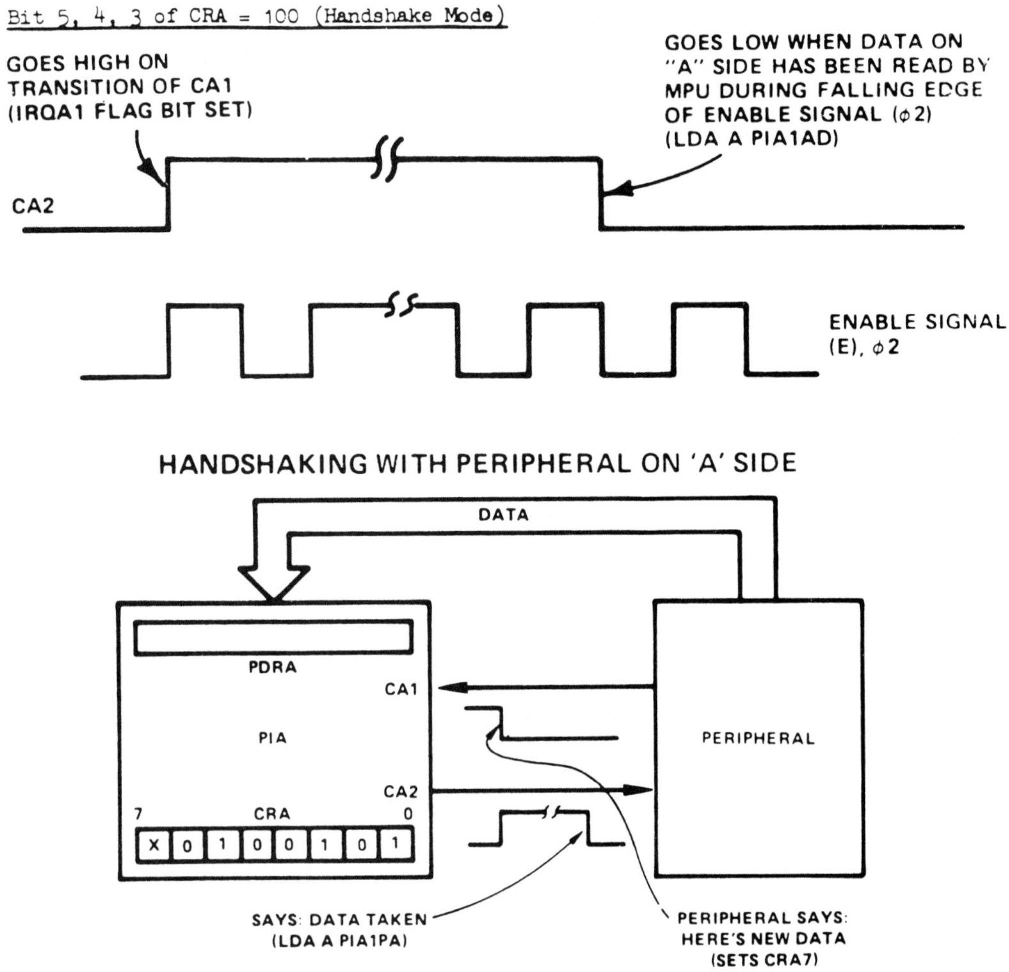

Figure 3-11. Handshaking with peripheral on "A" side.

signal from the receiving device. The appropriate signal at CB1 causes

- An interrupt, if programmed, to set status bit IRQB1.
- A positive transition on the CB2 output control line.

When CA2 is positive, it indicates that the interrupt is in progress but the data have not yet been output. The receiving device can know the status by sampling the state of the CB2 line. By virtue of executing a STORE instruction to Port B, the data are transferred to the output

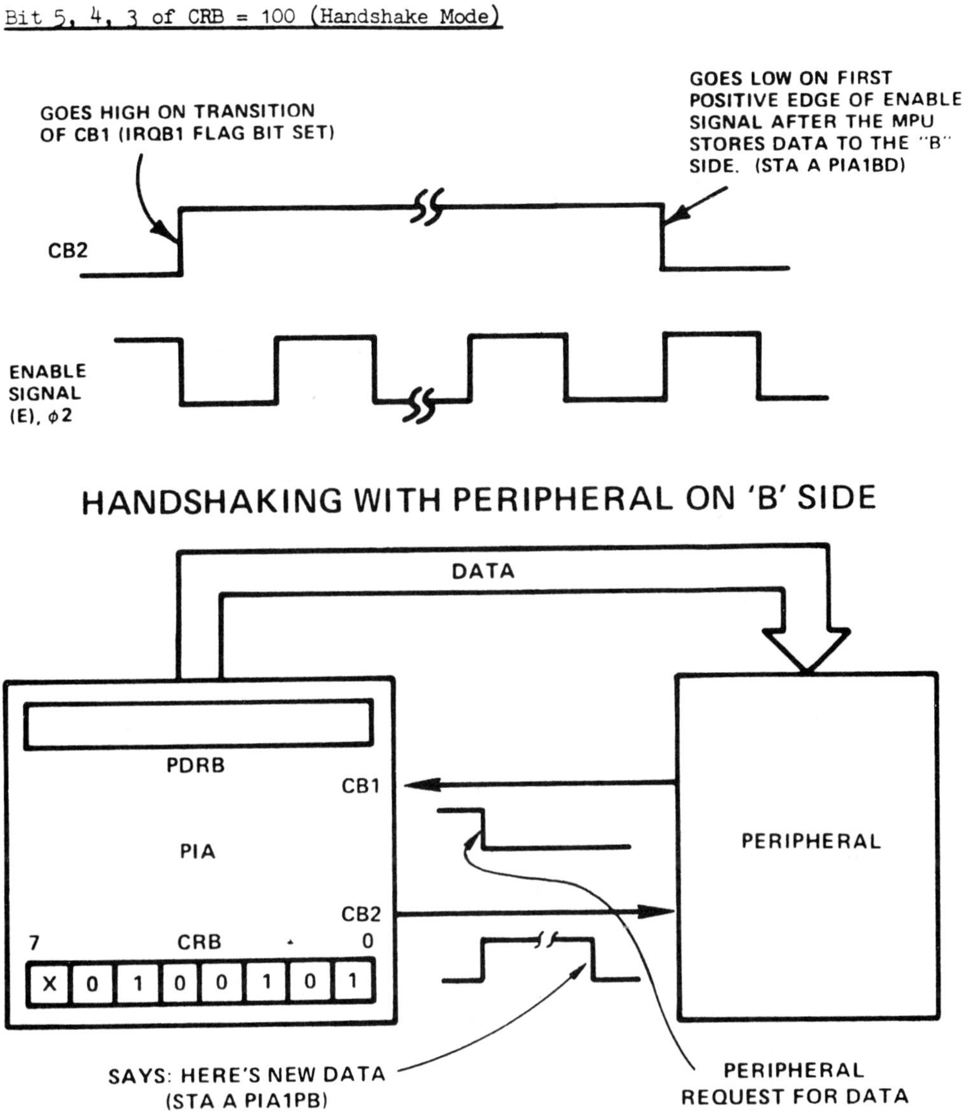

Figure 3-12. Handshaking with peripheral on "B" side. Bit 5, 4, 3, of CRB = 100 (handshake mode).

port, and the CB2 control line is pulled low, indicating to the receiving device that data are available. Executing a LOAD instruction from Port B is necessary to reset the IRQB1 status bit.

Following Mode (110 or 111)

In the pulse mode of operation, a negative pulse is output on the control lines CA2 and CB2. In the handshake mode, it is a positive control pulse output. The following mode offers the programmer the choice of outputting a positive or negative pulse at CA2 or CB2. The programmer selects the following mode by setting control bits CR-5 and CR-4 to 1's in the A or B control registers. Then the output line will follow the state of the CR-3 bit. To output a:

	Positive Pulse	Negative Pulse
Level	110	111
Pulse	111	110
Level	110	111

Examples of Parallel Communication

Two examples of parallel communication are described in this section, one using the pulse, and the second using the handshaking mode. Both examples are variations of a loop-back circuit. Loop-back circuits are convenient tutorial circuits where the output data are fed or looped back to the same device. It is analogous to a person who, having no one to play with, throws a ball against a wall and to have it bounce or loop back. Since Port B of the PIA is the output and Port A is the input port, then data are transferred out of Port B and back into Port A.

In the first example, when the pulse mode is used, the data are transferred through a first-in first-out (FIFO) buffer. This would vary the analogy of the person playing catch-a-ball against a wall by having the ball appear to be momentarily stuck against the wall before it bounces back. The FIFO is used because its response time is faster than the microcomputer, which is less than 1 μs, while it takes several microseconds to execute an input or output instruction. This is an ideal application of the pulse mode. The FIFO can store 40 bytes of data, and there is a ninth, a parity, bit, which is not used. In the example, 20 bytes of data are first loaded into the FIFO through Port B and then returned through Port A. Note that, when initializing the FIFO for the pulse mode, both control registers are loaded with the same code in bits 5, 4, and 3 (101) (see Figs. 3-13 and 3-14). Note that an inverter is necessary to invert the negative pulse from the microcomputer to a positive pulse required by the FIFO.

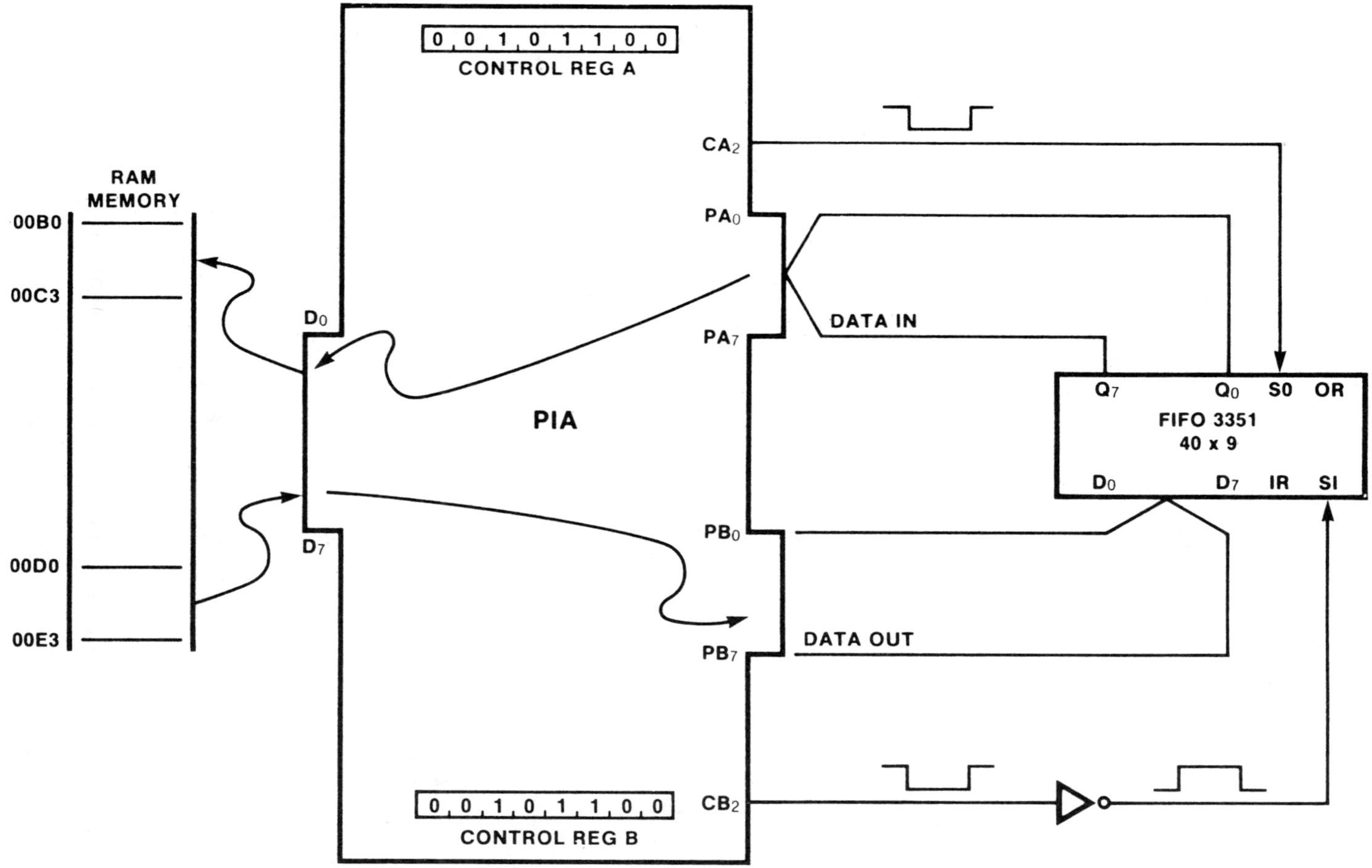

Figure 3-13. Pulse mode transfer of data through a FIFO.

Preliminary

```
PAGE  001    PULSE MO

                            NAM     PULSE     MODE 1
                      *ASSUME MEMORY LOCATIONS 00D0 THROUGH 00E3 HAVE DATA
                      *
                      *
                      *FIRST SET UP PIA
                      *
                      *
0100                        ORG     $100
0100 CE 8004 INIT           LDX     #$8004    POINT INDEX REG TO PIA
0103 4F      COND           CLR A
0104 A7 00                  STA A   0,X       DEFINE PORT A AS ALL INPUTS
0106 43                     COM A
0107 A7 02                  STA A   2,X       DEFINE PORT B AS ALL OUTPUTS
0109 86 2C                  LDA A   #$2C
010B A7 01                  STA A   1,X       CONTROL REG A TO PULSE MODE
010D A7 03                  STA A   3,X       CONTROL REG B TO PULSE MODE
                      *
                      *NOW MOVE DATA TO FIFO
                      *
010F CE 00D0 SETOUT         LDX     #$00D0    POINT TO FIRST MEMORY LOC
0112 A6 00   OUTTS          LDA A   0,X       GET DATA
0114 B7 8006                STA A   $8006     OUTPUT TO PORT B
0117 08                     INX
0118 8C 00E4                CPX     #$00E4    LAST MEMORY LOC?
011B 26 F5                  BNE     OUTTS     NO - LOOP TO OUTTS
                      *
                      *NOW INPUT WHAT HAS BEEN OUTPUTTED
                      *
011D CE 00B0 SETIN          LDX     #$00B0    POINT TO FIRST STORAGE LOC
0120 B6 8004 INNS           LDA A   $8004     INPUT FROM PORT A
0123 A7 00                  STA A   0,X       STORE DATA
0125 08                     INX               CPX #$00C4 LAST LOC?
0126 26 F8                  BNE     INNS      NO - LOOP TO INNS
                      *
                      *CONTINUE PROGRAM OR RETURN TO MAIN PROGRAM
                      *
                      *
     0000                   END

TOTAL ERRORS 00000
```

Figure 3-14. Program to transfer data through FIFO using the pulse mode.

Loop-Back Circuit Using the Handshake and Following Modes

In this configuration (Fig. 3-15), 20 bytes of data are transferred, starting from locations $00DO to $00BO through Port B to Port A. Port A is in control, indicating the transfer is initiated by Port A, with a

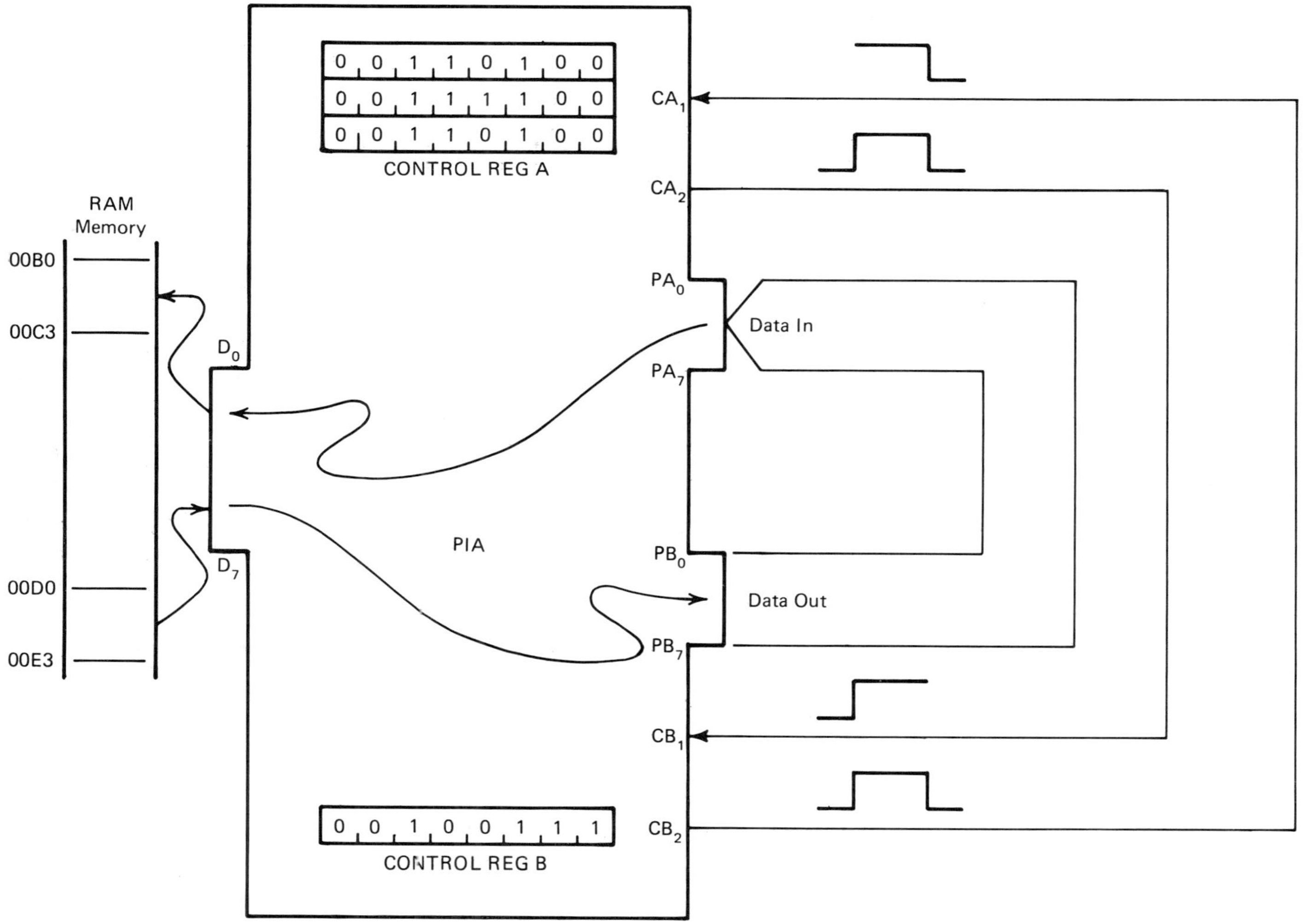

Figure 3-15. Loop-back circuit using handshake and following mode.

PROGRAM TITLE: LOOP-BACK USING THE HANDSHAKE/FOLLOWING MODES

PAGE OF | PROGRAMMER:

PC	MACHINE CODE	LABEL	MNEM	OPERAND	COMMENTS	N	Z	V	C
		* SEE FIG 3.15							
		* THE PIA IS AT LOCATION $8000							
		* PORT A IS AN INPUT & IN THE FOLLOWING MODE							
		* PORT B IS AN OUTPUT & IN THE HANDSHAKE MODE							
		*							
		PORTA	FDB	$8000					
		CONTRA	FDB	$8001					
		PORTB	FDB	$8002					
		CONTRB	FDB	$8003					
		*							
			LDS	#$00FF	LOAD STACK POINTER				
			LDX	#$00B0	LOAD INDEX POINTER				
		* INITIALIZE PIA, ASSUME THAT PIA IS RESET, ALL REGISTERS 0's							
			CLRA						
			STAA	PORTA	MAKE PORT A INPUT, DDR(A)=0s				
			COMA						
			STAA	PORTB	MAKE PORT B OUTPUT, DDR(B) = 1s				
			LDAA	#$27	MAKE PORT B HANDSHAKE & PIN CB1				
			STAA	CONTRB	CAUSE INTERRUPT WITH NEGATIVE TRANS.				
			LDAA	#$3C	MAKE PORT A FOLLOWING MODE				
			STAA	CONTRA	WITH OUTPUT CA2 HIGH				
			LDAB	#$14	BYTE COUNT = DECIMAL 20				

Figure 3-16. Loop-back configuration using handshake and modes listed above.

PROGRAM TITLE:

PAGE	OF	PROGRAMMER:							
PC	MACHINE CODE	LABEL	MNEM	OPERAND	COMMENTS	N	Z	V	C
		* DATA TRANSFE LOOP, 20 BYTES, FROM LOC $00D0 TO $00B0							
		DATA	LDAA	#$34	OUTPUT CA2 LOW				
			STAA	CONTRA	IN FOLLOWING MODE				
			LDAA	#$3C	OUTPUT CA2 HIGH				
			STAA	CONTRA	IN FOLLOWING MODE				
		* THE NEGATIVE TRANSITION AT INPUT CB1 CAUSES INTERRUPT							
		WAIT	LDAA	CONTRA	GET STATUS BIT IRQA-1				
			BPL	WAIT	TEST STATUS BIT				
			LDAA	PORTA	GET INPUT DATA				
			STAA	0,X	STORE DATA ($00B0 BLOCK)				
			INX		INC INDEX POINTER				
			DECB		DEC BYTE COUNT				
			BNE	DATA	GET NEXT BYTE				
			JMP	NEXTR	GO TO NEXT ROUTINE				
		*		INTERRUPT	ROUTINE				
		* THE INTERRUPT RESPONDS TO A POSITIVE TRANSITION AT							
		* PIN CB1. THE ADDRESS OF THE INTERRUPT VECTOR IS							
		* PRELOADED INTO LOCATION $FFF8 & FFF9.							
		INTERR	LDAA	$20,X	GET DATA FROM $00D0 BLOCK				
			STAA	PORTB	OUTPUT DATA				
			RTI		RETURN FROM INTERRUPT				

Figure 3-16. Continued.

positive request pulse from CA2 to the CB1 control/interrupt line. Port A is in the following mode, where the output signal at CA2 follows the state of CRA3 when CRA4 and 5 are 1's. Port B is programmed in the handshake mode when CRB bits 5, 4, and 3 are 100, and Port B is also programmed to respond to a positive transition with an interrupt when CRB bits 1 and 0 are 11. Two events occur when the positive input transition is received at pin CB1. First, an interrupt is initiated from Port B and, second, by virtue of handshake mode, the CB2 output pin is automatically pulled high. This indicates that the request for data has been received but not yet transmitted. When the data is outputted at Port B the CB2 line is automatically pulled low, indicating that the data is latched at the output port. At this time the CA1 input pin, which has been programmed to respond to a negative transition, receives the output signal for the CB2 pin indicating that the data is at port A ready to be inputted.

The program to execute this transfer of data is given in Fig. 3-16. It assumes that the PIA is at location $8000 and that the interrupt request vector at $FFF8 and $FFF9 has been loaded with the address of the interrupt routine $0150. The main routine

- Loads the stack pointer.
- Stores the source pointer at $10 to be used by the interrupt routine.
- Loads the index register with the destination pointer.
- Initializes the I/O ports.
- Initializes Port B to handshake mode.
- Loads accumulator B with the byte count.

The program then proceeds to the data transfer loop (DATA). A positive transition is put at the CA2 output, and the routine then waits for an indication that there are data at Port A. In the wait loop (WAITLO) the program continuously samples status bit IRQA1 for a 1 caused by a negative transition at CA1. Meanwhile, the positive transition causes an interrupt at Port A and pulls the CA2 output high.

The interrupt routine loads the index register with an address from the source block of data. The routine tests the IRQB1 status bit, which in this example may be redundant. The LOAD instruction from Port B resets the status bit IRQB1. Data are then transferred out through Port B, which automatically pulls the CB2 line low, and automatically resets the IRQA1 status bit. When the program returns from the interrupt, the main program, which is sampling the IRQA1 status bit, senses that there are new data at Port A. The new data are stored in the destination block, and the IRQA1 status bit is reset by virtue of executing a LOAD instruction from Port A.

4 A Computer on a Board/Debugging

This chapter describes how to build a typical microcomputer system from the various 6800 family of microprocessor devices. A microcomputer for training purposes, a kit, fits on one or two printed circuit boards. The Motorola MEK6800D2 Kit is the model described in this chapter and is generally referred to as the D-2 kit.

It is often assumed that the microcomputer contained only one program, the *user's program.* This is the case with most dedicated products, but kits are often used to test and debug programs before they are finalized and approved for production. This implies that there is another program for the purpose of testing and debugging the user's program, a *monitor*. The monitor in the D-2 kit is called JBUG. The monitor program in large computers is referred to as the *operating system* (OS). The monitor furnishes the means for initially loading, testing, and debugging the user program. Since both the monitor and the user programs share the microprocessor's registers, but have separate memory space, the reader should have an appreciation of how to allocate the memory space of the kit; this is called *memory mapping.*

The chapter concludes with a discussion of various 6800 microprocessor chips: 6801, 6802, and 6805.

4-1 MEMORY MAP AND WIRING DIAGRAM OF THE D-2 KIT

The memory map of the D-2 kit (Fig. 4-1) names the devices on the kit and indicates the allocation of the 64K memory space. The system layout worksheet (Fig. 4-2) is effectively a wire list used to indicate how the devices are connected to the 16-bit address bus of the schematic (see Appendix VI). These three diagrams are variations indicating how the microcomputer devices are connected to the address bus, and

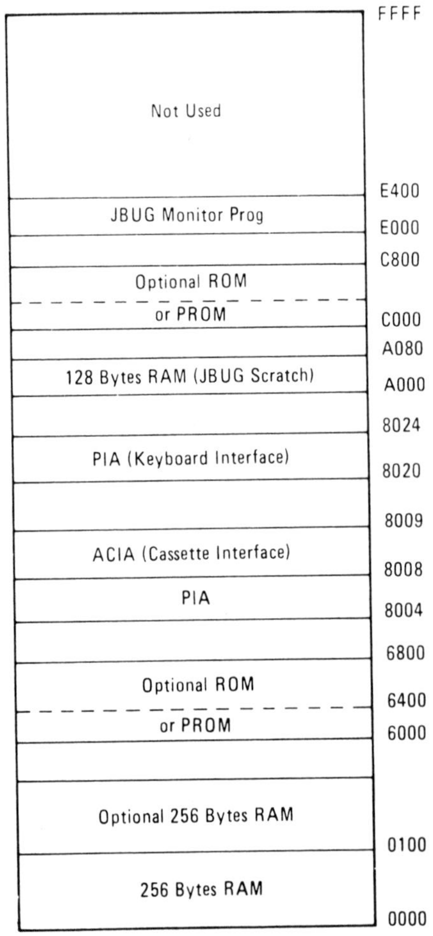

Figure 4-1. Memory map for MEK6800D2.

once the technique for wiring is understood, usually the memory map diagram is all that is required. This section illustrates how these three diagrams correlate with one another.

An examination of the memory map indicates 512 bytes of RAM—256 bytes of RAM and 256 bytes of optional RAM, from locations 0000 to \$01FF. The 6810 RAM devices are 128 × 8 bits of RAM. Therefore, two 6810 RAM devices are necessary to fill the 256 bytes of RAM. The devices are called by the lowest memory space occupied; thus, the first device is called RAM 0 and the second is called RAM \$80. As indicated by the two bottom lines of the system layout diagram, RAM 0 occupies the memory space from location 0000 to \$007F, and RAM \$80 occupies the memory space from location \$0080 to \$00FF. The optional 256 bytes of RAM on the memory map indicate that two additional sockets exist on the board to be filled with two 6810 RAM

		Address		MPU Address Lines (A0–A15)															
Device	Symbol*	From	To	15	14	13	12	11	10	9	8	7	6	5	4	3	2	1	0
ROM (JBUG)	$\overline{ROM}$	E000	E3FF		$\overline{CS1}$					A9	A8	A7	A6	A5	A4	A3	A2	A1	A0
RAM (JBUG)	$\overline{STACK}$	A000	A07F		$\overline{CS5}$						$\overline{CS2}$	$\overline{CS1}$	A6	A5	A4	A3	A2	A1	A0
PIA	$\overline{I/O}$	8020	8023		$\overline{CS2}$									CS1				RS1	RS0
ACIA	$\overline{I/O}$	8008	8009		$\overline{CS2}$											CS0			RS
PIA	$\overline{I/O}$	8004	8007		$\overline{CS2}$												CS1	RS1	RS0
USER	$\overline{4/5}$	4000	5FFF																
USER	$\overline{2/3}$	2000	3FFF																
RAM (USER)	$\overline{RAM}$	0180	01FF		$\overline{CS5}$						CS3	CS0	A6	A5	A4	A3	A2	A1	A0
RAM (USER)	$\overline{RAM}$	0100	017F		$\overline{CS5}$						CS0	$\overline{CS1}$	A6	A5	A4	A3	A2	A1	A0
RAM (USER)	$\overline{RAM}$	0080	00FF		$\overline{CS5}$						$\overline{CS2}$	CS0	A6	A5	A4	A3	A2	A1	A0
RAM (USER)	$\overline{RAM}$	0000	007F		$\overline{CS5}$						$\overline{CS2}$	$\overline{CS1}$	A6	A5	A4	A3	A2	A1	A0

Tie all CS lines to +5 V
Tie all $\overline{CS}$ lines to GND

Figure 4-2A. System layout worksheet

		Address		MPU Address Lines (A0–A15)															
Device	Symbol	From	To	15	14	13	12	11	10	9	8	7	6	5	4	3	2	1	0

Figure 4-2B.

*Symbol signal is formed from the A15, A14, and A13 address lines, and is tied to the chip select pin indicated.

devices at the user's option. These sockets occupy 256 bytes of memory space from locations $0100 to $01FF.

Connecting the address bus to the devices is referred to as *decoding* the address bus. Examining the schematic in Appendix VI, we see that the four RAMS, 0, $80, $0100 and $0180, are at sockets labeled U 14, U 16, U 18, and U 19. Each RAM occupies a unique memory space.

Before focusing on decoding the RAMs and continuing the examination of the memory map, the optional PROM and ROM at locations $6000 and $6400 indicate two additional sockets. There are two PIAs at location $8004 and $8020, with Port A, control register A, Port B, and control register B, at locations $8004, 5, 6 and 7, and $8020, 21, 22, 23, respectively. There is an ACIA occupying locations $8008 and $8009. A RAM used by the JBUG monitor is at location $A000, and the 1K-byte JBUG ROM occupies locations $E000 to $E3FF.

Address Decode

Since less than 2K of the 64K of memory space available is used by the kit, efficient decoding techniques are not necessary. As a consequence, note that address lines A10, A11, and A12 are not used.

The 64K of memory space is divided into eight 8K sections by decoding the three MSBs of the address bus, A15, A14, and A13, with the 1-of-8 decode device at schematic location U 11, whose outputs are labeled $\overline{\text{RAM}}$, $\overline{2/3}$, $\overline{4/5}$, $\overline{6/7}$, $\overline{\text{I/O}}$, $\overline{\text{STACK}}$, $\overline{\text{PROM}}$, and $\overline{\text{ROM}}$. These labels correspond to the tables of the system layout table. The valid memory address (VMA) control line functions as the chip select for the 1-of-8 decode device.

Each memory location is addressed by four hex characters. It should be appreciated that the most significant hex characters 0 to F divide the 64K space into sixteen 4K sections. When the 64K space is divided into eight sections, the most significant hex characters are 0/1, 2/3, 4/5, 6/7, 8/9, A/B, C/D, and E/F. These address spaces correlate with the output of the 1-of-8 decoder labeled $\overline{\text{RAM}}$, $\overline{2/3}$, $\overline{4/5}$, $\overline{6/7}$, $\overline{\text{I/O}}$, $\overline{\text{STACK}}$, $\overline{\text{PROM}}$ and $\overline{\text{ROM}}$.

RAM Decode

There are three parts to decoding the four user RAMs at locations 0 to $01FF: First, the seven address lines, A0 to A6, of the address bus are connected to address lines A0 to A6 of the 6810 (Fig. 4-3), which decodes 128 locations on each RAM chip. Second, the decode distinguishes and establishes a unique RAM space for each RAM by decoding address bus lines A7 and A8 with the chip select lines on each RAM. Third, the decode separates the RAM space as part of the

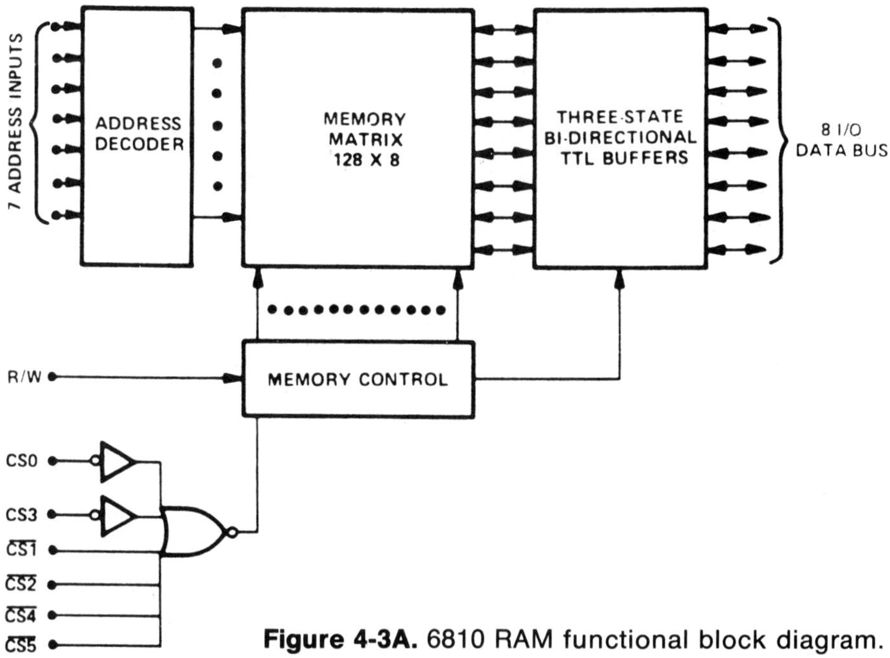

Figure 4-3A. 6810 RAM functional block diagram.

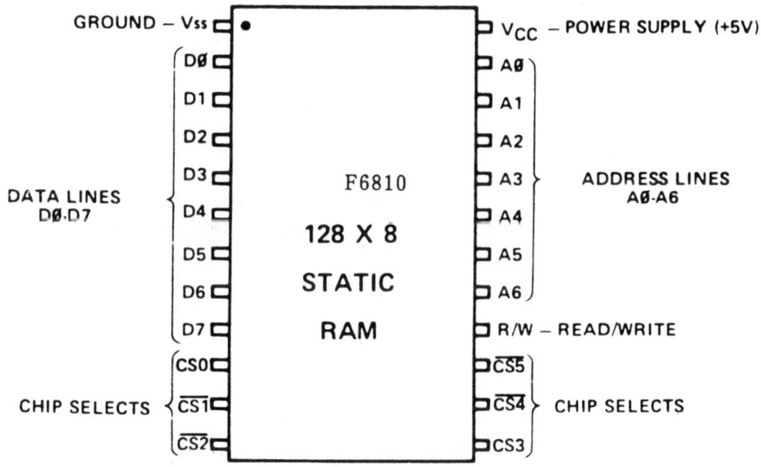

Figure 4-3B. 6810 pin assignment.

first 2000 memory locations from the rest of the 64K memory space by decoding the $\overline{\text{RAM}}$ line.

These wiring connections may be verified by examining the 6810 pins on the D-2 kit schematic. The microprocessor address lines A0 to

Table 4-1. Chip Select Decode Lines of User RAMs

	MSBs	A8	A7	RAM	No.	Pin No.	Pin
RAM 0000	0 0	$\overline{CS2}$	$\overline{CS1}$	$\overline{CS5}$	12	11	14
RAM 0080	0 1	$\overline{CS2}$	CS0	$\overline{CS5}$	12	10	14
RAM 0100	1 0	CS0	$\overline{CS1}$	$\overline{CS5}$	10	11	14
RAM 0180	1 1	CS3	CS0	$\overline{CS5}$	13	10	14

A6 are connected to the A0 to A6 pins of all four 6810 RAMs, starting from pins 23 to 17. The chip select pin assignments are listed in Table 4-1. The A8 and A7 address pins of each RAM are decoded from binary 0 to 3 by the chip select (CS) or chip select bar ($\overline{CS}$) pins. The chip select bar pins are logic-low signals and are connected where the 0 decode is required. The $\overline{RAM}$ signal is connected to the $\overline{CS5}$ pin 14 on each of the RAMs.

These pin connections are listed on the system layout worksheet (Fig. 4-2a). The system layout worksheet then is effectively the wiring list for the schematic and are two versions of the same information. Again, the memory map (Fig. 4-1), is a third version of the same information. The memory map then is the memory space assigned to each device without necessarily getting involved with each pin on the devices. Figure 4-2b is a blank system layout form.

The reader can trace the wiring on the two PIAs at locations $8004 and $8020 on the schematic, the system layout worksheet, and the memory map.

There are apparent contradictions for the address location of the JBUG ROM. On the memory map, JBUG occupies locations $E000 to $E3FF, while the interrupt vectors (see Table 3-3). RESET, NMI, SWI, and IRQ are in locations $FFF8 to $FFFF. As previously noted, address lines A10, A11, and A12 are not used, permitting inefficient decoding techniques, and effectively putting the ROM into eight different addresses.

Starting Address	End Address
E000	E3FF
E400	E7FF
E800	EBFF
EC00	EFFF
F000	F3FF
F400	F7FF
F800	FBFF
FC00	FFFF

Therefore, the JBUG and the interrupt vectors share eight common addresses. The notation used in the D-2 kit positions a device at the lowest memory location it occupies, which in this case is $E000.

4-2 MONITOR

Monitors like JBUG are used to load programs and aid the programmer in debugging the program. To find an error and correct the program, the programmer must be able to predict the expected data in each register and memory location throughout the program. The technique for finding an error requires stopping the program at suspected locations by setting a breakpoint. The data in the registers are then examined and compared to the expected data. If the data agree, the program is valid to that point. In cases where it does not agree, other breakpoints must be set prior to that point in the program until the critical point is located. Often the programmer single cycles through a critical point of the program to permit the programmer to examine the effect a sequence of instructions, not just a single instruction, has on the program.

The monitor offers features for loading and debugging programs:

- Examining memory and registers.
- Changing the data in memory and registers.
- Loading a program via keyboard, or storing and loading the program onto a cassette recorder.
- Setting breakpoints.
- Single cycling.

Software Interrupt (SWI)

There are two types of breakpoints, hardware and software. In the hardware breakpoint a comparison is made between a set of switches and the address of the program counter. When they are equal, the program stops.

The software interrupt is a special 6800 instruction specifically for setting software breakpoints. When the user sets a breakpoint into the D-2 kit, the monitor replaces the opcode with SW1 and saves the opcode in the JBUG RAM. At run time, if the program executes the SW1 (see Sec. 3-3), the data in the processor's registers are pushed onto the stack, and the program vectors to the address stored in locations $FFFA and $FFFB. The monitor's breakpoint routine restores the opcode at the breakpoint address, and then returns control to the user.

4-3 6800 FAMILY OF PROCESSORS

The everchanging, high-technology, semiconductor industry packages more and more transistors into a chip. Functions that in the past were packed with several chips are continually being merged into one chip. This process of packaging more capability onto fewer chips offers an economic advantage to the user, who can build the same system with fewer chips.

Two ways in which this evaluation is manifested are in the memory and the microprocessor chips. In memory chips, more and more bits are being packaged into one device, where the chips evolve from 1K to 2K to 4K to 16K bits of memory, and more. Note that the 128-byte 6810 RAM device has 128 × 8 bits, 1K bits of memory. In microcomputer chips, functions that were previously packaged onto separate devices are now being merged onto one device; the new chips are used to build microcomputer systems that are packaged differently but are not conceptually different systems. Chapters 11 and 12 discuss 8 and 16-bit microprocessors that are significantly different from the 6800.

Classic 6800 Microcomputer Family of Devices

The classic or, more accurately, the original seven-chip microcomputer system (Fig. 4-4) consists of the following:

6800 microprocessor	6800
Clock generator	
128-bytes of RAM	6810
2K of ROM	6830 (2 each)
PIA	6820/6846
Timer	6840/6846

The minimal system required five chips. The timer and 1-ROM chip might be eliminated. The advantage of this original system is that each device is functionally different from the other devices, and because of this convenience this book has described the original devices. This section describes not only the more recent devices that merge several functions, but attempts to indicate a continuously developing process.

Two-Chip 6802 and 6846 Microcomputer System

The seven-chip original system and most of the function capabilities are merged into a two-chip system as illustrated in Fig. 4-5a, where the first chip (6802 microprocessor) includes:

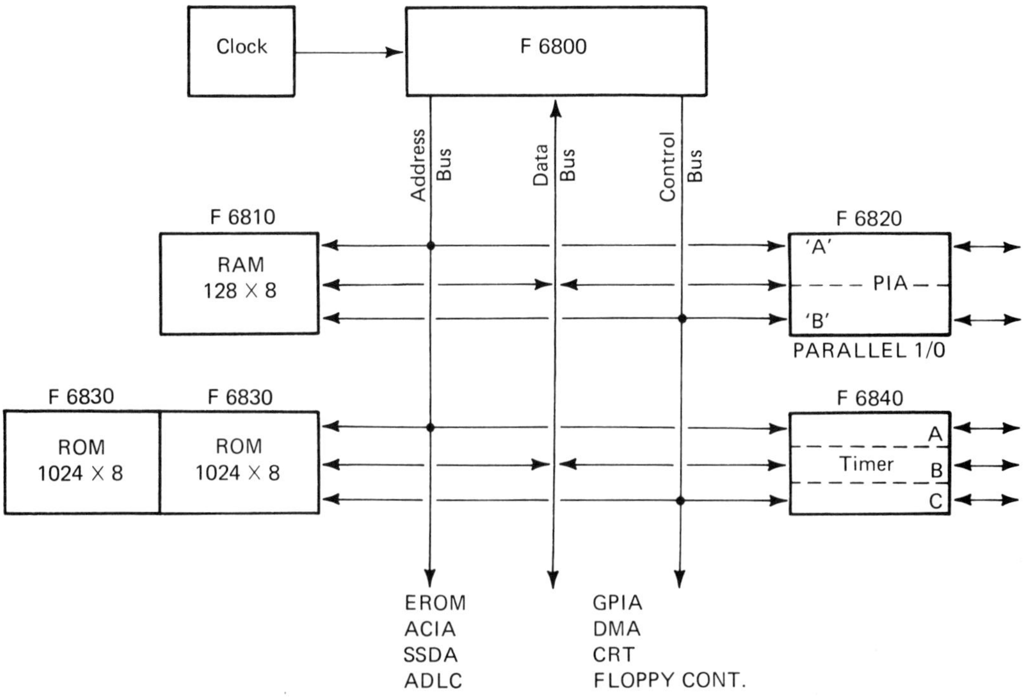

Figure 4-4. 7-chip 6800 microcomputer system.

- 6800 Microprocessor
- Internal clock
- 128-bytes of RAM (6810), including 32 bytes of retainable RAM

The second chip (6846 ROM-I/O-Timer) includes:

- 2K of ROM, two 6830s
- I/O port, one-half of a 6821
- Timer, one-third of a 6840

The 6802

With the internal clock and additional RAM, the 6802 microprocessor has virtually replaced the 6800 device in multichip as well as two-chip systems. One fault of RAMs is their *volatility*, the loss of data stored in the RAM when the voltage is turned off or power is inadvertently lost. To overcome this limitation, the first 32 of the 128 bytes are battery-backup retainable. That is, a 5-V battery may be attached to the Vcc STANDBY pin and save the data in the first 32 bytes with 8-mA drain on the battery. This implies that when a power loss is sensed the

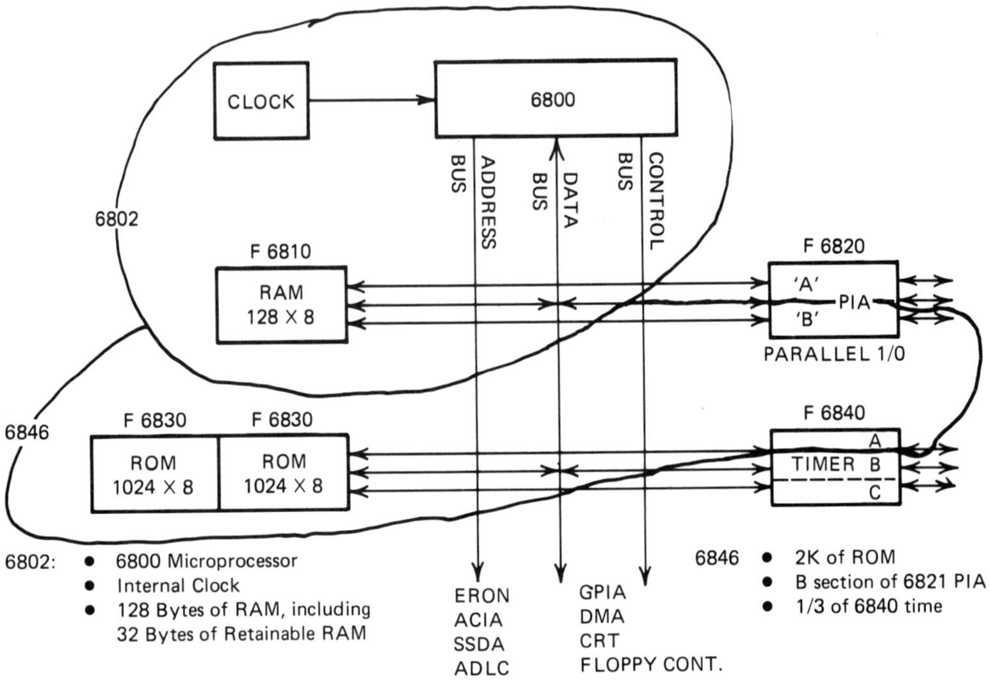

Figure 4-5A. 2-chip microcomputer systems: 6802 and 6846.

microcomputer system can invoke a nonmaskable interrupt (NMI) and quickly load the critical data into the first 32 bytes of data.

6801 Single-Chip Microcomputer

The multifunction 6801 may be used as a single-chip microcomputer or as a microprocessor in the multichip configuration (Fig. 4-6). The single-chip configuration, when compared to the original 6800 microcomputer, incorporates:

- The microprocessor with the 6800, plus 10 additional instructions (Fig. 4-2)
- 2K of ROM, two 6830s
- 128 bytes of RAM, one 6810
- Three I/O parallel I/O ports, one and a half 6821s
- Timer, one third of a 6840
- Serial communication interface (SCI), which has many of the features of the 6850

The 6801 programming model (Fig. 4-7) indicates a double (D) accu-

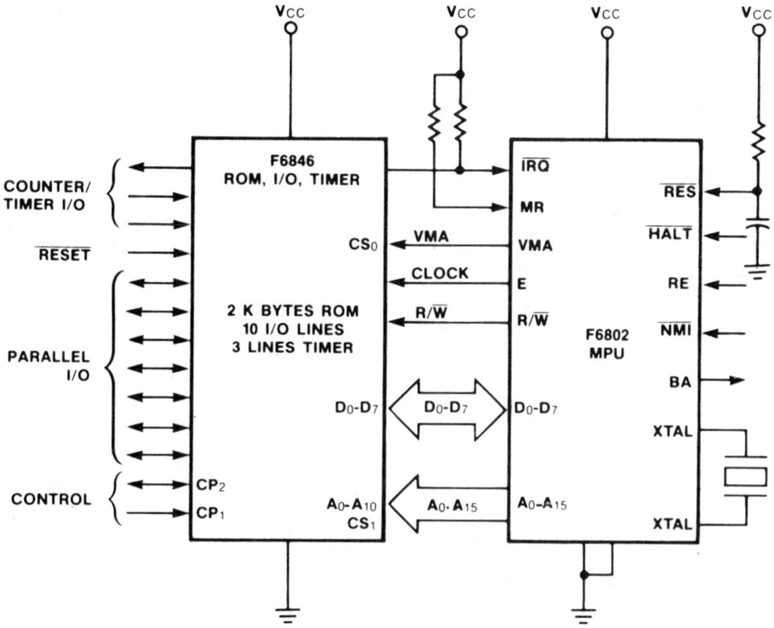

Figure 4-5B. 2-chip microcomputer system with 6802 and 6846.

mulator, which is physically the same as the A accumulator concatenated with the B accumulator so that any operation using accumulator D will destroy information in A and B. In addition to the 6800 instruction set, the 6801 has ten additional instructions (see Table 4-2).

4-4 DEBUGGING TECHNIQUES

After a program is written and before it is operational, Murphy's law states that if there is anything that can go wrong, it will. On the assumption that most programs are not completely correct when they are written, the process of finding the errors, or bugs, and correcting them is called *debugging*. The two basic debugging techniques are (1) by analyzing and (2) by using a debugger. The analyzing technique is the ability to think through the problem and find the error without any aids.

This chapter discusses the second alternative. The debugger is, in effect, a program used to debug another program and is part of a monitor program. So, for the sake of clarity, it is referred to as a monitor program that aids in debugging the user's program. This implies that

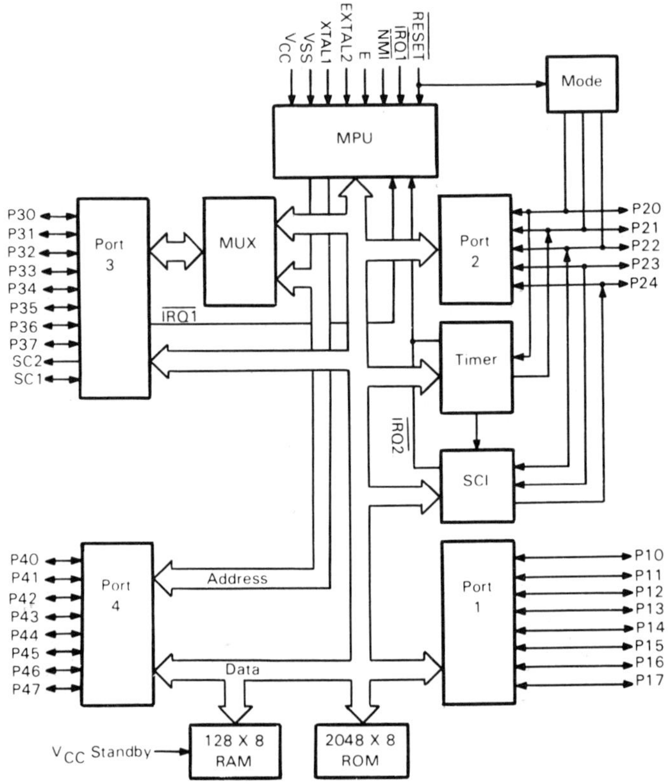

Figure 4-6. 6801 microcomputer block diagram.

there are at least two programs in the computer, the monitor with debugging capability and the user's program. Some features that are typical of monitor programs are follows:

- Loading the user programs.
- Examining the data in each register and memory location.
- Changing the data in each register and memory location, which is effectively the ability to load the program.
- Setting breakpoints and single-cycling through a program.

An additional feature of monitor programs is the ability to exercise these controls through a variety of I/O media, terminals being the most popular. The monitor program must, therefore, be in the computer memory before the user's program can be loaded and debugged. They are often stored in ROMs.

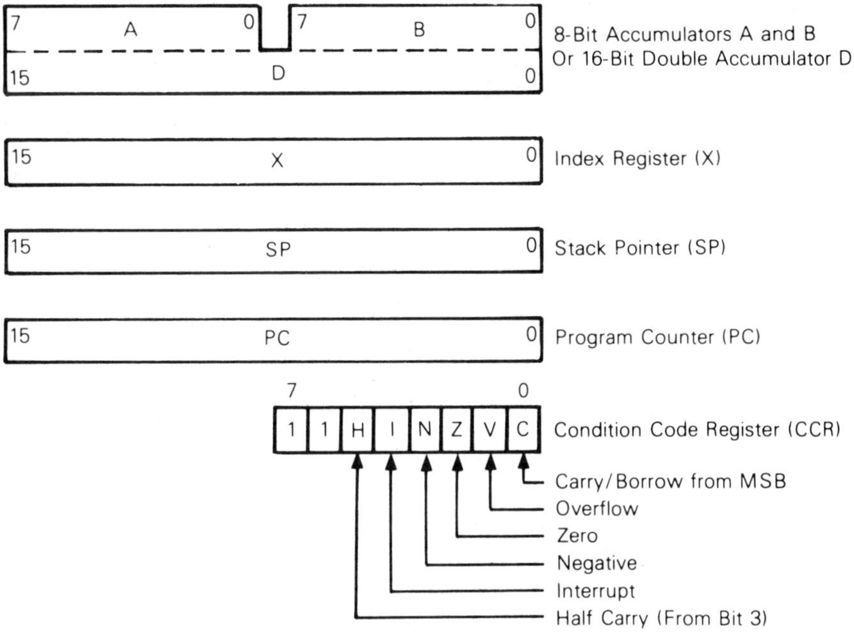

Figure 4-7. 6801 MCU programming model.

Breakpoint

The ultimate, but impractical, debugging technique is to trace or single-cycle through a program and examine the data in each register and memory location affected by that instruction. A more practical approach is to judiciously select places to stop a program and examine the data. The breakpoint serves that function.

There are two types of breakpoints, software and hardware. To implement the software breakpoint, the user indicates at which address to break or stop the program, and the address must be at the memory location of the opcode, the first byte of an instruction. The monitor program then saves the opcode from the address of the breakpoint and inserts a software interrupt (SW1 $3F) in its place. Then, as the program passes that location, the software interrupt is evoked. The software interrupt instruction loads the data in the general registers, except the stack pointer, onto the stack, and then executes the software interrupt routine, which transfers control back to the monitor. The monitor replaces the software interrupt with the opcode of the original instruction and makes the operation of inserting and replacing the

Table 4-2. 6801 Added Instructions

Instruction	Description
ABX	Unsigned addition of Accumulator B to Index Register
ADDD	Adds (without carry) the double accumulator to memory and leaves the sum in the double accumulator
ASLD or LSLD	Shifts the double accumulator left (towards MSB) one bit; the LSB is cleared and the MSB is shifted into the C-bit
BHS	Branch if Higher or Same; unsigned conditional branch (same as BCC)
BLO	Branch if Lower; Unsigned conditional branch (same as BCS)
BRN	Branch Never
JSR	Additional addressing mode: direct
LDD	Loads double accumulator from memory
LSL	Shifts memory or accumulator left (towards MSB) one bit; the LSB is cleared and the MSB is shifted into the C-bit (same as ASL)
LSRD	Shifts the double accumulator right (towards LSB) one bit; the MSB is cleared and the LSB is shifted into the C-bit
MUL	Unsigned multiply; multiplies the two accumulators and leaves the product in the double accumulator
PSHX	Pushes the Index Register to stack
PULX	Pulls the Index Register from stack
STD	Stores the double accumulator to memory
SUBD	Subtracts memory from the double accumulator and leaves the difference in the double accumulator
CPX	Internal processing modified to permit its use with any conditional branch instruction

software interrupt transparent to the user. Once the program is stopped at the breakpoint, the user can use the monitor to examine the data in the memory and the registers before either single-cycling or continuing to execute the program from the breakpoint. Since the data in the general registers were stored on the stack by the software interrupt, the data in the general registers are examined by accessing the stack.

The hardware breakpoint is the implementation of a logical circuit to compare the 16 address lines against the address of the breakpoint. The advantage of the hardware breakpoint is that it can stop the program at any location that the program passes, and it is not restricted to the opcode location, as with the software interrupt. The disadvantage of the hardware interrupt is the additional cost of building the computer circuit.

Monitor Command

A typical set of commands for a monitor are listed as follows:

Note: ×× or ×××× indicates either two or four hex characters.

M××××	Display the data in memory location displayed
H××	Change the data at the memory location displayed
I	Increment the memory location
D	Decrement the memory location
E	Exit to the monitor
G××××	Go load the program counter with address ×××× and begin executing the program
B××××	Set temporary breakpoint at location ×××× and it is cleared when breakpoint stops at location ××××
P××××	Set permanent breakpoint at location ××××
U××××	Clear breakpoint at location ××××
A	Clear all breakpoints
S	Single-cycle (trace) executes an instruction
R	Display next register PC, X, A, B, CC, SP
×××× or ××	Change the data in register displayed
C	Continue, to be used after a breakpoint or single-cycle

With some monitors, after the memory is opened with the M××××, the hex data are loaded into that location with an ××, which also increments the memory location. Some monitors have several temporary and permanent breakpoints. The temporary breakpoint (B) is removed when the program stops at the location of the temporary breakpoint. If the program does not pass the location of the breakpoint, then it is removed with one of the two REMOVE breakpoint commands U×××× or A. The permanent breakpoint (P) is removed by either the U×××× or A. The CONTINUE command (C) is used to continue running the program from a breakpoint or single-cycle command. It is, in effect, a return from software interrupt (RTI), where the data in the stack are returned to the general register and the program continues.

Troubleshooting Strategies

A program has a continuity and must be executed from either a start or from a know point, so that the data in the various registers are known and the condition code bits are predictable. When an error is detected, that is, either the program executed an incorrect branch or the data in a register or memory location are incorrect, it indicates that the previous instruction caused the error.

(A) If the program does not stop at the breakpoint, it implies the following:

- The breakpoint was not inserted at the opcode.
- The program branched before getting to the breakpoint.

In both cases move the breakpoint up or close to the start of the program.

(B) Generally, the breakpoint should be set at a branch instruction and then single-cycled to the next location. The programmer should, by examining the data in the registers and the condition code bits, predict whether the program will take the branch or advance to the next instruction. If the program takes the wrong branch, it implies the following:

- The relative address is incorrect.
- If the condition code bits are set correctly, then the wrong branch instruction was used.
- If the condition code bits are set incorrectly, then there is an error in one of the previously executed instructions that set the condition code bits.

Typical Application of the Breakpoint. The breakpoint is inserted after a program is loaded into memory and before it is executed.

B××××	Insert BP
G××××	Start executing program from location ××××

The program executes until the program passes the location of the breakpoint, at which time the program stops and the general registers are loaded onto the stack, PC, IX, Y, B, CC and SP.

R	Display data in index register
R	Display accumulator A
R	Display accumulator B
R	Display CC bits
R	Display SP
S	Single-cycle executes one instruction
RR	Display accumulator A (First R displays contents of index register)
R	Display accumulator B
B××××	Insert BP
C	Continue executing program

The program executes to the BP.

RR	Display accumulator A
R	Display accumulator B
C	Continue

(C) When data are modified by a program while executing a loop, or if an output routine is called, it is convenient to put a permanent breakpoint at a strategic place in the loop or at the output instruction. Then each time the program passes that location it breaks and the programmer can examine the data. A typical procedure after the program is loaded might be as follows:

P××××	Load permanent BP
G××××	Start program

When the program breaks:

RR	Examine data in accumulator A
R	Examine data in accumulator B
M××××	Examine data in memory bit ××××
E	Return to monitor
C	Continue; execute next loop

Other types of errors that cannot generally be detected with the aid of the breakpoint are caused when the various memory assignments for the program, the data, and the stack overlap.

5 Handling Blocks of Data Using the Index Register

This chapter deals with handling blocks of data, sometimes referred to as strings or arrays. Blocks of data are stored in contiguous memory locations and are moved or modified as a group. Since the 8-bit microprocessors handle 1 byte of data at a time, the block is moved or modified 1 byte at a time. The index register is used to point to the byte of data while the index addressing mode instruction indicates how the byte of data is moved or modified.

As noted previously, there are three parts of a loop (Fig. 5-1):

- Initialize for the loop.
- Execute the instructions that perform the function required.
- Test whether or not to exit from the loop.

The loop examples in Chapter 2 manipulated and modified 1 byte of data only, and the decision that determined when to exit from the loop tests the data itself.

Before writing routines with loops for handling blocks of data, it is necessary to understand how to control the index register. This is the primary objective of the chapter. The three parts of the loop are modified when referring to the index register. When initializing for the loop, an address is loaded into the index register. As the instructions are executed to perform the required function of the loop, the index register is either incremented or decremented to point to the byte of data being modified. That byte of data is modified by an index addressing mode instruction. There are three techniques for testing when to exit from the loop:

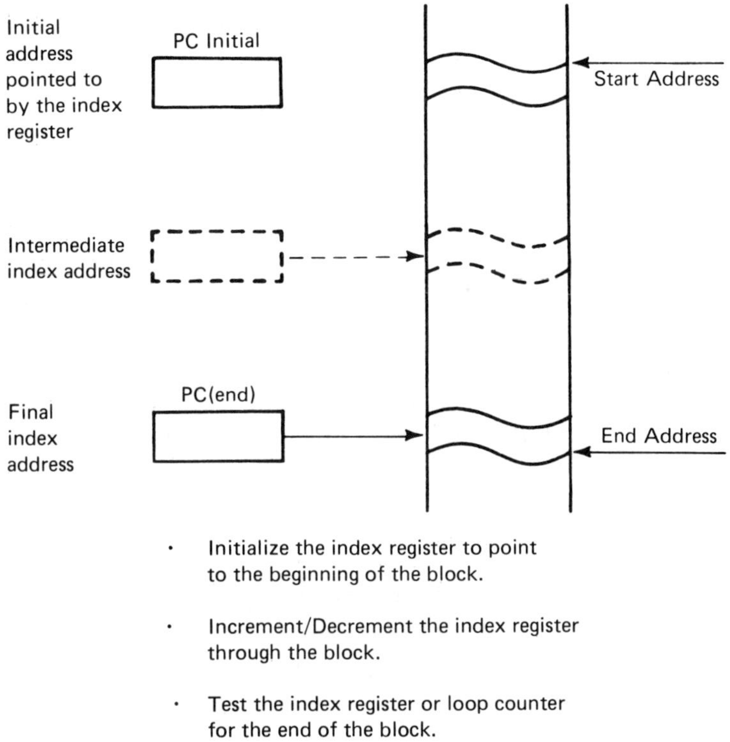

Figure 5-1. The three phases for controlling the index register: (a) Initialize the index register to point to the beginning if the block. (b) Increment/Decrement the index register through the block. (c) Test the index register or loop counter for the end of the block.

- Via a compare index register (CPX) instruction.
- Using a loop counter.
- The special case when the contents of the index register are equal to zero.

This chapter begins by discussing examples that handle one block of data and illustrate the necessary techniques for controlling the index register. The discussion proceeds to examples where two and three blocks of data are moved or modified simultaneously using one index register.

Examples that handle one block of data are the following:

- Test a RAM.
- Transmit or receive a message.
- Shift multibyte binary or decimal numbers.
- Left or right justify a multibyte number.

Examples that handle two blocks of data are the following:

- Move a block of data.
- Exchange two blocks of data.
- Add, subtract, a multibyte binary or decimal number.

Many of the arithmetic and shift routines in this chapter are called by the calculator system problem in Chapter 7. These routines are easily modified to become subroutines by adding the return from subroutine (RTS) instruction at the end of each routine. Good programming procedure dictates that there be only one exit or return from a subroutine, even when an error is detected within the subroutine. Techniques are discussed for detecting and setting an error flag before taking the one exit from the subroutine. The error flag is then tested and, if necessary, a branch to the error routine takes place in the main routine.

Index Register Instructions

The index register instructions are listed in Appendix IA, Table 2. The index register instructions are

CPX	compare	the index register
DEX	decrement	
INX	increment	
LDX	load	
STX	store	

The compare, load, and store the index register instructions move or compare the 16-bit address in the index register with data from two contiguous memory locations. For example, the load index register (LDX) instruction moves the two bytes of the address from memory locations M and (M + 1) to the index register high (IXH) and low bytes (IXL), respectively.

$$IXH \leftarrow M; \quad IXL \leftarrow (M + 1)$$

The addressing modes, immediate, direct, index, and extended, as with the accumulator instructions, are used to specify memory location (M). There is, however, no reference to the data in location (M + 1), which stores the low-byte (IXL) portion of the address.

The four addressing modes, immediate, direct, index, and extended, have the same function and use the same notation for specifying the memory location described in Chapter 1.

Immediate Addressing

The immediate addressing mode is used to initialize by introducing a 2-byte constant or *known* address into the index register. The 2-byte address is stored immediately behind the opcode.

CE 12 34 LDX #$1234

The opcode of this 3-byte instruction is CE, and the immediate address loaded into the Index Register is $1234.

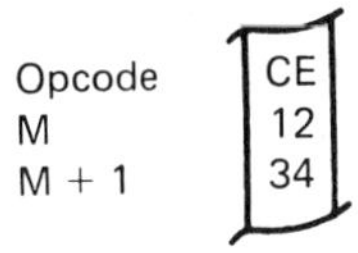

Direct Addressing

The 2-byte direct addressing mode is used for the quick and efficient access and storage of data (the address in the index register) to or from page 0 of memory. The contents of the index register must be stored in two contiguous memory locations, and the store direct instruction specifies the first memory location, M. To store the contents of the index register in locations 6 and 7, the instruction is written as follows:

DF 06 STX 06

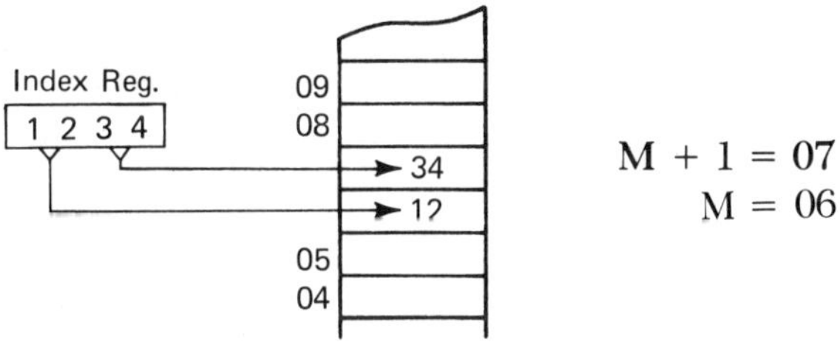

Extended Addressing

The 3-byte extended addressing mode is used to access or store the address in the index register anywhere in memory. The extended addressing mode instruction specifies the high-order byte (IXH) in memory location (M). To compare the contents of location $3000 and $3001 with the address in the index register, the instruction refers to location M at $3000:

BC 3000 CPX $3000

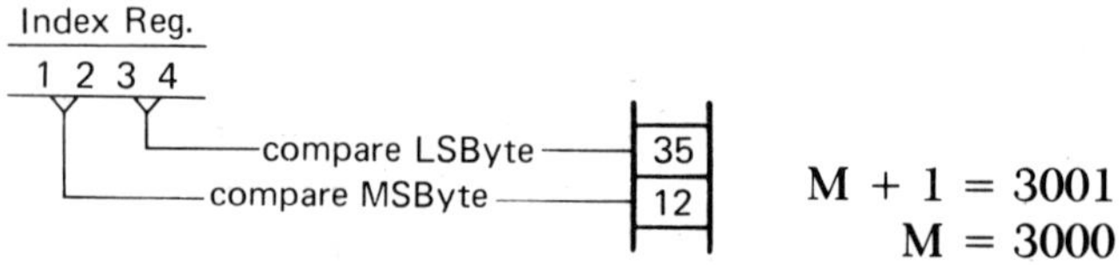

In this example the microprocessor compares:

$$IXH - M \qquad = 12 - 12 = 0$$

and

$$IXL - (M + 1) = 34 - 35 = -1 = \text{binary } 1111\ 1111$$

With a carry from the low-order byte to the high-order byte, the condition code bits are set:

1 2 3 4	0 0 0 1 0 0 1 0 0 0 1 1 0 1 0 0
−1 2 3 5	−0 0 0 1 0 0 1 0 0 0 1 1 0 1 0 1
F F F F	1 1 1 1 1 1 1 1 1 1 1 1 1 1 1 1
	↑ N

C = ● not affected
V = 0 no 2's complement overflow
Z = 0 nonzero result
N = 1 negative bit is set

The increment (INX) and decrement (DEX) index register instructions are 1-byte instructions. Once the index register is initialized, they are used to move the index register and point it to the next byte of data within the block to be accessed or modified. The 2 bit is the only condition code bit affected by the instruction.

5-1 TEST A RAM

A RAM is a random-access memory device used to read or write data to or from memory. The load and store instructions are used to execute the read and write data from memory. The 6810 is a 1K-bit RAM that is organized as 128 × 8 bits (see Appendix VII). It stores the data for 128 memory locations of 8 bits each. For example, four 6810 RAM devices store data for decimal 512 or $0200 memory locations (Fig. 5-2).

The load, store, and compare accumulator instructions (LDA, STA, and CMP), when used in the index addressing modes, are written

```
LDA  A   0,X
STA  A   0,X
CMP  A   0,X
```

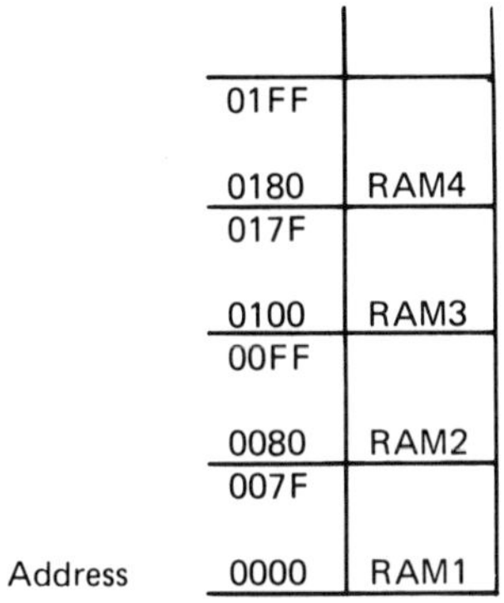

Figure 5-2. Four 6810 RAM devices occupying memory locations 0000 to 01FF.

RAM		Starting Address	Ending Address
1st	RAM 0000	\$0000	\$007F
2nd	RAM 0080	\$0080	\$00FF
3rd	RAM 0100	\$0100	\$017F
4th	RAM 0180	\$0180	\$01FF

where the X after the comma indicates the index addressing mode, and the 0 indicates a zero offset. They are written with the understanding that the index register has first been loaded, incremented, or decremented and is presently pointing to the appropriate address.

Programs used to test a RAM manipulate one block of data at a time. A test pattern is first loaded into the RAM as an original block of data, and then at a later time the pattern previously stored in the RAM is examined and compared to the original block of data. If there are any discrepancies, it is presumed that the RAM is faulty and failed the test. Each phase of the test is a separate routine. The index register is loaded with the starting address of the RAM to be tested and then loops through the routine, either loading or testing by comparing the pattern at the location pointed to by the index register.

Two variations of the RAM test are discussed; one test offers more flexibility than the other. The first RAM test tests a RAM of fixed size in a predetermined memory space with a predetermined test pattern. This less flexible test sets the parameters for memory size, location, and test pattern during the main routine and then calls the RAM test subroutine to execute the test.

Both tests test the RAM that occupies the memory 128 spaces from locations \$0080 to \$017F. Some typical test patterns are the following:

- All 1's
- All 0's
- A 1010 1010 pattern ($AA)
- A 0101 0101 pattern ($55)
- A checkerboard pattern

```
1010 1010
0101 0101
1010 1010
0101 0101
```

- A complementary checkerboard pattern

```
0101 0101
1010 1010
0101 0101
1010 1010
```

RAM Test 1

Test a 128 × 8 RAM in locations $0080 to $00FF with a $AA (1010 1010) test pattern (see Fig. 5-3). There are two parts of the test: the first loads the test pattern into the RAM and the second part examines and compares the data stored in memory with expected data. If the data in memory do not agree with the expected data, an error has been detected and the program branches to an error routine. The error routine is not defined, but generally can be expected to do the following:

- Turn on a red light indicating the test result to an operator.
- Drop the failed RAM into the appropriate bin.

LDX	#$0080	Load the index register IMMEDIATE with the starting address of the RAM
CLR	ERROR	Or CLR $000F is a clear direct location $F. This location will be tested on the return from the subroutine, and if there is a nonzero number at that location, it is an indication that the RAM failed the test.
STA A	0, X	Store the contents of Acc A in the memory location pointed to by the index register.
INX		Increment the index register to be pointing to the memory location next to be loaded with the test pattern.

CPX	#$0100	Compare the index register with the last address + 1.
BNE	TLOOP	Branch, if not equal to the last address T1, back to location labeled TLOOP. Stay in the loop and keep loading the test pattern.
LDX	#$0080	When the test pattern is loaded into RAM, reload the index register with the starting address.
CMP	0, X	Compare indexed (A-M), the contents of memory location pointed to by the index register, to the contents of accumulator A, which stores the original test pattern.
BNE	ERR	If they are unequal, indicates an error. Branch to ERROR routine R.
INX		Increment index register to examine the next memory location.
CPX	#$0100	Compare index register with the last address +1.
BNE	TSTCMP	If not equal, stay in loop and keep testing RAM.

RAM Test 2

The second example of a RAM test uses a subroutine to test a RAM. The parameters that define the location and size of the RAM and the test pattern are loaded into appropriate registers as part of the main routine and are then passed to the test subroutine. The parameters passed are the following:

- The test pattern via accumulator A.
- The location of the RAM via the index register.
- The size of the RAM via accumulator B, although it may be passed via a memory location.

This technique is more efficient than writing separate routines with every test pattern.

Exit from a Subroutine Due to an Error

Good programming practice requires that there be only one exit from a subroutine. *Nesting* a subroutine refers to one subroutine calling another and using the stack to keep track of which subroutine is

```
                           NAM     TESTRAM  SEC 5.1
                    * THIS ROUTINE FIRST LOAD A TEST PATTERN INTO RAM
                    * AND THEN GOES BACK TO THE STARTING ADDRESS AND
                    * TESTS THE DATA BY COMPARING THE DATA FROM MEMORY
                    * TO THE TEST PATTERN
                    *
                    * TEST MEMORY LOCATIONS $0080 TO $00FF
                    * LOAD TEST PATTERN $AA (1010 1010) INTO ACC A
                    *
0000 86 AA          TESTR  LDA A   #$AA      TST PATTERN 1010 1010
0002 CE 0080               LDX     #$0080    POINT INDEX R TO STARTING ADD
0005 7F 000F               CLR     $000F     CLR ERROR FLAG
0008 A7 00          TLOOP  STA A   0,X       START LOADING TEST PATTERN
000A 08                    INX               INC INDEX REG
000B 8C 0100               CPX     #$0100    TEST FOR EXIT FROM LOOP
000E 26 F8                 BNE     TLOOP     KEEP LOADING TEST PATTERN
                    * TEST PATTERN LOADED NOW START TESTING
                    *
0010 CE 0080               LDX     #$0080    RELOAD INDEX REG
0013 A1 00          TSTCMP CMP A   0,X       CMP TEST PATTERN
0015 26 08                 BNE     ERR1      BR TO SET ERR FLAG & EXIT
0017 08                    INX
0018 8C 0100               CPX     #$0100
001B 26 F6                 BNE     TSTCMP    TEST TO EXIT FROM LOOP
001D 20 03                 BRA     END1
001F 7C 000F        ERR1   INC     $0F       SET ERR FLAG TO NON ZERO NUM
0022 39             END1   RTS

TOTAL ERRORS 00000
```

Figure 5-3A. RAM test #1.

being called. When returning from these nested subroutines, it is imperative that the subroutine return through the stack in the same sequence in which the subroutines were called. This implies that there should be one exit from each subroutine, whether or not an error is detected.

This technique implies that an error flag is set during the subroutine and sensed after returning from the subroutine. The error flag is location $000E and, when clear, implies no error; when set to all 1's or a nonzero number, it implies an error.

5-2 INPUT AND OUTPUT A MESSAGE: ASCII

An input or output message that moves data between a terminal and microprocessor is handled as a block of data. These messages are often transmitted via an ASCII code. The ASCII code (Appendix V) is a list of 128 seven-bit alphanumeric and control characters.

```
                   * THIS IS THE MAIN PROGRAM FROM WHICH
                   * THE TEST RAM SUBROUTINE IS CALLED
                   *
0020                      ORG    $0020
                   *
0020 7F 000F              CLR    $000F     CLEAR ERROR FLAG
0023 CE 0080              LDX    #$0080    RAM LOCATION
0026 86 AA                LDA A  #$AA      TEST PATTERN 1010
0028 C6 7F                LDA B  #$7F      128 BYTE COUNT
002A BD 0040              JSR    TEST1     CALL TEST SUBROUTINE
002D 7D 000F              TST    $000F     CHECK ERROR FLAG?
0030 26 0D                BNE    ERRR      BR TO ERROR ROUTINE IF
0032 CE 0080              LDX    #$0080    IF NO ERROR THEN
0035 86 55                LDA A  #$55      LOAD NEXT TEST PATTERN
0037 C6 7F                LDA B  #$7F      128 BYTE COUNT
0039 BD 0040              JSR    TEST1     TEST PATTERN 0101
003C 7D 000F              TST    $000F     CHECK FOR ERRORS
                   *DUMMY INSTRUCTION
                   *
003F 01            ERRR   NOP
                   *
                   * TEST SUBROUTINE
                   *
                   * ASSUME THAT THE TEST PATTERN IS IN ACC A
                   *
0040 DF 02         TEST1  STX    $02       POINT INDEX R TO STARTING ADD
0042 D7 04                STA B  $04       SAVE RAM SIZE
0044 7F 000F              CLR    $000F     CLR ERROR FLAG
0047 A7 00         TLOOP  STA A  0,X       START LOADING TEST PATTERN
0049 08                   INX              INC INDEX REG
004A 8C 0100              CPX    #$0100    TEST FOR EXIT FROM LOOP
004D 26 F8                BNE    TLOOP     KEEP LOADING TEST PATTERN
                   * TEST PATTERN LOADED NOW START TESTING
                   *
004F DE 02                LDX    $02       RELOAD INDEX REG
0051 D6 04                LDA B  $04       GET RAM SIZE
0053 A1 00         TSTCMP CMP A  0,X       CMP TEST PATTERN
0055 26 08                BNE    ERR1      BR TO SET ERR FLAG & EXIT
0057 08                   INX
0058 8C 0100              CPX    #$0100
005B 26 F6                BNE    TSTCMP    TEST TO EXIT FROM LOOP
005D 20 03                BRA    END1
005F 7C 000F       ERR1   INC    $0F       SET ERR FLAG TO NON ZERO NUM
0062 39            END1   RTS

TOTAL ERRORS 00000
```

Figure 5-3B. RAM test #2.

The program initially points the index register to the beginning of the block, which is the memory location where the message is to be transferred to or from. A byte of data is then transferred between the appropriate I/O port and the memory location pointed to by the index register with each loop through the program. During each loop through the program, the index register is incremented or decremented pointing to the next word, actual memory location, of the message. When the end of transmission (EOT), which is coded $04, is detected, program DATAIN then exits from the loop.

This program presumes that the I/O device can handle the data rate, which is not necessarily a good assumption. In Chapter 9 this program is modified to test the I/O device before transferring data through it.

DATAIN

Write a program that stores an ASCII message starting in location $20 and in ascending memory locations until an EOT is detected. The input port is at location $8020.

```
DATAIN   LDX     #$0020   Load index starting add
CONT     LDA A   $8020    Input data
         STA A   0, X     Store 1 ASCII character
         INX              Increment index register
         CMPA    #$04     Test for EOT
         BNE     CONT     Br back if no EOT
```

5-3 SHIFTING MULTIBYTE NUMBERS

Numbers that must be expressed in 2, 3, 4, or more bytes, consisting of 16, 24, 32, or more bits, are multibyte numbers. They are handled as blocks of data and stored in contiguous memory locations. The index register points to the byte of data being shifted. This section discusses techniques for shifting 4-byte numbers both left and right.

The 6800 has five shift and rotate instructions (Fig. 5-4). Each shift and rotate instruction can be shifted in either accumulator or in a memory location. When shifted in a memory location, the data in the accumulator are not affected, but the carry bit is always affected. The shift instructions are used to modify either one byte of data standing alone or the first byte of a string of data. The rotate instructions, however, are used when shifting a bit of data through a block of data in memory (Fig. 5-5).

ASL The *arithmetic shift left* instruction is used to multiply a

1-byte number by 2, and shifts a zero into bit 0.

LSR The *logical shift right* instruction divides a positive 1-byte number by 2 and shifts a zero into bit 7.

ASR The *arithmetic shift right* instruction divides either a positive or negative 2's complement number by 2. Bit 7 is not changed and it is referred to as spreading the sign.

ROL and ROR The *rotate left* and *rotate right* instructions rotate the byte of data through the carry bit and are used when shifting multibyte numbers via the carry bit.

Example Shift a 4-byte number, stored in locations \$20 to \$23, left one bit. Shift zero into LSB.

SEE SHLEFT ROUTINE Care must be exercised that only the rotate instruction affect the carry bit, as illustrated in Fig. 5-6. This figure illustrates how data are rotated with each pass through the loop.

5-4 SHIFTING MULTIBYTE DECIMAL NUMBERS

The decimal number system is often used because it is convenient for inputting and outputting. It obviates the need to convert the decimal number to a binary or 2's complement form. Multibyte numbers used in arithmetic operations, such as addition, subtraction, multiplication, and division, must be shifted left or right during these operations and are handled as a block of data.

A typical example is to shift left by one digit a packed 8-digit decimal number, 02, 876, 195, stored in locations \$20 to \$23, when the most significant byte (MS byte) is stored in location \$23.

Before shift left

Loc \$23	Loc #22	Loc #21	Loc \$20	
0 2	8 7	6 1	9 5	←0

After shift left

2 8	7 6	1 9	5 0

Packed decimal or BCD numbers are two-decimal digits stored in a byte. In unpacked numbers there is one digit per byte. Shifting decimal numbers requires that each bit be shifted four times. This is implemented by executing the shift left or right bit routine four times.

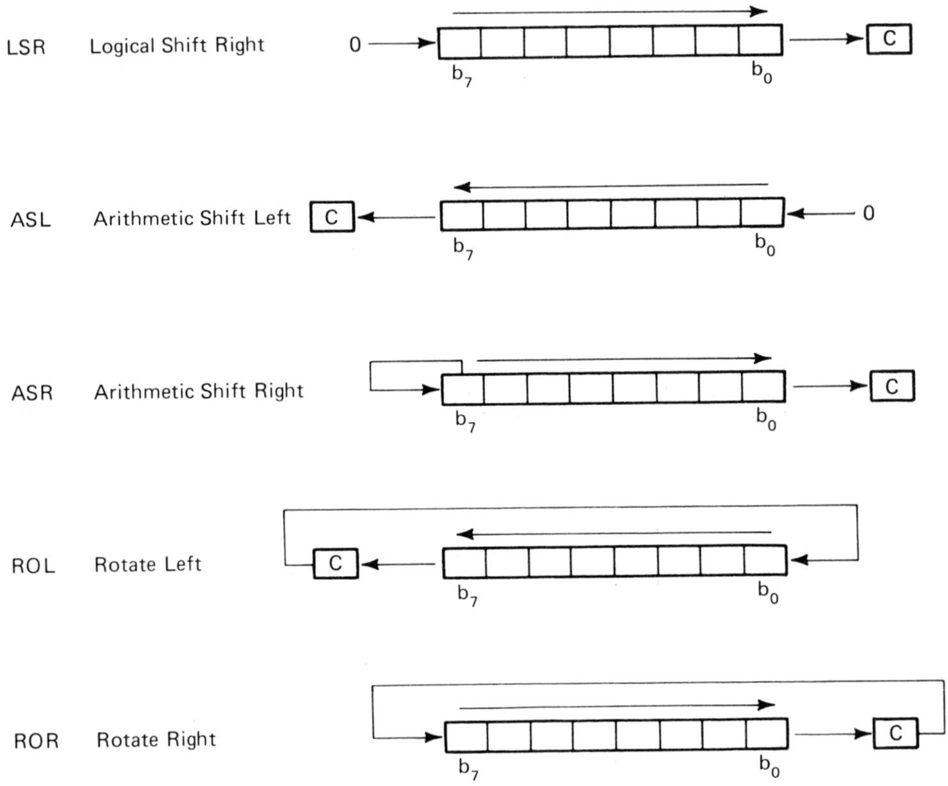

Figure 5-4. Shift and rotate instructions.

Therefore, shifting a digit left or right through a 4-byte number requires that each bit be shifted through the 4-byte number four times.

5-5 EXPONENT

Two types of number systems used in computers are fixed-length and floating-point numbers. Each number system has three components or fields: a mantissa, sign, and exponent. The exponent indicates the position of the decimal or binary point in the mantissa and is stored in its own memory location. In this section the examples used will have a packed 8-digit mantissa with a 1-byte 2's complement exponent. For example, the number 123.456 can be expressed three different ways that are all equal (see the figure at the top of page 145).

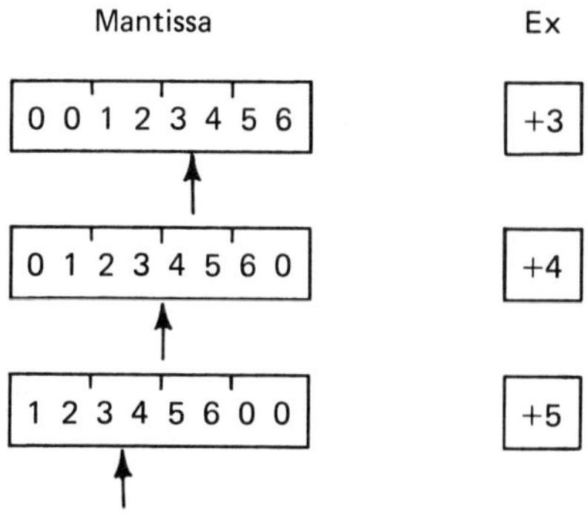

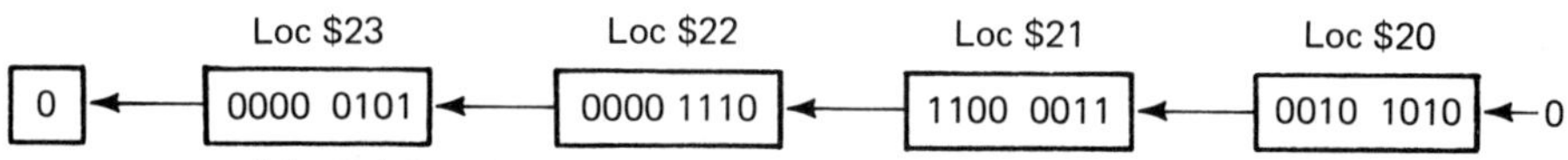

(a) A left shift through a 4-byte number effectively shifts the number.

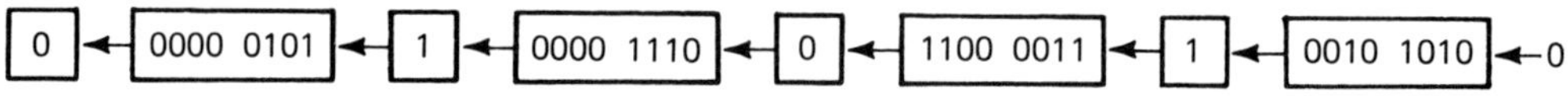

(b) They shift left "as if" a carry bit connects each byte.

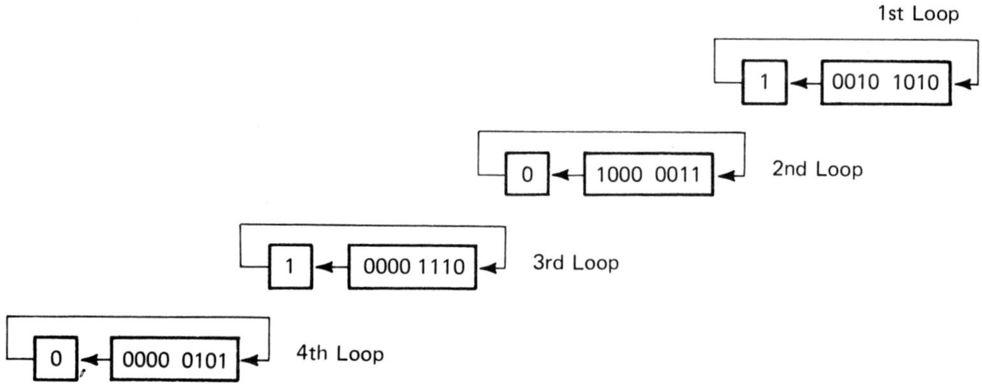

(c) The block shift is completed in a 4-LOOP program where 1-bit is shifted through the number.

Figure 5-5. Procedure by which bit is shifted through the carry bit.

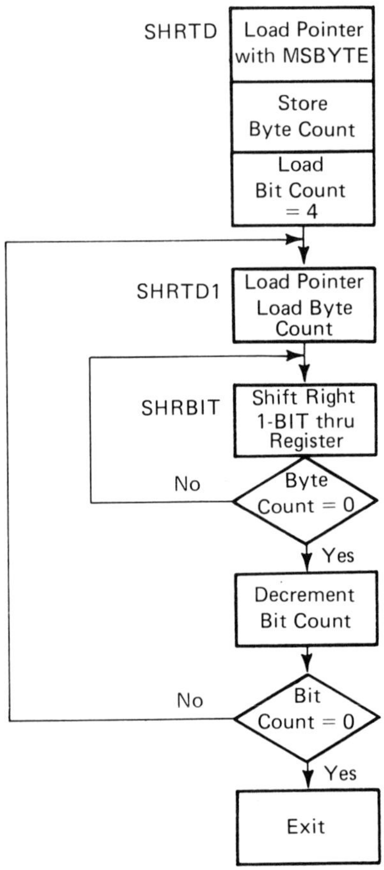

Figure 5-6. Digit shift right. The digit right routine shifts one digit 4 bits right. The index pointer is preloaded with the MSByte of the register to be shifted and the byte count is preloaded in accumulator B. The pointer and byte count are reloaded four times, once after each bit is shifted through the register.

Fixed-Length Number Notation

In fixed-length number notation, when the exponent is zero it is to the right of the least significant digit. When the exponent is 1, 2, 3, . . . , then the decimal point is moved to the left of either the first, second, third, . . . , position, respectively. For example,

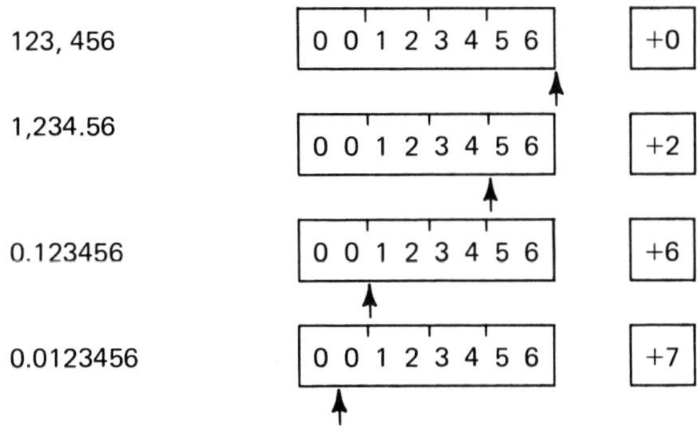

The range of a fixed length 8-digit number is from 0.000 000 01 to 99,999,999.

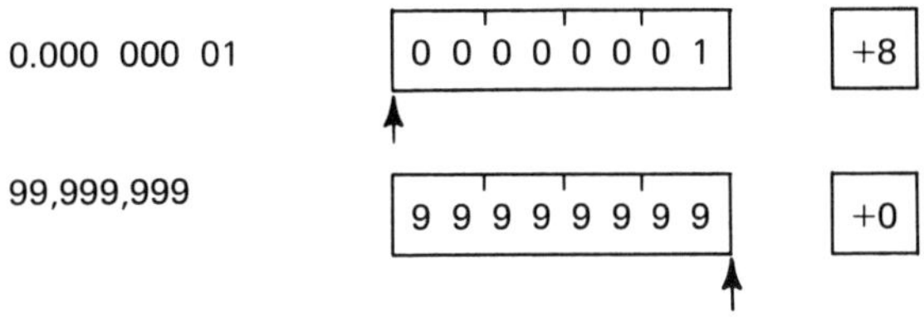

Floating-Point Number Notation

In floating-point notation the number is stored in normalized form, which means that the decimal point is to the left of the leftmost digit, and with an 8-digit number, no more than 8 digits of significance are stored. The size of the exponent is independent of the mantissa and can itself be a multibyte number. For a 1-byte 2's complement exponent, the range of the exponent is from +127 to −128. Some examples are as follows:

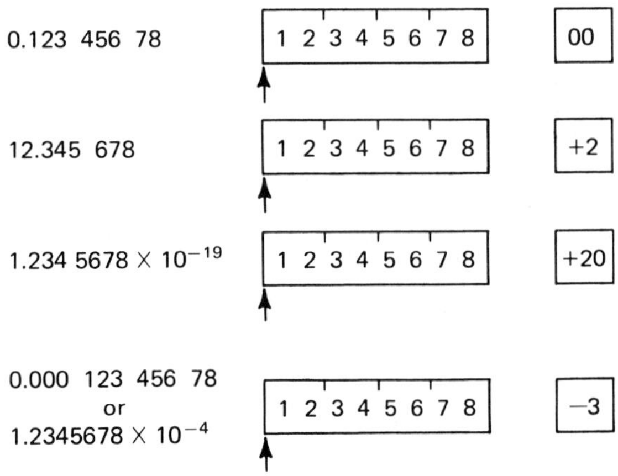

```
                          *
                          * IN THE DECIMAL SHIFT RIGHT ROUTINE THE INDEX
                          * REGISTER AND ACC B ARE PRELOADED WITH THE ADDR
                          * OF THE MSBYTE AND THE  NUMBER (SIZE) OF  BYTES
                          * TO BE SHIFTED, RESPECTIVELY
                          *
A 01E0 DF 10        A SHRTD   STX    $10       SAVE POINTER ADDR
A 01E2 D7 05        A         STAB   $05       SAVE SIZE
A 01E4 86 04        A         LDAA   #$04      BIT COUNT
A 01E6 97 00        A         STAA   $00       BIT COUNT TO LOC 00
                          * RELOAD POINTER & COUNT REGISTER
A 01E8 DE 10        A SHRTD1  LDX    $10
A 01EA D6 05        A         LDAB   $05       RELOAD BYTE CTOUNT
A 01EC BD 01F5      A         JSR    SHRBIT
A 01EF 7A 0000      A         DEC    $0000     DEC BIT COUNT
A 01F2 26 F4 01E8             BNE    SHRTD1
A 01F4 39                     RTS
                          *
                          * SUBROUTINE SHIFT RIGHT BIT
A 01F5 0C               SHRBIT CLC             CLEAR CARRY
A 01F6 66 00        A         ROR    0,X       ROTATE MENORY LOC
A 01F8 09                     DEX              DECREMENT POINTER
A 01F9 5A                     DECB             DEC BYTE COUNT
A 01FA 26 F9 01F5             BNE    SHRBIT
A 01FC 39                     RTS
                          *
```

5-6 LEFT AND RIGHT JUSTIFY A NUMBER

Left and right justify routines shift numbers left or right, removing either the leading or trailing zeros. This, of course, applies to nonzero numbers. As the number is left or right justified, the exponent is modified so that the value of the number is not affected. The exponent is incremented while left justifying and decremented while right justifying the number.

Left Justify Routine

Left justify or normalize routines permit the programmer to examine the number prior to an arithmetic operation. The programmer also knows the number of significant digits to the left of the decimal point. It calls the digital left shift subroutine and increments the exponent as each digit is shifted. The routine terminates when a nonzero number to the left of the decimal point is shifted into the MS digit position.

Two examples, 12.34 and 0.0678, of a left-justified, 7-digit, 4-byte number are illustrated on the next page.

The left justify routine (LEFTJ) tests if the MS digit is equal to zero by testing location \$23, and then testing if the exponent at location \$24 is less than 7. If either condition is met, the number is left justified and

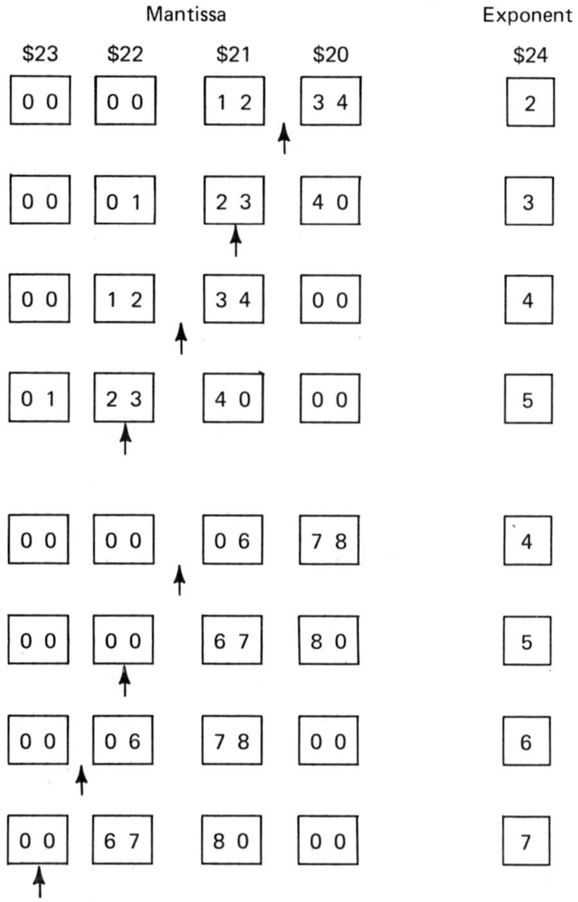

the routine exits from the subroutine. If the number is not left justified, the exponent is incremented and then branches back to the beginning of the routine (LEFTJ).

Right Justify Routine

Numbers are usually right justified after being modified by an arithmetic operation and before being displayed or examined for an error condition. Before displaying, and for cosmetic reasons, redundant zeros are eliminated to the right of the decimal point (see Fig. 5-7a and b).

When an arithmetic operation results in a number that is larger than the system can handle, an error is flagged and the program branches to an error routine. There are three basic criteria for determining an error condition:

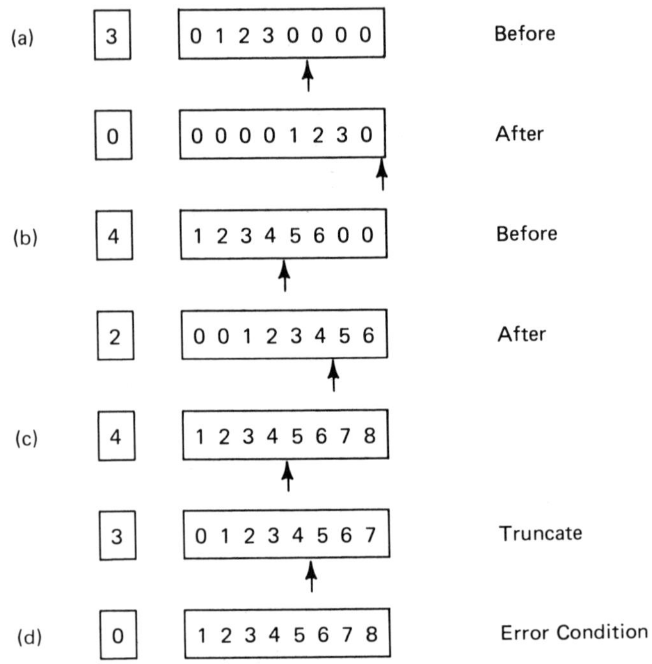

Figure 5-7. Examples of a right justified 7-digit number: (a) cosmetic, (b) cosmetic, (c) truncated number, (d) error condition, with an 8-digit nondecimal result.

- When a significant digit to the left of the decimal point is to be discarded before the number meets the system specifications; in this case a 7-digit number: 12345678.0.
- When the specification calls for two decimal digits to the right of the decimal point (e.g., dollars and cents), and the result must discard one of the two digits to the right of the decimal point to meet the system specifications; in this case when the result has 6 or more significant digits: 123456.78
- When any nonzero number is to be discarded: 12.345678

The right justify routine (RJUST) illustrated sets an error when the result has eight or more digits to the left of the decimal point. The routine can truncate and round-up:

- To truncate is to discard the least significant digits (see Fig. 5-7c). For example:

	12345.678
becomes	12345.67

```
                        * THE LEFT JUSTIFY ROUTINE, LEFT JUSTIFIES THE
                        * CONTENTS OF THE D-REGISTER PRIOR TO CALLING
                        * SHIFT LEFT DIGIT ROUTINE THE INDEX REGISTER
                        * & ACC B'ARE LOADED WITH THE LSBYTE OF REG D
                        * & THE BYTE COUNT (SIZE OF D REG).
                        *
                        * ASSUME THAT THE EXPONENT IS STORED IN LOC $2C &
                        * THE MSBYTE IS STORED N LOC $2B
                        *
02F8 7D 002B   A LEFTJ  TST    $002B    TEST MSBYE UNEQUAL TO 0
02FB 26 13 0310         BNE    ELEFT    EXIT IF MSBYTE NOT 0
02FD 86 13     A        LDAA   #$13     TEST MAX EXPONENT
02FF 91 2C     A        CMPA   $2C      AT LOC 2C
0301 2C 0D 0310         BGE    ELEFT    EXIT
                 *CONTINUE IF THE NUMBER IS NOT LEFT JUSTIFIED
0303 7C 002C   A        INC    $002C    INC EXPONNENT D
0306 CE 0028   A        LDX    #$0028   POINT TO D REG
0309 C6 04     A        LDAB   #$04     BYTE COUNT
030B BD 021A   A        JSR    SHLFD
030E 20 E8 02F8         BRA    LEFTJ    BR BACK TO TEST NEXT DIGIT
0310 39          ELEFT  RTS
                 *
                        END
```

```
                 *
                 * IN THE DECIMAL SHIFT LEFT ROUTINE THE INDEX
                 * REGISTER AND ACC B ARE PRELOADED WITH THE ADDR
                 * THE LSBYTE AND THE  NUMBER (SIZE) OF  BYTES
                 * TO BE SHIFTED, RESPECTIVELY
                 *
021A DF 10     A SHLFD  STX    $10      SAVE POINTER ADDR
021C D7 05     A        STAB   $05      SAVE SIZE
021E 86 04     A        LDAA   #$04     BIT COUNT
0220 97 00     A        STAA   $00      BIT COUNT TO LOC 00
                 * RELOAD POINTER & COUNT REGISTER
0222 DE 10     A SHLFD1 LDX    $10      RELOAD POINTER
0224 D6 05     A        LDAB   $05      RELOAD BYTE COUNT
0226 BD 022F   A        JSR    SHLBIT
0229 7A 0000   A        DEC    $0000    DEC BIT COUNT
022C 26 F4 0222         BNE    SHLFD1
022E 39                 RTS
                 *
                 * SUBROUTINE SHIFT LEFT BIT
022F 0C          SHLBIT CLC             CLEAR CARRY
0230 69 00     A        ROL    0,X      ROTATE MENORY LOC
0232 08                 INX             INCREMENT POINTER
0233 5A                 DECB            DEC BYTE COUNT
0234 26 F9 022F         BNE    SHLBIT
```

- To round-up is to add 1 to the least significant digit if the discard digit is 5 or greater.

The choice for determining the error and round-off technique is specified by the system.

5-7 MOVING BLOCKS OF DATA

"Blocks of data" refers to data that are stored in contiguous memory locations and are handled as a group. The block of data may refer to a program, message, multibyte number, or any other grouping. This section discusses two techniques for moving a block of data, 1 byte at a time, via an accumulator:

- In the most general case, from one memory location to another without restrictions.
- In the more restrictive case, when the data are moved less than 256 memory locations apart using the indexed capability of the index register.

When moving a block of data, as illustrated in Fig. 5-8, each byte of data pointed to by the index register is loaded from the source block into an accumulator. That byte of data is then stored in the memory location pointed to by the index register. It would be convenient to have two index registers to accomplish this operation, each pointing to the source and destination blocks, respectively. The 6800, however, has only one index register and, therefore, it becomes necessary to juggle the contents of the index register, where the contents must alternately point to the source and destination blocks. When not used, the contents of the index register are stored in memory. The subroutine to move data (MOOV) illustrates how the data of the block and the contents of the index register are transferred between memory, an accumulator, and the index register, respectively.

Three bits of information are necessary to move a block of data: the starting address of the source block (SOURAD), the starting address of the destination block (DESTAD), and the size of the block (SIZE). Assume that these three parameters have been passed to the subroutine by storing as follows:

- Starting address of the source block labeled SOURAD in location \$10.
- Starting address of the destination block labeled DISTAD in location \$12.
- Size of the block is stored in accumulator B, when the size is equal to, or less than, 256 bytes.

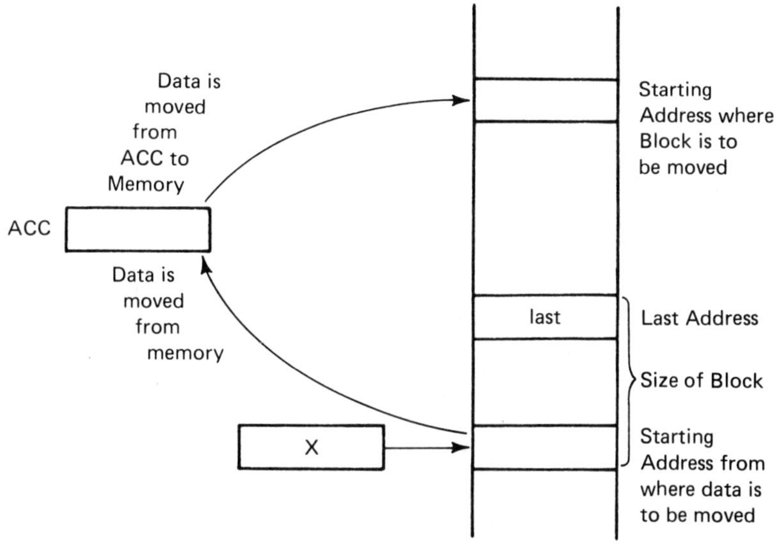

Figure 5-8. Moving a block of data.

Assume that a block of $20 bytes of data is moved from a source location $0020 to destination location $1234.

LDX	$10	The 16-bit address of the source location is transferred from memory locations $10 and $11 to the index register. The index register is pointing to a byte of data from the source block.
LDAA	0, X	The byte of data is loaded from the source block to accumulator A with an index addressing mode instruction.
INX		Increment the contents of the index register to point to the next byte of data to be moved.
STX	$10	Store the contents of the index register, which points to the byte of the source block to be moved next, back into locations $10 and $11.
LDX	$12	Load the 16-bit index register with the address of byte of data in the destination block.
STAA	0, X	Store the byte of data from accumulator A in the destination block with an index addressing mode instruction.

INX		Increment the contents of the index register to point to the next byte of data to be moved.
STX	$12	Store the 16-bit address of the index register back in memory locations $12 and $13.
DEC B		Test to exit from the loop by decrementing the size of the block.
BNE	MOOV	If the block of data has not been completely moved, stay in the loop and branch back to move the next byte of data. However, if the complete block has been moved, exit from the loop by advancing to the next instruction, which returns from the subroutine.

Moving Blocks of Data with More Than 256 Bytes

To move a block of more than 256 bytes of data, the size of the block is stored in two contiguous memory locations and decrements memory.

Example: To move 1K bytes of data, store the number, labeled size of 1K-hex 0200, in two contiguous memory locations, $14 and $15. Memory location $14 will contain 2, and location $15 will be cleared. This is part of the main routine, and the size is passed to the subroutine.

Replace	DEC B	
With	DEC	$15
	BNE	MOVED
	DEC	$14
	BNE	MOVED

It may, however, be convenient to store the size of the block in a memory location and keep accumulator B free, even when the size is less than 256 bytes.

Move a Block of Data Less Than 256 ($FF) Bytes, Using the Indexed (Offset) Capability of the Index Register

The indexing capability gives a single index register the ability to be pointing to two or more blocks of data when they are within the range of the offset ($FF) decimal 256. Where applicable, it is a very efficient technique.

Up to this point in the book the discussion of the index addressing mode has been limited to the zero offset, that is, the special case when the index register is pointing to the data in memory being addressed. The form of the index addressing mode instruction was

```
STA   A   0,X
LDA   A   0,X
```

where the zero to the left of the comma indicated the offset. The offset is added to the address contained in the index register to form an effective address (E). In the special case when the offset is equal to zero, the address in the index register points to the effecting address.

In the general case, the offset may have a 1-byte value from 00 to $FF. When the offset is nonzero, the effective address of the data being accessed is computed by adding the address in the index register to the offset, and the address in the index register is not affected.

Examples:

Effective Address	=	Index	+	Offset
$800	=	$800	+	0
$850	=	$800	+	$50
$8FF	=	$800	+	$FF
$1278	=	$1234	+	$44
$C08B	=	$C011	+	$7A

```
                    *
                    * MOVE A BLOCK OF DATA
                    * FROM A STARTING LOCATION  STORED IN $08
                    * TO A LOCATION STORED IN $0A
                    * THE SIZE OF THE BLOCK IS STORED IN ACCUMULATOR
                    *
A 0237 DE 08      A MOOV    LDX     $08       LOAD SOURCE BLOCK POINTER
A 0239 A6 00      A         LDAA    0,X       LOAD BYTE INTO ACC A
A 023B 08                   INX               INC SOURCE BLOCK ADDR
A 023C DF 08      A         STX     $08       STORE SOURCE BLOCK POINTER
A 023E DE 0A      A         LDX     $0A       GET DESTINATION BLOCK POIN
A 0240 A7 00      A         STAA    0,X       MOVE BYTE
A 0242 08                   INX               INC DEST BLOCK ADDR
A 0243 DF 00      A         STX     $0        STORE DEST BLOCK POINTER
A 0245 5A                   DECB              DEC SIZE COUNTER
A 0246 26 EF 0237           BNE     MOOV
A 0248 39                   RTS
                    *
```

The index addressing mode instructions are all 2-byte instructions, where the second byte is the offset.

The MOVOFF program moves a block of less than 256 bytes of data less than $FF memory locations. For example, if the main routine has

```
                       * MOVE A BLOCK OF DATA USING THE INDEX OFFSET
                       * FROM SOURCE BLOCK AT LOCATION $0800
                       * TO DEST BLOCK AT LOCATION $0850
                       * $20 BYTE COUNT IN ACC B
                       *
0000 8E 0800                   LDS     #$0800    LOAD POINTER
0003 C6 20                     LDA B   #$20      LOAD BYTE COUNT
0005 A6 00             MOVOFF  LDA A   0,X       GET BYTE FROM SOURCE BLOCK
0007 A7 50                     STA A   $50,X     STORE IN DEST BLOCK
0009 08                        INX               INC POINTER
000A 5A                        DEC B             DEC BYTE COUNT
000B 26 F8                     BNE     MOVOFF
                       *
                       *
```

to move a block of $20 bytes of data from a source location starting at $800 to destination location starting at $850. Assume that, before calling subroutine MOVOFF, the index register is loaded with the address $0800, and the size of the block is loaded into accumulator B.

The MOVOFF routine has 6 instructions, while the MOOV routine has 11 instructions, which indicates that, where it is applicable, it is twice as efficient.

MOVOFF	LDAA	0, X	Load a byte of data from source
	STAA	$50, X	Store the byte of data in the destination block
	INX		Increment the index register
	DECB		Decrement the sign counter
	BNE	MOVOFF	Bring back into the loop if the block of data is not moved
	RTS		Or else exit from the loop

5-8 EXCHANGE REGISTERS

The exchange routine is similar to the move routine with the added feature of simultaneously moving or exchanging two bytes of data. Both accumulators A and B are used, the first to move the byte of data in one direction, while the second accumulator is used to hold the byte being exchanged (Fig. 5-9).

```
                       * EXCHANGE TWO REGISTERS STARTING AT LOC $20 TO $
                       * INDEX REG IS PRELOADED WITH AN LOWEST ADDR (002
                       * SIZE OF REGISTERS IS PRELOADED IN LOC $05
                       *
0249 A6 00           A EXCH    LDAA    0,X        1ST REG TO ACC A
024B E6 08           A         LDAB    8,X        2ND REG TO ACC B
024D A7 08           A         STAA    8,X        FROM ACC A TO REG 2
024F E7 00           A         STAB    0,X        FROM ACC B TO REG 1
0251 7A 0005         A         DEC     $0005
0254 26 F3 0249                BNE     EXCH
0256 39                        RTS
                       *
```

The exchange subroutine (EXCHA) exchanges the two 4-byte data blocks, starting at location $20 and $28, respectively. The index register points initially to location $20, and moves the byte of data into accumulator A. The index addressing mode, with an offset of 8, loads the alternate byte of data into accumulator B. The size of the block of data is stored in location $14.

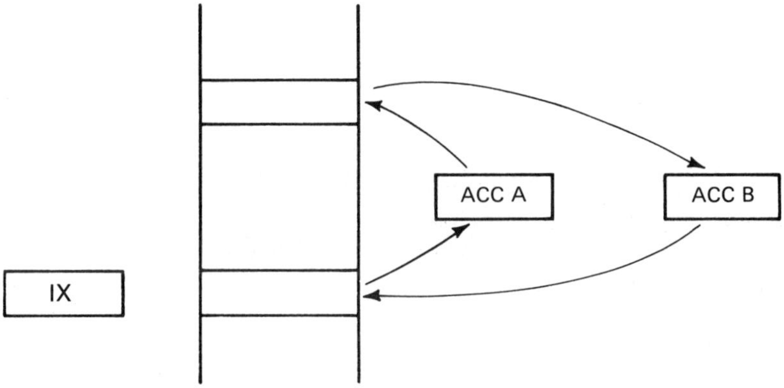

Figure 5-9. Exchange registers.

5-9 ALIGN ROUTINE

The alignment routine is discussed in this section in anticipation of arithmetic operations discussed in the next sections. In these sections first we align and then we add or subtract the two 4-byte decimal numbers, whose mantissas are stored in locations $20 to $23 and locations $28 to $2B, and the respective exponents are stored in locations $24 and $2C.

The alignment routine is used to align the decimal point of two numbers prior to executing an add and subtract routine. The ALIGN routine assumes that both numbers are left justified. The number is shifted one digit to the right with a shift right subroutine (SHRTH). By initially loading the index register with location $0020, the program presumes that the number in register $20 is shifted. If the result of the index compare instruction indicates that the exponent of register $20 is less than the exponent of register $28, then the branch, if less than (BLS) instruction, causes a branch around the next instruction. The next instruction loads the index register with location $28 so that the index register points to the appropriate register when the SHFT4 subroutine is called.

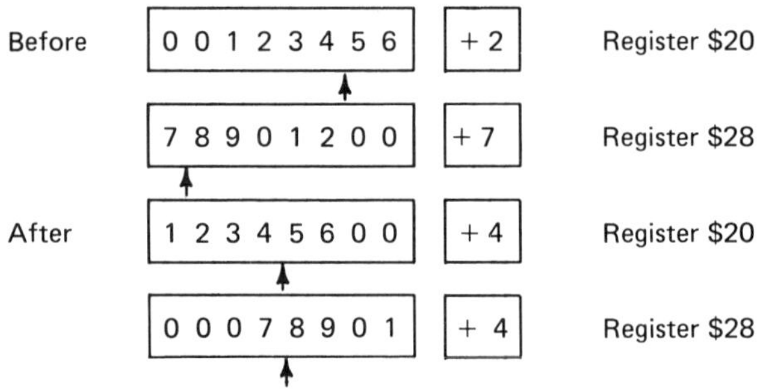

The align routine (Fig. 5-10) aligns the decimal point of both D and E registers. It assumes that both operands are left justified and that the contents of the register with the greater exponent are shifted right until the exponents are equal.

The routine starts by comparing both exponents. If they are equal the routine branches to the exit, or else it assumes that the exponent of register D is greater and loads the address of the MS byte of the D register into the index register. If, in fact, the D exponent is greater than the E exponent, the routine branches to ALIGN 1, or else the MS byte of the E register is loaded into the index register. The relevant exponent is decremented, and the contents are shifted right one digit.

```
                       *
                       * ALIGN TWO THE DECIMAL POINT OF TWO NUMBER THAT
                       * ARE TO BE LEFT JUSTIFIED ASSUME THAT BOTH
                       * ARE 4 BYTE NUMBERS AND THE EXPONENT IS IN
                       * THE FIFTH BYTE.  BOTH REGISTERS ARE 8-BYTES
                       * APART WHICH PUTS THE 2ND EXPONENT IN LOC $2C.
                       *
A 01CC CE 0020    A ALIGN   LDX     #$20       INDEX POINTER
A 01CF A6 04      A         LDAA    4,X        LOAD 1ST EXPON
A 01D1 A1 0C      A         CMPA    $C,X       CMP EXPON
```

```
00384A 01D3 27 0A 01DF          BEQ    ALIGEX    IF EQ THEN ALIGNED
00385A 01D5 23 03 01DA          BLS    ALIGN1    2'S COMP CMP RTSH $20
00386A 01D7 CE 0028   A         LDX    #$0028    ELSE RT SHIFT $28
00387A 01DA BD 01E0   A ALIGN1  JSR    SHRTD     CALL RT SHIFT BYTE
00388A 01DD 20 ED 01CC          BRA    ALIGN
00389A 01DF 39          ALIGEX  RTS
```

Branch Instructions for 2's Complement Numbers

The exponent is used to manipulate the mantissa, and in the ALIGN routine the exponents are compared to decide which number is to be shifted right. The decision is made with a branch instruction to test for

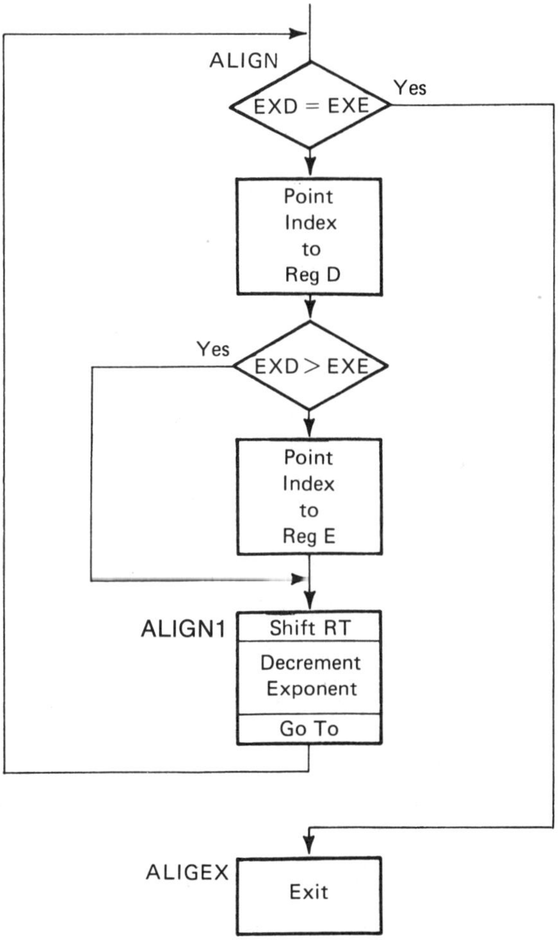

Figure 5-10. Align routine aligns the decimal point of two numbers. It is used prior to the add and subtract operations. It is assumed that both input operands are left justified, and that one of the operands is shifted right until the exponents are equal.

less than ($<$), less then or equal to ($\leq$), greater than ($>$) or greater than or equal to ($\geq$).

The 6800 microprocessor has 15 branch instructions, 6 of which test 2's complement numbers; they are identified by testing the V-bit (see Table 5-1). It has a more extensive group of branch instructions dedicated to handling 2's complement numbers than most 8-bit microprocessors.

Table 5-1(I) lists and compares eight instructions used for making the greater than, greater than or equal to, less than, or less than or equal to decisions.

Table 5-1(II) compares the four instructions. The branch if overflow set (BVS) and the branch if overflow clear (BVC) are used to detect a 2's complement overflow. They are comparable to the branch if carry set (BCS) or branch is clear (BCC) for binary numbers.

Two's Complement Exponents

A 1-byte 2's complement exponent has a range comparable to an 8-bit 2's complement number.

+127	is a 1-byte	80
0	is a 1-byte	00
−128	is a 1-byte	7F

The four 2's complement branch instructions are ideal for comparing 2's complement exponents.

Branch if greater than BGT	($>$)
Branch if greater than or equal to BGE	($\geq$)
Branch if less than BLT	($<$)
Branch if less than or equal to BLE	($\leq$)

5-10 MULTIBYTE DECIMAL ADDITION

The 6800 performs three types of add operations: binary, 2's complement, and decimal. The decimal operation could more accurately be described as a packed decimal number, which has two decimal numbers stored in 1 byte.

The advantage of having a microprocessor with decimal arithmetic capability negates the need for decimal-to-binary and binary-to-decimal routines between the internal operands and the I/O devices. For example, when not using decimal numbers, input devices, like keyboards and terminals, which conveniently input decimal numbers, would require a decimal-to-binary routine between the input device and the internal binary number system. Likewise, a binary-to-decimal routine is necessary when an internal binary number is to output to either 7-segment displays or terminals.

The add (ADD) or add with carry (ADC) instructions perform the same operation on either the binary or 2's complement number systems. The microprocessor sets both the carry (C) and the overflow (V) bits according to the rules for each number system being used, and selects the appropriate branch instructions to discern between them.

The decimal add operation, however, is executed by two contiguous instructions: first, a BINARY ADD (ADD or ADC) instruction and, second, the DECIMAL ADJUST in accumulator A (DAA), which adjusts or more accurately corrects the binary sum to a decimal sum for 1 byte.

Table 5-1. Suggested Application of Branch Instructions

I. After a COMPARE instruction where A − M:

If the decision is:	For 2's complement use:		For binary use use:	
		Test		TEST
A>	BGT	$Z \odot (N \oplus V) = 0$	BHI	$C \times Z = 0$
A≥M	BGE	$(N \oplus V) = 0$	BCS	$C = 1$
A<M	BLT	$(N \oplus V) = 1$	BCC	$C = 0$
A≤M	BLE	$Z \odot (N \oplus V) = 1$	BLS	$C \odot Z = 1$

II. After an add instruction where A + M:

For 2's complement number to detect an overflow V = 1:

- If +A + M > 7F, use BVS V = 1
- If −A − M < 80, use BVC V = 1

For binary unsigned number to detect the C = 1:

- If +A + M > FF, use BCS C = 1
- If −A − M < 0, use BCS C = 1

III. Five-branch instruction:

BRA	Branch	Always
BEQ	Z = 1	Apply to any number system
BNE	Z = 0	
BPL	N = 0	Apply to the sign bit of 2's complement or logic bit 7
BMI	N = 1	Apply to the sign bit of 2's complement or logic bit 7

Advantages of the Various Add Operations

In general, when considering which number system to use, the system programmer must consider the input device, the internal operations, and the output devices used with the system. Although the binary or 2's complement number system may be preferred for internal operation, the decimal number system is often more convenient for the I/O devices. If it is more convenient to use the decimal number for I/O, then the system programmer must decide whether to use the decimal number system internally, or to convert the I/O numbers to binary, which requires a decimal-to-binary and a binary-to-decimal converter routine at the input and output devices, respectively.

Decimal Addition and the Decimal Adjust (DAA) Instruction

To execute a decimal addition requires two contiguous instructions: first, a *binary add* and, second, the *decimal adjust* instructions (DAA), which corrects or adjusts the decimal add to reflect the result of a decimal addition. The decimal adjust instruction senses and uses the condition code bits set by the previous add instruction. As such, the decimal adjust instruction should immediately follow the add instruction before the condition code bits are disturbed. Caution should be exercised to use accumulator A for the add instruction, since the decimal adjust instruction operates on the data in accumulator A only. The decimal adjust instruction will add either 00, 06, 60, or 66 to result of the binary add instruction.

Example:	I	II	III	IV
	3 3	3 3	3 3	9 8
Binary add	+ 5 4	+ 8 4	+ 4 7	+ 9 9
Primary sum	8 7	3 7	7 A	[1] 3 1
DAA	+ 0 0	6 0	0 6	6 6
SUM	[0] 8 7	[1] 1 7	[0] 8 0	[1] 9 7

The 6800 processor provides the proper decimal sum with the DAA instruction.

```
                          * SUBTRACT KEY CHANGES THE SIGN OF THE D-REG
                          * AND PROCEEDS TO THE ADD KEY ROUTINE
       017A 86 FF      A SUBK    LDAA    #$FF
       017C 98 2D      A         EORA    DSIGN     CHANGE SIGN
       017E 97 2D      A         STAA    DSIGN
                          * ADD KEY ROUTINE
       0180 BD 01CC    A ADDK    JSR     ALIGN     ALIGN D & E REG'S
```

```
                         * TEST IF SIGNS ARE SAME OR DIFFRENT
0183 96 2D     A                LDAA   DSIGN
0185 98 25     A                EORA   ESIGN     COMPARE SIGNS
0187 27 0B 0194                 BEQ    ADD1      BR IF SAME
                         * ELSE SUBTRACT IF SIGNS ARE DIFFFERENT
                         * CALL DECIMAL SUBTRACT
0189 BD 01A1   A                JSR    SUBDEC
                         * TEST CARRY BIT
018C 25 0B 0199                 BCS    CHSIGD    & CHANGE DSIGN
                         * TAKE 10'S COMPLEMENT (RESTORE REG-D)
018E BD 01FD   A                JSR    TENS
0191 7E 00DA   A ADEXIT JMP    RESTOR
0194 BD 01BC   A ADD1   JSR    ADDDEC
0197 20 F8 0191                 BRA    ADEXIT
0199 86 FF     A CHSIGD LDAA   #$FF
019B 98 2D     A                EORA   DSIGN
019D 97 2D     A                STAA   DSIGN
019F 20 F0 0191                 BRA    ADEXIT
                         *
                         * THIS IS A ONE PASS SUBTRACT ROUTINE WHERE THE
                         * 10'S COMPLEMENT AND THE DECIMAL ADD ARE FORMED
                         * ONE BYTE OF DATA WITH EACH PASS THRU THE LOOP.
                         *      E - D -> D
                         * WHERE THE E REGISTER STARTS AT LOC $20 &
                         * THE D REGISTER STARTS AT LOC $28.
                         * THE NUMBER OF BYTES (SIZE) SUBTRACTED IS STORED
                         * LOC $05. THE TAP $ TPA INSTRUCTIONS ARE USED TO
                         * SAVE & RESTORE THE CC BITS IN ACC A WHILE THE 1
                         * IS FORMED SO THAT THE CARRY & HALF CARRY BITS U
                         * THE DECIMAL ADD PORTION OF THE ROUTINE ARE NOT
                         *
01A1 CE 0020   A SUBDEC LDX    #$0020    LOAD POINTER
01A4 86 04     A                LDAA   #$04
01A6 97 05     A                STAA   $05       STORE SIZE
01A8 0D                         SEC              SET CARRY, USED TO ADD 1 T
01A9 07          SUBBB  TPA              SAVE CC BITS IN ACC A
01AA C6 99     A                LDAB   #$99      CONSTANT $99 TO ACC B
01AC E0 08     A                SUBB   8,X       9'S COMP REG E
                         * THE SUBTRACT WITHOUT CARRY INSTRUCTION FORMS
                         * THE 9'S COMPLEMENT IN ACC B AFFECTS THE CARRY B
                         * USED BY THE DECIMAL ADD.
                         *
                         * NOW BRING BACK THE CARRY AND HALF CARRY BITS US
                         * BY THE ADD PART OF THE ROUTINE.
                         *
01AE 06                         TAP              REPLACE CC BITS
01AF 17                         TBA              TRANS ACCB TO A
                         * THE CARRY BITS ARE NOT AFFECTED
01B0 A9 00     A                ADCA   0,X       DECIMAL ADD TO REG E
01B2 19                         DAA              DECIMAL ADJUST IN ACC A ON
01B3 A7 08     A                STAA   8,X       STORE DIFF IN REG D
01B5 08                         INX              INCREMENT INDEX
01B6 7A 0005   A                DEC    $05       DEC SIZE COUNTER
                         * THE CARRY AND HALF CARRY BITS ARE NOT AFFFECTED
                         * THE INX & DEC INSTRUCTONS.
01B9 26 EE 01A9                 BNE    SUBBB
01BB 39                         RTS
```

There are two binary add instructions: (1) an add without carry (ADD), and (2) an add with carry (ADC). In a multibyte addition it is necessary to initially set the carry to zero and then execute the add with carry instruction. The add without carry (ADD) instruction is often used with a 1-byte number.

5-11 MULTIBYTE DECIMAL SUBTRACTION

The subtract instructions, SBC and SUB, execute a binary subtraction with and without a carry. The subtract with carry (SBC) instruction is used with multibyte numbers, while the subtract without carry (SUB) is on 1-byte operands. These instructions execute binary and 2's complement subtractions.

This section discusses the subtraction of multibyte decimal numbers, where the subtract instructions are *not* used. A decimal subtract is executed by adding the 10's complement of the subtrahend to the minuend.

$$\begin{array}{r} \text{Minuend} \\ -\text{Subtrahend} \\ \hline \text{Difference} \end{array}$$

In a decimal notation there are three parts of a number, the sign, an exponent, and a mantissa. The input operands were aligned by examining the exponent. The sign indicates whether each input operand is a positive or negative number. This section assumes that both input operands are positive numbers. The next section generalizes the problem by considering input operands of arbitrary signs.

	Sign	*EX*	*Mantissa*	
	2D	2C	2B … 28	
'E' Register				Minuend
'D' Register				Subtrahend/Diff.
	25	24	23 … 20	

There are two parts to the decimal subtract: (1) to obtain the difference, and (2) if the difference is negative, to take the 10's complement.

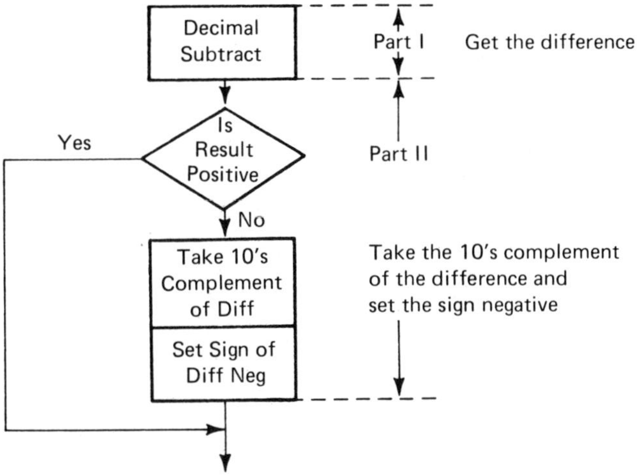

If the carry bit is clear, then take the 10's complement of the difference and set the sign negative.

When the minuend is larger than the subtrahend, the difference is positive, and if the subtrahend is greater than the minuend, the difference is negative. Two examples are illustrated, one yielding a positive and the other yielding a negative difference.

Once the procedure for decimal subtraction is established, a decimal subtract routine for positive or negative difference is as follows:

Example I Positive Difference	Example II Negative Difference
0 0 0 0 4 3 2 1	0 0 0 0 0 5 6 7
−0 0 0 0 0 5 6 7	−0 0 0 0 4 3 2 1
[+] 3 7 5 4	[−] 3 7 5 4

The 10's complement subtract routine is as follows:

A From the 10's complement of the subtrahend
B Add decimal
C Test for negative difference
D If required, form 10's complement of the difference

A. To form the 10's complement of the subtrahend, take the 9's complement and then add 1.

Example I	Example II	
99999999	99999999	
− 567	− 4321	
99999432	99995678	9's complement
+1	+1	
99999433	99995679	10's complement

B. Then do a decimal add.

00004321	00000567
+99999433	+99995679
[1] 00003754	[0] 99996246
One Carry	Zero Carry

C. Test the difference by testing the carry. If the carry = 1, then the result is positive; so exit from the routine. If the carry = 0, then the result is negative; so take the 10's complement to form the final difference.

D. Change sign of the subtrahend register, which now stores the difference = + 3754

99999999	
−99996246	
3753	9's complement
+1	
−3754	10's complement
Diff. = −3754	

Decimal Subtract Routine: E − D → D

The routine starts by taking the 10's complement of the D register, and then adding the contents of the D and E register and putting the difference into the D register. If the contents of the E register were initially greater than the contents of the D register, then the mantissa of the difference in the D register is positive, but the sign must be changed. If the contents of the D register were initially greater than the contents of the E register, then the mantissa in the D register is negative and is corrected by taking the 10's complement.

5-12 TEN'S COMPLEMENT

The 10's complement routine generates the negative or 10's complement of a decimal number, which is called by the decimal subtract routine. The 10's complement generates the following:

	General Case	Special Case
	9 9 9 9 9 9 9 9	9 9 9 9 9 9 9 9
Digit number	−d d d d d d d d	−0 0 0 0 1 2 3 4
9's complement	N N N N N N N N	9 9 9 9 8 7 6 5
	+1	+1
10's complement	T T T T T T T T	9 9 9 9 8 7 6 6

Two versions of the 10's complement are discussed. The first and more efficient version stores and juggles the carry bit of the condition code register, while the second version does not juggle the condition code bits. The routine efficiency is measured by the number of bytes, not instructions, per routine.

The 10's complement is generated in two steps: the first step is to generate the 9's complement, and the second step is to generate the 10's complement by adding 1 to the 9's complement. Subtracting the digital number dddd from 9999 forms the 9's complement NNNN, and a borrow is never generated or need be propagated during this part of the operation. The 10's complement is obtained by adding the 9's complement to a zero number and the 1 is introduced by initially setting the carry bit to 1. Care must be exercised that the relevant carry bit propagating through each byte is not affected by the other instructions in the loop (see Fig. 5-11).

Prior to writing this routine, it is helpful to review the instructions that offset the carry (out) bit, that use the carry (in) bit, and that transfer the condition code bits.

4th Loop		3rd Loop		2nd Loop		1st Loop	
	N N		N N		N N		N N
	0 0 Ci		0 0 Ci		0 0 Ci		0 0 1
Co	T T	Co	T T	Co	T T	Co	T T

Ci, carry in.
Co, carry out.

Figure 5-11. Generating 10's complement (TTTT) from 9's complement (NNNN).

The following is a list of instructions that are relevant to the 10's complement routine and their effect on the carry bit.

Affect Co	Affected by Ci (all affect Co)	No Effect on Carry
ABA	—	—
ADC	ADC	—
ADD	—	—
CLR	—	—
DAA	DAA	—
—	—	DEC
—	—	DEX
—	—	INC
—	—	INX
—	—	LDA
SUB	—	—
SBC	SBC	—
—	—	STA
TAP	—	—
—	—	TPA

Ten's Complement: Version I

Version I (Fig. 5-12) makes one loop through the routine, which makes it the most efficient version by saving on the overhead instructions. The routine assumes that the pointer and byte size register are preloaded. The initializing part (TENS) of the routine first loads the byte size, and, second, sets the carry bit, which is the plus 1 that is added to the 9's complement.

TENS1.	The 10's complement loop.
TPA	Transfer the condition code bits to accumulator A to store the relevant carry bit so that it is not inadvertently affected.
LDAB #$99	Loads the 99 into accumulator B.
SUBB 0, X	Subtract 99 − dd = NN. The carry bit in the CC register is affected.
STAB 0, X	Stores the 9's complement NN.
TAP	Transfer the relevant carry bit back to the condition code bits.
LDAA #00	Loads 00 into accumulator A. The CLEAR instruction, which affects the carry bit, *cannot* be used.

ADCA 0, X	Add 00 + NN + Ci = TT.
DAA	Decimal adjust must take place in accumulator A.
STAA 0, X	Store TT back in memory.
INX	Increment the pointer. Carry not affected.
DEC	Byte count. Carry not affected.
BNE	TENS1. Branch back if routine is not complete.

Version II

There are two passes or loops in version II. The relevant carry bit is not affected during the first pass while generating the 9's complement. Generating a 10's complement from a 9's complement does not require juggling the carry bit (see Fig. 5-13).

5-13 MULTIPLY ROUTINE

The multiply routine multiplies the 7-digit contents of the D and E registers to form a 14-digit product in the D and D-concatenated register (Fig. 5-14). This routine makes three assumptions:

- That the contents of the E register are saved prior to and restored after this routine is executed.
- That the input operands are left justified.
- That the 14-digit product is left in the D and D-concatenated register to be examined by the next routine for an error condition.

Four operations are executed prior to multiplying the mantissas of the input operand:

- Resolve the exponent of the result.
- Reassign the functions of the registers (Fig. 5-14) by moving the multiplier in the D register to the D-concatenated register.
- Clear the D register for the partial product.

The exponent of the result is formed by adding the input exponents and then subtracting seven.

$$\text{EEXP} + \text{DEXP} - 7 \rightarrow \text{REXP}$$

Subtracting the 7 is a consequence of shifting right the partial product (PP) seven times during the routine.

The sign of the result is formed by exclusive-ORing the signs of the input operands.

$$\text{ESIGN} \oplus \text{DSIGN} \rightarrow \text{RSIGN}$$

The 10's complement (TTTT) of a number (dddd) is obtained by getting the 9's complement (NNNN) and then adding one.

General Case	Special Case
9 9 9 9 9 9	9 9 9 9 9 9
− d d d d d d	− 0 0 1 2 3 4
N N N N N N	9 9 8 7 6 5
+ 1	+ 1
T T T T T T	9 9 8 7 6 6

Assuming that the index register points to the appropriate register and that the byte count is loaded in accumulator B.

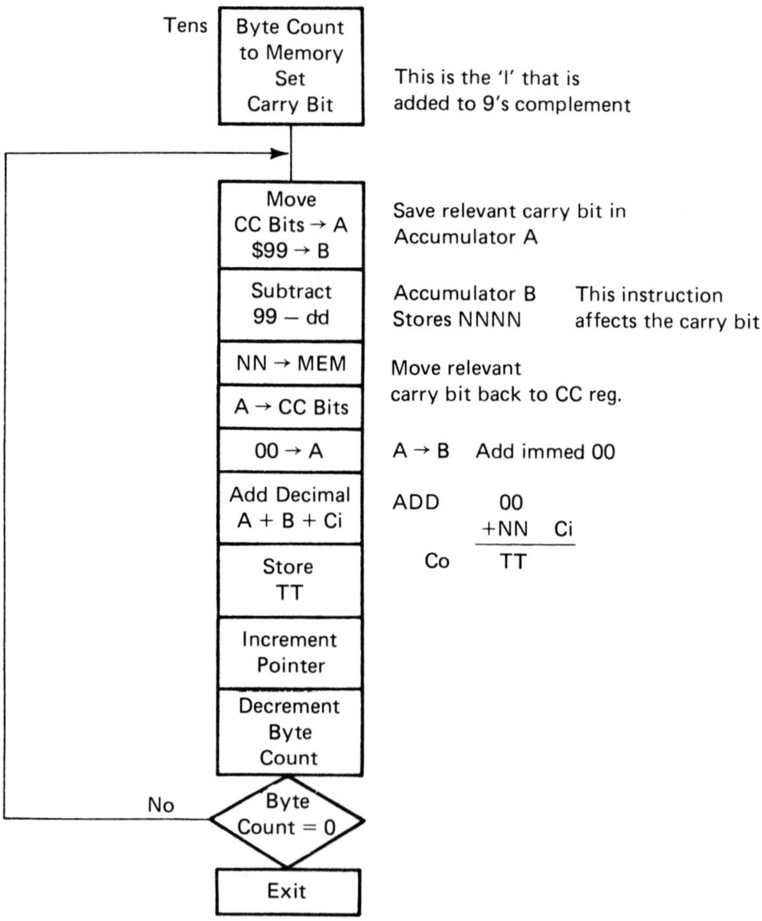

Figure 5-12. Ten's complement Version I.

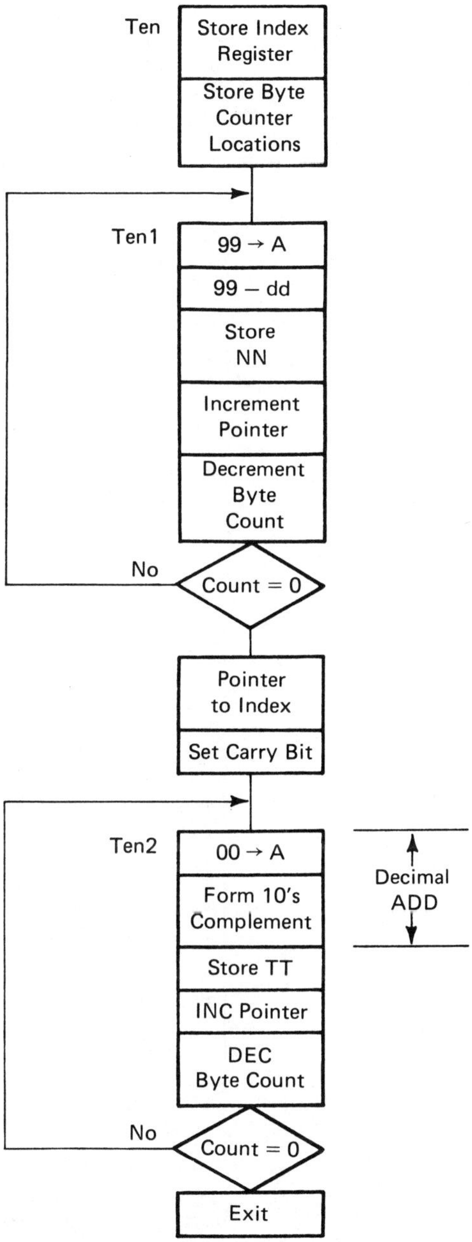

Figure 5-13. Ten's complement Version II. This version of the 10's complement makes two passes through the number. The pass generates the 9's complement and the second pass generates the 10's complement.

```
                   * TENS COMPLEMENT ROUTINE OF A 4-BYTE REGISTER
                   * WHOSE ADDRESS IS PRELOADED INTO THE INDEX REG
                   *
A 01FD DF 08     A TENS    STX    $08      SAVE INDEX POINTER
A 01FF C6 04     A         LDAB   #$04     SIZE IS 4-BYTES
A 0201 D7 05     A         STAB   $05      STORE SIZE
A 0203 7F 0007   A         CLR    $0007    ADD ZERO AT THIS LOC
A 0206 0D                  SEC             SET CARRY, ADDS +1
                   * THE CARRY IS USED TO ADD ONE TO THE 9'S COMP
                   * TO FORM THE 10'S COMP
                   *
A 0207 07          TENS1   TPA             SAVE CC BITS IN ACC A
A 0208 C6 99     A         LDAB   #$99
A 020A E0 00     A         SUBB   0,X      FORM 9'S COMP
A 020C 06                  TAP             RESTORE CC BITS
A 020D 17                  TBA             MOVE 9'S COMP TO ACC A
A 020E 99 07     A         ADCA   $07      ADD CARRY BIT TO FORM 10'S
A 0210 19                  DAA             DO DECIMAL ADJUST
A 0211 A7 00     A         STAA   0,X      STORE 10'S COMP
A 0213 08                  INX             INC INDEX
A 0214 7A 0005   A         DEC    $0005    DEC SIZE COUNTER
                   * THE INC & DEC INSTRUCTIONS DO NOT AFFECT THE CA
A 0217 26 EE 0207          BNE    TENS1
A 0219 39                  RTS
                   *
```

```
                 * THIS VERSION MAKES TWO PASSES, THE FIRST FORMS
                 * THE 9'S COMPLEMENT AND THE SECOND PASS FORMS THE
                 * 10'S COMPLEMENT.  THE INDEX REGISTER AND ACC B
                 * ARE PRELOADED WITH THE LEAST SIGNIFICANT ADDR AND
                 * SIZE OF THE REGISTER, RESPECTIVELY.
                 *
0000 DF 08       TEN     STX    $08      SAVE POINTER
0002 D7 05               STA B  $05      SAVE SIZE OF REGISTER
                 *
0004 86 99       TEN1    LDA A  #$99     99 -> A
0006 A0 00               SUB A  0,X      99 - DD = NN
0008 A7 00               STA A  0,X      SAVE 9'S COMP
000A 08                  INX
000B 5A                  DEC B
000C 26 F6               BNE    TEN1
                 *
                 * SECOND PASS, FORM 10'S COMP
                 *
000E DE 08               LDX    $08      GET POINTER
0010 D6 05               LDA B  $05      GET SIZE
0012 0D                  SEC             SET CARRY, ADD'S +1
0013 4F          TEN2    CLR A           00 -> A
0014 A9 00               ADC A  0,X      NN + CARRY = TT
0016 19                  DAA             DECIMAL ADJUST
0017 A7 00               STA A  0,X      SAVE 10'S COMP
0019 08                  INX
001A 5A                  DEC B
001B 26 F6               BNE    TEN2
001D 39                  RTS
```

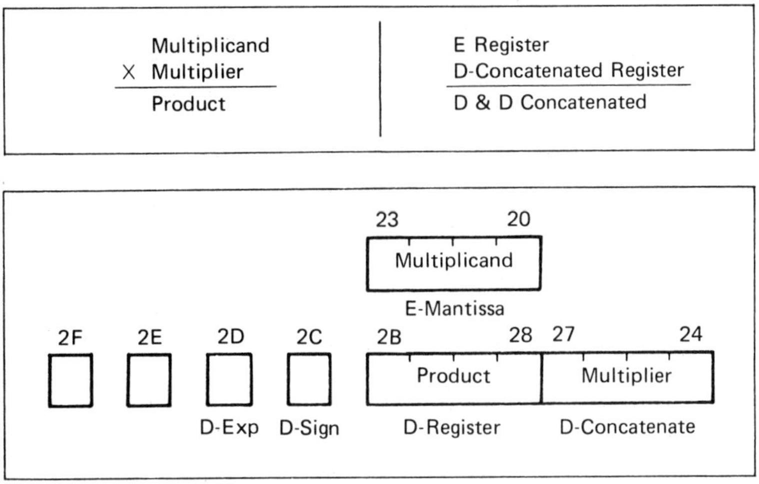

Figure 5-14. Register assignment for multiply.

The multiply routine is a sequence of add and shift routines (Fig. 5-15). The multiplicand in the E register is multiplied by the LS digit of the multiplier in the D-concatenated register. Actually, the multiplicand is added to the partial product as many times as is the LS digit of the multiplier. As the LS digit of the multiplier in location \$24 is decremented, the multiplicand is added to the partial product until the LS digit decrements to zero. When the LS digit of the multiplier equals zero, the partial product and the multiplier are both shifted right one digit. Then follows the process of adding the multiplicand to the partial product as many times as the present LS digit of the multiplier decrements to zero. As the 7-digit multiplier is shifted out, the 7-digit partial product in the D register expands to a 14-digit product in the D and D-concatenated register.

MULTK The exponent and sign of the product are generated and stored at the exponent and sign of the D register. Then the multiplier is moved to the D-concatenated register, and the D register is cleared to store the partial product.

MULOOP The multiply loop multiplies the two mantissas, and Fig. 5-16 illustrates the multiply sequence. The LS digit of the multiplier is tested. If it is a nonzero number, the program proceeds to decrement the LS digit at location \$24 and then jumps into the add subroutine, where the multiplicand is added to the partial product.

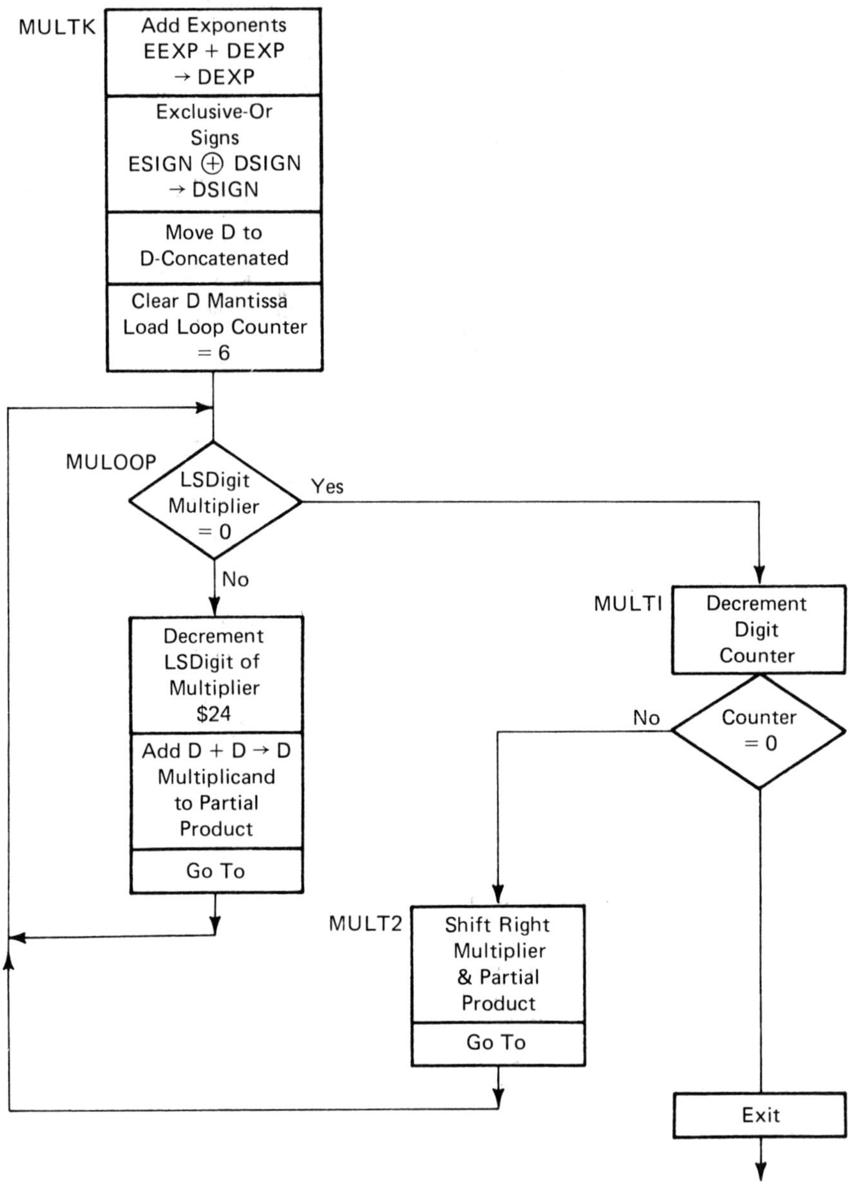

Figure 5-15. Multiplier flow chart.

		E-REGISTER	D-REGISTER
		MULTIPLICAND 23 20	
		0 4 5 6 7 0 0 0	
		2B PRODUCT 28	MULTIPLIER 27 24
		0 0 0 0 0 0 0 0	0 1 2 3 0 0 0 0
1st pass	Shift Multiplier		1 2 3 0 0 0
2nd pass	Shift Multiplier		1 2 3 0 0
3rd pass	Shift Multiplier		1 2 3 0
4th pass	Shift Multiplier		1 2 3
5th pass	Add Multiplicand	0 4 5 6 7 0 0 0	0 0 0 0 0 1 2 3
	Dec. Multiplier		1 2 2
	Add Multiplicand	0 9 1 3 4 0 0 0	0 0 0 0 0 1 2 2
	Dec. Multiplier		1 2 1
	Add Multiplicand	1 3 7 0 1 0 0 0	0 0 0 0 0 1 2 1
	Dec. Multiplier		1 2 0
	Shift Multiplier	0 1 3 7 0 1 0 0	0 0 0 0 0 0 1 2
6th pass	Add Multiplier	0 5 9 3 7 1 0 0	0 0 0 0 0 0 1 2
	Dec. Multiplier		1 1
	Add Multiplier	1 0 5 0 4 1 0 0	0 0 0 0 0 0 1 1
	Dec. Multiplier		1 0
	Shift Multiplier	0 1 0 5 0 4 1 0	0 0 0 0 0 0 0 1
7th pass	Add Multiplier	0 5 6 1 7 4 1 0	0 0 0 0 0 0 0 1
	Dec. Multiplier		0

Adjust exponent by subtracting 7.

Figure 5-16. Example of multiplying mantissa 123 × 4567 = 561741.

The program stays in this loop until the LS digit of the multiplier is decremented to zero.

When the LS digit of the multiplier is equal to zero, the program branches to the MULT1 loop.

MULT1 As the program passes through this loop, the digit counter at location $0000 is decremented six times, once as each digit is shifted right. The eighth and final pass through the loop does not shift out and loads the LS digit of the product.

MULT2 In MULT2 the partial product and multiplier are shifted right one digit.

5-14 DIVIDE ROUTINE

The divide routine divides two 7-digit numbers in the D and E registers to form a 7-digit quotient.

$$\frac{\text{Dividend}}{\text{Divisor}} = \text{Quotient}, \qquad \text{D/E} \rightarrow \text{D-concatenated}$$

This routine makes three assumptions:

- That the contents of the E register are saved prior to and restored after this routine is executed.
- That the input operands are left justified.
- That the 7-digit quotient is examined by the next routine for an error condition.

The mantissa of the dividend in the D register is divided by the mantissa of the divisor in the E register, and the quotient is formed in the D-concatenated register (see Fig. 5-17).

Three operations and one test are executed prior to dividing the mantissas, as follows (see Fig. 5-18):

- Resolving the exponents by DEXP − EEXP → QEXP.
- Resolve the sign of the quotient by exclusive-ORing the signs of the D and E registers.
- Clear the D-concatenated register.
- Test if the divisor is equal to zero.

In the divide operation a "divide by zero" yields the impossible result of infinity. To avoid this condition, the divisor is tested; if it is zero, the error flag is set and the program branches to exit.

There are two basic loops in the divide subroutine. The first and inner loop generates the value of each digit of the quotient, while iteratively subtracting the divisor from the dividend. The program exits from the inner loop when the dividend becomes negative. The condition, as in the subtract routine, is to test if the carry bit is clear (BCC).

In the second and outer loop the divisor is added back to restore the positive dividend. Next the dividend and quotient in the D and D-concatenated register are shifted left one digit. The program is routed through the outer loop seven times, once for each digit of the quotient. Then the quotient in the D-concatenated register is moved to the D register.

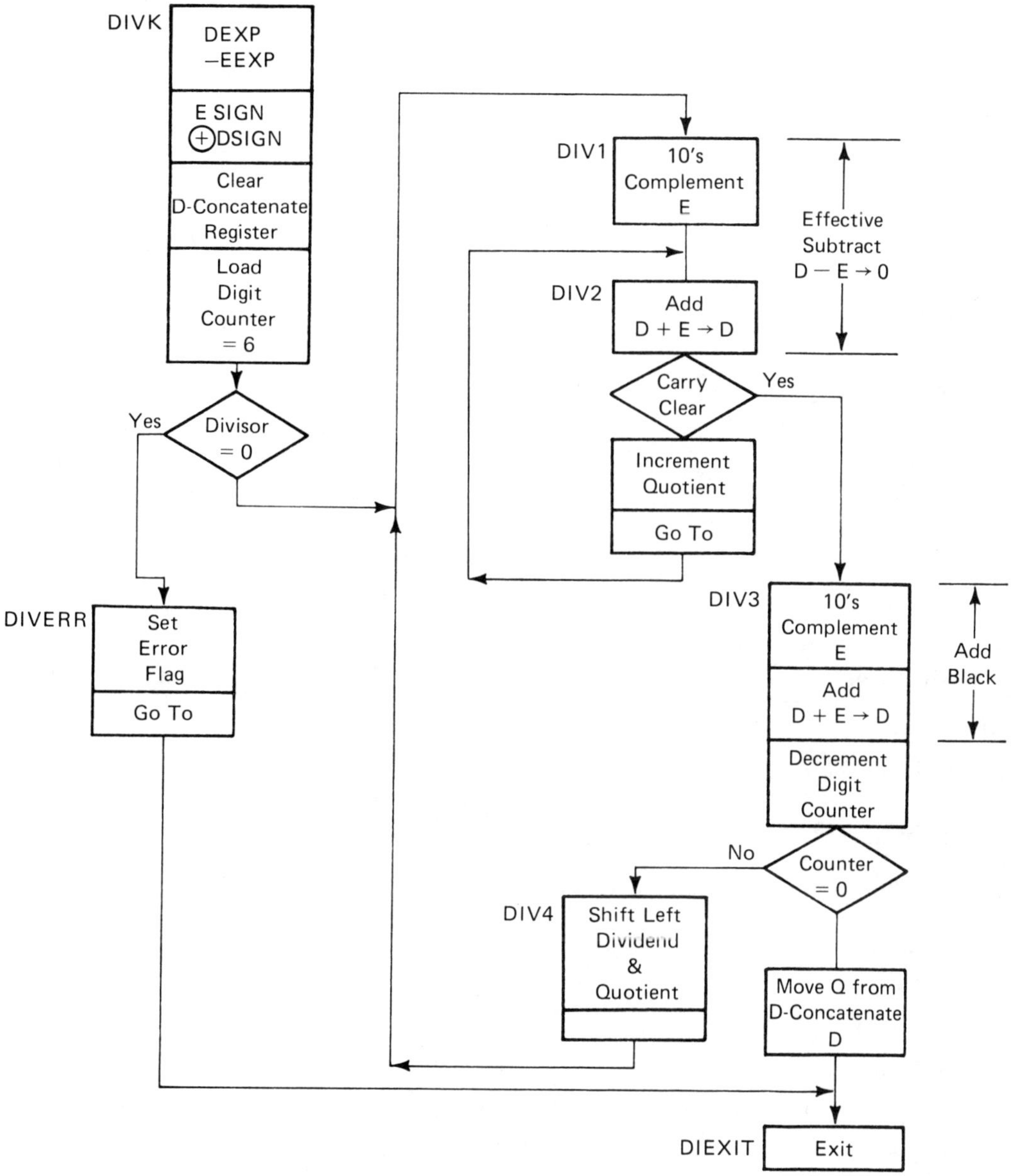

Figure 5-17. Divide flow chart.

			Dividend	
			0 1 2 3 0 0 0 0	
			Divisor	**Quotient**
			0 5 6 1 7 4 1 0	0 0 0 0 0 0 0 0
1st	Pass:			
	Subtract		−0 1 2 3 0 0 0 0	0 0 0 0 0 0 0 0
	Inc Q		0 4 3 8 7 4 1	1
	Subtract		− 1 2 3	
	Inc Q		0 3 1 5 7 4 1	2
	Subtract		− 1 2 3	
	Inc Q		0 1 9 2 7 4 1	3
	Subtract		− 1 2 3	
	Inc Q		0 0 6 9 7 4 1 0	0 0 0 0 0 0 0 4
	Subtract		− 1 2 3	
		Negative Result	9 9 4 6 7 4 1	
	Add Back		+ 1 2 3 0 0 0	
			0 0 6 9 7 4 1	
	Shift Left		0 6 9 7 4 1 0 0	0 0 0 0 0 0 4 0
2nd	Pass:			
	Subtract		− 1 2 3	
	Inc Q		5 7 4 4 1	4 1
	Subtract		− 1 2 3	
	Inc Q		4 5 1 4 1	4 2
	Subtract		− 1 2 3	
	Inc Q		3 2 8 4 1	4 3
	Subtract		− 1 2 3	
	Inc Q		2 0 5 4 1	4 4
	Subtract		− 1 2 3	
	Inc Q		0 0 8 2 4 1 0 0	0 0 0 0 0 0 4 5
	Subtract		− 1 2 3	
		Negative Result	9 9 6 9 4 1	
	Add Back		+ 1 2 3	
			0 0 8 2 4 1 0 0	0 0 0 0 0 0 4 5
	Shift Left		0 8 2 4 1 0 0 0	0 0 0 0 0 4 5 0

Figure 5-18. Example of dividing mantissa 561741 / 123 = 4567.

3rd Pass:			
Subtract		− 1 2 3	
Inc Q		7 0 1 1	4 5 1
Subtract		− 1 2 3	
Inc Q		5 7 8 1	4 5 2
Subtract		− 1 2 3	
Inc Q		4 5 5 1	4 5 3
Subtract		− 1 2 3	
Inc Q		3 3 2 1	4 5 4
Subtract		− 1 2 3	
Inc Q		0 2 0 9 1	4 5 5
Subtract		− 1 2 3	
Inc Q		0 8 6 1 0 0 0	0 0 0 0 0 4 5 6
Subtract		− 1 2 3	
	Negative Result	9 9 6 3	
Add Back		+ 1 2 3	
		0 0 8 6 1	
Shift Left		0 8 6 1 0 0 0 0	0 0 0 0 4 5 6 0
		Dividend	
		0 1 2 3 0 0 0 0	
		Divisor	Quotient
		0 5 6 1 7 4 1 0	0 0 0 0 0 0 0 0
4th Pass:		0 8 6 1 0 0 0 0	
Subtract		− 1 2 3	
Inc Q		7 3 8	4 5 6 1
Subtract		− 1 2 3	
Inc Q		6 1 5	4 5 6 2
Subtract		− 1 2 3	
Inc Q		4 9 2	4 5 6 3
Subtract		− 1 2 3	
Inc Q		3 6 9	4 5 6 4
Subtract		− 1 2 3	
Inc Q		2 4 6	4 5 6 5
Subtract		− 1 2 3	
		1 2 3	4 5 6 6
		− 1 2 3	
		0 0 0 0 0 0 0 0	0 0 0 0 4 5 6 7

Figure 5-18. continued.

	Subtract		− 1 2 3	
		Negative Result	9 8 7 7 0 0 0 0	
	Add Back		+ 1 2 3	
			0 0 0 0 0 0 0 0	
	Shift Left		0 0 0 0 0 0 0 0	0 0 0 4 5 6 7 0
5th	Pass:			
	Subtract		− 1 2 3	
		Negative Result	9 8 7 7	4 5 6 7 0
	Add Back		+ 1 2 3	
			0 0 0 0 0 0 0 0	
	Shift Left		0 0 0 0 0 0 0 0	0 4 5 6 7 0 0
6th	Pass:			
	Subtract		− 1 2 3	
		Negative Result	9 8 7 7	4 5 6 7 0 0
	Add Back		1 2 3	
			0 0 0 0 0 0 0 0	
	Shift Left		0 0 0 0 0 0 0 0	0 4 5 6 7 0 0 0
7th	Pass:			
	Subtract		− 1 2 3	
		Negative Result	9 8 7 7	0 4 5 6 7 0 0 0
	Add Back		+ 1 2 3	
			0 0 0 0 0 0 0 0	
Move D-Concatenated to D			0 4 5 6 7 0 0 0	0 4 5 6 7 0 0 0

Figure 5-18. continued.

```
                       * THE MULTIPLY ROUTINE
                       *
                       * THE EXPONENT OF THE RESULT = EEXP + DEXP - 7
                       *
0257 96 24      A MULTK  LDAA   $24        GET EEXP
0259 9B 2C      A        ADDA   $2C        EEXP + DEXP
025B 80 07      A        SUBA   #$07       EEXP + DEXP = 7
025D 97 2C      A        STAA   $2C        STORE RESULT EXP
                       * FORM SIGN OF THE PRODUCT
025F 96 25      A        LDAA   $25        ESIGN
0261 98 2D      A        EORA   $2D        EXCL-OR E & D SIGNS
0263 97 2D      A        STAA   $2D        STORE RESULT SIGN
                       * MOVE D TO D-CONCATINATE REGISTER
0265 CE 0024    A        LDX    #$0024
0268 DF 0A      A        STX    $0A        STORE IN DESTINATION POINT
026A CE 0028    A        LDX    #$0028
026D DF 08      A        STX    $08        SOURCE POINTER
026F C6 04      A        LDAB   #$04       BYTE COUNT
0271 BD 0237    A        JSR    MOOV
                       * CLEAR THE D MANTISSA,
                       * THE POINTER AND BYTE COUNT ARE LOAADED
0274 4F                  CLRA
0275 08                  INX
0276 5A                  DECB
                       * LOAD DIGIT COUNT = 6, 7-DIGIT MULTIPLY
0277 86 06      A        LDAA   #$06
0279 97 05      A        STAA   $05        SAVE SIZE
                       *
                       * MULTIPLY LOOP
                       * TEST LSDIGIT OF MULTIPLIER = 00
027B 7D 0024    A MULOOP TST    $0024
027E 27 08 0288          BEQ    MULT1      BR TO DIGIT COUNT
                       * ELSE DECREMENT LCDIGIT & PROCCEED TO ADD LOOP
0280 7A 0024    A        DEC    $0024
0283 BD 01BC    A        JSR    ADDDEC     ADD MULTIPLICAND TO PARTIA
0286 20 F3 027B          BRA    MULOOP
                       *
                       * DECREMENT DIGIT COUNT & SHIFT PARTIAL PRODUCT
0288 7A 0000    A MULT1  DEC    $0000
028B 26 03 0290          BNE    MULT2      BR TO SHIFT LOOP
                       * ELSE EXIT & RESTORE REGISTERS
028D 7E 00DA    A        JMP    RESTOR
                       * SHIFT LOOP
0290 CE 002B    A MULT2  LDX    #$002B     D & D-CONCATINATE
0293 C6 08      A        LDAB   #$08       BYTE COUNT
0295 BD 01E0    A        JSR    SHRTD      SHIFT DIGIT
0298 20 E1 027B          BRA    MULOOP
```

DIVK The divide routine forms the exponent of the quotient by subtracting the E exponent from the D exponent and stores it in the D-exponent location \$2D. The sign of the quotient is formed by exclusive-ORing the signs of the D and E registers and storing the result in the D sign location \$2D. The D-concatenated register is cleared to form the quotient, and the digit count of 7 is loaded into location \$0000. Next, the routine tests if the divisor is equal to zero and, if so, branches to set the error flag at location DIVERR, and it branches to divide the mantissas at DIV1.

DIV1 Take the 10's complement of the E register, the divisor.

DIV2 In the DIV2 loop the divisor is subtracted from the dividend until the result is negative. The quotient is incremented for each pass through the DIV2 loop. The routine adds the 10's complement of E, which is an effective subtract operation. The program exits from this loop when the result, the contents of the D register, is negative, as indicated by NO CARRY.

DIV3 The program loops through DIV3 seven times, once for each digit. The positive, 10's complement contents of the E register are added back to and set the dividend positive. The digit count is decremented, and the program loops through the shift left branch 7 times and exits on the eight digit. Finally, the quotient is moved from the D extended to the D register.

DIV4 The partial dividend and the quotient are shifted left 7 times.

```
                          *
                          * THE DIVIDE ROUTINE
                          *
                          * EXPONENT Q = DEXP - EEXP
                          *
029A 96 24        A DIVK     LDAA    $24        GET D EXP
029C 90 2C        A          SUBA    $2C        DEXP - EEXP
029E 97 2C        A          STAA    $2C        QEXP
                          * SIGN OF Q, EXCLUSIVE-OR SIGN D & E
02A0 96 25        A          LDAA    $25        ESIGN
02A2 98 2D        A          EORA    $2D        EXCLUSIVE-OR SIGNS
02A4 97 2D        A          STAA    $2D        QSIGN
                          * CLEAR D-CONCATINATE REGISTER
02A6 CE 0024      A          LDX     #$0024     LOAD POINTER
02A9 C6 04        A          LDAB    #$04       BYTE COUNT
02AB 4F                      CLRA
02AC A7 00        A DIVCL    STAA    0,X
02AE 08                      INX
02AF 5A                      DECB               BYTE COUNT
02B0 26 FA 02AC              BNE     DIVCL
```

```
                           * TEST DIVISOR, IF ZERO BR TO ERROR
A 02B2 CE 0028   A                LDX    #$0028   LOAD POINTER
A 02B5 C6 04     A                LDAB   #$04
A 02B7 6D 00     A DIVZRO TST     0,X
A 02B9 26 06 02C1                 BNE    DIV1     EXIT IF NONZERO
A 02BB 08                         INX             ELSE KEEP TESTING
A 02BC 5A                         DECB
A 02BD 26 F8 02B7                 BNE    DIVZRO   KEEP TESTING IF NONZERO
A 02BF 20 31 02F2                 BRA    DIVERR   IF 4-BYTES EQ ZERO
                           *
                           * DIVIDE LOOP
                           *
A 02C1 CE 0020   A DIV1   LDX     #$0020   POINT TO E REG
A 02C4 C6 04     A        LDAB    #$04     BYTE COUNT
A 02C6 D7 05     A        STAB    $05      SAVE SIZE
A 02C8 BD 01FD   A        JSR     TENS     10'S COMP REG E
A 02CB BD 01BC   A DIV2   JSR     ADDDEC   SUB D - E => D
A 02CE 24 05 02D5         BCC     DIV3     BR IF RESULT NEG
A 02D0 7C 0024   A        INC     $0024    ELSE INC Q
A 02D3 20 F6 02CB         BRA     DIV2     KEEP SUBTRACTING
                           *
                           * ELSE ADD BACK
A 02D5 CE 0020   A DIV3   LDX     #$0020   POINT TO E REG
A 02D8 C6 04     A        LDAB    #$04     BYTE COUNT
A 02DA BD 01FD   A        JSR     TENS     RESTORE E REG POSITIVE
A 02DD BD 01BC   A        JSR     ADDDEC   ADD BACK
A 02E0 7A 0005   A        DEC     $05      DEC SIZE
A 02E3 26 03 02E8         BNE     DIV4     BR & KEEP DIVIDNG
                           * ELSE EXIT & MOVE Q TO D REGISTER
A 02E5 7E 00DA   A DIEXIT JMP     RESTOR
                           *
                           * SHIFT D & D-CONCATINATE REGISTER LEFT
                           *
A 02E8 CE 0024   A DIV4   LDX     #$0024   POINT TO D & D CONCATINATE
A 02EB C6 08     A        LDAB    #$08     BYTE SIZE
A 02ED BD 021A   A        JSR     SHLFD    SHIFT LEFT DIGIT
A 02F0 20 CF 02C1         BRA     DIV1     RETURN TO DIV LOOP
                           *
                           * IF DIVISOR IS ZERO SET ERROR FLAG
A 02F2 86 FF     A DIVERR LDAA    #$FF
A 02F4 97 0E     A        STAA    $0E      SET ERROR FLAG
A 02F6 20 ED 02E5         BRA     DIEXIT
                           *
```

6 Keyboard and Seven-Segment Display

This chapter discusses I/O routines, the keyboard as an input device and the 7-segment display as an output device. The arithmetic routines from Chapter 5 and the I/O routines of this chapter are merged to build the calculator system discussed in the next chapter. In Chapter 9 a terminal is used to replace the keyboard and 7-segment display as the I/O devices.

Calculator systems are designed to continuously scan the input device for an input from the operator, at which time the program goes off to either enter some data or execute a function. The program then returns to scan the input device while waiting for the next entry from the operator. This implies that in calculator-type systems most of the time is spent in a program loop to interrogate the input device.

In this example of a keyboard 7-segment display the keyboard may be sampled as infrequently as once every 10 ms, and it still appears to be an instantaneous response to the operator. Between key scans, when there are no inputs, the microcomputer outputs the data to the 7-segment displays; that is, each digit is displayed on one of the 7-segment displays for a short period of time until all the digits are displayed. This sequence is repeated continuously, and a person's persistence of vision gives the illusion of a continuous display.

When a system has both a keyboard and 7-segment display, then the input and output functions are alternately executed. There are numerous techniques for time sharing the I/O functions. The technique used in this chapter is to output a digit on each of the displays and then to continuously sample the keyboard for an input. When outputting data the first part of the routine is to format or convert the internal data to a form that is acceptable by the display device, whether it is a

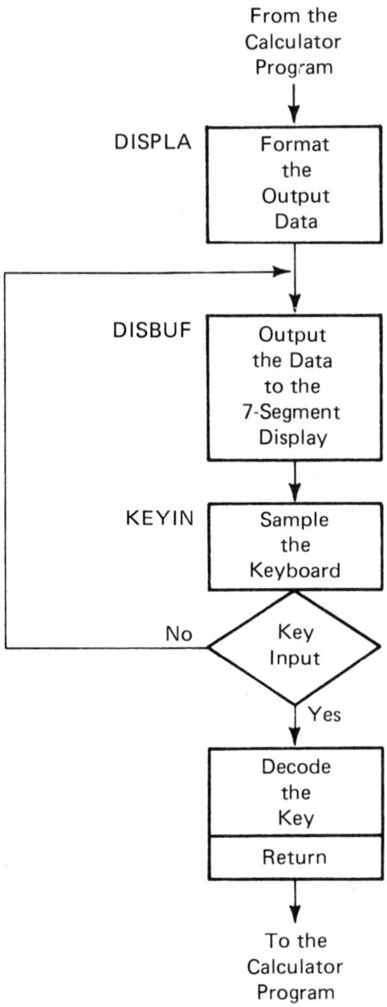

Figure 6-1. Keyboard/7-segment display loop.

7-segment display, printer, terminal, or some other computer; the second part is to output the data. Likewise, when data are coming into the microcomputer, the first part of the routine is to get the data. The second part is to decode or convert the input data, or control signals, into a form that is usable and compatible with the internal data of the microcomputer. Although the two aspects of each I/O routine execute clearly defined functions, they may not be written as two separate routines. The programmer, to save instructions, memory space, or time, may not necessarily write it as two separate routines. The strategy for handling the keyboard/7-segment display is illustrated in Fig. 6-1. First the output data are formatted and stored in the output register. Then the digits are sequentially output to each display, and the keyboard is sampled for an input. The program stays in this I/O loop until an input is sensed. The program then decodes the input data and returns to the system program to process the data.

6-1 SEVEN-SEGMENT DISPLAY

The 7-segment display is generally, but not necessarily, used to output alphanumeric data. The number of displays may vary from 1 to 20 and are a consequence of the system requirements. Before writing any output routines, the programmer must have an understanding of how the 7-segment device functions and how several display devices are tied together and to the output port of the microcomputer.

This is the area where the hardware and software disciplines merge, either within one person or a team of people. Three steps are necessary to bridge the hardware/software gap.

- Hardware: Understand the 7-segment displays and how they work.
- Hardware/software: Specify the signals required at the output ports to control the display.
- Software: Write the output routine that supplies the appropriate signals to the output port.

The primary purpose of 7-segment displays is for displaying the alphanumeric characters of calculators or number-crunching machines. Six 7-segment displays, however, furnish 42 LEDs and, for tutorial purposes or just for fun, can be used to play games with lights. These games may vary from imitating the lights on a movie marqueè to exercises in logic problems by turning LEDs on and off to simulate motors, switches, and valves.

6-2 SCHEMATIC OF THE 7-SEGMENT DISPLAY

A light-emitting diode (LED) is a diode that emits light when current is passing through. A 7-segment display has 8 LEDs in one package. In Fig. 6-2a, seven of the segments are geometrically arranged to display the number 8 when they are all conducting current, and the eighth segment is used to light the decimal point. The schematic for a common cathode 7-segment display is illustrated in Fig. 6-2b, show-

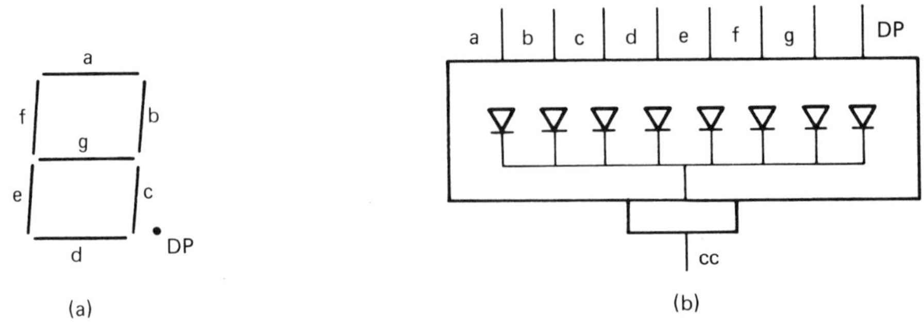

Figure 6-2. 7-segment display: (a) packaged, (b) schematic.

ing the 8-segment pins that are labeled a to g plus DP. Generally, the diodes in the package are not shown in the schematic. An example indicating which segments must be lit to display the number 2 or 1 or 4, plus the decimal point, is illustrated in Fig. 6-3.

Display Techniques

There are two basic techniques for displaying the three characters 4, 1, and 2. The first technique is to light all three displays independently. This requires nine I/O pins from the microcomputer per display, one pin for the digit and eight pins for the segment drivers. Each additional display requires nine additional I/O pins, for a total of 27 pins for three displays. The requirement for the large number of I/O pins tends to make this technique impractical.

Dynamic Display

The second technique for driving or turning on this display is referred to as the *dynamic display*. This technique requires a total of eight I/O pins to simultaneously drive the segments of all the displays, and one extra pin is assigned for each digit. Therefore, eleven I/O pins from the microcomputer are required to drive three digits, 8 segment and 3 digit pins, and only three more, or 14 pins, are required to drive six digits, 8 segment and 6 digit pins. The advantage of the dynamic technique is that it requires fewer I/O pins. The disadvantage is that since only one digit can be displayed at any instant of time the microcomputer must continuously be preoccupied to dynamically refresh the display (see Fig. 6-4).

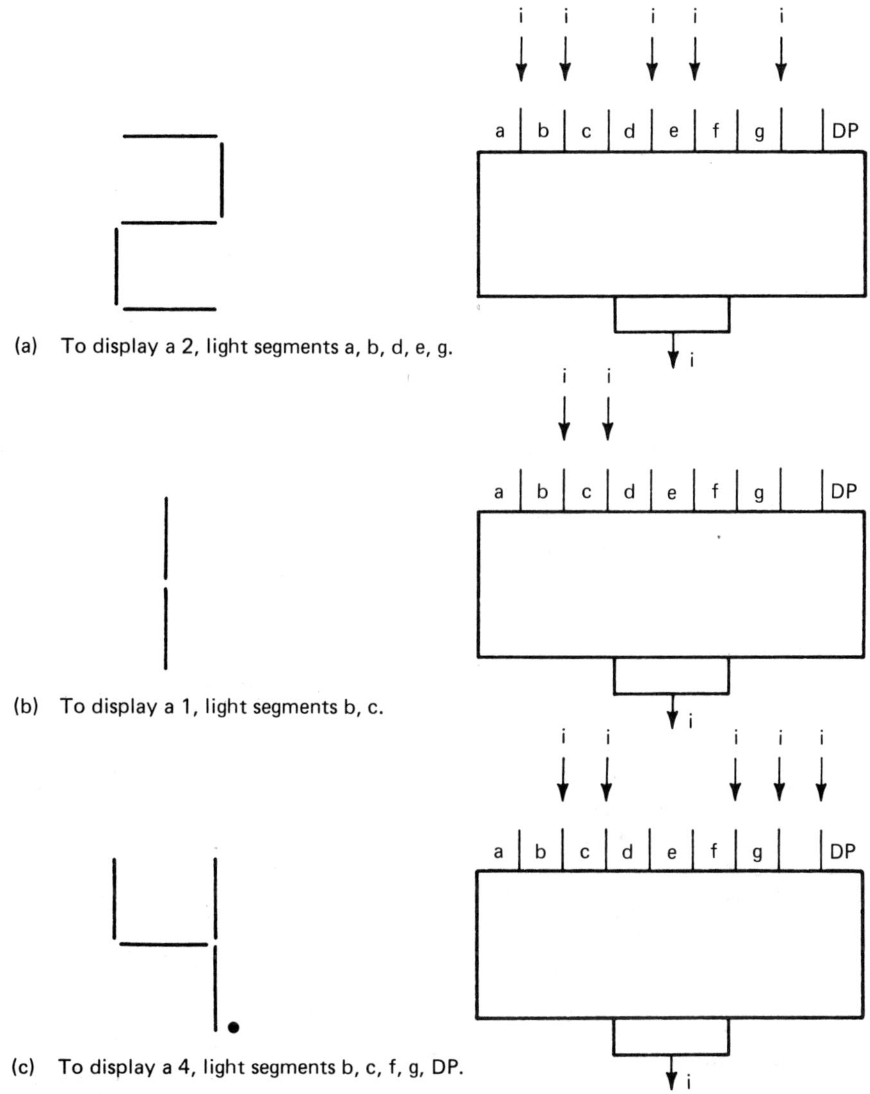

Figure 6-3. Indicates which segments are lit to display: (a) number 2, (b) number 1, (c) number 4.

Six-Digit 7-Segment Display Configuration of the D-2 Kit

The 6-digit 7-segment display configuration from the D-2 kit is typical of most dynamic-type displays (Fig. 6-5). The digits are labeled 1 to 6, and the 6-digit select lines are tied to pins PB0 to PB5 of the

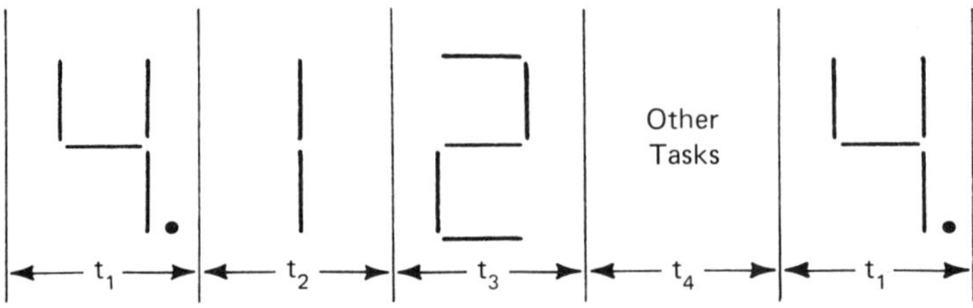

Figure 6-4. Dynamic display of the three characters 4., 1, and 2.

microcomputer through driver, NAND gates, U9A, U8B, U8A, U7A. The 7-segment select lines, a to g, are tied to pins PA0 to PA6 of the microcomputer through the transistor driver Q7 to Q1. The decimal point (DP) segment is not an output port.

Each segment emits light when current flows through the segment. The flow of the current through each segment is controlled by a combination of one segment and one digit driver. Segment A of digit 1 emits light when the output from pin PA0 causes transistor driver Q7 to conduct, and the output from pin PB0 causes the U9A NAND gate to conduct (see Fig. 6-6).

The Q7 transistor conducts when a low or logic 0 signal is output from pin PA0. When the second input of the U9A NAND gate is tied to +5 V, it is effectively reduced to an inverter that conducts when a high or logic 1 signal is output from pin PB0. In this circuit all the segment drivers conduct when output signals are low, and all the digit drivers conduct when output signals are high from the microcomputer.

In the D-2 kit the output pins PA0 to PA6 indicate pins 0 to 6 of Port A at location $8020, and the output pins PB0 to PB5 indicate the output pins of Port B at location $8022. Pins PA7, PB6, and PB7 of Ports A and B are used for scanning the keyboard.

Segment Codes for the Hex Characters

The segment output codes to display the 16 hex characters for the output schematic illustrated in Fig. 6-5 are listed in Table 6-1. The segment codes are a function of three conditions:

- Whether a logic 1 or 0 turns on the segment drivers.
- Which output pins are tied to which segment drivers.
- Whether the decimal point segment is used.

In this example,

- The segment drivers are turned on by a logic 0 signal.

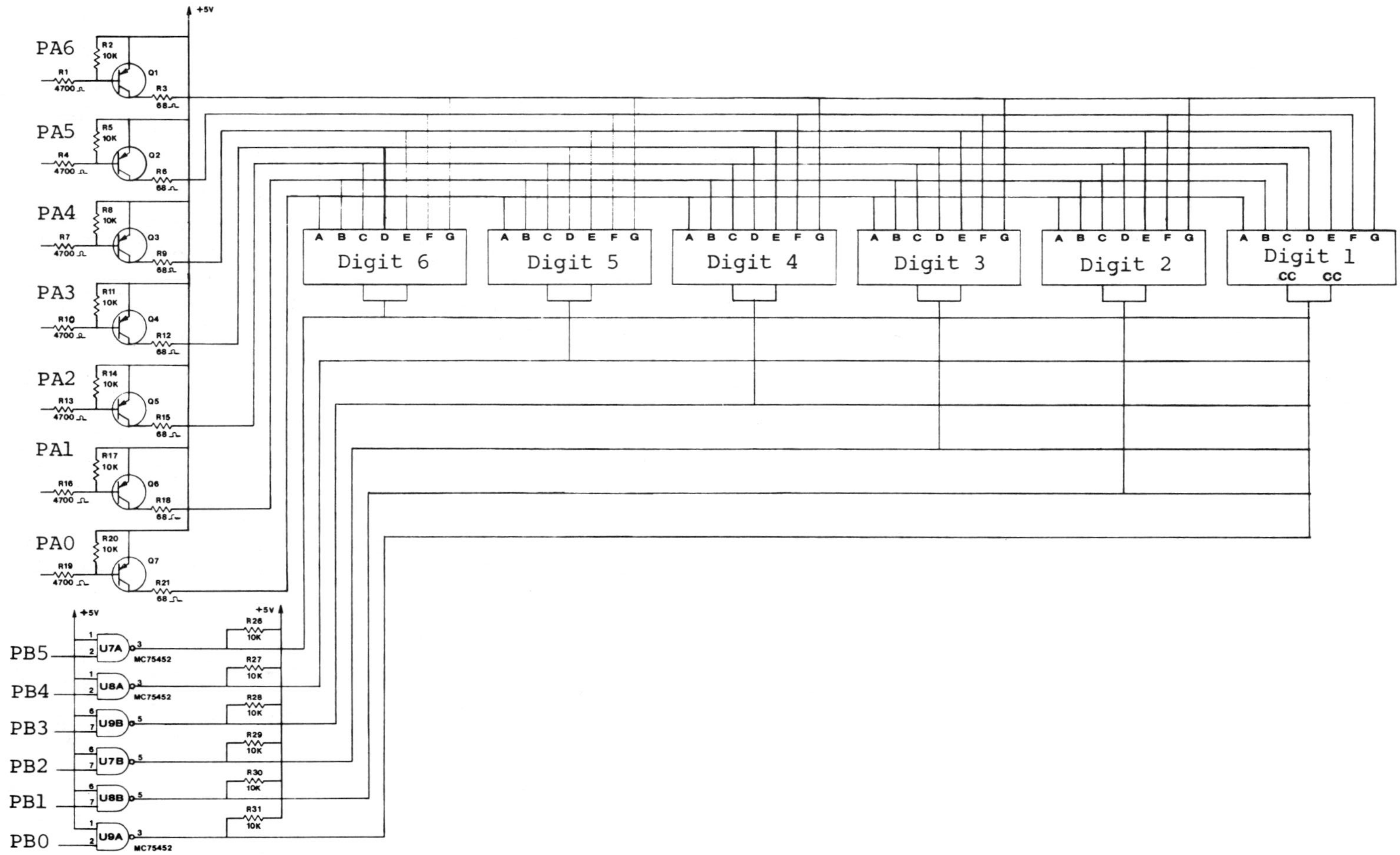

Figure 6-5. 6-digit 7-segment display configuration of the D2 kit.

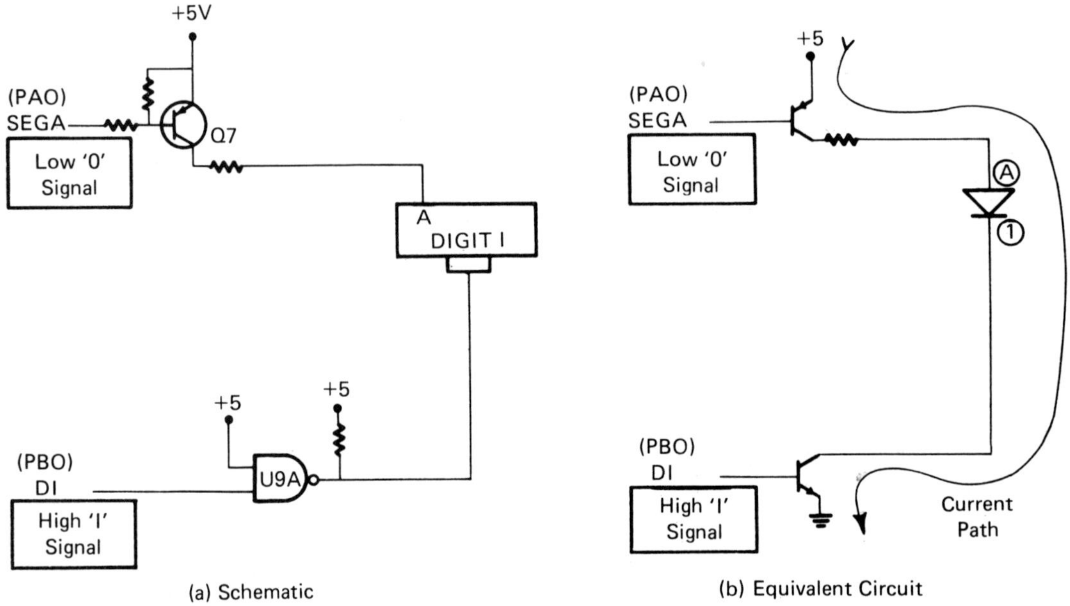

Figure 6-6. Schematic and equivalent circuit for turning-on segment A of digit I.

- The output pins PA0 to PA6 are tied to segments a to g, respectively.
- The decimal point segment is not used.

Bit 7 of Port A, PA7, is used by the keyboard scan routine not tied to the DP segment of the display. Table 6-1, therefore, lists two segment select codes, depending on whether or not the DP segment is used.

6-3 TECHNIQUE FOR HANDLING THE HARDWARE/SOFTWARE INTERFACE

Prior to writing an output software routine, the designer must know how the output device functions and what signals are required to control it, as described in Sec. 6-2. The next phase is the area where the hardware and software skills merge, either within one person or in a team. When two people, one hardware and one software, work together, the hardware person indicates, or specifies, the signals required at the output ports of the microcomputer to control the output device so that the software person can write the program that supplies the appropriate signals. This interface is the result of discussions between the hardware and software personnel.

Table 6-1. Listing of the Segment Select Code for Hex Characters 0 to F and Blank, with and without the DP Segment

	Segment Select Codes	
Hex	Without DP	With DP Segment
0	40	C0
1	79	F9
2	20	A4
3	30	B0
4	19	99
5	12	92
6	02	82
7	78	F8
8	00	80
9	18	98
A	08	88
B	03	83
C	46	C6
D	21	A1
E	06	86
F	0E	8E
Blank	7F	FF

The output data required to display the six characters blank, blank, A, 4, 1, 2 on displays D6 to D1 are listed in Table 6-2. BLANK is a valid character where no segment is lit. These data are required by the programmer to begin writing the program. The programmer, however, has the choice of selecting the sequence for displaying the digits, either D1 to D6 or D6 to D1. Caution must also be exercised by the programmer to blank the digits between each display or "ghosts," a faint trace of an adjacent digit, will inadvertently be displayed.

Examples

The following examples indicate the output codes from the microcomputer to light the 7-segment displays (refer to Fig. 6-7). They offer the reader an opportunity to practice lighting any of the 42 segments of the six displays.

Specify the output code at Ports A and B to:

A. Light segments a, d, g of digit II.
B. Light segment a of digits I, III, V.
C. Light segments c, f, g of digits I, II, III.
D. Display H's on all the digits.

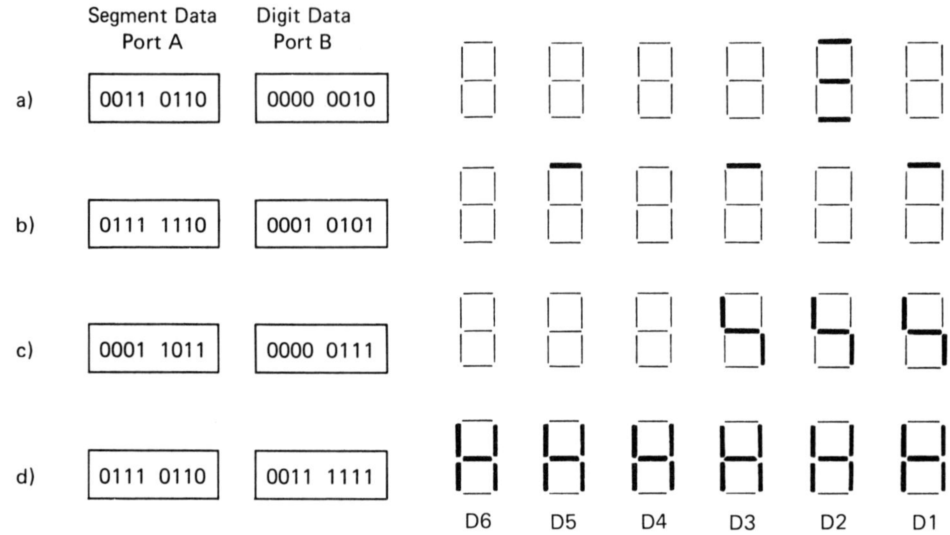

Figure 6-7A. Output data at ports A and B to light selected segments.

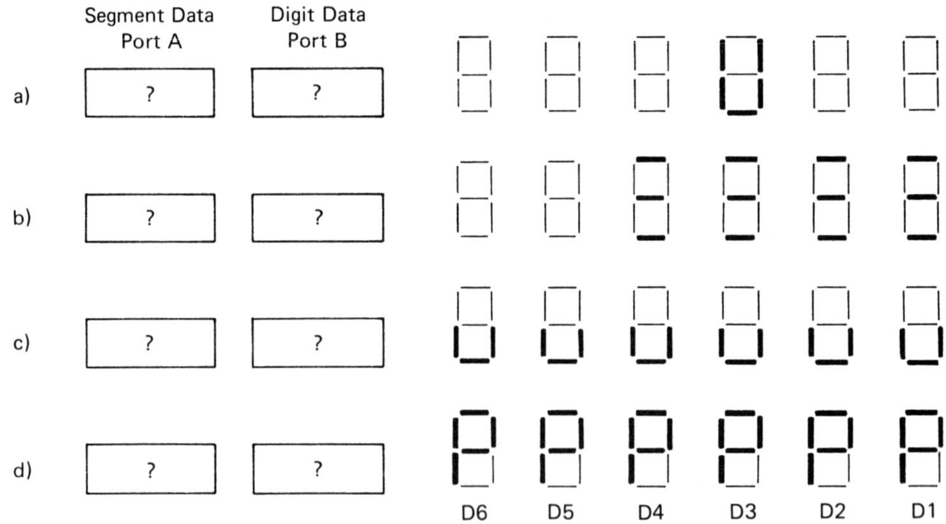

Figure 6-7B. Specify the output codes at ports A and B to display the segment pattern.

This type of exercise is meaningful to logic applications for controlling valves, switches, and motors, which may seem to be turned on in some random fashion.

Table 6-2. Output Codes to Display Six Characters: Blank, Blank, A, 4, 1, 2

	Binary Code		Hex Code	
	Segment Code	Digit Code		
Display	PORT A[a]	PORT B	Port A	Port B
2 at D1	1010 0100	0000 0001	A4	01
1 at D2	1111 1001	0000 0010	F9	02
4 at D3	1001 1001	0000 0100	99	04
A at D4	1000 1000	0000 1000	88	08
Blank at D5	1111 1111	0001 0000	FF	10
Blank at D6	1111 1111	0010 0000	FF	20

[a] The segment code is obtained from Table 6-1.

Problems

Refer to Fig. 6-7B. The reader should specify the output codes at Ports A and B to:

A. Light segments b, c, d, e, f on digit III.
B. Light a, d, g of digits I, II, V, VI.
C. Display ⊔ on all digits.
D. Display |] on odd digits.

6-4 FORMAT THE DISPLAY DATA

Formatting converts the display data to a form that is acceptable by the output device and must be done prior to the output of the data. There are four phases to formatting the output data:

1. Mantissa
   - Unpack the numbers in the D register.
   - Convert each digit to its 7-segment equivalent via a look-up table
   - Store 7-segment equivalents in the output register.
2. DP
   - Set the decimal point segment of the appropriate digit.
3. Blank leading zeros.

4. Sign
   - If appropriate, insert or light the negative sign segment of the appropriate digit.

The formatting of the number −123.4 is illustrated in Fig. 6-8. The display data are stored in the D register, with the mantissa packed into the 4 bytes starting at location $0028, and the exponent and sign stored in locations $002C and $002D, respectively.

Fig. 6-8a Unpack and convert each digit to its 7-segment equivalent and, via a look-up table, store it in the output register.

Fig. 6-8b The decimal point is inserted by setting the decimal point segment, bit 7. In this example the second digit is switched from $BO to $30.

Fig. 6-8c Blank leading zeros by inserting $FF.

Fig. 6-8d Insert a negative sign $BF left of the MS digit or the location of the least significant blanked digit.

Phase I: The Mantissa

In phase I the mantissa, the 8 packed BCD digits that are stored in 4 bytes starting at location $0028, are converted to the 7-segment codes and loaded into an 8-byte output register starting at location $0030. The routine starts at the location labeled DISPLA. See the flow chart of Fig. 6-9 and the listing on page 208.

DISPLA Four constants are used in this routine:

- The address of the source register, the D register at location $0028.
- The address of the destination register, the output register at location $0030.
- The byte count register, labeled SIZE at location $05.
- The odd/even indicator at location $0000.

The odd/even indicator indicates whether the rightmost or odd, or leftmost or even, packed digit is being converted to its 7-segment code. Even and odd codes are indicated by 00 and $FF, respectively. The odd/even indicator is sensed and simultaneously switched by an exclusive-OR of $FF.

DILOOP The DILOOP access, two packed digits from the D register, selects the odd or even digit in turn, converts the BCD digit to its 7-segment code, and stores it in the appropriate byte of the output

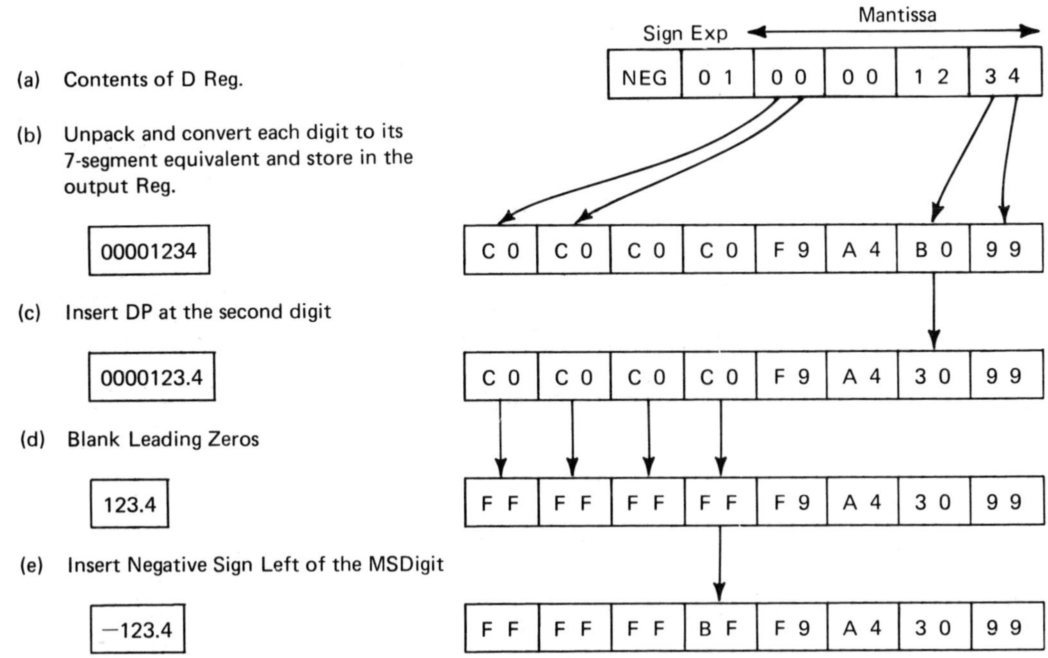

Figure 6-8. Example of the formatting sequence to display −123.4.

register. The routine stays in the DILOOP until all eight digits are converted and then proceeds to insert the decimal point.

ODD/EVEN BRANCH When the routine drops through to the odd digit, the odd digit is masked by ANDing the contents of accumulator A with a $OF. When the routine takes the even branch, labeled DEVEN, the even digit is shifted left 4 bits into the leftmost position. The source pointer is incremented in the DEVEN branch and then joins with the odd branch, where the digit in accumulator A is converted into its 7-segment code.

TSEGCD The 7-segment decode is listed under the label of Table for SEGMENT CODE, and is a copy of Table 6-1.

Phase II: Insert the Decimal Point

The index register is again pointed to location $0030, the LS byte of the output register, and the D exponent is loaded into accumulator A. If the exponent is equal to zero, then no decimal point is inserted, and the program exits from this phase of the routine.

If the exponent is unequal to zero, the program goes into the DIS11 loop, where the pointer is incremented and the exponent in accumu-

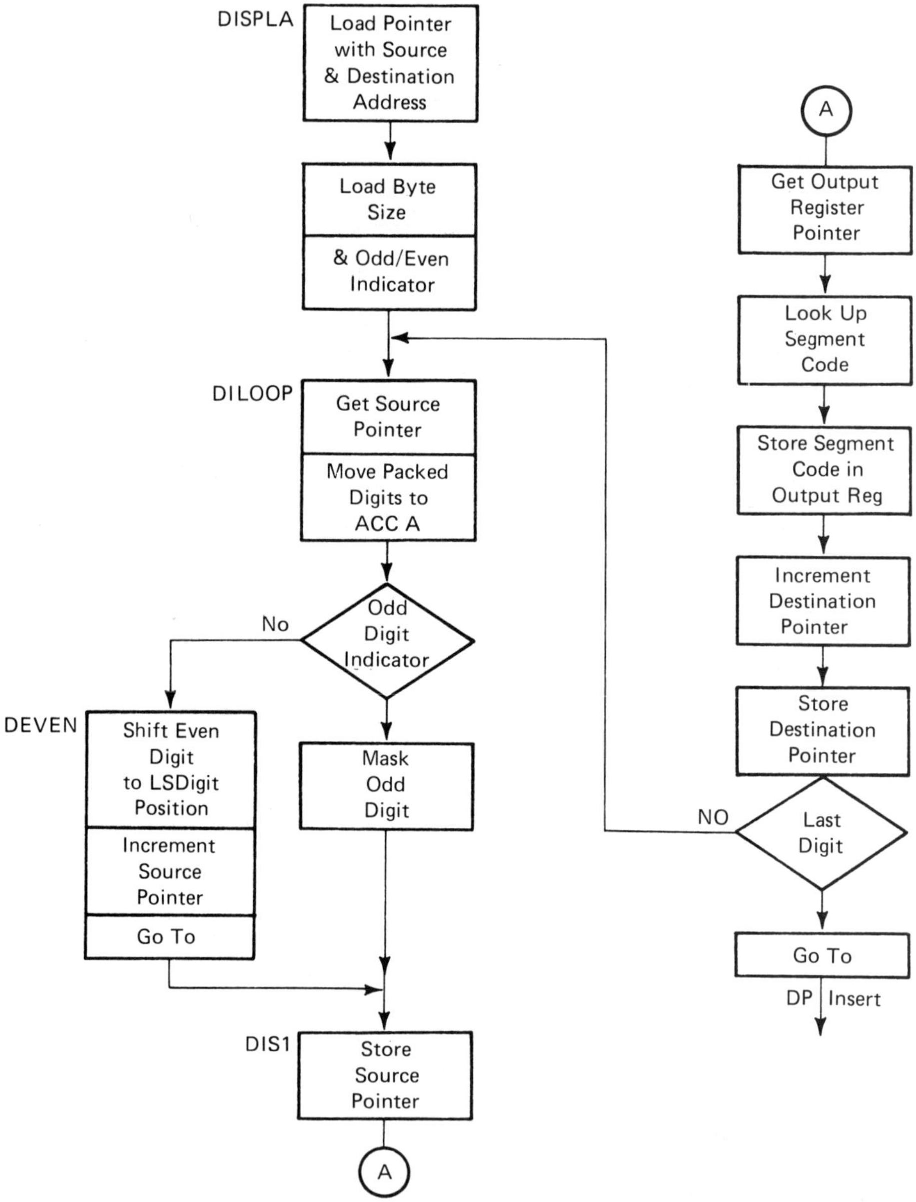

Figure 6-9. Flow chart to format data for 7-segment display load output register with segment select mode.

lator A is decremented. The pointer then has counted up to and now points to the byte whose decimal point (DP) segment is to be set. The 7-segment code is loaded into accumulator A, and bit 7 is reset by ORing accumulator A with a $75F and stored back to the output register. See Fig. 6-10.

Phases III and IV: Blank Leading Zeros and Insert the Sign

Blanking leading zeros not only makes for a cosmetically more appealing display, but also makes it easier to read. Leading zeros are all zeros left of the MS digit or the decimal point. For fractions, however, it is appropriate to display one zero left of the decimal point, as: 0.1234567. This implies that two extra 7-segment displays are required in addition to those needed for the mantissa, one to display the negative sign and one for a leading zero left of a fraction, when required (see Fig. 6-11). For example, to display a 7-digit fraction, −0.1234567, requires nine 7-segment displays and a 9-byte output register, $0030 to $0038.

DIS20 In phase III the MS byte at location $38 is loaded with the blank code, and the index register is initially set pointing to the eighth digit at location $37. Starting with the eighth digit, each byte is examined for the zero code ($C0), where the decimal point segment is not set. If a nonzero code is sensed, the program branches out of the loop to DIS30. Otherwise, the routine stays in the DIS21 loop as long as the segment code is $C0, and the pointer has not reached the last digit.

In the DIS21 loop leading zeros are replaced by the blank code, $FF, the index register is decremented, and the pointer examined. If it is pointing to the last digit, it branches to Phase IV to insert the negative sign if necessary.

DIS30 In phase IV the sign of the D register is examined, and if it is negative, the byte left of the pointer, at location pointer +1, is loaded with the negative.

Output the Data to the 7-Segment Display This routine is written to display data on six 7-segment displays of the D-2 kit. The abbreviated schematic of the D-2 kit is in Fig. 6-5, and the complete schematic is shown in Appendix VI. The routine, starting with the LS digit, displays the data in each digit for 1 ms and then branches to scan the keyboard for an input.

DISBUF The index pointer is loaded with the address of the LS digit of the output register $30, and the accumulator B is loaded with $01, selecting the LS display. The segment drivers are blanked by

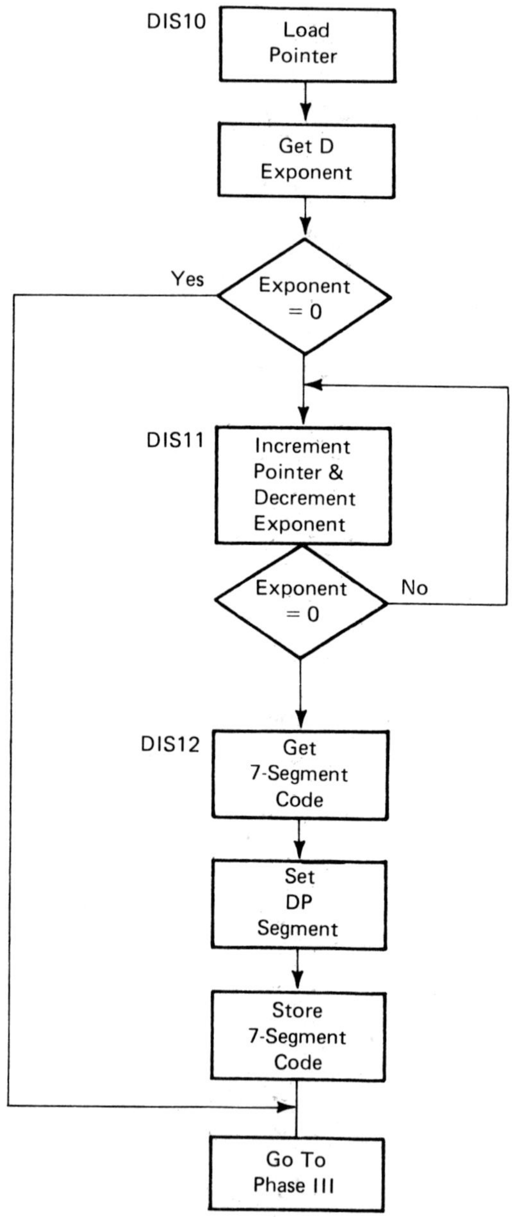

Figure 6-10. Flow chart to insert DP into appropriate 7-segment display code output register.

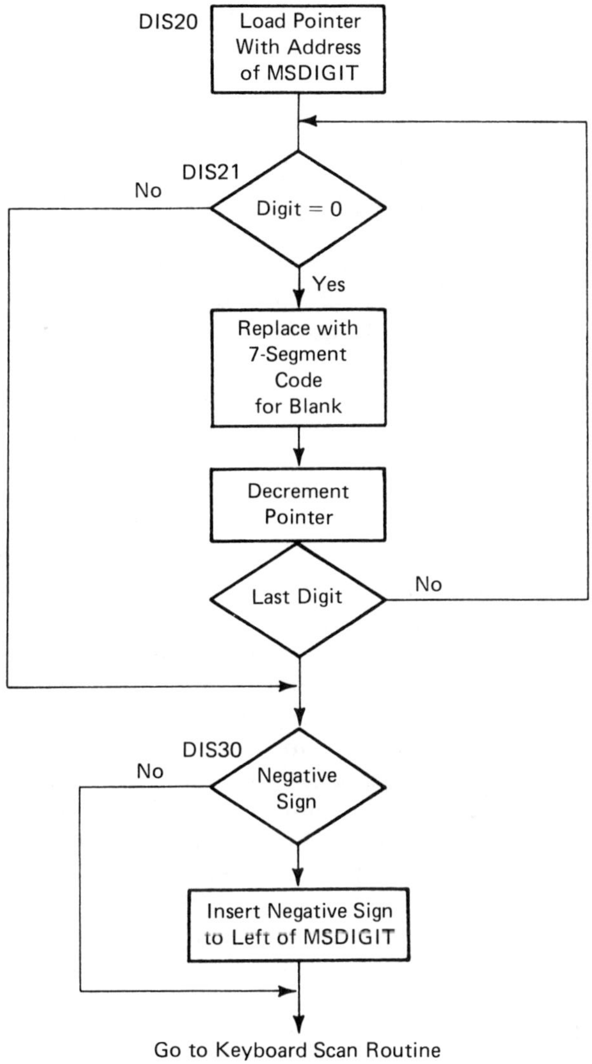

Figure 6-11. Flow chart to insert leading zeros and insert negative sign left of MSDIGIT.

loading accumulator A with $EF, which is then output to the segment driver (SDRIVE) at location $8020.

DISB1 Each digit is displayed with each pass through the DISB1 loop. The segment code is retrieved from the byte of the register pointed to by the index register and output to the segment driver (SDRIVE). The digit select in accumulator B is output to the digit driver (DDRIVE) at location $8022. At this point in the routine a digit is displayed.

The routine goes into a 1-ms delay loop. This delay may be shortened when more than six digits are displayed. The refresh cycle must be frequent enough to avoid display flicker. The segment code then is loaded with a blank code to avoid ghosts.

Next, the index pointer is incremented, the digit select in accumulator B is shifted left to select the next digit, and then the digit select is tested to determine when to stay in the DISB1 loop. After each digit is displayed, the program branches to the keyboard scan routine.

6-5 KEYBOARD INPUT

The two functions of a keyboard input routine are to sense a key entry and then to decode or convert the particular key entry into data that are meaningful to the system. This section describes two different keyboard routines: the first is referred to as the classic keyboard routine, for lack of a better title, and the second applies to the D-2 keyboard. These two routines present the variations that the reader might come across and offer a general understanding of keyboard routines.

The two criteria for most routines are (1) how many I/O pins are required and (2) how many instructions are used? However, when different keyboards are used as an input to a system, the keys must be decoded to the same value. Figure 6-12 indicates the keys and the equivalent decoded value required by the system.

The D-2 kit, or for that matter any other microcomputer with a keyboard, can be used as the calculator system described in Chapter 7. Each key of the D-2 keyboard may be reassigned, as indicated in Fig. 6-13b, by overlaying and remarking each key of Fig. 6-13a.

Technique for Scanning a Keyboard

The 4 × 5 keyboard in Fig. 6-12 has 5 rows and 4 columns, for a total of 20 key switches. The rows are generally tied to output, and the columns are tied to input pins of the microcomputer ports (Fig. 6-14). The rows and columns are connected only when one or more of the keys are depressed. Each key, however, is a switch that, when closed, electrically connects a row to a column at a particular intersection.

The technique for scanning the keyboard is to selectively put a low signal on one of the row lines at any moment of time and then to test the column lines for a low signal. A low signal on any of the column lines indicates that one of the keys in the selected row is closed, and

(a)

3	2	1	0
7	6	5	4
C/S	•	9	8
÷	X	—	+
CE	C	EX	E

(b)

3	2	1	0
7	6	5	4
B	A	9	8
F	E	D	C
13	12	11	10

Figure 6-12. (a) Keyboard. (b) Equivalent decode hex value.

(a) The D2 Keyboard

P	L	N	V	
7	8	9	A	M
4	5	6	B	E
1	2	3	C	R
0	F	E	D	G

(b) Reassigned Calculator Keyboard

CE	C	EX	E	
7	8	9	+	
4	5	6	—	
1	2	3	X	
0	CS	•	÷	

Figure 6-13. (a) D2 keyboard assignment. (b) Reassigned calculator keyboard.

the routine then proceeds to decode the key. This implies that the column lines are normally kept at a high state, either by an internal pull-up resistor in the port of the microcomputer or an external resistor tied to each column.

Nine I/O pins are used to scan the 4 × 5 keyboard: five output row pins from Port B and four input pins at Port A. The output pins are tied to the keyboard through inverter drivers and a logic 1 output pulls that row low.

Flow Chart and Listing for Keyboard Scan

The functions of the keyboard routine are as follows:

- Debounce: wait for the key switch to settle.

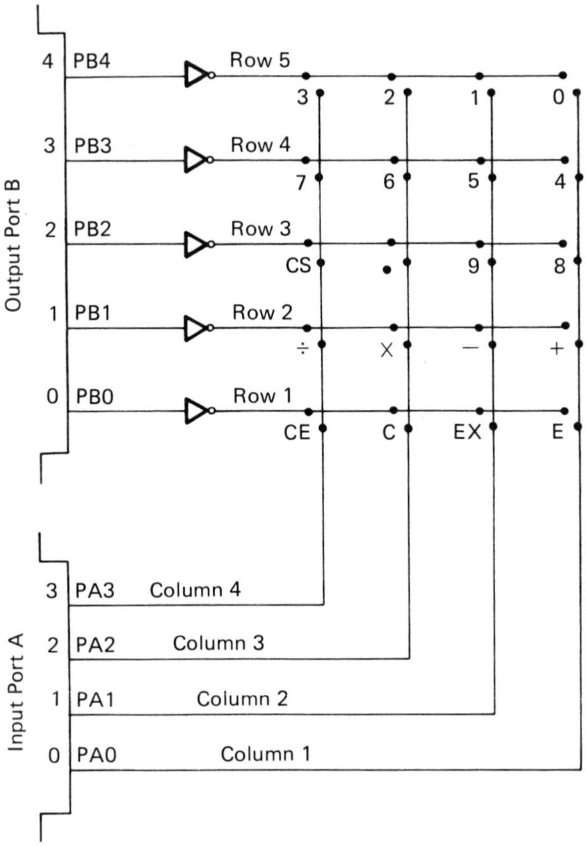

Figure 6-14. 4 x 5 keyboard.

- Select a row.
- Test for a key by examining the column inputs.
- Decode a 4-bit row input into a 2-bit code.
- Merge the row select and column code to a unique key code.
- Wait for key release.

See the flow chart in Fig. 6-15, and the listing in Fig. 6-16.

This routine assumes that only one key is depressed at any moment of time and does not test for key rollover.

KEYINN Since keys are mechanical switches, they bounce when they are closed. Bouncing describes an action that is a series of key-closures prior to the final close. Since the microcomputer operates at much higher speeds than the mechanical switch, a key bounce appears to be a series of depressions entered instead of a single key entry, and may, for example, interpret the closure of the 3 key as a series of 333

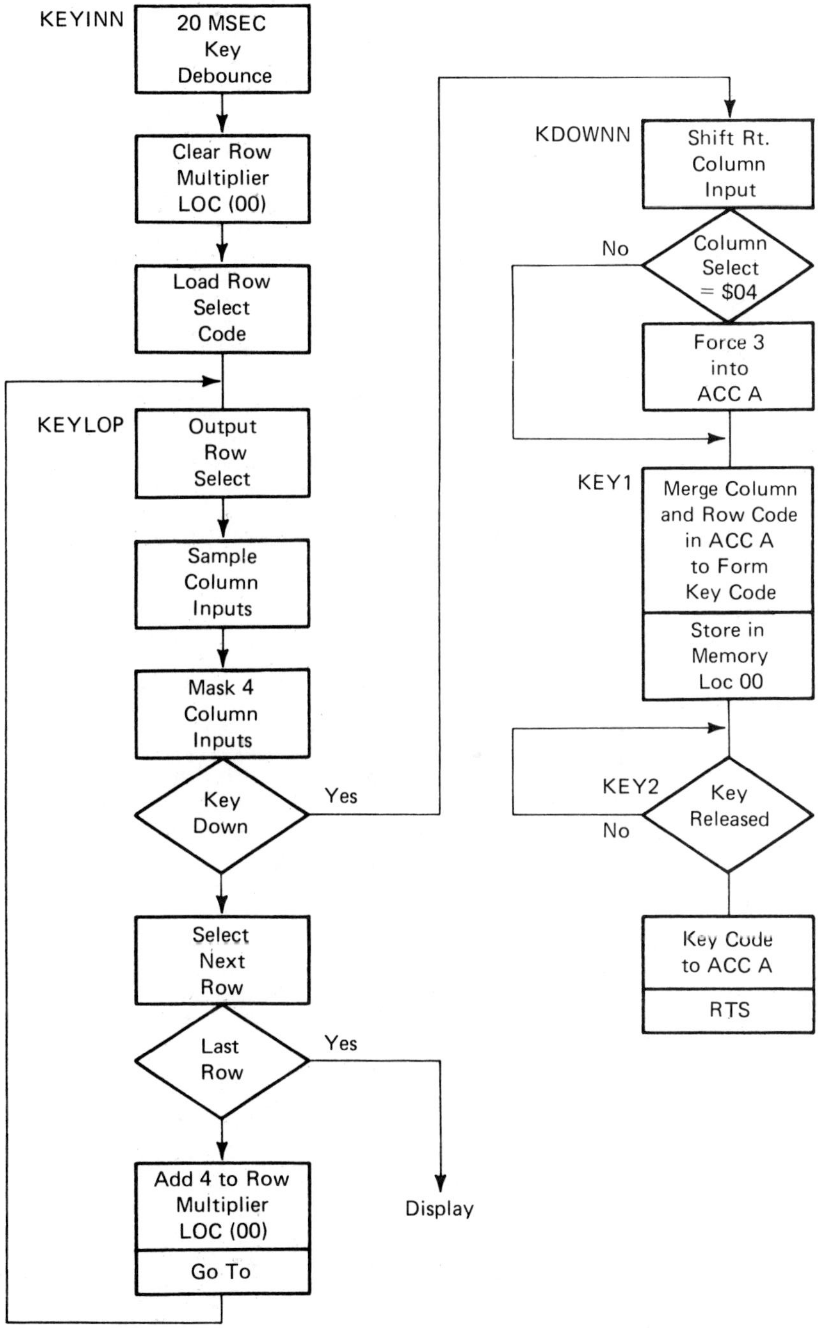

Figure 6-15. 4 x 5 keyboard scan flowchart.

Figure 6-16. Program listing for 4 x 5 keyboard.

```
                          *THIS PROGRAM HAS TWO PARTS:
                          *     INPUT...FROM A KEYBOARD
                          *     OUTPUT..TO A 7-SEGMENT DISPLAY
                          * WHEN THIS SUBROUTINE IS CALLED, IT
                          * ALTERNATELY SCANS THE KEYBOARD & THEN
                          * DISPLAYS OUTPUT DATA.  SEE FIG 6.1.
                          * THIS PROCESS CONTINUES UNTIL THERE IS
                          * A KEY INPUT, AND IS WHERE THE MICRO-
                          * PROCESSOR SPENDS MOST OF ITS TIME.
                          * WHEN A KEY INPUT IS DETECTED, THE CODE FOR
                          * THAT KEY IS PUT INTO ACC A BEFORE
                          * RETURNING TO THE MAIN ROUTINE.
                          *
                          * FOR KEYBOARD SCAN....SEE FIG 6.15.
                          * ASSUME THAT PORT A & PORT B AT LOCATIONS
                          * $8040 & $8042 ARE INITIALIZED AS
                          * INPUT AND OUTPUT PORTS, RESPECTIVELY.
                          * SEE SECTION 6.5.
                          *
A 0000 CE 0600    A KEYINN LDX    #$0600   DEBOUNCE CONSTANT
A 0003 09           KEYDEB DEX
A 0004 26 FD 0003          BNE    KEYDEB   TIME OUT
A 0006 7F 0000    A        CLR    $0000    CLR ROW MULTIPLIER
A 0009 C6 10      A        LDAB   #$10     ACTIVATE ROW 5 LOW
A 000B F7 8042    A KEYLOP STAB   $8042    OUTPUT ROW SELECT
A 000E B6 8040    A        LDAA   $8040    INPUT COLUMN CODE
A 0011 43                  COMA
A 0012 84 0F      A        ANDA   #$0F     MASK COLUMN DATA
A 0014 26 0B 0021          BNE    KDOWNN   BR TO KEY INPUT
A 0016 54                  LSRB            SELECT NEXT ROW
A 0017 27 32 004B          BEQ    DISPLA   BR TO DISPLAY
A 0019 96 00      A        LDAA   $00      GET MULTIPLIER
A 001B 8B 04      A        ADDA   #$04     # OF KEYS IN ROW
A 001D 97 00      A        STAA   $00      PROGRESSION 0.4.8.C.
A 001F 20 EA 000B          BRA    KEYLOP
                    * KEY INPUT
A 0021 47           KDOWNN ASRA            SHIFT RT INPUT CODE
                    * THIS SHIFT CODES THE 0, 1, & 2 KEYS
                    * CORRECTLY. NOW DETECT & CORRECT 3 KEY.
A 0022 81 04      A        CMPA   #$04     KEY FROM ROW 4?
A 0024 26 02 0028          BNE    KEY1
A 0026 86 03      A        LDAA   #$03     CORRECT 3 KEY
                    * MERGE ROW WITH COLUNM BY ADDING
                    * COLUMN MULTIPLIER TO 2-BIT ROW CODE
A 0028 9B 00      A KEY1   ADDA   $00
A 002A 97 00      A        STAA   $00      STORE KEY CODE
                    * WAIT FOR KEY RELEASE BEFORE PROCEEDING
                    * PULL ALL ROW LINES LOW
A 002C C6 1F      A        LDAB   #$1F
A 002E F7 8042    A        STAB   $8042
A 0031 B6 8040    A KEY2   LDAA   $8040    SAMPLE ROW INPUT
A 0034 43                  COMA
A 0035 95 0F      A        BITA   $0F      MASK
A 0037 26 F8 0031          BNE    KEY2     BR TILL KEY RELEASED
                    * GET KEY CODE
```

Figure 6-16. Continued.

```
                          * KEY CODE TO ACC A
A 0039 96 00     A              LDAA    $00
A 003B 39                       RTS
                          *
                          *
                          * THERE ARE FOUR PHASES TO FORMATTING OUTPUT DATA
                          *    1. CONVERT EACH DIGIT TO IT'S 7-SEGMENT
                          *       EQUIVALENT..SEE FIG 6.9.
                          *    2. LIGHT THE APPROPRIATE DP SEGMENT
                          *       ..SEE FIG 6.10.
                          *    3. BLANK THE LEADING ZEROS..SEE FIG 6.11.
                          *    4. INSERT A NEGATIVE SIGN, IF REQUIRED
                          *
                          * PHASE 1 CONVERTS THE 8 PACKED DIGITS TO THEIR
                          * 7-SEGMENT EQUIVALENT & STORES THEM IN 8-BYTES
                          * OF THE OUTPUT REGISTER STARTING AT LOCATION $30
                          *
A 0005                          ORG     $0005
A 0005        0001  A SIZE      RMB     1         BYTE COUNT
A 0008                          ORG     $0008
A 0008        0002  A SPOINT    RMB     2         SOURCE POINTER
A 000A        0002  A DPOINT    RMB     2         DESTINATION POINTER
A 0028                          ORG     $0028
A 0028        0004  A DMANN     RMB     4         4-BYTE D-MANTISSA
A 002C        0001  A DEXP      RMB     1         D-EXPONENT
A 002D        0001  A DSIGN     RMB     1
A 0030                          ORG     $0030
A 0030        0009  A OUTREG    RMB     9         9-BYTE OUTPUT REGISTER
                        * LIST LOOK-UP TABLE OF 7-SEGMENT DISPLAY CODES
                        * SEE TABLE 6.1.
A 0039        0C    A TABLE7    FCB     $0C       0
A 003A        F7    A           FCB     $F7       1
A 003B        A4    A           FCB     $A4       2
A 003C        B0    A           FCB     $B0       3
A 003D        99    A           FCB     $99       4
A 003E        92    A           FCB     $92       5
A 003F        82    A           FCB     $82       6
A 0040        F8    A           FCB     $F8       7
A 0041        80    A           FCB     $80       8
A 0042        98    A           FCB     $98       9
A 0043        88    A           FCB     $88       A
A 0044        83    A           FCB     $83       B
A 0045        C6    A           FCB     $C6       C
A 0046        A1    A           FCB     $A1       D
A 0047        86    A           FCB     $86       E
A 0048        8E    A           FCB     $8E       F
A 0049        BF    A           FCB     $BF       - NEGATIVE SIGN
A 004A        FF    A           FCB     $FF       BLANK
                        *
              8020  A SDRIVE    EQU     $8020     SEGMENT DRIVERS
              8022  A DDRIVE    EQU     $8022     DIGIT DRIVERS
                        *
                        * LOAD POINTER WITH SOURCE, DESTINATION ADDRESS,
                        * BYTE COUNT (9) OF THE OUTPUT REGISTER.
                        *
```

(Continued)

Figure 6-16. Continued.

```
00111A 004B CE 0030   A DISPLA LDX     #OUTREG   ADDR OF OUTPUT REG
00112A 004E DF 0A     A        STX     DPOINT    SAVE POINTER
00113A 0050 CE 0028   A        LDX     #DMANN    MANTISSA D-REG
00114A 0053 DF 08     A        STX     SPOINT    SAVE POINTER
00115A 0055 7F 0001   A        CLR     $0001     ODD/EVEN INDICATOR
00116A 0058 C6 09     A        LDAB    #$09      BYTE COUNT
00117A 005A D7 05     A        STAB    SIZE
00118                   * TEST ODD/EVEN INDICATOR, FOR UNPACKING
00119A 005C DE 08     A DILOOP LDX     SPOINT    GET POINTER
00120A 005E A6 00     A        LDAA    0,X       GET PACKED DIGIT
00121                   *
00122                   * IN THE ODD/EVEN INDICATOR
00123                   * 00 INDICATES ODD & FF INDICATES EVEN
00124                   * THE STATE OF THE FLAG IS FLIPPED WHEN TESTED
00125A 0060 C6 FF     A        LDAB    #$FF
00126A 0062 D8 01     A        EORB    $01       TEST & FLIP FLAG
00127A 0064 D7 01     A        STAB    $01
00128A 0066 26 1E 0086         BNE     DEVEN     BR TO EVEN DIGIT
00129                   * ELSE PROCESS ODD LSDIGIT
00130A 0068 84 0F     A        ANDA    #$0F
00131                   * MERGE WITH EVEN DIGIT BRANCH
00132A 006A DF 08     A DIS1   STX     SPOINT    SAVE POINTER
00133                   *
00134                   * LOOKUP DIGIT IN 7-SEGMENT DISPLAY TABLE
00135A 006C CE 0039   A        LDX     #TABLE7
00136A 006F 4D                 TSTA              TEST IF DIGIT EQ 0
00137A 0070 27 04 0076         BEQ     DIS3      BR IF DIGIT ZERO
00138                   * INCREMENT TABLE POINTER BY NUMBER TO DISPLAY
00139A 0072 08          DIS2   INX
00140A 0073 4A                 DECA              DEC DIGIT
00141A 0074 26 FC 0072         BNE     DIS2      KEEP INCREMENTING
00142                   * POINTER NOW POINTS TO PROPER 7-SEGMENT CODE
00143A 0076 A6 00     A DIS3   LDAA    0,X       GET 7-SEG MENT CODE
00144                   * LOAD POINTER WITH APPROPRIATE OUTPUT REGISTER
00145A 0078 DE 0A     A        LDX     DPOINT
00146A 007A A7 00     A        STAA    0,X       STORE 7-SEG CODE
00147A 007C 08                 INX
00148A 007D DF 0A     A        STX     DPOINT    SAVE POINTER
00149A 007F 8C 0038   A        CPX     #$0038    TEST FOR LAST DIGIT
00150A 0082 26 D8 005C         BNE     DILOOP    BR BACK FOR NEXT DIGIT
00151A 0084 20 07 008D         BRA     DIS10
00152                   * ELSE PROCEED TO PHASE 2 & INSERT DP
00153                   * EVEN DIGIT BRANCH, SHIFT DIGIT IN THE ACC A
00154                   * TO THE LSDIGIT POSITION
00155A 0086 44          DEVEN  LSRA
00156A 0087 44                 LSRA
00157A 0088 44                 LSRA
00158A 0089 44                 LSRA
00159A 008A 08                 INX               INC SOURCE POINTER
00160A 008B 20 DD 006A         BRA     DIS1      MERGE WITH ODD BRANCH
00161                   *
00162                   * PHASE 2.  LOAD DECIMAL POINT (DP)
00163A 008D CE 0030   A DIS10  LDX     #$0030    LOAD POINTER
00164A 0090 96 2C     A        LDAA    DEXP      GET EXPONENT
00165A 0092 4D                 TSTA              TEST IF DEXP EQ ZERO
```

Figure 6-16. Continued.

```
0093 27 0A 009F          BEQ    DIS20     BR IF ZERO EXP
                       * ELSE INCREMENT POINTER
0095 08                DIS11  INX              COUNT UP TO DIGIT
0096 4A                       DECA             COUNT DOWN EXP
0097 26 FC 0095               BNE    DIS11
0099 A6 00      A      DIS12  LDAA   0,X       GET 7-SEGMENT CODE
009B 8A 7F      A             ORAA   #$7F      LITE DP SEGMENT
009D A7 00      A             STAA   0,X       RESTORE CODE
                       *
                       * PHASE 3.  BLANK LEADING ZEROS
009F CE 0038    A      DIS20  LDX    #$0038    POINT TO MSBYTE
00A2 C6 FF      A             LDAB   #$FF      CODE FOR BLANK
00A4 D7 38      A             STAB   $38       BLANK MSBYTE
00A6 A6 00      A      DIS21  LDAA   0,X       GET SEGMENT CODE
00A8 81 C0      A             CMPA   #$C0      NON-DECIMAL ZERO
00AA 26 08 00B4               BNE    DIS30     EXIT
00AC E7 00      A             STAB   0,X       REPLACE WITH BLANK
00AE 09                       DEX
00AF 8C 0030    A             CPX    #$0030    TEST FOR LSBYTE
00B2 26 F2 00A6               BNE    DIS21     KEEP BLANKING
                       *
                       * PHASE 4.  TEST TO INSERT NEGATIVE SIGN
00B4 96 2D      A      DIS30  LDAA   DSIGN
00B6 27 04 00BC               BEQ    DISBUF    POSITIVE IS 00
00B8 86 BF      A             LDAA   #$BF      NEGATIVE SIGN
00BA A7 01      A             STAA   1,X       AT POINTER +1
                       *
                       * OUTPUT DATA FROM OUTREG TO 7-SEGMENT DISPLAY
00BC CE 0030    A      DISBUF LDX    #$0030
00BF C6 01      A             LDAB   #$01      DIGIT SELECT CODE
00C1 86 FF      A             LDAA   #$FF      BLANK
00C3 B7 8020    A             STAA   SDRIVE    BLANK SEGMENTS
                       * DISPLAY OUTPUT LOOP
00C6 A6 00      A      DISB1  LDAA   0,X       GET SEGMENT CODE
00C8 B7 8020    A             STAA   SDRIVE    OUTPUT SEG CODE
00CB F7 8022    A             STAB   DDRIVE    DIGIT SELECT
                       * THE SELECTED DIGIT IS LIT WITH APPROPRIATE
                       * SEGMENT CODE.  TIME DELAY..
00CE 86 70      A             LDAA   #$70      DELAY CONSTANT
00D0 4A                DISB2  DECA             DELAY LOOP
00D1 26 FD 00D0               BNE    DISB2
00D3 08                       INX
00D4 86 FF      A             LDAA   #$FF      BLANK CODE
00D6 B7 8020    A             STAA   SDRIVE    BLANK SEGMENT
00D9 58                       ASLB             SHIFT DIGIT SELECT
00DA C1 40      A             CMPB   #$40      TEST FOR LAST DIGIT
00DC 26 E8 00C6               BNE    DISB1
00DE 7E 0000    A             JMP    KEYINN
                              END
```

entries. The debounce routine is a time-delay routine that waits for the key to stop bouncing, or debounce, and takes typically about 20 ms.

Row Multiplier Each of the 15 keys is decoded into a 5-bit code from 0 to $13. The four columns are decoded into the 2LSBs and the row multiplier constitutes the 3MSBs. The multiplier is initialized to zero, and the program adds 4 to the multiplier at location $00 with each pass through the loop. In the KDOWN routine the 2LS column bits are merged with the 3MS row bits to form the 5-bit key decode value.

KEYLOP In the key scan loop, each row select and code is output through Port B and column inputs are sampled at the 4 LSBs of Port A. The input data are complemented, the 4 LSBs are masked, and the data are sampled for a high or nonzero number. If there is a key entry, the routine branches to the location labeled key down, KDOWN. If no key entry, the routine selects the next row select. If the last row has been sampled, then the routine branches to the 7-segment display routine; otherwise, 4 is added to the multiplier at location $00, and the routine continues to scan the keyboard by branching back to KEYLOP.

KDOWN When a key is depressed, the program branches to KDOWN, where the program decodes or converts a key closure to a form that is usable by the internal program (see Fig. 6-12).

The data in accumulator A, because it was complemented, should have a 1 set in one of the 4 LSBs that correspond to column 1, 2, 3, or 4. See Fig. 6-14.

Examples:

1. If ROW 5 is selected and bit 2 in accumulator A is high, then key 2 is closed.
2. If ROW 4 is selected and bit 0 in accumulator A is high, then key 4 is closed.
3. If ROW 2 is selected and bit 1 is high, then the subtract key is closed.
4. If ROW 1 is selected and bit 3 is high, then the CE key is closed.

The keys in ROW 5 are 0, 1, 2, and 3, corresponding to bits 0, 1, 2, and 3 in accumulator A. Shifting the column select data in accumulator A right 1 bit makes the binary data for 0, 1, and 2 agree with keys 0, 1, and 2, respectively. The data for key 3 must, however, be corrected. If the column select data is $04, it is connected to binary 03, so that the correct binary number for a column select is stored in the 2 LSBs of accumulator A.

KEY1 The key decode data are formed in accumulator A by merging the column data with the multiplier or row data in location $00, and then stored in location $00.

KEY2 The routine stays in the key release loop until the key is released by the operator. The key code is then transferred to accumulator A, and the program branches back to the main system program.

6-6 D-2 KEYBOARD SCAN

This section describes an alternate technique for scanning a keyboard, the D-2 keyboard. Prior to describing the keyboard scan, it is necessary to consider the number of I/O pins available. The primary constraint is that both display keyboard scan routines must be implemented with two ports, or 16 I/O pins. The six 7-segment displays require 7 segment select pins and 6 digit select pins, for a total of 13 I/O pins. This leaves three I/O pins for other functions. The 6 × 4 D-2 keyboard shares the six row drivers with the 6-digit select drivers of the 7-segment display. This leaves three I/O pins for sampling the four

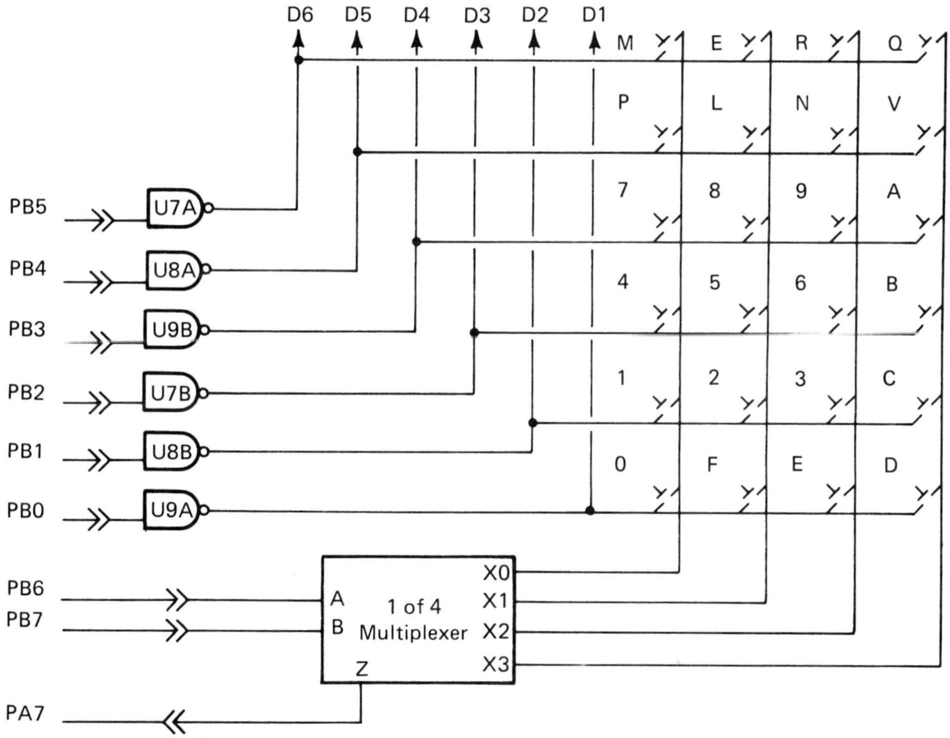

Figure 6-17. D2 keyboard and I/O port schematic.

column lines, which in themselves are not enough, but the addition of a 1 of 4 multiplexer does make it work. The four column lines of the keyboard are routed to one output, pin Z, of the multiplexer. Multiplexing refers to having one wire carry several different signals or information. In this case of time multiplexing, the wire connected to pin Z carries the information from each of the column lines at different times. The two column select pins from PB6 and PB7 control which column line is multiplexed to input pin PA7 of the microcomputer.

The key select code for outputting to the D-2 kit combines the six rows and two columns into one 8-bit key select code through Port B that permits each key to be individually examined. With this technique, therefore, each key is uniquely identified by the key select code, which, however, may not be compatible with the internal notation of the system. The key select code is then decoded, or converted, by a look-up table to a key decode that is compatible with the system.

By virtue of using a look-up table for decoding, the assigning of key values to key positions is not critical, whereas in the classic keyboard scan each key position is judiciously selected to coordinate with the decode algorithm.

Function of the D-2 Keyboard Scan Routine

The function of the D-2 keyboard scan routine is to adapt the D-2 keyboard for the calculator by reassigning the 27 keys in Fig. 6-13a to the 20 keys indicated in Fig. 6-13b. The key decodes are listed in Table 6-3. The program listing is on page 214.

KEYIN The flow chart and listing are given in Figs. 6-17 and 6-18.

Blank the Display The six-row select pins of the keyboard are shared with the six-digit select pins of the 7-segment display, and the segment drivers are “blanked” or turned off to prevent inadvertent flickers of the display while scanning the keyboard.

Debounce See Debounce, Sec. 6-5.

Select the First Key See Table 6-3. Putting the $01 code into the output key select code at Port B, $8022 selects the numeric 0 key to be examined. Bit 1 of the key select code activates row 1, and when bits 6 and 7 are 00 the column select code passes the signal from column 0 through the multiplexer. The status of the selected key is examined at pin 7 of Port A, $8020.

KEYSCN The keyboard scan loop sequences and tests each key as listed in Table 6-3.

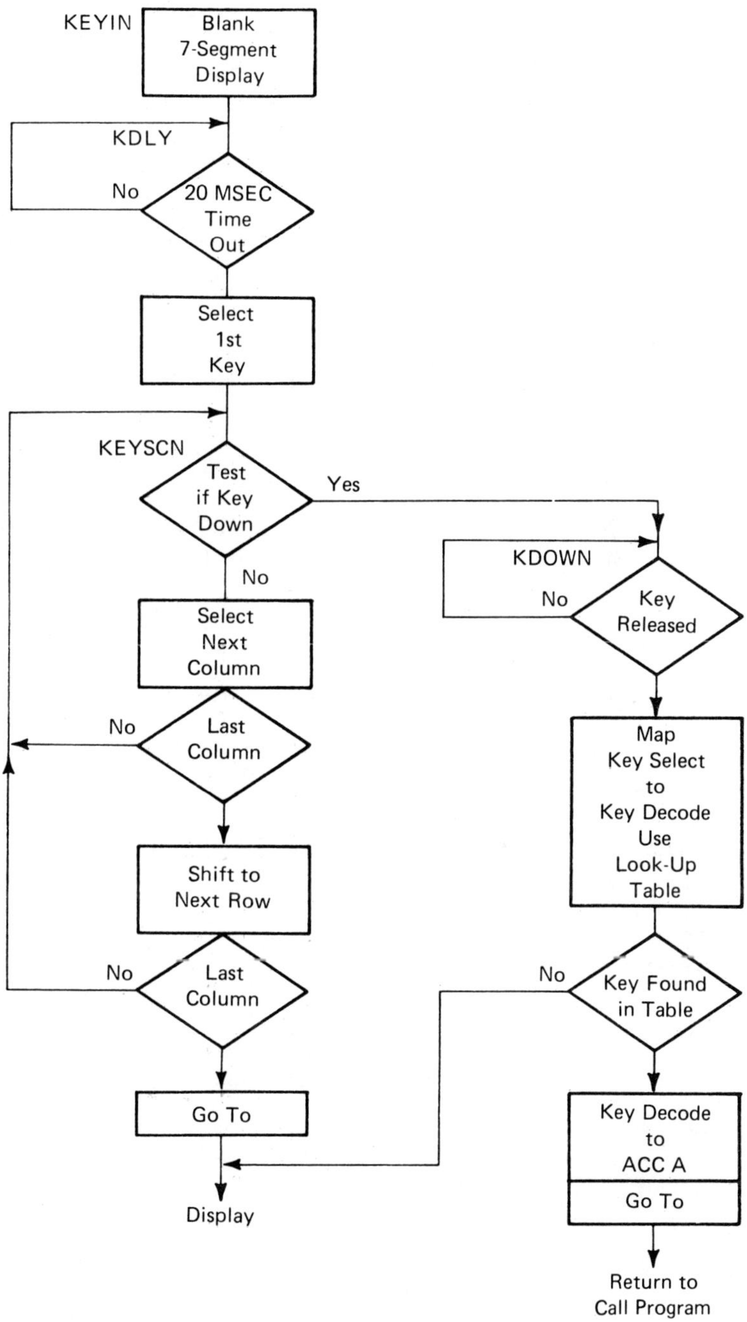

Figure 6-18. Flowchart for the D2 keyboard.

Figure 6-19.

```
                            * SCAN D-2 KEYBOARD, SEE SECTION 6.6, FIG 6.18.
A 0010                               ORG    $10
               8020   A SEGREG EQU    $8020    SEGMENT DRIVERS
               8022   A DIGREG EQU    $8022    DIGIT DRIVERS
                            *
                            * SEE TABLE 6.4, KEYS NOT IN THE TABLE ARE IGNORE
                            * CODE FOR THE DIGITS 0-9 AND THE FUNCTION KEYS
A 0010    01         A KTABLE FCB    $01,$02,$42,$82,
A 0015    04         A        FCB    $04,$44,$84,$08,
A 001A    48         A        FCB    $48,$88,
A 001D    81         A        FCB    $81      DP
A 001E    41         A        FCB    $41      CS CHANGE SIGN
A 001F    C8         A        FCB    $C8      +  ADD
A 0020    C4         A        FCB    $C4      -  SUBTRACT
A 0021    C2         A        FCB    $C2      X  MULTIPLY
A 0022    C1         A        FCB    $C1      /  DIVIIDE
A 0023    D0         A        FCB    $D0      E  ENTER
A 0024    90         A        FCB    $90      EX EXCHANGE
A 0025    50         A        FCB    $50      C  CLEAR
A 0026    10         A        FCB    $10      CE CLEAR ENTRY
                            *
A 0027 86 EF         A KEYIN  LDAA   #$EF     BLANK CODE
A 0029 B7 8020       A        STAA   SEGREG   BLANK SEGMENTS
A 002C CE 0600       A        LDX    #$0600   20 MSEC DELAY
A 002F 09              KDLY   DEX             DEBOUNCE DELAY
A 0030 26 FD 002F             BNE    KDLY
A 0032 CE 8020       A        LDX    #SEGREG  LOAD POINTER
A 0035 86 01         A        LDAA   #$01
                            * SCAN KEYBOARD
A 0037 A7 02         A KEYSCN STAA   2,X      ROW DRIVERS
A 0039 6D 00         A        TST    0,X      TEST COLUMN INPUTS
A 003B 2A 0C 0049             BPL    KDOWN    BR TO KEY DOWN
A 003D 8B 40         A        ADDA   #$40     ELSE UPDATE KEY CODE
A 003F 24 F6 0037             BCC    KEYSCN   SELECT NEXT COLUMN
A 0041 48                     ASLA            SELECT NEXT ROW
A 0042 81 40         A        CMPA   #$40     TEST FOR LAST KEY
A 0044 26 F1 0037             BNE    KEYSCN   SELECT NEXT ROW
A 0046 7E 0064       A        JMP    DISPLA   NO KEY DOWN
                            * KEY DOWN, KEY INPUT IS IN ACC A
                            * MORE APPROPRIATELY THE OUTPUT CODE IN
                            * ACC A SELECTED THE KEY WHICH WAS DOWN
                            * NOW DECODE IT
A 0049 6D 00         A KDOWN  TST    0,X      WAIT FOR KEY RELEASE
A 004B 2A FC 0049             BPL    KDOWN
                            * MAP KEY SELECT INTO KEY DECODE USING
                            * LOOK-UP TABLE
A 004D D6 14         A        LDAB   $14      KEY COUNT
A 004F D7 00         A        STAB   $00      SAVE KEY COUNT
A 0051 5F                     CLRB            CLEAR FOR KEY CODE
A 0052 CE 0010       A        LDX    #KTABLE
A 0055 A1 00         A KLOOK  CMPA   0,X
A 0057 27 09 0062             BEQ    KCODE    KEY FOUND
A 0059 7A 0000       A        DEC    $00      DEC KEY COUTNT
A 005C 27 06 0064             BEQ    DISPLA   GO TO DISPLAY
A 005E 08                     INX             INC TABLE POINTER
```

```
A 005F 5C                INCB              INC KEY DECODE
A 0060 20 F3 0055        BRA      KLOOK    EXAIMINE NEXT CODE
                    * TRANSFER KEY DECODE TO ACC A
A 0062 17           KCODE    TBA
A 0063 39                RTS               RETURN TO MAIN ROUTINE
                    *
                    * DUMMY INSTRUCTION
A 0064 01           DISPLA NOP
```

Algorithm for Sequencing through the Keyboard The column select bits, 7 and 6, control the multiplexer, which passes the signal from the selected column of the keyboard to PA7, the input pin of the microcomputer.

Bits	7	6	Column
	0	0	1
	0	1	2
	1	0	3
	1	1	4

The program sequences through each column by adding $40 to the contents of accumulator A, that is, adding 1 to bit 6. While the column select code sequences through 00, 01, 10, and 11, the row select bits are not affected. The program stays in the column select sequence by testing for NO CARRY, and then drops through to select the next row. The next row is selected by shifting the data in accumulator A left 1 bit (ASLA). The column select code at this time is 00 and is not affected by the arithmetic left shift instruction.

The program uses the test instruction (TST) index addressing mode to test all the bits of Port A, and branches, if positive, to key down (KDOWN) for a key closure.

Last Key If no key is closed, the program branches to refresh the 7-segment display.

KDOWN See KDOWN, Sec. 6-5.

Map the Key Select Code into the Key Code Mapping converts, or substitutes, the key select code required by the keyboard to the key decode used by the program. The map is a look-up table with the list of keys used by the calculator program listed in the order of their key decode value (see Table 6-4).

Accumulator B is cleared and the index register points to the top of the KTABLE, key table. A comparison is made between the key select

Table 6-3. Key Selector Code Sequence for D2 Keyboard

D2 Keyboard	Hex	Binary: Column Select Bits	Binary: Row Select Bits
0	0 1	0 0 0 0	0 0 0 1
F	4 1	0 1 0 0	0 0 0 1
E	8 1	1 0 0 0	0 0 0 1
D	C 1	1 1 0 0	0 0 0 1
1	0 2	0 0 0 0	0 0 1 0
2	4 2	0 1 0 0	0 0 1 0
3	8 2	1 0 0 0	0 0 1 0
C	C 2	1 1 0 0	0 0 1 0
4	0 4	0 0 0 0	0 1 0 0
5	4 4	0 1 0 0	0 1 0 0
6	8 4	1 0 0 0	0 1 0 0
B	C 4	1 1 0 0	0 1 0 0
7	0 8	0 0 0 0	1 0 0 0
8	4 8	0 1 0 0	1 0 0 0
9	8 8	1 0 0 0	1 0 0 0
A	C 8	1 1 0 0	1 0 0 0
P	1 0	0 0 0 1	0 0 0 0
L	5 0	0 1 0 1	0 0 0 0
N	9 0	1 0 0 1	0 0 0 0
V	D 0	1 1 0 1	0 0 0 0
M	2 0	0 0 1 0	0 0 0 0
E	6 0	0 1 1 0	0 0 0 0
R	A 0	1 0 1 0	0 0 0 0
G	E 0	1 1 1 0	0 0 0 0

code in accumulator A and the key select code in the location pointed to by the index register. Both accumulator B and the index register are incremented after each comparison. When the key select code is found in the table, key decode value in accumulator B has incremented to the proper key decode value.

If the key is not found, the program branches to the display routine. When the key is found in the table, the key decode is transferred to accumulator A and returns to the calculator program.

Table 6-4. Value Look-up Table to Map Key to Decoded Value

Key	D-2 Key Selector Code	Key Decode (in Acc A)
0	0 1	0 0
1	0 2	0 1
2	4 2	0 2
3	8 2	0 3
4	0 4	0 4
5	4 4	0 5
6	8 4	0 6
7	0 8	0 7
8	4 8	0 8
9	8 8	0 9
•	8 1	0 A
CS	4 1	0 B
+	C 8	0 C
−	C 4	0 D
×	C 2	0 E
÷	C 1	0 F
E	D 0	1 0
Ex	9 0	1 1
C	5 0	1 2
CE	1 0	1 3

6-7 QUICK SCAN OF THE KEYBOARD

There are occasions when it is preferable to make a quick preliminary scan of the keyboad, and if there is a key closure to go to the key scan procedures described in Secs. 6-5 and 6-6. The preliminary quick scan may be necessary when many, 10 or more, 7-segment displays are used and there is a need to increase the refresh cycle to eliminate flicker. Other occasions might be when the microcomputer has other important tasks to perform and cannot afford the extra time lost for a complete keyboard scan.

The quick scan examines all the keys of the keyboard simultaneously. To test the classic keyboard (Sec. 6-5) for a preliminary key closure, pull all the row select lines low and test all the input column lines for a closure.

To test the D-2 keyboard again, all the row select lines are pulled low, and then the routine must make four passes through a loop to test a key closure in each column.

7 The Calculator as a System

A system problem offers the reader an opportunity for understanding how to partition a problem for the purpose of writing smaller and more manageable routines, often referred to as *modules*. It also demonstrates the techniques for reassembling or calling the various routines to form a system. Another advantage for considering a system problem is to develop an appreciation of the impact of each routine on the system and, conversely, to indicate how to change the system specification by modifying, adding, or deleting routines. See the system flow chart in Fig. 7-6.

This chapter integrates the internal arithmetic and support routines developed in Chapter 5 and the I/O routines of Chapter 6 into a total system. A calculator is chosen as the system example because it is a generally understood system that needs little explanation. Hence, it is necessary to define and write the system specifications prior to writing the various routines required to support it. Effectively, then, this system chapter was written first, and then the routines of Chapters 5 and 6 were developed to support the system. This implies that it is necessary to have a functional understanding of the system prior to implementing a solution.

The objective of this chapter is to implement a system problem and to describe the interrelations between the routines. Other features of this chapter are to suggest a myriad of examples that can be used to modify the system. As soon as the system example is described, the general response often is, "Why do it that way?," which of course is the appropriate response, and readers are invited to modify or change the system. A discussion of suggested examples to modify the system is deferred to the end of the chapter in Sec. 7-5. These suggestions relate to the system but are more meaningful after the reader has gained familiarity with the system.

7-1 SYSTEM SPECIFICATION OF THE CALCULATOR

The four basic specifications of the four-function, 7-digit Reverse Polish calculator are as follows:

- Internal organization—Reverse Polish calculator
- Four-function keyboard—add, subtract, multiply, divide
- Range of 7-digit numbers
- Error detect routines, for number entry after an arithmetic operation

Reverse Polish-Type (RPT) Calculator

A calculator is a simple, two-register arithmetic unit. The registers are loaded with two operands, which, on command, form either a sum, difference, product, or quotient, and the user is not cognizant of the internal operations. In the reverse Polish-type calculator the user must be aware of the data in each of the registers. This calculator has two registers; the D register is the I/O register and E is the alternate register. Numbers are automatically loaded into the D register and the E, or ENTER key, moves the data into the E register (Fig. 7-1). The data in the D register are displayed after each operation. The essential difference between the RPT and other calculators is that it does not have an EQUAL key. The key sequence for other calculators is:

$$
\begin{array}{c}
23 + 56 = \\
23 - 56 = \\
23 \times 56 = \\
23 \div 56 =
\end{array}
$$

The key sequence for the RPT calculator is to load the appropriate operands into the D and E registers and then to execute the required function:

$$
\begin{array}{c}
23 \text{ E } 56 + \\
23 \text{ E } 56 - \\
23 \text{ E } 56 \times \\
23 \text{ E } 56 \div
\end{array}
$$

The RPT calculator executes the second function and stores the result to be displayed in the D register.

The RPT calculator is also referred to as a stack-type calculator. It should not be confused with the internal stack and stack pointer of the 6800. In the stack-type calculator there are a series of E registers, E1, E2, E3, E4, which constitutes a stack and is used for storing several operands. In this case, the E key is used to push data into the stack, which simultaneously moves data from

$$\begin{aligned} D &\rightarrow E1 \\ E1 &\rightarrow E2 \\ E2 &\rightarrow E3 \\ E3 &\rightarrow E4 \end{aligned}$$

Once the data are loaded into the registers, the function key executes the appropriate operation on the data in the D and E1 registers. The result is stored in the D register and the data are pulled from the stack, which simultaneously moves data from

$$\begin{aligned} E4 &\rightarrow E3 \\ E3 &\rightarrow E2 \\ E2 &\rightarrow E1 \end{aligned}$$

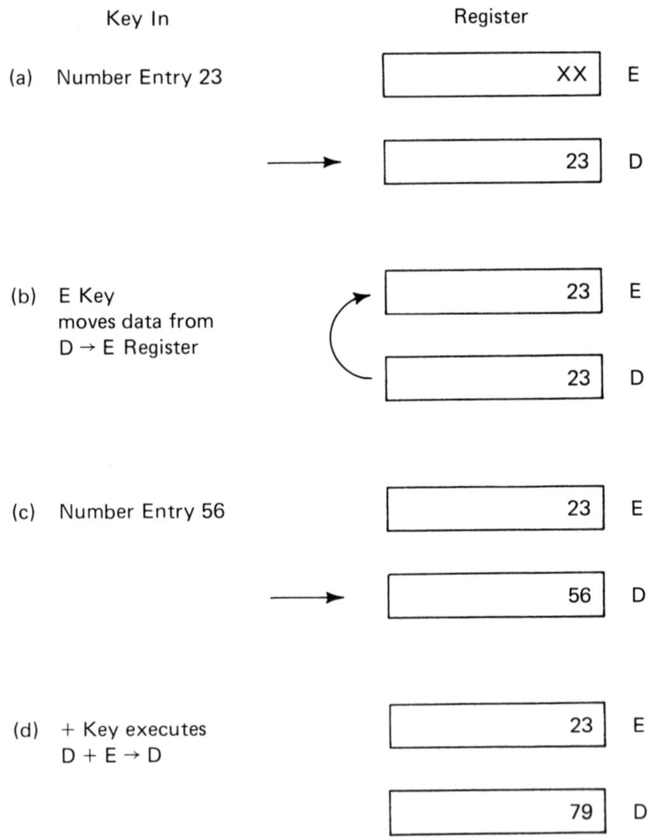

Figure 7-1. Sequence for adding 23 + 56 on the Reverse Polish calculator. The key sequence is 23 E 56 +.

Calculator Keyboard

The 20 keys of the calculator (Fig. 7-2) fall into three groups:

- 12 numeric keys
- 6 function keys
- 2 clear keys

The numeric keys load the three parts of the input operand, the mantissa, exponent, and sign, into the D register.

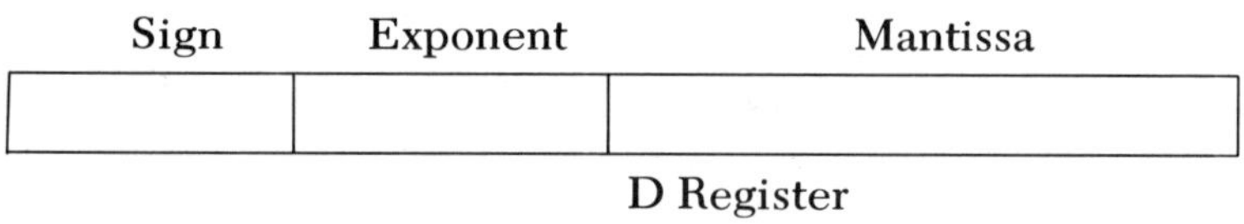

By entering a number after a function key, the D register is automatically cleared and a new number sequence begins. The numeric keys are the digits 0 through 9, the decimal point (DP), and the change sign (C/S) keys. The DP flag is set by the DP key, and the exponent, which indicates the position of the decimal point, increments as numbers are loaded after the DP flag is set. The change sign key changes the sign of the D register.

The six function keys indicate how data are modified or moved by the four arithmetic and two move or exchange keys. A person using a Reverse Polish-type calculator must know what data are in each register. The function keys execute

+	Add	$E + D \rightarrow D$
−	Subtract	$E - D \rightarrow D$
×	Multiply	$E \times D \rightarrow D$
÷	Divide	$D / E \rightarrow D$
E	Enter	$D \rightarrow E$
EX	Exchange	$D \leftrightarrow E$

There are two clear keys, clear (C) and clear entry (CE). The clear key clears the D register and the error flag, while the clear entry is used when loading a number because it clears the last number inserted.

Calculator Display

The numeric range of a 7-digit calculator is from 9 999 999 to −0.000 000, and requires nine 7-segment displays to show the 7 digits (Fig.

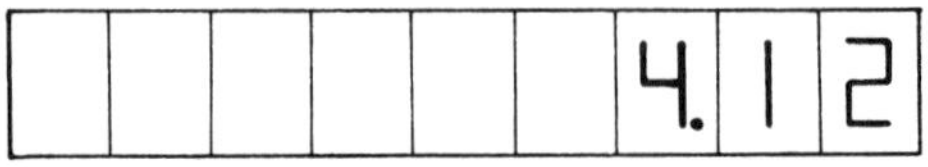

3	2	1	0
7	6	5	4
c/s	•	9	8
÷	×	−	+
CE	C	EX	E

Figure 7-2. 4-function keyboard with 9-digit display.

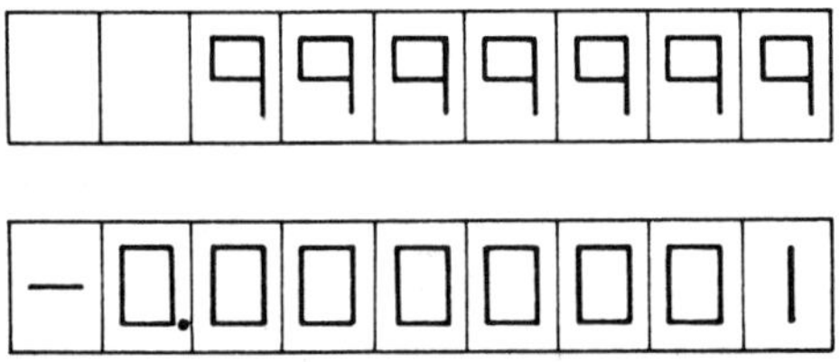

Figure 7-3. Range of numbers for digit from 9,999,999 to −0.0000001.

7-3). Of the two extra, one display shows the negative sign, and the second display is used to show a zero left of the decimal point for numbers less than 1.

Error Indicator

An error indicator indicates that a number too large for the calculator to handle has either been loaded through the keyboard or generated as a consequence of an arithmetic operation. A red light or an error message on the display may be used to indicate such an error. This calculator system does not have an error display routine. There is an error detect routine to test the result of the arithmetic operation, but not, however, for the number entry routine.

7-2 MEMORY MAP AND NOTATION

A memory map indicates the allocation of the memory space, and for the calculator there are four groups (Fig. 7-4):

- Variables at $0000
- Registers at $0020
- Program at $0040, discussed in Sec. 7-4
- I/O ports at $8000, discussed in Chapter 6

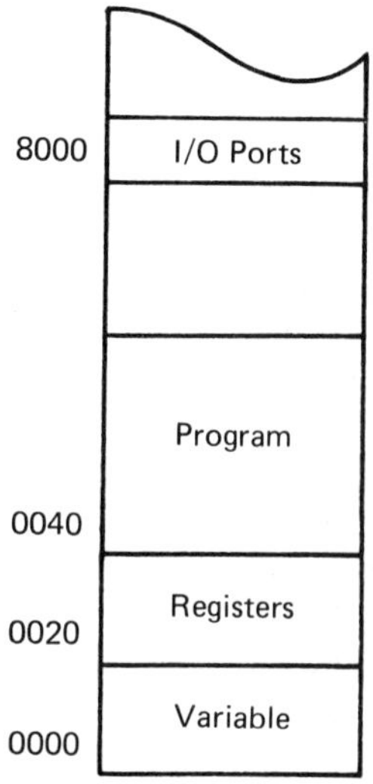

Figure 7-4. Memory map for the calculator.

Variables and Symbolic Names

It is convenient, when writing programs, to refer to the variables by their symbolic names (see Table 7-1). For example, there are 20 keys in the calculator keyboard or, restated, the last key entered is a variable that has 20 possibilities. For convenience, while examining and processing the last key entry, it is given the symbolic name of NEWKEY. On occasion it becomes necessary to examine the key entered prior to the NEWKEY, and that variable is given the symbolic name OLDKEY. Again, OLDKEY is a variable that represents 1 of the 20 keys of the keyboard. The memory location or locations that store the variable data are referred to by their symbolic names. For example, NEWKEY and OLDKEY refer to 1-byte variable data that are stored in locations $03 and $04, respectively.

The index register is used to point to a block of data, and as the pointer points to each location within the block, the address contained by the pointer varies. The pointer address is a 2-byte variable. When moving a block of data, two pointers are required: a source and a destination pointer. The symbolic names for the source and destination pointers are SPOINT and DPOINT, respectively, and these 2-byte variables are stored, starting at locations $08 and $0A.

Table 7-1 Symbolic Names of the Variables and Their Memory Locations

00	GP[a]	
01	GP	
02	GP	
03	NEWKEY	Last key entry
04	OLDKEY	Next to the last key entry
05	SIZE	Size or length of a block of data
06	WTABLE	Work space for table modification
07		
08,09	SPOINT	Source pointer
0A,0B	DPOINT	Destination pointer
0C,0D	JTABLE	Function key jump table
0E	ERROR	Error flag; zero indicates an error
0F		
10,11	ADDK	Contains address of ADD routine
12,13	SUBK	Contains address of SUBTRACT routine
14,15	MULTK	Contains address of MULTIPLY routine
16,17	DIVK	Contains address of DIVIDE routine
18,19	ENTERK	Contains address of ENTER routine
1A,1B	EXCHK	Contains address of EXCHANGE routine
1C,1D	CLEARK	Contains address of CLEAR routine
1E,1F	CENTK	Contains address of CLEAR ENTRY routine
20-23	EMANN	
24	EEXP	
25	ESIGN	
26		
27		
28-2B	DMANN	
2C	DEXP	
2D	DSIGN	
2E	DP flag	
2F		
30-38	OUTREG	Output register
39-3F		Spares

[a] General purpose.

The mantissa stored in the D register is a 7-digit variable that is stored in 4 bytes of memory. The symbolic name for the D register mantissa is DMANN, which refers to the LS byte of the register at location $28.

A symbolic name is made of six alphanumeric characters or less, with no spaces, and must start with an alpha character.

The Registers

The three registers of the calculator are the D, E, and output registers (Fig. 7-5a). The D and E registers start at locations $28 and $20, respectively, and store 7-decimal digits packed into the 4-byte mantissa, with the fifth and sixth bytes storing the exponents and signs, respectively.

The D register is the data input and output register, but before outputting the data it must be formatted or converted to a form that is compatible with the output device. The output register stores the formatted data.

The MULTIPLY operation generates a 14-digit product that is too large to be stored in the D register. During operations that require a larger register, the D register is extended to an 8-byte register by attaching the D-concatenated register (Fig. 7-5b). To clear the D-concatenated register, the E exponent and E sign are temporarily moved.

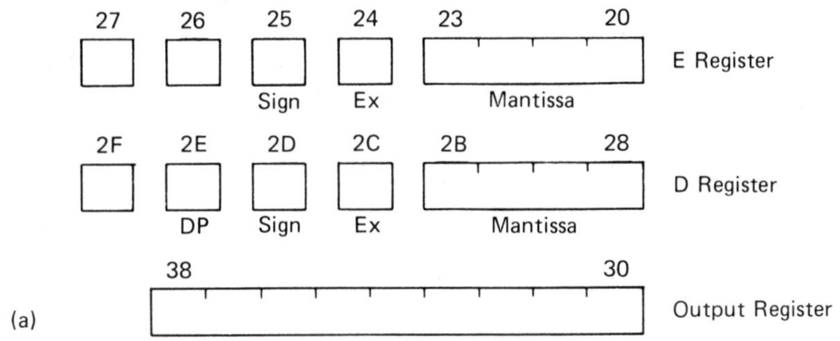

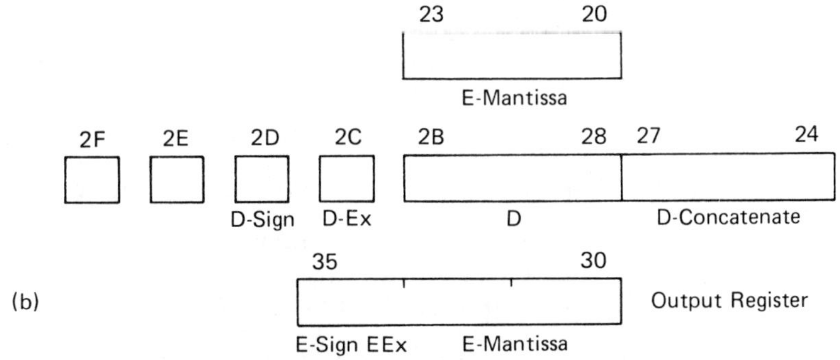

Figure 7-5. The calculator registers: (a) for general operation, (b) during the multiply and divide operation.

7-3 CALCULATOR FLOW CHART

This section describes the flow of data through the calculator (Fig. 7-6) and is a precursor for discussing the listing in Sec. 7-4, which details the program. After initializing, the calculator jumps to sample the keyboard for an input and stays in the loop until there is an input. The key input is examined and the program flow splits into two major paths: one for a numeric key, and the second for a function or clear key input. In the numeric path a new number with mantissa, sign, and exponent is loaded into the D register. The program then examines the D register for a number that is larger than 7 digits; if found, it ignores or rejects the input, sets no error flag, and returns the input routine waiting for the next key input.

In the function path, the key is examined and a jump table is used to route the program to the appropriate function routine. If the input is one of the six arithmetic, move, or exchange keys, then the operand in the D register is left justified. This assures that the operands in both the D and E registers are left justified prior to jumping into their respective function routines. On exiting from one of these six function routines, the program branches to the right justify routine. The right justify routine tests the operand in the D register for a result that is too large for the system to handle and, if found, sets the error flag. There is, however, no error routine in this program.

The new key is moved to become the old key and the program moves to the display routine. It then branches to the keyboard input routine, waiting for the next key input (see Chapter 6).

7-4 CALCULATOR PROGRAM

The listing of the calculator program is given on pages 238–248. This section describes the main program, and the reader is referred to Chapters 5 and 6 for a discussion of each of the individual routines. Omitted from this listing are the I/O and error display routines, which are functions of the particular microcomputer accessible to the reader.

INIT The three functions of the initializing routine are to

- Set the stack pointer.
- Clear and set the relevant memory locations.
- Initialize the I/O devices.

The relevant memory locations are cleared by calling the CLEAR subroutine, which has three entry points:

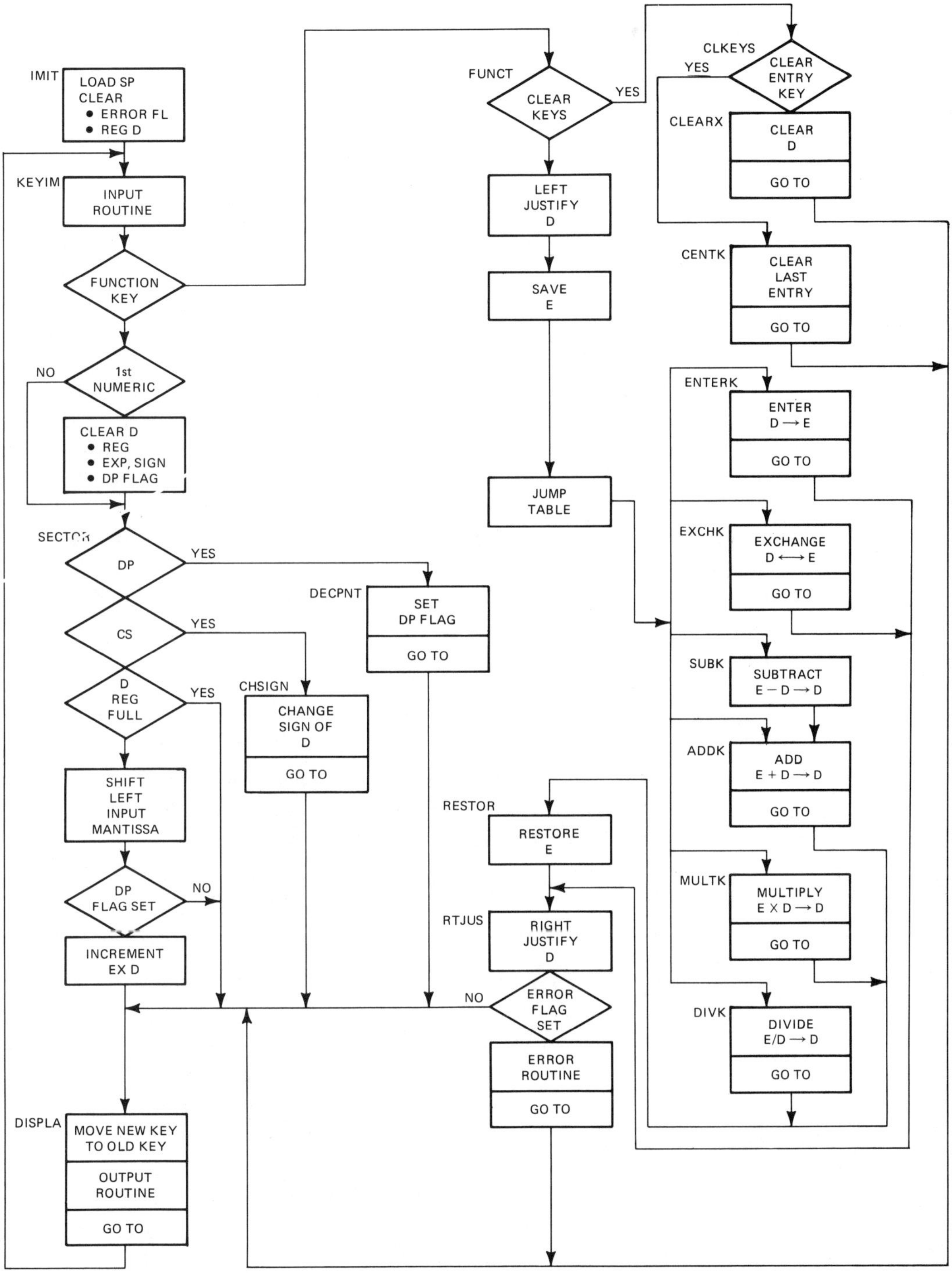

Figure 7-6. Calculator flow chart.

- From initializing.
- From the clear key input.
- When clearing D register for a new numeric input.

When called from the initializing routine, the CLEAR subroutine

- Loads the NEWKEY and OLDKEY.
- Clears the error flag.
- Clears the D register, which includes the mantissa, exponent, sign, and DP flag.

The I/O devices are not initialized by this program.

KEYIN The keyboard input routine accepts data from an output device. It should be appreciated that any number of input devices may be used, and, of course, each input device has an associated INPUT subroutine. All of the INPUT routines have two common characteristics:

- They sample the input device for an input.
- They convert each key input to a hex code according to Tables 6-3 and 6-4 and store that code in accumulator A.

Two keyboard INPUT routines are listed:

- Input from a keyboard in Sec. 6-5 and 6-6
- Input from a terminal in Sec. 9-2

KTYPE The new key input in accumulator A is transferred to the NEWKEY location and then compared to $0C. If the NEWKEY is greater than or equal to $0C, then the input is a function key and the program branches to FUNCT. If the input is a numeric key, the program drops through to process the number key.

Numeric Entry If the input is the first of a string of new numbers, the D register, mantissa, exponent, sign, and decimal point must be cleared. To test for the first of a string of numeric keys, the last key entry, OLDKEY, is examined for a numeric or function key. If OLDKEY is a numeric key, it indicates that a continued string of numbers is being loaded, and the program branches to SECNUM. If it is the first numeric input of the string, the program jumps to the clear subroutine and clears the D register and DP flag. The program then proceeds to enter the numeric key.

SECNUM The numeric keys are the numbers 0 to 9, the decimal point, and change sign. The program tests for the decimal point or change sign key entry, and if either key is entered, the program branches to DECPNT or CHSIGN, respectively. Otherwise, the program examines if the D register is full by testing for 7 digits or an exponent that is greater than or equal to 7. If either of these conditions are met, then this program discards the present input and branches to DISPLA. This program does not set or branch to an error routine, but other variations might be modified to include an error display routine.

If the D register is not full, the program calls the digit left shift subroutine, which shifts the digit of the D register left one digit. This permits loading the new number key into the LS digit position, packing or storing 2 digits per byte. Prior to calling the digit left shift subroutine, the index register is loaded to point to the DMANN, and the byte count of 4 is loaded into accumulator B.

Increment Exponent If the decimal point (DP) flag is set, then the D exponent is incremented; otherwise, the program branches to DISPLA.

DISPLA The display is located at a point in the program where all the various branches taken to modify the data in the D register merge together. The NEWKEY is moved to the OLDKEY location. The program then jumps to the display subroutines, where the modified data in the D register are displayed.

This program calls the display and keyboard routines in Chapter 6, which continually refresh the 7-segment display and scan the keyboard until there is a key entry. When a new key is entered, the program loops back to resolve which key type, KTYPE, was entered.

DECPNT This routine sets the DP flag to $FF. When the decimal point flag is cleared, it indicates that the decimal point key has not been entered.

CHSIGN A zero setting indicates a positive and a $FF setting indicates a negative sign. This routine changes the sign by exclusive-ORing the sign with $FF.

Function Branch The object of the function branch is to process the eight function keys. The four arithmetic functions are

+ KEY	$E + D \rightarrow D$
− KEY	$E - D \rightarrow D$
× KEY	$E \times D \rightarrow D$
÷ KEY	$E / D \rightarrow D$

The two move/exchange functions are

E KEY	$D \rightarrow E$	moves contents of D to E
Ex KEY	$D \leftrightarrow E$	exchanges contents of D and E

The two clear functions are

C KEY	$0 \rightarrow D$	clears the D register
CE KEY	clears the last number entered	

The two clear keys, C and CE, are each routed to execute their respective functions and then to branch and merge with the main program to display the modified data in the D register. As for the six remaining function keys, the contents of the D register are left justified prior to executing the various operations and then right justified before merging with the main program. Left justifying the contents of the D register assures that the contents of both the D and E registers are left justified prior to any of the arithmetic operations. This is particularly convenient for the ADD and SUBTRACT operations for which the data must be aligned prior to executing the operation. Aligning, however, may modify the data in the E register, which must be preserved, and so the contents of the E register are saved and then restored before and after the arithmetic function operations.

A jump table is used to route the arithmetic, move and exchange functions to their respective routines. The arithmetic routines merge at a location labeled RESTOR, where the contents of the E register are restored, and the move or exchange functions merge at RTJUS, where the contents of the D register are right justified and tested for an error condition. If no error condition exists, then the arithmetic, move, and exchange functions merge with the main program to display the modified data in the D register. If the error flag is set, the program is routed to an error display routine, which is omitted from this program.

FUNCT In the function branch the clear keys are separated from the other function keys and routed to CLKEYS. Before left justifying, the index register and accumulator B are loaded with the address and size of the D mantissa, respectively, which then calls the left justify subroutine. To save the contents of the E register, they are moved to the output register at location \$30 by calling the move subroutine after loading the source and destination addresses and the byte size of the register.

Jump Table A jump table is a programming technique for routing the program to one of several different routines. The table is a list in memory of the starting addresses of each of the function key routines. It is referred to by the label of the starting address of the table, which in this example is JTABLE. The six functions have key values from \$0C to \$11, and if \$0C is subtracted the modified key values become

Modified Key Value	
00	ADDK
01	SUBK
02	MULTK
03	DIVK
04	ENTERK
05	EXCHK

Since each address in the table is stored in two contiguous locations, the appropriate routine is selected by adding twice the modified key value to the table location.

Twice Modified Key Value	Address of Routine	Routine
00	JTABLE + 00	ADDK
02	JTABLE + 02	SUBK
04	JTABLE + 04	MULTK
06	JTABLE + 06	DIVK
08	JTABLE + 08	ENTERK
0A	JTABLE + 0A	EXCHK

The purpose of the jump table routine is to modify the JTABLE address to select the appropriate function key routine.

The JTABLE is stored in locations \$06 and \$07, where twice the modified key value is added to the LS byte of the address in location \$07. If a carry is generated, it must be added to the MS byte of the JTABLE address in location \$06. This is accomplished by an add with carry instruction in location \$06 to a cleared accumulator B. The jump table routine ends with a jump extended instruction to the address in locations \$06 and \$07.

RESTOR The arithmetic routines merge at a point in the program where the contents of the E register are restored. The contents of the E registers that were stored in the output register are now moved back.

Right Justify Routine The right justify routine (Fig. 7-7) tests the contents of the D register, and if there are eight or more digits left of the decimal point, an error flag is set. If, however, there are seven or less digits in the D register, all the zeros to the right of the decimal point are, for cosmetic appearances, shifted out. The error condition can easily be modified to test for a 7-digit number with two digits to the right of the decimal point.

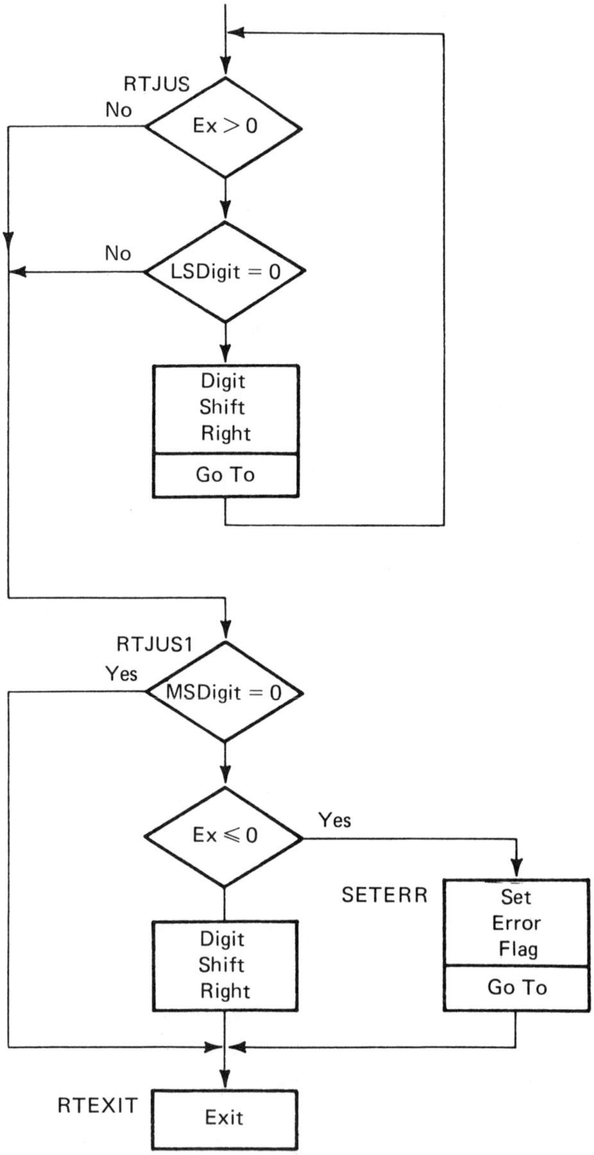

Figure 7-7. Right justify routine.

RTJUST The first part of the right justify routine tests for zero in the rightmost digit to the right of the decimal point. If found, the routine then jumps to the digit right shift subroutine. The second part of the routine makes one of three decisions:

1. If the MS digit is equal to zero, indicating less than 8 digits, then exit.
2. If the MS digit is not equal to zero and:
   (a) if the exponent is greater than zero, then the LS digit to the right of the decimal point is discarded.
   (b) if the exponent is less than or equal to zero, then the error flag is set.

Error Routine The function of the error routine is to indicate or display an error condition to the user. It may vary from turning on a red light to displaying an error message. There is no error routine in this program.

Strategy of the Add/Subtract Routine An add routine for signed numbers must include a subtract portion. When the signs of the operands are the same, then add the operands; when the signs are different, then subtract. The difference between the add and subtract keys is resolved for the subtract by changing the sign of the D register and then proceeding to the add operation (Fig. 7-8).

SUBK The subtract key routine changes the sign of the subtrahend in the D register and proceeds to the add key routine. The positive and negative signs are 0's and $FF, respectively, and are changed by exclusive-ORing them with $FF.

ADDK The decimal point of both operands must be aligned prior to the add/subtract operation. Since both operands are left justified when entering the add routine, the align routine shifts the operand with the larger exponent right until the exponents are equal.

The signs of the D and E registers are compared. If the signs are the same, then the program branches to the decimal add routine at ADD1. If the signs are different, the program proceeds to execute a decimal subtract. (see Sec. 5-11).

MULTK The multiply routine multiplies the contents of the E register, multiplicand, by the contents of the D register, and puts the product into the D register.

$$E \times D \rightarrow D$$

The result of multiplying two 7-digit mantissas is a 14-digit product that is stored in the D and D-concatenated registers. If the result is a product with more than 7 significant digits, the error is detected by the right justify routine.

The signs of the input signs are exclusive-ORed to form the sign of the product. If the signs of the input operands are the same, the sign of the product is positive; if the signs are different, the sign of the result is negative. The exponents of the input operands are added and

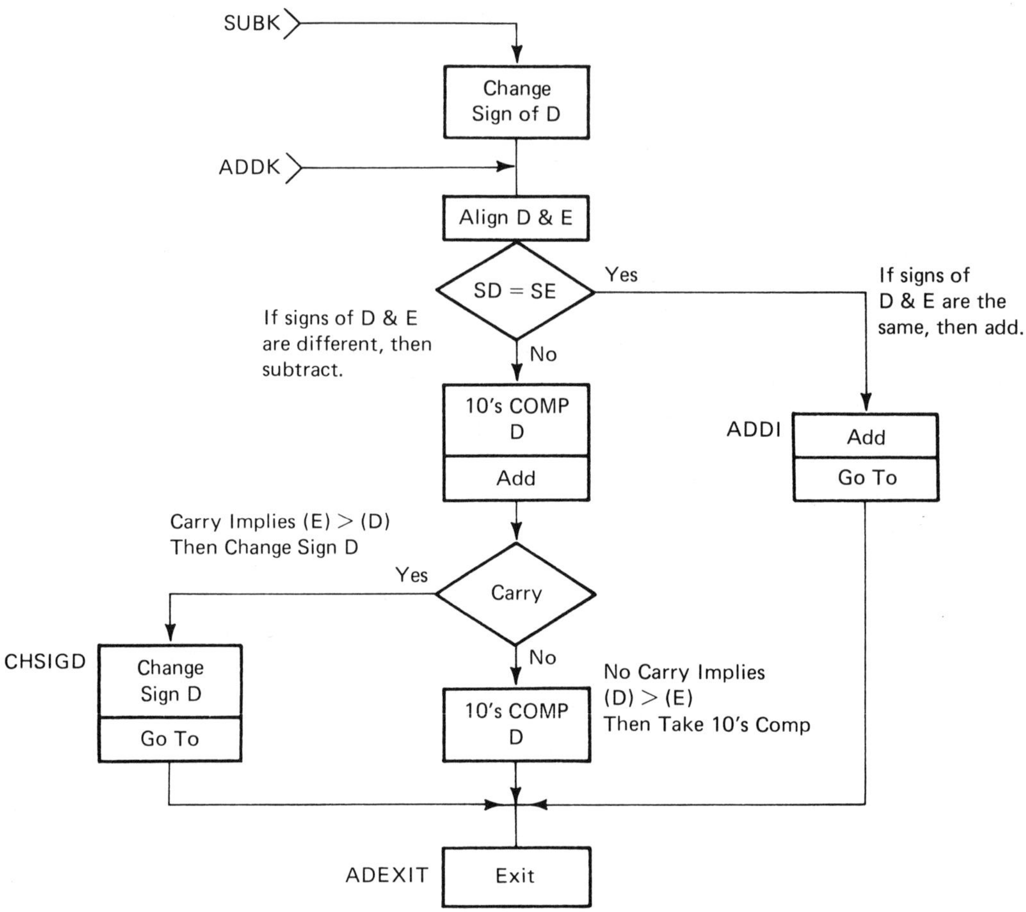

Figure 7-8. Add/subtract flow chart.

then 7 is subtracted, because this machine discards the 7 LS digits. See Sec. 5-13 for the multiply routine.

DIVK The divide routine divides the contents of the D register, the dividend, by the contents of the E register, the divisor, and puts the quotient into the D register.

$$D/E \rightarrow D$$

If there is a divide by zero, then the error flag is set. If the exponent of the quotient is a negative number, indicating that there are more than 7 significant digits of the quotient, the error is detected by the right justify routine, Sec. 5-6 for divide routine.

ENTERK The enter key moves the 6 bytes of data in the D register to the E register.

$$D \rightarrow E$$

The source and destination addresses are stored in locations $08 and $0A, respectively, and the byte count is loaded into the accumulator B. The program then calls the MOVE subroutine, MOOV.

EXCHK The exchange key exchanges the 6 bytes of data in the D and E registers.

$$D \leftrightarrow E$$

The exchange subroutine exchanges data from locations in memory that are eight addresses apart so that, prior to calling the subroutine, the address of the lowest memory location must be loaded into the index register, and the byte count of 6 is loaded into location $05, SIZE.

CLKEYS The two clear keys are routed to their respective routines by comparing the keys to $12. The clear last entry key is coded $13, and when compared to $12, branches if higher (BHI) to CENTK. If the CLEAR key is entered, the program proceeds to the clear routine.

Clear (Last) Key Entry The clear the last entry key (Fig. 7-9) is intended to correct the last numeric entry in a string of numbers. The routine accesses the last key entry, OLDKEY, for examination. If OLDKEY is a function key, it is ignored and branches to CKEY3. If it is either the change sign or the decimal point key, then the sign is changed, or the decimal point flag is reset, at locations labeled CKEY4 and CKEY5, respectively.

If OLDKEY is a numeric key between 0 and 9, the contents of the D register are shifted right one digit, discarding the last number entry. Then the exponent is examined, and if it is nonzero it is decremented.

The OLDKEY, or the last key entry, is moved to replace the NEWKEY, which in this case is the CKEY. This permits the replacing of several keys in correct numeric entry.

7-5 TUTORIAL ADVANTAGES OF SYSTEM PROBLEM WITH SUGGESTED PROBLEMS

The primary benefit of a system problem is to gain an appreciation of how the various routines affect the system. This implies that it becomes necessary for students to be able to read and find their way around a system program listing. The calculator system problem has

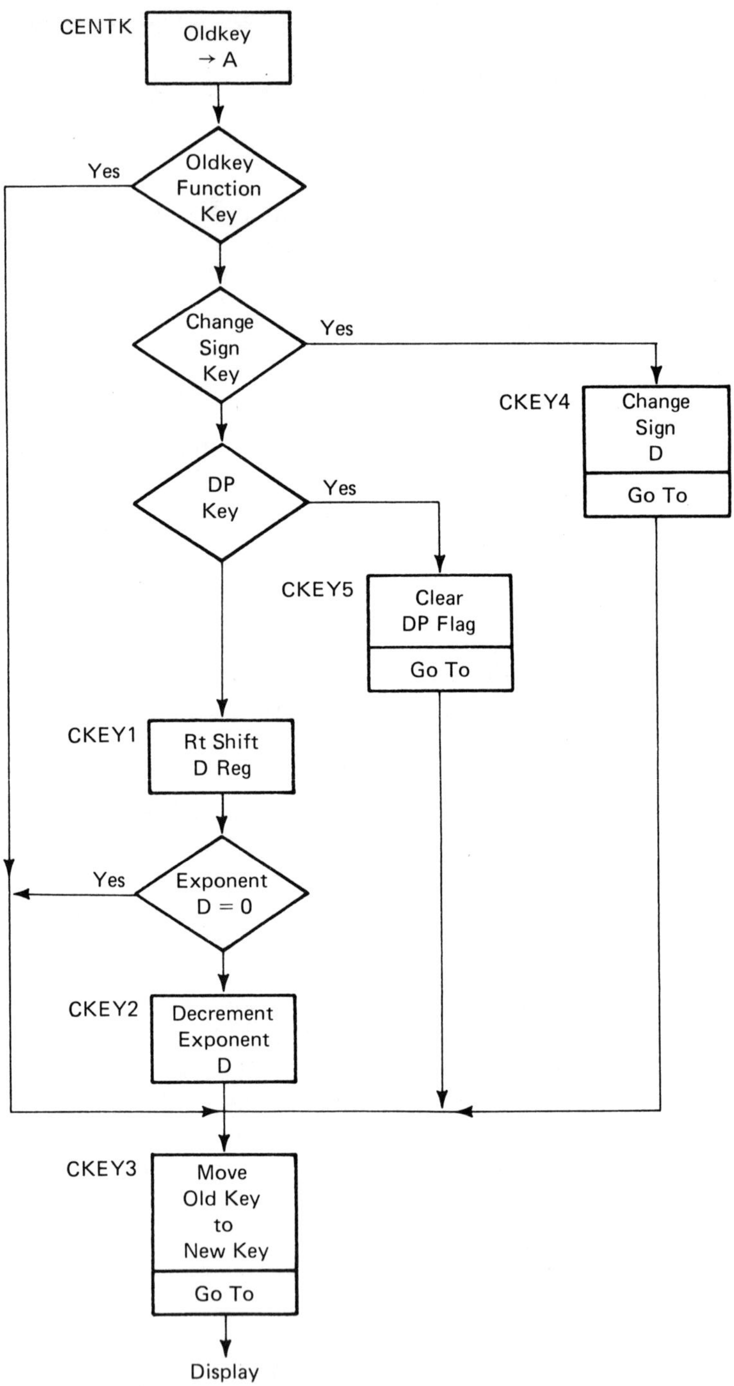

Figure 7-9. Clear last entry flow chart.

the magnitude of a term project. If each student writes his or her separate system program, there would be such a large variety of programs that an instructor would have difficulty in discussing and comparing. However, organizing the system problem into modules facilitates the instructor's ability to discuss each of the modules separately. This not only makes it more manageable for the instructor, but is the reason for writing and managing the development of large programs in industry. It has been the author's experience that students do not often focus on a system problem until they have an understanding of, and feel comfortable with, many of the parts of the system. This is the reason for discussing the parts, the routines, in Chapters 5 and 6 prior to discussing the system. At some point, it becomes necessary to shift the student's perspective from how each of the routines functions to how the system works. This occurs when the student gains confidence and realizes that he or she has the necessary background and could, when required and given sufficient time, understand each of the routines. At this point, the lessons should focus on modifying the system and the discussion should emphasize the impact that each routine has on the system. Some suggested system problems are easier to implement once the system with I/O routines are there:

- Add or modify key functions (i.e., sine, cosine keys) or modify the arithmetic routines.
- Expand the single E register into a stack, a group of perhaps four E registers, E_1, E_2, E_3, E_4.
- Extend the mantissa to 8, 9, 10, or more digits.
- Change the number format from fixed length to floating-point notation.
- Change the exponent from 2's complement to two-decimal digit notation.
- Change I/O formats.
- Change the I/O devices.
- Modify the right justify routine to set the error flag when 2, 3, 4, or 5 decimal digits must be discarded.
- Write an error display routine.
- Modify the program with an interlock so that only the clear key resets the system after an error.

```
                         * INITIALIZE THE CALCULATOR PROGRAM BY LOADING
                         * THE STACK POINTER, AND THEN CLEARING THE ERROR
                         * FLAG, THE DECIMAL POINT (DP) FLAG, AND THE
                         * D REGISTER.
                         * SINCE THIS PROGRAM IS WRITTEN TO BE USED
                         * WITH EITHER A KEYBOARD & 7-SEGMENT DISPLAY
                         * OR A TELETYPE, THE I/O ROUTINES ARE NOT
                         * INCLUDED IN THIS PROGRAM.
                         *
A 0003                          ORG    $0003
A 0003     0001   A NEWKEY RMB    1         LAST KEY ENTRY
A 0004     0001   A OLDKEY RMB    1         NEXT TO THE LAST KEY ENTRY
A 0005     0001   A SIZE   RMB    1         SIZE OF THE BLOCK OF DATA
A 0006     0002   A WSPACE RMB    2         WORK SPACE FOR TABLE
A 0008     0002   A SPOINT RMB    2         SOURCE POINTER
A 000A     0002   A DPOINT RMB    2         DESTINATION POINTER
A 000C     0002   A VTABLE RMB    2         VARIABLE TABLE ADDR
A 000E     0001   A ERROR  RMB    1         ADDR ERROR FLAG
                         *
                         * JUMP TABLE FOR THE FUNCTION KEYS
A 0010                          ORG    $0010
A 0010     0180   A JTABLE FDB    ADDK
A 0012     017A   A        FDB    SUBK
A 0014     0257   A        FDB    MULTK
A 0016     029A   A        FDB    DIVK
A 0018     011A   A        FDB    ENTERK
A 001A     012B   A        FDB    EXCHK
                         *
A 0020                          ORG    $0020
A 0020     0004   A EMANN  RMB    4         E REG MANTISSIA
A 0024     0001   A EEXP   RMB    1         E REG EXPONENT
A 0025     0001   A ESIGN  RMB    1         E REG SIGN
A 0028                          ORG    $0028
A 0028     0004   A DMANN  RMB    4         D REG MANTISSA
A 002C     0001   A DEXP   RMB    1         D REG EXPONENT
A 002D     0001   A DSIGN  RMB    1         D REG SIGN
A 002E     0001   A DP     RMB    1         DECIMAL POINT FLAG
A 0030                          ORG    $0030
A 0030     0009   A OUTREG RMB    9         OUTPUT DATA REG
                         *
A 0050                          ORG    $0050    THE PROGRAM STARTS HERE
                         *
                         * THE CLEAR SUBROUTINE HAS THREE ENTRY POINTS
                         *    * FROM INITIALIZATION (CLEAR)
                         *    * FROM THE CLEAR KEY (CLEARK)
                         *    * FOR A NEW NUMBER ENTRY (CLEAR2)
                         *
A 0050 8E 037F    A INIT   LDS    #$037F    LOAD SP
A 0053 BD 0163    A        JSR    CLEAR     INIT CLEAR
                         *
                         *  THE INPUT DATA MAY BE INPUT FROM EITHER A
                         * KEY BOARD OR A TERMINAL. ALTHOUGH THE ROUTINES
                         * ARE DIFFERENT THEY PERFORM THE SAME FUNCTION.
                         * WHEN CALLED THEY CONTINUOUSLY SCAN THE KEYBOARD
                         * FOR AN ENTRY.  THIS IMPLIES THEY MOST OF
                         * THE TIME IS SPENT IN THE INPUT ROUTINE,
                         * SCANNING KEYBOARD FOR AN INPUT.
                         * WHEN DATA IS INPUT, EACH ROUTINE CONVERTS THE
```

```
                      * DATA TO THE INTERNAL HEX CODE FOR THAT KEY INPU
                      * & LEAVES IT IN ACCUMULATOR A.
                      *
                      * THE HEX CODES ARE:
                      *      NUMERIC KEYS      0 TO 9
                      *      DP                $A
                      *      C/S KEY           $B    CHANGE SIGN
                      *      ADD KEY           $C
                      *      SUB KEY           $D
                      *      MULT KEY          $E
                      *      DIVIDE KEY        $F
                      *      E KEY             $10   ENTER KEY
                      *      EX KEY            $11   EXCHANGE KEY
                      *      C KEY             $12   CLEAR KEY
                      *      CE KEY            $13   CLEAR LAST ENTRY
                      *
                      * THE PROGRAM CALLS THE INPUT ROUTINE
0056 BD 0096   A KEYIN  JSR    KEYBD
                      *
0059 97 03     A KTYPE  STAA   NEWKEY    SAVE NEW KEY
005B 81 0C     A        CMPA   #$0C      FUNCTION OR NUMERIC
005D 25 4A 00A9         BCS    FUNCT     BR TO FUNCTION KEY
                      * ELSE CONTINUE FOR NUMERIC KEY INPUT
005F D6 04     A NUMBER LDAB   OLDKEY    GET OLD KEY
0061 C1 0C     A        CMPB   #$0C      IS OLDKEY NUMERIC?
0063 24 03 0068         BCC    SECNUM    BR AROUND 'CLEAR'
0065 BD 016C   A        JSR    CLEAR2    ELSE CLEAR REG D
0068 81 0A     A SECNUM CMPA   #$0A      NUM, DP, OR CSIGN KEY
006A 27 2C 0098         BEQ    DECPNT    BR TO DP IF EQUAL
006C 22 30 009E         BHI    CHSIGN    BR TO CHANGE SIGN
                      * ELSE IT MUST BE A NUMBER BETWEEN 0-9
                      * TEST IF THE D REGISTER IF FULL.  TEST IF THE
                      * 7TH DIGIT IS NONZERO OR IF THE EXPONENT
                      * IS EQ OR GREATER THEN 7.
006E 7D 002B   A        TST    $002B     TEST MSDIGIT NONZERO
0071 26 1A 008D         BNE    DISPLA    BR IF REG FULL
                      * TEST EXPONENT EQ OR GR THEN 7
0073 D6 2C     A        LDAB   DEXP      GET THE D-EXPONENT
0075 C1 07     A        CMPB   #$07
0077 2C 14 008D         BGE    DISPLA    BR IF REG FULL
                      * ELSE SHIFT IN THE NEW DIGIT
0079 CE 0028   A        LDX    #DMANN    LOAD POINTER
007C C6 04     A        LDAB   #$04      BYTE COUNT
007E BD 021A   A        JSR    SHLFD     CALL SHIFT LEFFT DIGIT
                      * INPUT NEW DIGIT & PACK NEW DIGIT
0081 9A 28     A        ORAA   DMANN     PACK DIGIT IN ACC A
0083 97 28     A        STAA   DMANN     & STORE AWAY
                      * IF PD FLAG IS SET?  THEN INCREMENT DEXP.
0085 7D 002E   A        TST    DP
0088 27 03 008D         BEQ    DISPLA    BR IF NOT SET
008A 7C 002C   A        INC    DEXP      ELSE INC DEXP
                      *
                      * ALL ROUTINES CONVERGE TO DISPLAY NEW DATA
008D 96 03     A DISPLA LDAA   NEWKEY    NEWKEY TO ACCA
008F 97 04     A        STAA   OLDKEY    & REPLACE OLDKEY
0091 BD 0097   A        JSR    DISOUT    DISPLAY OUTPUT DATA
                      *
0094 20 C0 0056         BRA    KEYIN
```

```
                        *  THIS COMPLETES THE NUMERIC INPUT BRANCH
                        *
                        *
0096 39                 KEYBD  RTS                 DUMMY INSTRUCTION
                        * THIS INSTRUCTION SHOULD BE REPLACED BY AN
                        * APPROPRIATE INPUT ROUTINE. SEE CHAPTERS 6 OR 9
                        * FOR A KEYBOARD OR TERMINAL INPUT ROUTINE.
                        *
0097 39                 DISOUT RTS                 DUMMY INSTRUCTION
                        * THIS INSTRUCTION SHOULD BE REPLACED BY AN
                        * APPROPRIATE 7-SEGMENT OR TERMINAL
                        * OUTPUT ROUTINE. SEE CHAPTERS 6 & 9.
                        *
                        * IF THE OUTPUT DEVICE MUST CONTINUOUSLY BE
                        * REFRESHED, THEN THE INPUT & OUTPUT
                        * ROUTINES MAY HAVE TO BE MERGED.
                        *
                        * SET THE DP FLAG
0098 86 FF            A DECPNT LDAA   #$FF      ALL 1'S, SETS FLAG
009A 97 2E            A        STAA   DP        SET DP FLAG
009C 20 EF 008D                BRA    DISPLA
                        * CHANGE THE SIGN OF D-REGISTER
009E 86 FF            A CHSIGN LDAA   #$FF
00A0 98 2D            A        EORA   DSIGN     FLIPS ALL 1'S TO ALL 0'S
00A2 97 2D            A        STAA   DSIGN
00A4 20 E7 008D                BRA    DISPLA
                        *
00A6 7E 0135          A CKEYS  JMP    CKEYK     JUMP > 128 LOCATIONS
                        *
                        * FUNCTION KEYS
                        * TEST FOR ONE OF THE CLEAR KEYS
00A9 81 12            A FUNCT  CMPA   #$12
00AB 2C F9 00A6                BGE    CKEYS     BR TO CLEAR KEYS
                        * ELSE, PREPARE DATA FOR ONE OF THE ARITHMETIC
                        * OPERATIONS AND LEFT JUSTIFY DATA IN THE D-REG
00AD CE 0028          A        LDX    #DMANN
00B0 C6 04            A        LDAB   #$04      BYTE COUNT
00B2 BD 02F8          A        JSR    LEFTJ
                        * SAVE DATA IN THE E-REG BY MOVING IT TO OUTPUT R
00B5 CE 0020          A        LDX    #EMANN
00B8 DF 08            A        STX    SPOINT    SAVE ADDR OF E-REG
00BA CE 0030          A        LDX    #OUTREG
00BD DF 0A            A        STX    DPOINT    SAVE ADDR OF OUTREG
00BF C6 06            A        LDAB   #$06      BYTE COUNT
00C1 BD 0237          A        JSR    MOOV
                        *
                        * JUMP TABLE FOR ONE OF THE ARITHMETIC ROUTINES
                        * SUBTRACT $0C FROM NEWKEY
00C4 96 03            A        LDAA   NEWKEY
00C6 80 0C            A        SUBA   #$0C      NEWKEY - $0C
00C8 48                        ASLA             2 X(NEWKEY - $0C)
                        * THIS MODIFIES THE FUNCTION KEY VALUE
                        * PROGRESSION TO 0.2.4.6.8...
                        * SINCE THE ADDRESS FOR EACH ROUTINE IS STORED IN
                        * TWO CONTIGUOUS LOCATIONS STARTING AT 'JTABLE'
                        * THE ADDRESS OF THE APPROPRIATE ROUTINE IS
                        * LOCATED BY ADDING THE MODIFIED FUNCTION KEY
                        * VALUE TO JTABLE.
```

```
                        *
                        * GET ADDRESS OF 'JTABLE'
00C9 CE 0010  A                LDX    #JTABLE
00CC DF 06    A                STX    $06       IN LOC 06 & 07
00CE 5F                        CLRB             ALSO CLEARS THE CARRY BIT
00CF 9B 07    A                ADDA   $07       MODIFY LSBYTE OF JTABLE
00D1 97 07    A                STAA   $07       SAVE MODIFIED ADDR
                        * NOW ADD CARRY TO MSBYTE OF JTABLE
00D3 D9 06    A                ADCB   $06
00D5 D7 06    A                STAB   $06
                        * THE ADDRESS OF THE ROUTINE TO JUMP TO
                        * IS NOW STORED IN LOCATIONS $06 & $07
                        *
00D7 7E 0006  A                JMP    $0006
                        *
                        * RESTORE THE CONTENTS OF THE E-REGISTER
                        * FROM THE OUTPUT REGISTER
00DA CE 0030  A RESTOR LDX    #OUTREG
00DD DF 08    A        STX    SPOINT    OUTPUT REG IS SOURCE
00DF CE 0020  A        LDX    #EMANN
00E2 DF 0A    A        STX    DPOINT    E-REG IS DESTINATION
00E4 C6 06    A        LDAB   #$06      BYTE COUNT
00E6 BD 0237  A        JSR    MOOV
                        *
                        * THE NUMBER IS RIGHT JUSTIFIED BEFORE BEING
                        * DISPLAYED.  THE ERROR FLAG IS SET IF THERE ARE
                        * 8 OR MORE DIGITS LEFT OF THE DP.
                        *
00E9 7D 002C  A RTJUS  TST    DEXP
00EC 23 10 00FE        BLS    RTJUS1    BR IF EX > 7
00EE 96 28    A        LDAA   DMANN     GET LSBYTE
00F0 85 0F    A        BITA   #$0F      MASK LSDIGIT
00F2 26 0A 00FE        BNE    RTJUS1
                        * RIGHT SHIFT D-REG IF EX > 0 AND LSD = 0
00F4 CE 002B  A        LDX    #$002B    LOAD POINTER
00F7 C6 04    A        LDAB   #$04      BYTE COUNT
00F9 BD 01E0  A        JSR    SHRTD
00FC 20 EB 00E9        BRA    RTJUS     BR BACK & TEST NEXT DIGIT
00FE 86 2B    A RTJUS1 LDAA   #$2B      GET MSBYTE
0100 85 F0    A        BITA   #$F0      MASK MSDIGIT
0102 27 0D 0111        BEQ    RTEXIT    EXIT IF MSD = 0
0104 7D 002C  A        TST    DEXP
0107 23 0B 0114        BLS    SETERR
                        * SET ERROR IF EXP LESS THEN OR EQ TO 0
                        * ELSE SHIFT LEFT ONE DIGIT
0109 CE 002B  A        LDX    #$002B    LOAD POINTER
010C C6 04    A        LDAB   #$04      BYTE COUNT
010E BD 01E0  A        JSR    SHRTD     SHIFT RT DIGIT
0111 7E 008D  A RTEXIT JMP    DISPLA
                        *  SET ERROR FLAG
0114 86 FF    A SETERR LDAA   #$FF
0116 97 0E    A        STAA   $0E       SET ERROR FLAG
0118 20 C0 00DA        BRA    RESTOR
                        *
                        * THE ENTER KEY MOVES THE DATA IN THE
                        * D -> E REGISTERS
011A CE 0028  A ENTERK LDX    #DMANN
011D DF 08    A        STX    SPOINT    SOURCE POINTER
```

```
011F CE 0020  A        LDX    #EMANN
0122 DF 0A    A        STX    DPOINT   DESTINATION POINTER
0124 C6 06    A        LDAB   #$06     BYTE COUNT
0126 BD 0237  A        JSR    MOOV
0129 20 BE 00E9        BRA    RTJUS
                *
                * EXCHANGE KEY'EXCHANGES THE DATA IN THE
                * D & E REGISTERS D <-> E
012B CE 0020  A EXCHK  LDX    #$0020   LOAD POINTER
012E C6 06    A        LDAB   #$06     BYTE COUNT
0130 BD 0249  A        JSR    EXCH
0133 20 B4 00E9        BRA    RTJUS
                *
                * THE CLEAR KEY OVERRIDES THE LAST KEY ENTRY
                * IF IT IS A NUMBER FROM 0 TO 9 THEN IT IS
                * SHIFTED OUT.  IF IT IS THE DP KEY OR THE
                * CHANGE SIGN KEY THEN THEY ARE UNDONE.
                * IF IT IS A FUNCTION KEY, IT IS IGNORED.
0135 96 04    A CKEYK  LDAA   OLDKEY   GET OLDKEY
0137 81 0C    A        CMPA   #$0C
0139 2C 16 0151        BGE    CKEY3    BR IF FUNCTION KEY
013B 81 10    A        CMPA   #$10
013D 2C 17 0156        BGE    CKEY4    BR IF CSIGN KEY
013F 27 1D 015E        BEQ    CKEY5    BR TO DP KEY
                * ELSE IT IS A NUMBER FROM 0 TO 9
                * RT SHIFT D REGISTER
0141 CE 0028  A        LDX    #$0028
0144 C6 04    A        LDAB   #$04     BYTE COUNT
0146 BD 01E0  A        JSR    SHRTD
0149 7D 002C  A        TST    $2C      TEST DEXP = 0
014C 27 03 0151        BEQ    CKEY3    BR IF DEXP = 0
                * ELSE DECREMENT D EXPONENT
014E 7A 002C  A        DEC    DEXP
0151 97 03    A CKEY3  STAA   NEWKEY   REPLACE NEWKEY
0153 7E 008D  A        JMP    DISPLA
                *
                * CHANGE SIGN
0156 C6 FF    A CKEY4  LDAB   #$FF
0158 D8 2D    A        EORB   DSIGN    CHANGE SIGN OF D
015A D7 2D    A        STAB   DSIGN
015C 20 F3 0151        BRA    CKEY3
015E 7F 002E  A CKEY5  CLR    $002E    CLEAR DP FLAG
0161 20 EE 0151        BRA    CKEY3
                *
                *
                * THE CLEAR SUBROUTINE HAS THREE ENTRY POINTS
                * ENTER FROM INITILIZATION
0163 86 12    A CLEAR  LDAA   #$12     CODE FOR CLEAR KEY
0165 97 03    A        STAA   NEWKEY   IS CLEAR KEY
0167 97 04    A        STAA   OLDKEY   IS CLEAR KEY
                * ENTER FROM CLEAR KEY
0169 7F 000E  A CLEARK CLR    ERROR    CLEAR ERROR FLAG
                * ENTER FROM START OF NEW MUMBER ENTRY
016C CE 0028  A CLEAR2 LDX    #DMANN
016F C6 08    A        LDAB   #$08     BYTE SIZE
0171 6F 00    A CLOOP  CLR    0,X      CLEAR D-REG
0173 08                INX
0174 5A                DECB
```

```
A 0175 26 FA 0171          BNE    CLOOP
A 0177 7E 008D  A          JMP    DISPLA
                         *
                         * SUBTRACT KEY CHANGES THE SIGN OF THE D-REG
                         * AND PROCEEDS TO THE ADD KEY ROUTINE
A 017A 86 FF    A SUBK     LDAA   #$FF
A 017C 98 2D    A          EORA   DSIGN     CHANGE SIGN
A 017E 97 2D    A          STAA   DSIGN
                         * ADD KEY ROUTINE
A 0180 BD 01CC  A ADDK     JSR    ALIGN     ALIGN D & E REG'S
                         * TEST IF SIGNS ARE SAME OR DIFFRENT
A 0183 96 2D    A          LDAA   DSIGN
A 0185 98 25    A          EORA   ESIGN     COMPARE SIGNS
A 0187 27 0B 0194          BEQ    ADD1      BR IF SAME
                         * ELSE SUBTRACT IF SIGNS ARE DIFFFERENT
                         * CALL DECIMAL SUBTRACT
A 0189 BD 01A1  A          JSR    SUBDEC
                         * TEST CARRY BIT
A 018C 25 0B 0199          BCS    CHSIGD    & CHANGE DSIGN
                         * TAKE 10'S COMPLEMENT (RESTORE REG-D)
A 018E BD 01FD  A          JSR    TENS
A 0191 7E 00DA  A ADEXIT JMP    RESTOR
A 0194 BD 01BC  A ADD1     JSR    ADDDEC
A 0197 20 F8 0191          BRA    ADEXIT
A 0199 86 FF    A CHSIGD LDAA   #$FF
A 019B 98 2D    A          EORA   DSIGN
A 019D 97 2D    A          STAA   DSIGN
A 019F 20 F0 0191          BRA    ADEXIT
                         *
                         * THIS IS A ONE PASS SUBTRACT ROUTINE WHERE THE
                         * 10'S COMPLEMENT AND THE DECIMAL ADD ARE FORMED
                         * ONE BYTE OF DATA WITH EACH PASS THRU THE LOOP.
                         *      E - D -> D
                         * WHERE THE E REGISTER STARTS AT LOC $20 &
                         * THE D REGISTER STARTS AT LOC $28.
                         * THE NUMBER OF BYTES (SIZE) SUBTRACTED IS STORED
                         * LOC $05. THE TAP $ TPA INSTRUCTIONS ARE USED TO
                         * SAVE & RESTORE THE CC BITS IN ACC A WHILE THE 1
                         * IS FORMED SO THAT THE CARRY & HALF CARRY BITS U
                         * THE DECIMAL ADD PORTION OF THE ROUTINE ARE NOT
                         *
A 01A1 CE 0020  A SUBDEC LDX    #$0020    LOAD POINTER
A 01A4 86 04    A          LDAA   #$04
A 01A6 97 05    A          STAA   $05       STORE SIZE
A 01A8 0D                  SEC              SET CARRY, USED TO ADD 1 T
A 01A9 07         SUBBB  TPA              SAVE CC BITS IN ACC A
A 01AA C6 99    A          LDAB   #$99      CONSTANT $99 TO ACC B
A 01AC E0 08    A          SUBB   8,X       9'S COMP REG E
                         * THE SUBTRACT WITHOUT CARRY INSTRUCTION FORMS
                         * THE 9'S COMPLEMENT IN ACC B AFFECTS THE CARRY B
                         * USED BY THE DECIMAL ADD.
                         *
                         * NOW BRING BACK THE CARRY AND HALF CARRY BITS US
                         * BY THE ADD PART OF THE ROUTINE.
                         *
A 01AE 06                  TAP              REPLACE CC BITS
A 01AF 17                  TBA              TRANS ACCB TO A
                         * THE CARRY BITS ARE NOT AFFECTED
```

```
A 01B0 A9 00     A          ADCA    0,X        DECIMAL ADD TO REG E
A 01B2 19                   DAA                DECIMAL ADJUST IN ACC A ON
A 01B3 A7 08     A          STAA    8,X        STORE DIFF IN REG D
A 01B5 08                   INX                INCREMENT INDEX
A 01B6 7A 0005   A          DEC     $05        DEC SIZE COUNTER
                   * THE CARRY AND HALF CARRY BITS ARE NOT AFFFECTED
                   * THE INX & DEC INSTRUCTONS.
A 01B9 26 EE 01A9           BNE     SUBBB
A 01BB 39                   RTS
                   *
                   * THIS ROUTINE ADDS TWO PACKED 7-DIGIT DECIMAL NU
                   * NUMBERS IN 4-BYTS EIGHT LOCATIONS APART
                   * THE POINTER AND BYTE COUNT WERE PRELOADED
                   * INTO LOCATIONS $0008 AND $0005, RESPECTIVELY
                   *
A 01BC DE 08     A ADDDEC LDX   $08
A 01BE D6 05     A          LDAB    $05        GET SIZE
A 01C0 0C                   CLC                CLEAR CARRY
A 01C1 A6 00     A ADDLOP LDAA  0,X        CARRY NOT EFFECTED
A 01C3 A9 08     A          ADCA    8,X        ADD WITH CARRY
A 01C5 19                   DAA                DEC ADJUST CARRY EFFECTED
A 01C6 A7 08     A          STAA    8,X        CARRY NOT EFFECTED
A 01C8 5A                   DECB               CARRY NOT ÉFFECTED
A 01C9 26 F6 01C1           BNE     ADDLOP     CARRY NOT EFFECTED
A 01CB 39                   RTS
                   *
                   * ALIGN TWO THE DECIMAL POINT OF TWO NUMBER THAT
                   * ARE TO BE LEFT JUSTIFIED ASSUME THAT BOTH
                   * ARE 4 BYTE NUMBERS AND THE EXPONENT IS IN
                   * THE FIFTH BYTE.  BOTH REGISTERS ARE 8-BYTES
                   * APART WHICH PUTS THE 2ND EXPONENT IN LOC $2C.
                   *
A 01CC CE 0020   A ALIGN  LDX   #$20       INDEX POINTER
A 01CF A6 04     A          LDAA    4,X        LOAD 1ST EXPON
A 01D1 A1 0C     A          CMPA    $C,X       CMP EXPON
A 01D3 27 0A 01DF           BEQ     ALIGEX     IF EQ THEN ALIGNED
A 01D5 23 03 01DA           BLS     ALIGN1     2'S COMP CMP RTSH $20
A 01D7 CE 0028   A          LDX     #$0028     ELSE RT SHIFT $28
A 01DA BD 01E0   A ALIGN1 JSR   SHRTD      CALL RT SHIFT BYTE
A 01DD 20 ED 01CC           BRA     ALIGN
A 01DF 39          ALIGEX RTS
                   *
                   * IN THE DECIMAL SHIFT RIGHT ROUTINE THE INDEX
                   * REGISTER AND ACC B ARE PRELOADED WITH THE ADDR
                   * OF THE MSBYTE AND THE  NUMBER (SIZE) OF  BYTES
                   * TO BE SHIFTED, RESPECTIVELY
                   *
A 01E0 DF 10     A SHRTD  STX   $10        SAVE POINTER ADDR
A 01E2 D7 05     A          STAB    $05        SAVE SIZE
A 01E4 86 04     A          LDAA    #$04       BIT COUNT
A 01E6 97 00     A          STAA    $00        BIT COUNT TO LOC 00
                   * RELOAD POINTER & COUNT REGISTER
A 01E8 DE 10     A SHRTD1 LDX   $10
A 01EA D6 05     A          LDAB    $05        RELOAD BYTE CTOUNT
A 01EC BD 01F5   A          JSR     SHRBIT
A 01EF 7A 0000   A          DEC     $0000      DEC BIT COUNT
A 01F2 26 F4 01E8           BNE     SHRTD1
A 01F4 39                   RTS
```

```
                          *
                          * SUBROUTINE SHIFT RIGHT BIT
 01F5 0C                  SHRBIT CLC                CLEAR CARRY
 01F6 66 00          A           ROR     0,X        ROTATE MENORY LOC
 01F8 09                         DEX                DECREMENT POINTER
 01F9 5A                         DECB               DEC BYTE COUNT
 01FA 26 F9 01F5                 BNE     SHRBIT
 01FC 39                         RTS
                          *
                          * TENS COMPLEMENT ROUTINE OF A 4-BYTE REGISTER
                          * WHOSE ADDRESS IS PRELOADED INTO THE INDEX REG
                          *
 01FD DF 08          A    TENS   STX     $08        SAVE INDEX POINTER
 01FF C6 04          A           LDAB    #$04       SIZE IS 4-BYTES
 0201 D7 05          A           STAB    $05        STORE SIZE
 0203 7F 0007        A           CLR     $0007      ADD ZERO AT THIS LOC
 0206 0D                         SEC                SET CARRY, ADDS +1
                          * THE CARRY IS USED TO ADD ONE TO THE 9'S COMP
                          * TO FORM THE 10'S COMP
                          *
 0207 07                  TENS1  TPA                SAVE CC BITS IN ACC A
 0208 C6 99          A           LDAB    #$99
 020A E0 00          A           SUBB    0,X        FORM 9'S COMP
 020C 06                         TAP                RESTORE CC BITS
 020D 17                         TBA                MOVE 9'S COMP TO ACC A
 020E 99 07          A           ADCA    $07        ADD CARRY BIT TO FORM 10'S
 0210 19                         DAA                DO DECIMAL ADJUST
 0211 A7 00          A           STAA    0,X        STORE 10'S COMP
 0213 08                         INX                INC INDEX
 0214 7A 0005        A           DEC     $0005      DEC SIZE COUNTER
                          * THE INC & DEC INSTRUCTIONS DO NOT AFFECT THE CA
 0217 26 EE 0207                 BNE     TENS1
 0219 39                         RTS
                          *
                          *
                          * IN THE DECIMAL SHIFT LEFT ROUTINE THE INDEX
                          * REGISTER AND ACC B ARE PRELOADED WITH THE ADDR
                          * THE LSBYTE AND THE  NUMBER (SIZE) OF  BYTES
                          * TO BE SHIFTED, RESPECTIVELY
                          *
 021A DF 10          A    SHLFD  STX     $10        SAVE POINTER ADDR
 021C D7 05          A           STAB    $05        SAVE SIZE
 021E 86 04          A           LDAA    #$04       BIT COUNT
 0220 97 00          A           STAA    $00        BIT COUNT TO LOC 00
                          * RELOAD POINTER & COUNT REGISTER
 0222 DE 10          A    SHLFD1 LDX     $10        RELOAD POINTER
 0224 D6 05          A           LDAB    $05        RELOAD BYTE COUNT
 0226 BD 022F        A           JSR     SHLBIT
 0229 7A 0000        A           DEC     $0000      DEC BIT COUNT
 022C 26 F4 0222                 BNE     SHLFD1
 022E 39                         RTS
                          *
                          * SUBROUTINE SHIFT LEFT BIT
 022F 0C                  SHLBIT CLC                CLEAR CARRY
 0230 69 00          A           ROL     0,X        ROTATE MENORY LOC
 0232 08                         INX                INCREMENT POINTER
 0233 5A                         DECB               DEC BYTE COUNT
 0234 26 F9 022F                 BNE     SHLBIT
```

```
A 0236 39                      RTS
                         *
                         * MOVE A BLOCK OF DATA
                         * FROM A STARTING LOCATION  STORED IN $08
                         * TO A LOCATION STORED IN $0A
                         * THE SIZE OF THE BLOCK IS STORED IN ACCUMULATOR
                         *
A 0237 DE 08       A MOOV  LDX    $08      LOAD SOURCE BLOCK POINTER
A 0239 A6 00       A       LDAA   0,X      LOAD BYTE INTO ACC A
A 023B 08                  INX             INC SOURCE BLOCK ADDR
A 023C DF 08       A       STX    $08      STORE SOURCE BLOCK POINTER
A 023E DE 0A       A       LDX    $0A      GET DESTINATION BLOCK POIN
A 0240 A7 00       A       STAA   0,X      MOVE BYTE
A 0242 08                  INX             INC DEST BLOCK ADDR
A 0243 DF 00       A       STX    $0       STORE DEST BLOCK POINTER
A 0245 5A                  DECB            DEC SIZE COUNTER
A 0246 26 EF 0237          BNE    MOOV
A 0248 39                  RTS
                         *
                         * EXCHANGE TWO REGISTERS STARTING AT LOC $20 TO $
                         * INDEX REG IS PRELOADED WITH AN LOWEST ADDR (002
                         * SIZE OF REGISTERS IS PRELOADED IN LOC $05
                         *
A 0249 A6 00       A EXCH  LDAA   0,X      1ST REG TO ACC A
A 024B E6 08       A       LDAB   8,X      2ND REG TO ACC B
A 024D A7 08       A       STAA   8,X      FROM ACC A TO REG 2
A 024F E7 00       A       STAB   0,X      FROM ACC B TO REG 1
A 0251 7A 0005     A       DEC    $0005
A 0254 26 F3 0249          BNE    EXCH
A 0256 39                  RTS
                         *
                         * THE MULTIPLY ROUTINE
                         *
                         * THE EXPONENT OF THE RESULT = EEXP + DEXP - 7
                         *
A 0257 96 24       A MULTK LDAA   $24      GET EEXP
A 0259 9B 2C       A       ADDA   $2C      EEXP + DEXP
A 025B 80 07       A       SUBA   #$07     EEXP + DEXP = 7
A 025D 97 2C       A       STAA   $2C      STORE RESULT EXP
                         * FORM SIGN OF THE PRODUCT
A 025F 96 25       A       LDAA   $25      ESIGN
A 0261 98 2D       A       EORA   $2D      EXCL-OR E & D SIGNS
A 0263 97 2D       A       STAA   $2D      STORE RESULT SIGN
                         * MOVE D TO D-CONCATINATE REGISTER
A 0265 CE 0024     A       LDX    #$0024
A 0268 DF 0A       A       STX    $0A      STORE IN DESTINATION POINT
A 026A CE 0028     A       LDX    #$0028
A 026D DF 08       A       STX    $08      SOURCE POINTER
A 026F C6 04       A       LDAB   #$04     BYTE COUNT
A 0271 BD 0237     A       JSR    MOOV
                         * CLEAR THE D MANTISSA,
                         * THE POINTER AND BYTE COUNT ARE LOAADED
A 0274 4F                  CLRA
A 0275 08                  INX
A 0276 5A                  DECB
                         * LOAD DIGIT COUNT = 6, 7-DIGIT MULTIPLY
A 0277 86 06       A       LDAA   #$06
A 0279 97 05       A       STAA   $05      SAVE SIZE
```

```
                            *
                            * MULTIPLY LOOP
                            * TEST LSDIGIT OF MULTIPLIER = 00
A 027B 7D 0024   A MULOOP TST    $0024
A 027E 27 08 0288         BEQ    MULT1     BR TO DIGIT COUNT
                            * ELSE DECREMENT LCDIGIT & PROCCEED TO ADD LOOP
A 0280 7A 0024   A        DEC    $0024
A 0283 BD 01BC   A        JSR    ADDDEC    ADD MULTIPLICAND TO PARTIA
A 0286 20 F3 027B         BRA    MULOOP
                            *
                            * DECREMENT DIGIT COUNT & SHIFT PARTIAL PRODUCT
A 0288 7A 0000   A MULT1  DEC    $0000
A 028B 26 03 0290         BNE    MULT2     BR TO SHIFT LOOP
                            * ELSE EXIT & RESTORE REGISTERS
A 028D 7E 00DA   A        JMP    RESTOR
                            * SHIFT LOOP
A 0290 CE 002B   A MULT2  LDX    #$002B    D & D-CONCATINATE
A 0293 C6 08     A        LDAB   #$08      BYTE COUNT
A 0295 BD 01E0   A        JSR    SHRTD     SHIFT DIGIT
A 0298 20 E1 027B         BRA    MULOOP
                            *
                            * THE DIVIDE ROUTINE
                            *
                            * EXPONENT Q = DEXP - EEXP
                            *
A 029A 96 24     A DIVK   LDAA   $24       GET D EXP
A 029C 90 2C     A        SUBA   $2C       DEXP - EEXP
A 029E 97 2C     A        STAA   $2C       QEXP
                            * SIGN OF Q, EXCLUSIVE-OR SIGN D & E
A 02A0 96 25     A        LDAA   $25       ESIGN
A 02A2 98 2D     A        EORA   $2D       EXCLUSIVE-OR SIGNS
A 02A4 97 2D     A        STAA   $2D       QSIGN
                            * CLEAR D-CONCATINATE REGISTER
A 02A6 CE 0024   A        LDX    #$0024    LOAD POINTER
A 02A9 C6 04     A        LDAB   #$04      BYTE COUNT
A 02AB 4F                 CLRA
A 02AC A7 00     A DIVCL  STAA   0,X
A 02AE 08                 INX
A 02AF 5A                 DECB             BYTE COUNT
A 02B0 26 FA 02AC         BNE    DIVCL
                            * TEST DIVISOR, IF ZERO BR TO ERROR
A 02B2 CE 0028   A        LDX    #$0028    LOAD POINTER
A 02B5 C6 04     A        LDAB   #$04
A 02B7 6D 00     A DIVZRO TST    0,X
A 02B9 26 06 02C1         BNE    DIV1      EXIT IF NONZERO
A 02BB 08                 INX              ELSE KEEP TESTING
A 02BC 5A                 DECB
A 02BD 26 F8 02B7         BNE    DIVZRO    KEEP TESTING IF NONZERO
A 02BF 20 31 02F2         BRA    DIVERR    IF 4-BYTES EQ ZERO
                            *
                            * DIVIDE LOOP
                            *
A 02C1 CE 0020   A DIV1   LDX    #$0020    POINT TO E REG
A 02C4 C6 04     A        LDAB   #$04      BYTE COUNT
A 02C6 D7 05     A        STAB   $05       SAVE SIZE
A 02C8 BD 01FD   A        JSR    TENS      10'S COMP REG E
A 02CB BD 01BC   A DIV2   JSR    ADDDEC    SUB D - E => D
A 02CE 24 05 02D5         BCC    DIV3      BR IF RESULT NEG
```

```
02D0 7C 0024   A        INC    $0024     ELSE INC Q
02D3 20 F6 02CB         BRA    DIV2      KEEP SUBTRACTING
                 *
                 * ELSE ADD BACK
02D5 CE 0020   A DIV3   LDX    #$0020    POINT TO E REG
02D8 C6 04     A        LDAB   #$04      BYTE COUNT
02DA BD 01FD   A        JSR    TENS      RESTORE E REG POSITIVE
02DD BD 01BC   A        JSR    ADDDEC    ADD BACK
02E0 7A 0005   A        DEC    $05       DEC SIZE
02E3 26 03 02E8         BNE    DIV4      BR & KEEP DIVIDNG
                 * ELSE EXIT & MOVE Q TO D REGISTER
02E5 7E 00DA   A DIEXIT JMP    RESTOR
                 *
                 * SHIFT D & D-CONCATINATE REGISTER LEFT
                 *
02E8 CE 0024   A DIV4   LDX    #$0024    POINT TO D & D CONCATINATE
02EB C6 08     A        LDAB   #$08      BYTE SIZE
02ED BD 021A   A        JSR    SHLFD     SHIFT LEFT DIGIT
02F0 20 CF 02C1         BRA    DIV1      RETURN TO DIV LOOP
                 *
                 * IF DIVISOR IS ZERO SET ERROR FLAG
02F2 86 FF     A DIVERR LDAA   #$FF
02F4 97 0E     A        STAA   $0E       SET ERROR FLAG
02F6 20 ED 02E5         BRA    DIEXIT
                 *
                 * THE LEFT JUSTIFY ROUTINE, LEFT JUSTIFIES THE
                 * CONTENTS OF THE D-REGISTER PRIOR TO CALLING
                 * SHIFT LEFT DIGIT ROUTINE THE INDEX REGISTER
                 * & ACC B ARE LOADED WITH THE LSBYTE OF REG D
                 * & THE BYTE COUNT (SIZE OF D REG).
                 *
                 * ASSUME THAT THE EXPONENT IS STORED IN LOC $2C &
                 * THE MSBYTE IS STORED N LOC $2B
                 *
02F8 7D 002B   A LEFTJ  TST    $002B     TEST MSBYE UNEQUAL TO 0
02FB 26 13 0310         BNE    ELEFT     EXIT IF MSBYTE NOT 0
02FD 86 13     A        LDAA   #$13      TEST MAX EXPONENT
02FF 91 2C     A        CMPA   $2C       AT LOC 2C
0301 2C 0D 0310         BGE    ELEFT     EXIT
                 *CONTINUE IF THE NUMBER IS NOT LEFT JUSTIFIED
0303 7C 002C   A        INC    $002C     INC EXPONNENT D
0306 CE 0028   A        LDX    #$0028    POINT TO D REG
0309 C6 04     A        LDAB   #$04      BYTE COUNT
030B BD 021A   A        JSR    SHLFD
030E 20 E8 02F8         BRA    LEFTJ     BR BACK TO TEST NEXT DIGIT
0310 39          ELEFT  RTS
                 *
                        END
```

8 The 3870: A Single-Chip Microcomputer with Interrupt

This chapter discusses an alternate, single-chip microcomputer with the intent of both reviewing the basics and giving the reader a broader perspective of microprocessors and microcomputers. Knowledge of only one microprocessor, or microcomputer system, often limits or restricts an individual to the designs and applications with that system, while comprehending a second system enables the reader to generalize his or her understanding of the subject. The intent of this chapter is to illustrate that there are more similarities than differences between the various microprocessors, and that programs written with one instruction set are easily translated into an equivalent program written in a second instruction set. After understanding two microcomputer systems, the multichip 6800 and the singlechip 3870, the reader should not feel captive by any one microprocessor family, and should be able to approach any microcomputer system available in the marketplace.

The single-chip 3870 represents a microcosm of a multichip microcomputer family, and the topics in this chapter are discussed in roughly the same sequence as those of the first five chapters.

The 3870 has both external and internal interrupt capabilities, and previews of the interrupt mechanism of the 6800 peripheral devices are discussed in Chapters 3 and 9. Section 8-1 discusses the parts of the microcomputer system and Sec. 8-2 discusses the instruction set. Section 8-3 discusses a logic-type program for a counter and 8-bit bouncing balls, which includes a delay loop subroutine and I/O instructions.

Section 8-4 previews the interrupt and then illustrates how the timer interrupt is used to replace the delay loop subroutine. An example of a switch being tied to the interrupt, rather than the input port pin, illustrates how the program must be modified to accommodate the difference.

8-1 PARTS OF THE 3870

The three basic parts of a microcomputer are the processor, the memory and the I/O circuits. The 3870 meets all these requirements; it also includes two interrupts, an external and an internal, or timer, interrupt. This section discusses the architecture of the 3870 as illustrated in Fig. 8-1. This includes the following:

- General registers
- Memory
    - ROM, 2 K bytes
    - RAM, 64 bytes of scratchpad
- Six ports
    - Four I/O ports
    - Interrupt control register
    - Timer

The three parts of the 3870 are separated into four fields, each with a group of instructions to control the data flow through each field:

- General register
- Memory (ROM)
- ISAR (RAM)
- I/O ports

This is in contrast to the 6800, which has only two fields, the six general registers and 64K of memory.

General Registers

There are seven general registers:

A	Accumulator	8 bits
PC	Program counter	16 bits
P	Stack register	16 bits
DC	Data counter	16 bits
DCI	Auxiliary data counter	16 bits

ISAR	Indirect scratchpad address register	6 bits of 8 bits
W	Status register	5 bits of 8 bits

Accumulator (A) The accumulator has two primary functions: the first is to act as the crossroads and main intersection through which all data is routed into and out from the I/O ports, scratchpad register, or memory; the second is that all the data manipulation takes place in the accumulator.

Program Counter (PC) The program counter is a 16-bit register that points to the instruction of the program being executed. Although the 3870 has only 2K of memory, the 16-bit program counter enables future developments of the 3870 memory to be expanded to a 64K memory.

Stack Register (P) The 3870 has a single-level stack. The K-pair are two adjacent locations of the scratchpad registers that may, if accessed properly, be considered a second-level stack register. The 3870 has no stack pointer, but a software stack may be programmed using some of the scratchpad registers.

Data Counter (DC) and the Auxiliary Data Counter (DC1) The data counter is used to indirectly address data from memory. It is referred to as a pointer, pointing to a memory location. Indirect addressing is a two-step process, where the pointer must be loaded with a memory address before accessing the data at that location. It is similar to the index register of the 6800, but without the offset capability. The auxiliary data counter is used to exchange and store the contents of the data counter.

Indirect Scratchpad Address Register (ISAR) The indirect scratchpad address register is a 6-bit pointer used to indirectly access data from one of the 64 scratchpad registers. It is comparable to the data counter and performs the same function for the scratchpad registers as the data counter does for memory.

Status Register (W) There are five status bits: sign (S), carry (C), zero (Z), overflow (O), and an interrupt control bit (ICB). The first four status bits, S, C, Z, and O, indicate the status of new data as a result of a processor operation. They perform identical functions to the four condition code bits, N, C, Z, and V of the 6800. The decision instructions that alter the program flow are as a consequence of examining one or more of the status bits by the branch instructions.

A note of caution concerning the status or condition code bits of the various microprocessors. When they are set, the rules that set them are generally the same, but there is no universal rule as to which bits are

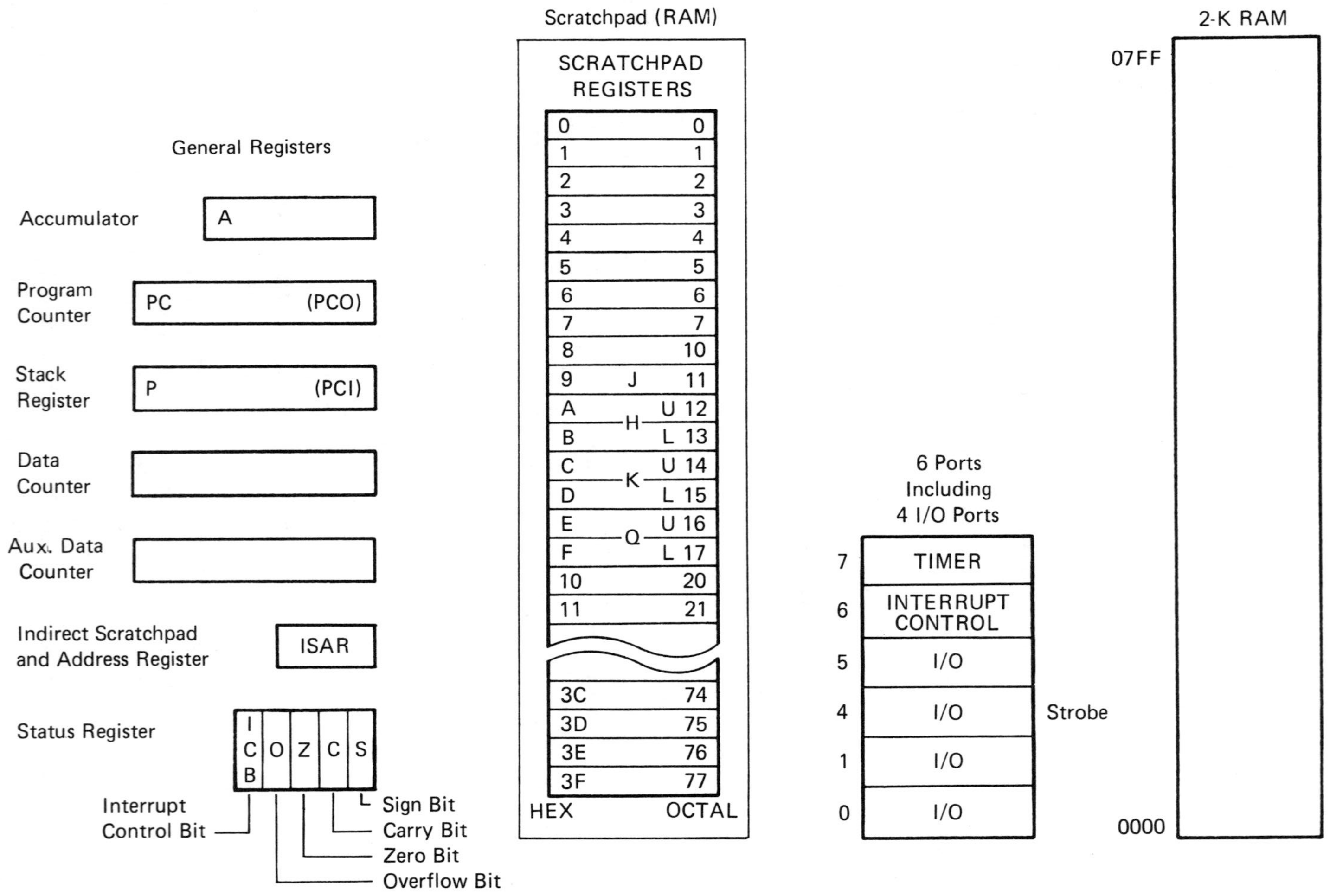

Figure 8-1. Programming model of the 3870.

set by the various instructions. The user must examine the instruction set to identify which of the status bits are affected by each instruction.

The interrupt control bit, ICB, is used to enable or disable the interrupt from affecting the program, and it is identical to the I-bit of the 6800.

Sixty-Four-Byte Scratchpad Registers and ISAR

The RAM for the 3870 consists of 64 bytes of the scratchpad registers. The first decimal 12 registers, R0 to R11, can be directly addressed, and all the 64 registers can be indirectly addressed through ISAR. Decimal 64 is equal to octal 77. The scratchpad registers are organized in an 8 × 8 matrix and are addressed by 6 bits (see Fig. 8-2).

ISAR has two independent parts, upper and lower, each consisting of 3 bits or 2 octal numbers, with no carry bit connecting them. For example, if ISAR is loaded with octal 35 and continuously incremented, it counts through 36, 37, and then to 30. Likewise, when starting with 35 and continuously decrementing, ISAR counts through 34, 33, 32, 31, 30, and then to 37.

Memory

The 3870 has 2K of ROM memory for storing programs, constants, and look-up or jump tables. Future developments in the 3870 single-chip family of devices will probably expand the memory to include 4K of ROM and additional RAM memory.

ISAR UPPER

0's array	07	06	05	04	03	02	01	00
10's array	17	16	15	14	13	12	11	10
20's array	27							20
30's array	37							30
40's array	47							40
50's array	57							50
60's array	67							60
70's array	77	76	75	74	73	72	71	70
	7	6	5	4	3	2	1	0

ISAR LOWER

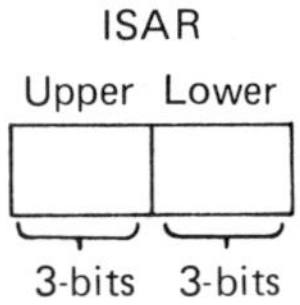

Figure 8-2. 8 x 8 bytes of scratchpad register, 64 decimal or 77 octal bytes.

The user, however, must be aware that the ROM code, or program that is stored in the ROM, is generated by the user. This program must be furnished by the customer to the manufacturer, who custom codes each 3870 to specifications. The 38E70 is a 3870 single-chip device with an electronically programmable ROM (PROM) that is used to verify customer codes.

I/O Ports

The input and output instructions control the data flow to and from the I/O ports. Four of the I/O ports are, in fact, I/O ports, while the two additional ports are for the interrupt control register and the timer.

In the 6800 a portion of the 64K memory field is allocated for I/O ports, as opposed to the 3870, which has a separate field of registers for I/O. When the I/O ports are a part of the memory field, it is referred to as *memory-mapped* I/O, and the same instructions are used that move and control the data flow between the I/O ports and the accumulator.

I/O and Miscellaneous Pins

The 3870 is a single-chip microcomputer in a 40-pin package, 32 of which are allocated to the four I/O ports, referred to as Ports 0, 1, 4, and 5. See Fig. 8-3.

The 8 additional pins are the following:

Pin 1, Pin 2	Crystal or timer inputs
Pin 38	External Interrupt input
Pin 39	Reset
Pin 7	Strobe
Pin 21	Test
Pin 40	VCC (+5 V)
Pin 20	GND (0 V)

The four I/O ports consist of eight latches through which data pass into and out from the microcomputer. When outputted from the accumulator, data are latched or stored in the port. When inputted, however, data are not latched. The inputting device must store the data until transferred into the microcomputer.

Data are inverted as they flow between the accumulator and the I/O pins. Therefore, a 1 in the accumulator appears as a low voltage at the I/O pin, and, conversely, a 0 in the accumulator appears as a high voltage. This inversion applies to both incoming and outgoing data.

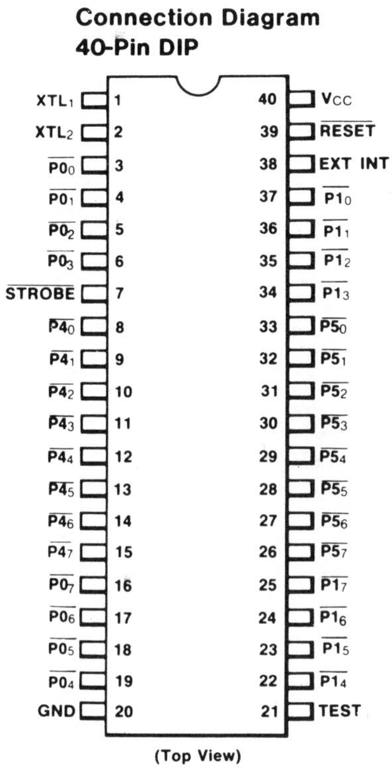

Figure 8-3. 3870 pin assignments.

8-2 3870 INSTRUCTION SET

The 76 instructions listed in Appendix II are in six chatagories:

- Accumulator Instructions
- Branch Instructions
- Memory Reference Instructions
- Address Register Group Instructions
- Scratchpad Register Instructions
- Miscellaneous Instructions

There are two factors in an instruction set: (1) the number of instructions, and (2) the number of bytes per instruction. The 6800 has approximately twice as many instructions, most of which are 2-byte instructions. Most of the instructions of the 3870 are 1-byte instructions. Program efficiency can be measured either by the number of instructions it takes to write a program or by the number of memory locations it takes to store the program. In comparing programs that are written with both the 6800 and 3870 instructions sets, often the 6800 program requires fewer instructions to execute, but storing requires a larger memory space.

To program any computer in assembly language, it is necessary to first know all the registers, memory locations, and the instruction set. Familiarity with the instruction set implies that the user can predict the following:

- Which registers and memory locations are affected by each instruction.
- How the data in these registers and memory locations are modified by each instruction.
- The execution time for each instruction.

The programming model (Fig. 8-4) indicates the data flow and the paths associated with each instruction.

The instruction set (Appendix II) has all the necessary data listed under the various headings:

Accumulator Group Instructions

OPERATION	MNEMONIC OP CODE	OPERAND	FUNCTION	MACHINE CODE	BYTES	CYCLES	STATUS BITS OVF	ZERO	CRY	SIGN
ADD CARRY	LNK		ACC ← (ACC) + CRY	19	1	1	1/0	1/0	1/0	1/0
ADD IMMEDIATE	AI	ii	ACC ← (ACC) ∧ H'ii'	24 ii	2	2.5	1/0	1/0	1/0	1/0
AND IMMEDIATE	NI	ii	ACC ← (ACC) H 'ii'	21 ii	2	2.5	0	1/0	0	1/0

Operation and Function The operation is a word descriptive equivalent of the programming notation stated in the function column.

Mnemonic and Operand The mnemonic is the name of the instruction used by the programmer for assembler language programming. The operand column indicates when there is an operand and which form it takes:

i	is a hex data character of ½ byte
ii	are two hex data characters of 1 byte
aa	are two hex address characters of 1 byte
aaaa	are four hex address characters of 2 bytes
r	is a hex character for one of the first 12 scratchpad registers, or 1 of 3 characters S, I, or D used for the indirect addressing of scratchpad registers by ISAR

For the 3870 a hex number is indicated as H'ii' (enclosed by single quotes and preceded by an upper case H). A number is assumed to be a decimal number if there is no hex notation.

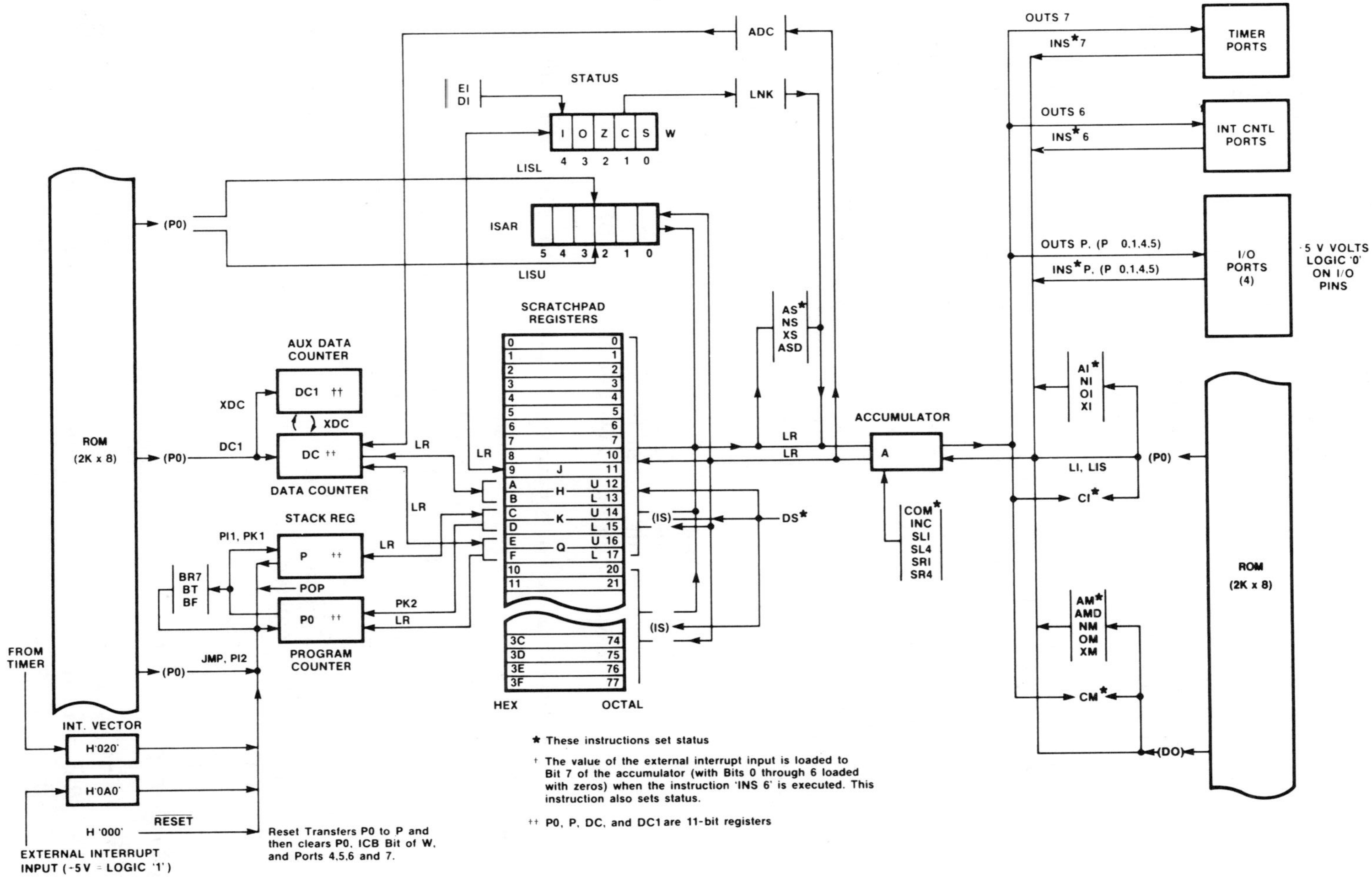

* These instructions set status

† The value of the external interrupt input is loaded to Bit 7 of the accumulator (with Bits 0 through 6 loaded with zeros) when the instruction 'INS 6' is executed. This instruction also sets status.

†† P0, P, DC, and DC1 are 11-bit registers

Note
The instructions PI and PK are shown in two sequential parts (PI1, PI2, and PK1, PK2).

Figure 8-4. Programming model.

Operands with commas, such as A,r, imply a transfer of data. The data are transferred from r to A (A ← r). For example, if r is replaced by 3, then A,3 reads that data are transferred from register 3 to the accumulator. More specifically, the instruction LR A,r reads "load or move data from register r to accumulator." When r is replaced by 3, then LR A,3 reads "load the accumulator with the contents of scratchpad register 3." Conversely, LR 3,A reads "load scratchpad register 3 with the contents of the accumulator."

Machine Code and Bytes The machine code is the program in hex notation. The bytes heading indicates the number of bytes in each instruction, and as the program is executed the program counter will increment by the number of bytes in each instruction.

Cycles Cycles indicate the time it takes to execute each instruction. The basic machine cycle is the clock period at pins 1 and 2 multiplied by 8. For example, for a 4-MHz clock frequency the period is 250 ns. The basic machine cycle is derived by multiplying the clock period by 8. A 250-ns clock period times 8 equals 2 μs. Thus, one-cycle instructions take 2 μs to execute and two-cycle instructions take 4 μs.

Status Bits There are four status bits:

S	for	SIGN	BIT 0
C	for	CRY carry	BIT 1
Z	for	ZERO	BIT 2
O	for	OVG overflow	BIT 3

The status bits affected by each instruction are indicated by the following:

I/O	Determined by the status of the data
1	Forced to a 1 state
0	Forced to a 0 state
—	Not affected if blank

Note that the sign bit of the accumulator is complemented when stored in the status register, and the shift instructions shift 0's into the accumulator.

Accumulator Group Instructions

There are two types of accumulator group instructions, the 1 and 2-byte instructions (see Appendix II). The 1-byte instructions modify the contents of the accumulator. The 2-byte instructions are all *imme-*

diate instructions that introduce constants into the program. The exception is the load immediate short (LIS), which is a 1-byte instruction that introduces a hex constant, 0-F, into the program. The load immediate (LI), a 2-byte instruction, performs the same function as the LIS instruction, but requires 1 byte of code.

The 1-byte instructions are comparable to the 1-byte accumulator instructions of the implied addressing mode of the 6800 family. The 2-byte instructions are comparable to the immediate addressing mode of the 6800. See Sec. 1-6 for a discussion of immediate instructions.

Three instructions included in this group are not part of the 6800 family:

LINK (LNK)
SHIFT LEFT 4 (SL4)
SHIFT RIGHT 4 (SR4)

The link instruction adds the carry bit to the accumulator and it is used by the add and subtract routines, which is necessary because the 3870 does not have an add with carry or a subtract with borrow instruction. The shift left and shift right 4 bits are used to shift hex characters.

As an example of reading the instruction from the instruction set, we will use LNK (link the carry). Three registers are affected by this instruction: the program counter, the accumulator, and the status register. Reading across the instruction listing:

Operation Add carry (to the accumulator)

MNEMONIC LNK

Function Acc ← (ACC) + CRY
The function is a mathematic notation that describes the operation of the instruction and reads: The contents of the accumulator are replaced by the contents of the accumulator plus the carry bit. By the 3870 convention the brackets to the left of the replace sign (←) are omitted. It indicates that the contents of the accumulator are affected by this instruction.

Machine Code The machine code for this 1-byte instruction is 19.

Bytes This is a 1-byte instruction, and the program counter is incremented by 1.

Cycles The time to execute this instruction is one cycle and is calculated by multiplying the period of the input clock by 8. In the general case, multiply the number of cycles by 8 times the period of the input clock.

Status bits: All four status bits are affected by this instruction.

Table 8-1 Accumulator Group Instructions

F3870 Instruction Set
F8 Compatible

OPERATION	MNEMONIC OP CODE	OPERAND	FUNCTION	MACHINE CODE	BYTES	CYCLES	STATUS BITS OVF	ZERO	CRY	SIGN
ADD CARRY	LNK		ACC ← (ACC) + CRY	19	1	1	1/0	1/0	1/0	1/0
ADD IMMEDIATE	AI	ii	ACC ← (ACC) ∧ H'ii'	24 ii	2	2.5	1/0	1/0	1/0	1/0
AND IMMEDIATE	NI	ii	ACC ← (ACC) H 'ii'	21 ii	2	2.5	0	1/0	0	1/0
CLEAR	CLR		ACC ← H'00'	70	1	1				
COMPARE IMMEDIATE	CI	ii	H 'ii' + $\overline{(ACC)}$ + 1	25 ii	2	2.5	1/0	1/0	1/0	1/0
COMPLEMENT	COM		ACC ← (ACC) ⊕ H'FF'	18	1	1	0	1/0	0	1/0
EXCLUSIVE OR IMMEDIATE	XI	ii	ACC ← (ACC) ⊕ H 'ii'	23 ii	2	2.5	0	1/0	0	1/0
INCREMENT	INC		ACC ← (ACC) + 1	1F	1	1	1/0	1/0	1/0	1/0
LOAD IMMEDIATE	LI	ii	ACC ← H 'ii'	20 ii	2	2.5	—	—	—	—
LOAD IMMEDIATE SHORT	LIS	i	ACC ← H'0i'	7i	1	1	—	—	—	—
OR IMMEDIATE	OI	ii	ACC ← (ACC) ∨ H 'ii'	22 ii	2	2.5	0	1/0	0	1/0
SHIFT LEFT ONE	SL	1	SHIFT LEFT 1	13	1	1	0	1/0	0	1/0
SHIFT LEFT FOUR	SL	4	SHIFT LEFT 4	15	1	1	0	1/0	0	1/0
SHIFT RIGHT ONE	SR	1	SHIFT RIGHT 1	12	1	1	0	1/0	0	1
SHIFT RIGHT FOUR	SR	4	SHIFT RIGHT 4	14	1	1	0	1/0	0	1

Table 8-2. Scratchpad Register Instructions

OPERATION	MNEMONIC OP CODE	OPERAND	FUNCTION	MACHINE CODE	BYTES	CYCLES	STATUS BITS OVF	ZERO	CRY	SIGN
ADD BINARY	AS	r	ACC ← (ACC) + (r)	Cr	1	1	1/0	1/0	1/0	1/0
ADD DECIMAL	ASD	r	ACC ← (ACC) + (r)	Dr	1	2	1/0	1/0	1/0	1/0
DECREMENT	DS	r	r ← (r) + H'FF'	3r	1	1.5	1/0	1/0	1/0	1/0
LOAD	LR	A,r	ACC ← (r)	4r	1	1	—	—	—	—
LOAD	LR	A,KU	ACC ← (r12)	00	1	1	—	—	—	—
LOAD	LR	A,KL	ACC ← (r13)	01	1	1	—	—	—	—
LOAD	LR	A,QU	ACC ← (r14)	02	1	1	—	—	—	—
LOAD	LR	A,QL	ACC ← (r15)	03	1	1	—	—	—	—
LOAD	LR	r,A	r ← (ACC)	5r	1	1	—	—	—	—
LOAD	LR	KU,A	r12 ← (ACC)	04	1	1	—	—	—	—
LOAD	LR	KL,A	r13 ← (ACC)	05	1	1	—	—	—	—
LOAD	LR	QU,A	r14 ← (ACC)	06	1	1	—	—	—	—
LOAD	LR	QL,A	r15 ← (ACC)	07	1	1	—	—	—	—
AND	NS	r	ACC ← (ACC) $\wedge$ (r)	Fr	1	1	0	1/0	0	1/0
EXCLUSIVE OR	XS	r	ACC ← (ACC) $\oplus$ (r)	Er	1	1	0	1/0	0	1/0

*Privileged instruction
‡Contents of ACC Destroyed

Scratchpad Register Instructions and the Load ISAR and Branch if ISAR Is Lower Than 7

The scratchpad registers are 64 bytes of RAM memory that are controlled by the scratchpad register instructions (see Appendix II), plus the load ISAR and branch if ISAR is lower than 7 instructions. They are probably the most used group of instructions. They are all 1-byte instructions. This permits programs that can be stored in limited ROM memory.

The first 12 scratchpad registers are directly addressable and are generally used to store 1-byte variables, while ISAR is used to point to and indirectly address all 64 RAM locations, which is preferable for handling blocks of data. Seven of the registers, hex 9 to F, are reserved to store the status register and the 16-bit pointer registers. Caution should be exercised when using them for other purposes. The following seven registers are hex:

9	Referred to as the J register and used to store the status bits
A and B	Referred to as the H pair
C and D	Referred to as the K pair
E and F	Referred to as the Q pair

Controlling ISAR To write programs using the scratchpad registers, it is first necessary to control ISAR. The indirect addressing mode of the scratchpad register instructions is powerful, which means that a 1-byte instruction can modify the ISAR pointer and also access the data in the registers. To write a program with the scratchpad instructions, it is necessary to first load ISAR and then to test when to exit from a loop.

The four instructions from the Miscellaneous Instructions that control ISAR are used to load and move an address into and from ISAR. They are as follows:

LR	IS,A	Load ISAR
LR	A,IS	Store ISAR
LISU	a	Load ISAR upper
LISL	a	Load ISAR lower

The load and store ISAR instructions move an address from and to the accumulator. The two load ISAR instructions, upper and lower, are immediate instructions that load a constant into ISAR. ISAR is a 6-bit register with two octal numbers, and the 2 MSBs of ISAR are not used. Each octal number is loaded with an instruction, and it should be noted that the notation for the numbers between 0 and 7 is the same in octal, decimal, and hex notation.

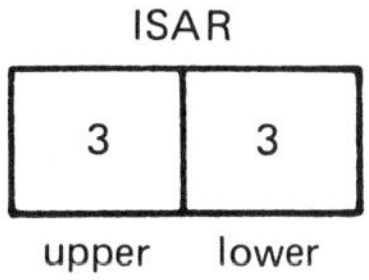

Example: To load ISAR with octal 33, the assembler instructions are

```
LISU    3
LISL    3
```

Converting the assembler notation of these two instructions to machine code, where the 3 LSBs represent an octal operand, is unique to these two instructions.

The machine code for

LISU	a	is	0110	1aaa
LISL	a	is	0110	0aaa

To load ISAR with octal 33 the 3 LSBs are 011. This makes the machine code:

LISU	3	is	0110	1011	for a machine code of hex 6B
LISL	3	is	0110	0011	for a machine code of hex 63

Distinguishing between scratchpad direct and indirect notation. Some of the scratchpad register instructions have an r as part of the operand. When the scratchpad register instruction is used in the direct addressing mode, then r is replaced by the hex address from 0 to H'B'.

Examples of Direct Addressing:

1. To transfer the contents of register 3 (R3) to the accumulator, LR A,r is written as LR A,3
2. To decrement the contents of R8, DS r is written as DS 8.
3. To AND the contents of R H'A', decimal 10, to the accumulator, NS r is written as NS H'A'.
4. To ADD the contents of R5 to the accumulator, AS r is written as AS 5.

5. To transfer the contents of the accumulator to R H'B', decimal 11, LR r,A is written as LR H'B', A.

For indirect scratchpad notation, the r that appears as part of the operand is replaced by an S, I, or D. These three variations first execute the instructions with the data pointed to by ISAR, and then either

	Mnem Notation	Machine Code
Leave ISAR the same	S	H'C'
Increment ISAR	I	H'D'
Decrement ISAR	D	H'E'

Branch if ISAR lower is less than 7 (BR7) Most of the branch instructions make a decision to take the branch or not by examining one of the status bits. The BR7 instruction makes a decision based on which of the scratchpad registers ISAR is pointing to. There are three parts to a program using a loop:

- Initialize the loop.
- Execute the instructions of the loop.
- Test to exit from the loop.

The BR7 instruction is useful in exiting from the loop, especially when the scratchpad register is organized as an 8 x 8 array (see Fig. 8-2). The BR7 instruction is effectively a branch and return to the loop if ISAR lower is unequal to 7. Since the indirect mode of the scratchpad instructions first execute the instruction and then either decrement or increment ISAR, the MS byte of the array may be either X0 or X7, depending on whether ISAR is decrementing or incrementing (Fig. 8-5). An array may have two to eight registers, and for an eight-register array ISAR initially points to X7 and is decremented to X0 (Fig. 8-5a). When ISAR is incremented, each array is limited to seven registers (Fig. 8-5b). A 3-byte array is illustrated in Fig. 8-5c, storing the decimal number 012345, and Fig. 8-5d illustrates a 3-byte array storing the decimal number 667789.

Branch Instructions

These are 2-byte instructions with relative addressing mode (see Appendix II). They examine one or more of the status bits, S, C, Z or O, and then may execute a branch. When the branch is taken, the 8-bit 2's complement relative address plus 1 is added to the 16-bit program counter. Conversely, when the branch is not taken, the program

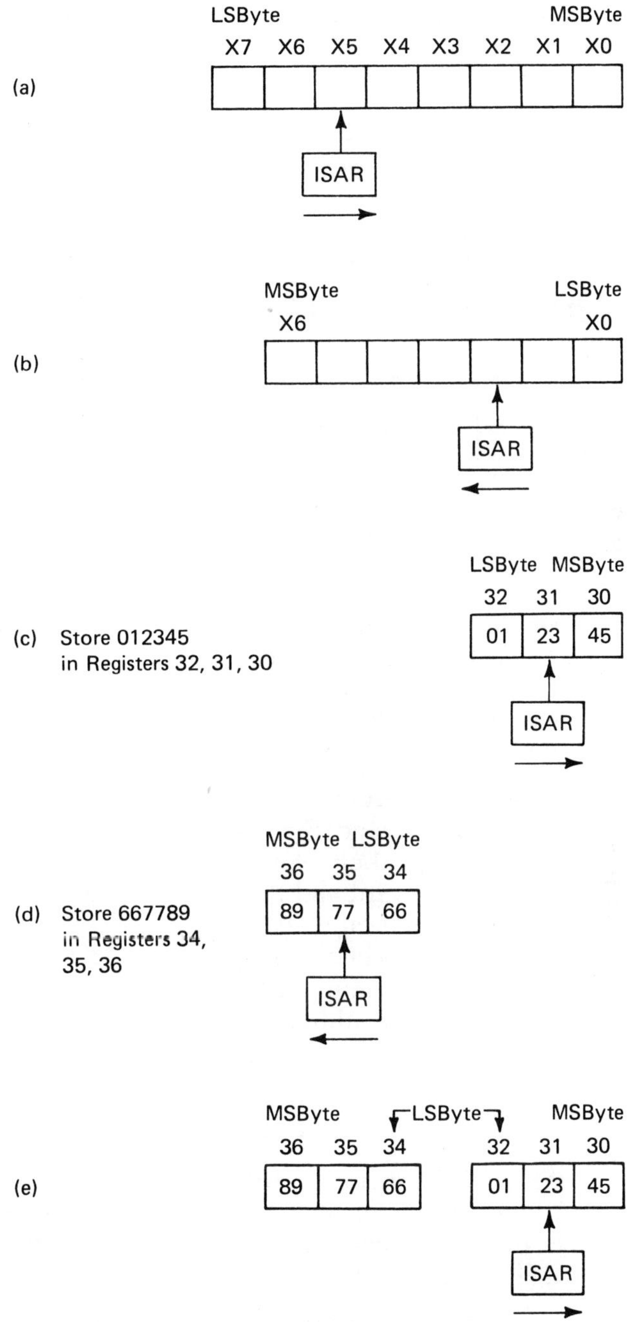

Figure 8-5. Examples for organizing scratchpad register using BR7. The control byte X7 is not used.

PC	MACHINE CODE	LABEL	MNEM	OPERAND
1000	80 15	LOOPB	BR	LOOPA
	– – –			
	– – –			
	– – –			
	– – –			
1006	80 E9	LOOPA	BR	LOOPB
	– – –			
	– – –			
	– – –			

Figure 8-6. Example of relative addressing.

counter is incremented by 2, and the program continues by executing the next instruction. See Chapter 1 regarding the condition code bits, S, C, Z and O, and how they are set, and 2's complement numbers. An exception for determining the branch address of the 3870 is to add 1 plus the relative address to the program counter.

Relative addressing. The relative address is used to modify the program counter, and Fig. 8-6 is an example of a program that continuously loops between two branch instructions. One instruction branches forward and the second branches back.

The location labeled LOOPB has a 2-byte branch always (BR) instruction in locations H'1000' and H'1001'. The operand, LOOPA, indicates that the program should branch to location H'1016' by adding the relative address of hex 15 plus 1 to the program counter.

$$\text{PCO} \leftarrow ((\text{PC0}) + 1) + \text{H'aa'}$$
$$\text{PCO} = 1000 + 1 + 0015$$
$$\text{PCO} = 1016$$

When the program branches to the location labeled LOOPA, the 2-byte branch always instruction routes the program back to location H'1000'. The operand LOOPB indicates that the relative address is H-E9' (equal to hex 16).

$$\text{PCO} \leftarrow ((\text{PCO}) + 1) + \text{H'aa'}$$
$$\text{PCO} = 1016 + 1 + \text{FFE9}$$
$$\text{PCO} = 1017 + \text{FFE9}$$

Hex FFE9	= binary	1111	1111	1110	1001
Hex 1017	= binary	0001	0000	0001	0111
		0001	0000	0000	0000
PCO	= 1000				

General form of the 3870 branch instruction The special cases of the branch instructions test only one status bit per instruction, while the general case permits the programmer to branch by testing two or more of the status bits.

Operation	General Form of the Instruction	2-Byte Machine Code
Branch on true	BT t,aaa	8t aa
Branch on false	BF t,aa	9t aa

The status bits are stored in the 4 LSBs of the status register as 0, Z, C, and S, where

S is selected with binary 0 0 0 1	Hex 01
C is selected with binary 0 0 1 0	Hex 02
Z is selected with binary 0 1 0 0	Hex 04
0 is selected with binary 1 0 0 0	Hex 08

In the special cases where only one status bit is tested, the symbol t is restricted to the hex values of 1, 2, 4, and 8, but in the general case the value of the symbol t can vary from 0 to F. For example,

Hex	Binary O Z C S	Tests
when t = 3 then	0 0 1 1	Carry and sign bits
when t = 5 then	0 1 0 1	Zero and sign bits
when t = 6 then	0 1 1 0	Zero and carry bits
when t = 7 then	0 1 1 1	Zero, carry, and sign bits

Note of caution for the branch when true:

- The symbol t is restricted to vary from 0 to 7.
- Test for an OR condition; branch if any of the test bits are 1.

Note of caution for branch when false:

- The symbol t can vary from O to F.
- Test for an AND condition; branch if all the test bits are O.

Table 8-3. Branch Instructions

In all conditional branches P0 (P0) + 2 if the test conditions are not met. Execution is complete in 30 cycles.

OPERATION	MNEMONIC OP CODE	OPERAND	FUNCTION	MACHINE CODE	BYTES	CYCLES	STATUS BITS OVF	ZERO	CRY	SIGN
BRANCH ON CARRY	BC	aa	P0 ← [(P0) + 1] + H'aa' if CRY = 1	82 aa	2	3.5	—	—	—	—
BRANCH ON POSITIVE	BP	aa	P0 ← [(P0) + 1] + H'aa' if SIGN = 1	81 aa	2	3.5	—	—	—	—
BRANCH ON ZERO	BZ	aa	P0 ← [(P0) + 1] + H'aa' if ZERO = 1	84 aa	2	3.5	—	—	—	—
BRANCH ON TRUE	BT	t,aa	P0 ← [(P0) + 1] + H'aa' if any test is true	8t aa	2	3.5	—	—	—	—

t - TEST CONDITION

2^2	2^1	2^0
ZERO	CRY	SIGN

OPERATION	MNEMONIC OP CODE	OPERAND	FUNCTION	MACHINE CODE	BYTES	CYCLES	OVF	ZERO	CRY	SIGN
BRANCH IF NEGATIVE	BM	aa	P0 ← [(P0) + 1] + H'aa' if SIGN = 0	91 aa	2	3.5	—	—	—	—
BRANCH IF NO CARRY	BNC	aa	P0 ← [(P0) + 1] + H'aa' if CARRY ≠ 0	92 aa	2	3.5	—	—	—	—
BRANCH IF NO OVERFLOW	BNO	aa	P0 ← [(P0) + 1] + H'aa' if OVF = 0	98 aa	2	3.5	—	—	—	—
BRANCH IF NOT ZERO	BNZ	aa	P0 ← [(P0) + 1] + H'aa' if ZERO = 0	94 aa	2	3.5	—	—	—	—
BRANCH IF FALSE TEST	BF	t,aa	P0 ← [(P0) + 1] + H'aa' if all false test bits	9t aa	2	3.5	—	—	—	—

t = TEST CONDITION

2^3	2^2	2^1	2^0
OVF	ZERO	CRY	SIGN

OPERATION	MNEMONIC OP CODE	OPERAND	FUNCTION	MACHINE CODE	BYTES	CYCLES	OVF	ZERO	CRY	SIGN
BRANCH IF ISAR (LOWER) 7	BR7	aa	P0 ← [(P0) + 1] + H'aa' if ISARL ≠ 7	8F aa	2	2.5	—	—	—	—
			P0 ← (P0) + 2 if ISARL = 7			2.0	—	—	—	—
BRANCH RELATIVE	BR	aa	P0 ← [(P0) + 1] + H'aa'	90 aa	2	3.5	—	—	—	—
JUMP*	JMP	aaaa	P0 ← H'aaaa'	29 aaaa	3	5.5	—	—	—	—

*Privileged instruction

Note
JMP and PI change accumulator contents to the HIGH byte address.

Table 8-4. Memory Reference Instructions

In all Memory Reference Instructions, the Data Counter is incremented DC ← DC − 1.

OPERATION	MNEMONIC OP CODE	OPERAND	FUNCTION	MACHINE CODE	BYTES	CYCLES	STATUS BITS OVF	ZERO	CRY	SIGN
ADD BINARY	AM		ACC ← (ACC) + [(DC)]	88	1	2.5	1/0	1/0	1/0	1/0
ADD DECIMAL	AMD		ACC ← (ACC) + [(DC)]	89	1	2.5	1/0	1/0	1/0	1/0
AND	NM		ACC ← (ACC) ∧ [(DC)]	8A	1	2.5	0	1/0	0	1/0
COMPARE	CM		[(DC)] + ($\overline{ACC}$) + 1	8D	1	2.5	1/0	1/0	1/0	1/0
EXCLUSIVE OR	XM		ACC ← (ACC) ⊕ [(DC)]	8C	1	2.5	0	1/0	0	1/0
LOAD	LM		ACC ← [(DC)]	16	1	2.5	—	—	—	—
LOGICAL OR	OM		ACC ← (ACC) ∨ [(DC)]	8B	1	2.5	0	1/0	0	1/0
STORE	ST		(DC) ← (ACC)	17	1	2.5	—	—	—	—

Table 8-5. Instructions

	Accumulator Immediate	Scratchpad Registers	Memory Reference
LOAD	LIii/LIi	LR A,r	LM
STORE	—	LR r,A	ST[a]
ADD	AI ii	AS r	AM
ADD DECIMAL	—	ASD r	AMD
AND	NI ii	NS r	NM
Logical-OR	OI ii	—	OM
Exclusive-OR	XF ii	XS r	XM
COMPARE	CI ii	—	CM
LINK	LNK		
CLEAR	CLR		
COMPLEMENT	COM		
INCREMENT	INC		
DECREMENT		DS r	

[a] Does not apply when the memory is ROM only.

Memory Reference Instructions

The memory reference instructions (see Appendix II) use the indirect addressing mode. The data counter must first be loaded with, and pointing to, the memory location before a memory reference instruction is executed. The data counter is incremented each time one of these instructions is executed. Table 8-5 is a matrix of the instructions and how they relate to the accumulator, scratchpad, and memory.

Address Register Group Instructions

The address register group of instructions (see Appendix II) are loosely comparable to the index register and stack manipulating instructions and the jump and return from subroutine instructions of the 6800 family.

Add to Data Counter (ADC) The add to data counter instruction is an ideal instruction for look-up and jump tables. It adds the 8-bit 2's complement value in the accumulator to the 16-bit data counter and puts the result in the data counter.

Load and Store the Data Counter Instructions The load and store the data counter instructions are comparable to the load index register

Table 8-6. Address Register Group Instructions

OPERATION	MNEMONIC OP CODE	OPERAND	FUNCTION	MACHINE CODE	BYTES	CYCLES	STATUS BITS OVF	ZERO	CRY	SIGN
ADD to DATA COUNTER	ADC		DC ← (DC) + (ACC)	8E	1	2.5	—	—	—	—
CALL to SUBROUTINE	PK		P ← P0 ; P0U ← r12 ; PL ← (r13)	0C	1	4	—	—	—	—
CALL TO SUBROUTINE IMMEDIATE	PI	aaaa	P ← P ; P0 ← H'aaaa' ‡	28 aaaa	3	6.5	—	—	—	—
EXCHANGE DC	XDC		DC ↔ DC1	2C	1	2	—	—	—	—
LOAD DATA COUNTER	LR	DC,Q	DCU ← (r14); DCL ← (r15)	0F	1	4	—	—	—	—
LOAD DATA COUNTER	LR	DC,H	DCU ← (r10); DCL ← (r11)	10	1	4	—	—	—	—
LOAD DC IMMEDIATE	DCI	aaaa	DC ← H'aaaa'	2A aaaa	3	6	—	—	—	—
LOAD PROGRAM COUNTER	LR	P0,Q	P0U ← (r14); P0L ← (r15)	0D	1	4	—	—	—	—
LOAD STACK REGISTER	LR	PU	PU ← (r12); PL ← (r13)	09	1	4	—	—	—	—
RETURN FROM SUBROUTINE	POP		P0 ← P	1C	1	2	—	—	—	—
STORE DATA COUNTER	LR	Q,DC	r14 ← (DCU); r15 ← (DCL)	0E	1	4	—	—	—	—
STORE DATA COUNTER	LR	H,DC	r10 ← (DCU); r11 ← (DCL)	11	1	4	—	—	—	—
STORE STACK REGISTER	LR	K,P	r12 ← (PU) ; r13 ← (PL)	08	1	4	—	—	—	—

direct and the store index register instructions of the 6800 family. The four load and store data counter instructions are 1-byte instructions that move the data counter to or from either the Q or H register pairs. The load immediate instruction puts a constant address into the data counter.

Exchange DC (XDC) The exchange data counter is applicable when blocks of data are to be moved in a RAM. Each of the data counters, DC1 and DC2, may store the address of the source and destination blocks.

Jump and Return from Subroutines and Stack Instructions The 3870 has a stack register (PCI), and the K-register pair can be considered as a pseudo second-level stack. When the call to subroutine immediate (PI aaaa) instruction is executed, two transfers occur simultaneously: PCI ← (PCO); PCO ← H'aaaa'. The immediate address, the location of the subroutine, is transferred into the program counter which forces the program to subroutine. Simultaneously, the contents of the program counter plus 3, the return address, are transferred to the stack (PCI).

A note of caution: when 16-bit immediate instructions are executed, the contents of the accumulator are replaced by the high address byte of the immediate instruction.

Return from Subroutine or Interrupt (POP) The POP instruction transfers the return address from the stack to the program counter.

Store Stack Register (LR K,P) The LR K,P moves the address in the stack to the K-pair. The K-pair is a pseudo second-level stack (see Fig. 8-7).

Call to Subroutine (PK) The PK instruction (see Fig. 8-7) has two primary applications. The first is to call a subroutine whose address is stored in the K-pair and is comparable to the 6800 call to subroutine direct instruction. The instruction simultaneously transfers the address of the subroutine stored in the K-pair to the program counter and saves the return address from the subroutine in the stack. The second application of the PK instruction is a return from subroutine. This is useful when the return address from the subroutine has been transferred to the K-pair by the LR K,P instruction. The address that is stored in the stack is expendable.

Miscellaneous Instructions, Input and Output The four I/O instructions are IN, INS, OUT, and OUTS. They input and output data through the four I/O ports, 0, 1, 4 and 5, and to the timer at port 7 and the interrupt control register at port 6. The 2-byte IN and OUT instructions are redundant for the 3870. The 1-byte input short (INS) and output short (OUTS) are sufficient.

Each of the 32 pins of the 4 ports can either be an input or output pin.

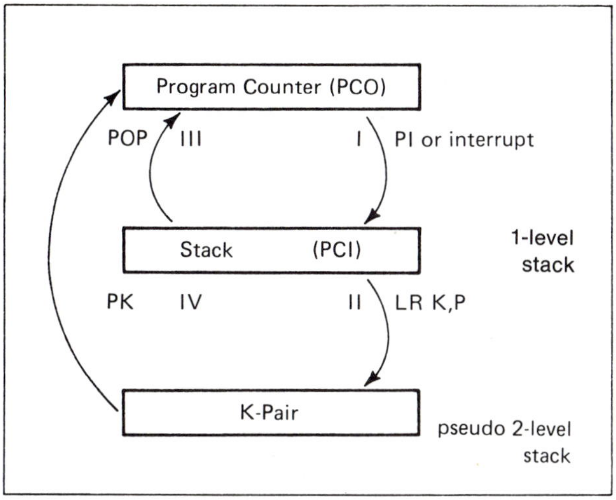

Recommended stack organization for 1-level subroutine and 1-level interrupt:

I	PI push immediate is a call to subroutine.
II	The first instruction in the subroutine should be an LR K,P which pushes the return address from the 1st to the pseudo second-level stack.
III	If an interrupt occurs it pushes the return address into the stack and the POP is effectively a return from interrupt.
IV	PK is the return from the subroutine.

Figure 8-7. Suggested call and return from subroutine organization.

Before a pin can be an input pin, it must first be cleared by outputting a 0 to that pin. All ports are initially cleared by the power-on sequence, but when a pin is alternately used as an input and output pin during a program, it must also be cleared before it can be reused as an input pin. During the execution of an input/output instruction, the logical signal is inverted. Therefore, a 1 in the accumulator appears as a 0, or low voltage, at the output pin. Conversely, a 0, or low voltage, at the input pin is a logic 1 in the accumulator. See Appendix II.

Store and Load Status Register The store and load status register instructions (LR J,W) and (LR W,J) are used to save and restore the status register in scratchpad register R9. These instructions are illustrated in the example of a binary add routine.

Enable and Disable Interrupt The enable and disable interrupt

Table 8-7. Miscellaneous Instructions

OPERATION	MNEMONIC OP CODE	OPERAND	FUNCTION	MACHINE CODE	BYTES	CYCLES	STATUS BITS OVF	ZERO	CRY	SIGN
DISABLE INTERRUPT	DI		RESET ICB	1A	1	2	—	—	—	—
ENABLE INTERRUPT*	EI		SET ICB	1B	1	2	—	—	—	—
INPUT	IN	aa	ACC ← (INPUT PORT aa)	26 aa	2	4	0	1/0	0	1/0
INPUT SHORT	INS	a	ACC ← (INPUT PORT a)	Aa	1	4***	0	1/0	0	1/0
LOAD ISAR	LR	IS,A	ISAR ← (ACC)	0B	1	1	—	—	—	—
LOAD ISAR LOWER	LISL	a	ISARL ← a	01101a**	1	1	—	—	—	—
LOAD ISAR UPPER	LISU	a	ISARU ← a	01100a**	1	1	—	—	—	—
LOAD STATUS REGISTER*	LR	W,J	W ← (r9)	1D	1	2	1/0	1/0	1/0	1/0
NO-OPERATION	NOP		P0 ← (P0) + 1	2B	1	1	—	—	—	—
OUTPUT	OUT	aa	OUTPUT PORT aa ← (ACC)	27 aa	2	4	—	—	—	—
OUTPUT SHORT	OUTS	a	OUTPUT PORT a ← (ACC)	Ba	1	4***	—	—	—	—
STORE ISAR	LR	A,IS	ACC ← (ISAR)	0A	1	1	—	—	—	—
STORE STATUS REG	LR	J,W	r9 ← (W)	1E	1	1	—	—	—	—

*Privileged instruction
**3-bit octal digit
***Two machine cycles for CPU ports

instructions (EI and DI) are identical to the clear and set interrupt mask instructions of the 6800 family.

8-3 LOGIC PROGRAM WITH SUBROUTINES

This section describes an abbreviated version of the logic program discussed in Chapter 2 with the 6800 instruction set. This program with the 3870 instruction set consists of the following:

- An input routine
- Two logic routines, a counter and a bouncing ball
- A delay loop subroutine

The microcomputer is tied to the I/O devices, as illustrated in Fig. 8.8 with associated listing on pages 278-279. There are no substantial

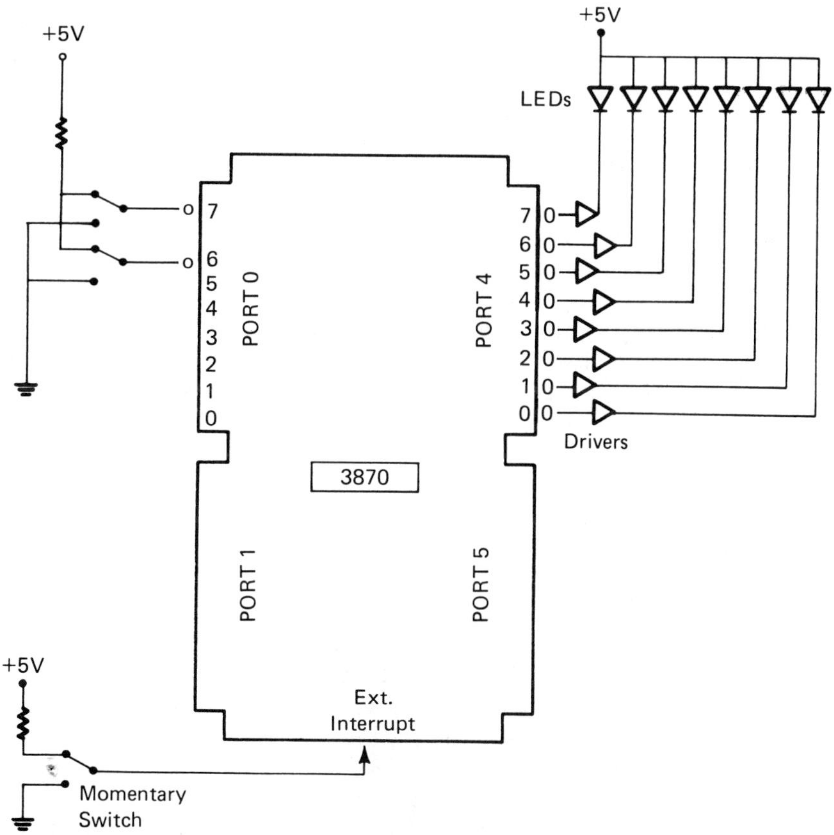

Figure 8-8. The 3870 with input switch and LEDs.

differences between the program written in the 6800 and the 3870 instruction sets, but because of only one accumulator, care must be exercised to store its contents as the program passes through each section.

The input switches are tied to Port O, pins 7 and 6, where switch 7 selects the count and switch 6 selects the bouncing ball routine. Since the input signals are inverted, a +5-V signal inputs a 0 to the accumulator and is considered an open switch, while the 0 V inputs a 1 and is considered a closed switch.

The input routine examines, or polls, the accumulator, and if there are no closed switches, the program stays in the tight little loop just waiting for an input. If there is an input, then each switch, starting with pin 7, is examined, and if there is a closed switch, the program branches to that routine. Each routine makes a pass through the program, and then the input switches are polled again.

Both logic routines, the counter and the bouncing ball, use the same eight LEDs to display the output pattern and the same delay-time subroutine. See Sec. 2-4.

This is a program limited to a one-level subroutine. The push immediate (PI) calls the subroutine and the POP returns the program to the main routine.

8-4 LOGIC PROGRAM WITH SUBROUTINE AND INTERRUPT

This section augments the logic program from the previous section by introducing both interrupts. The two types of interrupt, external and timer interrupt, are introduced separately, with a one-level subroutine. Included on pages 279-280 is the listing (IIA) for a program where an external interrupt interrupts a routine in which is included a subroutine.

The two techniques for inputting to a microcomputer are to *poll the input* or to *interrupt*. Polling is the technique where the program periodically scans the input devices, as illustrated in Sec. 8-3. This technique is analogous to periodically lifting the phone and asking if anyone is calling, while working at a desk. The second technique is to keep a person working, have the telephone ring, and interrupt as necessary. The advantage of an interrupt is that it is, timewise, more efficient, but the disadvantage is that when an interrupt occurs a person must remember what he was doing and how to get back to work without the appearance of having been interrupted. This suggests then that an interrupt is similar to calling a subroutine. It is, except that the programmer knows when to call a subroutine and has more control, but does not know when the interrupt will occur. The interrupt has five functions:

- To store away the contents of the general registers
- To execute the function for the interrupt routine
- To replace the contents of the general registers
- To enable the interrupt
- To return from the interrupt

The five parts of the interrupt routine are analogous to my responding to the telephone. First, I must put away the papers I am working at, so as not to mark them inappropriately. Second, I must respond to the telephone message. Third, I must replace the papers I was working with back into the place they were prior to the interrupt, fourth is to re-enable the interrupt, which has no human analogy, and, fifth, I can return to that task. When the interrupt, by a transition at the external interrupt pin, occurs, the address in the program counter is transferred to the stack, and the address of the external interrupt routine 00A0 is stuffed into the program counter. This is effectively a call to a subroutine at location 00A0, but it is caused by a transition at the external interrupt pin rather than a call to a subroutine.

When the interrupt occurs, the address of the next instruction is stored in the program counter, and the address H'00A0' is stuffed into the program counter. This is effectively a call to subroutine at location H'00A0', but it is caused by a pulse at the external interrupt pin, rather than a call instruction.

The example in this section has the interrupt input select the bouncing dark spot routine as soon as the switch is closed. The microcomputer then returns to continue whatever it was doing prior to the interrupt. However, since the interrupt is similar to a subroutine and there is only one stack, a technique is necessary that converts the K-pair registers to a pseudo-second stack (see Fig. 8-6). The main program in Sec. 8-3 calls a subroutine, and the interrupt routine may occur when the main program is in the subroutine. The interrupt then is effectively the second subroutine. Since it is the effective second subroutine, the interrupt itself cannot call a subroutine.

The subroutine is modified by having the first instruction of the subroutine transfer the return address from the stack to the K-pair by the LR K,P instruction. The return from the subroutine then becomes the PK instruction, while the POP instruction is used to return from the interrupt routine (see program listing IIB on pages 280-281).

Timer Interrupt

In these programs most of the time is spent in the delay subroutine waiting while displaying the logic pattern. This is a very inefficient use of a microcomputer. The analogy of a timer may be an alarm clock. When waiting, a person can either just watch the clock until the appropriate amount of time passes or set an alarm. The person who sets the alarm may use the time more efficiently until interrupted by the alarm. To use a timer, the programmer must set the timer and store the timer interrupt routine at Location H'0020'. Care must be exercised to turn off the timer or it may recur at an inappropriate time. See program listing III on page 281.

I

```
ERRS  LOC OBJECT ADDR        SOURCE STATEMENT

                        * SEE SECTION 8.3.
                        * THIS PROGRAM SCANS A KEYBOARD & EITHER BRANCHES
                        * TO THE COUNT OR THE BOUNCING BALL ROUTINE.
                        * IT USES A SINGLE LEVEL SUBROUTINE.
                        *
                        * THE PROGRAM STARTS BY SCANNING THE INPUT SWITCHES
                        * AT PORT 0:
                        *      IF SWITCH 7 IS CLOSED BRANCH TO 'COUNT'
                        *      IF SWITCH 6 IS CLOSED BRANCH TO 'BBALL'
                        *
      0000 A0           START INS 0      INPUT PORT 0
      0001 84FE    0000       BZ  START BR BACK IF NO INPUT
      0003 9107    000B       BM  COUNT IF SW 7
      0005 2140               NI H'40'   'AND' TEST SW 6
      0007 940F    0017       BNZ BBALL
      0009 90F6    0000       BR START   ELSE GO BACK
                        *
      000B 70           COUNT CLR
      000C B4           LOOP  OUTS       4 OUTPUT 0'S
      000D 280029 0029        PI  DTIME  JUMP TO SUBROUTINE
      0010 1F                 INC        INC ACC
      0011 250B               CI H'0B'   CMP FOR LAST COUNT
      0013 94F8    000C       BNZ LOOP   KEEP COUNTING
      0015 90EA    0000       BR START   ELSE SAMPLE INPUT
                        *
      0017 2002         BBALL LI H'02'   LITE 2ND LED
      0019 B4           LEFT  OUTS 4     OUTPUT LITE PATTERN
      001A 280029 0029        PI DTIME   JMP SUBROUTINE TIME DELAY
      001D 13                 SL 1       SHIFT LEFT 1
      001E 81FA    0019       BP LEFT    BR STAY IN LEFT SHIFT LOOP
      0020 B4           RITE  OUTS 4     ELSE BOUNCE BACK
      0021 280029 0029        PI DTIME
      0024 12                 SR 1       SHIFT RIGHT 1
      0025 94FA    0020       BNZ RITE   STAY IN RT SHIFT LOOP
      0027 90D8    0000       BR START   ELSE GO TO SAMPLE SWITCHES
                        *
                        * SUBROUTINE DELAY TIME
      0029 53           DTIME LR 3,A     SAVE ACC
      002A 70                 CLR
      002B 50                 LR  0,A    CLR REG 0
      002C 51                 LR  1,A    CLR REG 1
      002D 30           DELAY DS 0       DEC REG #0
      002E 94FE    002D       BNZ DELAY
```

I (Continued)

```
0030 31              DS 1       DEC REG #1
0031 43              LR A,3     RESTORE ACC
0032 1C              POP
                *
                *
                     END
 0 ERRS
```

IIA

```
ERRS  LOC OBJECT ADDR LINE           SOURCE STATEMENT

                          * SEE SECTION 8.4.
                          * THIS PROGRAM USES THE EXTERMAL INTERRUUPT
                          * & A SUBROUTINE.  THE MAIN ROUTINE IS SIMILAR
                          * TO THE PREVIOUS ROUTINE WITH ONE EXCEPTION.
                          * TO MAKE THE ONE-LEVEL STACK RESPOND AS A PSUEDO
                          * TWO LEVEL STACK, THE RETURN ADDRESS FROM THE
                          * SUBROUTINE IS PUSHED INTO THE K-REGISTER PAIR.
                          *        . THE RETURN FROM THE INTERRUPT IS THE POP INSTRUCTION
                          *        . THE RETURN FROM THE SUBROUTINE IS THE PK INSTRUCTION
                          *
                          * THE INTERRUPT IS INITIALIZED AT THE BEGINNING OF THE
                          * PROGRAM & IT STARTS AT LOCATION H'00A0'.
                          * WHEN THE EXTERNAL INTERRUPT IS ACTIVATED, THE
                          * 3870 JUMPS TO THE INTERRUPT ROUTINE & EXECUTES
                          * THE DSPOT PROGRAM.
                          *
      0000 2003           INIT LI H'03'  LOAD INTERRUPT
      0002 B6                  OUTS 6    CONTROL REG
                          * THE EXTERMAL INTERRUT RESPONDS TO A POSITIVE PULSE
                          * NOW ENABLE THE ICB BIT.
      0003 1B                  EI        ENABLE INTERRUPT
                          *
                          *
                          *
                          * THIS PROGRAM SCANS A KEYBOARD & EITHER BRANCHES
                          * TO THE COUNT OR THE BOUNCING BALL ROUTINE.
                          * IT USES A SINGLE LEVEL SUBROUTINE.
                          *
                          * THE PROGRAM STARTS BY SCANNING THE INPUT SWITCHES
                          * AT PORT 0:
                          *       IF SWITCH 7 IS CLOSED BRANCH TO 'COUNT'
                          *       IF SWITCH 6 IS CLOSED BRANCH TO 'BBALL'
                          *
      0004 A0             START INS 0     INPUT PORT 0
      0005 84FE    0004         BZ  START BR BACK IF NO INPUT
      0007 9107    000F         BM  COUNT IF SW 7
      0009 2140                 NI H'40'  'AND' TEST SW 6
      000B 940F    001B         BNZ BBALL
      000D 90F6    0004         BR START  ELSE GO BACK
                          *
```

IIA (Continued)

```
000F 70             COUNT CLR
0010 B4             LOOP  OUTS      4 OUTPUT 0'S
0011 28002D 002D          PI  DTIME JUMP TO SUBROUTINE
0014 1F                   INC       INC ACC
0015 250B                 CI H'0B'  CMP FOR LAST COUNT
0017 94F8   0010          BNZ LOOP  KEEP COUNTING
0019 90EA   0004          BR START  ELSE SAMPLE INPUT
                    *
001B 2002           BBALL LI H'02'  LITE 2ND LED
001D B4             LEFT  OUTS 4    OUTPUT LITE PATTERN
001E 28002D 002D          PI DTIME  JMP SUBROUTINE TIME DELAY
0021 13                   SL 1      SHIFT LEFT 1
0022 81FA   001D          BP LEFT   BR STAY IN LEFT SHIFT LOOP
0024 B4             RITE  OUTS 4    ELSE BOUNCE BACK
0025 28002D 002D          PI DTIME
0028 12                   SR 1      SHIFT RIGHT 1
0029 94FA   0024          BNZ RITE  STAY IN RT SHIFT LOOP
002B 90D8   0004          BR START  ELSE GO TO SAMPLE SWITCHES
                    *
                    * SUBROUTINE DELAY TIME
002D 08             DTIME LR  K,P  PUSH RETURN ADDR TO K-PAIR
```

IIB

```
ERRS  LOC OBJECT ADDR LINE          SOURCE STATEMENT

     002E 53                    LR 3,A      SAVE ACC
     002F 70                    CLR
     0030 50                    LR  0,A     CLR REG 0
     0031 51                    LR  1,A     CLR REG 1
     0032 30              DELAY DS 0        DEC REG #0
     0033 94FE   0032           BNZ DELAY
     0035 31                    DS 1        DEC REG #1
     0036 43                    LR A,3      RESTORE ACC
     0037 0C                    PK
                          *
                          *
                          *
                          * THE INTERRUPT ROUTINE
                              ORG H'00A0'
                          * ROTATING DARK SPOT OUTPUTS THE COMPLEMENT OF
                          * OUTPUT OF THE BOUNCING BALL PROGRAM.
                          *
                          * STORE CONTENTS OF ACC & STATUS REGISTER
     00A0 56                    LR  6,A      SAVE ACC
     00A1 1E                    LR  J,W   SAVE STATUS REG
                          *
     00A2 2002            DSPOT LI H'02'   LITE 2ND LED
     00A4 18              LLEFT COM
     00A5 B4                    OUTS 4   OUTPUT LITE PATTERN
     00A6 33              TYME  DS 3     DEC REG#3
     00A7 94FE   00A6           BNZ  TYME
     00A9 34                    DS 4     DEC REG#4
     00AA 94FB   00A6           BNZ  TYME
     00AC 18                    COM
     00AD 13                    SL 1
     00AE 81F5   00A4           BP LLEFT
                          *
```

IIB (Continued)

```
                     * RETURN FROM INTERRUPT ROUTINE
                     * REPLACE CONTENTS OF ACC & STATUS REGISTER
        00B0 1D           LR   W,J    STATUS REG
        00B1 46           LR   A,6  ACC
                     * ENABLE ICB (INTERRUPT CONTROL BIT)
        00B2 1B           EI
        00B3 1C           POP      RETURN FROM INTERRUPT
                     *
                     *
                        END
    00 ERRS
```

III

```
ERRS  LOC OBJECT ADDR LINE           SOURCE STATEMENT

                    * THIS PROGRAM USES THE TIMER INTERRUPT IN LIEU OF
                    * THE DELAY TIME SUBROUTINE, FOR THE COUNTER ROUTINE.
                    * USING A TIMER PERMITS A MORE EFFICIENT USE OF
                    * THE MICROPROCESSOR.
                    *
                    * IN THIS EXAMPLE THE COUNT, COUNTS FOREVER.
                    * IN THE TIMER INTERRUPT ROUTINE, THE COUNT IS ADVANCED
                    * TO NEW NUMBER & OUTPUT TO PORT 4 BEFORE
                    * RETURNING TO THE MAIN PROGRAM.
                    *
                    * THE COUNT IS STORED IN REG 5
                    *
                    * INITIALIZE THE TIMER INTERRUPT
      0000 20EA          LI H'EA'   SET TIMER INTERRUT
      0002 B6            OUTS 6     LOAD CONTROL REG
      0003 20FF          LI H'FF'   LOAD
      0005 B7            OUTS 7       TIMER
                    * NOW GO THAT THE TIMER IS SET THE PROGRAM AND
                    * BE FREE TO DO OTHER FUNCTIONS.
                    *
                    *
                        ORG H'0020'
                    * COUNTER INTERRUPT ROUTINE
                    * SAVE CONTENTS OF ACC & STATUS BITS
      0020 1E       TIMINT LR J,W
      0021 56              LR 6,A
                    * GET THE COUNT
      0022 45              LR A,5
      0023 1F              INC        INC COUNT
      0024 B4              OUTS 4     OUTPUT COUNT
      0025 55              LR 5,A     SAVE COUNT
                    * REPLACE CONTENTS OF ACC & STATUS REG
      0026 46              LR A,6      RESTORE ACC
      0027 1D              LR W,J      RESTORE STATUS BITS
                    * ENABLE INTERRUPTS
      0028 1B            EI
                    * RETURN TO MAIN PROGRAM
      0029 1C           POP
                    *
                    *
                       END
00 ERRS
```

9 Interfacing a Microcomputer With a Terminal: The Asynchronous Communication Interface Adapter (6850) and the Programmable Timer, PTM, (6840)

This chapter discusses techniques for interfacing a microcomputer with a terminal or teletype (TTY). Initially, the asynchronous communication interface adapter (ACIA) is described, and then it is used as the I/O for the calculator example described in Chapter 7. The example is developed in Sec. 9-2, where the ASCII data are input and then converted to the hex number notation, which is the internal notation used by the calculator. Prior to outputting data from the microcomputer to the terminal, the data must first be converted to their ASCII equivalent. Second, the data are formatted, which implies that the decimal point and the arithmetic operation (plus, minus, multiply, or divide signs) must be inserted with the appropriate spacing. The programmable timer (PTM) is programmed to supply the necessary time base.

After using the ACIA, which is designed to interface a microcomputer to a terminal, the PIA, in conjunction with the timer, is used to perform the same task. This not only offers an alternate technique for implementing the same solution, but also illustrates some additional capabilities of the PIA:

- Keyboard / 7-segment display (Chapter 6)

- ACIA to interface between a microcomputer and a terminal (Sec. 9-2)
- PIA/timer to interface between a microcomputer and a terminal (Sec. 9-3)

Both peripheral devices, the ACIA and the timer, are discussed according to the rules in Chapter 3:

- Understanding the basic function of the device
- Defining the function and address of each register on the peripheral device
- Examining the pins
- Defining the fields of the control register
- Defining the bits of the status register
- Illustrating the features of the device with an example

9-1 FUNCTION OF THE ACIA

The terminal has two modes of operation, local and automatic. In the local mode it functions much like a typewriter, where the letters corresponding to each key depressed are displayed on the screen. In the automatic mode, however, the keyboard and screen are two separate machines. The keyboard is tied to the input line of the ACIA, and the output line of the ACIA is tied to the screen. When a key is depressed, the data are transmitted to the microcomputer through the ACIA, and then retransmitted or 'echoed' back to the screen, giving the impression that the terminal is functioning like the typewriter. However, because the microcomputer is in the path of the data flow, the data are also examined and stored in the computer's memory and are available for examination by the programmer.

Effectively, when a key is depressed, each key is coded, formatted, and converted to a serial string and transmitted to the ACIA over a single line or channel. The receiver that accepts the data inputs the data at a random or asynchronous rate. The function of the receiving section of the ACIA is, first, to detect the beginning of a new string of data, then to extract the ASCII or equivalent code, and last, to convert it to an 8-bit parallel data for the microcomputer. The same procedure is followed when transmitting data from the microcomputer through the ACIA's transmitting section to the screen of the terminal. Prior to transmitting, the ACIA and the terminal must be coordinated to use the same code, the same format, and the same rate of transmission.

The two most popular codes are the ASCII and the EBCDIC codes. The ASCII code listed in Appendix V is used throughout this book.

Format

Of the large variety of asynchronous formats (see Fig. 9-1), there are four basic parts:

Start bit	1 bit
Character	7 or 8 bits
Parity bit	1 bit
Stop bit	1 or 2 bits

Start Bit Prior to starting a transmission, the signal is in the mark or logic 1 state. Detecting the mark to space, or logic 1 to logic 0, transition synchronizes the receiving unit to transmitting unit for that one character.

Character There are two common character codes, ASCII and EBCDIC, which use 7 and 8 bits, respectively. The character is transmitted LSB first.

ASCII example (Fig. 9-2)

	ASCII Code	Direction of Flow
Number 3	33	0011 0011
Alpha H	48	0100 1000
EOT (end of transmission)	04	0000 0100

Parity Bit Parity is a technique for verifying the accuracy of the data, and it is particularly good for detecting a 1-bit error. There are two types of parity, odd or even, which check for either an odd or even number of 1's in the code. For odd, the parity bit is set so that the total number of 1's in the character, plus the parity bit, add up to an odd number, and, conversely, the total number of 1's in the character, plus the parity bit, are an even number.

Example:

	ASCII Code	Binary 1's	Even Parity Bit	Odd Parity Bit
Number 3	33	4	0	1
Alpha H	48	2	0	1
EOT	04	1	1	0

When the user selects the odd parity, then for the 3, H, and EOT the parity bits are set to a 1, 1, and 0, respectively.

110 BAUD
SERIAL ASCII DATA TIMING

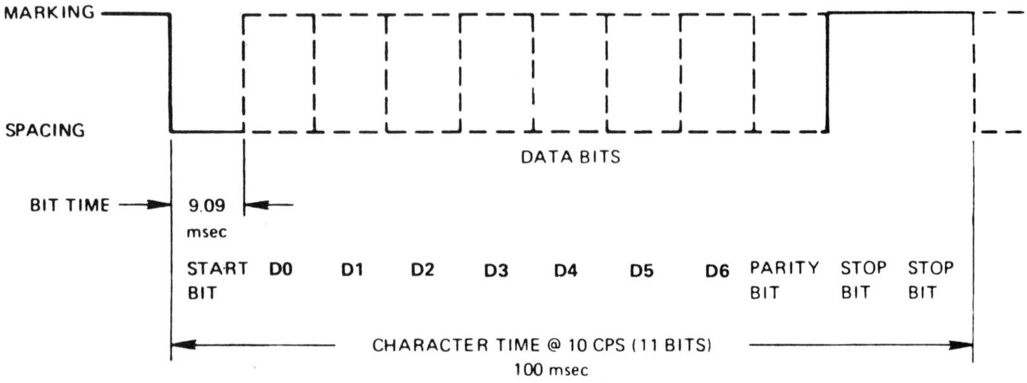

(a) Format with one start, seven character bits, one parity, and two stop bits.

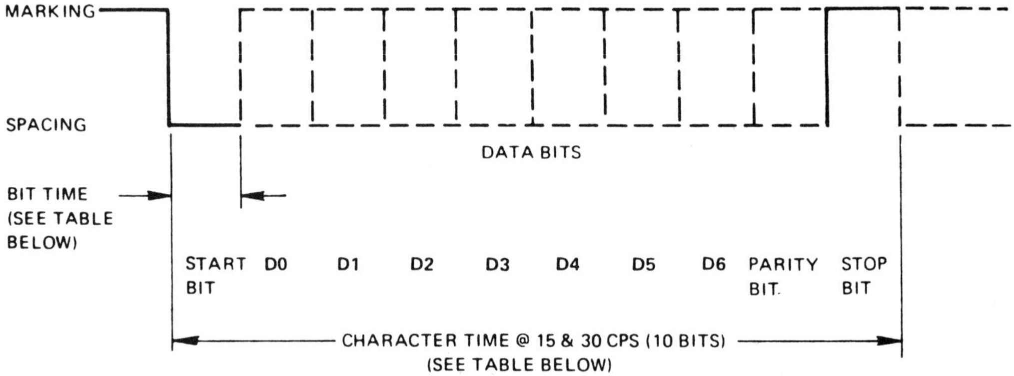

BAUD RATE	150	300
CHARACTERS/SEC	15	30
BIT TIME (msec)	6.67	3.33
CHARACTER TIME (msec)	66.7	33.3

$$\text{BIT TIME} = \frac{\text{SEC}}{\text{BAUD RATE}}$$

150 & 300 BAUD SERIAL ASCII DATA TIMING

(b) Format with one start, seven character bits, one parity, and one stop bit.

Figure 9-1. Two of the eight ACIA formats.

SEND A 7 BIT ASCII CHAR. "H"
EVEN PARITY — 2 STOP BITS
$H = 48_{16} = 1001000_2$

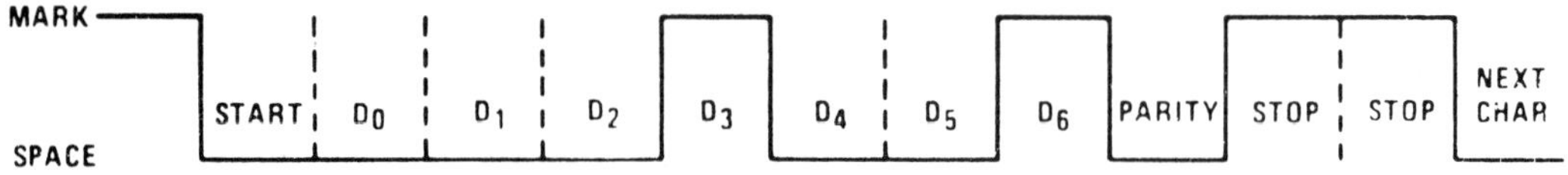

Figure 9-2. Example of ASCII code.

Stop Bit During the one or two stop bits, the signal returns to the mark, or logic 1, state, indicating an end of transmission. This leaves the signal in the mark state, which permits the easy detection of the start of the next character, the mark to space transition.

Baud Rate Timing

The baud rate is the number of bits transmitted per second.

150 baud = 150 bits/s
300 baud = 300 bits/s of transmission

The time or period to transmit each bit is the reciprocal of the baud rate.

150 baud = 6.67 ms/bit
300 baud = 3.33 ms/bit

Often the more important parameter is the rate of character transmission, which is

$$\text{Character transfer rate} = \frac{\text{baud rate}}{\text{number of bits per character}}$$

Since there are generally 10 bits per character transfer at a 300-baud rate transmission, it implies that 30 characters are transmitted per second, and that it takes 33.3 ms to transmit a character. The baud rate selections are 75, 110, 150, 300, 600, 1200, 1800, 2400, 4800, 9600 and 19,200. Note that many of the choices are multiples of 2 and the slowest Baud rate is 75.

Converting Data from Serial to Parallel and Parallel to Serial Form

The ACIA (Fig. 9-3) is used to interface a TTY or terminal that may be either a few feet or many miles away from the microcomputer system. For great distances there is a trade-off between the expensive, parallel, eight-channel (wires) high-speed version, versus the less expensive, slower, single-channel version. The ACIA with two serial channels, one for transmitting and one for receiving, offers a cost-effective solution. In addition, the ACIA provides the parallel to serial, or serial to parallel, conversion of the parallel formatted data on the data bus to the serial I/O lines.

The ACIA is separated into two separate sections, one for transmitting and one for receiving data. To output the ASCII or equivalent coded data, they are loaded into the transmit data register (Fig. 9-3). The data are then automatically transferred by the ACIA to the output shift register if it is empty, and the formatted data are shifted out through the transmit data (TXD) pin. Independently, the formatted serial data are input at the received data (RXD) pin. When all the bits are received, the ASCII, or equivalent data, are transferred to the received data register (RDR), where they are accessible to the program.

Defining and Addressing the Registers of the ACIA

The four registers of the ACIA are the data input and output registers (referred to as the receive and transmit data registers) and the control and status registers. These four registers occupy two memory locations, which implies that the four registers share two memory locations. The receive and transmit data registers share one address, and the control and status registers share the other. The apparent incompatibility is resolved because the receive data register is a read only and the transmit data register is a write only register. The same applies to the control and status registers. The status register is a read only and the control register is a write only register.

The register select (RS) pin selects or addresses the I/O data or the control/status registers. The control/status registers are addressed when the address (Ao) line, which is usually tied to the RS pin, is logic 0, or low, and the I/O data line is addressed when the Ao is 1.

Example: If the ACIA is at locations $8000 and $8001, then

- A write or store into location $8000 loads the control register.
- A read or load from location $8000 accesses the status word.
- To output, store data at location $8001.
- To input, load data from location $8001.

Defining the ACIA Registers

There are four registers in the ACIA: the data input and output registers (sometimes referred to as the I/O buffers) and the control and

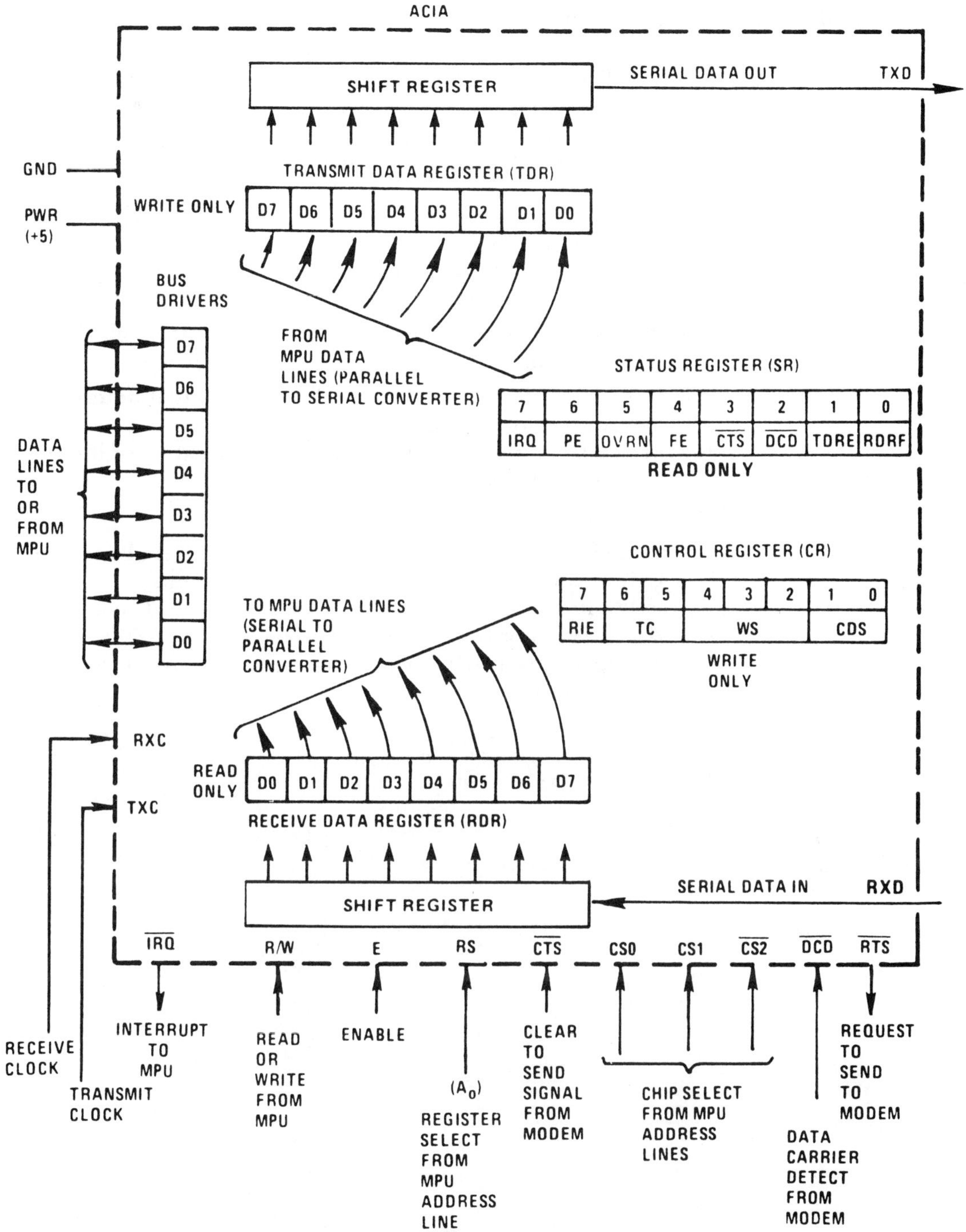

Figure 9-3. Functional diagram of the ACIA (Asynchronous Communications Interface Adapter).

status registers. The data-in register and the control registers are write only registers, where data move from an accumulator to the ACIA. The data-out register and the status registers are read only registers where data move from the ACIA to an accumulator only.

The 24 Pins of the ACIA

The ACIA comes in a 24-pin package (Fig. 9-4):

- Eight data lines that are tied to the data bus D9 through D8.
- Four addressing pins:

  Three chip select lines, CS0, CS1 and CS2, that determine the address of the device.

  One register select pin RS to select the registers of the device. It is tied to address line Ao.
- Three control bus lines:

  Enable (E) line ties to clock 02 and keeps the ACIA in synchronization with the microcomputer system.

  Read/write (R/W) pin, which determines the direction of data flow to or from the microprocessor.

  Interrupt request (IRQ), which passes the interrupt from the ACIA on to the microprocessor.

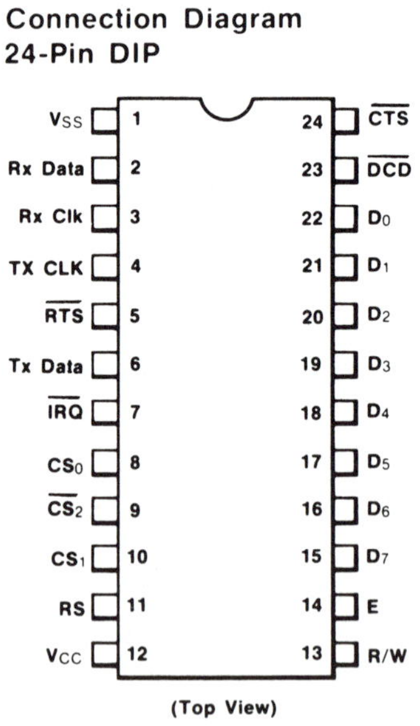

Figure 9-4. The 8 pins of the ACIA.

- Two data I/O lines:

  Serial data out: TXD, TRANSMIT DATA
  Serial data in: RXD, RECEIVE DATA

- Two baud rate clocks, the transmit and receive sections of the ACIA, are independent and have separate clock input pins:

  Receive clock.
  Transmit clock.

- Three ACIA or MODEM interconnection control pins that tie ACIAs together, or the ACIA to a MODEM. These interconnect pins are used to interrogate and test if the terminal they are tied to is active. They are:

  Request to send (RTS), used to indicate to the terminal that the microcomputer system is active, and that the ACIA has been initialized to send and receive characters.
  Clear to send (CTS), used to sense that the terminal is active.
  Data carrier detect (DCD), used to detect that the carrier signal from the MODEM is present.

- Two power pins, +5 V and ground.

Strategy for Programming the ACIA

Prior to using the ACIA, the code, the format, and the baud rate must be agreed upon, and the selector switches in the terminal must be set accordingly. The baud rate is set primarily by the clock input at the receive and transmit clock pins, RXC and TXC, respectively. Two functions of the control register are to select the appropriate format and to select or modify the baud rate.

When terminals are located at great distances from, or just out of sight of, the microcomputer, it might be judicious to confirm that the terminal is turned on and ready to accept data prior to transmitting. Again, the technique must also sense if, during a transmission, either the line breaks down or the terminal is turned off, or either the terminal or the line has broken down. Three lines, the data carrier detect (DCD), the clear to send (CTS) and the request to send (RTS), are tied between the terminal and the microcomputer and are used to sense and control the data flow. The request to send signal is set or reset through the control register and the input signals; the data carrier detect and the clear to send are sensed at the status register. Part of the initializing routine, therefore, is to confirm that the terminal is turned on, and an interrupt may be set to detect that the terminal has been turned off or that either the terminal or the line has broken down.

After the ACIA has been initialized, and during the transmitting, the status register must be examined to find out if the previous output data have been transmitted and that the output register is ready to accept the new data. The status register must also be examined to find out if new input data have been received.

ACIA Control Register

The ACIA control register (Table 9-1) has four fields:

- Character transmit format select bits 2, 3, and 4.
- Counter divide select bits 0 and 1.
- Transmitter control bits 5 and 6.
- Interrupt enable bit 7.

Character Transmit Format Select The ACIA offers the user eight different transmit formats, listed in Table 9-1(c). In each case the programmer must coordinate the selection with the terminal or the communicating device. The 7-bit character is generally reserved for ASCII characters and the 8-bit character for EBCDIC code, respectively.

Counter Divide Select Bits 0 and 1 The counter divide selection bits (Table 9-1b) offer the user three programmable choices: divide by 1, 16, or 64. The basic, or divide by 1, selection is the input transmit (TXC) and receive (RXC) clocks. For example, if the basic input clock is 9600 Hz, the divide by 16 selects a 600-baud rate and the divide by 64 selects a 150-Baud rate.

The ACIA is reset by programming the counter divide select bits to 1's. The ACIA is reset by resetting the status register to 0's, except for the $\overline{CTS}$ and $\overline{DCD}$ bits, which are tied directly to and reflect the status of the $\overline{CTS}$ and $\overline{DCD}$ input pins.

Transmitter Control Bits 5 and 6 ($\overline{RTS}$) The transmit control bits (Table 9-1d) are used in systems where modems and other computers of the system are not in proximity with the microcomputer, and the user requires a means to confirm that they are connected and operating. In these cases the program must first test the transmitter control bits before commencing the transmission. This function is performed with the $\overline{RTS}$ output signal in conjunction with the input $\overline{CTS}$ and $\overline{DCD}$ signals.

During normal transmission, the ACIA is programmed to pull the $\overline{RTS}$ signal low and senses that the $\overline{CTS}$ and $\overline{DCD}$ signals are pulled low by the terminal or other device. If either the $\overline{CTS}$ or $\overline{DCD}$ signals goes high, it indicates that either the terminal has shut down or broken down. Likewise, the microcomputer indicates that it is shut down by forcing the $\overline{RTS}$ signal high.

A typical sequence by the transmitter control bits might be as follows:

Table 9-1. ACIA Control Register (CR)

(a) Bits of the Control Register

7	6	5	4	3	2	1	0
RIE	Transmitter Control		Word Select			Counter Divide	

(b) Counter Divide Field

CR_1	CR_0	Function
0	0	÷1
0	1	÷16
1	0	÷64
1	1	Master Reset

(c) Word Select Field

CR_4	CR_3	CR_2	Function
0	0	0	7 Bits + Even Parity + 2 Stop Bits
0	0	1	7 Bits + Odd Parity + 2 Stop Bits
0	1	0	7 Bits + Even Parity + 1 Stop Bit
0	1	1	7 Bits + Odd Parity + 1 Stop Bit
1	0	0	8 Bits + 2 Stop Bits
1	0	1	8 Bits + 1 Stop Bit
1	1	0	8 Bits + Even Parity + 1 Stop Bit
1	1	1	8 Bits + Odd Parity + 1 Stop Bit

(d) Transmitter Control Bits

CR_6	CR_5	Function
0	0	$\overline{RTS}$ = LOW, Transmitting Interrupt Disabled
0	1	$\overline{RTS}$ = LOW, Transmitting Interrupt Enabled
1	0	$\overline{RTS}$ = HIGH, Transmitting Interrupt Disabled
1	1	$\overline{RTS}$ = LOW, Transmits a Break Level on the Transmit Data Output. Transmitting Interrupt Disabled.

- Start with the $\overline{\text{RTS}}$ low, indicating that the ACIA is on, but not yet ready to respond. The interrupt is inhibited. Bits 6 and 5 are 00.
- Interrogate the $\overline{\text{CTS}}$ or $\overline{\text{DCD}}$ for a low signal to test if the terminal/modem is active.
- If active, then force bits 6, 5, to 01, and enable interrupts if the terminal or modem becomes inactive. This is the normal operating mode. When bits 6 and 5 are coded 10, it sets the $\overline{\text{RTS}}$ signal high, indicating that the microcomputer is shut down.

Receive Interrupt Enable Bit 7 A 1 in bit 7 enables an interrupt when:

- The receive data register is full; status bit 0 is set.
- An overrun occurred; status bit 5 is set.
- The transmit/receiving device becomes inactive, a low-to-high transit at the $\overline{\text{DCD}}$ pin; status bit 2 is set.

Status Register

The status register, a read only register, is used to check the status of the ACIA:

Bit 0	RDRF	Receive data register full indicates that the input buffer stores input data when set. It is cleared by a load from the receive data register.
Bit 1	TDRE	Transmit data register empty indicates that the output buffer is empty and can accept the next output byte of data when set. It is automatically cleared by a store to transmit data register until the data have been transmitted.
Bit 2	$\overline{\text{DCD}}$	Data carrier detect indicates the state of input pin $\overline{\text{DCD}}$.
Bit 3	$\overline{\text{CTS}}$	Clear to send indicates the state of the input pin $\overline{\text{CTS}}$.
Bit 4	FE	Framing error indicates that a discrepancy in the baud rate has been detected by the absence of the first stop bit.
Bit 5	RO	Receive overrun error indicates that the next data word started through the input RXD pin before the data in the serial input data register were transferred to the input buffer, and overran and invalidated. The overrun error is set after the valid input data in the input buffer are read.
Bit 6	PE	Parity error indicates a parity error.
Bit 7	IRQ	Interrupt request bit indicates that either:

- the input data buffer is full, or
- there is an overrun error, or
- a positive transition at the $\overline{\text{DCD}}$ pin.

9-2 EXAMPLE OF USING AN ACIA TO INTERFACE A TERMINAL AS THE I/O DEVICE TO THE MICROCOMPUTER PROGRAMMED AS A CALCULATOR

This section describes how to interface a microcomputer to a terminal using an ACIA. The calculator system program in Chapter 7 is used with the keyboard and 7-segment display for the I/O devices, and they are here replaced by a terminal. The terminal offers two advantages for expanding the system, first by having many more function keys available and, second, by easily displaying more than twice the number of digits of the 7-segment display.

This section describes three routines:

- Initializing routine
- ASCII input routine
- ASCII ECHO and output routine

Each routine is part of a practical example, and the I/O programs particularly are supported by the necessary formatting routines.

Initializing the ACIA

Before initializing, the code, the format, and the baud rate to be used between the terminal and the ACIA must be agreed upon. In this example the baud rate is 1200 and the receive and transmit clocks are set at 18,400 Hz, requiring that the count divide field be set to 16. Generally, clock drives function more effectively at the higher frequencies, and the countdown field makes the clock compatible with the desired lower baud rate. The field selected has the following:

- 7-bit ASCII code
- Odd parity
- 2 stop bits

Assume that the control and status registers at location $8008 are labeled ACIACS and that the transmit and receive registers at location $8009 are labeled ACIATR. The initializing routine begins by resetting the status register, that is, all but the $\overline{\text{DCD}}$ and $\overline{\text{CTS}}$ status bits, which are tied to their respective input pins. This clears the error status bits and the transmit and receive indicators.

Next, the divide counter and the word select field set the baud rate and the appropriate format. During this time the transmitter control bits pull the $\overline{\text{RTS}}$ line low, indicating to the terminal that the microcomputer is ready to transmit and receive data. The interrupt is inhibited from occurring during this time.

The $\overline{\text{DCD}}$ and $\overline{\text{CTS}}$ bits are examined; if they are low, the program stays in the TERMUP loop forever, without indicating the reason for the holdup to the operator. By building an indicator onto a microcomputer, the operator can be informed of the reason for the impasse. If, however, the $\overline{\text{DCD}}$ and $\overline{\text{CTS}}$ lines, which are not included in this routine, are pulled low, the transmitter control bits are set to permit interrupts and the ACIA is initialized.

Terminal Input Data Routine

This subroutine (Fig. 9-5 and listing on page 298, line 48,) senses an input from a terminal, stores it to be ECHOed back to the terminal, and then converts it from an ASCII to a hex code, which is compatible with the internal code used by the calculator described in Chapter 7. It then stores that code in accumulator A before returning from the subroutine. The ECHO is transmitted back to the terminal screen in the terminal output routine. The terminal input data routine labeled TERM described in this section may be used to replace the KEYIN subroutine from Chapter 7, which inputs data from a keyboard. The calculator system is described in Chapter 7. Table 9-2 lists the 20 permissible key inputs, the ASCII, and equivalent hex code used by the calculator. All other input keys are ignored.

The routine starts by examining the receive data register full (RDRF) status bits. Most of the time this program remains in this loop searching for an input. Next, the three error bits are tested. If there is an error, the program branches to an error routine, which is not described, or proceeds. The routine tests for a number input, which is the ASCII code from \$30 to \$39. If there is a number input, the program branches to number and is labeled NUMBIN. The ten remaining keys have random ASCII codes, which must be converted to an ordered hex number from \$0A to \$13. The ASCII codes for the input keys are listed in the table TERKEY in the same order as the hex codes for the function keys. Accumulator A is loaded with the \$0A constant, which is at the top of Table 9-2. The input ASCII code in accumulator B is then sequentially compared to the ASCII keys listed in the table, while the contents of accumulator A are incremented. When the ASCII input matches the code for the key in the table, then the contents of accumulator A would have been incremented to the appropriate hex code used by the calculator. The program then branches to a valid key input labeled TERMIN. If, however, there is no match with any of the

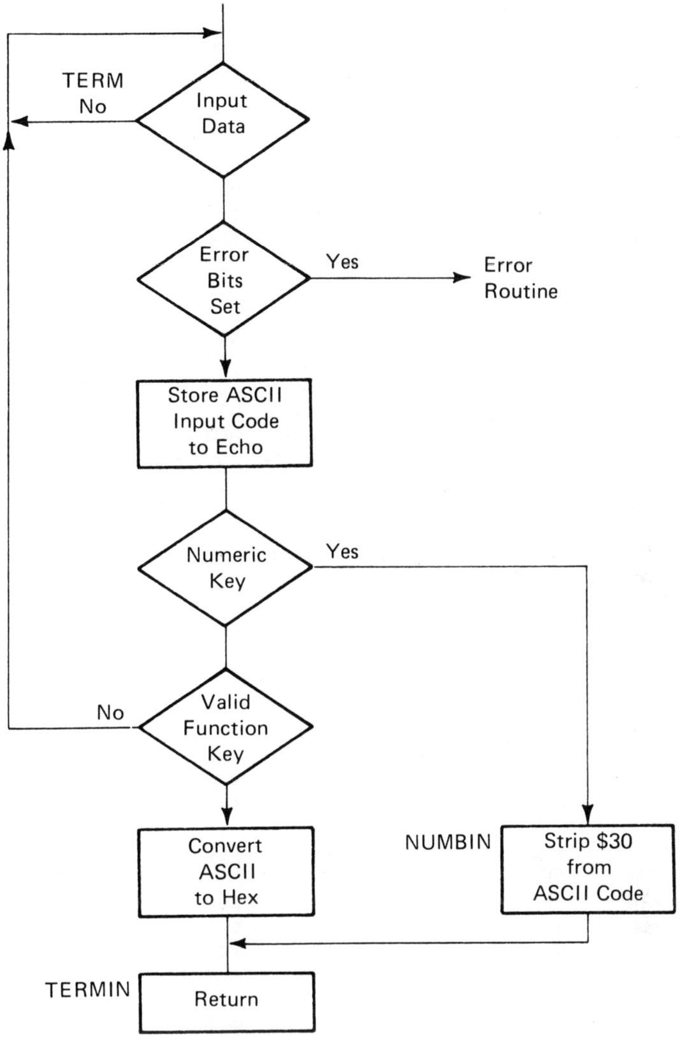

Figure 9-5. ASCII input routine.

ten permissible input keys, the program branches back to TERM and continues to scan for a key input.

If the input is a numeric key and the program has branches to NUMBIN, then $30 is masked from the ASCII code for the number key leaving its hex code equivalent; the code is then transferred from accumulator B to A.

```
                        * INITIALIZE THE ACIA: TO DIVIDE THE CLOCK BY 16,
                        * 7-BITS OF DATA, ODD PARITY, & 2 STOP-BITS.
                        * SEE SECTION 9.2
                        *
            8008   A ACIACS EQU    $8008    CONTROL/STATUS REGISTERS
            8009   A ACIATR EQU    $8009    DATA TRANSFER (I/O) REG
                        *
0003                          ORG    03
0003        0001   A NEWKEY RMB    1        KEY CODE FOR CALCULATOR
0008                          ORG    $08
0008        0002   A SPOINT RMB    2        SAVE SOURCE POINTER
000A        0002   A DPOINT RMB    2        SAVE DESTINATION POINTER
                        *   ORG $50
000C 86 03         A ACIA   LDAA   #$03     0000 0011
000E B7 8008       A        STAA   ACIACS   INIT STATUS REG
                        * SELECT CLOCK DIVIDE COUNT AND FORMAT
0011 86 05         A        LDAA   #$05     0000 0101
0013 B7 8008       A        STAA   ACIACS
                        * CHECK IF THE TERMINAL IS UP & RUNNING
0016 B6 8008       A TERMUP LDAA   ACIACS   TEST DCD & CTS BITS
0019 85 0C         A        BITA   #$0C     0000 1100
001B 26 F9 0016             BNE    TERMUP   KEEP CHECKING
                        * SET CONTROL BIT TO ENABLE AN INTERRUPT
001D 86 25         A        LDAA   #$25     0010 0101
001F B7 8008       A        STAA   ACIACS
                        * THE ACIA IS READY
                        *
0022 20 0D 0031             BRA    TERM     GO TO TERMINAL INPUT
                        *
                        * THE ASCII CODE FOR NUMBERS 0-9 ARE $30-$39
                        * LOOK-UP TABLE FOR KEYBOARD FUNCTIONS
0024        2E     A TERKEY FCB    $2E      DP          (.)
0025        53     A        FCB    $53      CHANGE SIGN (S)
0026        2B     A        FCB    $2B      ADD         (+)
0027        2D     A        FCB    $2D      SUBTRACT    (-)
0028        58     A        FCB    $58      MULTIPLY    (X)
0029        2F     A        FCB    $2F      DIVIDE      (/)
002A        45     A        FCB    $45      ENTER       (E)
002B        47     A        FCB    $47      EXCHANGE    (G)
002C        43     A        FCB    $43      CLEAR       (C)
002D        08     A        FCB    $08      BACK SPACE
002E        60     A        FCB    $60      BLANK (SPACE)
002F        0D     A        FCB    $0D      CARRIAGE RETURN (CR)
0030        0A     A        FCB    $0A      LINE FEED (LF)
                        *
                        *
                        *
                        * TERMINAL INPUT DATA ROUTINE. SEE FIG 9.5.
                        * TEST STATUS REGISTER FOR INPUT DATA
0031 B6 8008       A TERM   LDAA   ACIACS   GET STATUS WORD
0034 85 01         A        BITA   #$01     TEST RECEIVE DATA REG FULL
0036 27 F9 0031             BEQ    TERM     KEEP TESTING FOR DATA
0038 85 70         A        BITA   #$70     TEST 3 ERROR BITS
003A 26 25 0061             BNE    ERRO     BR TO ERROR ROUTINE
                        * INPUT KEY DATA
```

```
                         * & SAVE TO ECHO BACK DURING OUTPUT ROUTINE
A 003C B6 8009  A              LDAA   ACIATR   GET INPUT DATA
A 003F 97 00    A              STAA   $00      SAVE INPUT DATA
                         * TEST FOR NUMBER KEY FROM $30 TO #39
A 0041 81 30    A              CMPA   #$30     CMP FOR LESS THEN $30
A 0043 25 04 0049              BCS    FUNKEY   BR TO FUNCTION KEY
A 0045 81 39    A              CMPA   #$39     CMP FOR GT THEN $3A
A 0047 23 12 005B              BLS    NUMBIN   BR TO NUMBER KEY
                         * FUNCTION KEY INPUT
A 0049 16                FUNKEY TAB            INPUT CODE => ACC B
A 004A 86 10    A              LDAA   #$10     LOWEST FUNCTION KEY CODE
A 004C CE 0024  A              LDX    #TERKEY  ADDR OF LOOK-UP TABLE
A 004F E1 00    A        FUNK1 CMPB   0,X      CMP INPUT & TABLE CODES
A 0051 27 0A 005D              BEQ    TERMIN   DATA IN VALID, EXIT
A 0053 4C                      INCA            INC KEY CODE
A 0054 08                      INX             INC POINTER
A 0055 81 20    A              CMPA   #$20     END OF TABLE
A 0057 26 F6 004F              BNE    FUNK1    TEST NEXT KEY CODE
A 0059 20 D6 0031              BRA    TERM     ELSE KEEP SAMPLING KEYBD
                         * MUMERIC INPUT KEY
A 005B 84 0F    A        NUMBIN ANDA  #$0F     STRIP #$30 FROM ASCII CODE
                         * RETURN TO MAIN ROUTINE WITH KEY CODE IN ACC A
A 005D 39                TERMIN RTS
                         *
A 005E 7E 0110  A        ECEXIT JMP   EEXIT    JMP > 128 LOCATIONS
A 0061 7E 013B  A        ERRO   JMP   ERRRO    JMP > 128 LOCATIONS
                         *
                         *
                         *
                         * DATA OUTPUT ROUTINE, SEE FIG 9.6
                         * CHECK STATUS REGISTER IF OUTPUT REGISTER FULL
                         *
A 0064 F6 8008  A        ECHO   LDAB  ACIACS   GET STATUS REGISTER
A 0067 C5 02    A               BITB  #$02     TEST TRANSMIT REG
A 0069 26 F9 0064               BNE   ECHO     KEEP TESTING
                         * GET ASCII INPUT CODE TO ECHO
A 006B D6 00    A               LDAB  $00
A 006D F7 8009  A               STAB  ACIATR   ECHO INPUT DATA
                         * TEST INPUT KEY FOR: NUMERIC, DP, CHANGE SIGN,
                         * OR BACK SPACE
                         * TEST (NEWKEY) THE CONVERTED ASCII CODE
A 0070 96 03    A               LDAA  NEWKEY   GET CONVERTED CODE
A 0072 81 0B    A               CMPA  #$0B     TEST FOR NUMBER
A 0074 23 E8 005E               BLS   ECEXIT   EXIT IF NUMBER KEY
A 0076 81 13    A               CMPA  #$13     BACK SPACE
A 0078 27 E4 005E               BEQ   ECEXIT
                         * OUTPUT CR,LF, & 10 BLANKS
A 007A BD 0111  A               JSR   LFEED    LINE FEED
                         * TEST FOR ENTER, EXCHANGE, OR CLEAR KEYS
A 007D 81 10    A               CMPA  #$10
A 007F 23 DD 005E               BLS   ECEXIT
A 0081 BD 0111  A               JSR   LFEED    LINE FEED
                         * IF THE INPUT WAS A ARIITHMETIC FUNTTION KEY
                         * FORMAT THE OUTPUT DATA
                         * THERE ARE FOUR PHASES FOR FORMATTING
```

```
                        *   1. TRANSFER DATA TO THE OUTPUT REGISTER
                        *   2. INSERT THE DP IF APPROPRIATE
                        *   3. BLANK THE LEADING ZEROS
                        *   4. INSERT A NEGATIVE SIGN IF APPROPRIATE
                        *
                        * PHASE 1.  UNPACK 8-DIGITS FROM D-REGISTER
                        * LOCATIONS $28 TO $2B, & TRANSFER TO OUTREG
                        * AT LOCATIONS $30 TO $39
A 0084 CE 0030   A AFORM   LDX    #$0030   DESTINATION REG
A 0087 DF 0A     A         STX    DPOINT   SAVE
A 0089 CE 0028   A         LDX    #$0028   SOURCE REG
A 008C DF 08     A         STX    SPOINT   SAVE
A 008E 7F 0000   A         CLR    $0000    CLEAR ODD/EVEN INDICATOR
A 0091 C6 08     A         LDAB   #$08     BYTE COUNT
A 0093 D7 05     A         STAB   $05      SAVE SIZE
                        * GET PACKED DATA FROM SOURCE REG
A 0095 DE 08     A AFORM1  LDX    SPOINT
A 0097 A6 00     A         LDAA   0,X      GET PACKED DIGITS
                        * TEST ODD/EVEN INDICATOR
                        * 00 INDICATES ODD & FF INDICATES EVEN
                        * THE STATE OF THE FLAG IS FLIPPED WHEN TESTED
A 0099 C6 FF     A         LDAB   #$FF
A 009B D8 00     A         EORB   $00      TEST & FLIP FLAG
A 009D D7 00     A         STAB   $00      SAVE O/E FLAG
A 009F 26 18 00B9          BNE    ADEVEN   BR TO EVEN DIGIT
                        * ELSE PROCESS ODD DIGIT
A 00A1 84 0F     A         ANDA   #$0F     MASK ODD DIGIT
                        * MERGE WITH EVEN BRANCH
A 00A3 DF 08     A ADIS1   STX    SPOINT   SAVE POINTER
                        *
                        * CONVERT NUMBERS TO ASCII EQUIVALENT BY ORING $3
A 00A5 9A 30     A         ORAA   $30
                        * GET OUTPUT REGISTER POINTER
A 00A7 DE 0A     A         LDX    DPOINT
A 00A9 A7 00     A         STAA   0,X      STORE ASCII CODE IN OUTREG
A 00AB 08                  INX             INC D POINTER
A 00AC DF 0A     A         STX    DPOINT   SAVE POINTER
A 00AE 8C 0039   A         CPX    #$0039   TEST FOR LAST DIGIT
A 00B1 26 E2 0095          BNE    AFORM1
                        * INSERT ASCII LEADING ZERO IN MSDIGIT
A 00B3 86 30     A         LDAA   #$30
A 00B5 A7 00     A         STAA   0,X
A 00B7 20 07 00C0          BRA    ADIS10   BR TO PHASE 2
                        * EVEN DIGIT
A 00B9 44          ADEVEN  LSRA
A 00BA 44                  LSRA
A 00BB 44                  LSRA
A 00BC 44                  LSRA
A 00BD 08                  INX             INC SOURCE POINTER
A 00BE 20 E3 00A3          BRA    ADIS1
                        *
                        * PHASE 2. LOAD DP
A 00C0 96 2C     A ADIS10  LDAA   $2C      GET D-EXPONENT
A 00C2 4D                  TSTA            TEST EXP EQ ZERO
A 00C3 27 17 00DC          BEQ    ADIS20   EXIT IF ZERO
```

```
                           * DETERMINE WHERE TO INSERT THE DP
                           * LOAD INDEX REGISTER WITH $0030 PLUS EXPONENT
                           * LOAD NUMBER OF DIGITS LEFT OF DP INTO ACC B
00C5 CE 0030   A                  LDX    #$0030
00C8 C6 09     A                  LDAB   #$09      SIZE OF OUTPUT REG
00CA 08                    ADIS11 INX              INC POINTER TO $30 + EXP
00CB 5A                           DECB             DEC SIZE OF OUTREG - EXP
00CC 4A                           DECA             DEC TO ZERO & STOP
00CD 26 FB 00CA                   BNE    ADIS11
00CF D7 05     A                  STAB   $05       SAVE NUMBER OF DIGITS
00D1 DF 08     A                  STX    SPOINT    SAVE LOCATION OFF DP
                           * JUMP TO SHIFT LEFT DIGIT SUBROUTINE, CHAPTER 6
00D3 BD 013C   A                  JSR    SHLFD
                           * INSERT DP
00D6 DE 08     A                  LDX    SPOINT
00D8 86 2E     A                  LDAA   #$2E      ASCII CODE FOR DP
00DA A7 00     A                  STAA   0,X       INSERT DP
                           *
                           * PHASE 3. BLANK LEADING ZEROS
00DC CE 0039   A ADIS20 LDX    #$39      POINTER TO MSDIGIT
00DF C6 60     A                  LDAB   #$60      ASCII BLANK (SPACE BAR)
                           * REPLACE ZERO ($30) WITH BLANK ($60)
00E1 A6 00     A ADIS21 LDAA   0,X       GET LEADING DI CHARACTERS
00E3 81 30     A                  CMPA   #$30      TEST FOR ASCII ZERO
00E5 26 08 00EF                   BNE    ADIS30    EXIT IF NON-ZERO
00E7 E7 00     A                  STAB   0,X       ELSE REPLACE
00E9 09                           DEX
00EA 8C 0030   A                  CPX    #$0030    TEST LSDIGIT
00ED 26 F2 00E1                   BNE    ADIS21    KEEP INSERTING BLANKS
                           *
                           * PHASE 4. TEST FOR NEGATIVE
00EF 96 2D     A ADIS30 LDAA   $2D       GET SIGN OF D
00F1 4D                           TSTA             TEST FOR POSITIVE SIGN
00F2 27 04 00F8                   BEQ    ADIS31    EXIT IF POSITIVE
00F4 86 2D     A                  LDAA   #$2D      ASCII NEGATIVE SIGN
00F6 A7 01     A                  STAA   1,X       INSERT AT POINTER + 1
                           *
                           * OUTPUT ASCII DATA
00F8 CE 0039   A ADIS31 LDX    #$39      MSDIGIT
00FB B6 8008   A                  LDAA   ACIACS    GET STATUS REG
00FE 85 02     A                  BITA   #$02      TEST OUTREG READY
0100 27 F6 00F8                   BEQ    ADIS31    KEEP TESTING
0102 A6 00     A                  LDAA   0,X       GET DATA
0104 B7 8009   A                  STAA   ACIATR    OUTPUT DATA
0107 09                           DEX
0108 8C 002F   A                  CPX    #$2F      TEST FOR LAST DIGIT
010B 26 EB 00F8                   BNE    ADIS31
010D BD 0111   A                  JSR    LFEED     LINE FEED
0110 39                    EEXIT  RTS
                           *
                           * SUBROUTINE LINE FEED
0111 B6 8008   A LFEED  LDAA   ACIACS    GET STATUS REG
0114 85 02     A                  BITA   #$02      TEST OUTPUT REG READY
0116 26 F9 0111                   BNE    LFEED     KEEP TESTING
0118 86 0D     A                  LDAA   #$0D      CARRIAGE RETURN
```

```
00221A 011A B7 8009   A          STAA    ACIATR    OUTPUT CR
00222A 011D B6 8008   A LFEED1 LDAA    ACIACS
00223A 0120 85 02     A          BITA    #$02
00224A 0122 26 F9 011D           BNE     LFEED1
00225A 0124 86 0A     A          LDAA    #$0A      LINE FEED
00226A 0126 B7 8009   A          STAA    ACIATR    OUTPUT LF
00227                   * INSET TEN BLANKS
00228A 0129 C6 0A     A          LDAB    #$0A
00229A 012B B6 8008   A LFEED2 LDAA    ACIACS
00230A 012E 95 02     A          BITA    02
00231A 0130 26 F9 012B           BNE     LFEED2
00232A 0132 86 60     A          LDAA    #$60      LOAD BLANK
00233A 0134 B7 8009   A          STAA    ACIATR    OUTPUT BLANK
00234A 0137 5A                   DECB              DEC COUNT
00235A 0138 26 F1 012B           BNE     LFEED2
00236A 013A 39                   RTS
00237                   *
00238                   * DUMMY INSTRUCTIONS
00239                   *
00240A 013B 01          ERRRO  NOP
00241A 013C 39          SHLFD  RTS
00242                   *
```

Table 9-2. Keyboard to Terminal to ASCII to Hex Code Equivalent

Key Name	Keyboard Key	Terminal Key	ASCII Code	Calculator Hex Code
0	0	0	30	00
1	1	1	31	01
2	2	2	32	02
3	3	3	33	03
4	4	4	34	04
5	5	5	35	05
6	6	6	36	06
7	7	7	37	07
8	8	8	38	08
9	9	9	39	09
Decimal point	.	.	2E	0A
Change sign	C/S	S	53	0B
Add	+	+	2B	0C
Subtract	−	−	2D	0D
Multiply	×	×	58	0E
Divide	÷	/	2F	0F
Enter	E	E	45	10
Exchange	EX	G	47	11
Clear	C	C	43	12
Clear entry	CE	Back space	08	13

Table 9-3. Output Only ASCII Codes

Key Name	Keyboard Key	Terminal Key	ASCII Code	Calculator Hex Code
Space	—	Blank	60	14
Carriage return	—	CR	0D	15
Line feed	—	LF	0A	16

ASCII Output Routine

There are three different paths in the ASCII output routine (Fig. 9-6 and listing on page 299, line 85), that respond to the last input key for the following:

Path I	Numeric keys and clear entry
Path II	Enter, exchange, and clear keys
Path III	Arithmetic keys

All the input keys pass through path I, whereas the ASCII input code that was stored away is retrieved from memory and ECHOed or output to the terminal. If the input key is a numeric key, which includes the decimal point, or change sign key, or the backspace key, then exit from the routine. When the routine continues after echoing, the subroutine is called, which outputs the carriage return (CR), line feed (LF), and ten blanks to center the numbers on the display. (See Table 9-3.) At this point, if either the enter, exchange, or clear keys were entered, path II exits from the routine. After echoing and outputting the carriage return, line feed, and ten blanks, the terminal is positioned to output the result of the arithmetic operation nearer the center of the screen. If not, then more than ten blanks should be used. In path III the result of the arithmetic operation is output, and then the routine outputs another carriage return, line feed, and ten blanks to position the next display near the center of the screen.

Output Format Routine

The output format routine (Fig. 9-7) converts the decimal data in the D register at memory locations \$28 to \$2D, mantissa, and exponent and sign, to ASCII code in the output register, locations \$30 to \$39. See Chapter 6, where decimal data in the D register are converted to 7-segment data in the output register. The output format has four phases (Fig. 9-7):

- Unpack the mantissa and insert leading zeros in output register.
- Insert decimal point.

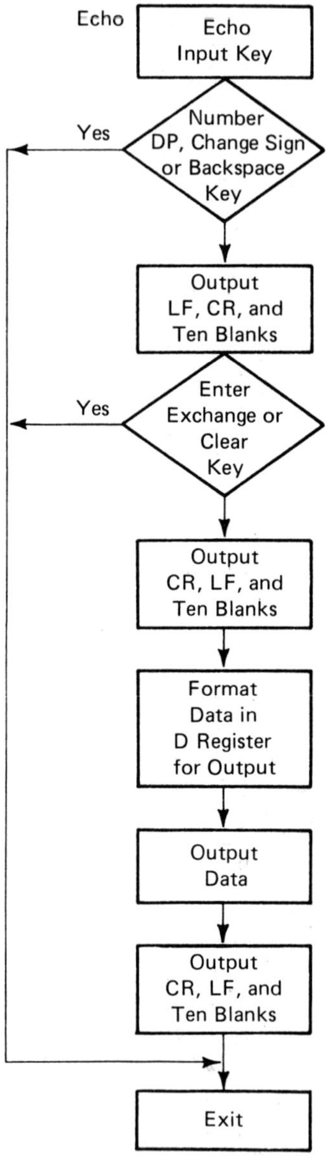

Figure 9-6. ASCII output routine.

- Blank leading zeros.
- Insert negative sign, if required.

After the output data are formatted, the ASCII data are output after the ten blanks center the data on the display. The line feed routine is then called again, which outputs a carriage return, line feed, and ten blanks.

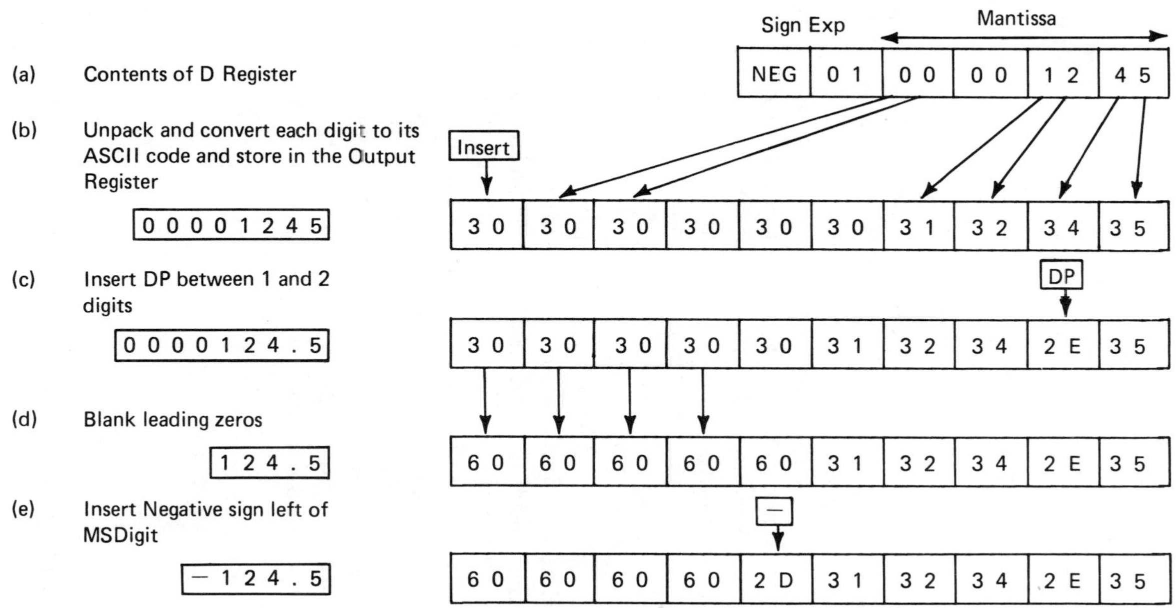

Figure 9-7. Example of the formatting sequence to display −123.4.

9-3 USING THE PIA AS THE INTERFACE WITH A TERMINAL

This section describes how to use a PIA as the interface device between a terminal and the microcomputer (Fig. 9-8 and listing on page 308) in lieu of the ACIA. The two objectives of this section are, first, to serve as an example of the PIA in Chapter 3, and, second, to illustrate the benefits of the ACIA that otherwise might not be appreciated. The three routines in this section are as follows:

- Initializing the PIA
- Receiving data routine
- Transmitting data routine

In the transmit routine the ASCII character stored in accumulator A is imbedded appropriately between the start and parity bits, plus the stop bits. However, the receive routine, first sensing the start of a new character, strips the start, parity, and stop bits, leaving the ASCII character in accumulator A. A timer is used to measure the bit time, which is the reciprocal of the baud rate. During the transmit routine, as each bit is output, a time subroutine measures the bit time before outputting the next bit. With the receive routine, after the start of transmission is sensed, each input bit is sensed at the midpoint of the bit as measured by half the bit time.

Port B of the PIA is used for the parallel-to-serial and the serial-to-parallel conversion of data for outputting and inputting data between a terminal and the microcomputer, respectively. Pin 0 of Port B is the outpin pin and pin 7 of Port B is the input pin. When data are not being transmitted from pin 0, it should be at the high or mark state, and care must be exercised not to disturb it while data are being received at pin 7. The remaining pins, 1 to 6, of Port B are used for the serial-to-parallel and the parallel-to-serial conversion.

The organization of this machine is such that it responds to an input from the terminal keyboard and then goes to a loop that samples the input line and waits for the next input. It presumes that the operator does not input another key before the ECHO is displayed. The sequence of events is as follows:

Receiving	Transmitting
Sense the beginning of a character	
Wait half the baud period—to sense at the middle of each bit	
Test start bit	Output a start bit
	Load Port B with ASCII code bits 0 to 6
Load Port B with $FF	

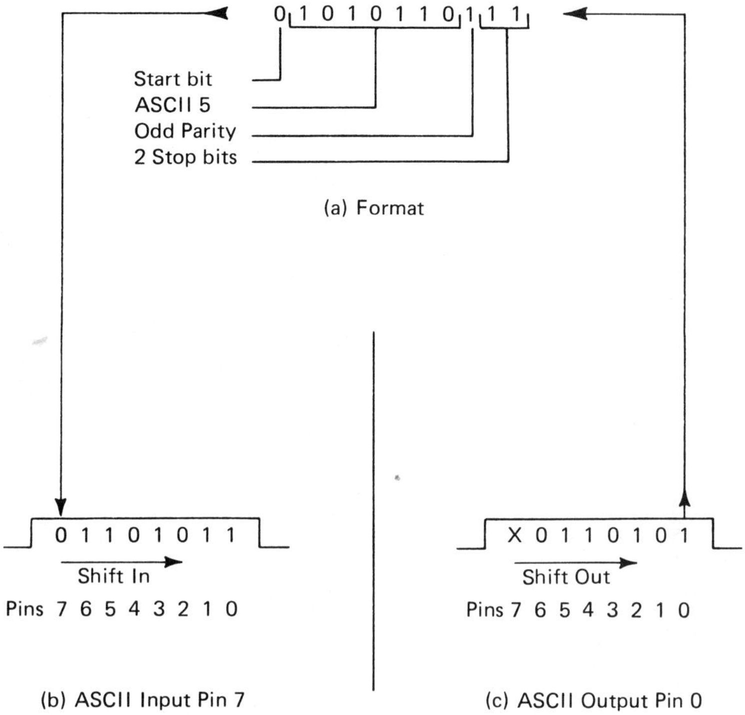

Figure 9-8. Using a PIA port to interface with a terminal.

Input loop	Output loop
Input ASCII bit at Port B, pin 7	Output ASCII bit at Port B, pin 6
Generate parity	Generate parity
Wait baud period	Wait baud period
Shift right ASCII code in Port B	Shift right ASCII code in Port B
If seven ASCII bits not yet received, branch back to input loop	If seven ASCII bits not yet transmitted, branch back to output loop
Input parity bit	Output parity bit
Compare input parity bit with generated parity bit	
Input stop bits	Output stop bits

```
                         * THESE SUBROUTINES USE A PIA AS THE INTERFACE
                         * BETWEEN A TERMINAL & THE MICROPROCESSOR.
                         * SEE SECTION 9.3 & FIG 9.8.
                         * USE PORT B AT LOCATION $8002.
                         * THE PIA IS AT LOCATION $8000, & CONTROL
                         * REGISTER B IS AT LOCATION &8003.
                         *
0010                             ORG     $10
            8002   A PORTB   EQU     $8002     THE I/O PORT
            8003   A PORTBC  EQU     $8003     CONTROL REG, PORT B
                         *
                         * PIN 7 IS THE INPUT PIN FROM THE TERMINAL,
                         * PINS 0 - 6 ARE OUTPUT PINS, & OUTPUT
                         * DATA FLOWS TO THE TERMINAL THRU PIN 0.
                         * PORT B HAS A BUFFERED OUTPUT, SO THAT DATA
                         * AT PINS 0 - 6 ARE NOT AFFECTED BY ANY ACTIVITY
                         * AT THE I/O PINS.   PIN 7 IS THE ONLY INPUT.
                         * INITIALIZE THE PIA
                         *
0010 7F 8003   A PIAINT  CLR     PORTBC    CLEAR CONTROL REG
0013 86 7F     A         LDAA    #$7F
0015 B7 8002   A         STAA    PORTB     LOAD DATA DIRECTION REG
0018 C6 04     A         LDAB    #$04
001A F7 8003   A         STAB    PORTBC    SET BIT CRB-2
001D B6 8002   A         LDAA    PORTB     OUTPUT A MARK
0020 39                  RTS
                         *
                         *
                         * TRANSMIT ASCII CHARACTER AT PORT B, PIN 0, PB0
                         * THE ASCII CHARACTER IS IN ACC A, WITH
                         * A START BIT, 7-BITS, ODD PARITY, 2-STOP BITS.
                         *
0021 7F 8002   A PIATR   CLR     PORTB     OUTPUT START BIT
                         * CALL BIT TIME SUBROUTINE
0024 BD 0085   A         JSR     PERIOD    BIT TIME
0027 B7 8002   A         STAA    PORTB     ASCII CHAR TO PORT B
                         * THE LSBIT IS OUTPUT
002A C6 07     A         LDAB    #$07      BIT COUNT
002C BD 0085   A PIATR1  JSR     PERIOD    BIT TIME
002F 74 8002   A         LSR     PORTB     SH LEFT, OUTPUT NEXT BIT
0032 B8 8002   A         EORA    PORTB     GENERATE PARITY IN ACCA
0035 5A                  DECB              DEC BIT COUNT
0036 26 F4 002C          BNE     PIATR1
                         * NOW OUTPUT PARITY BIT
0038 43                  COMA              COMPLEMENT PARITY BIT
0039 B7 8002   A         STAA    PORTB
003C BD 0085   A         JSR     PERIOD    PARITY TIME
                         * OUTPUT TWO STOP BITS
003F 86 01     A         LDAA    #$01
0041 B7 8002   A         STAA    PORTB
0044 BD 0085   A         JSR     PERIOD    1ST STOP BIT
0047 BD 0085   A         JSR     PERIOD    2ND STOP BIT
004A 39                  RTS
                         *
                         *
```

```
                          * RECEIVE ASCII CHARACTER AT PORT B, PIN 7, PB7
                          * ASSUME THAT THE INPUT PIN IS AT MARK '1'
                          * PUT ASCII CHARACTER IN ACC A BEFORE RETURING
                          * TO MAIN ROUTINE
                          *
A 004B B6 8002   A PIARC  LDAA   PORTB
A 004E 2B FB 004B         BMI    PIARC    BR BACK IF AT MARK
                          * PROCEED AT MARK TO SPACE TRANSITION
A 0050 BD 0086   A        JSR    HALFP    WAIT HALF BIT TIME
                          * TEST FOR VALID START BIT
A 0053 B6 8002   A        LDAA   PORTB
A 0056 2B F3 004B         BMI    PIARC    BR BACK IF INVALID
                          * INPUT CHARACTER AT PORT B & GENERATE
                          * PARITY IN ACC B.
                          * INPUT BIT AT HALF BIT TIME.
A 0058 5F                 CLRB
A 0059 86 07     A        LDAA   #$07     BIT COUNT
A 005B BD 0085   A PIARC1 JSR    PERIOD
A 005E F8 8002   A        EORB   PORTB    GENERSTE PARITY
A 0061 74 8002   A        LSR    PORTB    SHIFT IN NEXT BIT
A 0064 4A                 DECA            DEC BIT COUNT
A 0065 26 F4 005B         BNE    PIARC1
                          *
A 0067 B6 8002   A        LDAA   PORTB    ASCII CHAR TO ACC A
                          * TEST FOR PARITY
A 006A BD 0085   A        JSR    PERIOD
A 006D F8 8002   A        EORB   PORTB    COMPARE PARITY BITS
A 0070 2B D9 004B         BMI    PIARC    RESTART IF INVALID
                          * ELSE TEST FOR TWO 2-STOP BITS
A 0072 BD 0085   A        JSR    PERIOD   1ST STOP BIT
A 0075 F6 8002   A        LDAB   PORTB
A 0078 2A D1 004B         BPL    PIARC    RESTART IF INVALID
A 007A BD 0085   A        JSR    PERIOD   2ND STOP BIT
A 007D F6 8002   A        LDAB   PORTB
A 0080 2A C9 004B         BPL    PIARC    RESTART IF INVALID
                          *
                          * RESET BIT 7 OF ASCII CHARACTER & EXIT
A 0082 84 7F     A        ANDA   #$7F
A 0084 39                 RTS
                          *
                          *
                          * SUBROUTINES
                          * TIME DELAY SUBROUTINES, SEE CHAPTER 2.
                          * TIME IS A FUNCTION OF BAUD RATE & CLOCK RATE
A 0085 39          PERIOD RTS
A 0086 39          HALFP  RTS
```

9-4 PROGRAMMABLE TIMER (PTM) 6840

A clock or timer is a required part of many systems. The timer is a unique type of peripheral device in that it is not necessarily used to interface the processor to other devices. Rather, it is often used as a variable clock or timer to generate a variety of baud rates, often for communication devices under program control. The timer is utilized in such tasks as an interval timer, frequency measurement, or event counter, or as a pulse clock generator for square waves and single or grated pulses. The PTM is described and then two routines are developed: (1) to generate the baud rate clock for the ACIA, and (2) to generate the baud rate timing for the PIA by setting the status bit, which may be used to interrupt the microprocessor.

A timer is a counter where the period of each count in real time is well defined. For example, in a digital watch the period of each count is an accurate one, and when the watch counts 60 counts, or seconds, it indicates that a 1-minute interval of time has passed. The timer then is used to measure or indicate an interval of time that is incrementally larger than the period where the interval is indicated by a number or count. An alarm clock indicates or measures an interval of time that is the difference between the present and some future time. The alarm clock then continuously compares the present time, as indicated by the clock hands, against the time indicated by the alarm hand. As another example, industrial timers, which are often attached to ovens, are set by turning a knob to an interval of time, and when the clock has counted down to the zero number, a bell rings. The 6840 timer operates much like the industrial timer, where a count indicating a time is loaded into the timer. The counter then counts down to zero count, where

- A status bit is set.
- An interrupt flag may also be set.
- A pulse output is generated of either a continuous pulse train or a single shot.

The continuous pulse train may be used as the baud rate generator for the ACIA and the PIA, and will illustrate how to use the timer as a baud rate generator.

Another application of the Timer is to digitize or express a wave form in terms of a number. The wave form may be a square wave, since a wave or any other wave form with a well-defined start and end point is used to start and stop the timer. Often, however, the sine wave or continuous-pulse wave form is measured by the period that is the reciprocal of the frequency ($1/f$). The higher the frequency of the timer clock relative to the wave form that is digitized, the higher will be the resolution of the digitized number. When the timer is used to compare either a pulse width or a frequency, the wave form or period is first digitized, and the digitized count that is stored in the timer is compared to the wave form or period. The digitized count is stored in the timer and at the start of the wave form the counter begins to count down. The timer may be programmed to generate an interrupt if either:

- The digitized number counts down to zero before the occurrence of the end of the pulse, indicating that the digitized count is shorter than the external wave form.
- The external wave form ends before the digitized number counts to zero, indicating that the external wave form is longer than the digitized count.

Registers of the Timer

The 6840 programmable timer has three 16-bit counters that are interchangeably referred to as the timers, with three corresponding 16-bit latches and three 8-bit control registers. Three additional registers that are shared are the status register, the MSB buffer and the LSB buffer (Fig. 9-9). To initialize the timer, a binary number or count is first loaded and stored in the corresponding latches and then transferred into the timer. The timer continuously counts down to zero, at which time an output may be masked or enabled at the corresponding output pin 0, and the corresponding interrupt flag in the status register is set. It is intuitively obvious that a 16-bit number should be loaded into the timer at the same instant. Yet the 6800 is a byte-oriented machine, so when 2 bytes of data, which represent a 16-bit contiguous number, are loaded through the accumulator there is an inherent delay. To overcome this objection, the first byte of data is loaded from the accumulator into the appropriate MSB buffer. The second byte of data is then loaded into the appropriate set of latches, and the PTM chip loads the 16-bit number into the latches simultaneously, that is, the 8 MSBits from the MSB buffer and the 8 LSBits from the accumulator (see Fig. 9-10). A 16-bit number may be transferred to the appropriate latches from either the index register or stack pointer. The 16-bit number in the latches is then transferred into the 16-bit timer, which counts down to zero, at which time the number in the latches is again transferred into the timer. Each time the counter crosses the zero count, an output may be enabled and the respective interrupt bit is set. This process continues indefinitely or until another number is loaded into the latches.

To read the timer it is necessary to transfer the everchanging 16-bit

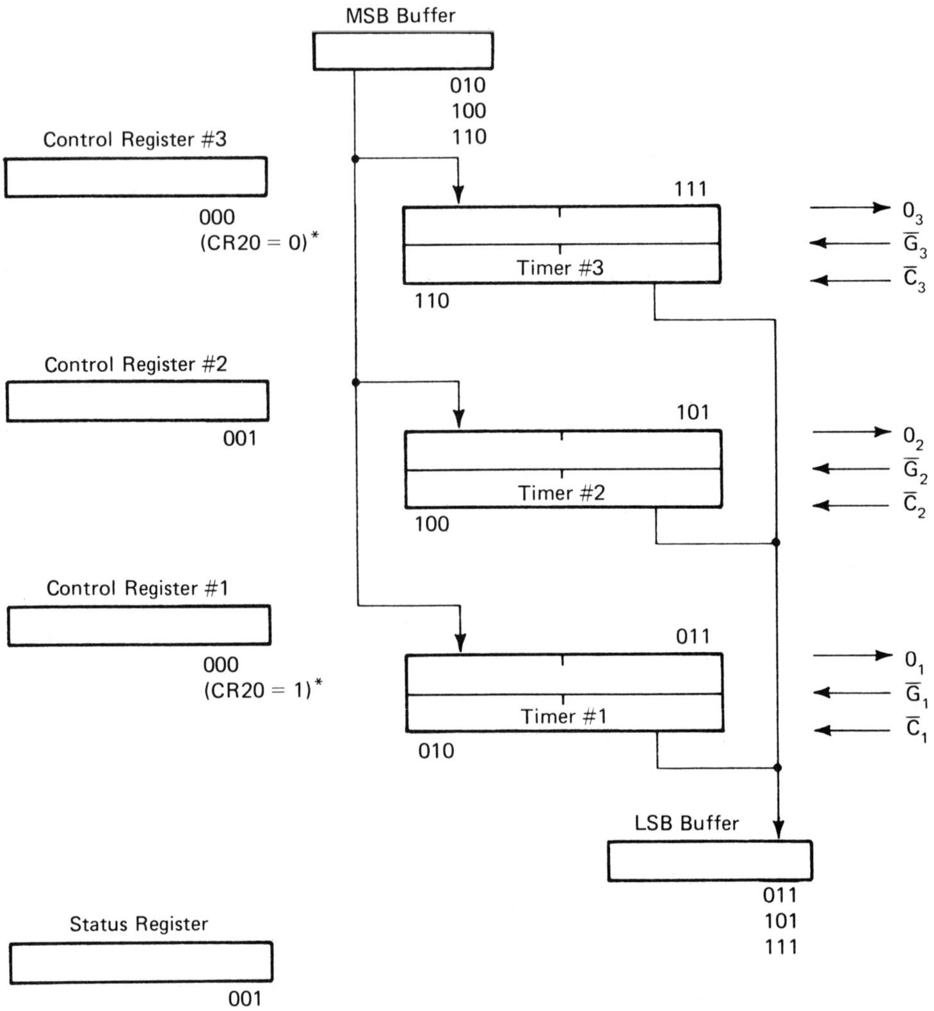

Figure 9-9. Registers of the 6840 programmable timer.

number out of the timer, so that with a read or load from the MSByte of the timer the LSByte in the timer is simultaneously transferred to the LSB buffer, from where it may be read.

Control Registers

The addresses of the control and other registers are listed in Table 9-4, and bits CRX_3, CRX_4, and CRX_5, which select the operating modes, are listed in Tables 9-5. Table 9-6 defines the interrupt control

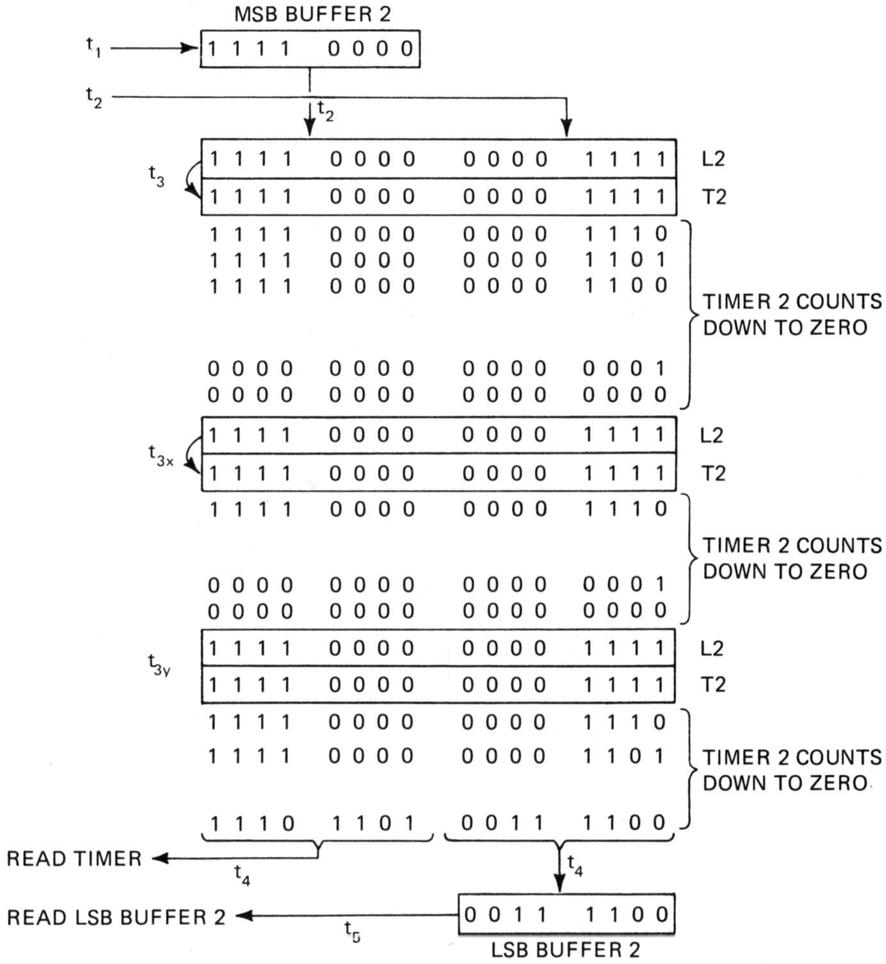

t_1	Loads MSB BUFFER 2 with MSByte
t_2	(a) Loads LSByte of LATCH 2
	(b) MSB BUFFER transfers to MSByte of LATCH 2
t_3	16-bit count in LATCH 2 transfers to Timer 2
t_{3x}, t_{3y}	(a) 16-bit count in LATCH 2 transfers to Timer 2
	(b) Set interrupt bit 2
	(c) Output Timer Out (TO)
t_4	(a) Read Timer 2
	(b) LSByte Timer 2 to LSB BUFFER 2
t_5	Read LSB BUFFER 2

Figure 9-10. Loading and reading 16-bit timer 2.

Table 9-4. Register Selection

Register Select Inputs			Operations	
RS2	RS1	RS0	$R/\overline{W} = 0$	$R/\overline{W} = 1$
0	0	0	CR20 = 0 Write Control Register #3 CR20 = 1 Write Control Register #1	No Operation
0	0	1	Write Control Register #2	Read Status Register
0	1	0	Write MSB Buffer Register	Read Timer #1 Counter
0	1	1	Write Timer #1 Latches	Read LSB Buffer Register
1	0	0	Write MSB Buffer Register	Read Timer #2 Counter
1	0	1	Write Timer #2 Latches	Read LSB Buffer Register
1	1	0	Write MSB Buffer Register	Read Timer #3 Counter
1	1	1	Write Timer #3 Latches	Read LSB Buffer Register

Table 9-5. Operating Modes

Control Register			Timer Operating Mode	
CRX3	CRX4	CRX5		
0	*	0	Continuous	Synthesizer
0	*	1	Single-Shot	
1	0	*	Frequency Comparison	Measurement
1	1	*	Pulse Width Comparison	

*Defines Additional Timer Function Selection.

Table 9-6. Timer Interval Modes

CRX3 = 1			
CRX4	CRX5	Application	Condition for Setting Individual Interrupt Flag
0	0	Frequency Comparison	Interrupt Generated if $\overline{\text{Gate}}$ Input Period (1/F) is less than Counter Time Out (TO)
0	1	Frequency Comparison	Interrupt Generated if $\overline{\text{Gate}}$ Input Period (1/F) is greater than Counter Time Out (TO)
1	0	Pulse Width Comparison	Interrupt Generated if $\overline{\text{Gate}}$ Input "Down Time" is less than Counter Time Out (TO)
1	1	Pulse Width Comparison	Interrupt Generated if $\overline{\text{Gate}}$ Input "Down Time" is greater than Counter Time Out (TO)

for the frequency and pulse width comparison modes. Bits 1 through 7 of each control register select functions that are common to the three control registers, while bit 0 of the respective register control has a unique function:

- Control register 2, bit 0 ($CR2_0$). Since control registers 1 and 3 share the same register address of 000, the control Register 1 is addressed when bit $CR2_0 = 0$, and control register 3 is addressed when bit $CR2_0 = 1$.
- Control register 1, bit 0 ($CR1_0$), either lets all the timers operate or holds them in the present state when $CR1_0$ is 0 and 1, respectively.
- Control register 3, bit 0 ($CR3_0$), lets timer 3 count normally or is prescaled by 8 when bit $CR3_0$ is 0 and 1, respectively.

Status Register

Only four of the status bits shown in Fig. 9-11 are used. Bits 0, 1, and 2 are set when timers 1, 2, and 3 count down to zero, respectively. The interrupt bit is activated when the respective timer counts down to zero and control register bit 6, CRX_6, is set. When any of the individual interrupts is set, then status bit 7 is also set, and the interrupt request pin ($\overline{IRQ}$) pin is pulled low. When the interrupt control bit, CRX_6, is clear, the respective status bit is set when the timer counts down to zero. Each of the interrupt bits is cleared with both a read from the status register and a read from the respective timer. The status bits are also cleared by either a reset by bit $CR1_0 = 1$ or loading the latches of the respective timer.

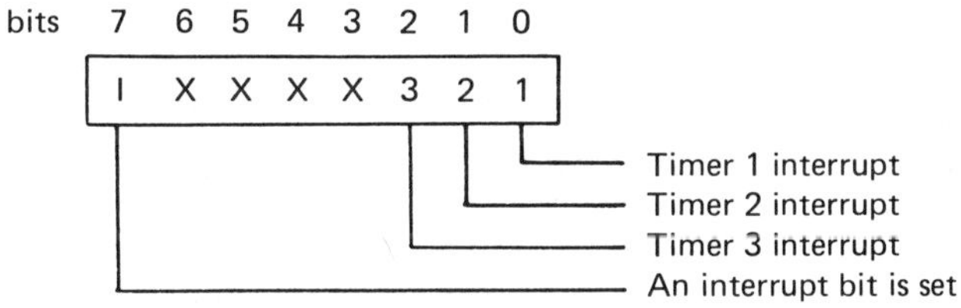

Figure 9-11. Timer status register.

Timer Clock Input, Output, and Gate Input Pins

Each timer has three pins associated with it:

Clock input pins	$\overline{C1}, \overline{C2}, \overline{C3}$
Clock output pins	01, 02, 03
Gate input pins	$\overline{G1}, \overline{G2}, \overline{G3}$

The clock output 0 and input $\overline{C}$ permit the three 16-bit timers to be used separately or as one long 48-bit timer. Bit 1 of the respective control register permits the selection of the external clock, or the system enable clock, to drive the timer. The gate inputs to control the input clock, $\overline{C}$. Control bit 7, CRX_7, masks or enables the output clock at the respective 0 pin.

9-5 TIMER AS A BAUD-RATE GENERATOR

This section describes the timer in two examples as a baud-rate generator:

- To generate a square wave for the ACIA of 1200 baud. (See listing on page 317.)
- To set the interrupt status bit at the bit time period of 1200 baud for the PIA. (See listing on page 317.)

In both cases timer 2 (see Figure 9-9) is used as follows:

- With the enable clock at 1 MHz
- With the 16-bit configuration
- In the continuous mode
- For inhibiting the interrupt
- To enable the output clock for the ACIA or inhibit the output clock for the PIA

The bit time is the reciprocal of the baud rate:

$$\text{Bit Time} = \frac{\text{second}}{\text{baud rate}}$$

$$= \frac{1}{1200} = 833\ \mu\text{s}$$

for a bit count of 833 at a 1 MHz clock. When generating a square wave, the time is loaded with half of the bit period for a count of 416. To generate a square wave of 1200 baud for the ACIA, the control register 2 is loaded as follows:

```
1 0 0 0 0 0 1 0                    Hex 82
| | \___/ | | |
| |   |   | | |_______ don't care
| |   |   | |_________ enable clock
| |   |   |___________ 16-bit configuration
| |   |_______________ continuous mode
| |___________________ mask interrupt
|_____________________ enable output clock at time out (TO)
```

The count is as follows:

Count	Binary	Hex
833	0 0 0 0 0 0 1 1 0 1 0 0 0 0 0 1	0341
416	0 0 0 0 0 0 0 1 1 0 1 0 0 0 0 0	01A0

For the PIA there is no output wave form, but the status bit is set.

```
                          * SEE SECTION 9.5,
                          * USE THE TIMER AS A BAUD RATE GENERATOR FOR THE
                          * ACIA. THE TIMER OUTPUT, O2, DRIVES THE ACIA
                          * TRANSMIT & RECEIVE CLOCKS, TXCLK & RXCLK.
                          * ASSUME THAT THE SYSTEM CLOCK DRIVERS THE
                          * TIMER AT 1MHZ.  THEN AN 833 USEC PERIOD
                          * GENERATES A 1200 BAUD RATE.  SINCE THE TIMER
                          * IN THE CONTINUOUS MODE MUST BE FLIPPED
                          * TWICE PER CYCLE.  THE TIMER REGISTER 2 IS
                          * LOADED WITH HALF THE COUNT OF HEX $01A0 FOR
                          * 416 USEC.
                          *
                          * ASSUME THAT THE TIMER IS AT LOCATION $8000,
                          * & OCCUPIES THE MEMORY LOCATIONS THRU TO $8007.
                          * THE ACIA IS AT LOCATIONS $8008 & $8009.
                          *
                          * TO INITIALIZE THE TIMER REGISTER 2 IN THE
                          * CONTINUOUS MODE, 16-BIT CONFIGURATION,
                          * INHIBITING INTERRUPTS,  LOAD CONTROL REGISTER
                          * REGISTER 2 WITH $82.
                          *
A 0000 86 82        A BAUDG  LDAA   #$82
A 0002 B7 8001      A        STAA   $8001     LOAD CONTROL REG 2
                          * LOAD 16-BIT TIMER 2 WITH $01A0
A 0005 86 01        A        LDAA   #$01
A 0007 B7 8004      A        STAA   $8004     MSB BUFFER 2
A 000A 86 A0        A        LDAA   #$A0
A 000C B7 8005      A        STAA   $8005     TIMER LATCH 2
A 000F 39                    RTS
                          *
                          *
                          *
                          * SEE SECTION 9.5.
                          * USE THE TIMER TO GENERATE A BAUD RATE PERIOD
                          * & HALF PERIOD FOR THE PIA EXAMPLE OF SECTION 9.
                          * TIMER OUTPUT, O2, DRIVES  PIA INPUT PIN, CAI.
                          * THE PIA MAY BE PROGRAMMED TO BE INTERRUPTED
                          * BY THE INPUT PULSE, OR TO POLE THE IRQA1
                          * STATUS BIT FOR A TIME OUT.
                          *
```

```
                           * THIS ROUTINE MAY BE A SUBROUTINE FOR THE
                           * PROGAM WHERE THE PIA IS USED TO IN LIEU OF
                           * AN ACIA TO INTERFACE THE MICROPROCESSOR TO
                           * A TERMINAL & THE IRQA1 STATUS BIT IS POLLED.
                           *
                           * ASSUME THAT THE PIA IS AT LOCATION $8000 &
                           * THE TIMER IS AT LOCATION $8004.
                           *
0000 86 82       A PERIOD LDAA    #$82
0002 B7 8005     A        STAA    $8005     LOAD CONTROL REG 2
                           * LOAD 16-BIT TIMER 2 WITH $0341
0005 86 03       A        LDAA    #$03
0007 B7 8008     A        STAA    $8008     MSB BUFFER 2
000A 86 41       A        LDAA    #$41
000C B7 8009     A        STAA    $8009     TIMER LATCH 2
000F 20 0F 0020           BRA     WAIT
                           *
                           *
0011 86 82       A HALFP  LDAA    #$82
0013 B7 8005     A        STAA    $8005     LOAD CONTROL REG 2
                           * LOAD 16-BIT TIMER 2 WITH $01A0
0016 86 01       A        LDAA    #$01
0018 B7 8008     A        STAA    $8008     MSB BUFFER 2
001B 86 A0       A        LDAA    #$A0
001D B7 8009     A        STAA    $8009     TIMER LATCH 2
                           *
                           *
0020 B6 8001     A WAIT   LDAA    $8001     GET PIA CONTROL REG
0023 2B FB 0020           BMI     WAIT      SAMPLE IRQA1
0025 86 02       A        LDAA    #$02
0027 B7 8005     A        STAA    $8005     DISABLE TIMER OUTPUT
002A 39                   RTS
```

10 Interfacing for Synchronous Data Communication Systems:

The Synchronous Protocol Communication Controller

In the movie "Star Wars" there are two robot characters that constitute the computer system. The first, ARTOO DETOO (R2D2), is the thinking part of the computer, which must communicate with the world through the second part, SEE THREEPIO, (C3PIO), the human-appearing part of the system. C3PIO is the voice interface between a human and the computer, and because people do not like to talk to and be answered by black boxes, C3PIO is in human form.

People talk to C3PIO, while C3PIO communicates with R2D2 via shrills, howls, and whistles. The point is that C3PIO is the ideal interface device. Humans simply tell or give the data to C3PIO, the interface device, and it passes the data and adds all the necessary procedural and protocol information that is required to communicate with R2D2, the computer. When C3PIO is threatened with extinction, it justifies its existence by indicating all the protocols familiar to it, implying that there are many types of computers that require an I/O interface device with C3PIO's capabilities for handling protocols. The synchronous communication controllers offer the user many of the advantages performed by SEE THREEPI0 by furnishing parts of protocol previously handled by the programmer, which are necessary for getting data into and out from a computer over a channel.

Synchronous communication is used to transfer blocks of data, as contrasted to asynchronous communication, which is used to transmit one character at a time. The data may be transferred between two or more computers, a computer and a smart terminal, where a line of data rather than a character is transmitted, or between a computer and a data-reducing or data-gathering station. Care must then be exercised to assure that the data received are, in fact, the same as the data transmitted. If the data are transmitted to one of several stations, there must be assurance that they are received by the station addressed.

Protocol, then, is a formal and predetermined agreed-upon procedure that governs any information transfer, and its function is to assure a proper transfer of data. The data link controllers (DLC) that interface computers, smart terminals, or data-gathering machines via communication lines are measured much as SEE THREEPIO by two primary functions: (1) by how much of the protocol they manage, thereby alleviating the programmer of the task, and (2) by their flexibility, or how many different protocols they handle.

This chapter does not include a general discussion of synchronous communication, but is limited to how the data link controller is used in two versions, two protocols, of the same example. The first example uses the IBM BISYNC, byte control protocol (BCP), and the second example uses the bit-oriented protocol (BOP).

The point of this chapter is to illustrate that the programs that control the two different transmissions are more similar because of the communication controller than they would be without it. Compare listing BISYNC (pages 338-341) and BOP (pages 347-351). As the communication controllers are further developed they will handle more of the protocol chores, and the software that controls the transmissions for the various protocols will be more alike. The ideal, of course, is a C3PIO-type controller that is voice-activated, knows which protocol to use, and then handles the interface.

The synchronous protocol communication controller (SPCC) 6856 is the programmable peripheral device used in the examples. All the 6800 family of devices discussed in the previous chapters are manufactured by Motorola and second-sourced by Fairchild Semiconductor. However, the SPCC 6856 is the first device that, at this writing, is manufactured by Fairchild Semiconductor only. It was selected because it has both the BCP and BOP protocols, making it a flexible device and characteristic of future devices. The advantage of having a controller with many protocols is that, in a fast-changing field, it can be programmed to handle a variety of protocols without a hardware change. For example, if the central computer in a bank has to communicate with a variety of branch banks, each with terminals that were purchased over a period of years and each using a different protocol, it need not be obsoleted. The most flexible communication device can be programmed to interface with the greatest number of other computers, terminals, and networks.

Communication Configuration

Two common communication configurations, the point-to-point and the multipoint, are illustrated in Fig. 10-1. A more detailed diagram of the network (Fig. 10-2) indicates that each station consists of the following:

- Communication controller, usually with computing power.
- The data link controller (DLC), which is the interface between the line and the computer.
- A modem is usually included.
- The line, which may be a wire or a microwave link.

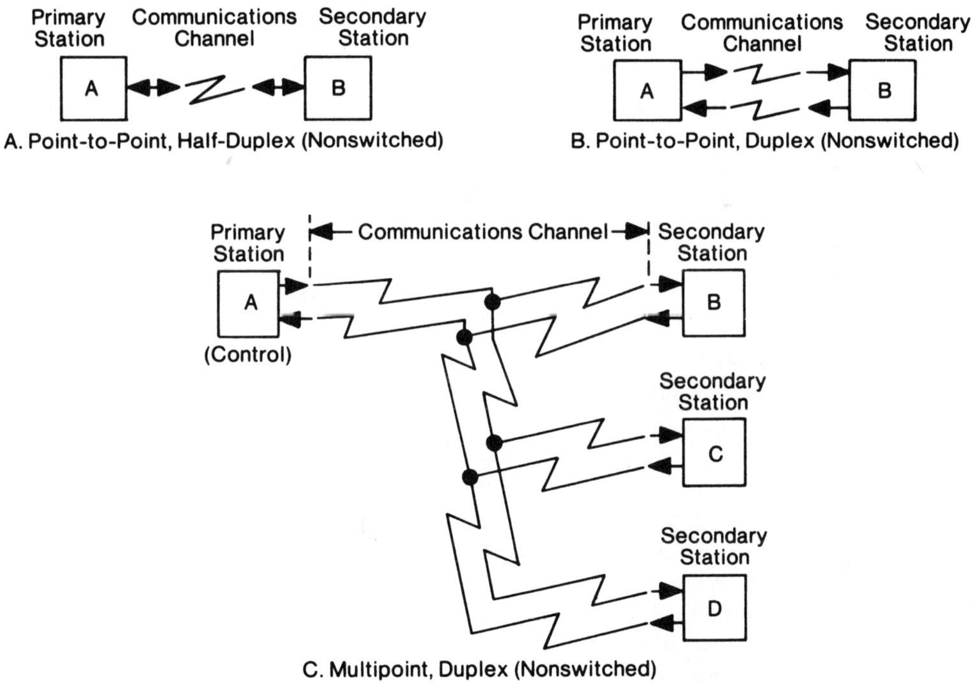

Figure 10-1. Communication configurations.

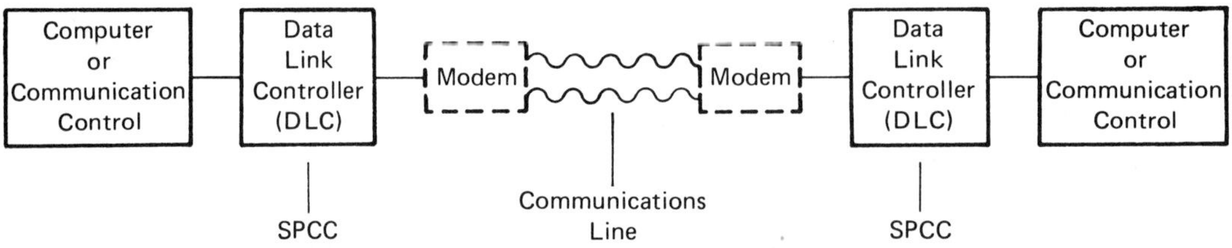

Figure 10-2. Data link including the controller.

The communication network may be assembled in a laboratory environment with two 6800-type single-board computers as the communication controllers connected by two SPCC units as the DLC interfaces. The modems would be optional. The system would be connected in the duplex mode, giving both stations the ability to transmit and receive simultaneously.

This chapter describes a typical program used by both the transmit and receive stations and indicates some of the functions performed by the SPCC in simplifying the programmer's task. The data link described is the general configuration and is independent of the protocol used.

The synchronous protocol communication controller (SPCC) is designed to satisfy the major interface requirements for both the BCP and BOP. Among the byte control protocols (BCP) are the following:

BISYNC	IBM's Binary Synchronous Communication
DDCMP	DEC's Digital Data Communication Message Protocol

Among the bit-oriented protocols are the following:

SDLC	IBM's Synchronous Data Link Control
ADCCP	ANSI's Advanced Data Communication Control Procedure
HDLC	ISO's High-level Data Link Control

Message

There are three parts to the message, the start of message (SOM), the data or text, and the end of message (EOM) (Fig. 10-3a). Ideally, the DCL should generate the start and end of message and the computer or program transmit the data with no more effort than would be required to output data through any port. In practice the program is often expected to generate parts of the start and the end of message (Fig.

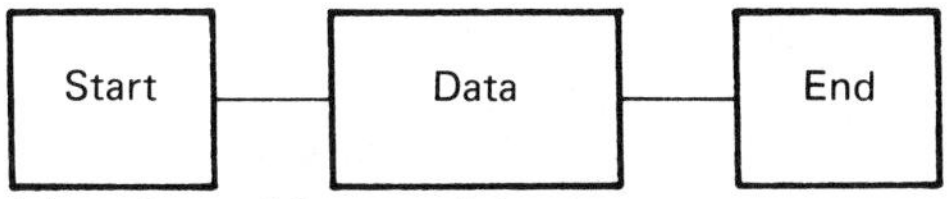

(a) General format of the message:
- Start of message
- Data
- End of message

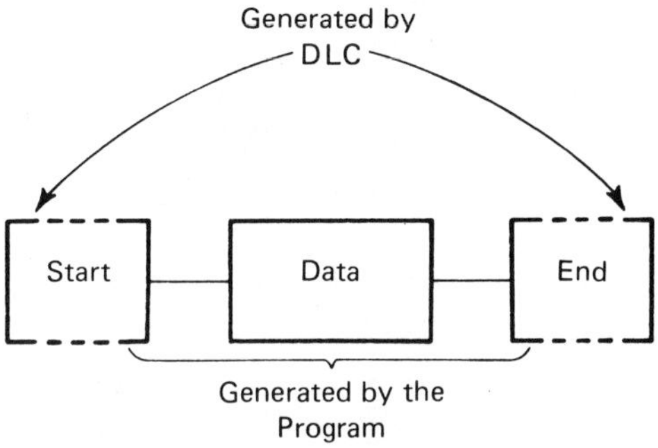

(b) Practical format of the message:
- Start of message under DLC control
- Start of message under program control
- Data
- End of message under program control
- End of message under DLC control

Figure 10-3. Message format and control.

10-3b). This varies with the protocols and whether transmitting in a multipoint or in a point-to-point configuration.

Parts of the message and other tasks required at the transmit and receive stations are as follows:

Start of message

- Synchronize the receiver to the incoming character.
- Address field, is often the address of the secondary station.
- Control field.

Data or Text

- At the transmit station the data must be converted from parallel-to-serial form and from serial-to-parallel at the receiver.
- In some protocols, the data and control characters are assigned

different codes, while in other protocols the data and control characters may have the same codes. To distinguish or make the data transparent from the control characters, they are modified and restored at the transmit and receive stations, respectively.

In the BISYNC format, the data link escape (DLE) character is inserted prior to control characters, and in the BOP a 0 is inserted when a string of five 1's appears in the data string.

- The frame check sequence is used to validate transmission accuracy, and an FSC character is generated at both the transmit and receive stations on the respective data.
- Detect underrun error when the controller is ready to transmit the data, but the microprocessor has not yet put or stored the data into the controller's transmit register. An underrun error is an interruption or lack of continuity in the transmission.
- Detect overrun error. At the receive station, an overrun error occurs when the microprocessor does not load or take the data from the controller's receive data register before the next byte of data arrives. The incoming data then overruns and destroys the data in the receive buffer.

End of message

- Indicates end of data.
- The transmitter sends the FCS character while the receiver compares the generated to the received FCS character. An error is generated if they do not compare.
- Indicates end of message.

The variations in the messages are a function of the protocols and are best discussed in specific examples (Secs. 10-2 and 10-3). The SPCC is described in Sec. 10-1.

10-1 PIN ASSIGNMENTS AND THE REGISTERS OF THE SPCC

The 40 pins of the SPCC (see Fig. 10-4) are described in groups:

- Data Bus:

  16 data bus pins D_0 to D_{15} (this configuration is not discussed)
  For an 8-bit bus, D_0 to D_7 are connected to D_8 to D_{15}

Byte when high selects the 8-bit bus

- Address Bus:

  A_0 to A_2 register select pins
  $\overline{CE}$, chip enable

- Control Bus:

  R/$\overline{W}$, read/write
  DBE, data bus enable, enables the transfer of data to/from the data bus

- Chip initialize, $\overline{CI}$
- Baud rate clock generator:

  TCLK, transmit clock
  RCLK, receive clock

- Station active: controls and feedback

  $\overline{DSR}$, data set ready
  $\overline{DTR}$, data terminal ready
  $\overline{RTS}$, request to send
  $\overline{CTS}$, clear to send
  $\overline{CD}$, carrier detect
  RSOF, receive sync or flag: goes high for one clock period each time a SYNC or FLAG is detected. It is generally used to detect that a SYNC or FLAG signal has not been received for 1 or 2 full seconds, indicating that there is a problem with the transmit station. It is tied to a time-out clock, which is reset with each SYNC or FLAG, and sets an alarm when the 1- or 2-s clock times out.

- Transmit and Receive:

  TSO, transmit serial output
  RSI, receive serial input

- Interrupt Request:

  $\overline{IRQ}$, interrupt request
  RDA, receive data available. It is also a bit in the receive status register giving the user the option of sensing the pin or the status bit.
  TBMT, transmit buffer empty. It is also a bit in the transmit status register giving the user the option of sensing the pin or the status bit.

- Power Pins:

  VCC, +5 V
  VSS, ground, 0 V

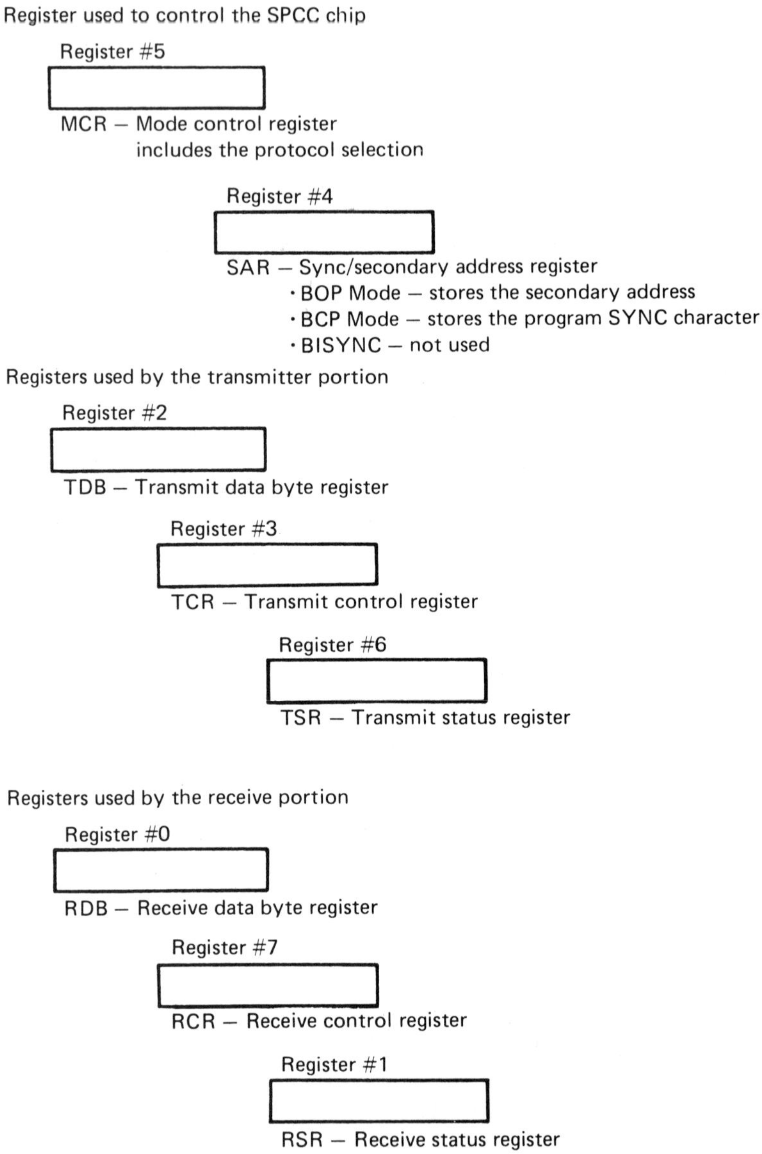

Figure 10-4. The eight-bit registers of the SPCC.

Registers and Addresses of the SPCC

In the byte mode, which is controlled by the input pin "byte," there are eight 8-bit registers, separated into three functional categories associated with the following:

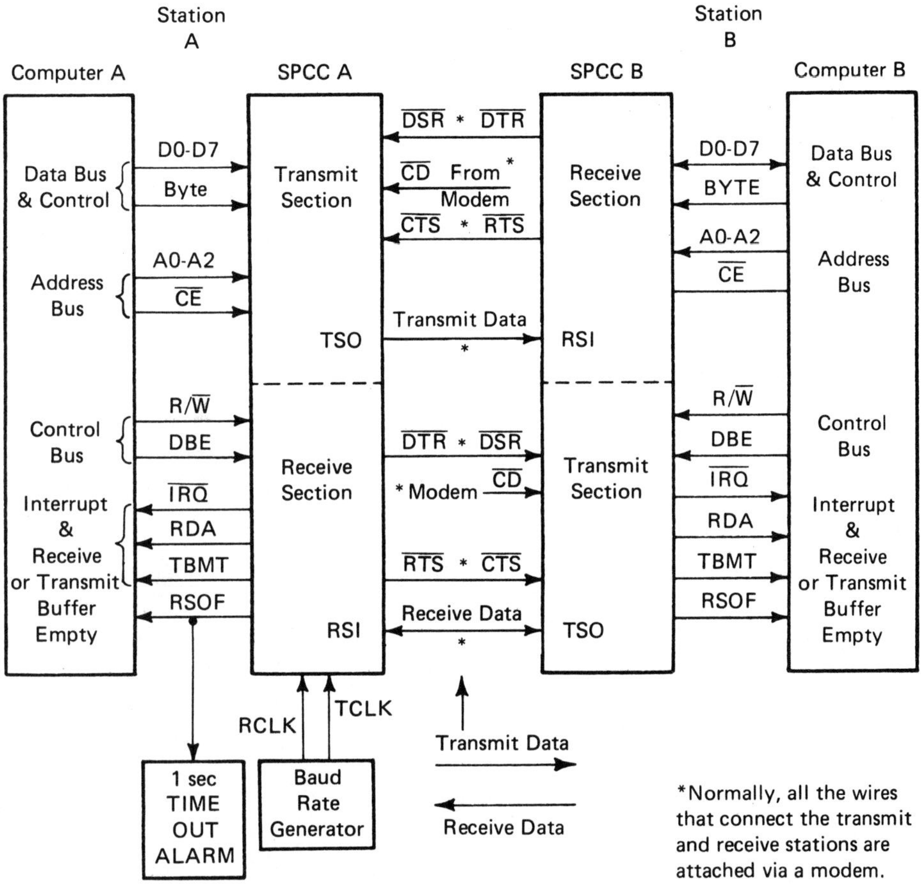

Figure 10-5. Pin assignment of the SPCC.

- Overall control
- The transmitter operation
- The receiver operation

The names and addresses of the registers, listed in Table 10-1 to 10-8, are as follows:

- Associated with controlling the SPCC:

  MCR register 5 is the mode control register, which contains

control information for the transit and receive sections, that is, the protocol select bits.

SAR register 4 sync/secondary address register for the:

BOP mode stores the secondary station address
BCP mode stores the programmed SYNC character
BISYNC is not used

- Associated with the transmit function:

  TDB register 2 is the transmitter data buffer
  TCR register 3 is the transmitter control register
  TSR register 6 is the transmitter status register

- Associated with the receive function:

  RDB register 0 is the receiver data buffer
  RCR register 7 is the receiver control register
  RSR register 1 is the receiver status register

10-2 EXAMPLES USED TO DEMONSTRATE HOW TO USE A DLC

As stated in Chapter 3, the variety of applications for any of the programmable peripheral devices (PPDs) are so numerous that they cannot be covered in any one chapter. As previously recommended, after describing the pins and the registers of the device, the next step is to work through practical examples. The reader may then expand the example in the direction of most interest. To demonstrate how to use the SPCC and to appreciate its advantages, the same data, 256 bytes coded from 0 to $FF, are transmitted via two protocols, point-to-point BISYNC and multipoint BOP, in Secs. 10-3 and 10-4, respectively.

The two examples are then contrasted, and the advantages of a data link controller for the user are summarized in Sec. 10-5.

Four different programs are discussed:

- Transmit program using BISYNC
- Receive program using a BISYNC
- Transmit program using BOP
- Receive program using BOP

The discussion follows each part of the message from:

- Transmit program
- Action of the transmit SPCC
- Action of the receiver SPCC
- Receiver program

Some terms and concepts should be defined before discussing the examples:

- Transparent data
- Control character versus control field
- Baud rate
- FCS, frame check sequence
- ABORT ERROR
- Strategy for transmitting data
- Strategy for receiving data

Transparent Data

There are two kinds of information being sent on the data link: message data and link control. In the BISYNC protocol there are control characters, and in the BOP protocol there are flags, addresses, and other controls. The text or data part of the message in the examples is to transmit 256 bytes of code with every possible 8-bit combination from 0 to $FF, which could be a program or raw data. This implies that the data and the flags, or control characters, may have the same 8-bit code as the data, and that there must be some technique used by the receive station to distinguish between the data and the flags or control characters. Historically, the BISNYC protocol was designed to send only printable ASCII or EDCDIC character codes as message data. The special control characters available in each of these character sets were used to control the data link. Later, BISYNC was extended to permit the transmission of control characters as message data. This is known as "transparent text" mode.

In BISYNC, transparent data transmission is achieved by examining each data byte for $40, and inserting an extra data link escape (DLE) character prior to the $40 code. When, at the receive station, a DLE pair is received, one of the DLE characters is removed and the data are restored to their original form. In BOP, the data are modified by inserting and removing a 0 after five consecutive 1's at the transmit and receive stations, respectively. The communication controllers are ideally suited to alleviate the programmer from modifying and restoring the data at the transmit and receiving stations. However, there must be a procedure for the controller to know when control information is to be modified prior to transmission. It is accomplished by setting the control bits that direct the controller to generate and transmit the control characters. Data that are modified to be transparent move through the data buffers.

Control Characters versus Control Field

Control characters are generally used to control the transmission and are as follows:

SPECIAL CHARACTERS

CHARACTER	BIT PATTERN	FUNCTION
BOP		Frame
FLAG	01111110	Message
ABORT	11111111 Generated 11111110 Detected	Terminate a message prematurely
GA	11111110	Close frame in Store Loop Mode
ADDRESS	SAR	Secondary station address
BISYNC		
SYNC	00010110 USASCII 00110010 EBCDIC	Start a message and fill character
PAD	11111111	End of frame pad
DLE	00010000	Data link escape
SOH	00000001	Start of heading
STX	00000010	Start of text
ITB	00011111	End of intermediate transmission block
ETB	00010111 USASCII 00100110 EBCDIC	End of transmission block
ETX	00000011 ETX	End of transmission
BCP		
SYNC	SAR	Start a message and fill character
PAD	11111111	End of frame pad, selectable fill character for DDCMP.

The information in the control field is used in BOP to identify a successful transmission and for a secondary station to request to transmit. It is discussed in Sec. 10-4.

Baud Rate

The bit rate indicates how many bits are transmitted per second. The period is the reciprocal of the baud rate and indicates the time needed to transmit each bit of data.

$$\text{Period} = \frac{1\text{ s}}{\text{baud rate}} = \frac{1}{9600} = 0.104\text{ ms}$$

For a baud rate of 9600, the period is 0.104 ms, and the time required to transmit an 8-bit character is 0.832 ms. Some typical times for transmitting characters are as follows:

Baud Rate	Period	8-Bit Character	7-Bit Character
300	3.33	26.64 ms	23.310 ms
600	1.67	13.350	11.690
1200	0.835	6.680	5.705
2400	0.417	3.336	2.939
4800	0.208	1.664	1.456
9600	0.104	0.832	0.728

Frame Check Sequence (FCS) Field

The 16-bit frame check sequence field is used to validate the accuracy of the transmission, and the SPCC is admirably suited to generate and check it. The FCS is generated by the transmitter and calculated by the receiver on the same data, yielding the same result unless the data have been changed by noise or other distortions in the data line. It is transmitted as part of the end of message sequence prior to the closing flag. The receiver then compares the received to the generated FCS field, and if they agree it validates the transmission. If not, it indicates an error.

ERROR CONTROL

BOP	A Frame Check Sequence (FCS) is transmitted/received as a 16-bit character following the last data character of a frame. The CRC polynomial used to generate/check the FCS is CRC-CCITT ($X^{16} + X^{12} + X^5 + 1$) with the dividend preset to "0" or "1"s.
BISYNC	A Block Check Character (BCC) is transmitted/received as a 16-bit character following an ITB, ETB or ETX character. The CRC polynomial used to generate/check the BCC is either CRC-16 ($X^{16} + X^{15} + X^2 + 1$) or CRC-CCITT with the dividend preset to "0"s.
BCP	A BCC, twice the data character length is transmitted/received following the last data character of a message if CRC is selected. The CRC polynomial used to generate/check the CRC changes with character length. These polynomials are listed below. 5 Bit $X^{10} + X^9 + X^3 + X^2 + 1$ 6 Bit $X^{12} + X^{11} + X^3 + X^2 + 1$ (CRC-12) 7 Bit $X^{14} + X^{12} + X^4 + X^2 + 1$ 8 Bit $X^{16} + X^{15} + X^2 + 1$ (CRC-16 or CRC-CCITT) The dividend is always preset to "0"s.

Abort

An abort is a BOP concept only. When mark (all 1's) are sent between frames it indicates an inactive data link, which usually implies that the data link is down and must be restored. A message that is terminated by an abort indicates an unsuccessful transmission. The message is aborted by transmitting 7 or more consecutive 1's instead of the flag. The abort may be generated under the control of the program by setting the transmit abort/CRC generate (TACG) bit, or it may be generated automatically by the SPCC device.

Error

The three basic errors are the following:

- Underrun
- Overrun
- FCS character

The status bits indicate which of the various errors have occurred. In the examples the programs test for an error prior to transmitting or receiving data. If an error is detected, the program branches to an error routine. The error routine, or the technique for recovering from an error, is not discussed in this chapter. The technique used by the programs is to load the status bits into accumulator B and use the BIT test instruction to examine but not destroy the status bits. They are required by the error routine to recover from an error.

Strategy for Transmitting Data: TSR

The transmit status register (TSR) is examined in much the same manner for the BISYNC and BOP protocols prior to transmitting data. Six of the eight status bits are used:

- Three bits are tied directly to pin input lines and are used to sense if the modem and channel are connected and ready:
  DSR, data set ready
  CD, carrier detect
  CTS, clear to send
- Two bits are used to detect errors:
  TOR, transmitter overrun
  TUR, transmitter underrun
- One bit is used to indicate when the transmitter buffer is empty:
  TBMT

Prior to transmitting each byte of data, the status bits are tested, and if any of the five bits indicates a problem with the transmission line or with the receiver, the program branches to an error routine. In the error routine each of the five status bits is tested to determine the source of the error and the procedure to follow. If there is no error, the TBMT bit is tested to determine if either the buffer is empty to transmit the next byte of data or to load the control register to transmit the next control character. It is, however, impractical to continuously loop and wait for the SPCC to request the next character to be transmitted or received. For example, at a 9600-baud rate of an 8-bit character there are 104 μs between character transfers. If it takes, on the average, 3 μs to execute each instruction, then the microcomputer could easily process data, receive data, and perform other tasks in addition to transmitting, which happens in the practical example.

Strategy for Receiving Data: RSR

The receive status register (RSR) is examined in much the same manner by the BISYNC and BOP protocols prior to receiving data. The eight status bits are used:

- Three bits are used to detect errors:
  ROVR, receiver overrun error
  RERR, CRC error occurred on receive message
  ABGA, (BOP only) receive abort
- One bit senses end of message.
  REOM
- One bit is used to indicate when the receive buffer has data or is available.
  RDA, receive data available
- Three bits are used in BOP only, which indicates the number of bits or character lengths from 0 to 8 in the last character received.
  RDL_0, RDL_1, RDL_2, received last character length

Prior to receiving data, the error status bits are tested, and if an error bit is set, then the program branches to an error routine. Next the routine tests for a received end of message (REOM), and then tests for received data (RDA). The three received character lengths (RDLs) are used when the data being transmitted may be any number of bits. This is a legal but seldom used feature of the HDLE protocol.

10-3 BISYNC TRANSMISSION OF TRANSPARENT DATA IN A POINT-TO-POINT CONFIGURATION

This section describes two programs, one for transmitting and one for receiving transparent data in a point-to-point configuration via the BISYNC protpcol. The programs are listed. (See pages 338-341.) The discussion tracks each part of the message, start, data, and end, as it originates with the transmit program, the function of the transmit SPCC, the function of the SPCC receiver, and the receive program (see Table 10-9). The text is 256 bytes of data from 0 to $FF, and the message format is illustrated in Fig. 10-6: SYN, SYN; DLE; STX; transparent data; DLE; ETX; BCC; PAD.

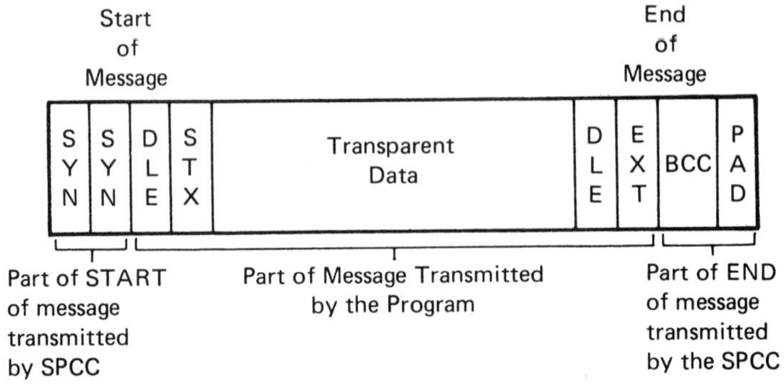

Figure 10-6. BISYNC message format used in example. The DLE is transmitted by the SPCC, but only when ordered to do so by setting the GATD bit of the TCR.

Initialize the SPCC

To initialize the SPCC, the control registers are loaded with appropriate constants. There are three control registers:

MCR	Mode control register
TCR	Transmit control register
RCR	Receive control register

The sync/secondary address register is not used in BISYNC. The addresses of each register in this example are as follows:

Location:	\$8100	RDB	Receive data buffer	Read only
	\$8101	RSR	Receive status register	Read only
	\$8102	TDB	Transmit data buffer	Write only
	\$8103	TCR	Transmit control buffer	Write only
	\$8104	SAR	Sync/secondary address register	Write only
	\$8105	MCR	Mode control register	Write only
	\$8106	TSR	Transmit status register	Read only
	\$8107	RCR	Receive control register	Write write

The TCR is a write only register. During the transmit program some of the bits of the TCR must be modified. Since the data in the TCR are inaccessible, the same data are also stored at memory location TCRBUF. To modify a bit in the TCR, the bits in the TCRBUF are ORed by the program and then reload l into the TCR.

The MCR register is initializea with a $C1 (1100 0001):

Bit 0	EC	1	Error control; presets CCITT to all 0's
Bit 1	Loop	0	Not in the self-test mode
Bit 2	NRZI	0	NRZ data
Bit 3	CC	0	Number of control characters (not used)
Bit 4	LRSS	0	Loop repeat/sync strip (not used)
Bits 5,6,7		110	Protocol select, BISYNC USASCII

The TCR is initialized with $48 (0100 1000):

Bits 0,1,2		000	Transmitter character length; defaults to 8 bits
Bit 3	RTS	1	Request to send; pin is output low
Bit 4	EOM	0	End of message
Bit 5	GATD	0	Go ahead/transmit DLE
Bit 6	TACG	1	Enables BCC at end of message
Bit 7	SOM	0	Start of message

The RCR is initialized with $8C (1000 1100):

Bits 0,1	RCL	00	Receive character length, 8 bits
Bit 2	RE	1	Receive enable
Bit 3	CRC	1	Selected
Bits 4,5		00	Not used
Bit 6	MISC	0	Controls the MISC bar output pin
Bit 7	DTR	1	Data terminal ready, output pin low

Start of Message: SYN, SYN; DLE; STX

The SYN, SYN part of the message enables the receive station to character sync the message. The STX is start of text, and the DLE, STX indicates the start of transparent text or data.

Transmit Station

The start of message, SOM, starts at label TB102 by examining the status register for the following:

- An overrun or underrun error: bits 5 and 7
- Testing if the transmit buffer is empty

If there is an error, the program branches to an error routine with the ability to recover from the error. This error routine is not discussed. If no error is detected, the start of message sequence SYN, SYN, DLE, STX is transmitted. As mentioned, most control characters are transmitted via the TCR. Two bits of the control register are set simultaneously: start of message (SOM) and go-ahead transmit DLE (GATD). When the SPCC detects that the start of message control bit (SOM) is set and that the mode control register (MCR) has selected the BISYNC protocol, then the SYN, SYN control characters are transmitted. The DLE control characters immediately follow the SYN, SYN characters, and since the transmission of the SYN, SYN, DLE characters is initiated by the control registers, the data buffer is still empty. The STX character ($02) is loaded into the data buffer, and the SPCC transmits it next in the sequence.

Receive Station

The receive routine starts at label RB102. When the receiver SPCC senses the SYN, SYN, it sequences and tests for the STX control character. On sensing the DLE, STX it prepares to receive transparent data. The receive program tests for an STX or DLE, STX and either clears or sets the transparent data flag.

Transmitting Transparent Data

The SPCC, when transmitting transparent data, starts generating the CRC beginning with the character following STX, the message data. The programmer need not be concerned with this operation. Prior to transmitting each byte of data the program at location TB104 tests the status register, first, for an error and, second, for an empty transmit buffer.

To transmit transparent data, the data cannot inadvertently contain the code for DLE, $40; and if it does, then a DLE pair must be transmitted. The program must then examine each byte of data for the code $40. If the data equals $40, then the data are transmitted via the data buffer and the GATD control bit is set, which causes the SPCC to transmit another DLE, thus completing the pair.

Receiving Transparent Data

The receive SPCC starts to accumulate the CRC on the received data.

The program at location RB104 starts by loading the index register with the location in memory to store the received data. Then, before the system reads the data from the read data buffer (RDB), it reads the receive status register and tests for the following:

- Errors, ROVR bit 7
- End of message, REOM bit 5
- Receive buffer full, RDA bit 6

If an overflow error is sensed, the program branches to the error routine. If an end of message is sensed, then the program branches to label RB106 to determine if noise on the transmission line may have caused the message to be improperly received. Otherwise, the program waits to receive the data and tests for a DLE pair. The first of the DLE pair is discarded.

Transmitting End of Message: DLE, ETX, BCC, PAD

After testing the status bits for an available transmit buffer and no error, the program transmits the end of message control characters at location TB106. Two control bits are set, GATD and EOM, bits 5 and 4, and then control character end of transmission, ETX ($03), is loaded into the transmit buffer.

The SPCC first transmits the DLE, ETX control characters and, second, transmits the BCC. The SPCC then transmits:

- DLE, ETX after sensing the GATD control bit.
- The BCC character, a 16-bit block check character that was generated as a function of the transmit data.
- The PAD, a string of 1's.

Receiving End of Message

The SPCC receiver senses the DLE, ETX which detects an end of message. Prior to setting the REOM status bit, the SPCC receiver compares the received BCC against its own generated BCC character.

- If they are equal, then the SPCC sets the REOM status bit only.
- If they are not equal, the RERR status bit is set.

In the end of message portion of the routine at location RB106, the RERR status bit is tested to determine if there is an error, and the program branches to the error routine. If not, the received message is valid.

```
                           NAM     BISYNC
                     * THIS PROGRAM USES THE SYNCHRNOUS PROTOCOL
                     * COMMUNICATION CONTROLLER (SPCC) SEE SECTION 0.3
                     * IN THE BISYNC PROTOCOL TO TRANSMIT 256 BYTES
                     * OF DATA  -00 TO $FF-  IN THE TRANSPARENT DATA
                     * MODE.
                     * THE MESSAGE CONSISTS OF SYN, SYN, DLE, SYN,
                     * TRANSPARENT DATA, DLE, ETX, BCC, & PAD.
                     *
                     * ASSUME THAT THE SPCC IS IN LOCATION $8100,
                     * THEN THE REGISTERS OF THE SPCC ARE AT:
            8100   A RDB    EQU    $8100     RECEIVE DATA BUFFER
            8102   A RSR    EQU    $8102     RECEIVE STATUS REGISTER
            8102   A TDB    EQU    $8102     TRANSMIT DATA BUFFER
            8103   A TCR    EQU    $8103     TRANSMIT CONTROL REGISTER
            8104   A SAR    EQU    $8104     SYNC/SECONDARY ADDRESS REG
            8105   A MCR    EQU    $8105     MODE CONTROL REGISTER
            8106   A TSR    EQU    $8106     TRANSMIT STATUS REGISTER
            8107   A RCR    EQU    $8107     RECEIVE CONTROL REGISTER
                     *
                     * BECAUSE THE TCR IS A WRITE ONLY REGISTER,
                     * WHICH MAKES IT'S DATA INACCESSABLE, THAT DATA
                     * IS ALSO STORED IN THE TCRBUF.
            0010   A TCRBUF EQU    $0010     TRANSMIT CONTROL BUFFER
            1000   A TDATA1 EQU    $1000     TRANSMIT DATA IS STORED AT
                     *                     LOCATIONS $1000 TO $10FF
            1100   A RDATA1 EQU    $1100     RECEIVE DATA IS STORED AT
                     *                     LOCATIONS $1100 TO $11FF
                     *
                     * THE BISYNC TRANSMIT ROUTINE
                     *
                     * INITIALIZE THE MODE CONTROL REGISTER (MCR),
                     * THE TRANSMIT CONTROL REGISTER (TCR), &
                     * THE RECEIVE CONTROL REGISTER (RCR).
                     *
A 0040                      ORG    $40
A 0040 86 C1       A TBI01  LDAA   #$C1      INIT MCR
A 0042 B7 8105     A        STAA   MCR       FOR BISYNC
                     * BIT 0    EC    ERROR CONTROL, PRESETS CCITT
                     * BIT 1    LOOP  NOT IN SELF TEST MODE
                     * BIT 2    NRZI  NRZ DATA
                     * BIT 3    CC    NUMBER OF CONTROL CHARACTERS
                     * BIT 4    LRSS  LOOP REPEAT/ SYNC STRIP

                     * BIT 567  PROTOCOL SELECT - BISYNC USASCII
                     *
                     * INITIALIZE THE TCR
```

```
A 0045 86 48     A         LDAA   #$48
A 0047 B7 8103   A         STAA   TCR
A 004A 97 10     A         STAA   TCRBUF
                  * BIT 012 TRANS CHAR LENGTH, DEFAULT 8-BITS
                  * BIT 3   RTS   REQUEST TO SEND
                  * BIT 4   EOM   END OF MESSAGE
                  * BIT 5   GATD  GO AHEAD/ TRANSMIT DLE
                  * BIT 6   TACG  BISYNC   CRC ON TRANSMIT MESSAGE
                  * BIT 7   SOM   START OF MESSAGE
                  *
                  * INITIALIZE THE RCR
A 004C 86 8C     A         LDAA   #$8C
A 004E B7 8107   A         STAA   RCR
                  * BIT 01  RCL  RECEIVE CHARACTER LENGTH
                  * BIT 2   RE   RECEIVE ENABLE
                  * BIT 3   CRC  SELECT
                  * BIT 45  NOT USED
                  * BIT 6   MISC CONTROLS THE MISC BAR OUTPUT PIN
                  * BIT 7   DTR  DATA TRANSMIT READY
                  *
                  * SOM - TRANSMIT SYN, SYN, DLE, STX.
                  * TEST TOR & TUR ERROR STATUS BITS
                  *
A 0051 F6 8106   A TBI02   LDAB   TSR       GET STATUS REG
A 0054 C5 A0     A         BITB   #$A0      TEST ERROR BITS
A 0056 26 4F 00A7          BNE    ERROA     BR IF ERROR
                  * TEST IF TRANSMIT DATA BUFFER EMPTY
A 0058 C5 40     A         BITB   #$40      TBMT
A 005A 27 F5 0051          BEQ    TBI02     WAIT TILL BUFFER EMPTY
                  * ELSE OUTPUT SYN, SYN, DLE, STX
                  *      SET SOM  BIT - TRANSMIT SYN, SYN
                  *      SET GATA BIT - TRANSMITS DLE BEFORE DATA
                  *      LOAD STX INTO DATA BUFFER
                  *
A 005C 96 10     A         LDAA   TCRBUF    GET CONTROL CHARACTER
A 005E 8A A0     A         ORAA   #$A0      SET SOM & GATD BITS
A 0060 B7 8103   A         STAA   TCR       LOAD CONTROL REG
A 0063 86 02     A         LDAA   #$02      LOAD STX
A 0065 B7 8102   A         STAA   TDB       INTO DATA BUFFFER
                  *
                  * OUTPUT TRANSPARENT DATA - 256 BYTES
                  * INSERT DLE CHAR ($40) PRIOR TO DATA CODE $40
                  *
A 0068 CE 1000   A TBI03   LDX    #TDATA1   LOAD POINTER
A 006B 7F 0000   A         CLR    $0000     SET DATA COUNTER
A 006E F6 8106   A TBI04   LDAB   TSR       GET STATUS BITS
A 0071 C5 A0     A         BITB   #$A0      TEST ERROR BITS
A 0073 26 32 00A7          BNE    ERROA     BR TO ERROR
A 0075 C5 40     A         BITB   #$40      TEST TBMT BIT
A 0077 27 F5 006E          BEQ    TBI04
                  * GET & TEST DATA FOR DLE ($40)
A 0079 A6 00     A         LDAA   0,X


A 007B 81 40     A         CMPA   #$40
A 007D 26 07 0086          BNE    TBI05     BR AROUNT DLE INSERT
```

```
                             * INSERT DLE CODE BY SETTING GATD BIT
A 007F D6 10      A                LDAB   TCRBUF
A 0081 CA 20      A                ORAB   #$20      SET GATD BIT
A 0083 F7 8103    A                STAB   TCR
                             * TRANSMIT DATA
A 0086 B7 8102    A TBI05          STAA   TDB
A 0089 08                          INX              INC POINTER
A 008A 7C 0000    A                INC    $0000     INC DATA COUNTER
A 008D 26 DF 006E                  BNE    TBI04
                             *
                             * END OF MESSAGE, TRANSMIT DLE, ETX, BCC, & PAD
                             * TO TRANSMIT END OF MESSAGE, SET CONTROL BITS
                             *         EOM  - END OF MESSAGE BIT TCR-3
                             *         GATD - GO AHEAD/ TRANSMIT DLE BEFORE ET
                             * THEN LOAD THE TDB WITH ASCII CODE FOR ETX ($03)
                             * THE SPCC THEN TRANSMITS THE BCC CHARACTER
                             *
A 008F F6 8106    A TBI06          LDAB   TSR
A 0092 C5 A0      A                BITB   #$A0
A 0094 26 6B 0101                  BNE    ERROR
A 0096 C5 40      A                BITB   #$40
A 0098 27 F5 008F                  BEQ    TBI06
                             * SET CONTROL BITS DLE & EOM
A 009A 96 10      A                LDAA   TCRBUF
A 009C 8A 18      A                ORAA   #$18
A 009E B7 8103    A                STAA   TCR       LOAD CONTROL REG
                             * LOAD TRANSMIT DATA BUFFER WITH ETX ($03)
A 00A1 86 03      A                LDAA   #$03
A 00A3 B7 8102    A                STAA   TDB
                             * THE SPCC THEN AUTOMATICLLY TRANSMITS THE BCC
                             * CHARACTER & PAD
A 00A6 39                          RTS
                             *
                             *
                             * EXTEND THE BRANCH TO ERROR RANGE
A 00A7 7E 0101    A ERROA          JMP    ERROR
                             *
                             *
                             * THE BISYNC RECEIVE ROUTINE
                             *
                             * START OF MESSAGE:
                             *      ..FOR TRANSPARENT DATA - SYN, SYN, DEL, STX
                             *      ..FOR NON-TRANSPARENT DATA - SYN, SYN, STX
                             * THE SOFTWARE DETECT THE STX OR DLE, STX
                             * CHARACTERS & EITHER CLEARS OR SETS THE
                             * TRANSPARENT DATA FLAG AT LOC $0001
                             *
A 00AA 7F 0001    A RBI02          CLR    $0001     CLEAR TRANS DATA FLAG
A 00AD F6 8102    A                LDAB   RSR       GET STATUS BITS
A 00B0 C5 40      A                BITB   #$40      DATA AVAILABLE ?
A 00B2 27 F6 00AA                  BEQ    RBI02
A 00B4 B6 8100    A                LDAA   RDB       GET DATA
A 00B7 81 40      A                CMPA   #$40      CMP FOR DLE CHARACTER


A 00B9 26 0D 00C8                  BNE    RBI03     NON-TRANSPARENT DATA
                             * ELSE THE DATA IS TRANSPARENT & SET FLAG
```

```
00BB 7A 0001   A        DEC    $0001     SET FLAG
                      * GET SECOND CHARACTER
00BE F6 8102   A RBI02A LDAB   RSR       GET STATUS BITS
00C1 C5 40     A        BITB   #$40      DATA AVAILABLE ?
00C3 27 F9 00BE         BEQ    RBI02A
00C5 B6 8100   A        LDAA   RDB       GET DATA
                      * TEST FOR STX CHARACTER
00C8 81 20     A RBI03  CMPA   #$20
00CA 26 DE 00AA         BNE    RBI02     BR BACK
                      * ELSE PROCEED IF STX CHARACTER
                      *
00CC CE 1100   A RECBIS LDX    #RDATA1   LOAD POINTER
00CF F6 8102   A RBI04  LDAB   RSR       GET STATUS BITS
00D2 2B 2D 0101         BMI    ERROR     BR TO ERROR ROUTINE
00D4 C5 20     A        BITB   #$20      TEST REOM
00D6 26 24 00FC         BNE    RBI06     BR TO EOM
00D8 C5 40     A        BITB   #$40      TEST RDA
00DA 27 F3 00CF         BEQ    RBI04     BR IF DATA NOT AVALIABLE
                      * DATA AVALIAABLE
00DC B6 8100   A        LDAA   RDB       GET DATA
                      * TEST FOR DLE CHARACTER
00DF 81 40     A        CMPA   #$40      TEST FOR DLE
00E1 26 14 00F7         BNE    RBI05A    BY-PASS & ACCEPT DATA
                      * ELSE TEST FOR SECOND DLE CHARACTER
00E3 F6 8102   A RBI05  LDAB   RSR
00E6 2B 19 0101         BMI    ERROR
00E8 C5 20     A        BITB   #$20      TEST ROEM
00EA 26 10 00FC         BNE    RBI06     BR TO EOM
00EC C5 40     A        BITB   #$40      TEST RDA BIT
00EE 27 F3 00E3         BEQ    RBI05
00F0 B6 8100   A        LDAA   RDB       GET DATA
00F3 81 40     A        CMPA   #$40      TEST FOR DLE
00F5 26 0A 0101         BNE    ERROR     BR IF NOT DLE
                      * ELSE INPUT ONE DLE CHARACTER
                      *
00F7 A7 00     A RBI05A STAA   0,X       STORE DATA
00F9 08                 INX
00FA 20 D3 00CF         BRA    RBI04     GET NEXT BYTE
                      * AT EOM TEST RERR BIT FOR BCC ERROR
00FC C5 01     A RBI06  BITB   #$01
00FE 26 01 0101         BNE    ERROR
0100 39                 RTS
                      *
                      * DUMMY INSTRUCTION
0101 01           ERROR NOP
                      *
                        END
TOTAL ERRORS 00000--00000
```

10-4 BOP TRANSMISSION IN A MULTIPOINT CONFIGURATION

This section describes two programs, one for transmitting and one for receiving data from a master to a secondary station in a multipoint configuration via a bit-oriented protocol (BOP). The discussion tracks each part of the message, start, data, and end as it originates with the transmit program, the function of the transmit SPCC, the function of the receive SPCC, and the receive program (see Table 10-10). The text is 256 bytes of data from 0 to $FF, and the message format is illustrated in Fig. 10-7: flag, address field, control field, data, BCC and closing flag.

Some terms are unique to the multipoint configuration in BOP:

- Primary station
- Secondary station
- Address field
- Control field

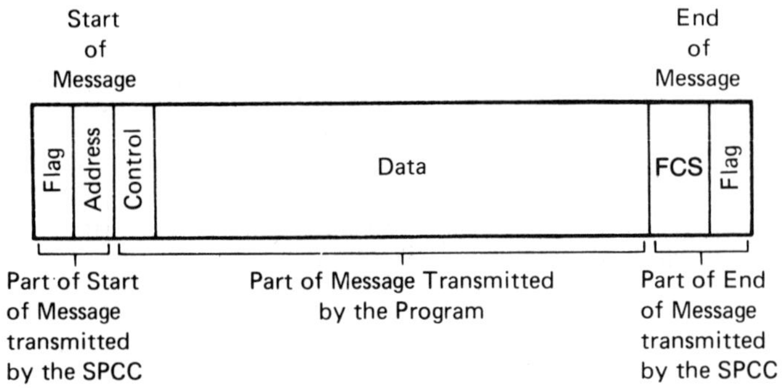

Figure 10-7. BOP message format used in example.

Primary Station

In a multipoint configuration, one primary station controls the network and decides when and which secondary station should be the transmitter and the receiver. It may do the following:

- Transmit to one or more secondary stations.
- Receive from a secondary station.
- Poll a secondary for a query on how many successful messages have been received.
- Poll a secondary to determine if a station wants to transmit.

Secondary Station

There may be up to 255 secondary stations, each with a unique address, and the address $FF addresses all secondaries. The sync/secondary address register of the SPCC stores the address of each secondary station and is loaded during the initializing process. The sync/secondary address register is not used by the primary station.

Address Field

After a flag character is received, the first non-flag character, the address field, signals the beginning of message. It is a 1-byte position dependent field that addresses up to 255 stations, and the global address $FF addresses all the secondary stations.

All secondary stations continuously scan the special input data for a flag character (0111 1110). Then each secondary station examines the received address field to test if it is addressed. If addressed, the secondary station proceeds to receive the message. If the address does not match either the secondary station address or a global address $FF, the serial data of the message are ignored and the SPCC resumes its search for flags.

Control Field

The primary station controls and commands the secondary stations on how to respond via the control field. There are three control field formats (Table 10-11):

	Addressed by Accumulator Bits 1	0
Information format	X	0
Supervisory format	0	1
Nonsequence format	1	1

When an information format has a data field, it is identified by a zero in accumulator bit 0. The N(S) field, accumulator bits 1, 2, and 3, indicates the number of messages sent to that station. In the N(R) field, accumulator bits 5, 6, and 7 indicate the number of messages received by that station. If a frame is received incorrectly, that is, the number in the N(R) field disagrees with the bookkeeping account of the receive station, then corrective action is taken by the system.

The poll/final (P/F) bit (bit 4) has two meanings, depending on whether a primary or secondary initiates transmission of the frame. It is used by the primary to solicit responses from the secondary station and, in this case, is called a *poll bit*. It is used by the secondary to indicate to the primary that this is the last (final) frame to be transmitted. Thus a P/F bit is sent to the secondary requesting transmission and is sent to the primary by the secondary ending transmission of the requested data. Some communication systems can operate with the information format alone.

The supervisory and nonsequence formats are identified by a 0 and 1 respectively in the 2 and 3 serial bits of the control field. The supervisory frames are used to acknowledge the reception of error-free frames, to request retransmission of information frames, and to inhibit the sending of information frames.

Nonsequenced frames are used for data-link management. Data-link management includes activating and initializing secondary stations, controlling the response mode of secondary stations, and reporting procedural errors.

Initializing the SPCC

The mode control (MCR) and the sync/secondary address registers are initialized with different codes for the primary and secondary stations, whereas the transmit (TCR) and receive (RCR) control registers are initialized with the same code. The addresses of the register in this example are as follows:

Location:	\$8100	RDB	Receive data buffer	Read only
	\$8101	RSR	Receive status register	Read only
	\$8102	TDB	Transmit data buffer	Write only
	\$8103	TCR	Transmit control buffer	Write only
	\$8104	SAR	Sync/secondary address register	Write only
	\$8105	MCR	Mode control register	Write only
	\$8106	TSR	Transmit status register	Read only
	\$8107	RCR	Receive control register	Write only

The TCR is a write only reigster. During the transmit program some of the bits of the TCR must be modified. Since the data in the TCR are inaccessible, the same data are also stored at memory location TCRBUF. To modify a bit in the TCR, the bits in the TCRBUF are accessed by the program and then reloaded into the TCR.

The MCR register of the primary station is initialized with a 00, and the secondary station with $41 (0100 0001):

Bit 0	EC	1	Error control; presets CCITT to all 1's
Bit 1	Loop	0	Not in the self-test mode
Bit 2	NRZI	0	NRZ data
Bit 3	CC	0	Number of control characters (not used)
Bit 4	LRSS	0	Loop repeat/sync strip (not used)
Bits 5,6,7		010	Protocol select: BOP primary, 000 BOP secondary, 010

The sync/secondary address register is not used in the primary station and is set to $42 in the secondary station.

The TCR is initialized with $08 (0000 1000):

Bits 0,1,2		000	Transmitter character length, 8 bits, 000
Bit 3	RTS	1	Request to send, pin is output low
Bit 4	EOM	0	End of message
Bit 5	GATD	0	(Go-ahead) not used in this protocol mode
Bit 6	TACG	0	Transmit ABORT
Bit 7	SOM	0	Start of message

The RCR is initialized with $8C (1000 1100):

Bits 0,1	RCL	00	Receive character length, 8 bits
Bit 2	RE	1	Receive enable
Bit 3	CRC	1	Selected
Bits 4,5		00	Not used
Bit 6	MISC	0	Controls the MISC bar output pin
Bit 7	DTR	1	Data terminal ready output pin low

Transmitting the Flag (0111 1110) To transmit the flag, the transmit program, at location labeled TBOPO2, sets the SOM control bit. The status register is tested for an error condition, TOR or TUR, and for the transmit buffer's availability. The transmit SPCC senses the SOM bit and transmits two flags (0111 1110). The flag code, or any code with six consecutive 1's cannot be transmitted via the data buffer. It is transmitted automatically by the chip and this is controlled by the microprocessor system via the control register.

Receiving the Flag The SPCC receiver senses the flag, then sequences and prepares to test the address field. The receive program takes no action.

Transmitting the Address Field The transmit program first tests the status bits for an error and then for an empty data buffer. Second, it loads the address of the secondary station into the data buffer for transmission. The SPCC then tests the data it is transmitting, and if there are five consecutive 1's, inserts a 0. The SPCC also starts to accumulate the CRC character on the transmitted data.

Receiving the Address Field The SPCC receiver removes the 0 if it follows the five consecutive 1's, and starts to accumulate the CRC character on the received data. The SPCC compares the received address against the address in the secondary address register and, if they are equal, the SPCC for that secondary station sequences to receive data. If the addresses do not match, then the secondary SPCC returns to search for the flag (0111 1110).

Transmitting the Control Field The transmit program tests the status register for a NO error and an empty buffer. It then loads the control field. The SPCC transmits the control field, just as any other data, unless the data character length is less than 8 bits.

Receiving the Control Field The SPCC receiver passes the control field through to the receive buffer as data. The receive program, however, examines the control field to determine the nature of the message and branches to one of the several routines for the appropriate response. In this example, which is to receive data, the index register is loaded with the location in memory to store the received data.

Transmitting the Data The transmit program at location labeled TBOPO6 accesses the data from memory and loads it into the data buffer after testing the status bits. The SPCC transmits the data.

Receiving the Data The SPCC passes the data to the receive buffer, and the receive program at location labeled RBOPO6 loads it into memory. The receive status register is tested for the following:

- An error
- Receive data buffer full
- An end of message (REOM)

Transmitting the FCS Character and Flag The transmit program at location labeled TBOPO8 simply sets the end of message (EOM) control bit immediately after the last character of the end of message is loaded into the transmitter data buffer. This causes the SPCC to transmit the CRC character and the closing flag.

Receiving the FCS Character and Flag The SPCC receiver compares its own generated CRC character against the one from the transmit station. If they agree, the SPCC senses the flag and indicates a successful message received by setting the REOM status bit and not setting an error status bit. If the CRC characters are not equal, then the SPCC sets the receive error bit, RERR, and the receive end of message, REOM. For a successful message, the receive program at location labeled RBOPO8 tests the status register for an REOM bit, and no error bit is set. If either the RERR or the receive abort (ABGA) bit is set, the program branches to the error routine.

```
                              NAM     BOP
                    * THIS PROGRAM USES THE SYNCHRNOUS PROTOCOL
                    * COMMUNICATION CONTROLLER (SPCC) SECTION 10.3.
                    * IN THE BISYNC PROTOCOL TO TRANSMIT 256 BYTES
                    * OF DATA  -00 TO $FF-  IN THE TRANSPARENT DATA
                    * MODE.
                    * THE MESSAGE CONSISTS OF SYN, SYN, DLE, SYN,
                    * TRANSPARENT DATA, DLE, ETX, BCC, & PAD.
                    *
                    * ASSUME THAT THE SPCC IS IN LOCATION $8100,
                    * THEN THE REGISTERS OF THE SPCC ARE AT:
          8100   A RDB      EQU    $8100     RECEIVE DATA BUFFER
          8102   A RSR      EQU    $8102     RECEIVE STATUS REGISTER
          8102   A TDB      EQU    $8102     TRANSMIT DATA BUFFER
          8103   A TCR      EQU    $8103     TRANSMIT CONTROL REGISTER
          8104   A SAR      EQU    $8104     SYNC/SECONDARY ADDRESS REG
          8105   A MCR      EQU    $8105     MODE CONTROL REGISTER
          8106   A TSR      EQU    $8106     TRANSMIT STATUS REGISTER
          8107   A RCR      EQU    $8107     RECEIVE CONTROL REGISTER
                    *
                    * BECAUSE THE TCR IS A WRITE ONLY REGISTER,
                    * WHICH MAKES IT'S DATA INACCESSABLE, THAT DATA
                    * IS ALSO STORED IN THE TCRBUF.
          0010   A TCRBUF EQU    $0010     TRANSMIT CONTROL BUFFER
          1000   A TDATA1 EQU    $1000     TRANSMIT DATA IS STORED AT
                    *                    LOCATIONS $1000 TO $10FF
          1100   A RDATA1 EQU    $1100     RECEIVE DATA IS STORED AT
                    *                    LOCATIONS $1100 TO $11FF
                    *
                    * THE BOP TRANSMIT ROUTINE
                    *

                    * INITIALIZE THE MODE CONTROL REGISTER (MCR),
                    * THE TRANSMIT CONTROL REGISTER (TCR), &
                    * THE RECEIVE CONTROL REGISTER (RCR).
                    *
A 0040                      ORG    $40
A 0040 86 00     A TBOP01 LDAA   #$00      INIT MCR
A 0042 B7 8105   A        STAA   MCR       FOR BOP
```

```
                            * BIT 0    EC    ERROR CONTROL, PRESETS CCITT
                            * BIT 1    LOOP  NOT IN SELF TEST MODE
                            * BIT 2    NRZI  NRZ DATA
                            * BIT 3    CC    SELECT A CONTROL CHARACTER
                            * BIT 4    LRSS  LOOP REPEAT/ SYNC STRIP
                            * BIT 567  PROTOCOL SELECT - BOP PRIMARY STATION
                            *
                            * INITIALIZE THE TCR
0045 86 48      A                 LDAA   #$48
0047 B7 8103    A                 STAA   TCR
004A 97 10      A                 STAA   TCRBUF
                            * BIT 012 BOP PRIMARY
                            * BIT 3    RTS   REQUEST TO SEND
                            * BIT 4    EOM   END OF MESSAGE
                            * BIT 5    GATD  TRANSMIT MARKS BETWEEN FRAMES
                            * BIT 6    TACG  NO TRANSMIT ABORT SET INITIALLY
                            * BIT 7    SOM   START OF MESSAGE
                            *
                            * INITIALIZE THE RCR
004C 86 8C      A                 LDAA   #$8C
004E B7 8107    A                 STAA   RCR
                            * BIT 01   RCL  RECEIVE CHARACTER LENGTH
                            * BIT 2    RE   RECEIVE ENABLE
                            * BIT 3    CRC  SELECT
                            * BIT 45   NOT USED
                            * BIT 6    MISC CONTROLS THE MISC BAR OUTPUT PIN
                            * BIT 7    DTR  DATA TRANSMIT READY
                            *
                            * INITALIZE THE SYNC ADDRESS REGISTER FOR PRIMARY
                            * STATION, WHERE THE SECONDARY STATION ADDR - $42
0051 86 42      A                 LDAA   #$42
0053 B7 8104    A                 STAA   SAR
                            * OUTPUT MESSAGE: FLAG, ADDRESS FIELD,
                            * CONTROL FIELD, DATA, BCC, FLAG.
                            * THE ADDRESS OF THE SECONDARY ADDRESS IN THIS
                            * EXAMPLE IS $42.
                            * THE CONTROL FIELD IS A I-BYTE 00, & IS IGNORED
                            * IN THIS EXAMPLE BY THE RECEIVING STATION
                            * THE CONTROL FIELD GENERALLY INDICATES THE TYPE
                            * OFF MESSAGE BEING TRANSMITTED.
                            *
0056 CE 1000    A           TBOP02 LDX    #TDATA1   LOAD POINTER
0059 7F 0000    A                  CLR    $0000     CLEAR DATA COUNTER
                            *
                            * SOM   CHECK STATUS REGISTER
005C F6 8106    A           TBOP03 LDAB   TSR       GET STATUS REG
005F C5 A0      A                  BITB   #$A0      TEST TOR & TUR
0061 26 48 00AB                    BNE    ERROR1    BR TO ERROR ROUTINE
                            * TEST FOR TRANSMITTER EMPTY - TBMT
0063 C5 40      A                  BITB   #$40
0065 27 F5 005C                    BEQ    TBOP03    WAIT
                            * ELSE TRANSMIT FLAG
0067 D6 10      A                  LDAB   TCRBUF    GET CONTROL REG
0069 CA 80      A                  ORAB   #$80      SET SOM
006B F7 8103    A                  STAB   TCR
                            * TRANSMIT ADDRESS OF SECONDARY STATION
```

```
A 006E 86 42      A        LDAA   #$42
A 0070 B7 8102    A        STAA   TDB
                    * THE CONTROL FIES FIELD GENERALLY INDICATES TYPE
                    * OF MESSAGE
A 0073 4F                  CLRA
                    * TEST STATUS REG
A 0074 F6 8106    A TBOP04 LDAB   TSR
A 0077 C5 A0      A        BITB   #$A0
A 0079 26 30 00AB          BNE    ERROR1
A 007B C5 40      A        BITB   #$40
A 007D 27 F5 0074          BEQ    TBOP04
A 007F B7 8102    A        STAA   TDB
                    *
                    * TRANSMIT 256 -BYTES OF DATA
                    *
A 0082 F6 8106    A TBOP06 LDAB   TSR
A 0085 C5 A0      A        BITB   #$A0
A 0087 26 22 00AB          BNE    ERROR1
A 0089 C5 40      A        BITB   #$40
A 008B 26 F5 0082          BNE    TBOP06
                    * BUFFER EMPTY, TRANSMIT DATA
A 008D A6 00      A        LDAA   0,X
A 008F B7 8102    A        STAA   TDB
A 0092 08                  INX
A 0093 7C 0000    A        INC    $0000     INC DATA COUNTER
A 0096 26 EA 0082          BNE    TBOP06
                    *
                    * TRANSMIT EOM: BCC & CLOSING FLAG
A 0098 F6 8106    A TBOP08 LDAB   TSR
A 009B C5 A0      A        BITB   #$A0
A 009D 26 0C 00AB          BNE    ERROR1
A 009F C5 40      A        BITB   #$40
A 00A1 27 F5 0098          BEQ    TBOP08
                    * SET EOM FLAG - TCR BIT 4
A 00A3 96 10      A        LDAA   TCRBUF
A 00A5 8A 10      A        ORAA   #$10
A 00A7 B7 8103    A        STAA   TCR
                    *
A 00AA 39                  RTS
                    *
                    *
A 00AB 7E 0105    A ERROR1 JMP    RRROR
                    *
                    * THE BOP RECEIVE ROUTINE
                    * SECONDARY STATION ADDRESS $42
                    *
A 00AE 86 00      A RBOP01 LDAA   #00
A 00B0 B7 8105    A        STAA   MCR
A 00B3 86 4A      A        LDAA   #$4A
A 00B5 B7 8103    A        STAA   TCR
A 00B8 86 8C      A        LDAA   #$8C
A 00BA B7 8107    A        STAA   RCR
A 00BD 86 42      A        LDAA   #$42
A 00BF B7 8104    A        STAA   SAR
                    *
                    * RECEIVE MESSAGE: FLAG, ADDRESS FIELD,
```

```
                          * CONTROL FIELD, DATA, BCC, FLAG.
                          *
                          * . THE SPCC SENSES THE STARTING FLAG & COMPARES
                          *   THE RECEIVED AGAINST THE SECONDAY ADDRESS IN
                          *   THE SAR REGISTER.
                          * . THE SPCC FIRST RECEIVES THE CONTROL FIELD,
                          *   & THEN THE DATA.
                          * . A 0 FOLLOWING FIVE CONSECUTIVE 1'S IS
                          *   AUTOMATICALLY DELETED.
                          * . THE CRC CHARACTER IS GENERATED AS THE
                          *   DATA MOVES THRU THE RECEIVE DATA BUFFER.
                          * . THE STATUS BITS ARE TESTED PRIOR TO READING
                          *   THE DATA.
                          *     ROVR   ERROR OVERRUN
                          *     REAM   END OF MESSAGE
                          *     RDA    RECEIVE DATA AVAILABLE
                          *
                          * GET ADDRESS AND DISCARD
00C2 F6 8102  A RBOP04 LDAB    RSR
00C5 2B 3E 0105        BMI     RRROR
00C7 C5 20    A        BITB    #$20      TEST REOM
00C9 26 35 0100        BNE     RBOP08    BR TO EOM
00CB C5 40    A        BITB    #$40      TEST RDA BIT
00CD 27 F3 00C2        BEQ     RBOP04
00CF B6 8100  A        LDAA    RDB       DISCARD ADDRESS
                * GET CONTROL WORD AND DISCARD
00D2 F6 8102  A RBOP05 LDAB    RSR
00D5 2B 2E 0105        BMI     RRROR
00D7 C5 20    A        BITB    #$20      TEST REOM
00D9 26 25 0100        BNE     RBOP08    BR TO EOM
00DB C5 40    A        BITB    #$40      TEST RDA
00DD 27 F3 00D2        BEQ     RBOP05
00DF B6 8100  A        LDAA    RDB       DISCARD CONTROL FIELD
                * GET DATA
00E2 CE 1100  A        LDX     #RDATA1   LOAD POINTER
00E5 7F 0000  A        CLR     $0000     DATA COUNTER
                *
00E8 F6 8102  A RBOP06 LDAB    RSR
00EB 2B 18 0105        BMI     RRROR
00ED C5 20    A        BITB    #$20
00EF 26 0F 0100        BNE     RBOP08
00F1 C5 40    A        BITB    #$40
00F3 27 F3 00E8        BEQ     RBOP06
00F5 B6 8100  A        LDAA    RDB       GET DATA
00F8 A7 00    A        STAA    0,X       STORE DATA
00FA 08                INX               INC POINTER
00FB 7C 0000  A        INC     $0000     DATA COUNT
00FE 20 E8 00E8        BRA     RBOP06
                *
                * EOM
                * THE RECEIVED AND GENERATED CRC CHARACTERS
                * ARE COMPARED. THE RERR & ABGA STATUS
                * BITS ARE TESTED AND IF THERE THEY DON'T
```

```
                          * INDICATE AN ERROR, THEN THE MESSAGE IS
                          * ASSUMED TO BE CORRECT.
                          *
 0100 C5 01             A RBOP08 BITB   #$01      TEST RERR
 0102 26 01 0105                 BNE    RRROR
 0104 39                         RTS
                          *
                          * DUMMY INSTRUCTION
 0105 01                  RRROR  NOP
                          *
                                 END
TOTAL ERRORS 00000--00000
```

10-5 SUMMARY

There are five primary advantages of the SPCC:

- The parallel-to-serial and serial-to-parallel conversion of transmit and receive data
- Inserting extra bits or characters required for transparency
- Calculating the error check code (BCC)
- Transmitting some control characters
- Detecting special control characters or bit sequences

If these operations were not performed by the transmit and receive SPCCs, they would be a part of the transmit and receive program. The ability of the SPCC to handle BCP and BOP protocols makes the programs for the BISYNC and BOP receive stations more similar.

Table 10-1. Defining the Bits of the MCR (Mode Control Register), Address 5

7	6	5	4	3	2	1	0
PROTOCOL SELECT			LRSS	CC	NRZI	LOOP	EC

Bit	Name	Mode	Function
0	EC		Error control
		BOP	0 = CCITT preset to all 0's 1 = CCITT preset to all 1's
		Bisync	0 = CRC-16 preset to all 0's 1 = CCITT preset to all 0's
		BCP	Same as Bisync for 8-bit characters length *only*
1	LOOP	All	Self-test loop mode; TSO loop to RSI internally
2	NRZI	All	0 = NRZ data 1 = NRZI, zero complementing
3	CC	BOP	0 = 1 control byte, 1 = 2 control bytes
		Bisync	Not used
		BCP	Not used
4	LRSS		Loop repeater/sync strip
		BOP	0 = Normal mode 1 = Loop repeater mode
		Bisync	Not used
		BCP	0 = Tx mark for FILL character Strip Leading SYNC's only 1 = Tx SYNC for FILL character Strip all SYNC
5-7		All	Protocol select 7 6 5 0 0 0 BOP, primary 0 1 0 BOP, secondary 0 1 1 BOP, secondary global 1 0 0 BCP 1 1 0 Bisync, USASCII 1 1 1 Bisync, EBCDIC 0 0 1 Reserved 1 0 1 Reserved

Table 10-2. The SAR: Sync/Secondary Address Register

7	6	5	4	3	2	1	0
Sync/Secondary Address							

Bit	Name	Mode	Function
0-7	SAR		Sync/address register
		BOP	Secondary address for secondary station mode
		Bisync	Not used
		BCP	SYNC character

Table 10-3. The TDB: Transmitter Data Buffer

7	6	5	4	3	2	1	0
Transmitter Data Buffer							

Bit	Name	Mode	Function
0-7	TDB	All	Transmitter data buffer

Table 10-4. TCR: Transmitter Control Register

7	6	5	4	3	2	1	0
SOM	TACG	GATD	EOM	RTS	TCL_2 – TCL_0		

Bit	Name	Mode	Function
0-2	TCL_0-TCL_2		Transmitter character length
		BOP/BCP	0 1 2
			0 0 0 8-bits
			1 0 0 1
			0 1 0 2
			1 1 0 3
			0 0 1 4
			1 0 1 5
			0 1 1 6
			1 1 1 7
		BISYNC	Character length automatically 8 bits
3	RTS	All	Request to send. 0 = 1 on $\overline{RTS}$ output; 1 = 0 on $\overline{RTS}$ output.
4	EOM	All	End of message. 1 defines character in TBD as last data character of message. This bit is self-canceling.
5	GATD		Go-ahead/transmit DLE
		BOP	0 = FLAGs transmitted between frames
			1 = Marks transmitted between frames
		BISYNC	1 = Transmit DLE character ahead of character in TDB. Enter transparent mode
		BCP	Not used
6	TACG		Transmit abort/CRC generate
		BOP	1 = Transmit abort
		BISYNC	0 = No CRC on transmitted message
		BCP	1 = Transmit block check character after last data character.
7	SOM	All	Start of message. Initiates start of message causing SYNCs or FLAGs to be transmitted. This bit is self-canceling

Table 10-5. TSR: Transmitter Status Register

7	6	5	4	3	2	1	0
TUR	TBMT	TOR	Not Used		CTS	CD	DSR

Bit	Name	Mode	Function
0	DSR	All	Data set ready. Equals 1 when $\overline{DSR}$ input is low
1	CD	All	Carrier detect. Equals 1 when $\overline{CD}$ input is low
2	CTS	All	Clear to send. Equals 1 when $\overline{CTS}$ input is low
3-4			Not used
5	TOR	All	Transmitter overrun. 1 = CPU updated TCDR before the SPCC was ready
6	TBMT	All	Transmitter buffer empty. 1 = CPU may load new data and/or control information in TCDR
7	TUR	All	Transmitter underrun. 1 = CPU failed to load TDB in time. Abort is transmitted in BOP mode. When TUR occurs, fill characters are transmitted in BISYNC or BCP. TUR occurs along with a low level of $\overline{IRQ}$ output.

Table 10-6. RDB: Receive Data Buffer

7	6	5	4	3	2	1	0
Receiver Data Buffer							

Bit	Name	Mode	Function
0-7	RDB	All	Receiver data buffer

Table 10-7. RCR: Receive Control Register

7	6	5	4	3	2	1	0
DTR	MISC	Not Used		CRC	RE	RCL_1-RCL_0	

Bit	Name	Mode	Function
0-1	RCL_0-RCL_1	All	Receiver character length 8 9 0 0 8-bits 1 0 5 0 1 6 1 1 7
2	RE	All	Receiver enable. 1 enables receiver
3	CRC	All	0 = No CRC (transmit/receive) 1 = CRC selected
4-5			Not used
6	MISC	All	Miscellaneous. 0 = 1 on $\overline{MISC}$ output 1 = 0 on $\overline{MISC}$ output
7	DTR	All	Data terminal ready. 0 = 1 on DTR output 1 = 0 on DTR output

Table 10-8. RSR: Receive Status Register

7	6	5	4	3 2 1	0
ROVR	RDA	REOM	ABGA	ROL_2-ROL_0	RERR

Bit	Name	Mode	Function
0	RERR	All	Received error. 1 = CRC error occurred on received message. Asserted when last character is in RDB.
1-3	RDL_0-RDL_2	BOP only	Received last character length. Corresponds to the number of bits in last character. 000 = 8 bits, 100 = 1 bit, 010 = 2 bits, etc.
4	ABGA	BOP only	Abort/go-ahead corresponds to received abort if RERR = 1 or go-ahead if RERR = 0
5	REOM	 BOP BISYNC	Received end of message 1 = Received flag, abort or go-ahead 1 = Received ITB, ETB, or ETX (preceded by DLE in transparent mode)
6	RDA	All	Received data available. 1 indicates valid data available in RDB
7	ROVR	All	Receiver overrun. 1 indicates CPU failed to read data in RDB before next character was assembled. Accompanied by a low on $\overline{IRQ}$ output

Table 10-9. BISYNC Protocol

Part of Message	Transmitter Program	Transmitter SPCC	Receiver SPCC	Receiver Program
1. Start of message SYN, SYN, DLE, STX	1(A) Set control bits • SOM (TCR7) = 1 • GATD (TCR5) = 1 (B) Transmit STX = $02 through data buffer	1(A) SOM bit transmits SYN, SYN (B) GATD bit transmits DLE (C) Transmit thru data buffer STX DLE, STX indicates transparent data	1(A) Sense SYN, SYN (B) Sense transparent data being transmitted	Sense for DLE, STX, and set transparent data flag.
2. Transparent data	2(A) Test status bits • TOR (overrun error) • TUR (underrun error) • TBMT (transmit buffer empty) (B) Test data = DLE ($40) (i) If not equal, transmit data (ii) If equal, set control bit GATD and transmit data	2(A) No error sensed (B) (i) Transmit data (ii) Transmits DLE pair (C) Generate FSC on transmitted data	2(A) For overrun error set ROVE status bit (B) Remove first of DLE pairs (C) Generate BCC on received data	2(A) Sense status bit • ROVE (overrun error) = 0 • RDA (receive buffer empty) = 1 (B) Read data (C) Test REOM status bit Branch to exit
3. End of message DLE, ETX, BCC, PAD	3(A) Set control bit • EOM (TCR4) = 1 • GATD (TCR5) = 1 (B) Transmit ETX = $03 thru data buffer	3(A) GATD bit transmit DLE (B) Transmit ETX thru data buffer (C) Transmit BCC (D) Transmit PAD	3(A) Sense DLE, ETX (B) Compare received and generated BCC characters (C) • Set REOM • Set RERR if received and generated BCC characters not equal	3. Test for BCC error Status bit RERR

Table 10-10. BOP Message Transmission

Part of Message	Transmit Program	Transmit SPCC	Receive SPCC	Receiver Program
1. Flag (0111 1110)	1(A) Test status bits for error (B) Set SOM control bit	1. SOM bit causes SPCC to transmit flag (0111 1110)	1. Sense flag	1. No action
2. Address field	2(A) Test status bits for error and TBMT (B) Load address for secondary station into transmit buffer	2(A) (B) Transmits address field (C) SPCC starts to insert 0's after five 1's (D) SPCC starts to accumulate the FCS character on transmitted data	2(A) (B) Tests address received against the address in the secondary address register (C) SPCC removes inserted 0's (D) SPCC starts to accumulate CRC character on received data (E) Puts address in RDB	2. Receives the address field through the RDB and ignores it
3. Control field	3(A) Test status bits for error and TBMT (B) Load control field into the transmit buffer	3(A) (B) Transmit control field	3(A) For overrun error set ROVR status bit (B) Receive control word	3(A) Read control field (B) The control field in this example, has an address that is loaded into the index register of where the data is stored.
4. Data (information) field	4(A) Test status bits for error and TBMT (B) Load one byte of data into transmit buffer	4(A) (B) Transmit data	4(A) For overrun error set ROUL (B) Receive data	4. Get data from receive buffer
5. BCC field and flag	5. Set EOM control bit	5(A) Transmit the FCS character (B) Transmit flag (0111 1110)	5(A) Detect flag (B) Compare received and generated FCS (C) Set RERR if they don't compare	5(A) Test REOM for end of message (B) Test RERR and ABGA for error or successful message received.

Table 10-11. Control Field Formats

	7 6 5	4	3 2 1	0	Accumulator bits
Information format	N(R)	P/F	N(S)	0	
Supervisory format	N(R)	P/F	-S-	0 1	
Nonsequence format	-N-	P/F	-N-	1 1	

N(S)	Transmitted sequence frame count
N(R)	Received sequence from count
P/F	Poll/final frame
S	Supervisory codes command/respond
N	Nonsequenced codes command/respond

11 The 6809: An Advanced Eight-Bit Microprocessor

Computers are machines defined by their organization, which consists of a processor, memory, I/O, and an instruction set. Understanding the 6800 forms a basis for examining and appreciating the additional capabilities of the more advanced and sophisticated 8- and 16-bit microprocessors. This dynamic, expanding field of microprocessors that have characteristics previously found only in the mini- and the larger-scale computers offers a greater variety of programmable solutions to many problems. It should be appreciated that new terminology has been introduced describing these expanded capabilities.

The earlier microprocessors, however, offer the reader an opportunity to acquire basic concepts in computer programming and organization. This chapter describes the 6809 and its enhanced characteristics of the 6800 family. These additional features are discussed with reference to the earlier chapters, which provided a foundation for the reader to advance to the 6809 microprocessor.

The 6809 offers convenient software advantages for writing multitask programs with relocatable or position-independent codes. Multitask refers to several programs that are executed on the same microcomputer, as opposed to a dedicated microcomputer that executes only one program. There are two basic variations of multitasking. The first combination is a one-user program and a monitor, which is used to load and debug the main program. This is typical of a user program loaded onto the D-2 kit and the J-BUG monitor, which is used to load and debug it (see Chapter 4). In this case it is convenient for each program to have its own stack pointer, which makes it easier to write monitor-type programs. The second version of multitasking is when several tasks or programs are executed on the same microcomputer, apparently independently of each other. In this case, there is one program, the *supervisor*, which is in control of the other user programs.

Relocatable programs are source-code programs that are put into specified memory locations by the assembler at assembly time while generating object code. These programs may be moved or relocated at a different place in memory, but before they are moved the program must be reassembled and each label assigned a new memory location.

Position-independent code is written with the intent of putting the routine anywhere in memory. The program is written where all labels are identified by relative addressing modes, often referenced to the starting address of the routine. Position-independent code has two major applications. The first is with microcomputers with external mass storage, typically disc or magnetic tape, which store many programs and where each program may be loaded anywhere in the RAM memory of the microcomputer. Programs may not only be transferred from mass storage but can also be "down loaded" from larger to smaller computers via synchronous communication lines. The second application is for code stored in ROMs that can be positioned anywhere in the memory space.

The technique of organizing an instruction set in matrix form, instructions/mnemonics, and addressing modes used by the 6800 has been carried over to the 6809 instruction set. It is becoming the standard format for listing an instruction set. Note that the word "instruction" is a misnomer, or perhaps has a double meaning. An instruction often has two parts, a mnemonic and an addressing mode, which are sometimes referred to as the opcode or operand. This technique enables the 6809 programmer to memorize 59 instructions/mnemonics and 10 addressing modes, rather than the 1464 possible unique instructions. It also facilitates a separate discussion of the instruction set and the addressing modes. The reader must appreciate that many of the mnemonics are modified by the addressing modes to form an instruction.

Section 11-1 describes the 6809 programming model and the new 6809 registers. Section 11-2 discusses the 6809 machine code format, which includes the opcode, the postbyte, and the operand. Since an instruction is not completely described until all its parts are discussed, this section functions as a guide to the remainder of the chapter. The 6809 is an enhanced version of the 6800 instruction set and is contrasted with it, and each instruction is described in both its assembler language and machine code form.

Section 11-3 describes the new 6809 instructions and the register addressing mode of operation. Section 11-4 briefly describes the inherent addressing mode. Section 11-5, the non-index addressing modes, describes the immediate, direct, extended, and extended indirect addressing modes. Section 11-6 discusses the variations of the index addressing modes, zero, constant, and accumulator offsets, and the autoincrement/decrement. The relative addressing modes are described in Secs. 11-7 and 11-8, whereas relative addressing, as it pertains to branch instructions, is discussed in Sec. 11-7. Accessing data at an address relative to the program counter is discussed in Sec. 11-8.

11-1 THE 6809 PROGRAMMING MODEL

The 6809 microprocessor's registers (Fig. 11-1) consist of the following:

- Two 8-bit accumulators, A and B, which can be concatenated into one 16-bit accumulator D
- Two 16-bit index registers, X and Y
- Two 16-bit stack pointers, U and S
- Program counter (PC)
- 8-Bit condition code register (CC)
- 8-Bit direct page register (DP)

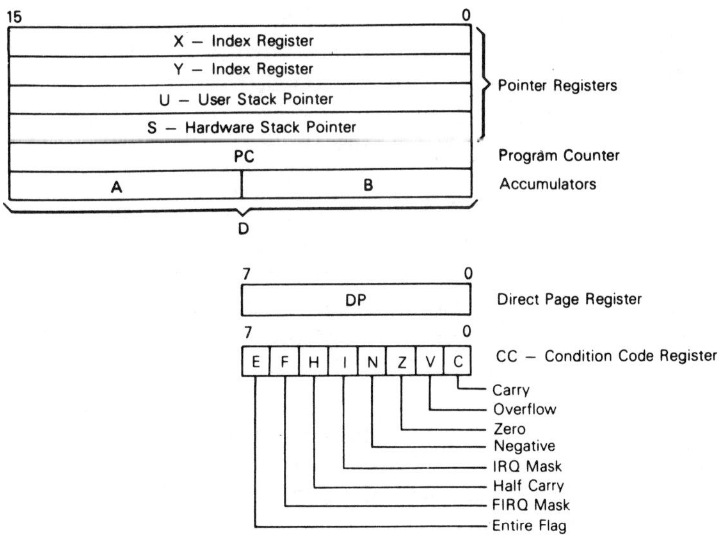

Figure 11-1 6809 programming model. (Courtesy Motorola Semiconductor Products Inc.)

Accumulator

The two 8-bit accumulators, A and B, can be concatenated to form one 16-bit accumulator, D, where accumulator A is in the MSB position. This gives the 6809 the capability for 16-bit or double precision arithmetic.

Pointer Registers

There are X and Y index registers and the U and S stack pointers. Two registers have been added to the 6809, an extra index register (Y) and an extra stack pointer (U). The extra stack pointer makes multitasking more convenient, where the U and S stack pointers are reserved for the user programs and the supervisor programs, respectively. For example, the JBUG monitor program described in Chapter 4 may now be written more conveniently, where the JBUG monitor, a supervisor-type program, uses the S, and the user program utilizes the U stack pointer. The two index registers, X and Y, make it more convenient to write programs that handle several arrays or blocks of data. Another advantage of the 6809 pointer registers is that they can act interchangeably as index or stack pointer registers.

Condition Code Register

The six condition code bits of the 6800 remain unchanged, and two bits, E and F, in bit positions 7 and 6, have been added to the 6809. During interrupts, the data in the processor's registers are loaded into the S stack, sometimes referred to as the hardware stack.

The I bit, bit position 4, blocks or permits the interrupt request signal from initiating an interrupt. When the I bit equals 0, the interrupt sequence is initiated by a low signal, the $\overline{\text{IRQ}}$ pin, and the contents of all but the S stack of the processor's registers are stored onto the S stack. Loading the contents of four 8-bit and four 16-bit registers slows the processor's response to an interrupt and may defeat the purpose of the interrupt response. The F bit, in bit position 6, is introduced into the 6809 to facilitate a *fast* response to an interrupt by loading the contents of program counter and the condition code registers only onto the S stack during an interrupt. The F bit blocks or permits a low signal at the fast interrupt request ($\overline{\text{FIRQ}}$) pin from initiating the fast interrupt sequence.

The E bit, in bit position 7, stores and remembers which interrupt sequence occurred in IRQ or FIRQ. This information is necessary when returning from an interrupt (RTI), at which time the contents of the condition code register are pulled from the stack and the E bit is examined. The processor then knows whether to continue with a return from a fast or normal interrupt.

Direct Page Register

The direct addressing mode is a more limited and, where applicable, a more efficient variation of the extended addressing mode. In the 6800 the direct addressing mode is limited to accessing data from the first 256 memory locations referred to as page 0, while the extended addressing mode data may be accessed anywhere in the 64K memory space. When initializing the 6809 microprocessor, the direct page register is loaded with a $00 and the direct addressing modes of the 6800 and the 6809 function identically. However, with the direct page register, the efficiency of the direct addressing mode of the 6809 may be used throughout the 64K memory space.

When loaded, the direct page register furnishes the 2 MS hexadecimal characters, and the direct addressing mode specifies the 2 LS hexadecimal characters of a 4 hexadecimal address anywhere in the memory space.

11-2 INSTRUCTION FORMAT AND ASSEMBLER LANGUAGE NOTATION

The 6800 instruction set has two fields, the opcode and the operand, whereas the 6809 instruction format, in order to accommodate the 1,464 instructions, has been extended to three fields:

Opcode	Always the first byte or first 2 bytes
Postbyte	1-Byte field, when required
Operand	One or two bytes, when required

For 1-byte opcodes the instruction word varies from 1 to 4 bytes in length (Fig. 11-2). The 1-byte postbyte, when required, is the second field, and the operand, when required, is the last byte or two.

Opcode or Mnemonic

There are two definitions of an instruction. The first refers to the total instruction, consisting of an opcode and operand, or a mnemonic and operand, which specifies the addressing mode. The second definition of an instruction is one of the 59 basic instructions listed in Table 11-1.

In assembler language notation, the mnemonic specifies the machine opcode. The machine opcode hex 9B for the ADD DIRECT

OPCODE
1-BYTE

INHERENT, includes accumulator, instructions

OPCODE	OPERAND
2-BYTE	

REGISTER ADDRESSING, the post byte specifies a register or CC bit

TFR EXG	Register to be transferred to or exchanged with
PUSH PULL	Registers to be pushed or pulled from the stack
AND CC OR CC	CC bits to be set or reset
CWAI	Clear either or both the I or F interrupt masks prior to an interrupt

OPCODE	OPERAND
2-BYTE	

The 1-byte operand specifies a memory location or immediate data

- Immediate addressing
- Direct addressing
- Short relative branch addressing

OPCODE	OPERAND	
3-BYTE		

16-Bit operand specifies a 16-bit address

- Extended Addressing
- Immediate Addressing

OPCODE	POST BYTE
2-BYTE	

INDEX ADDRESSING, specifies on memory location pointed to by a, x, y, u, s pointers

- Zero offset
- 5-bit offset
- Accumulator offset
- Auto increment/Decrement

OPCODE	POST BYTE	OPERAND
3-BYTE		

Index addressing, the operand is the 8-bit offset for the program counter or any pointer register

OPCODE	POST BYTE	OPERAND	
4-BYTE			

Index addressing, the operand is the 16-bit offset for program counter or any pointer register

Figure 11-2. 6809 instruction format for 1-byte OP codes.

Table 11-1. Equivalent Instructions for 6800 and 6809

6800 mnemonics, which are not included in the 6809 assembly language, are handled by automatically translating the 6800 instructions into functionally equivalent 6809 instructions, as described:

6800 Instruction	6809 Equivalent			
ABA	PSHS	B;	ADDA	,S+
CBA	PSHA	B;	CMPA	,S+
CLC	ANDCC	#$FE		
CLI	ANDCC	#$EF		
CLV	ANDCC	#$FD		
CPX	CMPX	P		
DES	LEAS	−1,S		
DEX	LEAX	−1,X		
INS	LEAS	1,S		
INX	LEAX	1,X		
LDAA	LDA			
LDAB	LDB			
ORAA	ORA			
ORAB	ORB			
PSHA	PSHS	A		
PSHB	PSHS	B		
PULA	PULS	A		
PULB	PULS	B		
SBA	PSHS	B;	SUBA	,S+
SEC	ORCC	#$01		
SEI	ORCC	#$10		
SEV	ORCC	#$02		
STAA	STA			
STAB	STB			
TAB	TFR	A,B;	TST	A
TAP	TFR	A,CC		
TBA	TFR	B,A;	TST	A
TPA	TFR	CC,A		
TSX	TFR	S,X		
TXS	TFR	X,S		
WAI	CWAI[a]	#$FF		

[a] The interrupt structure on the 6809 has been extensively analyzed and improved compared to the 6800. While with the 6800 it was useful to execute the sequence CLI, WAI, the 6809 logically equivalent sequence ANDCC #$EF, CWAI, #$FF would allow an IRQ interrupt to occur after the ANDCC instruction. If this is not desired, the 6809 instruction CWAI #$EF should be used to replace the logically equivalent sequence.

instruction specifies three things, the basic operation, the register affected, and the addressing mode used to interpret the operand. Because of the additional 6809 mnemonic and addressing modes, some of the instructions have 2-byte opcodes. The first of the 2-byte opcodes is always either a \$10 or \$11, and often specifies the same opcode function as the 1-byte opcodes, but refers to an alternate register. The 2-byte opcodes include all the "long branch" instructions, LBXX, plus the following:

1st Byte is	\$10	\$11
	SW12	SW13
	LDY	CMPU
	LDS	CMPS
	STY	
	STS	
	CMPY	
	CMPD	
(Long branch)	LBXX	

The 6809 and their 6800 equivalent instructions are listed in Table 11-1, and the hexadecimal values of machine codes are listed in Appendix IIIB.

There are four significant advantages of the 6809 addressing modes over the 6800 (see Fig. 11-3 for comparison of the 6800 and 6809 addressing modes):

- The 6800 index addressing mode, with a 1-byte constant offset, has been expanded to five variations, which facilitate a 16-bit constant offset and a variable offset stored in an accumulator.
- Long relative branch instructions permit a branch to any location in the 64K memory space and are not limited to +127 and −128 locations.
- Relative addressing of data, which permits the referencing of data in a memory location relative to the program counter, enabling the writing of position-independent code.
- Memory indirect, in addition to register indirect, addressing. The 6800 was limited to register indirect addressing, which referred to the address in the index register as pointing to the memory location of the data to be accessed. With memory indirect addressing there are as many pointers indirectly addressing data as there are memory locations.

Figure 11-3. Comparison of the 6800 and 6809 addressing modes.

6800	6809	Section
Inherent addressing	Inherent addressing	11.4
	Register addressing	11.3
Immediate	Immediate	11.5
Direct	Direct	11.5
Extended	Extended	11.5
	Extended indirect	11.5
	Index	
	Zero offset	11.6
Index (8-bit constant)	Constant offset	11.6
	Accumulator offset	11.6
	Autoincrement/decrement	11.6
	Index indirect	
Relative addressing (1-byte)	Relative addressing (1 and 2-byte) for Branch instructions	11.7
	Relative addressing for accessing data from memory	11.8

Postbyte

The postbyte has been introduced into the 6809 instruction format to accommodate the coding of the additional addressing modes, which specifies how to decode the operand.

Operand

The operand specifies a register or memory address.

Assembler Language Notation

Assembler language is a source language notation for each instruction. Generally, there are two parts to an instruction, referred to either as instruction and addressing mode or opcode and operand.

LDA		> $1234	reads: load Acc. A
↑		↑	extended with
instruction		addressing mode	the contents
			of memory lo-
	or		cation hex 1234
opcode		operand	

The 6809 mnemonics vary slightly from those of the 6800 (see Table 11-1). The 6809 does not permit any spaces in the mnemonic field.

	6809	6800		
Load accumulator A	LDA	LDA A	or	LDAA
Load accumulator B	LDB	LDA B	or	LDAB
Add Acc A	ADDA	ADD A	or	ADDA
Add Acc A with carry	ADCA	ADC A	or	ADCA

The operand field uses symbols as follows:

Hexidecimal number	$
Decimal number	(Default)
Immediate addressing	#
Direct addressing	<
Extended addressing	>
Index	offset, register
Memory indirect addressing	[ ]

11-3 THE 6809 INSTRUCTION SET, INCLUDING THE REGISTER ADDRESSING MODE

The 6809 instruction set is similar to that of the 6800. The discussion in this section presumes that the reader is familiar with the 6800 instruction set described in the first three chapters, and so continues on with the new instructions and variations. The instruction set is listed in Tables 11-2 to 11-6. The equivalent 6800 and 6809 instructions are listed in Table 11-1. The hexadecimal values of machine codes, including the mnemonics and the number of bytes for each variation of an instruction, are listed in Appendix IIIB. The instructions are modified by the addressing modes discussed in the remainder of the chapter.

The register addressing mode is new to the 6809 and indicates how to specify the operand for three types of instructions:

TFR and EXG The "transfer and exchange" are new instructions that permit the transfer and exchange of data between any two like-size registers, 8-bit to 8-bit, 16-bit to 16-bit, and the register addressing mode indicates which registers are involved.

Push and Pull The "push and pull" instructions of the 6800 push and pull data from one of the accumulators to or from the stack. In the

6809 the data in any or all of the registers may be pushed or pulled from the stack as specified by the register addressing mode.

ANDCC or ORCC In the 6800 only three of the condition code bits may be set or reset with the six condition code manipulation instructions, whereas all eight of the 6809's condition code bits may be set or reset with the ANDCC or ORCC instructions. The register addressing mode specifies which of the CC bits arc modified.

CWAI In the clear and wait for interrupt instruction the register addressing mode ANDs the operand with the condition code register and may clear either or both the I or F interrupt masks.

Accumulator Instructions

The A and B accumulators of the 6809 may be concatenated into one 16-bit D accumulator, and the 8- and 16-bit instructions that refer to either the A and B or the D accumulator are listed in Tables 11-2 and 11-3.

The D accumulator facilitates 16-bit or double precision arithmetic, and improves the microcomputer through-put by reducing the computing time of many examples. This improved computing time is a consequence of reducing the number of times a routine sequences through a loop. This applies to binary arithmetic and logic operations, but not to decimal arithmetic operations, which require the 8-bit decimal adjust instructions (DAA). A scan of the instructions indicates four additional 6809 instructions:

Transfer	TFR	Applies to 8- and 16-bit instructions
Exchange	EXG	Applies to 8- and 16-bit instructions
Sign extend	SEX	Applies to 16-bit instructions only
Multiply	MUL	Applies to 8-bit instructions only

TFR/EXG The "transfer and exchange" instructions facilitate the transfer or exchange of data with other registers of the same size, all 8- to 8-bit registers, and the transfer or exchange of the data in the D accumulator with other 16-bit registers. For 8-bit registers,

TFR	R1,R2	Transfer R1 to R2
EXG	R1,R2	Exchange R1 with R2

where either the R1 or the R2 registers are A, B, CC, or DP.

For 16-bit registers there are two forms of the transfer instructions: the first, which transfers data from the D accumulator, and the second, which transfers data to the D accumulator from the other 16-bit registers, X, Y, S, U or PC. The general form of the instructions is

Table 11-2. 68098-Bit Accumulator and Memory Instructions

Mnemonic(s)	Operation
ADCA, ADCB	Add memory to accumulator with carry
ADDA, ADDB	Add memory to accumulator
ANDA, ANDB	And memory with accumulator
ASL, ASLA, ASLB	Arithmetic shift of accumulator or memory left
ASR, ASRA, ASRB	Arithmetic shift of accumulator or memory right
BITA, BITB	Bit test memory with accumulator
CLR, CLRA, CLRB	Clear accumulator or memory location
CMPA, CMPB	Compare memory from accumulator
COM, COMA, COMB	Complement accumulator or memory location
DAA	Decimal adjust A accumulator
DEC, DECA, DECB	Decrement accumulator or memory location
EORA, EORB	Exclusive or memory with accumulator
EXG R1, R2	Exchange R1 with R2 (R1, R2 = A, B, CC, DP)
INC, INCA, INCB	Increment accumulator or memory location
LDA, LDB	Load accumulator from memory
LSL, LSLA, LSLB	Logical shift left accumulator or memory location
LSR, LSRA, LSRB	Logical shift right accumulator or memory location
MUL	Unsigned multiply (A × B → D)
NEG, NEGA, NEGB	Negate accumulator or memory
ORA, ORB	Or memory with accumulator
ROL, ROLA, ROLB	Rotate accumulator or memory left
ROR, RORA, RORB	Rotate accumulator or memory right
SBCA, SBCB	Subtract memory from accumulator with borrow
STA, STB	Store accumulator to memory
SUBA, SUBB	Subtract memory from accumulator
TST, TSTA, TSTB	Test accumulator or memory location
TFR R1, R2	Transfer R1 to R2 (R1, R2 = A, B, CC, DP)

NOTE: A, B, CC or DP may be pushed to (pulled from) either stack with PSHS, PSHU (PULS, PULU) instructions.

Table 11-3. 6809: 16-Bit Accumulator and Memory Instructions

Mnemonic(s)	Operation
ADDD	Add memory to D accumulator
CMPD	Compare memory from D accumulator
EXG D, R	Exchange D with X, Y, S, U or PC
LDD	Load D accumulator from memory
SEX	Sign Extend B accumulator into A accumulator
STD	Store D accumulator to memory
SUBD	Subtract memory from D accumulator
TFR D, R	Transfer D to X, Y, S, U or PC
TFR R, D	Transfer X, Y, S, U or PC to D

NOTE: D may be pushed (pulled) to either stack with PSHS, PSHU (PULS, PULU) instructions.

TFR	D,R	Transfer D to X, Y, S, U or PC
TFR	R,D	Transfer X, Y, S, U, PC to D

Bits 7 to 4 of the operand specify the source register, and bits 3 to 0 specify the destination register:

16-Bit Registers		8-Bit Registers	
0 0 0 0	D	1 0 0 0	A
0 0 0 1	X	1 0 0 1	B
0 0 1 0	Y	1 0 1 0	CCR
0 0 1 1	US	1 0 1 1	DPR
0 1 0 0	SP		
0 1 0 0	PC		

For example, to transfer the data in the condition code register to the accumulator, the instruction is written

```
IF A9     TFR     CC,B
```

To exchange the contents of the accumulator A with the direct page register, the instruction is written

```
IE 88     EXG     A,DP
```

To transfer data from the D accumulator to the program counter, the instruction is written

```
IF 04     TFR     D,PC
```

To transfer data to accumulator D from the X index register, the instruction is written

```
IF 10     TFR     X,D
```

Sign Extend (SEX) When concatenating the 8-bit accumulators, it may be necessary to convert the 8-bit 2's complement number in accumulator B to a 16-bit 2's complement number. The SEX instruction extends the sign in accumulator B through the MSBs in accumulator A.

Multiply The MULTIPLY instruction executes an unsigned multiplication of two 8-bit numbers in accumulators A and B, and puts the result in accumulator D.

Pointer Registers: The X and Y Index Registers and the U and S Stack Pointers

The most significant enhancements of the 6809 are manifested in the four 16-bit pointer registers (Table 11-4):

- The X and Y index registers
- The U and S stack pointer registers

Two additional registers of the 6809, one index and one stack pointer, permit a program to point to a greater number and variety of memory locations simultaneously. The added index register and stack pointer facilitates multitasking where the U and S stack pointers are reserved for the user program and supervisor program, respectively. For example, the JBUG monitor described in Chapter 4 may now be written more conveniently, where the JBUG monitor, a supervisor-type program, uses the S, and the user program utilizes the U stack pointer.

The second major advantage of the 6809 pointer registers is that they can interchangeably act as index or stack pointer registers. The primary function of the index register is indirect addressing of blocks or arrays of data, and having two index registers facilitates writing programs where two blocks or arrays of data located anywhere in the 64K of memory space may interact more conveniently (i.e., block move or add routines).

Another convenient feature is the autoincrementing/decrementing of the index register by the index addressing mode (Sec. 11-5), which eliminates the need to increment and decrement the 6800 index register instructions. This feature makes the index register pointer function like a stack pointer when executing a load and decrement or a store and increment the index register instruction.

Three new 6809 instructions are added to the index register and stack pointer instructions (Table 11-4):

Table 11-4. 6809: Index Register/Stack Pointer Instructions

Mnemonic(s)	Operation
CMPS, CMPU	Compare memory from stack pointer
CMPX, CMPY	Compare memory from index register
EXG R1, R2	Exchange D, X, Y, S, U or PC with D, X, Y, S, U or PC
LEAS, LEAU	Load effective address into stack pointer
LEAX, LEAY	Load effective address into index register
LDS, LDU	Load stack pointer from memory
LDX, LDY	Load index register from memory
PSHS	Push A, B, CC, DP, D, X, Y, U, or PC onto hardware stack
PSHU	Push A, B, CC, DP, D, X, Y, S, or PC onto user stack
PULS	Pull A, B, CC, DP, D, X, Y, U or PC from hardware stack
PULU	Pull A, B, CC, DP, D, X, Y, S or PC from hardware stack
STS, STU	Store stack pointer to memory
STX, STY	Store index register to memory
TFR R1, R2	Transfer D, X, Y, S, U or PC to D, X, Y, S, U or PC
ABX	Add B accumulator to X (unsigned)

Load effective address	LEA
Push/Pull	PSH/PUL
Add accumulator B to index register X	ABX

Two instructions, the 16-bit transfer and exchange, are also listed as accumulator instructions, and four 6800 instructions, which were used to increment and decrement the index and stack pointer, are replaced by the autoincrement and decrement addressing modes.

Load Effective Address, (LEA) In writing programs the pointer registers must initially be loaded with a memory location. The index addressing modes form an effective address (EA) and the load effective address (LEA) instructions both form and load the effective address into one of the pointer registers. The four LEA instructions, one for each pointer register, offer the programmer a much greater variety of choices for initializing the pointer registers. The variety of effective addresses (EA) is described in Sec. 11-5.

Pull/Push The pull and push accumulator group instructions of the 6800 have been expanded to modify both the U or S stack pointers. In the 6800, only data from an accumulator is pushed or pulled onto the stack, while in the 6809 any or all of the processor registers are pushed or pulled onto either stack.

The three functions of the 6800 stack pointer (Chapter 2) are as follows:

- To store the return address from a subroutine in the stack.
- To store the return address from an interrupt, plus the processor registers in the stack.
- The quick and sequential storing of data to and from the accumulator onto the stack, modified to include any and all the registers.

In the four variations of the 6809 2-byte push and pull instructions, the first byte indicates which stack to push or pull data from, and the second byte, the operand, indicates which register or registers are pushed or pulled from the stack.

PSHS	Push onto the S stack
PSHU	Push onto the U stack
PULS	Pull from the S stack
PULU	Pull from the U stack

In response to an interrupt, data are stacked on the hardware stack S with two interrupt stacking sequences, fast and regular. The fast response stacks only the program counter and condition code registers, while, when responding to a regular interrupt, the stacking sequence is as follows:

- Program counter
- U stack pointer
- Y index register
- X index register
- Direct page register
- Accumulator B
- Accumulator A
- Condition code register

Any combination of the eight registers is stacked as indicated by a 1 in the appropriate bit position of the operand. The bit positions are

Bit Positions	Register
7	PC
6	U stack pointer
5	Y
4	X
3	DP
2	B
1	A
0	CC

Opcode	Mnemonic	
36	PSHU	Push onto the user stack
34	PSHS	Push onto the hardware stack
37	PULU	Pull from the user stack
35	PULS	Pull from the hardware stack

For example;

Machine Code	Mnem	Operand	
3693	PSHU	PC, Y, A, CC	Push the contents of registers PC, Y, A, CC onto stack U in the order indicated (1001 0011)

3471	PSHS	U, Y, X, CC	Push the contents of registers U, Y, X, CC onto stack S in the order indicated (0111 0001)
37FF	PULU	$FF	Pull the contents of all the registers PC, S, Y, X, DP, B, A, CC from stack U in the order indicated (1111 1111)
3581	PULS	PC, CC	Pull the contents of registers PC and CC from stack S in the order indicated (1000 0001)

In the 6800, after stacking, the stack pointer points to the next empty location of the stack, whereas in the 6809 the stack pointer points to the address of the last location of the data pushed onto the stack.

ABX Add the 8-bit contents of accumulator B to the contents of the 16-bit index register X, and replace the modified address into index register X.

$$X \leftarrow (X) + A$$

This is an ideal instruction for a look-up and jump table. The contents of accumulator A are not affected.

Program Counter and Branch Instructions

The program counter points to the instruction being executed, and the address in the program counter is generally incremented as the program executes a sequence of instructions. Branch instructions (Table 11-5), however, are the decision instructions that cause the program to branch by adding a 2's complement relative address to the program counter. The 6809 has two types of relative addresses, regular and long, which add a one- or two-byte relative address to the program counter. This enables branches of ± 128 or ± 32K locations, the full microcomputer memory space.

The short branch instructions are similar to the 6800 branch instructions and use the same mnemonics. The mnemonics for the long branch instructions are the same as the regular mnemonics, but are prefaced with an L. For example, the branch if equal mnemonics is written

BEQ or LBEQ

There are three new BRANCH instructions:

BRN	or	LBRN
BHS	or	LBHS
BLO	or	LBLO

The branch never (BRN), a new instruction, is effectively a no-op instruction. The branch if carry clear (BCC) and branch if carry set (BCS) instructions have new and dual redundant mnemonics. The new mnemonics are more meaningful than the existing ones. The branch on higher or same (BHS) tests for the carry clear bit and is used for unsigned binary where the contents of the accumulator are greater than, or equal to, the contents of memory ($A \geq M$). The branch if lower (BLO) tests the carry set bit and is used when the contents of the accumulator are less than the contents of memory ($A < M$).

Table 11-5. 6809: Branch Instructions

Mnemonic(s)	Operation
	SIMPLE BRANCHES
BEQ, LBEQ	Branch if equal
BNE, LBNE	Branch if not equal
BMI, LBMI	Branch if minus
BPL, LBPL	Branch if plus
BCS, LBCS	Branch if carry set
BCC, LBCC	Branch if carry clear
BVS, LBVS	Branch if overflow set
BVC, LBVC	Branch if overflow clear
	SIGNED BRANCHES
BGT, LBGT	Branch if greater (signed)
BGE, LBGE	Branch if greater than or equal (signed)
BEQ, LBEQ	Branch if equal
BLE, LBLE	Branch if less than or equal (signed)
BLT, LBLT	Branch if less than (signed)
	UNSIGNED BRANCHES
BHI, LBHI	Branch if higher (unsigned)
BHS, LBHS	Branch if higher or same (unsigned)
BEQ, LBEQ	Branch if equal
BLS, LBLS	Branch if lower or same (unsigned)
BLO, LBLO	Branch if lower (unsigned)
	OTHER BRANCHES
BSR, LBSR	Branch to subroutine
BRA, LBRA	Branch always
BRN, LBRN	Branch never

Condition Code Registers and the Miscellaneous Instructions

The first 6 bits, bits 0 to 5 of the condition code register, remain unchanged. Bits 6 and 7, the F and E bits, respectively, are new and are used during interrupts. The hardware stack S is the only stack used for interrupts. The 6809 has two interrupt request pins, $\overline{\text{IRQ}}$ and $\overline{\text{FIRQ}}$, for interrupt request and fast interrupt request at pins 3 and 2, respectively. During an interrupt request the contents of all processor registers but the hardware stack are stored in the S stack. For a fast interrupt request response, however, only the contents of the program counter and the condition code register are stored in the S stack. The contents of the condition code register are always last to be stored in the stack.

The E bit is set and reset when an interrupt occurs and indicates which interrupt, $\overline{\text{IRQ}}$ or $\overline{\text{FIRQ}}$, occurred and whether all the registers, or only the program counter and condition code registers, are stored in the stack. This information is necessary when returning from an interrupt (RTI). The processor pulls the contents of the condition code register first and examines the E bit to determine which register sequence follows for unstacking.

The F bit performs the same function for a fast interrupt request ($\overline{\text{FIRQ}}$) on pin 2 as does the I bit for the interrupt request (IRQ) on pin 3. The F and I bits permit or inhibit the respective interrupts from occurring.

There are seven new miscellaneous instructions (Table 11-6):

ANDCC	AND condition code register
ORCC	OR condition code register
CWAI	Clear and wait for interrupt
SW11, SW12, SW13	Software interrupts 1, 2, and 3
SYNC	Synchronize

Table 11-6. 6809: Miscellaneous Instructions

Mnemonic(s)	Operation
ANDCC	AND condition code register
CWAI	AND condition code register, then wait for interrupt
NOP	No operation
ORCC	OR condition code register
JMP	Jump
JSR	Jump to subroutine
RTI	Return from interrupt
RTS	Return from subroutine
SWI, SWI2, SWI3	Software interrupt (absolute indirect)
SYNC	Synchronize with interrupt line

ANDCC and ORCC Most of the 6800 miscellaneous instructions are 1-byte instructions that modify one of the condition code bits. The comparable 6809 instructions are replaced by two 2-byte instructions:

ANDCC	AND immediate data with the condition code register
ORCC	OR immediate data with the condition code register

where the second byte, the operand, indicates which condition code bit or bits are to be ANDed or ORed. This permits any condition code bit to be set or reset.

Condition Code Register

E	F	H	I	N	Z	V	C

The CC bits are set by ORing with 1's and reset by ANDing with 0's the appropriate bits of the postbyte.

Examples

Machine Code	Mnem	Operand	
1A 80	ORCC	#$80	Set E bit
1A D1	ORCC	#$DI	Set E, F, I, and C bits
1C 7F	ANDCC	#$7F	Reset E bit
1C DC	ANDCC	#$DC	Reset the H, V, and C bits

CWAI The clear and wait for interrupt instruction ANDs immediate data with the condition code register, usually to clear one of the two interrupt request bits, F or I, to enable an interrupt. Then either all the registers, or just the program counter and condition code register, are stored in the stack, and the microprocessor waits for an interrupt. This instruction is comparable to the 6800 wait for interrupt instruction, but offers the programmer a choice of waiting for either an FIRQ or IRQ interrupt. The operand is first ANDed with the condition code register, which offers the programmer a choice of inhibiting an IRQ or FIRQ by ANDing and CC register with either a $BF or $EF.

Examples

3C 00	CWAI	#$00	Clears the F bit
3C 40	CWAI	#$40	Leaves the F bit alone

Then all the appropriate registers are pushed onto the stack and the processor stops and waits for a fast or regular IRQ interrupt. The processor then responds to the interrupt more quickly, not having spent time stacking the registers.

SYNC The SYNC instruction is used to synchronize the microcomputer to I/O data. After a SYNC instruction the microcomputer enters the WAIT state, much as in the CWAI instruction, and waits for an interrupt, which clears the WAIT state and executes the appropriate interrupt, NMI, FIRQ, or IRQ.

SW11, SW12, SW13 The 6809 has three software interrupts, two more than the 6800, furnishing the user and supervisor programs with independent software interrupts.

11-4 INHERENT, ACCUMULATOR, AND REGISTER ADDRESSING MODES

The inherent addressing modes are instructions that have no addressing options (i.e., MUL, SW1 instructions), or the accumulator addressing modes, which operate on data in an accumulator, A, B, or D only, (i.e., CLRA, CLRB, COMA).

11-5 NON-INDEX ADDRESSING MODES

The four addressing modes discussed in this section are separated into two groups:

Group I: immediate addressing, direct addressing, and extended addressing

Group II: Extended indirect addressing

The three addressing modes in group I are similar to those of the 6800. The instruction format has two parts, an opcode and operand.

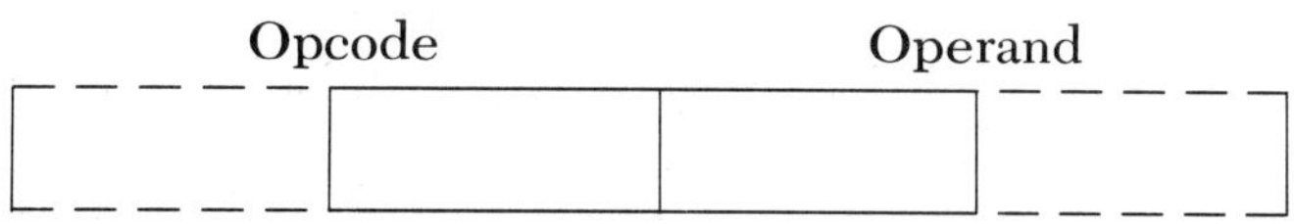

In the extended indirect addressing mode the postbyte is code #9F. The instruction format has three parts, an opcode, postbyte, and operand.

Opcode	Postbyte	Operand
	9F	

Immediate Addressing Mode

The immediate addressing mode is used to introduce an 8- or 16-bit constant into the program.

Examples

86 3F	LDA	#$3F	Load immediate 3F into Acc A
BE 04C6	LDX	#$04C6	Load immediate 04C6 into index reg X
84 B3	ANDA	#$B3	AND immediate Acc A with B3

Direct Addressing Mode

The 2-byte direct addressing mode instruction of the 6800 is a quick and efficient technique for accessing data stored in page 0, the first 256 memory locations. This is accomplished by having the microprocessor force 00's into the two most significant hex characters of the address. During the power-on sequence, the direct page register of the 6809 is set to zero, and the direct addressing modes of both the 6800 and the 6809 processors are identical. The direct page register of the 6809 makes the advantages of the direct addressing mode applicable through the total memory space. The 6809 microprocessor forces the 8 bits in the direct page register into the MS byte of the address.

In multitask programs the supervisor program might assign each user program its own page of memory space for direct addressing. This is a technique for relocating a user program by the supervisor. Two instructions, transfer and exchange (TFR and EXG), load the 8-bit direct page register.

Examples of Direct Addressing Instruction

Machine Code	Mnem	Operand	
96 34	LDA	$34	Load Acc A from loc. 34
94 44	ANDA	$44	AND Acc A with data from loc. 44
97 34	STA	$34	Store Acc A in loc. 34
C6 10	LDB	#$10	Load immed. 10 to Acc B
1F 9B	TFR	B,DP	Transfer Acc B to DP

96	34	LDA	$34	Load Acc A from loc. 1034
94	44	ANDA	$44	AND A Acc A in loc. 1034
97	34	STA	$34	Store Acc A in loc. 1034
10DF	FF	STS	$FF	Store address in stack S into locations 10FF and 10FE

Extended Addressing Mode

The extended mode of the 6809 is identical to that of the 6800 and is sometimes referred to as *absolute addressing*. The extended addressing mode is often used for I/O devices. For example,

B7 8020	> STA	$8020	Output to Port A of PIA 8020
BT 8022	> LDA	$8022	Input from Port B of PIA 8020

Extended Indirect Addressing Mode

The extended indirect addressing mode (Fig. 11-4) is a single-level memory indirect addressing that enables a memory location to be used as a pointer to a data location. It is useful for supervisory programs to assign one of several I/O ports, attached to one of several PIAs or ACIAs, to each user program. A system convention must be agreed upon by the supervisor and user programs, which specifies the location within the user's memory space to be used as I/O ports. The user program addresses those I/O ports with extended indirect addressing mode, while the supervisory program loads the user's assigned location with the absolute address of the assigned I/O ports. For example, the supervisory program assigns ACIA tied to locations 8004 and 8005 to the user program by storing locations 8004 and 8005 in locations 64, 65, 66, and 67. Remember that the supervisory program may also be responsible for loading the direct page register.

The program is assigned to ACIA 8004 through locations 0064 and 0066.

B6 9F 0064	BACK	LDA	>[0064]	Test ACIA status bit
2A FA		BPL	BACK	If bit 7 = 0, BR BACK
F7 9F 0066		STB	>[0066]	Outdate through ACIA

Note: The extended direct instructions are 4-byte instructions, where the postbyte (9F) indicates the variation of the index addressing mode.

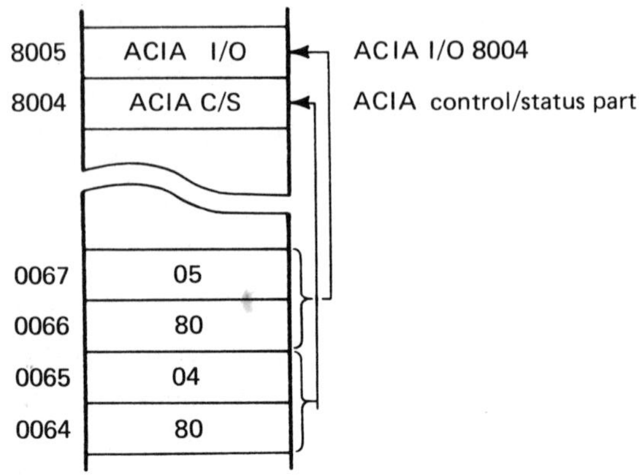

Figure 11-4. Extended indirect addressing mode.

11-6 INDEX ADDRESSING MODE

There are 23 variations of the index addressing mode specified by the postbyte as listed in Table 11-7. Approximately half of these addressing modes are nondirect and will be referred to simply as the index addressing mode, while the remaining half are the index indirect addressing mode. The index addressing modes access data, while the index indirect addressing modes first access an address from memory, which then indirectly references the data. The distinction is determined by bit 4 of the postbyte.

For convenience, the 23 variations are separated into four categories:

- Constant, including zero offset
- Accumulator or variable offset
- Autoincrement/decrement of a pointer register
- Constant offset from program counter, which is referred to as relative addressing for the accessing of data

Note that there are index and indirect index variations for each of these four categories.

In the index addressing mode the address of the data to be accessed is referred to as the *effective address* (EA) and is computed by adding the address in one of the 16-bit registers to an offset:

$$EA = (R) + \text{offset}$$

The address in the register R may be one of five registers, X, Y, U, S,

Table 11-7. Indexed Addressing Modes

Type	Forms	Non Indirect				Indirect			
		Assembler Form	Postbyte OP Code	+ ~	+ #	Assembler Form	Postbyte OP Code	+ ~	+ #
Constant Offset From R	No Offset	,R	1RR00100	0	0	[,R]	1RR10100	3	0
(2's Complement Offsets)	5 Bit Offset	n, R	0RRnnnnn	1	0	defaults to 8-bit			
	8 Bit Offset	n, R	1RR01000	1	1	[n, R]	1RR11000	4	1
	16 Bit Offset	n, R	1RR01001	4	2	[n, R]	1RR11001	7	2
Accumulator Offset From R	A Register Offset	A, R	1RR00110	1	0	[A, R]	1RR10110	4	0
(2's Complement Offsets)	B Register Offset	B, R	1RR00101	1	0	[B, R]	1RR10101	4	0
	D Register Offset	D, R	1RR01011	4	0	[D, R]	1RR11011	7	0
Auto Increment/Decrement R	Increment By 1	,R+	1RR00000	2	0	not allowed			
	Increment By 2	,R++	1RR00001	3	0	[,R++]	1RR10001	6	0
	Decrement By 1	,−R	1RR00010	2	0	not allowed			
	Decrement By 2	,−−R	1RR00011	3	0	[,−−R]	1RR10011	6	0
Constant Offset From PC	8 Bit Offset	n, PCR	1xx01100	1	1	[n, PCR]	1xx11100	4	1
(2's Complement Offsets)	16 Bit Offset	n, PCR	1xx01101	5	2	[n, PCR]	1xx11101	8	2
Extended Indirect	16 Bit Address	—	—	—	—	[n]	10011111	5	2

R = X, Y, U or S
x = Don't Care

RR:
00 = X
01 = Y
10 = U
11 = S

$\overset{+}{\sim}$ and $\overset{+}{\#}$ indicate the number of additional cycles and bytes for the particular variation.

(Courtesy Motorola Semiconductor Products Inc.)

and PC, and the offset may be either a constant stored in the postbyte or a 1- or 2-byte operand, or a variable stored in one of the accumulators, A, B, or D.

$$EA = (R) + \text{offset}$$

$$EA = \left\{\begin{matrix}(X)\\(Y)\\(U)\\(S)\\(PC)\end{matrix}\right\} + \left\{\begin{matrix}\left\{\begin{matrix}\text{5-bit}\\\text{8-bit}\\\text{6-bit}\end{matrix}\right\} & \begin{matrix}\text{constant}\\\text{constant}\\\text{constant}\end{matrix}\\ \left\{\begin{matrix}A\\B\\C\end{matrix}\right\} & \text{accumulator}\end{matrix}\right\}$$

When forming the effective address (EA), the address in the register referenced is not affected.

Postbyte

There are three basic fields in the postbyte (Table 11-8):

Bits 6 and 5 are the register field.
Bit 4 is the indirect field.
Bits 3, 2, 1, and 0 are the addressing mode field.

The register (R) specified by the register field refers to one of the four, X, Y, U, and S, registers, which are discussed in this section. The index addressing modes that refer to the program counter,

$$EA = (PC) + \text{offset}$$

are referred to as program counter relative addressing and are discussed in Sec. 11-7.

The assembler language notation for the index addressing mode generally is

```
MNEMONIC    offset, register
```

Examples of direct index addressing notation:

```
LDA     $24,X
STB     $1234,Y
ANDA    4, U
LDAD    $4567,S
STB     $-A,X
STB     A,X
LDA     $B,Y
LDB     B,Y
```

```
LDA     $3456,PC
ANDA    $89AB,PC
```

Indirect index addressing notation includes brackets:

```
LDA     [$24,X]
STB     [$1234,Y]
```

The index addressing instruction word format:

Opcode, Postbyte	2-Byte index instruction Zero offset 5-Bit (4-bit plus sign) constant offset Accumulator offset Autoincrement/decrement
Opcode, Postbyte, Operand	3-Byte index instruction 8-Bit constant offset
Opcode, Postbyte, Operand (2 bytes)	4-Byte index instruction 16-Bit constant offset

Zero and Constant Offset

The index addressing mode of the 6800, sometimes referred to as register indirect addressing, is ideal for handling several blocks or arrays of data with one pointer. The 1-byte, 8-bit constant offset of the 6800 was restrictive by requiring that the blocks of data not be separated by more than 256 memory locations. The 6809 offers the program two degrees of freedom for manipulating blocks or arrays of data anywhere in the memory space, first, by having two index registers, X and Y, and, second, by having a 0, 5, 8, and 16-bit signed or 2's complement offset.

Initializing the Pointer Register with Immediate Addressing Mode The pointer registers must be initialized by loading an address into the register before the index addressing mode is used. For the examples in this section, it will be assumed that these are the addresses in the pointer registers.

Table 11-8. Indexed Addressing Postbyte

Post-Byte Register Bit								Indexed Addressing Mode
7	6	5	4	3	2	1	0	
0	R	R	d	d	d	d	d	EA = ,R + 5 Bit Offset
1	R	R	0	0	0	0	0	,R+
1	R	R	i	0	0	0	1	,R+ +
1	R	R	0	0	0	1	0	,– R
1	R	R	i	0	0	1	1	,– – R
1	R	R	i	0	1	0	0	EA = ,R +0 Offset
1	R	R	i	0	1	0	1	EA = ,R + ACCB Offset
1	R	R	i	0	1	1	0	EA = ,R + ACCA Offset
1	R	R	i	1	0	0	0	EA = ,R +8 Bit Offset
1	R	R	i	1	0	0	1	EA = ,R +16 Bit Offset
1	R	R	i	1	0	1	1	EA = ,R +D Offset
1	x	x	i	1	1	0	0	EA = ,PC +8 Bit Offset
1	x	x	i	1	1	0	1	EA = ,PC +16 Bit Offset
1	R	R	i	1	1	1	1	EA = [,Address]

Addressing Mode Field (bits 3–0)

Indirect Field (bit 4)
(Sign bit when b_7 = 0)

Register Field: RR (bits 6–5)
00 = X
01 = Y
10 = U
11 = S

x = Don't Care
d = Offset Bit
i = 0 = Not Indirect
1 = Indirect

Examples

8E 0000	LDX	#$0000	Load immediate reg. X with 0000
108E 1000	LDY	#$1000	Load immediate reg. Y with 1000
CE 2000	LDU	#$2000	Load immediate reg. U with 2000
10CE A000	LDS	#$A000	Load immediate reg. S with A000

Zero Offset In the 2-byte zero offset only the register must be specified by the postbyte; it is coded

1 R R 1 0 1 0 0

where the registers specified by RR field in bits 6 and 5 are as follows:

Register	Bits 6 5	Postbyte Code
X	0 0	94
Y	0 1	B4
U	1 0	D4
S	1 1	F4
Don't care	X X	

Examples of zero offset:

A6 94	LDA	,X	Load data pointed to by X register into Acc A
A6 94	LDA	0,X	
A7 B4	STA	,Y	Store contents of Acc A to location pointed to by Y
AE D4	LDX	,U	Load address pointed to by U into register X
A4 94	ANDA	,X	AND data pointed to by X register with data in Acc A
10AF 94	STY	,X	Load data pointed to by X register into Y register
E1 B4	CMPB	,Y	Compare data pointed to by Y register with data in Acc B
10A3 B4	CMPD	,Y	Compare address pointed to by Y register with data in Acc D

Five-Bit Constant Offset The range of the offset is from +15 to −16. The postbyte of this 2-byte instruction specifies both the register and the offset. The postbyte is coded

0 R R X X X X

where

- 0 at bit 7 indicates a 5-bit constant offset
- RR specifies the register
- X's at bits 4 to 0 specify the offset

Examples of 5-bit offset:

Assume address in

X is $0000
Y is $1000
U is $2000
S is $A000

A6 84	LDA	4,X	Loan contents from loc. 4 into Acc A
A4 8F	ANDA	$F,X	AND data from loc. F, or 15, with data in Acc A
108E E	LDY	−2,X	Load address from loc. FFFE/F into register Y
E7 A3	STB	3,Y	Store data from Acc B into loc. 1003
9B BC	ADDA	−3,Y	Add the data from loc. OFFD with the contents of Acc A
10EE CA	LDS	$A,U	Load the address of loc. 200A/B into reg. S

Eight and 16-Bit Constant Offsets The 8- and 16-bit constant offsets are 3- and 4-byte instructions, where the 2's complement offset is specified by a 1- or 2-byte operand, respectively. The postbyte is coded

R + 7-bit offset	1 R R 0 1 0 0 0
R + 15-bit offset	1 R R 0 1 0 0 1

Example with 8-bit offset:

A698 64	LDA	$64,X	Load the contents from loc. 64 into Acc A
A498 F6	ANDA	$F6,X	AND the contents from loc. F6 with data in Acc A
108E98 EE	LDY	$−11,X	Load the address from loc. FFEE/F into reg. Y
E7B8 33	STB	$33,Y	Store contents of Acc B into loc. 0033
9BB8 CC	ADDA	$−33,Y	Add the data from loc. FFCC with the contents of Acc A
10EE F82A	LDS	$2A,U	Load the address from loc. 202A/B into reg. S

Examples of 16-bit offset:

A6 99 0164	LDA	\$164,X	Load the contents from loc. 0164 into Acc A
A4 99 12E6	ANDA	\$12E6,X	AND the contents from loc. 12E6 with the data in Acc A
108E 99 EEEE	LDY	\$−1111,X	Load the address from loc. EEEE/F into reg. Y
E7 B9 3345	STB	\$3345,Y	Store the contents of Acc B into loc. 3345
9B B9 CCBB	ADDA	\$−3345,Y	ADD the contents of loc. CCBB with the concents of Acc A
10EE F9 012A	LDS	\$12A,U	Load the address from loc. 012A/B into reg. S

Accumulator Offset Index Instructions

The accumulator offset forms an effective address by adding the contents of the accumulator, a variable, to one of the pointer registers. With the constant offset, the offset had to be decided on when the program was written. In the accumulator offset, the contents of one of the pointer registers are added to one of the accumulators to form an effective address at program execution time. The program computes the variables stored in an accumulator and enables the dynamic addressing of data in memory. This makes the accumulator offset ideal for look-up and jump tables. The accumulator offset forms an effective address by adding the 2's complement contents of the 8-bit or sign extended 16-bit accumulator to the address in a pointer register.

Load Effective Address (LEA) Instruction

The address in the pointer register of the 6800 was loaded with a constant by a load immediate instruction or an address from memory. The 6809 has an abundant variety of index addressing modes that compute an effective address and do not disturb the address in the pointer register. The load effective address (LEA) (Table 11-9) permits

Table 11-9. LEA Examples

Instruction	Operation	Comment
LEAX 10, X	X + 10 → X	Adds 5-bit constant 10 to X
LEAX 500, X	X + 500 → X	Adds 16-bit constant 500 to X
LEAY A, Y	Y + A → Y	Adds 8-bit A accumulator to Y
LEAY D, Y	Y + D → Y	Adds 16-bit D accumulator to Y
LEAU – 10, U	U – 10 → U	Subtracts 10 from U
LEAS – 10, S	S – 10 → S	Used to reserve area on stack
LEAS 10, S	S + 10 → S	Used to 'clean up' stack
LEAX 5, S	S + 5 → X	Transfers as well as adds

the programmer to take advantage of the greatly expanded index addressing modes, and loads one of the pointer registers with an address formed by one of the index addressing modes. The advantage of the LEA instruction is the convenient setting of an address into a pointer register.

There are four 2-byte load effective instructions:

Machine Code		Mnem	Operand		
30	ii	LEAX	Postbyte	EA	X
31	ii	LEAY	Postbyte	EA	Y
32	ii	LEAU	Postbyte	EA	U
33	ii	LEAS	Postbyte	EA	S

Autoincrement/Decrement

The 2-byte autoincrement/decrement 6809 instructions obviate the four increment/decrement index and stack pointer registers of the 6800. They merge two features required to step through a block of data: in the autoincrement variation the data are accessed and then the pointer is (post) incremented, while, when decrementing, the pointer is (pre) decremented and then the data are accessed. The four variations of the autoincrement/decrement instructions permit the incrementing/decrementing by 1 to access data and by 2 to address addresses. The postbyte is coded as follows:

	Direct	Indirect
R+	1 RR 00000	1 RR not allowed
R++	1 RR 00001	1 RR 1 000 1
R–	1 RR 00010	1 RR not allowed
R––	1 RR 00011	1 RR 1 0011

11-7 RELATIVE ADDRESSING

The relative addressing modes reference an address in memory location relative to the address in the program counter. The relative address indicates the distance or number of locations the address is from the program counter and is ideal for writing position-independent programs. The two variations of relative addressing are for branching or decision-making instructions and for accessing data. The relative addressing mode, when used for decisions, causes a branch as a consequence of the state of one or more of the condition codes. The two variations are short and long branch instructions, with 1- or 2-byte relative addresses, which branch from −218 to +127 or −32000 to +32000 locations. The mnemonics for the long branch instructions have an L in front of the same short branch mnemonics (Table 11-5).

The technique for calculating the 2-byte relative address branch instructions is similar to that of the 6800. In the 6800 the relative address is computed by

$$PC \leftarrow ((PC) + 2) + REL$$

The 2 is added because the program counter is incremented by 2 when the relative address is accessed and added to the program counter. The branch address for the 6809 is computed by

$$PC \leftarrow ((PC) + \text{no. of bytes of instruction}) + REL$$

where the number of bytes in instruction is 2 or 3 for short and long branch instructions, respectively.

11-8 PROGRAM COUNTER RELATIVE

Constant offset from the program counter should more appropriately be called relative addressing for the data access. The relative address, a constant determined at program assembler time, indicates the distance of the data location from the program. The addressing mode is ideal for position-independent code.

Example:

```
LDA     $1234, PC
STB     $56, PC
ANDA    $9A, PC
CLR     $9F, PC
```

The pointer register can be loaded with an address relative to the program counter with the load effective address (LEA) instruction.

```
LEAX    $4C, PC
LEAY    $5678, PC
```

12 The 68000 Microprocessor

The 68000 microprocessor offers the speed and versatility previously found only in large and minicomputers. Here, where the large, mini, and microcomputer worlds meet, it becomes necessary to be aware of the applications that were previously reserved for large computers before appreciating some of the features of the 68000.

The 68000, with a 24-bit address bus, can access a 16-megaword (16,777,256) or 32-megabyte memory. With access to that large a memory the 68000 can be used in time-shared applications where many users share the same computers. In such systems a supervisor program is required to manage and assign a memory space to each of the user programs. A function of the supervisor program, sometimes called the operating system (OS), is to protect the integrity and memory space of each user program from being destroyed by other user programs. This implies that there is a hierarchy of programs, with the supervisor program having privileges denied the user programs. The user programs that may be assigned any memory space determined by the supervisor must be written in position-independent code. Speed and throughput are two measures of the higher computing power. Speed is measured by how rapidly an instruction is executed, and the 68000 has an 8 MH_Z clock, while still retaining independent address and data buses, a feature not characteristic of other 16-bit microprocessors. Typically, these higher speeds are critical in communication systems.

While high throughput is a measure of the volume of data to be processed and is a necessary feature of time-shared data processing, it is achieved in the 68000 with a 16-bit instruction word and 32-bit data registers.

The 68000 and 6800 instructions are similar by having two parts, the opcode or function to be performed, and the addressing mode, which specifies the register or memory locations whose data are to be moved or modified. The 16-bit instructions have a large enough size to accommodate a greater variety of choices for accessing and moving data to or between any register and memory location and memory locations. These additional addressing modes make the instruction set more powerful by saving program instructions that are otherwise required to move data to accommodate a more restrictive instruction set.

The 32-bit registers of the 68000 can process a byte, a 16-bit word, or a 32-bit long word format. Higher throughput is achieved in data-processing application with the long word format. Processing 32 bits of data often saves unnecessary accessing of data. When executing programs with loop counters, it cuts down the number of times required to cycle through a loop and the time required to execute the overhead instruction of the loop.

The supervisor requires and has additional capability not available to the user program, as follows:

- Privileged instructions are a group of instructions accessible to the supervisor program only.
- Exception processing consists of a variety of conditions often encountered by the user program that the supervisor program is called on to resolve. Interrupts are examples of actions outside normal processing that call on exceptional processing. Traps are caused by user programs that encounter conditions (e.g., divide by zero) that need to be resolved by exception programs.
- Supervisory stack.
- Supervisory byte, the MS byte of the status register.

These features, in conjunction with 56 instruction types with 14 addressing modes, greatly expand the range of applications for the microprocessor. These new and more complex programs necessitate the need for preparing these programs in high-level languages.

Historically, the maintenance and program-writing costs for the large IBM UNIVAC and GE-type computers were extraordinarily high. These computers were maintained by teams, with specialists in the separate software and hardware areas. High-level languages such as FORTRAN and OGAL were developed originally to reduce the high costs of software development. These high-level languages offered the added advantage that the programmer did not need to be aware of the architecture of the computer on which the program was to be executed. High-level language programs are compiled, which is to translate each instruction into machine code prior to run time. A compiler is a program written for a specific computer that translates the high-level language program into a machine code program, where each high-level instruction is translated into a series of machine-coded instructions.

The high-price-tag large computers evolved into a series of smaller minicomputes from DEC and Data General. Often these computers were programmed with high-level languages.

On the low end, a new family of 4-bit microprocessors emerged from the semiconductor industry and quickly evolved into 8-bit machines with some calculator or data-processing applications. The microprocessors were often used initially to replace logic elements by engineers who had acquired the necessary programming techniques. Many of these so-called logic problems had real-time applications, where outputs must respond to inputs within a specified time.

With the 68000 the two worlds of the large and minicomputers merge with the world of the microprocessors, where many architectural features of the minicomputer world are incorporated into a microprocessor with applications previously considered reserved for the minicomputer.

12-1 PROGRAMMING MODEL: REGISTER SET

The 68000 has seventeen 32-bit registers, a 32-bit program counter, and a 16-bit status register (Fig. 12-1).

The eight data registers (D0 to D7) handle data fields by (Fig. 12-2)

Bytes, 8 bits
Words, 16 bits
Long words, 32 bits

The advantage of having the 32-bit long data word is that it improves throughput. By handling larger groups, the data are processed in less time. The technique for handling blocks or arrays of data implies that the program is written using loops. These loops are required to manage additional instructions by counting the number of loops or events and then comparing and testing when to exit from the loop, all of which requires additional time to execute. Processing larger data fields obviates the time required to execute these overhead instructions and improves throughput, the overtime to input, process, and output the finished data.

For example, the computer problem discussed in Chapter 7 processed a 7-digit, or 28-bit, number. The addition of a 28-bit number is accomplished by the 68000 with a single instruction, while in the 6800 it required a routine. This is a tremendous reduction of processing time and high throughput.

The advantage of having a variety of data field lengths, bit, byte, and

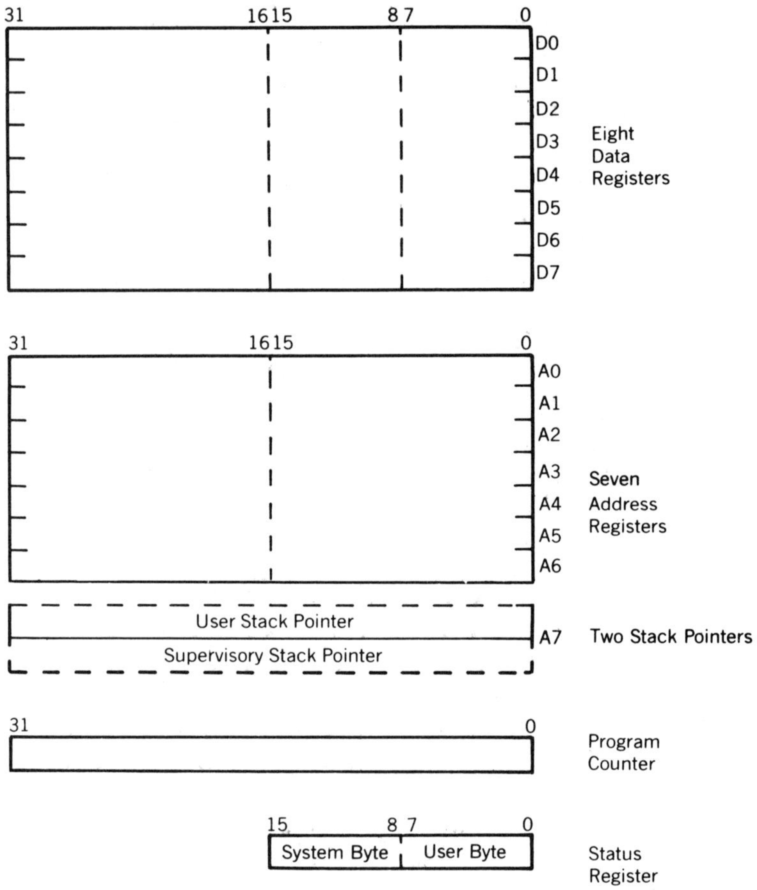

Figure 12-1. 68000 register set—programming model.

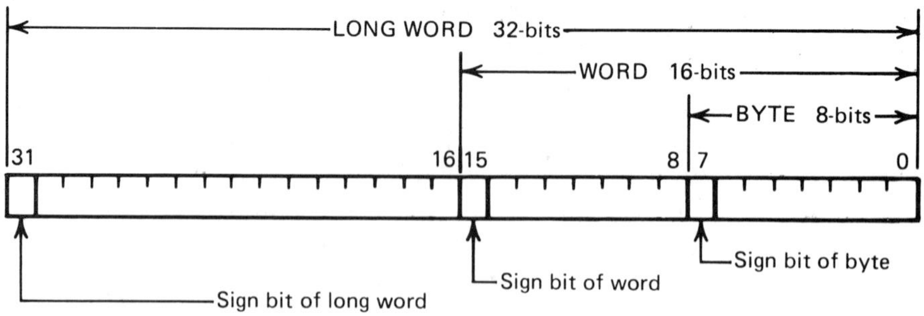

Figure 12-2. Sign bit for byte, word, and long word.

word, offers the programmer the option of choosing the ideal field length for a particular application. Another correlating feature of the variable data word is to set the sign bit by bit 7, 15, or 31, depending on whether the instruction operates on a byte, word, or long word, respectively (Fig. 12-2). Likewise, the carry bit for byte or word lengths does not propagate to bits 8 or 16 and beyond.

Of the nine address registers, A0 to A7 and A7′, only eight, either A0 to A7 or A0 to A6 and A7′, are accessible to a programmer at any one time. The 68000 has two states: the supervisor state uses stack A7′ and the user state uses stack A7. During subroutine calls, the return address is stored in the respective user or supervisor stack. The supervisor stack, however, is used exclusively by the operating system (OS), which includes exceptional processing (e.g., interrupts).

The eight 32-bit address or pointer registers, A0 to A7 and A7′, are used as index registers, base registers, and stack pointers to form an effective address (EA) as specified by the addressing mode. When a 32-bit address is modified by an offset that is less than 32-bits, the carry bit propagates, or is signed extended, through to the MSB of the address.

To Add	Processor Executes
A negative number \$8000	FFFF 8000
to a positive number \$3000	0000 3000
	FFFF 5000

Status Register

The 16-bit status register (Fig. 12-3) has two parts, system and user byte. The status register instructions affect all 16-bits, while the condition code instructions affect the 8 LSBs only. The system byte, MS byte, is for the exclusive use of the supervisor program, and the condition code register, LS byte, which is used for decision making by the branch instructions, is comparable to the 6800 branch instructions. The condition code bits are carry (C), overflow (V), zero (Z), negative (N), and extend (X) (see Fig. 12-3). The extend (X) bit is new. It is similar to and is often used in lieu of the carry bit to execute an add with carry or subtract with borrow function.

In executing multibyte arithmetic operations, there are two distinct functions: (1) to execute the arithmetic operation, and (2) to count and test to exit from the loop. In most instruction sets the carry bit is set by both an arithmetic operation in the conventional method, used to propagate the carry, and, again, by the compare instruction used to test to exit from the loop. In these cases, two instructions of the loop affect the

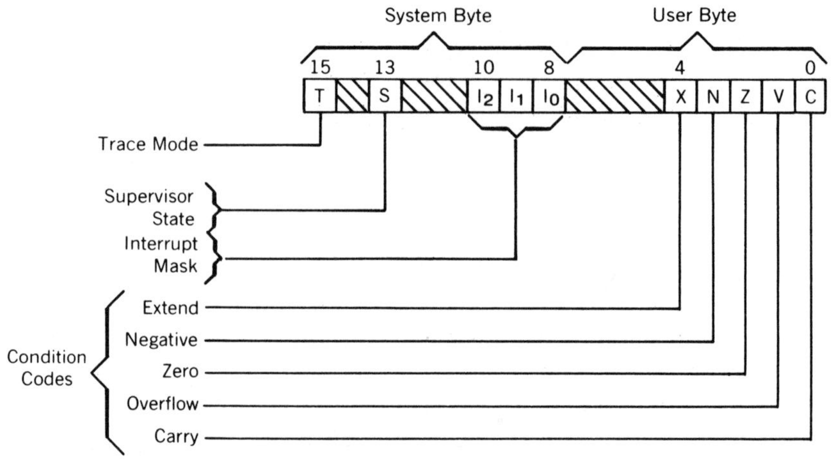

Figure 12-3. User byte is also the condition code register.

carry bit for different purposes. The X bit is used to resolve such conflicts. It is set by an arithmetic operation, but not by the compare instruction.

In the 68000 the add with X is used in lieu of the add with C, which might be affected by another instruction. Three examples of the add with carry in the 6800, 6809, and 68000 are illustrated in Fig. 12-4.

System Byte

Three parts of the system byte are under the exclusive control of supervisor state:

Interrupt priority	I_0, I_1, I_2
Supervisor	S bit
Trace	T bit

The three interrupt bits indicate the priority of the interrupt. An input priority number from 1 to 7 indicates an interrupt, and zero indicates no interrupt. If the input has a higher priority number than that being executed, then the priority is executed, except for a level 7 priority, which cannot be blocked and is comparable to a nonmaskable interrupt (NMI).

The priority input lines are inverted when they are transferred into the status register, where 1's at the input pins represent a level 7 priority, indicating the highest priority.

Restrictions on Using the C Bit to Propagate a Carry

6800	6809	68000
Clear carry	Clear carry Push CC register into stack	Clear X
Loop	Loop Pull CC register from stack	Loop
Add with carry	Add with carry	Add with X affects both C and X bits
(use no instruction that affects the carry bit)	Push CC register into stack Compare affects C	Compare affects C only
Branch back to loop	Branch back to loop	Branch back to loop
In the 6800, generally, care is exercised not to let any other instruction of the loop affect the carry bit. Generally, the loop or event counter decrements to zero and the decrement instruction does not affect the carry bit. An alternate method is to temporarily transfer the CC bits into Acc with the TPA instruction.	In the 6809, if another instruction of the loop affects the carry, then push the CC bits onto the stack prior to the compare or other instruction that affects the CC bits and pull them from the stack at the appropriate time.	In the 68000 the X and C bits are affected by arithmetic and shift instructions, while only the C bit is affected by the compare-type instruction.

Figure 12-4. Convenience of using the X bit of the 68000 compared to the 6800 or 6809.

		System Byte	Input Pins	
		I_2 I_1 I_0	I_2 I_1 I_0	
Interrupt request	Highest priority	0 0 0	1 1 1	Level 7
		0 0 1	1 1 0	6
		0 1 0	1 0 1	5
		0 1 1	1 0 0	4
		1 0 0	0 1 1	3
		1 0 1	0 1 0	2
	Lowest priority	1 1 0	0 1 0	1
No interrupt		1 1 1	0 0 0	0

The supervisor (S) bit indicates when the user or system stack pointer is used.

S = 0	S = 1
user stack A7	supervisor stack A7′

Trace mode (T bit) is a debugging tool. It is used to single cycle through a program and to trace, top read out the data in the selective registers, before executing the next instruction.

12-2 THE 64-PIN PACKAGE

The power and flexibility of the 68000 microprocessor is reflected in the 64 pins of the package. Traditionally, a microprocessor has three buses, data, address, and control, where data flow over the data bus to or from a memory location or I/O port selected by the address bus. The control bus controls the system timing and direction of data flow. The 68000 has two control buses, synchronous and asynchronous. The asynchronous control bus is for large memories with indeterminate response times; the synchronous control bus is for 6800 compatible synchronous peripheral devices with fixed or known response times, (Fig. 12-5).

- 23-pin address bus for 16 megabytes of memory (A_1 to A_{23})
- 16-pin data bus (D_0 to D_{15})
- Synchronous control bus
- Asynchronous control bus
- Other control signals

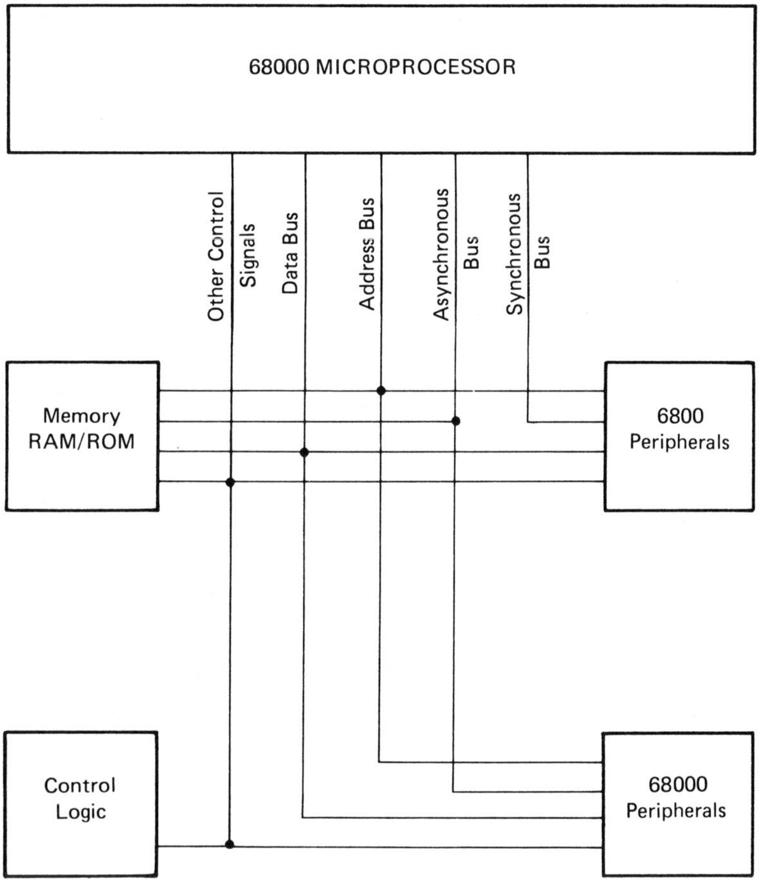

Figure 12-5. Basic system diagram.

These other control signals may be referred to as parts of the control bus (Fig. 12-6).

Clock and Power Pins The input clock pin permits a maximum 8 MHz clock. There are four power pins, two for Vcc at +5 V and two for ground pins.

Data Bus The 16-bit data bidirectional data bus carries the data to and from memory.

Address Bus and Data Organization in Memory The 23-pin address bus (A_1 to A_{23}) addresses an 8-megaword memory, where each 16-bit word consists of an even and odd byte (Fig. 12-7). To access a byte of data, R0, the LSB of the address register, selects the even and odd byte but is not part of the address bus. Rather, R0 drives two lines

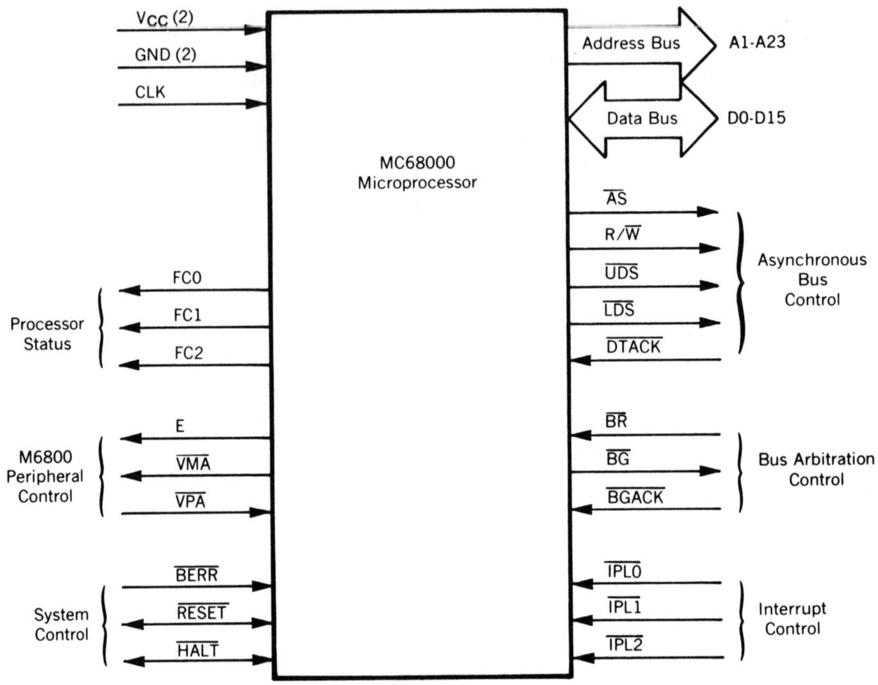

Figure 12-6. Input and output signals of the control buses.

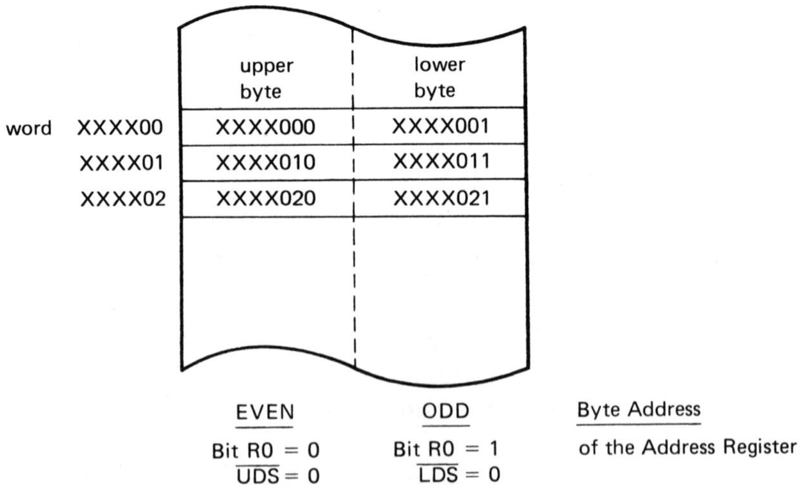

Figure 12-7. Byte addressing and word organization in memory.

of the asynchronous control bus; the upper data strobe ($\overline{UDS}$) selects the even byte and the lower data strobe ($\overline{LDS}$) selects the odd byte of the word addressed. To access a word or long word of data, both the upper and lower data strobe barred signals are low.

Control Buses The rest of the I/O pins of the 68000 are grouped into six control buses (Fig. 12-6):

- Asynchronous bus control
- Synchronous bus control
- Processor status bits
- Bus arbitration or DMA control
- Interrupt control
- System control

Asynchronous Control Bus The 8-bit 6800 family of microprocessors are all synchronous microcomputer systems. Synchronous systems imply that all the components, the processor, memory, and peripheral chips of the family are selected to run at a maximum specified clock frequency of 1, 1.5, or 2 MHz. The designers of the 6800 chips solved all the user's timing problems by specifying the speed and access time of the memory and I/O devices. The propagation time, or the time it takes to move data between the chips of the family, has been anticipated within fixed timing cycles. Synchronous systems are generally restricted to small systems with selected devices.

Asynchronous systems, however, are more applicable to large memory systems where not all memory devices must meet critical response times. Also, large memory systems are packaged on several printed circuit boards, making it difficult to anticipate the time it takes the data to propagate along the bus, especially for high-frequency clocks.

The pins of the asynchronous bus are as follows:

$\overline{AS}$	Address strobe indicates that a valid address is on the address bus
$R/\overline{W}$	Read/not write when high specifies a read and when low specifies a write cycle
$\overline{LDS}$	Lower data strobe
$\overline{UDS}$	Upper data strobe
$\overline{DTACK}$	Data transfer acknowledge is the asynchronous response signal from the memory, indicating that the data transfer is complete; is generated by memory control logic

Synchronous/Peripheral Control Bus There are three peripheral control signals, two of which emulate the 6800 control bus, enable (E) and valid memory address (VMA).

E The enable clock synchronizes 6800 devices to the 68000 microprocessor. The time period for this output is six clocks low and four clocks high.

$\overline{VPA}$ The valid peripheral input indicates that data flow from a 6800-type synchronous peripheral device. It is generated by control logic, which senses that a section of memory assigned to 6800 devices is addressed. It also indicates an interrupt request ($\overline{IRQ}$) as defined by the 6800 system. See Sec. 3-3.

$\overline{VMA}$ The valid memory address responds to a $\overline{VPA}$ input signal and emulates a 6800 control signal.

Interrupt Bus The three input interrupt lines indicate the priority assigned to the I/O device requesting an interrupt where zero indicates an interrupt. A process of autovectoring is initiated if the $\overline{VPA}$ accompanies the interrupt request number. See Interrupt Request ($\overline{IRQ}$), Sec. 3-3. In autovectoring, the priority numbers 1 to 6 are mapped to vectors 25 to 31 (decimal).

The 68000 has 192 additional interrupt vector addresses when not asserting VPA. Each of up to 192 interrupting devices is assigned an 8-bit interrupt address transmitted on the address bus and mapped into one of the 192 vector interrupt addresses.

Processor Status Bits FC0, FC1, FC2 The processor status or function control bits report what operation the processor is engaged in as indicated by Function Code Outputs (Table 12-1). They are valid when the address status (AS) output is low. In multiprocessor systems, the processor status bits are sensed by the bus arbitrator of memory management devices.

Bus Arbitration or DMA Control Pins The bus arbitration control signals determine which device will control the bus. The bus may be controlled by another processor or a direct memory access (DMA) device. Data throughput with a DMA device is increased over data moving through an I/O port. The DMA device is tied to the control line and senses when there is a request to input or output, read or write, data to or from the processor. Under appropriate conditions, described later, the DMA device requests, and when the processor indicates, takes control of the buses to transfer data between an I/O device and memory.

Peripheral Control Bus for Synchronous Operations The 68000 is designed to operate asynchronously with memory and I/O devices,

Table 12-1. Function Code Outputs

FC0	FC1	FC2	Cycle Type
Low	Low	Low	(Undefined, Reserved)
Low	Low	High	User Data
Low	High	Low	User Program
Low	High	High	(Undefined, Reserved)
High	Low	Low	(Undefined, Reserved)
High	Low	High	Supervisor Data
High	High	Low	Supervisor Program
High	High	High	Interrupt Acknowledge

whereas the 6800 family was designed to operate with synchronous devices. The function of the peripheral control bus is to permit the interface of synchronous 6800 devices with the 68000 system. This is accomplished by essentially slowing down the 68000 response to meet the 6800 response time specifications.

There are three bus arbitration control lines:

$\overline{\text{BR}}$	The bus request is a wired-ORed input of all interrupting devices. When low it indicates that a device is requesting to control the bus.
$\overline{\text{BG}}$	The bus grant is an output signal indicating that the processor will relinquish control of the bus at the end of the current bus cycle.
$\overline{\text{BGACK}}$	The bus grant acknowledge is an input signal indicating that the interrupting device is in control of the bus.

System Control The system control bus is used to reset the processor, the peripheral devices, single-cycling operations, or to indicate a variety of system errors. There are three signals:

$\overline{\text{BERR}}$	Bus error
$\overline{\text{RES}}$	Bidirectional reset signal
$\overline{\text{HLT}}$	Bidirectional halt signal

12-3 ADDRESSING MODES

The 68000 has 56 basic instructions, or functions, and five addressing modes with 14 variations, for more than 1000 effective instructions. The technique of separating the instructions into a function, expressed

Table 12-2. Instruction Set

Mnemonic	Description
ABCD	Add Decimal with Extend
ADD	Add
AND	Logical And
ASL	Arithmetic Shift Left
ASR	Arithmetic Shift Right
B_{CC}	Branch Conditionally
BCHG	Bit Test and Change
BCLR	Bit Test and Clear
BRA	Branch Always
BSET	Bit Test and Set
BSR	Branch to Subroutine
BTST	Bit Test
CHK	Check Register Against Bounds
CLR	Clear Operand
CMP	Compare
DB_{CC}	Test Condition, Decrement and Branch
DIVS	Signed Divide
DIVU	Unsigned Divide
EOR	Exclusive Or
EXG	Exchange Registers
EXT	Sign Extend
JMP	Jump
JSR	Jump to Subroutine
LEA	Load Effective Address
LINK	Link Stack
LSL	Logical Shift Left
LSR	Logical Shift Right
MOVE	Move
MOVEM	Move Multiple Registers
MOVEP	Move Peripheral Data
MULS	Signed Multiply
MULU	Unsigned Multiply
NBCD	Negate Decimal with Extend
NEG	Negate
NOP	No Operation
NOT	One's Complement
OR	Logical Or
PEA	Push Effective Address
RESET	Reset External Devices
ROL	Rotate Left without Extend
ROR	Rotate Right without Extend
ROXL	Rotate Left with Extend
ROXR	Rotate Right with Extend
RTE	Return from Exception
RTR	Return and Restore
RTS	Return from Subroutine
SBCD	Subtract Decimal with Extend
S_{CC}	Set Conditional
STOP	Stop
SUB	Subtract
SWAP	Swap Data Register Halves
TAS	Test and Set Operand
TRAP	Trap
TRAPV	Trap on Overflow
TST	Test
UNLK	Unlink

by a mnemonic, and an addressing mode, started with the 6800 family for the convenience of having the programmer remember fewer instruction variations (Sec. 1-6). There are two parts of the instruction: (1) the function performed, expressed by the operation code (opcode), which is the first word of the instruction, generally referred to as "the instruction" (Table 12-2), and (2) the addressing mode, which indicates the location of the data to be modified by the opcode.

The 68000 opcode generally has three fields: the instruction (function), the size, byte, word, and long word, and the effective address. The effective address field has two basic meanings. It specifies a register or the addressing mode as listed in Table 12-3. The effective address field is not to be confused with the effective address (EA), which is the actual or computed address of the data in memory. The addressing mode specifies the technique for computing the actual or effective address of the memory location.

The 68000 has eight data registers with no reference to an accumulator. The two basic restrictions of the accumulator in the 6800 (Sec. 1-4) do not apply to the data registers. First, all data that flow to and

Table 12-3. Data Addressing Modes

Mode	Generation
Register Direct Addressing	
Data Register Direct	EA = Dn
Address Register Direct	EA = An
Absolute Data Addressing	
Absolute Short	EA = (Next Word)
Absolute Long	EA = (Next Two Words)
Program Counter Relative Addressing	
Relative with Offset	$EA = (PC) + d_{16}$
Relative with Index and Offset	$EA = (PC) + (Xn) + d_8$
Register Indirect Addressing	
Register Indirect	EA = (An)
Postincrement Register Indirect	EA = (An), An ← An + N
Predecrement Register Indirect	An ← An − N, EA = (An)
Register Indirect with Offset	$EA = (An) + d_{16}$
Indexed Register Indirect with Offset	$EA = (An) + (Xn) + d_8$
Immediate Data Addressing	
Immediate	DATA = Next Word(s)
Quick Immediate	Inherent Data
Implied Addressing	
Implied Register	EA = SR, USP, SP, PC

NOTES:

EA = Effective Address
An = Address Register
Dn = Data Register
Xn = Address or Data Register used as Index Register
SR = Status Register
PC = Program Counter
( ) = Contents of
d_8 = Eight-bit Offset (displacement)
d_{16} = Sixteen-bit Offset (displacement)
N = 1 for Byte, 2 for Words and 4 for Long Words
← = Replaces

from memory, or in and out of the processor, move through the accumulator. In the 68000, data move from one memory location to another, or to and from memory to an I/O port, without passing through the data register.

The second restriction of the 6800 is typically described by

$$A \leftarrow (A) + (M)$$

where the contents of the accumulator are replaced after being modified by the arithmetic logic unit (ALU) with data from a memory location. The general form of the ALU operation of the 68000 refers to a source (S) and destination (D) data:

$$D \leftarrow (S) + (D)$$

where either the source or destination may specify a data register or a memory location. Eliminating these restrictions makes the 68000 a more powerful microprocessor.

Table 12-4. Effective Address Field

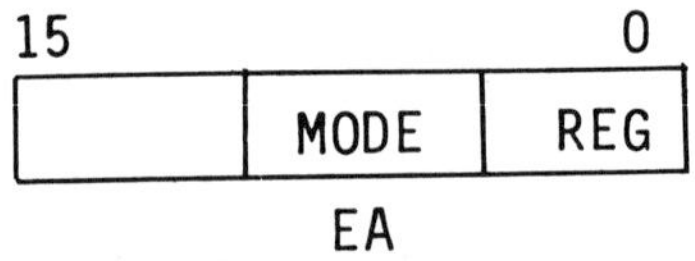

	EA MODE	EA REG	ADDRESSING MODE	
1	000	REG#	DATA REGISTER DIRECT	Dn
2	001	REG#	ADDRESS REGISTER DIRECT	An
3	010	REG#	ADDRESS REGISTER INDIRECT (ARI)	(An)
4	011	REG#	ARI WITH POSTINCREMENT	(An)+
5	100	REG#	ARI WITH PREDECREMENT	-(An)
6	101	REG#	ARI WITH DISPLACEMENT	d(An)
7	110	REG#	ARI WITH INDEX	d(An,Rm)
8	111	000	ABSOLUTE SHORT	SXXXX
9	111	001	ABSOLUTE LONG	SXXXXXXXX
10	111	010	PC WITH DISPLACEMENT	d(PC)
11	111	011	PC WITH INDEX	d(PC, R+)
12	111	100	IMMEDIATE STATUS REGISTER	#, SR, CCR
13	111	101	(UNUSED)	
14	111	110	(UNUSED)	
15	111	111	(UNUSED)	

Addressing Modes

There are five addressing modes:

Register direct	2 variations
Immediate	2 variations
Register indirect	5 variations
Absolute	2 variations
Program counter	2 variations

The effective address is coded in two fields of the opcode, the mode and register fields. The effective address field and the assembler language notation are listed in Table 12-4. The mode and register fields of the effective address may at times invert positions. All but the move instructions have one effective address, whereas the move instruction has two, a source and destination effective address field.

The general assembler notation of a move instruction is:

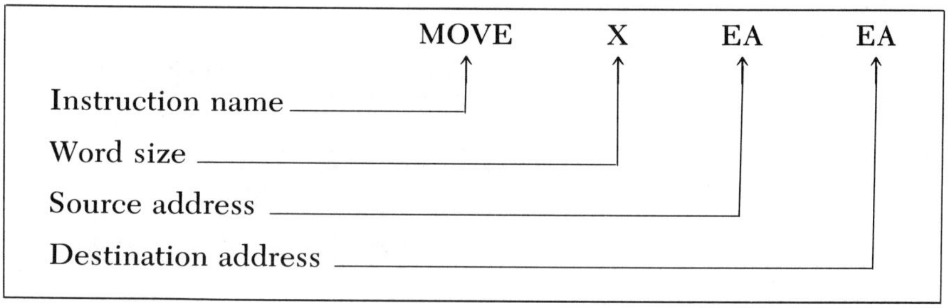

The instruction format of the move instruction is:

15	14	13	12	11	10	9	8	7	6	5	4	3	2	1	0
0	0	Size		Destination						Source					
				Reg			Mode			Mode			Reg		

Size		
	01	Byte
	11	Word
	10	Long word

Register Direct Addressing

In the direct register addressing mode, the data in one of the registers are moved or modified.

- D_0 to D_7: Data register direct is coded 000
- A_0 to A_7: Address register direct is coded 001
- Status or condition code register: Status register 8 MSBs; condition code register 8 LSBs

The move instruction moves data between registers, between memory locations, or between a register and a memory location. The move instruction is the only instruction with two effective addressing fields and is ideal for illustrating the various forms of the effective addressing fields (see Table 12-5).

Table 12-5. Move Instruction Format

MOVE INSTRUCTION

MOVE .X ⟨ea⟩, ⟨ea⟩

SOURCE DESTINATION

*** WHERE X SPECIFIES LENGTH OF DATA BEING TRANSFERRED**

B — BYTE
W — WORD (DEFAULT)
L — LONG WORD

Example: Assembler Notation and Equivalent Machine Code

1. The one-word move instruction to move a byte of data from register DO → A3.

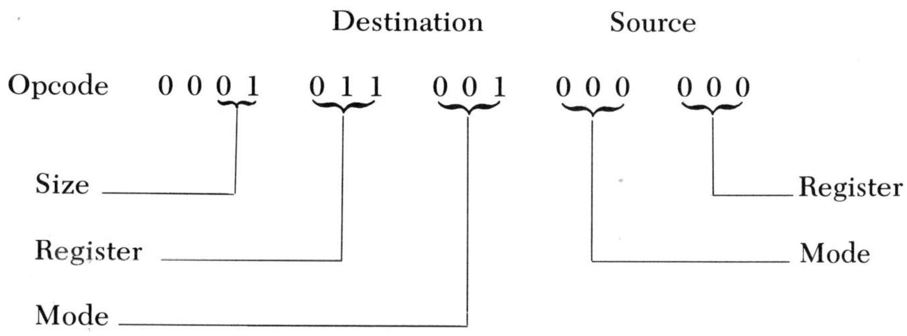

ASM* 1640 MOVEB D_0,A_3

2. The one-word move instruction to move a word of data from register A3 → DO.

Opcode 0 0 1 1 0 0 0 0 0 0 0 0 1 0 1 1

ASM 300B MOVE A3,DO

3. The two-word move instruction to move a byte of data from register D1 to the absolute short location $1234.

Opcode 0 0 0 1 0 0 0 1 1 1 0 0 0 0 0 1

ASM 11C1 1234 MOVE.B D1,$1234

4. The three-word move instruction to move a word of data from absolute long location $56789A to address register A4.

Opcode 0 0 1 1 1 0 0 0 0 1 1 1 1 0 0 1

ASM C879 0056 789A MOVE $56789A,A4

Immediate Addressing

Two variations of the immediate addressing mode are used to introduce constants into the processing registers (Sec. 1-6). In the first, the quick immediate, 1 byte of data is contained within the opcode, making it inherent data, and is loaded into one of the data registers. Move (or load) 1 byte of data $24 into data register D5.

* ASM, machine code and assembler language notation.

0111 101 0 00100100

Move quick — 0111
Data register # — 101
Immediate data — 00100100

ASM 7A24 MOVE #$24,D5

The second version of the immediate addressing, used to load a word or long word of data, may be loaded into the data or address registers.

The effective address of the immediate addressing mode is coded 111 011. With a two-word move immediate instruction load address #$79BD into address register A6.

Opcode 0 0 11 110 001 111 100

Word size — 11
Address reg. A6 — 110 001
Immediate addressing — 111 100

ASM 3C7C 79BD MOVE #$79BD,A6

With a three-word immediate instruction, load address #$123479BD into address register A6.

Opcode 0010 110 001 111 100

ASM 2C7C 1234 79BD MOVE #$123479BD,A6

Register Indirect Addressing

There are five register indirect addressing modes:

- Address register indirect where the effective address mode field is coded 010
  EA = (An)
- Address register indirect with postincrement where the effective address mode field is coded 011
  EA = An; An + M* → An
- Address register indirect with predecrement where the effective address is coded 100
  An − M → An; EA = (An)

* M, the increment, is 1, 2, or 4 for a byte, word, or long word size, respectively.

- Address register indirect with displacement where the effective address mode field is coded 101
  EA = An + d16
- Address register indirect with index where the effective address mode field is coded 110
  EA = Xm + d8

The register indirect addressing mode enables the move instruction to address two memory locations, source and destination, effectively making it an I/O instruction. The postincrement and predecrement modes are ideal for moving blocks of data.

Address Register Indirect, EA = (An)

1. A one-word instruction moves data indirectly in memory to or from a register. Move a byte of data from register D3 to the memory location pointed to by address register (A4).

Opcode 0 0 0 1 1 0 0 0 1 0 0 0 0 0 1 1

ASM 1883 MOVE.B D3,(A4)

2. Move a word of data between memory locations pointed to by address register (A1) to a location pointed to by address register (A3).

Opcode 0 0 1 1 1 0 0 0 1 0 0 1 0 0 0 1

ASM 3891 MOVE (A1),(A4)

3. Use a two-word instruction to move a byte of data from location $1234 using an absolute short effective address to the location pointed to by address register (A4). The absolute short address is stored in the operand, the second word of the instruction.

Opcode 0 0 0 1 1 0 0 0 1 0 1 1 1 0 0 0

ASM 18B8 1234 MOVE.B $1234,(A4)

Address Register Indirect Postincrement/Predecrement

1. Use a one-word instruction to move a word of data from a location pointed to by address register (A2) to (A4) and then increment both pointers by 2, so they are pointing to the location of the next word.

Opcode 0 0 1 1 1 0 0 0 1 1 0 1 1 0 1 0

ASM 38DA MOVE (A2)+,(A4)+

2. Use a two-word instruction to move a byte of data from a location

pointed to by address register (A3) to location \$8000, and then decrement address register A3 by 1. This instruction is applicable when location \$8000 is an output port and address register (A3) is pointing to the message. The operand, the second byte, stores 0001 absolute short address location \$8000.

Opcode		0 0 0 1	0 1 1	1 0 0	1 1 1	0 0 0
ASM	1738 8000	MOVE.B		\$8C00,−(A3)		

Address Register Indirect with Displacement

In this addressing mode the displacement, sign extended, is added to the address register to form an effective address. The displacement is either the source or destination address.

1. Use a two-word instruction to move a byte of data from data register D4 to an address register A5, plus a displacement of \$1000. The term displacement in the 68000 is comparable to offset for the 6800 (Sec. 1-6).

Opcode		0 0 0 1	1 0 1	1 0 1	0 0 0	1 0 0
ASM	1B44 1000	MOVE.B		D4,\$1000(A5)		

2. Use a three-word instruction to move a byte of data from location \$1234, the operand stored in the third byte, to the address register (A5) plus a displacement of \$1000, stored in the second byte.

Opcode		0 0 0 1	1 0 1	1 0 1	1 1 1	0 0 0
ASM	1B78 1000 1234	MOVE.B		\$1234,\$1000(A5)		

Address Register Indirect with Index

In this addressing mode, the effective address (EA) is the sign extended sum of three numbers contained in:

- an address register (An)
- an index register (Xm) and
- an 8-bit displacement (d8), which is the operand.

The indirect address with index is either the source or destination address. The displacement is stored in the second byte of the instruction and is followed by other bytes of operand, when required.

1. Use a two-word instruction to move a word of data from the effective address formed by adding A5 + D7 + \$100 to data register D2.

Opcode	0 0 1 1	0 1 0	0 0 0	1 1 0	1 0 1

ASM 3435 0100 MOVE #$100(A5,D7),D2

2. Use a three-word instruction to move a byte of data from the effective address formed by adding A5 + D6 + $100 to absolute long location $1234.

31F5	0 0 1 1	0 0 0	1 1 1	1 1 0	1 0 1

ASM 31F5 0100 1234 MOVE.B #$100(A5,D7),$1234

Absolute Addressing

The two variations of the absolute addressing mode are short and long, specifying a 16- or 24-bit address, respectively. The absolute short addressing mode coded 111 000 has a 1-byte operand, and the absolute long addressing mode code 111 001 requires a 2-byte operand. The 16-bit address is sign extended.

1. Use a two-word instruction to move a byte of data from data register R3 to location $8000.

Opcode	0 0 0 1	0 0 1	1 1 1	0 0 0	0 1 1

ASM 13C3 8000 MOVE.B R3,$8000

2. Use a three-word instruction to move a byte of data from data register R3 to location $89ABCD.

Opcode	0 0 0 1	0 1 0	1 1 1	0 0 0	0 1 1

ASM 15C3 0089 ABCD MOVE.B R3,$89ABCD

The move instruction is an exception by having two effective addresses in the opcode. When transferring data from one memory location to another using the absolute short instruction, the source operand precedes the destination operand.

3. The three-word instruction to move a byte of data from location $1234 to $8000, using the absolute addressing mode is:

Opcode	0 0 0 1	0 0 0	1 1 1	1 1 1	0 0 0

11F8 1234 8000 MOVE.B $1234,$8000

Program Counter

There are two variations of the program counter addressing mode:

- Program counter with displacement
- Program counter with index

The program counter addressing modes are used with position-independent code, and the program counter with index is used with a position-independent look-up table where the table is less than 256 or 8 bits away from the program counter.

1. Use a two-word instruction to move a byte of data from register R3 to location \$1234, which is above the program counter at the start of the instruction. Assume that the program counter is pointing to location \$1000 before executing the instruction.

$$\begin{aligned} \text{Addr} &= \text{PC} + 2 + \text{d16} \\ 1234 &= 1000 + 2 + \text{d16} \\ 1234 - 1000 - 2 &= \text{d16} \\ 232 &= \text{d16} \end{aligned}$$

The 16-bit displacement is stored in the operand.

Opcode	0 0 0 1	0 1 0	1 1 1	0 0 0	0 1 1

15C3 0232 MOVE.B R3,(\$0232)

2. Use a two-word instruction to look up the position in the table indicated by address register (A3), when the table is located 235 locations above the program counter, before the instruction is executed.

$$\begin{aligned} &\text{Assume PC at \$1000} \\ &\text{A3} = (0009) \\ &\text{Table at \$1235} \\ &1240 = 1000 = 2 = 9 = 235 \end{aligned}$$

The operand, the second word, contains the RX register number in the 6 MSBs and the displacement is the 8 LSB:

Opcode	0 0 0 1	1 0 1	0 0 0	1 1 1	0 1 1
Operand	0 0 0 1	0 1 0 0	0 0 1 1	0 0 1 0	

ASM 1A33 1432 MOVE.B TABLE,DR

12-4 INSTRUCTION SET

The fifty-six 68000 instructions listed in Table 12-2 use many of the same mnemonics of the 6800/9 instruction set and perform the same basic functions. The 6800/9 instructions, however, are restricted to replacing the data modified by the arithmetic and logic instructions in an accumulator only. The 68000 instructions permit the modified data to replace the contents of either a register or a memory location.

The instructions listed should more appropriately be referred to as the function expressed by the mnemonic, which, with an addressing mode, specifies the register or memory location of the data constituting the instruction. But, by convention, the term "instruction" will be used interchangeably.

This section begins by discussing the branch instructions and the relative addressing mode associated with the program control instructions. The instructions are highlighted with comments on the instructions that are unique to the 68000. The instruction categories are:

- Program control
- Integer arithmetic
- BCD
- Logic
- Shift and rotate
- Bit manipulation
- Data movement

Branch Instructions and Relative Addressing

The branch instructions make decisions by examining one or more of the five condition code bits, X, N, Z, V, and C; if the conditions are met the program takes the branch by adding the 8 or 16-bit 2's complement relative address to the program counter. If the conditions are not met, the program continues and executes the next instruction. The 68000 branch instructions are similar to the 6800 branch instructions (see Sec. 1-9), with one basic difference: a 16-bit branch capability permitting a branch of +/− 32K. The X bit is not tested by the branch instructions, but it is used by some instructions in lieu of the carry bit.

Program Control Instructions

The program control instructions (Table 12-6) modify the program flow by modifying the contents of the program counter, rather than autoincrementing the program counter to the next instruction. The stop, reset, and No-op (NOP) or no-operation instructions are exceptions. The reset instruction resets external devices. The stop instruction stops the computer. That is a drastic action used during program debugging. The NOP is used as a filler to either waste time or, during debugging, to reserve memory space.

Three branch instructions are similar to the 6800 branch instructions (Section 1-8 and 1-9).

Bcc	The 14 conditional branch instructions 8- and 16-bit displacement
BRA	Branch always
BSR	Branch to subroutine

Table 12-6. Program Control Instructions

Instruction	Operation
Conditional	
Bcc	Branch conditionally (14 conditions) 8- and 16-bit displacement
DBcc	Test condition, decrement counter, and branch. 16-bit displacement
Scc	Set byte conditionally (16 conditions)
Unconditional	
BRA	Branch always 8- and 16-bit displacement
BSR	Branch to subroutine 8- and 16-bit displacement
JMP	Jump
JSR	Jump to subroutine
Returns	
RTR	Return and restore condition codes
RTS	Return from subroutine

Two new 68000 instructions test the condition code bits:

DBcc   Decrement and branch
Scc   Set byte according to a condition code bit

The decrement and branch (DBcc) instruction is ideal for counting the number of loops the program must execute. The instruction incorporates a decrement loop, or event counter feature, into the condition of branch instruction. The instruction first tests the condition code bits and, if the conditions are met, decrements a specified data register, storing the count, and takes the branch if both the conditional test is met and the count is unequal to -1 ($\neq -1$). When neither the conditional test is met nor the count equals -1, the program continues to the next instruction.

The DBcc instruction is always a two-word instruction where the operand is a 16-bit displacement, sign extended, with eight 1's to the 24 bits. This 2's complement negative number always forces the instruction to branch back in the program.

The second instruction, set according to conditions (Scc), is used to set a flag byte according to one of the condition code bits tested. If the test is true, then the byte in memory specified by the effective address is set to all (eight) 1's. If the test is false, then the byte in memory is set to all 0's.

There are three return from subroutine instructions:

RTS   Return from subroutine

RTR	Return and restore condition code
RTE	Return from exception (privileged instruction)

The return from subroutine (RTS) pulls only the program counter from the appropriate stack when returning from a subroutine (Sec. 2-2). The return and restore condition codes pull and restore both the program counter and condition code register from the respective stack. The contents of the other selected register are pulled from the stack with the move multiple register (MOVEM) instruction.

Integer Arithmetic Instruction

In the 68000 instruction the result may replace the contents of the register or a memory location, depending on which is the destination of the data (D). The add extend (ADDX) instruction adds the contents of the X bit rather than the carry bit to form the sum. The add quick (ADDQ) instruction is a one-word add immediate instruction that adds a 3-bit operand, with a range from 1 to 8, to the destination data. There is a comparable set of subtract instructions. See Table 12-7.

There are two multiply and divide instructions each, signed and unsigned. The product/quotient, the destination operand, is always returned to a date register (Dn). The multiplying of two 16-bit operands yields a 32-bit result. In the divide operation the quotient and remainder are stored in the destination data register, where the quotient is in the lower 16-bit word and the remainder is in the upper 16-bit word. A trap is called for either a divide by zero or an overflow.

The arithmetic compare instructions subtract the (destination)/(source) operands and set the condition codes accordingly. The test an operand (TST) instruction is part of the 68000 instruction set. It, like the compare instruction, sets only the condition code bit to be used by a branch instruction.

BCD Instructions

The test and set operand (TAS) instruction is similar to the test an operand instruction, with the exception that the high-order bit, the seventh bit of the byte, data tested is set to 1. It is useful for multiprocessors or operations where it is necessary to leave a signature indicating that the data have been examined. There are three decimal or binary code decimal instructions:

ABCD	Add decimal
NBCD	Negate decimal
SBCD	Subtract decimal

Table 12-7. Integer Arithmetic Instruction

Instruction	Operand Size	Operation
ADD	8, 16, 32 16, 32	Dn + (EA) → Dn (EA) + Dn → EA (EA) + #xxx → EA An + (EA) → An
ADDX	8, 16, 32 16, 32	Dx + D6 + X → Dx Ax@- Ay@- + X → Ax@
CLR	8, 16, 32	0 → EA
CMP	8, 16, 32 16, 32	Dn - (EA) (EA) - #xxx Ax@+ - Ay@+ An - (EA)
DIVS	32 ÷ 16	Dn/(EA) → Dn
DIVU	32 ÷ 16	Dn/(EA) → Dn
EXT	8 → 16 16 → 32	$(Dn)_8$ → Dn_{16} $(Dn)_{16}$ → Dn_{32}
MULS	16 * 16 → 32	Dn * (EA) → Dn
MULU	16 * 16 → 32	Dn * (EA) → Dn
NEG	8, 16, 32	0 - (EA) → EA
NEGX	8, 16, 32	0 - (EA) - X → EA
SUB	8, 16, 32 16, 32	Dn - (EA) → Dn (EA) - Dn → EA (EA) - #xxx → EA An - (EA) → An
SUBX	8, 16, 32	Dx - Dy - X → Dx Ax@- - Ay@- - X → Ax@
TAS	8	(EA) - 0, 1 → EA[7]
TST	8, 16, 32	(EA) - 0

Note:
[ ] = bit number

They operate on pack, two BCD characters per byte, numbers with a carry using the X bit. These are single operations, as opposed to the 6800/9, which require a second decimal adjust instruction to complete the operation.

Logic Instructions

The logic instructions are similar to those of the 6800.

Shift and Rotate Instructions

Shift and rotate instructions (Table 12-8) are similar to those of the 6800/9, with two exceptions: first, the byte, word, or long word may be shifted by a count from 1 to 8, which obviates the need for a loop counter. The assembler notation, for example, is

Table 12-8. Shift and Rotate Instructions

Instruction	Operand Size	Operation
ASL	8, 16, 32	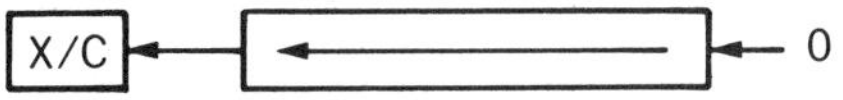
ASR	8, 16, 32	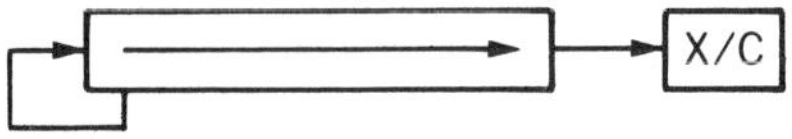
LSL	8, 16, 32	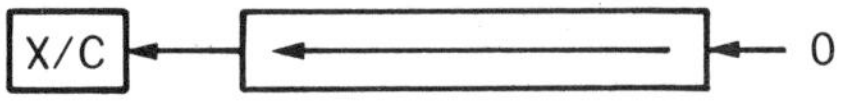
LSR	8, 16, 32	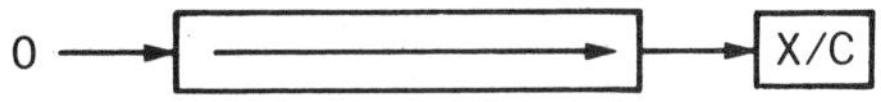
ROL	8, 16, 32	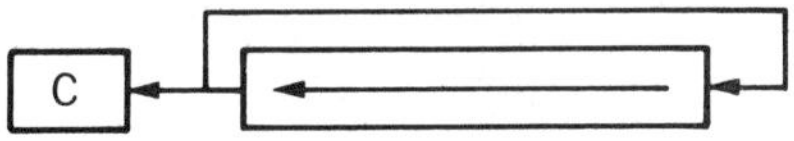
ROR	8, 16, 32	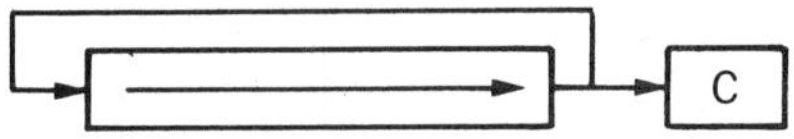
ROXL	8, 16, 32	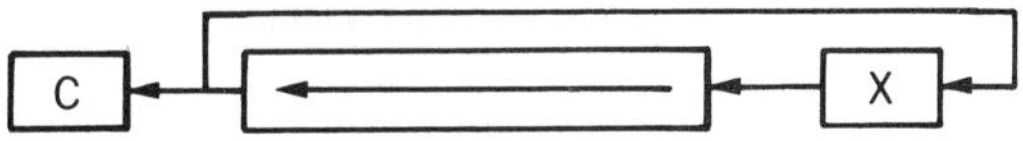
ROXR	8, 16, 32	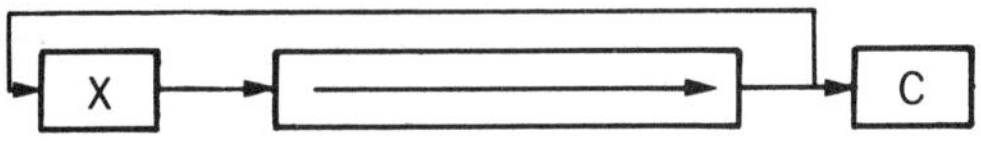

ASL DX,DY

where DX is the register to be shifted by the count stored in register DY.

A second difference of the 68000 shift/rotate instructions is that the X bit is modified with the same setting as the C bit.

Bit Manipulation

The bit manipulator instructions (Table 12-9) have been expanded from the single-bit test instruction of the 6800 to four instructions, which give the 68000 bit manipulation capabilities. These four instructions all test the specified bit and set the Z bit accordingly. In the bit test instruction (BTST) the data are not modified. The test bit and change instruction (BCNG) first tests the specified bit and then changes or inverts it. The clear and set instructions (BCLR and BSET) each test the specified bit and, after setting the Z bit accordingly, either clear or set the specified bit, respectively.

Table 12-9. Bit Manipulation Instructions

Instruction	Operand Size	Operation
BTST	8, 32	~ bit of (EA) → Z
BSET	8, 32	~ bit of (EA) → Z 1 → bit of EA
BCLR	8, 32	~ bit of (EA) → Z 0 → bit of EA
BCHG	8, 32	~ bit of (EA) → Z ~ bit of (EA) → bit of EA

Table 12-10. Data Movement Instructions

Instruction	Operand Size	Operation
EXG	32	Rx → Ry
LEA	32	EA → An
LINK	—	An → SP@- SP → An SP + d → SP
MOVE	8, 16, 32	$(EA)_s$ → EA_d
MOVEM	16, 32	(EA) → An, Dn An, Dn → EA
MOVEP	16, 32	(EA) → Dn Dn → EA
MOVEQ	8	#Imm → Dn
PEA	32	EA → SP@-
SWAP	32	Dn [31:16] ↔ Dn [15:0]
UNLK	—	An → SP SP @+ → An

Notes:
s = source
d = destination
[ ] = bit numbers

Data Movement Instruction

The move instructions (Table 12-10) are the only instructions with two effective addresses and have replaced the load and store instructions of the 6800 family. The indirect addressing modes permit the movement of data from one memory location to another and function as I/O instructions.

The move to and from the status register and move to user stack pointer are privileged instructions. The move address (MOVEA) moves the contents of a register or memory location specified by an effective address to an address register.

The move multiple registers (MOVEM) are the push and pull instructions. They function as a push instruction when the destination

Table 12-11. Move Multiple Registers Are Used to Push and Pull from the Stack

For the postincrement mode addresses, the mask correspondence is

15	14	13	12	11	10	9	8	7	6	5	4	3	2	1	0
A7	A6	A5	A4	A3	A2	A1	A0	D7	D6	D5	D4	D3	D2	D1	D0

while for the predecrement mode addresses, the mask correspondence is

15	14	13	12	11	10	9	8	7	6	5	4	3	2	1	0
D0	D1	D2	D3	D4	D5	D6	D7	A0	A1	A2	A3	A4	A5	A6	A7

in an effective address and a comparable pull instruction when the effective address is in the source position. These instructions are comparable to the 6809 push and pull instructions, where the operand indicates the list of registers to be stacked. A 1 in the appropriate bit position indicates which register(s) are to be pushed and pulled. Caution should be exercised in that the bit positions that specify which register(s) are to be pushed or pulled are reversed (see Table 12-11).

In the move peripheral data (MOVEP) I/O data are transferred between a data register and alternates bytes of memory. This is convenient when inputting or outputting data from a peripheral interface adaptor (PIA), where the I/O ports are assigned alternate memory locations.

The exchange and load effective address (EXG and LEA) are carried over from the 6809 instruction set (Sec. 11-6). In the 6800 the effective address (EA) specifies the memory location where data are accessed, but is itself not stored in a register. The load effective address instruction loads the address register with the effective address. This is an ideal way to set a pointer to the beginning of a block of data.

The push effective address (PEA) is an extension of the LEA instruction, which pushes the effective address onto the stack.

The load and unload instructions are paired where the link (LINE) instruction is used to link a table or data bank. The link instruction pushes the contents of the address onto the stack, and then the update stack address is loaded into the address register.

The swap register halves (SWAP) exchanges the 16 MSBs of a data register with the 16 LSBs.

Privileged Instructions

The two operating states of the processor are the supervisory state, when the S bit equals 1, and the user mode. The supervisory state has access to a group of privileged instructions not available to the user program:

RESET	Reset external devices
RTE	Return from exception
STOP	Stop program execution
ORI to SR	Logical OR to status register
MOVE USP	Move user stack pointer
ANDI to SR	Logical AND to status register
EORI to SR	Logical Exclusive-OR to status register
MOVE EA to SR	Load new status register
TRAP	Trap
TRAP V	Trap to overflow
CHK	Check register against bounds

Since only the supervisor program can modify the system byte of the status register, four of the privileged instructions that modify the status register are OR, AND, EOR and MOVE. Data are normally moved in and out of, or pointed to, the user or supervisor stack pointer A7 or A7′, when the program is in the respective state. The move to the status register instruction is an exception, where the supervisor program can modify the user stack pointer or the data being pointed to.

The return from exception (RTE) is a privileged instruction and is one method of transferring control from the supervisor program back to the user program. The contents of the status register and the program counter are pulled from the system stack. It is most likely used when returning from a trap.

The check register against bounds (CHK) instruction is used to assure that a program does not access memory beyond a boundary specified by a data register. The low-order word of the data register is compared against the upper bound of an address specified by the effective address. If the register value is less than zero or greater than the upper bound specified by the effective address, then TRAP. The processor branches to exception processing, and a vector number is generated to reference the CHK instruction exception vector.

The trap or trap on overflow (TRAPV) instructions specify a trap vector for a particular trap condition or, specifically, an overflow condition. Traps are often used in many places in a program, each calling the supervisor program and its corresponding trap vector. This can resolve one of many particular errors or other unresolved conditions.

Effective Addressing Mode Categories

Generally, each instruction can be modified by each of the addressing modes. The permissible combinations of instruction types and addressing modes are listed in Table 12-12.

Table 12-12. Effective Addressing Mode Categories

Effective Address Modes	Mode	Register	Addressing Categories				Assembler Syntax
			Data	Memory	Control	Alterable	
Dn	000	register number	X			X	Dn
An	001	register number				X	An
An@	010	register number	X	X	X	X	(An)
An@+	011	register number	X	X		X	(An)+
An@-	100	register number	X	X		X	-(An)
An@(d)	101	register number	X	X	X	X	d(An)
An@(d, ix)	110	register number	X	X	X	X	d(An, Ri)
xxx.W	111	000	X	X	X	X	xxx
xxx.L	111	001	X	X	X	X	xxxxxx
PC@(d)	111	010	X	X	X		PC relative
PC@(d, ix)	111	011	X	X	X		PC rel. + Ri
#xxx	111	100	X	X			#xxx

Appendices

Appendix IA
6800
Instruction Set

Table 1 Accumulator and Memory Instructions

OPERATIONS	MNEMONIC	IMMED			DIRECT			INDEX			EXTND			IMPLIED			BOOLEAN/ARITHMETIC OPERATION (All register labels refer to contents)	5 H	4 I	3 N	2 Z	1 V	0 C
		OP	~	=	OP	~	=	OP	~	=	OP	~	=	OP	~	=							
Add	ADDA	8B	2	2	9B	3	2	AB	5	2	BB	4	3				A + M → A	↕	•	↕	↕	↕	↕
	ADDB	CB	2	2	DB	3	2	EB	5	2	FB	4	3				B + M → B	↕	•	↕	↕	↕	↕
Add Acmltrs	ABA													1B	2	1	A + B → A	↕	•	↕	↕	↕	↕
Add with Carry	ADCA	89	2	2	99	3	2	A9	5	2	B9	4	3				A + M + C → A	↕	•	↕	↕	↕	↕
	ADCB	C9	2	2	D9	3	2	E9	5	2	F9	4	3				B + M + C → B	↕	•	↕	↕	↕	↕
And	ANDA	84	2	2	94	3	2	A4	5	2	B4	4	3				A · M → A	•	•	↕	↕	R	•
	ANDB	C4	2	2	D4	3	2	E4	5	2	F4	4	3				B · M → B	•	•	↕	↕	R	•
Bit Test	BITA	85	2	2	95	3	2	A5	5	2	B5	4	3				A · M	•	•	↕	↕	R	•
	BITB	C5	2	2	D5	3	2	E5	5	2	F5	4	3				B · M	•	•	↕	↕	R	•
Clear	CLR							6F	7	2	7F	6	3				00 → M	•	•	R	S	R	R
	CLRA													4F	2	1	00 → A	•	•	R	S	R	R
	CLRB													5F	2	1	00 → B	•	•	R	S	R	R
Compare	CMPA	81	2	2	91	3	2	A1	5	2	B1	4	3				A − M	•	•	↕	↕	↕	↕
	CMPB	C1	2	2	D1	3	2	E1	5	2	F1	4	3				B − M	•	•	↕	↕	↕	↕
Compare Acmltrs	CBA													11	2	1	A − B	•	•	↕	↕	↕	↕
Complement, 1s	COM							63	7	2	73	6	3				$\overline{M}$ → M	•	•	↕	↕	R	S
	COMA													43	2	1	$\overline{A}$ → A	•	•	↕	↕	R	S
	COMB													53	2	1	$\overline{B}$ → B	•	•	↕	↕	R	S
Complement, 2s (Negate)	NEG							60	7	2	70	6	3				00 − M → M	•	•	↕	↕	①	②
	NEGA													40	2	1	00 − A → A	•	•	↕	↕	①	②
	NEGB													50	2	1	00 − B → B	•	•	↕	↕	①	②
Decimal Adjust, A	DAA													19	2	1	Converts Binary Add. of BCD Characters into BCD Format	•	•	↕	↕	↕	③
Decrement	DEC							6A	7	2	7A	6	3				M − 1 → M	•	•	↕	↕	4	•
	DECA													4A	2	1	A − 1 → A	•	•	↕	↕	4	•
	DECB													5A	2	1	B − 1 → B	•	•	↕	↕	4	•
Exclusive OR	EORA	88	2	2	98	3	2	A8	5	2	B8	4	3				A ⊕ M → A	•	•	↕	↕	R	•
	EORB	C8	2	2	D8	3	2	E8	5	2	F8	4	3				B ⊕ M → B	•	•	↕	↕	R	•
Increment	INC							6C	7	2	7C	6	3				M + 1 → M	•	•	↕	↕	⑤	•
	INCA													4C	2	1	A + 1 → A	•	•	↕	↕	⑤	•
	INCB													5C	2	1	B + 1 → B	•	•	↕	↕	⑤	•
Load Acmltr	LDAA	86	2	2	96	3	2	A6	5	2	B6	4	3				M → A	•	•	↕	↕	R	•
	LDAB	C6	2	2	D6	3	2	E6	5	2	F6	4	3				M → B	•	•	↕	↕	R	•
Or, Inclusive	ORAA	8A	2	2	9A	3	2	AA	5	2	BA	4	3				A + M → A	•	•	↕	↕	R	•
	ORAB	CA	2	2	DA	3	2	EA	5	2	FA	4	3				B + M → B	•	•	↕	↕	R	•
Push Data	PSHA													36	4	1	A → M_{SP}, SP − 1 → SP	•	•	•	•	•	•
	PSHB													37	4	1	B → M_{SP}, SP − 1 → SP	•	•	•	•	•	•
Pull Data	PULA													32	4	1	SP + 1 → SP, M_{SP} → A	•	•	•	•	•	•
	PULB													33	4	1	SP + 1 → SP, M_{SP} → B	•	•	•	•	•	•
Rotate Left	ROL							69	7	2	79	6	3				M / A / B: C ← b7 ← b0	•	•	↕	↕	⑥	↕
	ROLA													49	2	1		•	•	↕	↕	⑥	↕
	ROLB													59	2	1		•	•	↕	↕	⑥	↕
Rotate Right	ROR							66	7	2	76	6	3				M / A / B: C → b7 → b0	•	•	↕	↕	⑥	↕
	RORA													46	2	1		•	•	↕	↕	⑥	↕
	RORB													56	2	1		•	•	↕	↕	⑥	↕
Shift Left, Arithmetic	ASL							68	7	2	78	6	3				M / A / B: C ← b7 ← b0 ← 0	•	•	↕	↕	⑥	↕
	ASLA													48	2	1		•	•	↕	↕	⑥	↕
	ASLB													58	2	1		•	•	↕	↕	⑥	↕
Shift Right, Arithmetic	ASR							67	7	2	77	6	3				M / A / B: b7 → b0 → C	•	•	↕	↕	⑥	↕
	ASRA													47	2	1		•	•	↕	↕	⑥	↕
	ASRB													57	2	1		•	•	↕	↕	⑥	↕
Shift Right, Logic	LSR							64	7	2	74	6	3				M / A / B: 0 → b7 → b0 → C	•	•	R	↕	⑥	↕
	LSRA													44	2	1		•	•	R	↕	⑥	↕
	LSRB													54	2	1		•	•	R	↕	⑥	↕
Store Acmltr	STAA				97	4	2	A7	6	2	B7	5	3				A → M	•	•	↕	↕	R	•
	STAB				D7	4	2	E7	6	2	F7	5	3				B → M	•	•	↕	↕	R	•
Subtract	SUBA	80	2	2	90	3	2	A0	5	2	B0	4	3				A − M → A	•	•	↕	↕	↕	↕
	SUBB	C0	2	2	D0	3	2	E0	5	2	F0	4	3				B − M → B	•	•	↕	↕	↕	↕
Subtract Acmltrs	SBA													10	2	1	A − B → A	•	•	↕	↕	↕	↕

		OP	~	#	OP	~	#	OP	~	#	OP	~	#	OP	~	#		H	I	N	Z	V	C
Subtr. with Carry	SBCA	82	2	2	92	3	2	A2	5	2	B2	4	3				A − M − C → A	•	•	↕	↕	↕	↕
	SBCB	C2	2	2	D2	3	2	E2	5	2	F2	4	3				B − M − C → B	•	•	↕	↕	↕	↕
Transfer Acmltrs	TAB													16	2	1	A → B	•	•	↕	↕	R	•
	TBA													17	2	1	B → A	•	•	↕	↕	R	•
Test, Zero	TST							6D	7	2	7D	6	3				M − 00	•	•	↕	↕	R	R
or Minus	TSTA													4D	2	1	A − 00	•	•	↕	↕	R	R
	TSTB													5D	2	1	B − 00	•	•	↕	↕	R	R

LEGEND:

OP Operation Code (Hexadecimal);
~ Number of MPU Cycles;
= Number of Program Bytes;
+ Arithmetic Plus;
− Arithmetic Minus;
· Boolean AND;
M_{SP} Contents of memory location pointed to be Stack Pointer;

+ Boolean Inclusive OR;
⊕ Boolean Exclusive OR;
$\overline{M}$ Complement of M;
→ Transfer Into;
0 Bit = Zero;
00 Byte = Zero;

Note − Accumulator addressing mode instructions are included in the column for IMPLIED addressing

CONDITION CODE SYMBOLS:

H Half-carry from bit 3;
I Interrupt mask
N Negative (sign bit)
Z Zero (byte)
V Overflow, 2s complement
C Carry from bit 7
R Reset Always
S Set Always
↕ Test and set if true, cleared otherwise
• Not Affected

Table 2 Index Register and Stack Manipulation Instructions

POINTER OPERATIONS	MNEMONIC	IMMED			DIRECT			INDEX			EXTND			IMPLIED			BOOLEAN/ARITHMETIC OPERATION	COND. CODE REG.					
																		5	4	3	2	1	0
		OP	~	#	OP	~	#	OP	~	#	OP	~	#	OP	~	#		H	I	N	Z	V	C
Compare Index Reg	CPX	8C	3	3	9C	4	2	AC	6	2	BC	5	3				X_H − M, X_L − (M + 1)	•	•	⑦	↕	⑧	•
Decrement Index Reg	DEX													09	4	1	X − 1 → X	•	•	•	↕	•	•
Decrement Stack Pntr	DES													34	4	1	SP − 1 → SP	•	•	•	•	•	•
Increment Index Reg	INX													08	4	1	X + 1 → X	•	•	•	↕	•	•
Increment Stack Pntr	INS													31	4	1	SP + 1 → SP	•	•	•	•	•	•
Load Index Reg	LDX	CE	3	3	DE	4	2	EE	6	2	FE	5	3				M → X_H, (M + 1) → X_L	•	•	⑨	↕	R	•
Load Stack Pntr	LDS	8E	3	3	9E	4	2	AE	6	2	BE	5	3				M → SP_H, (M + 1) → SP_L	•	•	⑨	↕	R	•
Store Index Reg	STX				DF	5	2	EF	7	2	FF	6	3				X_H → M, X_L → (M + 1)	•	•	⑨	↕	R	•
Store Stack Pntr	STS				9F	5	2	AF	7	2	BF	6	3				SP_H → M, SP_L → (M + 1)	•	•	⑨	↕	R	•
Indx Reg → Stack Pntr	TXS													35	4	1	X − 1 → SP	•	•	•	•	•	•
Stack Pntr → Indx Reg	TSX													30	4	1	SP + 1 → X	•	•	•	•	•	•

Table 3 Jump and Branch Instructions

OPERATIONS	MNEMONIC	RELATIVE OP	RELATIVE ~	RELATIVE #	INDEX OP	INDEX ~	INDEX #	EXTND OP	EXTND ~	EXTND #	IMPLIED OP	IMPLIED ~	IMPLIED #	BRANCH TEST	5 H	4 I	3 N	2 Z	1 V	0 C
Branch Always	BRA	20	4	2										None	•	•	•	•	•	•
Branch If Carry Clear	BCC	24	4	2										C = 0	•	•	•	•	•	•
Branch If Carry Set	BCS	25	4	2										C = 1	•	•	•	•	•	•
Branch If = Zero	BEQ	27	4	2										Z = 1	•	•	•	•	•	•
Branch If ⩾ Zero	BGE	2C	4	2										N ⊕ V = 0	•	•	•	•	•	•
Branch If > Zero	BGT	2E	4	2										Z + (N ⊕ V) = 0	•	•	•	•	•	•
Branch If Higher	BHI	22	4	2										C + Z = 0	•	•	•	•	•	•
Branch If ⩽ Zero	BLE	2F	4	2										Z + (N ⊕ V) = 1	•	•	•	•	•	•
Branch If Lower Or Same	BLS	23	4	2										C + Z = 1	•	•	•	•	•	•
Branch If < Zero	BLT	2D	4	2										N ⊕ V = 1	•	•	•	•	•	•
Branch If Minus	BMI	2B	4	2										N = 1	•	•	•	•	•	•
Branch If Not Equal Zero	BNE	26	4	2										Z = 0	•	•	•	•	•	•
Branch If Overflow Clear	BVC	28	4	2										V = 0	•	•	•	•	•	•
Branch If Overflow Set	BVS	29	4	2										V = 1	•	•	•	•	•	•
Branch If Plus	BPL	2A	4	2										N = 0	•	•	•	•	•	•
Branch To Subroutine	BSR	8D	8	2										} See Special Operations	•	•	•	•	•	•
Jump	JMP				6E	4	2	7E	3	3					•	•	•	•	•	•
Jump To Subroutine	JSR				AD	8	2	BD	9	3					•	•	•	•	•	•
No Operation	NOP										01	2	1	Advances Prog. Cntr. Only	•	•	•	•	•	•
Return From Interrupt	RTI										3B	10	1	} See Special Operations	(10)					
Return From Subroutine	RTS										39	5	1		•	•	•	•	•	•
Software Interrupt	SWI										3F	12	1		•	•	•	•	•	•
Wait for Interrupt*	WAI										3E	9	1		•	(11)	•	•	•	•

*WAI puts Address Bus, R/W, and Data Bus in the 3-state mode while VMA is held LOW.

Table 4 Condition Code Register Manipulation Instructions

OPERATIONS	MNEMONIC	IMPLIED OP	IMPLIED ~	IMPLIED #	BOOLEAN OPERATION	5 H	4 I	3 N	2 Z	1 V	0 C
Clear Carry	CLC	0C	2	1	0 → C	•	•	•	•	•	R
Clear Interrupt Mask	CLI	0E	2	1	0 → I	•	R	•	•	•	•
Clear Overflow	CLV	0A	2	1	0 → V	•	•	•	•	R	•
Set Carry	SEC	0D	2	1	1 → C	•	•	•	•	•	S
Set Interrupt Mask	SEI	0F	2	1	1 → I	•	S	•	•	•	•
Set Overflow	SEV	0B	2	1	1 → V	•	•	•	•	S	•
Acmltr A → CCR	TAP	06	2	1	A → CCR	(12)					
CCR → Acmltr A	TPA	07	2	1	CCR → A	•	•	•	•	•	•

CONDITION CODE REGISTER NOTES: (Bit set if test is true and cleared otherwise)

1 (Bit V) Test: Result = 10000000?

2 (Bit C) Test: Result = 00000000?

3 (Bit C) Test: Decimal value of most significant BCD Character greater than nine? (Not cleared if previously set.)

4 (Bit V) Test: Operand = 10000000 prior to execution?

5 (Bit V) Test: Operand = 01111111 prior to execution?

6 (Bit V) Test: Set equal to result of N ⊕ C after shift has occurred.

7 Bit N) Test: Sign bit of most significant (MS) byte = 1?

8 (Bit V) Test: 2s complement overflow from subtraction of MS bytes?

9 (Bit N) Test: Result less than "0"? (Bit 15 = 1)

10 (All) Load Condition Code Register from Stack. (See Special Operations)

11 (Bit I) Set when interrupt occurs. If previously set, a Non-Maskable Interrupt is required to exit the wait state.

12 (All) Set according to the contents of Accumulator A.

Appendix IB
6800
Operation
Summary

ADDRESS MODE AND INSTRUCTIONS	CYCLES	CYCLE #	VMA LINE	ADDRESS BUS	R/W LINE	DATA BUS
IMMEDIATE						
ADC EOR ADD LDA AND ORA BIT SBC CMP SUB	2	1	1	Op Code Address	1	Op Code
		2	1	Op Code Address + 1	1	Operand Data
CPX LDS LDX	3	1	1	Op Code Address	1	Op Code
		2	1	Op Code Address + 1	1	Operand Data (High Order Byte)
		3	1	Op Code Address + 2	1	Operand Data (Low Order Byte)
DIRECT						
ADC EOR ADD LDA AND ORA BIT SBC CMP SUB	3	1	1	Op Code Address	1	Op Code
		2	1	Op Code Address + 1	1	Address of Operand
		3	1	Address of Operand	1	Operand Data
CPX LDS LDX	4	1	1	Op Code Address	1	Op Code
		2	1	Op Code Address + 1	1	Address of Operand
		3	1	Address of Operand	1	Operand Data (High Order Byte)
		4	1	Operand Address + 1	1	Operand Data (Low Order Byte)
STA	4	1	1	Op Code Address	1	Op Code
		2	1	Op Code Address + 1	1	Destination Address
		3	0	Destination Address	1	Irrelevant Data (Note 1)
		4	1	Destination Address	0	Data from Accumulator
STS STX	5	1	1	Op Code Address	1	Op Code
		2	1	Op Code Address + 1	1	Address of Operand
		3	0	Address of Operand	1	Irrelevant Data (Note 1)
		4	1	Address of Operand	0	Register Data (High Order Byte)
		5	1	Address of Operand + 1	0	Register Data (Low Order Byte)
INDEXED						
JMP	4	1	1	Op Code Address	1	Op Code
		2	1	Op Code Address + 1	1	Offset
		3	0	Index Register	1	Irrelevant Data (Note 1)
		4	0	Index Register Plus Offset (w/o Carry)	1	Irrelevant Data (Note 1)
ADC EOR ADD LDA AND ORA BIT SBC CMP SUB	5	1	1	Op Code Address	1	Op Code
		2	1	Op Code Address + 1	1	Offset
		3	0	Index Register	1	Irrelevant Data (Note 1)
		4	0	Index Register Plus Offset (w/o Carry)	1	Irrelevant Data (Note 1)
		5	1	Index Register Plus Offset	1	Operand Data
CPX LDS LDX	6	1	1	Op Code Address	1	Op Code
		2	1	Op Code Address + 1	1	Offset
		3	0	Index Register	1	Irrelevant Data (Note 1)
		4	0	Index Register Plus Offset (w/o Carry)	1	Irrelevant Data (Note 1)
		5	1	Index Register Plus Offset	1	Operand Data (High Order Byte)
		6	1	Index Register Plus Offset + 1	1	Operand Data (Low Order Byte)
STA	6	1	1	Op Code Address	1	Op Code
		2	1	Op Code Address + 1	1	Offset
		3	0	Index Register	1	Irrelevant Data (Note 1)
		4	0	Index Register Plus Offset (w/o Carry)	1	Irrelevant Data (Note 1)
		5	0	Index Register Plus Offset	1	Irrelevant Data (Note 1)
		6	1	Index Register Plus Offset	0	Operand Data

ADDRESS MODE AND INSTRUCTIONS	CYCLES	CYCLE #	VMA LINE	ADDRESS BUS	R/W LINE	DATA BUS
INDEXED (Continued)						
ASL LSR ASR NEG CLR ROL COM ROR DEC TST INC	7	1	1	Op Code Address	1	Op Code
		2	1	Op Code Address + 1	1	Offset
		3	0	Index Register	1	Irrelevant Data (Note 1)
		4	0	Index Register Plus Offset (w/o Carry)	1	Irrelevant Data (Note 1)
		5	1	Index Register Plus Offset	1	Current Operand Data
		6	0	Index Register Plus Offset	1	Irrelevant Data (Note 1)
		7	1/0 (Note 3)	Index Register Plus Offset	0	New Operand Data (Note 3)
STS STX	7	1	1	Op Code Address	1	Op Code
		2	1	Op Code Address + 1	1	Offset
		3	0	Index Register	1	Irrelevant Data (Note 1)
		4	0	Index Register Plus Offset (w/o Carry)	1	Irrelevant Data (Note 1)
		5	0	Index Register Plus Offset	1	Irrelevant Data (Note 1)
		6	1	Index Register Plus Offset	0	Operand Data (High Order Byte)
		7	1	Index Register Plus Offset + 1	0	Operand Data (Low Order Byte)
JSR	8	1	1	Op Code Address	1	Op Code
		2	1	Op Code Address + 1	1	Offset
		3	0	Index Register	1	Irrelevant Data (Note 1)
		4	1	Stack Pointer	0	Return Address (Low Order Byte)
		5	1	Stack Pointer – 1	0	Return Address (High Order Byte)
		6	0	Stack Pointer – 2	1	Irrelevant Data (Note 1)
		7	0	Index Register	1	Irrelevant Data (Note 1)
		8	0	Index Register Plus Offset (w/o Carry)	1	Irrelevant Data (Note 1)
EXTENDED						
JMP	3	1	1	Op Code Address	1	Op Code
		2	1	Op Code Address + 1	1	Jump Address (High Order Byte)
		3	1	Op Code Address + 2	1	Jump Address (Low Order Byte)
ADC EOR ADD LDA AND ORA BIT SBC CMP SUB	4	1	1	Op Code Address	1	Op Code
		2	1	Op Code Address + 1	1	Address of Operand (High Order Byte)
		3	1	Op Code Address + 2	1	Address of Operand (Low Order Byte)
		4	1	Address of Operand	1	Operand Data
CPX LDS LDX	5	1	1	Op Code Address	1	Op Code
		2	1	Op Code Address + 1	1	Address of Operand (High Order Byte)
		3	1	Op Code Address + 2	1	Address of Operand (Low Order Byte)
		4	1	Address of Operand	1	Operand Data (High Order Byte)
		5	1	Address of Operand + 1	1	Operand Data (Low Order Byte)
STA A STA B	5	1	1	Op Code Address	1	Op Code
		2	1	Op Code Address + 1	1	Destination Address (High Order Byte)
		3	1	Op Code Address + 2	1	Destination Address (Low Order Byte)
		4	0	Operand Destination Address	1	Irrelevant Data (Note 1)
		5	1	Operand Destination Address	0	Data from Accumulator
ASL LSR ASR NEG CLR ROL COM ROR DEC TST INC	6	1	1	Op Code Address	1	Op Code
		2	1	Op Code Address + 1	1	Address of Operand (High Order Byte)
		3	1	Op Code Address + 2	1	Address of Operand (Low Order Byte)
		4	1	Address of Operand	1	Current Operand Data
		5	0	Address of Operand	1	Irrelevant Data (Note 1)
		6	1/0 (Note 3)	Address of Operand	0	New Operand Data (Note 3)

ADDRESS MODE AND INSTRUCTIONS	CYCLES	CYCLE #	VMA LINE	ADDRESS BUS	R/W LINE	DATA BUS
EXTENDED (Continued)						
STS STX	6	1	1	Op Code Address	1	Op Code
		2	1	Op Code Address + 1	1	Address of Operand (High Order Byte)
		3	1	Op Code Address + 2	1	Address of Operand (Low Order Byte)
		4	0	Address of Operand	1	Irrelevant Data (Note 1)
		5	1	Address of Operand	0	Operand Data (High Order Byte)
		6	1	Address of Operand + 1	0	Operand Data (Low Order Byte)
JSR	9	1	1	Op Code Address	1	Op Code
		2	1	Op Code Address + 1	1	Address of Subroutine (High Order Byte)
		3	1	Op Code Address + 2	1	Address of Subroutine (Low Order Byte)
		4	1	Subroutine Starting Address	1	Op Code of Next Instruction
		5	1	Stack Pointer	0	Return Address (Low Order Byte)
		6	1	Stack Pointer – 1	0	Return Address (High Order Byte)
		7	0	Stack Pointer – 2	1	Irrelevant Data (Note 1)
		8	0	Op Code Address + 2	1	Irrelevant Data (Note 1)
		9	1	Op Code Address + 2	1	Address of Subroutine (Low Order Byte)
INHERENT						
ABA DAA SEC ASL DEC SEI ASR INC SEV CBA LSR TAB CLC NEG TAP CLI NOP TBA CLR ROL TPA CLV ROR TST COM SBA	2	1	1	Op Code Address	1	Op Code
		2	1	Op Code Address + 1	1	Op Code of Next Instruction
DES DEX INS INX	4	1	1	Op Code Address	1	Op Code
		2	1	Op Code Address + 1	1	Op Code of Next Instruction
		3	0	Previous Register Contents	1	Irrelevant Data (Note 1)
		4	0	New Register Contents	1	Irrelevant Data (Note 1)
PSH	4	1	1	Op Code Address	1	Op Code
		2	1	Op Code Address + 1	1	Op Code of Next Instruction
		3	1	Stack Pointer	0	Accumulator Data
		4	0	Stack Pointer – 1	1	Accumulator Data
PUL	4	1	1	Op Code Address	1	Op Code
		2	1	Op Code Address + 1	1	Op Code of Next Instruction
		3	0	Stack Pointer	1	Irrelevant Data (Note 1)
		4	1	Stack Pointer + 1	1	Operand Data from Stack
TSX	4	1	1	Op Code Address	1	Op Code
		2	1	Op Code Address + 1	1	Op Code of Next Instruction
		3	0	Stack Pointer	1	Irrelevant Data (Note 1)
		4	0	New Index Register	1	Irrelevant Data (Note 1)
TXS	4	1	1	Op Code Address	1	Op Code
		2	1	Op Code Address + 1	1	Op Code of Next Instruction
		3	0	Index Register	1	Irrelevant Data
		4	0	New Stack Pointer	1	Irrelevant Data
RTS	5	1	1	Op Code Address	1	Op Code
		2	1	Op Code Address + 1	1	Irrelevant Data (Note 2)
		3	0	Stack Pointer	1	Irrelevant Data (Note 1)
		4	1	Stack Pointer + 1	1	Address of Next Instruction (High Order Byte)
		5	1	Stack Pointer + 2	1	Address of Next Instruction (Low Order Byte)

ADDRESS MODE AND INSTRUCTIONS	CYCLES	CYCLE #	VMA LINE	ADDRESS BUS	R/W LINE	DATA BUS
INHERENT (Continued)						
WAI	9	1	1	Op Code Address	1	Op Code
		2	1	Op Code Address + 1	1	Op Code of Next Instruction
		3	1	Stack Pointer	0	Return Address (Low Order Byte)
		4	1	Stack Pointer – 1	0	Return Address (High Order Byte)
		5	1	Stack Pointer – 2	0	Index Register (Low Order Byte)
		6	1	Stack Pointer – 3	0	Index Register (High Order Byte)
		7	1	Stack Pointer – 4	0	Contents of Accumulator A
		8	1	Stack Pointer – 5	0	Contents of Accumulator B
		9	1	Stack Pointer – 6 (Note 4)	1	Contents of Cond. Code Register
RTI	10	1	1	Op Code Address	1	Op Code
		2	1	Op Code Address + 1	1	Irrelevant Data (Note 2)
		3	0	Stack Pointer	1	Irrelevant Data (Note 1)
		4	1	Stack Pointer + 1	1	Contents of Cond. Code Register from Stack
		5	1	Stack Pointer + 2	1	Contents of Accumulator B from Stack
		6	1	Stack Pointer + 3	1	Contents of Accumulator A from Stack
		7	1	Stack Pointer + 4	1	Index Register from Stack (High Order Byte)
		8	1	Stack Pointer + 5	1	Index Register from Stack (Low Order Byte)
		9	1	Stack Pointer + 6	1	Next Instruction Address from Stack (High Order Byte)
		10	1	Stack Pointer + 7	1	Next Instruction Address from Stack (Low Order Byte)
SWI	12	1	1	Op Code Address	1	Op Code
		2	1	Op Code Address + 1	1	Irrelevant Data (Note 1)
		3	1	Stack Pointer	0	Return Address (Low Order Byte)
		4	1	Stack Pointer – 1	0	Return Address (High Order Byte)
		5	1	Stack Pointer – 2	0	Index Register (Low Order Byte)
		6	1	Stack Pointer – 3	0	Index Register (High Order Byte)
		7	1	Stack Pointer – 4	0	Contents of Accumulator A
		8	1	Stack Pointer – 5	0	Contents of Accumulator B
		9	1	Stack Pointer – 6	0	Contents of Cond. Code Register
		10	0	Stack Pointer – 7	1	Irrelevant Data (Note 1)
		11	1	Vector Address FFFA (Hex)	1	Address of Subroutine (High Order Byte)
		12	1	Vector Address FFFB (Hex)	1	Address of Subroutine (Low Order Byte)
RELATIVE						
BCC BHI BNE BCS BLE BPL BEQ BLS BRA BGE BLT BVC BGT BMI BVS	4	1	1	Op Code Address	1	Op Code
		2	1	Op Code Address + 1	1	Branch Offset
		3	0	Op Code Address + 2	1	Irrelevant Data (Note 1)
		4	0	Branch Address	1	Irrelevant Data (Note 1)
BSR	8	1	1	Op Code Address	1	Op Code
		2	1	Op Code Address + 1	1	Branch Offset
		3	0	Return Address of Main Program	1	Irrelevant Data (Note 1)
		4	1	Stack Pointer	0	Return Address (Low Order Byte)
		5	1	Stack Pointer – 1	0	Return Address (High Order Byte)
		6	0	Stack Pointer – 2	1	Irrelevant Data (Note 1)
		7	0	Return Address of Main Program	1	Irrelevant Data (Note 1)
		8	0	Subroutine Address	1	Irrelevant Data (Note 1)

Note 1. If device which is addressed during this cycle uses VMA, then the Data Bus will go to the high-impedance 3-state condition. Depending on bus capacitance, data from the previous cycle may be retained on the Data Bus.
Note 2. Data is ignored by the MPU.
Note 3. For TST, VMA = 0 and Operand data does not change.
Note 4. While the MPU is waiting for the interrupt, Bus Available will go HIGH indicating the following states of the control lines: VMA is low; Address Bus, R/W, and Data Bus are all in the high-impedance state.

Appendix II
3870
Instruction Set

F3870 Instruction Set
F8 Compatible

Accumulator Group Instructions

OPERATION	MNEMONIC OP CODE	OPERAND	FUNCTION	MACHINE CODE	BYTES	CYCLES	STATUS BITS OVF	ZERO	CRY	SIGN
ADD CARRY	LNK		ACC ← (ACC) + CRY	19	1	1	1/0	1/0	1/0	1/0
ADD IMMEDIATE	AI	ii	ACC ← (ACC) ∧ H'ii'	24 ii	2	2.5	1/0	1/0	1/0	1/0
AND IMMEDIATE	NI	ii	ACC ← (ACC) H'ii'	21 ii	2	2.5	0	1/0	0	1/0
CLEAR	CLR		ACC ← H'00'	70	1	1				
COMPARE IMMEDIATE	CI	ii	H'ii' + $(\overline{ACC})$ + 1	25 ii	2	2.5	1/0	1/0	1/0	1/0
COMPLEMENT	COM		ACC ← (ACC) ⊕ H'FF'	18	1	1	0	1/0	0	1/0
EXCLUSIVE OR IMMEDIATE	XI	ii	ACC ← (ACC) ⊕ H'ii'	23 ii	2	2.5	0	1/0	0	1/0
INCREMENT	INC		ACC ← (ACC) + 1	1F	1	1	1/0	1/0	1/0	1/0
LOAD IMMEDIATE	LI	ii	ACC ← H'ii'	20 ii	2	2.5	—	—	—	—
LOAD IMMEDIATE SHORT	LIS	i	ACC ← H'0i'	7i	1	1	—	—	—	—
OR IMMEDIATE	OI	ii	ACC ← (ACC) ∨ H'ii'	22 ii	2	2.5	0	1/0	0	1/0
SHIFT LEFT ONE	SL	1	SHIFT LEFT 1	13	1	1	0	1/0	0	1/0
SHIFT LEFT FOUR	SL	4	SHIFT LEFT 4	15	1	1	0	1/0	0	1/0
SHIFT RIGHT ONE	SR	1	SHIFT RIGHT 1	12	1	1	0	1/0	0	1
SHIFT RIGHT FOUR	SR	4	SHIFT RIGHT 4	14	1	1	0	1/0	0	1

Branch Instructions

In all conditional branches PO (PO) + 2 if the test conditions are not met. Execution is complete in 30 cycles.

OPERATION	MNEMONIC OP CODE	OPERAND	FUNCTION	MACHINE CODE	BYTES	CYCLES	STATUS BITS OVF	ZERO	CRY	SIGN
BRANCH ON CARRY	BC	aa	P0 ← [(P0) + 1] + H'aa' if CRY = 1	82 aa	2	3.5	—	—	—	—
BRANCH ON POSITIVE	BP	aa	P0 ← [(P0) + 1] + H'aa' if SIGN = 1	81 aa	2	3.5	—	—	—	—
BRANCH ON ZERO	BZ	aa	P0 ← [(P0) + 1] + H'aa' if ZERO = 1	84 aa	2	3.5	—	—	—	—
BRANCH ON TRUE	BT	t,aa	P0 ← [(P0) + 1] + H'aa' if any test is true	8t aa	2	3.5	—	—	—	—

t - TEST CONDITION

2^2	2^1	2^0
ZERO	CRY	SIGN

OPERATION	MNEMONIC OP CODE	OPERAND	FUNCTION	MACHINE CODE	BYTES	CYCLES	STATUS BITS OVF	ZERO	CRY	SIGN
BRANCH IF NEGATIVE	BM	aa	P0 ← [(P0) + 1] + H'aa' if SIGN = 0	91 aa	2	3.5	—	—	—	—
BRANCH IF NO CARRY	BNC	aa	P0 ← [(P0) + 1] + H'aa' if CARRY ≠ 0	92 aa	2	3.5	—	—	—	—
BRANCH IF NO OVERFLOW	BNO	aa	P0 ← [(P0) + 1] + H'aa' if OVF = 0	98 aa	2	3.5	—	—	—	—
BRANCH IF NOT ZERO	BNZ	aa	P0 ← [(P0) + 1] + H'aa' if ZERO = 0	94 aa	2	3.5	—	—	—	—
BRANCH IF FALSE TEST	BF	t,aa	P0 ← [(P0) + 1] + H'aa' if all false test bits	9t aa	2	3.5	—	—	—	—

t = TEST CONDITION

2^3	2^2	2^1	2^0
OVF	ZERO	CRY	SIGN

OPERATION	MNEMONIC OP CODE	OPERAND	FUNCTION	MACHINE CODE	BYTES	CYCLES	STATUS BITS OVF	ZERO	CRY	SIGN
BRANCH IF ISAR (LOWER) 7	BR7	aa	P0 ← [(P0) + 1] + H'aa' if ISARL ≠ 7	8F aa	2	2.5	—	—	—	—
			P0 ← (P0) + 2 if ISARL = 7			2.0	—	—	—	—
BRANCH RELATIVE	BR	aa	P0 ← [(P0) + 1] + H'aa'	90 aa	2	3.5	—	—	—	—
JUMP*	JMP	aaaa	P0 ← H'aaaa'	29 aaaa	3	5.5	—	—	—	—

*Privileged instruction

Note
JMP and PI change accumulator contents to the HIGH byte address.

Memory Reference Instructions In all Memory Reference Instructions, the Data Counter is incremented DC ← DC − 1.

OPERATION	MNEMONIC OP CODE	OPERAND	FUNCTION	MACHINE CODE	BYTES	CYCLES	STATUS BITS			
							OVF	ZERO	CRY	SIGN
ADD BINARY	AM		ACC ← (ACC) + [(DC)]	88	1	2.5	1/0	1/0	1/0	1/0
ADD DECIMAL	AMD		ACC ← (ACC) + [(DC)]	89	1	2.5	1/0	1/0	1/0	1/0
AND	NM		ACC ← (ACC) ∧ [(DC)]	8A	1	2.5	0	1/0	0	1/0
COMPARE	CM		[(DC)] + ($\overline{ACC}$) + 1	8D	1	2.5	1/0	1/0	1/0	1/0
EXCLUSIVE OR	XM		ACC ← (ACC) ⊕ [(DC)]	8C	1	2.5	0	1/0	0	1/0
LOAD	LM		ACC ← [(DC)]	16	1	2.5	—	—	—	—
LOGICAL OR	OM		ACC ← (ACC) ∨ [(DC)]	8B	1	2.5	0	1/0	0	1/0
STORE	ST		(DC) ← (ACC)	17	1	2.5	—	—	—	—

Address Register Group Instructions

OPERATION	MNEMONIC OP CODE	OPERAND	FUNCTION	MACHINE CODE	BYTES	CYCLES	STATUS BITS			
							OVF	ZERO	CRY	SIGN
ADD to DATA COUNTER	ADC		DC ← (DC) + (ACC)	8E	1	2.5	—	—	—	—
CALL to SUBROUTINE	PK		P ← (P0); P0U ← r12 ; PL ← (r13)	0C	1	4	—	—	—	—
CALL TO SUBROUTINE IMMEDIATE	PI	aaaa	P ← (P); P0 ← H'aaaa' ‡	28 aaaa	3	6.5	—	—	—	—
EXCHANGE DC	XDC		DC ↔ DC1	2C	1	2	—	—	—	—
LOAD DATA COUNTER	LR	DC,Q	DCU ← (r14); DCL ← (r15)	0F	1	4	—	—	—	—
LOAD DATA COUNTER	LR	DC,H	DCU ← (r10); DCL ← (r11)	10	1	4	—	—	—	—
LOAD DC IMMEDIATE	DCI	aaaa	DC ← H'aaaa	2A aaaa	3	6	—	—	—	—
LOAD PROGRAM COUNTER	LR	P0,Q	P0U ← (r14); P0L ← (r15)	0D	1	4	—	—	—	—
LOAD STACK REGISTER	LR	PU	PU ← (r12); PL ← (r13)	09	1	4	—	—	—	—
RETURN FROM SUBROUTINE	POP		P0 ← P	1C	1	2	—	—	—	—
STORE DATA COUNTER	LR	Q,DC	r14 ← (DCU); r15 ← (DCL)	0E	1	4	—	—	—	—
STORE DATA COUNTER	LR	H,DC	r10 ← (DCU); r11 ← (DCL)	11	1	4	—	—	—	—
STORE STACK REGISTER	LR	K,P	r12 ← (PU); r13 ← (P)	08	1	4	—	—	—	—

Scratchpad Register Instructions (Refer to Scratchpad Addressing Modes.)

OPERATION	MNEMONIC OP CODE	OPERAND	FUNCTION	MACHINE CODE	BYTES	CYCLES	STATUS BITS			
							OVF	ZERO	CRY	SIGN
ADD BINARY	AS	r	ACC ← (ACC) + (r)	Cr	1	1	1/0	1/0	1/0	1/0
ADD DECIMAL	ASD	r	ACC ← (ACC) + (r)	Dr	1	2	1/0	1/0	1/0	1/0
DECREMENT	DS	r	r ← (r) + H'FF'	3r	1	1.5	1/0	1/0	1/0	1/0
LOAD	LR	A,r	ACC ← (r)	4r	1	1	—	—	—	—
LOAD	LR	A,KU	ACC ← (r12)	00	1	1	—	—	—	—
LOAD	LR	A,KL	ACC ← (r13)	01	1	1	—	—	—	—
LOAD	LR	A,QU	ACC ← (r14)	02	1	1	—	—	—	—
LOAD	LR	A,QL	ACC ← (r15)	03	1	1	—	—	—	—
LOAD	LR	r,A	r ← (ACC)	5r	1	1	—	—	—	—
LOAD	LR	KU,A	r12 ← (ACC)	04	1	1	—	—	—	—
LOAD	LR	KL,A	r13 ← (ACC)	05	1	1	—	—	—	—
LOAD	LR	QU,A	r14 ← (ACC)	06	1	1	—	—	—	—
LOAD	LR	QL,A	r15 ← (ACC)	07	1	1	—	—	—	—
AND	NS	r	ACC ← (ACC) ∧ (r)	Fr	1	1	0	1/0	0	1/0
EXCLUSIVE OR	XS	r	ACC ← (ACC) ⊕ (r)	Er	1	1	0	1/0	0	1/0

*Privileged instruction
‡Contents of ACC Destroyed

Miscellaneous Instructions

OPERATION	MNEMONIC OP CODE	OPERAND	FUNCTION	MACHINE CODE	BYTES	CYCLES	STATUS BITS OVF	ZERO	CRY	SIGN
DISABLE INTERRUPT	DI		RESET ICB	1A	1	2	—	—	—	—
ENABLE INTERRUPT*	EI		SET ICB	1B	1	2	—	—	—	—
INPUT	IN	aa	ACC ← (INPUT PORT aa)	26 aa	2	4	0	1/0	0	1/0
INPUT SHORT	INS	a	ACC ← (INPUT PORT a)	Aa	1	4***	0	1/0	0	1/0
LOAD ISAR	LR	IS,A	ISAR ← (ACC)	0B	1	1	—	—	—	—
LOAD ISAR LOWER	LISL	a	ISARL ← a	01101a**	1	1	—	—	—	—
LOAD ISAR UPPER	LISU	a	ISARU ← a	01100a**	1	1	—	—	—	—
LOAD STATUS REGISTER*	LR	W,J	W ← (r9)	1D	1	2	1/0	1/0	1/0	1/0
NO-OPERATION	NOP		P0 ← (P0) + 1	2B	1	1	—	—	—	—
OUTPUT	OUT	aa	OUTPUT PORT aa ← (ACC)	27 aa	2	4	—	—	—	—
OUTPUT SHORT	OUTS	a	OUTPUT PORT a ← (ACC)	Ba	1	4***	—	—	—	—
STORE ISAR	LR	A,IS	ACC ← (ISAR)	0A	1	1	—	—	—	—
STORE STATUS REG	LR	J,W	r9 ← (W)	1E	1	1	—	—	—	—

***Privileged instruction**
****3-bit octal digit**
*****Two machine cycles for CPU ports**

Note
Each lower case character represents a Hexadecimal digit
Each cycle equals four machine clock periods
Lower case denotes variables specified by programmer

Function Definitions

←	is replaced by
( )	the contents of
(-)	Binary "1"s complement of
+	Arithmetic Add (Binary or Decimal)
⊕	Logical "OR" exclusive
∧	Logical "AND"
∨	Logical "OR" inclusive
H'#'	Hexadecimal digit

Register Names

a	Address Variable
A	Accumulator
DC	Data Counter (Indirect Address Register)
DC1	Data Counter #1 (Auxiliary Data Counter)
DCL	Least significant eight bits of Data Counter Addressed
DCU	Most significant eight bits of Data Counter Addressed
H	Scratchpad Register #10 and #11
i and ii	Immediate operand
ICB	Interrupt Control Bit
IS	Indirect Scratchpad Address Register
ISAR	Indirect Scratchpad Address Register
ISARL	Least Significant three bits of ISAR
ISARU	Most Significant three bits of ISAR
J	Scratchpad Register #9
K	Registers #12 and #13
KL	Register #13
KU	Register #12
P0	Program Counter
P0L	Least Significant eight bits of Program Counter
P0U	Most Significant eight bits of Program Counter
P	Stack Register
PL	Least Significant eight bits of Program Counter
PU	Most Significant eight bits of Active Stack Register
Q	Registers #14 and #15
QL	Register #15
QU	Register #14
r	Scratchpad Register (any address thru 11)
W	Status Register

Scratchpad Addressing Modes (Machine Code Format)

r = C	(Hexadecimal) Register Addressed by ISAR (Unmodified)
r = D	(Hexadecimal) Register Addressed by ISAR; ISARL Incremented
r = E	(Hexadecimal) Register Addressed by ISAR; ISARL Decremented
r = F	(No operation performed)
r = 0-B	(Hexadecimal) Register 0 thru 11 addressed directly from the Instruction

Status Register

-	No change in condition
1/0	is set to "1" or "0" depending on conditions
CRY	Carry Flag

Appendix IIIA
6809
Instruction Set

Instruction	Forms	Immediate Op	Immediate ~	Immediate #	Direct Op	Direct ~	Direct #	Indexed Op	Indexed ~	Indexed #	Extended Op	Extended ~	Extended #	Inherent Op	Inherent ~	Inherent #	Description	5 H	3 N	2 Z	1 V	0 C
ABX														3A	3	1	B + X → X (Unsigned)	•	•	•	•	•
ADC	ADCA	89	2	2	99	4	2	A9	4+	2+	B9	5	3				A + M + C → A	↕	↕	↕	↕	↕
	ADCB	C9	2	2	D9	4	2	E9	4+	2+	F9	5	3				B + M + C → B	↕	↕	↕	↕	↕
ADD	ADDA	8B	2	2	9B	4	2	AB	4+	2+	BB	5	3				A + M → A	↕	↕	↕	↕	↕
	ADDB	CB	2	2	DB	4	2	EB	4+	2+	FB	5	3				B + M → B	↕	↕	↕	↕	↕
	ADDD	C3	4	3	D3	6	2	E3	6+	2+	F3	7	3				D + M:M + 1 → D	•	↕	↕	↕	↕
AND	ANDA	84	2	2	94	4	2	A4	4+	2+	B4	5	3				A Λ M → A	•	↕	↕	0	•
	ANDB	C4	2	2	D4	4	2	E4	4+	2+	F4	5	3				B Λ M → B	•	↕	↕	0	•
	ANDCC	1C	3	2													CC Λ IMM → CC					7
ASL	ASLA													48	2	1	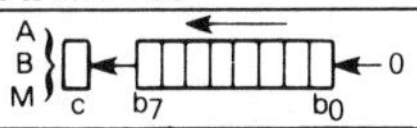	8	↕	↕	↕	↕
	ASLB													58	2	1		8	↕	↕	↕	↕
	ASL				08	6	2	68	6+	2+	78	7	3					8	↕	↕	↕	↕
ASR	ASRA													47	2	1	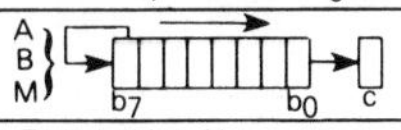	8	↕	↕	•	↕
	ASR													57	2	1		8	↕	↕	•	↕
	ASR				07	6	2	67	6+	2+	77	7	3					8	↕	↕	•	↕
BIT	BITA	85	2	2	95	4	2	A5	4+	2+	B5	5	3				Bit Test A (M Λ A)	•	↕	↕	0	•
	BITB	C5	2	2	D5	4	2	E5	4+	2+	F5	5	3				Bit Test B (M Λ B)	•	↕	↕	0	•
CLR	CLRA													4F	2	1	0 → A	•	0	1	0	0
	CLRB													5F	2	1	0 → B	•	0	1	0	0
	CLR				0F	6	2	6F	6+	2+	7F	7	3				0 → M	•	0	1	0	0
CMP	CMPA	81	2	2	91	4	2	A1	4+	2+	B1	5	3				Compare M from A	8	↕	↕	↕	↕
	CMPB	C1	2	2	D1	4	2	E1	4+	2+	F1	5	3				Compare M from B	8	↕	↕	↕	↕
	CMPD	10	5	4	10	7	3	10	7+	3+	10	8	4				Compare M:M + 1 from D	•	↕	↕	↕	↕
		83			93			A3			B3											
	CMPS	11	5	4	11	7	3	11	7+	3+	11	8	4				Compare M:M + 1 from S	•	↕	↕	↕	↕
		8C			9C			AC			BC											
	CMPU	11	5	4	11	7	3	11	7+	3+	11	8	4				Compare M:M + 1 from U	•	↕	↕	↕	↕
		83			93			A3			B3											
	CMPX	8C	4	3	9C	6	2	AC	6+	2+	BC	7	3				Compare M:M + 1 from X	•	↕	↕	↕	↕
	CMPY	10	5	4	10	7	3	10	7+	3+	10	8	4				Compare M:M + 1 from Y	•	↕	↕	↕	↕
		8C			9C			AC			BC											
COM	COMA													43	2	1	A → A	•	↕	↕	0	1
	COMB													53	2	1	B → B	•	↕	↕	0	1
	COM				03	6	2	63	6+	2+	73	7	3				M → M	•	↕	↕	0	1
CWAI		3C	20	2										3C	20	2	CC Λ IMM → CC Wait for Interrupt					7
DAA														19	2	1	Decimal Adjust A	•	↕	↕	0	↕
DEC	DECA													4A	2	1	A − 1 → A	•	↕	↕	↕	•
	DECB													5A	2	1	B − 1 → B	•	↕	↕	↕	•
	DEC				0A	6	2	6A	6+	2+	7A	7	3				M − 1 → M	•	↕	↕	↕	•
EOR	EORA	88	2	2	98	4	2	A8	4+	2+	B8	5	3				A V M → A	•	↕	↕	0	•
	EORB	C8	2	2	D8	4	2	E8	4+	2+	F8	5	3				B V M → B	•	↕	↕	0	•
EXG	R1, R2													1E	7	2	R1 ↔ R2[2]	•	•	•	•	•
INC	INCA													4C	2	1	A + 1 → A	•	↕	↕	↕	•
	INCB													5C	2	1	B + 1 → B	•	↕	↕	↕	•
	INC				0C	6	2	6C	6+	2+	7C	7	3				M + 1 → M	•	↕	↕	↕	•
JMP					0E	3	2	6E	3+	2+	7E	4	3				EA[3] → PC	•	•	•	•	•
JSR					9D	7	2	AD	7+	2+	BD	8	3				Jump to Subroutine	•	•	•	•	•
LD	LDA	86	2	2	96	4	2	A6	4+	2+	B6	5	3				M → A	•	↕	↕	0	•
	LDB	C6	2	2	D6	4	2	E6	4+	2+	F6	5	3				M → B	•	↕	↕	0	•
	LDD	CC	3	3	DC	5	2	EC	5+	2+	FC	6	3				M:M + 1 → D	•	↕	↕	0	•
	LDS	10	4	4	10	6	3	10	6+	3+	10	7	4				M:M + 1 → S	•	↕	↕	0	•
		CE			DE			EE			FE											
	LDU	CE	3	3	DE	5	2	EE	5+	2+	FE	6	3				M:M + 1 → U	•	↕	↕	0	•
	LDX	8E	3	3	9E	5	2	AE	5+	2+	BE	6	3				M:M + 1 → X	•	↕	↕	0	•
	LDY	10	4	4	10	6	3	10	6+	3+	10	7	4				M:M + 1 → Y	•	↕	↕	0	•
		8E			9E			AE			BE											
LEA	LEAS							32	4+	2+							EA[3] → S	•	•	•	•	•
	LEAU							33	4+	2+							EA[3] → U	•	•	•	•	•
	LEAX							30	4+	2+							EA[3] → X	•	•	↕	•	•
	LEAY							31	4+	2+							EA[3] → Y	•	•	↕	•	•

Legend:

- OP Operation Code (Hexadecimal)
- ~ Number of MPU Cycles
- # Number of Program Bytes
- \+ Arithmetic Plus
- − Arithmetic Minus
- • Multiply
- M Complement of M
- → Transfer Into
- H Half-carry (from bit 3)
- N Negative (sign bit)
- Z Zero (byte)
- V Overflow, 2's complement
- C Carry from bit 7
- ↕ Test and set if true, cleared otherwise
- • Not Affected
- CC Condition Code Register
- : Concatenation
- V Logical or
- Λ Logical and
- V Logical Exclusive or

Instruction	Forms	Immediate Op	Immediate ~	Immediate #	Direct Op	Direct ~	Direct #	Indexed[1] Op	Indexed[1] ~	Indexed[1] #	Extended Op	Extended ~	Extended #	Inherent Op	Inherent ~	Inherent #	Description	5 H	3 N	2 Z	1 V	0 C
LSL	LSLA													48	2	1	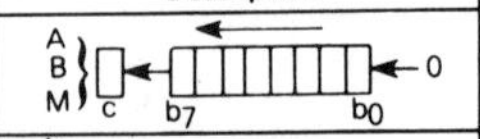	•	↕	↕	↕	↕
	LSLB													58	2	1		•	↕	↕	↕	↕
	LSL				08	6	2	68	6+	2+	78	7	3					•	↕	↕	↕	↕
LSR	LSRA													44	2	1	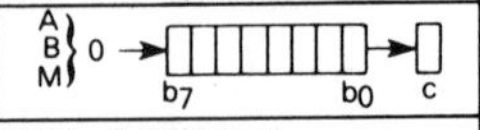	•	0	↕	•	↕
	LSRB													54	2	1		•	0	↕	•	↕
	LSR				04	6	2	64	6+	2+	74	7	3					•	0	↕	•	↕
MUL														3D	11	1	A × B → D (Unsigned)	•	•	↕	•	9
NEG	NEGA													40	2	1	A + 1 → A	8	↕	↕	↕	↕
	NEGB													50	2	1	B + 1 → B	8	↕	↕	↕	↕
	NEG				00	6	2	60	6+	2+	70	7	3				M + 1 → M	8	↕	↕	↕	↕
NOP														12	2	1	No Operation	•	•	•	•	•
OR	ORA	8A	2	2	9A	4	2	AA	4+	2+	BA	5	3				A V M → A	•	↕	↕	0	•
	ORB	CA	2	2	DA	4	2	EA	4+	2+	FA	5	3				B V M → B	•	↕	↕	0	•
	ORCC	1A	3	2													CC V IMM → CC				7	
PSH	PSHS	34	5+[4]	2													Push Registers on S Stack	•	•	•	•	•
	PSHU	36	5+[4]	2													Push Registers on U Stack	•	•	•	•	•
PUL	PULS	35	5+[4]	2													Pull Registers from S Stack	•	•	•	•	•
	PULU	37	5+[4]	2													Pull Registers from U Stack	•	•	•	•	•
ROL	ROLA													49	2	1	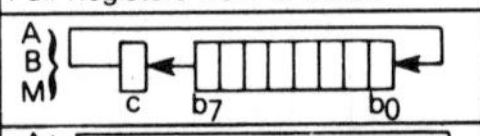	•	↕	↕	↕	↕
	ROLB													59	2	1		•	↕	↕	↕	↕
	ROL				09	6	2	69	6+	2+	79	7	3					•	↕	↕	↕	↕
ROR	RORA													46	2	1	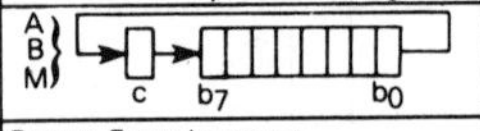	•	↕	↕	•	↕
	RORB													56	2	1		•	↕	↕	•	↕
	ROR				06	6	2	66	6+	2+	76	7	3					•	↕	↕	•	↕
RTI														3B	6/15	1	Return From Interrupt					7
RTS														39	5	1	Return from Subroutine	•	•	•	•	•
SBC	SBCA	82	2	2	92	4	2	A2	4+	2+	B2	5	3				A − M − C → A	8	↕	↕	↕	↕
	SBCB	C2	2	2	D2	4	2	E2	4+	2+	F2	5	3				B − M − C → B	8	↕	↕	↕	↕
SEX														1D	2	1	Sign Extend B into A	•	↕	↕	0	•
ST	STA				97	4	2	A7	4+	2+	B7	5	3				A → M	•	↕	↕	0	•
	STB				D7	4	2	E7	4+	2+	F7	5	3				B → M	•	↕	↕	0	•
	STD				DD	5	2	ED	5+	2+	FD	6	3				D → M:M + 1	•	↕	↕	0	•
	STS				10 DF	6	3	10 EF	6+	3+	10 FF	7	4				S → M:M + 1	•	↕	↕	0	•
	STU				DF	5	2	EF	5+	2+	FF	6	3				U → M:M + 1	•	↕	↕	0	•
	STX				9F	5	2	AF	5+	2+	BF	6	3				X → M:M + 1	•	↕	↕	0	•
	STY				10 9F	6	3	10 AF	6+	3+	10 BF	7	4				Y → M:M + 1	•	↕	↕	0	•
SUB	SUBA	80	2	2	90	4	2	A0	4+	2+	B0	5	3				A − M → A	8	↕	↕	↕	↕
	SUBB	C0	2	2	D0	4	2	E0	4+	2+	F0	5	3				B − M → B	8	↕	↕	↕	↕
	SUBD	83	4	3	93	6	2	A3	6+	2+	B3	7	3				D − M:M + 1 → D	•	↕	↕	↕	↕
SWI	SWI[6]													3F	19	1	Software Interrupt 1	•	•	•	•	•
	SWI[6]													10 3F	20	2	Software Interrupt 2	•	•	•	•	•
	SWI[6]													11 3F	20	1	Software Interrupt 3	•	•	•	•	•
SYNC														13	≥2	1	Synchronize to Interrupt	•	•	•	•	•
TFR	R1, R2													1F	7	2	R1 → R2[2]	•	•	•	•	•
TST	TSTA													4D	2	1	Test A	•	↕	↕	0	•
	TSTB													5D	2	1	Test B	•	↕	↕	0	•
	TST				0D	6	2	6D	6+	2+	7D	7	3				Test M	•	↕	↕	0	•

Notes:

1. This column gives a base cycle and byte count. To obtain total count, add the values obtained from the INDEXED ADDRESSING MODE table, Table 2.
2. R1 and R2 may be any pair of 8 bit or any pair of 16 bit registers.
   The 8 bit registers are: A, B, CC, DP
   The 16 bit registers are: X, Y, U, S, D, PC
3. EA is the effective address.
4. The PSH and PUL instructions require 5 cycles plus 1 cycle for each **byte** pushed or pulled.
5. 5(6) means: 5 cycles if branch not taken, 6 cycles if taken (Branch instructions).
6. SWI sets I and F bits. SWI2 and SWI3 do not affect I and F.
7. Conditions Codes set as a direct result of the instruction.
8. Vaue of half-carry flag is undefined.
9. Special Case — Carry set if b7 is SET.

Branch Instructions

Instruction	Forms	Addressing Mode Relative OP	~[5]	#	Description	5 H	3 N	2 Z	1 V	0 C
BCC	BCC	24	3	2	Branch C=0	•	•	•	•	•
	LBCC	10 24	5(6)	4	Long Branch C=0	•	•	•	•	•
BCS	BCS	25	3	2	Branch C=1	•	•	•	•	•
	LBCS	10 25	5(6)	4	Long Branch C=1	•	•	•	•	•
BEQ	BEQ	27	3	2	Branch Z=0	•	•	•	•	•
	LBEQ	10 27	5(6)	4	Long Branch Z=0	•	•	•	•	•
BGE	BGE	2C	3	2	Branch ≥ Zero	•	•	•	•	•
	LBGE	10 2C	5(6)	4	Long Branch ≥ Zero	•	•	•	•	•
BGT	BGT	2E	3	2	Branch > Zero	•	•	•	•	•
	LBGT	10 2E	5(6)	4	Long Branch > Zero	•	•	•	•	•
BHI	BHI	22	3	2	Branch Higher	•	•	•	•	•
	LBHI	10 22	5(6)	4	Long Branch Higher	•	•	•	•	•
BHS	BHS	24	3	2	Branch Higher or Same	•	•	•	•	•
	LBHS	10 24	5(6)	4	Long Branch Higher or Same	•	•	•	•	•
BLE	BLE	2F	3	2	Branch ≤ Zero	•	•	•	•	•
	LBLE	10 2F	5(6)	4	Long Branch ≤ Zero	•	•	•	•	•
BLO	BLO	25	3	2	Branch lower	•	•	•	•	•
	LBLO	10 25	5(6)	4	Long Branch Lower	•	•	•	•	•

Instruction	Forms	Addressing Mode Relative OP	~[5]	#	Description	5 H	3 N	2 Z	1 V	0 C
BLS	BLS	23	3	2	Branch Lower or Same	•	•	•	•	•
	LBLS	10 23	5(6)	4	Long Branch Lower or Same	•	•	•	•	•
BLT	BLT	2D	3	2	Branch < Zero	•	•	•	•	•
	LBLT	10 2D	5(6)	4	Long Branch < Zero	•	•	•	•	•
BMI	BMI	2B	3	2	Branch Minus	•	•	•	•	•
	LBMI	10 2B	5(6)	4	Long Branch Minus	•	•	•	•	•
BNE	BNE	26	3	2	Branch Z≠0	•	•	•	•	•
	LBNE	10 26	5(6)	4	Long Branch Z≠0	•	•	•	•	•
BPL	BPL	2A	3	2	Branch Plus	•	•	•	•	•
	LBPL	10 2A	5(6)	4	Long Branch Plus	•	•	•	•	•
BRA	BRA	20	3	2	Branch Always	•	•	•	•	•
	LBRA	16	5	3	Long Branch Always	•	•	•	•	•
BRN	BRN	21	3	2	Branch Never	•	•	•	•	•
	LBRN	10 21	5	4	Long Branch Never	•	•	•	•	•
BSR	BSR	8D	7	2	Branch to Subroutine	•	•	•	•	•
	LBSR	17	9	3	Long Branch to Subroutine	•	•	•	•	•
BVC	BVC	28	3	2	Branch V=0	•	•	•	•	•
	LBVC	10 28	5(6)	4	Long Branch V=0	•	•	•	•	•
BVS	BVS	29	3	2	Branch V=1	•	•	•	•	•
	LBVS	10 29	5(6)	4	Long Branch V=1	•	•	•	•	•

SIMPLE BRANCHES

	OP	~	#
BRA	20	3	2
LBRA	16	5	3
BRN	21	3	2
LBRN	1021	5	4
BSR	8D	7	2
LBSR	17	9	3

SIMPLE CONDITIONAL BRANCHES (Notes 1-4)

Test	True	OP	False	OP
N=1	BMI	2B	BPL	2A
Z=1	BEQ	27	BNE	26
V=1	BVS	29	BVC	28
C=1	BCS	25	BCC	24

SIGNED CONDITIONAL BRANCHES (Notes 1-4)

Test	True	OP	False	OP
r>m	BGT	2E	BLE	2F
r≥m	BGE	2C	BLT	2D
r=m	BEQ	27	BNE	26
r≤m	BLE	2F	BGT	2E
r<m	BLT	2D	BGE	2C

UNSIGNED CONDITIONAL BRANCHES (Notes 1-4)

Test	True	OP	False	OP
r>m	BHI	22	BLS	23
r≥m	BHS	24	BLO	25
r=m	BEQ	27	BNE	26
r≤m	BLS	23	BHI	22
r<m	BLO	25	BHS	24

Notes:

1. All conditional branches have both short and long variations.
2. All short branches are 2 bytes and require 3 cycles.
3. All conditional long branches are formed by prefixing the short branch opcode with $10 and using a 16-bit destination offset.
4. All conditional long branches require 4 bytes and 6 cycles if the branch is taken or 5 cycles if the branch is not taken.

Appendix IIIB 6809 Hexadecimal Values of Machine Codes

HEXADECIMAL VALUES OF MACHINE CODES

OP	Mnem	Mode	~	#	OP	Mnem	Mode	~	#	OP	Mnem	Mode	~	#
00	NEG	Direct	6	2	30	LEAX	Indexed	4+	2+	60	NEG	Indexed	6+	2+
01	•				31	LEAY		4+	2+	61	•			
02	•				32	LEAS		4+	2+	62	•			
03	COM		6	2	33	LEAU	Indexed	4+	2+	63	COM		6+	2+
04	LSR		6	2	34	PSHS	Inherent	5+	2	64	LSR		6+	2+
05	•				35	PULS		5+	2	65	•			
06	ROR		6	2	36	PSHU		5+	2	66	ROR		6+	2+
07	ASR		6	2	37	PULU		5+	2	67	ASR		6+	2+
08	ASL, LSL		6	2	38	•				68	ASL, LSL		6+	2+
09	ROL		6	2	39	RTS		5	1	69	ROL		6+	2+
0A	DEC		6	2	3A	ABX		3	1	6A	DEC		6+	2+
0B	•				3B	RTI		6, 15	1	6B	•			
0C	INC		6	2	3C	CWAI		20	2	6C	INC		6+	2+
0D	TST		6	2	3D	MUL		11	1	6D	TST		6+	2+
0E	JMP		3	2	3E	•				6E	JMP		3+	2+
0F	CLR	Direct	6	2	3F	SWI	Inherent	19	1	6F	CLR	Indexed	6+	2+
10	Page 2	–	–	–	40	NEGA	Inherent	2	1	70	NEG	Extended	7	3
11	Page 3	–	–	–	41	•				71	•			
12	NOP	Inherent	2	1	42	•				72	•			
13	SYNC	Inherent	2	1	43	COMA		2	1	73	COM		7	3
14	•				44	LSRA		2	1	74	LSR		7	3
15	•				45	•				75	•			
16	LBRA	Relative	5	3	46	RORA		2	1	76	ROR		7	3
17	LBSR	Relative	9	3	47	ASRA		2	1	77	ASR		7	3
18	•				48	ASLA, LSLA		2	1	78	ASL, LSL		7	3
19	DAA	Inherent	2	1	49	ROLA		2	1	79	ROL		7	3
1A	ORCC	Immed	3	2	4A	DECA		2	1	7A	DEC		7	3
1B	•	–			4B	•				7B	•			
1C	ANDCC	Immed	3	2	4C	INCA		2	1	7C	INC		7	3
1D	SEX	Inherent	2	1	4D	TSTA		2	1	7D	TST		7	3
1E	EXG		8	2	4E	•				7E	JMP		4	3
1F	TFR	Inherent	6	2	4F	CLRA	Inherent	2	1	7F	CLR	Extended	7	3
20	BRA	Relative	3	2	50	NEGB	Inherent	2	1	80	SUBA	Immed	2	2
21	BRN		3	2	51	•				81	CMPA		2	2
22	BHI		3	2	52	•				82	SBCA		2	2
23	BLS		3	2	53	COMB		2	1	83	SUBD		4	3
24	BHS, BCC		3	2	54	LSRB		2	1	84	ANDA		2	2
25	BLO, BCS		3	2	55	•				85	BITA		2	2
26	BNE		3	2	56	RORB		2	1	86	LDA		2	2
27	BEQ		3	2	57	ASRA		2	1	87	•			
28	BVC		3	2	58	ASLB, LSLB		2	1	88	EORA		2	2
29	BVS		3	2	59	ROLB		2	1	89	ADCA		2	2
2A	BPL		3	2	5A	DECB		2	1	8A	ORA		2	2
2B	BMI		3	2	5B	•				8B	ADDA		2	2
2C	BGE		3	2	5C	INCB		2	1	8C	CMPX	Immed	4	3
2D	BLT		3	2	5D	TSTB		2	1	8D	BSR	Relative	7	2
2E	BGT		3	2	5E	•				8E	LDX	Immed	3	3
2F	BLE	Relative	3	2	5F	CLRB	Inherent	2	1	8F	•			

LEGEND:

~ Number of MPU cycles (less possible push pull or indexed-mode cycles)
# Number of program bytes
• Denotes unused opcode

HEXADECIMAL VALUES OF MACHINE CODES (CONTINUED)

OP	Mnem	Mode	~	#
90	SUBA	Direct	4	2
91	CMPA		4	2
92	SBCA		4	2
93	SUBD		6	2
94	ANDA		4	2
95	BITA		4	2
96	LDA		4	2
97	STA		4	2
98	EORA		4	2
99	ADCA		4	2
9A	ORA		4	2
9B	ADDA		4	2
9C	CMPX		6	2
9D	JSR		7	2
9E	LDX		5	2
9F	STX	Direct	5	2
A0	SUBA	Indexed	4+	2+
A1	CMPA		4+	2+
A2	SBCA		4+	2+
A3	SUBD		6+	2+
A4	ANDA		4+	2+
A5	BITA		4+	2+
A6	LDA		4+	2+
A7	STA		4+	2+
A8	EORA		4+	2+
A9	ADCA		4+	2+
AA	ORA		4+	2+
AB	ADDA		4+	2+
AC	CMPX		6+	2+
AD	JSR		7+	2+
AE	LDX		5+	2+
AF	STX	Indexed	5+	2+
B0	SUBA	Extended	5	3
B1	CMPA		5	3
B2	SBCA		5	3
B3	SUBD		7	3
B4	ANDA		5	3
B5	BITA		5	3
B6	LDA		5	3
B7	STA		5	3
B8	EORA		5	3
B9	ADCA		5	3
BA	ORA		5	3
BB	ADDA		5	3
BC	CMPX		7	3
BD	JSR		8	3
BE	LDX		6	3
BF	STX	Extended	6	3

NOTE: All unused opcodes are both undefined and illegal

OP	Mnem	Mode	~	#
C0	SUBB	Immed	2	2
C1	CMPB		2	2
C2	SBCB		2	2
C3	ADDD		4	3
C4	ANDB		2	2
C5	BITB	Immed	2	2
C6	LDB	Immed	2	2
C7	•			
C8	EORB		2	2
C9	ADCB		2	2
CA	ORB		2	2
CB	ADDB		2	2
CC	LDD		3	3
CD	•			
CE	LDU	Immed	3	3
CF	•			
D0	SUBB	Direct	4	2
D1	CMPB		4	2
D2	SBCB		4	2
D3	ADDD		6	2
D4	ANDB		4	2
D5	BITB		4	2
D6	LDB		4	2
D7	STB		4	2
D8	EORB		4	2
D9	ADCB		4	2
DA	ORB		4	2
DB	ADDB		4	2
DC	LDD		5	2
DD	STD		5	2
DE	LDU		5	2
DF	STU	Direct	5	2
E0	SUBB	Indexed	4+	2+
E1	CMPB		4+	2+
E2	SBCB		4+	2+
E3	ADDD		6+	2+
E4	ANDB		4+	2+
E5	BITB		4+	2+
E6	LDB		4+	2+
E7	STB		4+	2+
E8	EORB		4+	2+
E9	ADCB		4+	2+
EA	ORB		4+	2+
EB	ADDB		4+	2+
EC	LDD		5+	2+
ED	STD		5+	2+
EE	LDU		5+	2+
EF	STU	Indexed	5+	2+
F0	SUBB	Extended	5	3
F1	CMPB		5	3
F2	SBCB		5	3
F3	ADDD		7	3
F4	ANDB		5	3
F5	BITB		5	3
F6	LDB		5	3
F7	STB		5	3
F8	EORB		5	3
F9	ADCB		5	3
FA	ORB		5	3
FB	ADDB	Extended	5	3
FC	LDD	Extended	6	3
FD	STD		6	3
FE	LDU		6	3
FF	STU	Extended	6	3

Page 2 and 3 Machine Codes

OP	Mnem	Mode	~	#
1021	LBRN	Relative	5	4
1022	LBHI		5(6)	4
1023	LBLS		5(6)	4
1024	LBHS, LBCC		5(6)	4
1025	LBCS, LBLO		5(6)	4
1026	LBNE		5(6)	4
1027	LBEQ		5(6)	4
1028	LBVC		5(6)	4
1029	LBVS		5(6)	4
102A	LBPL		5(6)	4
102B	LBMI		5(6)	4
102C	LBGE		5(6)	4
102D	LBLT		5(6)	4
102E	LBGT		5(6)	4
102F	LBLE	Relative	5(6)	4
103F	SWI2	Inherent	20	2
1083	CMPD	Immed	5	4
108C	CMPY		5	4
108E	LDY	Immed	4	4
1093	CMPD	Direct	7	3
109C	CMPY		7	3
109E	LDY		6	3
109F	STY	Direct	6	3
10A3	CMPD	Indexed	7+	3+
10AC	CMPY		7+	3+
10AE	LDY		6+	3+
10AF	STY	Indexed	6+	3+
10B3	CMPD	Extended	8	4
10BC	CMPY		8	4
10BE	LDY		7	4
10BF	STY	Extended	7	4
10CE	LDS	Immed	4	4
10DE	LDS	Direct	6	3
10DF	STS	Direct	6	3
10EE	LDS	Indexed	6+	3+
10EF	STS	Indexed	6+	3+
10FE	LDS	Extended	7	4
10FF	STS	Extended	7	4
113F	SWI3	Inherent	20	2
1183	CMPU	Immed	5	4
118C	CMPS	Immed	5	4
1193	CMPU	Direct	7	3
119C	CMPS	Direct	7	3
11A3	CMPU	Indexed	7+	3+
11AC	CMPS	Indexed	7+	3+
11B3	CMPU	Extended	8	4
11BC	CMPS	Extended	8	4

Appendix IV MC68000 Instruction Set

			Condition Codes				
Mnemonic	**Operation**	**Assembler Syntax**	**X**	**N**	**Z**	**V**	**C**
ABCD	Add Decimal with Extend	ABCD Dy,Dx ABCD -(Ay),-(Ax)	*	U	*	U	*
ADD	Add Binary	ADD <ea>,Dn ADD Dn,<ea>	*	*	*	*	*
ADDA	Add Address	ADDA <ea>,An	—	—	—	—	—
ADDI	Add Immediate	ADDI #<data>,<ea>	*	*	*	*	*
ADDQ	Add Quick	ADDQ #<data>,<ea>	*	*	*	*	*
ADDX	Add Extended	ADDX Dy,Dx ADDX -(Ay),-(Ax)	*	*	*	*	*
AND	AND Logical	AND <ea>,Dn AND Dn,<ea>	—	*	*	0	0
ANDI	AND Immediate	ANDI #<data>,<ea>	—	*	*	0	0
ASL, ASR	Arithmetic Shift	ASd Dx,Dy ASd #<data>,Dy ASd<ea>	*	*	*	*	*
Bcc	Branch Conditionally	Bcc <label>	—	—	—	—	—
BCHG	Test a Bit and Change	BCHG Dn,<ea> BCHG #<data>,<ea>	—	—	*	—	—
BCLR	Test a Bit and Clear	BCLR Dn,<ea> BCLR #<data>,<ea>	—	—	*	—	—
BRA	Branch Always	BRA <label>	—	—	—	—	—
BSET	Test a Bit and Set	BSET Dn,<ea> BSET #<data>,<ea>	—	—	*	—	—
BSR	Branch to Subroutine	BSR <label>	—	—	—	—	—
BTST	Test a Bit	BTST Dn,<ea> BTST #<data>,<ea>	—	—	*	—	—

Mnemonic	Operation	Assembler Syntax	Condition Codes				
			X	N	Z	V	C
CHK	Check Register Against Bounds	CHK <ea>,Dn	—	*	U	U	U
CLR	Clear an Operand	CLR <ea>	—	0	1	0	0
CMP	Arithmetic Compare	CMP <ea>,Dn	—	*	*	*	*
CMPA	Arithmetic Compare Address	CMPA <ea>,An	—	*	*	*	*
CMPI	Compare Immediate	CMPI #<data>,<ea>	—	*	*	*	*
CMPM	Compare Memory	CMPM (Ay)+,(Ax)+	—	*	*	*	*
DBcc	Test Condition, Decrement and Branch	DBcc Dn, <label>	—	—	—	—	—
DIVS	Signed Divide	DIVS <ea>,Dn	—	*	*	*	0
DIVU	Unsigned Divide	DIVU <ea>,Dn	—	*	*	*	0
EOR	Exclusive OR Logical	EOR Dn,<ea>	—	*	*	0	0
EORI	Exclusive OR Immediate	EORI #<data>,<ea>	—	*	*	0	0
EXG	Exchange Registers	EXG Rx,Ry	—	—	—	—	—
EXT	Sign Extend	EXT Dn	—	*	*	0	0
JMP	Jump	JMP <ea>	—	—	—	—	—
JSR	Jump to Subroutine	JSR <ea>	—	—	—	—	—
LEA	Load Effective Address	LEA <ea>,An	—	—	—	—	—
LINK	Link and Allocate	LINK An,#<displacement>	—	—	—	—	—
LSL, LSR	Logical Shift	LSd Dx,Dy LSd #<data>,Dy LSd <ea>	*	*	*	0	*
MOVE	Move Data from Source to Destination	MOVE <ea>,<ea>	—	*	*	0	0
MOVE to CCR	Move to Condition Codes	MOVE <ea>,CCR	*	*	*	*	*
MOVE to SR	Move to the Status Register	MOVE <ea>,SR	*	*	*	*	*
MOVE from SR	Move from the Status Register	MOVE SR,<ea>	—	—	—	—	—
MOVE USP	Move User Stack Pointer	MOVE USP,An MOVE An,USP	—	—	—	—	—
MOVEA	Move Address	MOVEA <ea>,An	—	—	—	—	—
MOVEM (see note)	Move Multiple Registers	MOVEM <register list>,<ea> MOVEM <ea>,<register list>	—	—	—	—	—
MOVEP	Move Peripheral Data	MOVEP Dx,d(Ay) MOVEP d(Ay),Dx	—	—	—	—	—
MOVEQ	Move Quick	MOVEQ #<data>,Dn	—	*	*	0	0
MULS	Signed Multiply	MULS <ea>,Dn	—	*	*	0	0
MULU	Unsigned Multiply	MULU <ea>,Dn	—	*	*	0	0
NBCD	Negate Decimal with Extend	NBCD <ea>	*	U	*	U	*
NEG	Two's Complement Negation	NEG <ea>	*	*	*	*	*
NEGX	Negate with Extend	NEGX <ea>	*	*	*	*	*

Mnemonic	Operation	Assembler Syntax	Condition Codes				
			X	N	Z	V	C
NOP	No Operation	NOP	—	—	—	—	—
NOT	Logical Complement	NOT <ea>	—	*	*	0	0
OR	Inclusive OR Logical	OR <ea>,Dn OR Dn,<ea>	—	*	*	0	0
ORI	Inclusive OR Immediate	ORI #<data>,<ea>	—	*	*	0	0
PEA	Push Effective Address	PEA <ea>	—	—	—	—	—
RESET	Reset External Devices	RESET	—	—	—	—	—
ROL, ROR	Rotate (without extend)	ROd Dx,Dy ROd #<data>,Dy ROd <ea>	—	*	*	0	*
ROXL, ROXR	Rotate with Extend	ROXd Dx,Dy ROXd #<data>,Dy ROXd <ea>	*	*	*	0	*
RTE	Return from Exception	RTE	*	*	*	*	*
RTR	Return and Restore Condition Codes	RTR	*	*	*	*	*
RTS	Return from Subroutine	RTS	—	—	—	—	—
SBCD	Subtract Decimal with Extend	SBCD Dy,Dx SBCD -(Ay),-(Ax)	*	U	*	U	*
Scc	Set according to Condition	Scc <ea>	—	—	—	—	—
STOP	Stop Program Execution	STOP #<data>	—	—	—	—	—
SUB	Subtract Binary	SUB <ea>,Dn SUB Dn,<ea>	*	*	*	*	*
SUBA	Subtract Address	SUBA <ea>,An	—	—	—	—	—
SUBI	Subtract Immediate	SUBI #<data>,<ea>	*	*	*	*	*
SUBQ	Subtract Quick	SUBQ #<data>,<ea>	*	*	*	*	*
SUBX	Subtract with Extend	SUBX Dy,Dx SUBX -(Ay),-(Ax)	*	*	*	*	*
SWAP	Swap Register Halves	SWAP Dn	—	*	*	0	0
TAS	Test and Set an Operand	TAS <ea>	—	*	*	0	0
TRAP	Trap	TRAP #<vector>	—	—	—	—	—
TRAPV	Trap on Overflow	TRAPV	—	—	—	—	—
TST	Test and Operand	TST <ea>	—	*	*	0	0
UNLK	Unlink	UNLK An	—	—	—	—	—

Note:

<register list> specifies the registers selected for transfer to or from memory.

<register list> may be:

Rn — a single register.

Rn-Rm — a range of consecutive registers with m being greater than n.

Any combination of the above separated by a slash.

Appendix V
ASCII Code

BITS 4 thru 6	—	0	1	2	3	4	5	6	7
	0	NUL	DLE	SP	0	@	P		p
	1	SOH	DC1	!	1	A	Q	a	q
	2	STX	DC2	”	2	B	R	b	r
	3	ETX	DC3	#	3	C	S	c	s
	4	EOT	DC4	$	4	D	T	d	t
	5	ENQ	NAK	%	5	E	U	e	u
BITS 0 thru 3	6	ACK	SYN	&	6	F	V	f	v
	7	BEL	ETB	'	7	G	W	g	w
	8	BS	CAN	(	8	H	X	h	x
	9	HT	EM	)	9	I	Y	i	y
	A	LF	SUB	*	:	J	Z	j	z
	B	VT	ESC	+	;	K	[	k	{
	C	FF	FS	,	<	L	/	l	/
	D	CR	GS	-	=	M	]	m	}
	E	SO	RS	.	>	N	∧	n	≈
	F	SI	US	/	?	O	—	o	DEL

Appendix VI
D-2 Kit
Schematic

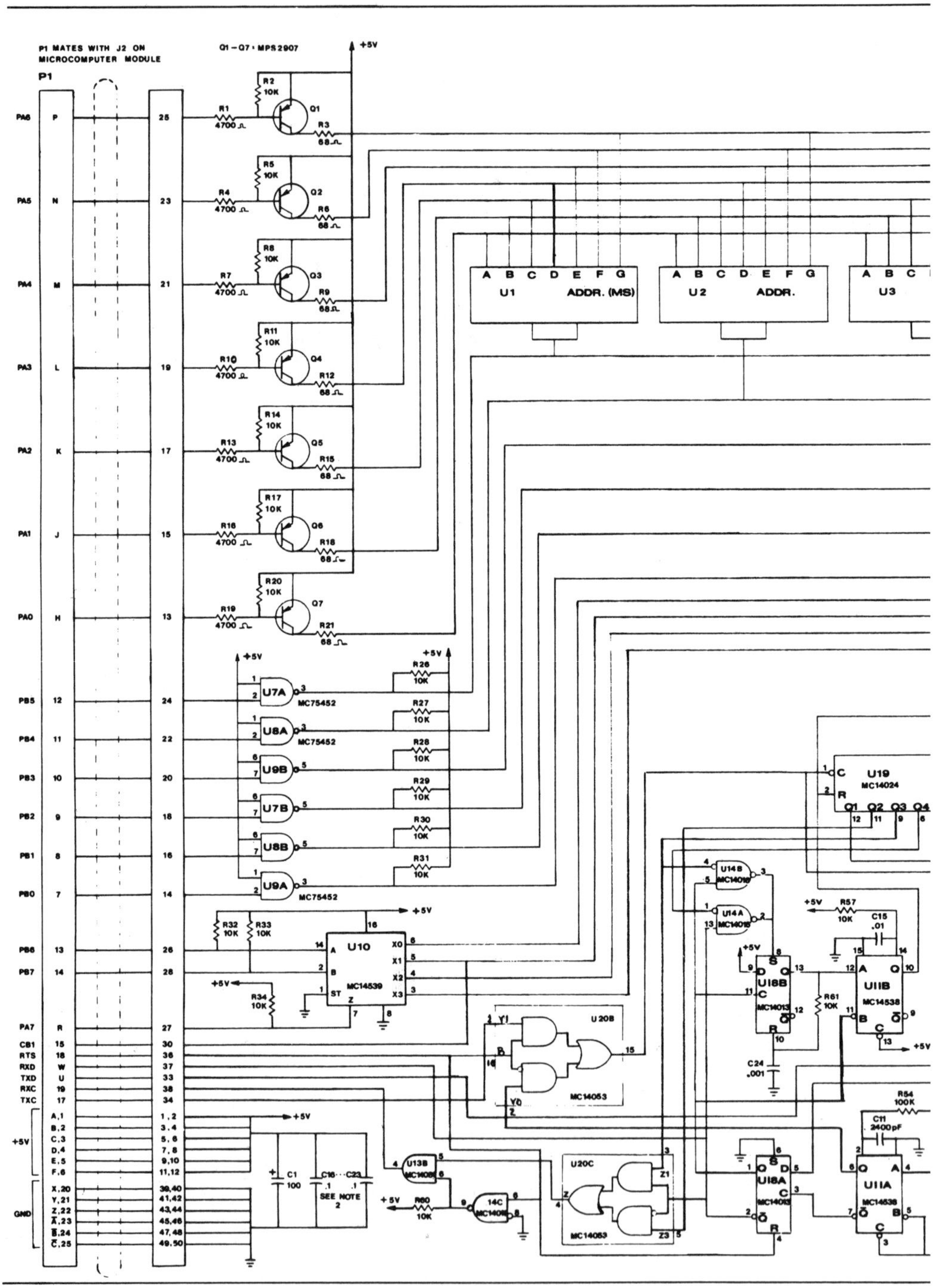

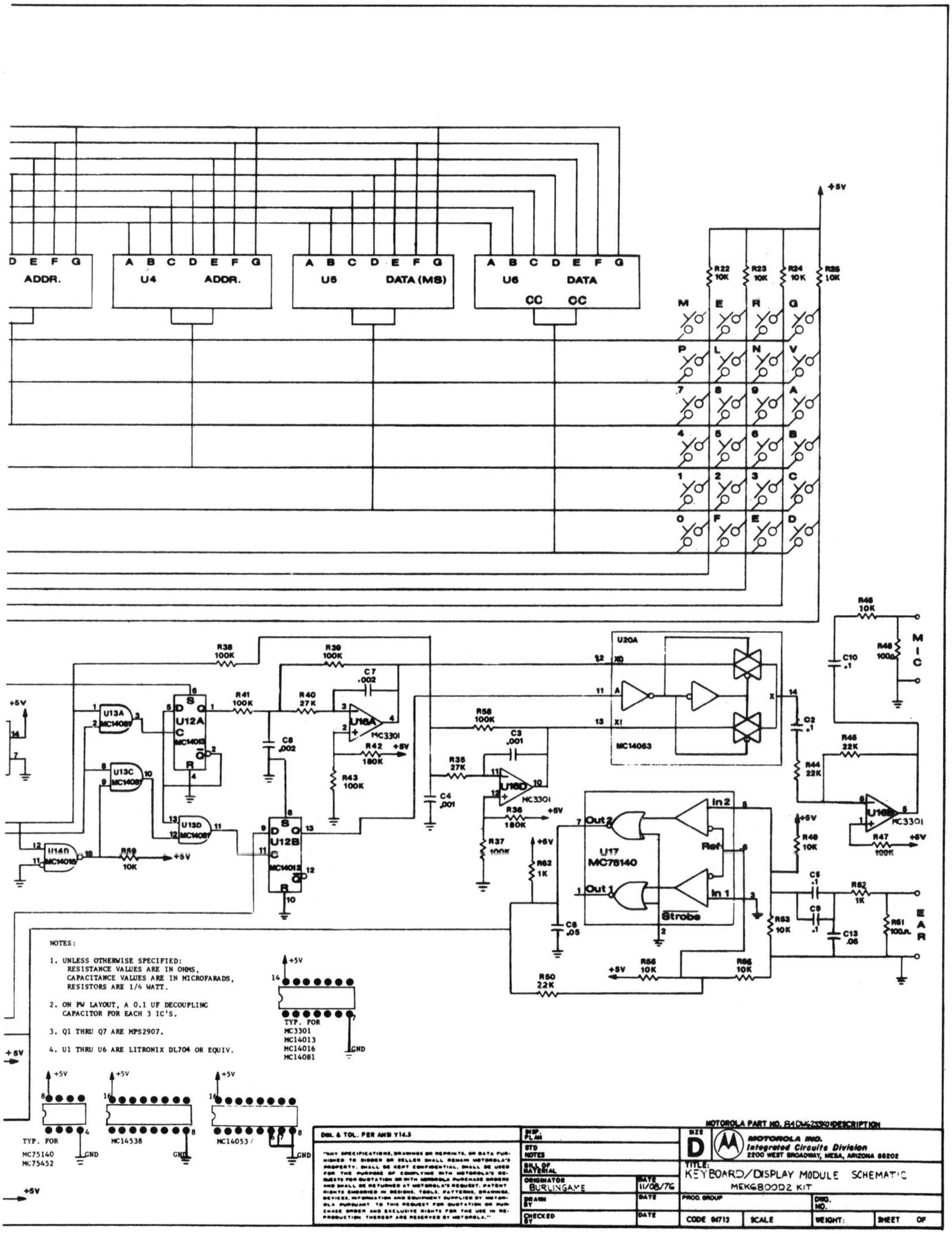
ADDR.
U4 ADDR.
U5 DATA (MS)
U6 DATA
CC CC
+5V
R22 10K
R23 10K
R24 10K
R25 10K
M E R G
P L N V
7 8 9 A
4 5 6 B
1 2 3 C
0 F E D
R38 100K
R39 100K
C7 .002
R41 100K
R40 27K
U13A MC14081
U12A MC14013
U13C MC14081
U16A MC3301
R42 180K
R43 100K
C8 .002
U13D MC14081
U12B MC14013
U14D MC14016
R59 10K
R58 100K
C3 .001
R35 27K
C4 .001
U16D MC3301
R36 180K
R37 100K
U20A
MC14053
R46 10K
R48 100Ω
C10 .1
MIC
C2 .1
R45 22K
R44 22K
U16B MC3301
R49 10K
R47 100K
U17 MC75140
In 2
Ref
In 1
Out 2
Out 1
Strobe
R62 1K
C6 .05
R53 10K
C5 .1
C9 .1
R52 1K
C13 .05
R51 100Ω
EAR
R50 22K
R55 10K
R56 10K
NOTES:
1. UNLESS OTHERWISE SPECIFIED:
RESISTANCE VALUES ARE IN OHMS,
CAPACITANCE VALUES ARE IN MICROFARADS,
RESISTORS ARE 1/4 WATT.
2. ON PW LAYOUT, A 0.1 UF DECOUPLING CAPACITOR FOR EACH 3 IC'S.
3. Q1 THRU Q7 ARE MPS2907.
4. U1 THRU U6 ARE LITRONIX DL704 OR EQUIV.
TYP. FOR
MC3301
MC14013
MC14016
MC14081
GND
TYP. FOR
MC75140
MC75452
MC14538
MC14053
DIM. & TOL. PER ANSI Y14.5
MOTOROLA INC.
Integrated Circuits Division
2200 WEST BROADWAY, MESA, ARIZONA 85202
SIZE D
TITLE: KEYBOARD/DISPLAY MODULE SCHEMATIC
MEK6800D2 KIT
ORIGINATOR BURLINGAME
DATE 11/08/76
DRAWN BY
CHECKED BY
PROD. GROUP
DWG. NO.
CODE 94713
SCALE
WEIGHT:
SHEET OF

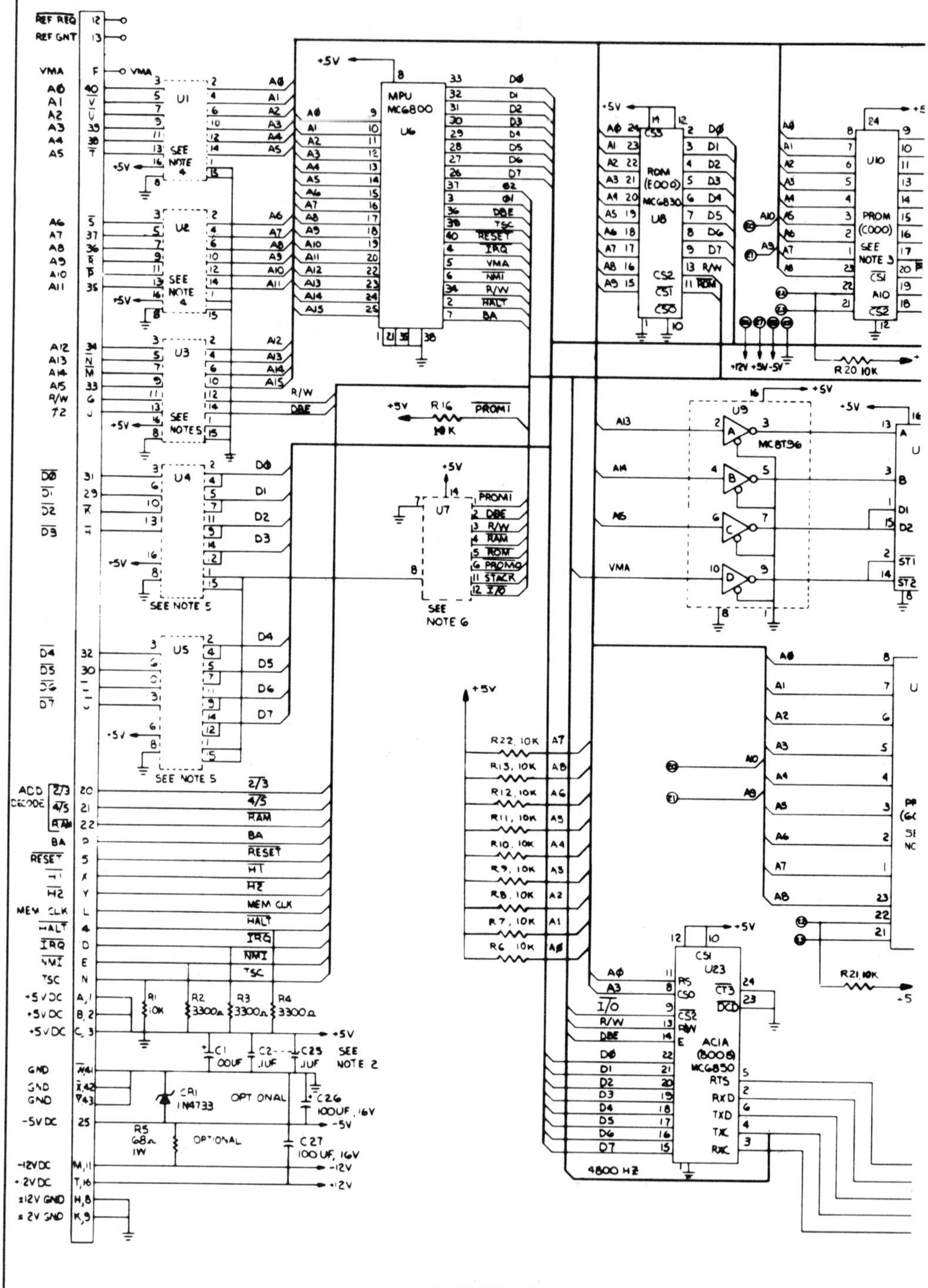

NOTES:

1. UNLESS OTHERWISE SPECIFIED: RESISTANCE VALUES ARE IN OHMS. CAPACITANCE VALUES ARE IN MICROFARADS. RESISTORS ARE $\frac{1}{4}$ WATT, ± 10%
2. CAPACITOR FOR EVERY 3 PACKS
3. OPTIONAL PROMS

MC68708	MCM7641	MCM68317
E1 TO E2	E3 TO E9	E0 TO E4
E3 TO E8	E4 TO E7	E1 TO E2
E4 TO E6	E5 TO E7	E5 TO E9
E5 TO E9		

4. MC8T97
5. MC8T26
6. MC74301

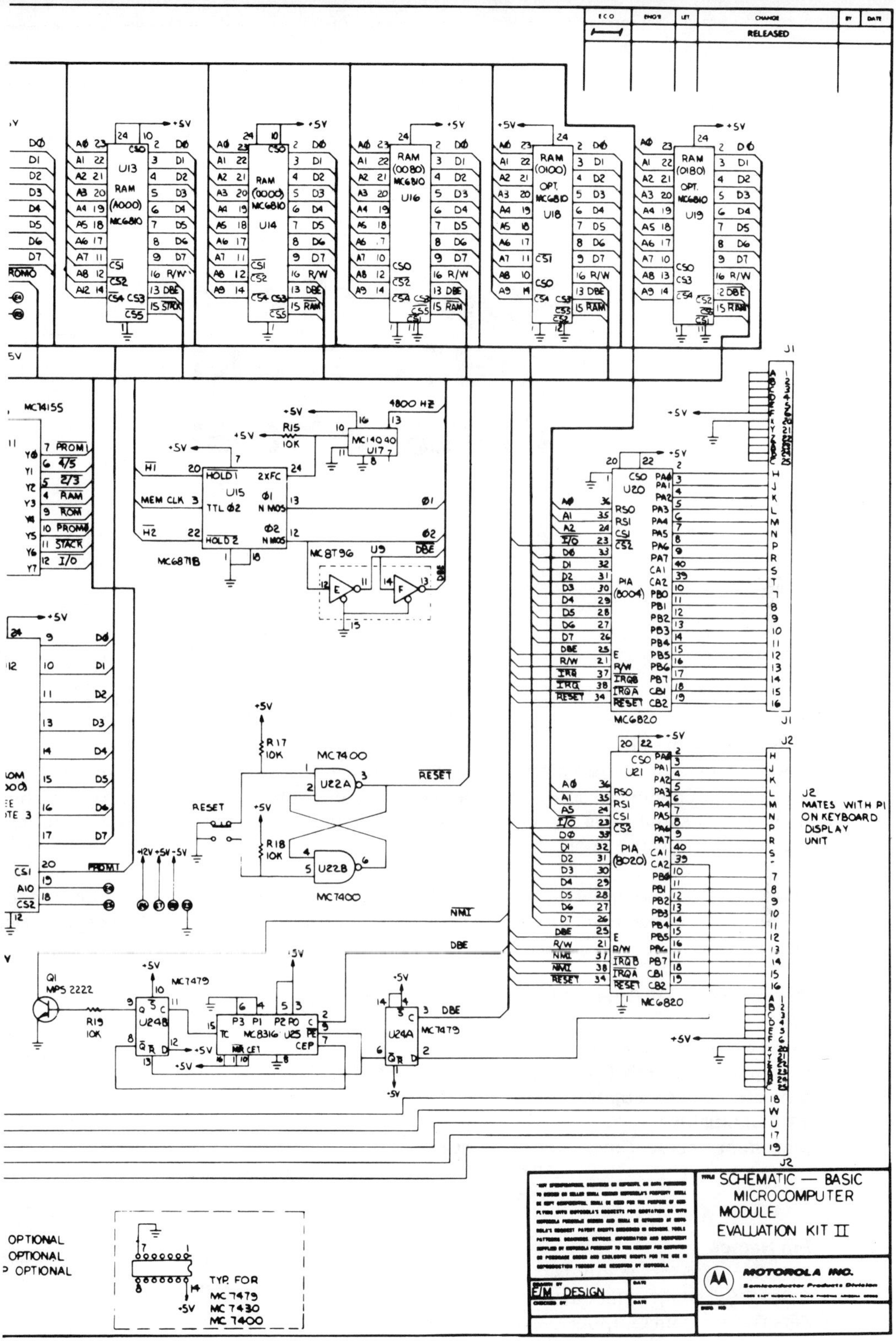
ECO
CHANGE
RELEASED
RAM (A000) MC6810 U13
RAM (0000) MC6810 U14
RAM (0080) MC6810 U16
RAM (0100) OPT. MC6810 U18
RAM (0180) OPT. MC6810 U19
MC74155
MC14040 U17
4800 HZ
R15 10K
MC6871B U15
MEM CLK
MC8T96 U9
PIA (8004) U20 MC6820
PIA (8020) U21 MC6820
J1
J2
J2 MATES WITH P1 ON KEYBOARD DISPLAY UNIT
R17 10K
MC7400
U22A
U22B
RESET
R18 10K
Q1 MPS 2222
R19 10K
MC7479 U24B
MC8316 U25
MC7479 U24A
NMI
DBE
OPTIONAL
OPTIONAL
OPTIONAL
TYP. FOR MC7479 MC7430 MC7400
SCHEMATIC — BASIC MICROCOMPUTER MODULE EVALUATION KIT II
MOTOROLA INC.
Semiconductor Products Division
E/M DESIGN

Appendix VII
6810 RAM
Data Sheet

General Description

F6810 is a byte-organized memory designed for use in bus-organized systems. It is fabricated with n-channel silicon-gate technology. For ease of use, the device operates from a single power supply, has compatibility with TTL and DTL, and needs no clocks or refreshing because of static operation.

The memory is compatible with the F6800 Microcomputer Family, providing random storage in byte increments. Memory expansion is provided through multiple Chip Select inputs.

Organized As 128 Bytes of Eight Bits
Static Operation
Bidirectional 3-State Data Input/Output
6 Chip Select Inputs (4 Active LOW, 2 Active HIGH)
Single 5 V Power Supply
TTL Compatible
Maximum Access Time = 450 ns — F6810
360 ns — F68A10
250 ns — F68B10

Pin Names

A_0 - A_6	Address Inputs
CS_0 - CS_5	Chip Select Inputs
D_0 - D_7	Data Outputs

Connection Diagram

24-Pin Plastic DIP

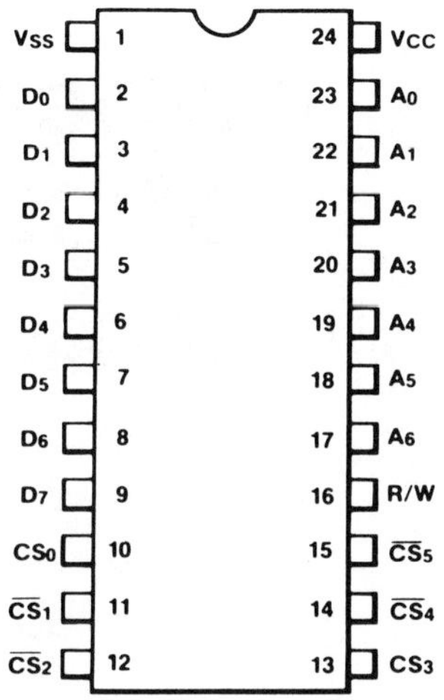

(TOP VIEW)

Block Diagram

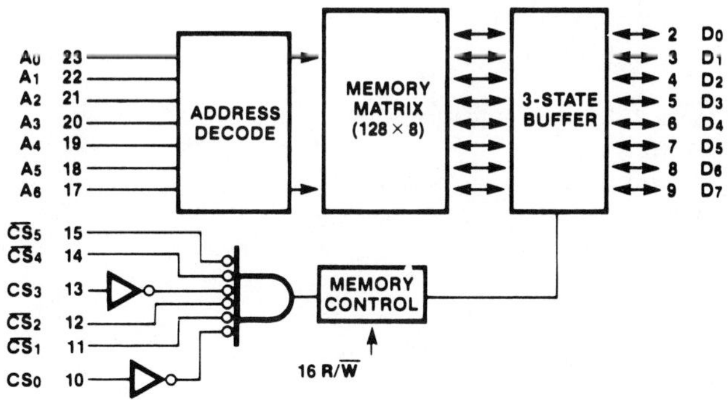

VCC = PIN 24
VSS = PIN 1

Appendix VIII MC68000 Instruction Set

ABCD — Add Decimal with Extend — ABCD

Operation: $(\text{Destination})_{10} + (\text{Source})_{10} + X \rightarrow \text{Destination}$
ABCD Dy TO Dx
ABCD Ay@- TO Ax@-

Assembler Syntax:
ABCD Dy,Dx
ABCD -(Ay),-(Ax)

Attributes: Size = (Byte)

Description: Add the source operand to the destination operand along with the extend bit, and store the result in the destination location. The addition is performed using binary coded decimal arithmetic. The operands may be addressed in two different ways:

1. Data register to data register: The operands are contained in the data registers specified in the instruction.
2. Memory to memory: The operands are addressed with the predecrement addressing mode using the address registers specified in the instruction.

This operation is a byte operation only.

Condition Codes:

X	N	Z	V	C
*	U	*	U	*

N — Undefined.
Z — Cleared if the result is non-zero. Unchanged otherwise.
V — Undefined.
C — Set if a carry (decimal) was generated. Cleared otherwise.
X — Set the same as the carry bit.

Instruction Format:

15	14	13	12	11	10	9	8	7	6	5	4	3	2	1	0
1	1	0	0	Register Rx			1	0	0	0	0	R/M	Register Ry		

Instruction Fields:

Register Rx field — Specifies the destination register:
If R/M = 0, specifies a data register.
If R/M = 1, specifies an address register for the predecrement addressing mode.

R/M field — Specifies the operand addressing mode:
0 — The operation is data register to data register.
1 — The operation is memory to memory.

Register Ry field — Specifies the source register:
If R/M = 0, specifies a data register.
If R/M = 1, specifies an address register for the predecrement addressing mode.

ADD — Add Binary — ADD

Operation: (Destination) + (Source) → Destination
ADD <ea> TO Dn
ADD Dn TO <ea>

Assembler Syntax: ADD <ea>,Dn
ADD Dn,<ea>

Attributes: Size = (Byte, Word, Long)

Description: Add the source operand to the destination operand, and store the result in the destination location. The size of the operation may be specified to be byte, word or long. The mode of the instruction indicates which operand is the source and which is the destination as well as the operand size.

Condition Codes:

X	N	Z	V	C
*	*	*	*	*

N — Set if the result is negative. Cleared otherwise.
Z — Set if the result is zero. Cleared otherwise.
V — Set if an overflow is generated. Cleared otherwise.
C — Set if a carry is generated. Cleared otherwise.
X — Set the same as the carry bit.

Instruction Format:

15	14	13	12	11 10 9	8 7 6	5 4 3 2 1 0
1	1	0	1	Register	Op-Mode	Effective Address

Instruction Fields:

Register field — Specifies any of the eight data registers.

Op-Mode field —

Byte	Word	Long	Operation
000	001	010	(<Dn>) + (<ea>) → <Dn>
100	101	110	(<ea>) + (<Dn>) → <ea>

Effective Address field — Determines addressing mode:

a. If the location specified is a source operand, then all addressing modes are allowed. If the operation size is byte, then the address register direct addressing mode is not allowed.

b. If the location specified is a destination operand, then only alterable memory addressing modes are allowed.

ADDA — Add Address — ADDA

Operation: (Destination) + (Source) → Destination
ADD <ea> TO An

Assembler Syntax: ADD <ea>,An

Attributes: Size = (Word, Long)

Description: Add the source operand to the destination address register, and store the result in the address register. The size of the operation may be specified to be word or long.

Condition Codes:

X	N	Z	V	C
—	—	—	—	—

N — Not affected.
Z — Not affected.
V — Not affected.
C — Not affected.
X — Not affected.

Instruction Format:

15	14	13	12	11	10	9	8	7	6	5	4	3	2	1	0
1	1	0	1	Register			Op-Mode			Effective Address					

Instruction Fields:

Register field — Specifies any of the eight address registers. This is always the destination.

Op-Mode field — Specifies the size of the operation:

011 — word operation. The source operand is sign-extended to a long operand and the operation is performed on the address register using all 32 bits.

111 — long operation.

Effective Address field — Specifies the source operand. All addressing modes are allowed.

ADDI **Add Immediate** ADDI

Operation: (Destination) + Immediate Data → Destination
ADD #<data> TO <ea>

Assembler Syntax: ADDI #<data>,<ea>

Attributes: Size = (Byte, Word, Long)

Description: Add the immediate data to the destination operand, and store the result in the destination location. The size of the operation may be specified to be byte, word or long. The size of the immediate data matches the operation size.

Condition Codes:

X	N	Z	V	C
*	*	*	*	*

N — Set if the result is negative. Cleared otherwise.
Z — Set if the result is zero. Cleared otherwise.
V — Set if an overflow is generated. Cleared otherwise.
C — Set if a carry is generated. Cleared otherwise.
X — Set the same as the carry bit.

Instruction Format:

<table>
<tr><th>15</th><th>14</th><th>13</th><th>12</th><th>11</th><th>10</th><th>9</th><th>8</th><th>7</th><th>6</th><th>5</th><th>4</th><th>3</th><th>2</th><th>1</th><th>0</th></tr>
<tr><td>0</td><td>0</td><td>0</td><td>0</td><td>0</td><td>1</td><td>1</td><td>0</td><td colspan="2">Size</td><td colspan="6">Effective Address</td></tr>
<tr><td colspan="8">Word Data (16 bits)</td><td colspan="8">Byte Data (8 bits)</td></tr>
<tr><td colspan="16">Long Data (32 bits, including previous word)</td></tr>
</table>

Instruction Fields:

Size field — Specifies the size of the operation:
- 00 — byte operation.
- 01 — word operation.
- 10 — long operation.

Effective Address field — Specifies the destination operand. Only data alterable addressing modes are allowed.

Immediate field — (Data immediately following the instruction):
- If size = 00, then the data is the low order byte of the immediate word.
- If size = 01, then the data is the entire immediate word.
- If size = 10, then the data is the next two immediate words.

ADDQ — Add Quick — ADDQ

Operation: (Destination) + Immediate Data → Destination
ADDQ #<data> TO <ea>

Assembler Syntax: ADDQ #<data>,<ea>

Attributes: Size = (Byte, Word, Long)

Description: Add the immediate data to the operand at the destination location. The data range is from 1 to 8. The size of the operation may be specified to be byte, word or long. Word and long operations are also allowed on the address registers.

Condition Codes:

X	N	Z	V	C
*	*	*	*	*

N — Set if the result is negative. Cleared otherwise.
Z — Set if the result is zero. Cleared otherwise.
V — Set if an overflow is generated. Cleared otherwise.
C — Set if a carry is generated. Cleared otherwise.
X — Set the same as the carry bit.

The condition codes are not affected if an addition to an address register is made.

Instruction Format:

15	14	13	12	11	10	9	8	7	6	5	4	3	2	1	0
0	1	0	1	Data			0	Size		Effective Address					

Instruction Fields:

Data field — Three bits of immediate data, 0, 1-7 representing a range of 8, 1 to 7 respectively.

Size field — Specifies the size of the operation:
- 00 — byte operation.
- 01 — word operation.
- 10 — long operation.

Effective Address field — Specifies the destination location. Only alterable addressing modes are allowed. If the operation size is byte, the address register direct addressing mode is not allowed.

ADDX — Add Extended — ADDX

Operation: (Destination) + (Source) + X → Destination
ADDX Dy TO Dx
ADDX Ay@- TO Ax@-

Assembler Syntax: ADDX Dy,Dx
ADDX -(Ay),-(Ax)

Attributes: Size = (Byte, Word, Long)

Description: Add the source operand to the destination operand along with the extend bit, and store the result in the destination location. The operands may be addressed in two different ways:

1. Data register to data register: the operands are contained in data registers specified in the instruction.
2. Memory to memory: the operands are addressed with the predecrement addressing mode using the address registers specified in the instruction.

The size of the operation may be specified to be byte, word or long.

Condition Codes:

X	N	Z	V	C
*	*	*	*	*

N — Set if the result is negative. Cleared otherwise.
Z — Cleared if the result is non-zero. Unchanged otherwise.
V — Set if an overflow is generated. Cleared otherwise.
C — Set if a carry is generated. Cleared otherwise.
X — Set the same as the carry bit.

Instruction Format:

15	14	13	12	11	10	9	8	7	6	5	4	3	2	1	0
1	1	0	1	Register Rx			1	Size		0	0	R/M	Register Ry		

Instruction Fields:

Register Rx field — Specifies the destination register:
If R/M = 0, specifies a data register.
If R/M = 1, specifies an address register for the predecrement addressing mode.

Size field — Specifies the size of the operation:
00 — byte operation.
01 — word operation.
10 — long operation.

R/M field — Specifies the operand addressing mode:
0 — The operation is data register to data register.
1 — The operation is memory to memory.

Register Ry field — Specifies the source register:
If R/M = 0, specifies a data register.
If R/M = 1, specifies an address register for the predecrement addressing mode.

AND — AND Logical — AND

Operation: (Destination) ∧ (Source) → Destination
AND <ea> TO Dn
AND Dn TO <ea>

Assembler Syntax: AND <ea>,Dn
AND Dn,<ea>

Attributes: Size = (Byte, Word, Long)

Description: AND the source operand to the destination operand, and store the result in the destination location. The size of the operation may be specified to be byte, word or long. The contents of an address register may not be used as an operand.

Condition Codes:

X	N	Z	V	C
—	*	*	0	0

N — Set if the most significant bit of the result is set. Cleared otherwise.
Z — Set if the result is zero. Cleared otherwise.
V — Always cleared.
C — Always cleared.
X — Not affected.

Instruction Format:

15	14	13	12	11 10 9	8 7 6	5 4 3 2 1 0
1	1	0	0	Register	Op-Mode	Effective Address

Instruction Fields:

Register field — Specifies any of the eight data registers.

Op-Mode field —

Byte	Word	Long	Operation
000	001	010	(<Dn>) ∧ (<ea>) → <Dn>
100	101	110	(<ea>) ∧ (<Dn>) → <ea>

Effective Address field — Determines addressing mode:

If the location specified is a source operand then only data addressing modes are allowed.

If the location specified is a destination operand then only alterable memory addressing modes are allowed.

ANDI **AND Immediate** ANDI

Operation: (Destination) ∧ Immediate Data → Destination
AND #<data> TO <ea>

Assembler Syntax: ANDI #<data>,<ea>

Attributes: Size = (Byte, Word, Long)

Description: AND the source operand to the destination operand, and store the result in the destination location. The size of the operation may be specified to be byte, word or long. The size of the immediate data matches the operation size. Access to the status register is available in two modes:

1. If the operation size is byte, the operation affects only the low order byte of the status register, which contains the condition codes.
2. If the operation size is word, the operation is performed on the whole status register. This is a privileged operation.

Condition Codes:

X	N	Z	V	C
—	*	*	0	0

N — Set if the most significant bit of the result is set. Cleared otherwise.
Z — Set if the result is zero. Cleared otherwise.
V — Always cleared.
C — Always cleared.
X — Not affected.

When accessing the status register the condition codes are affected according to the operation.

Instruction Format:

<table>
<tr><th>15</th><th>14</th><th>13</th><th>12</th><th>11</th><th>10</th><th>9</th><th>8</th><th>7</th><th>6</th><th>5</th><th>4</th><th>3</th><th>2</th><th>1</th><th>0</th></tr>
<tr><td>0</td><td>0</td><td>0</td><td>0</td><td>0</td><td>0</td><td>1</td><td>0</td><td colspan="2">Size</td><td colspan="6">Effective Address</td></tr>
<tr><td colspan="8">Word Data (16 bits)</td><td colspan="8">Byte Data (8 bits)</td></tr>
<tr><td colspan="16">Long Data (32 bits, including previous word)</td></tr>
</table>

Instruction Fields:

Size field — Specifies the size of the operation:
- 00 — byte operation.
- 01 — word operation.
- 10 — long operation.

Effective Address field — Specifies the destination operand. Only data alterable or the status register addressing modes are allowed.

Immediate field — (Data immediately following the instruction):
- If size = 00, then the data is the low order byte of the immediate word.
- If size = 01, then the data is the entire immediate word.
- If size = 10, then the data is the next two immediate words.

ASL, ASR — Arithmetic Shift — ASL, ASR

Operation: (Destination) Shifted by <count> → Destination
ASd Dy BY Dx
ASd Dy BY #<data>
ASd <ea>

Assembler Syntax:
ASd Dx,Dy
ASd #<data>,Dy
ASd <ea>

Attributes: Size = (Byte, Word, Long)

Description: Arithmetically shift the bits of the operand in the direction specified. The carry bit receives the last bit shifted out of the operand. The shift count for the shifting of a register may be specified in two different ways:

1. Immediate: the shift count is specified in the instruction (shift range, 1-8).
2. Register: the shift count is contained in a data register specified in the instruction.

The size of the operation may be specified to be byte, word or long. The content of memory may be shifted one bit only and the operand size is restricted to a word.

For ASL, the operand is shifted left; the number of positions shifted is the shift count. Bits shifted out of the high order bit go to both the carry and the extend bits; zeroes are shifted into the low order bit. The overflow bit indicates if any sign changes occur during the shift.

ASL:

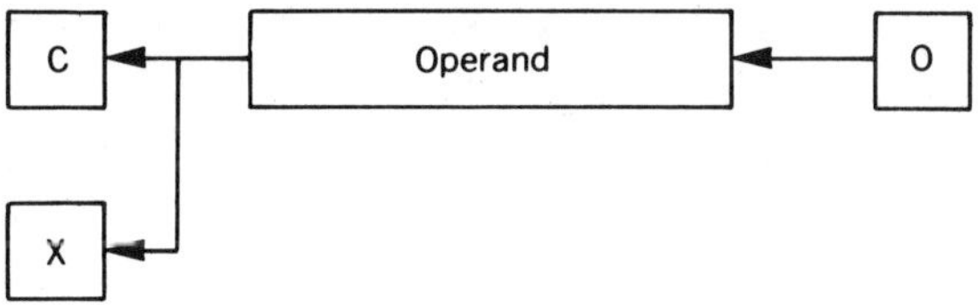

For ASR, the operand is shifted right; the number of positions shifted is the shift count. Bits shifted out of the low order bit go to both the carry and the extend bits; the sign bit is replicated into the high order bit.

ASR:

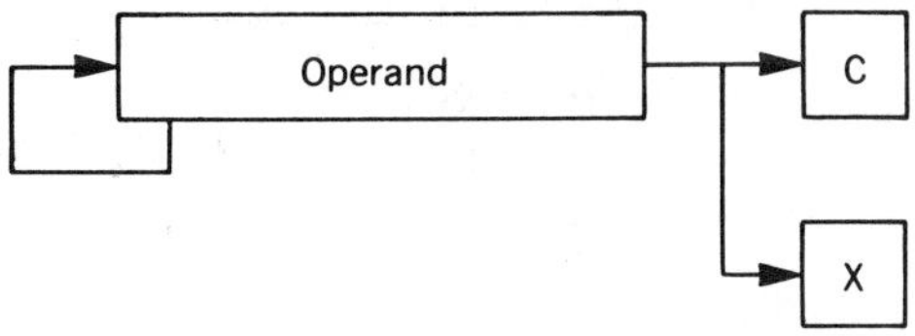

ASL, ASR **Arithmetic Shift** ASL, ASR

Condition Codes:

X	N	Z	V	C
*	*	*	*	*

N — Set if the most significant bit of the result is set. Cleared otherwise.
Z — Set if the result is zero. Cleared otherwise.
V — Set if the most significant bit is changed at any time during the shift operation. Cleared otherwise.
C — Set according to the last bit shifted out of the operand. Cleared for a shift count of zero.
X — Set according to the last bit shifted out of the operand. Unaffected for a shift count of zero.

Instruction Format (Register Shifts):

15	14	13	12	11 10 9	8	7 6	5	4	3	2 1 0
1	1	1	0	Count/ Register	dr	Size	i/r	0	0	Register

Instruction Fields (Register Shifts):

Count/Register field — Specifies shift count or register where count is located:
If i/r = 0, the shift count is specified in this field. The values 0, 1-7 represent a range of 8, 1 to 7 respectively.
If i/r = 1, the shift count (modulo 64) is contained in the data register specified in this field.

dr field — Specifies the direction of the shift:
0 — shift right.
1 — shift left.

Size field — Specifies the size of the operation:
00 — byte operation.
01 — word operation.
10 — long operation.

i/r field —
If i/r = 0, specifies immediate shift count.
If i/r = 1, specifies register shift count.

Register field — Specifies a data register whose content is to be shifted.

Instruction Format (Memory Shifts):

15	14	13	12	11	10	9	8	7	6	5 4 3 2 1 0
1	1	1	0	0	0	0	dr	1	1	Effective Address

Instruction Fields (Memory Shifts):

dr field — Specifies the direction of the shift:
0 — shift right.
1 — shift left.

Effective Address field — Specifies the operand to be shifted. Only memory alterable addressing modes are allowed.

Bcc — Branch Conditionally — Bcc

Operation: If cc then PC + d → PC
Bcc <label>

Assembler Syntax: Bcc <label>

Attributes: Size = (Byte, Word)

Description: If the specified condition is met, program execution continues at location (PC) + displacement. Displacement is a two's complement integer which counts the relative distance in bytes. The value in PC is the current (instruction) location plus two. If the 8-bit displacement in the instruction word is zero, then the 16-bit displacement (word immediately following the instruction) is used. "cc" may specify the following conditions:

CC — carry clear	LS — low or same
CS — carry set	LT — less
EQ — equal	MI — minus
GE — greater or equal	NE — not equal
GT — greater	PL — plus
HI — high	VC — no overflow
LE — less or equal	VS — overflow

Condition Codes:

X	N	Z	V	C
—	—	—	—	—

N — Not affected.
Z — Not affected.
V — Not affected.
C — Not affected.
X — Not affected.

Instruction Format:

15	14	13	12	11–9 (11 10 9)	8–0 (8 7 6 5 4 3 2 1 0)
0	1	1	0	Condition	8-bit Displacement
16-bit Displacement if 8-bit Displacement = 0					

Instruction Fields:

Condition field — One of fourteen conditions:

CC — 0100	LS — 0011
CS — 0101	LT — 1101
EQ — 0111	MI — 1011
GE — 1100	NE — 0110
GT — 1110	PL — 1010
HI — 0010	VC — 1000
LE — 1111	VS — 1001

8-bit Displacement field — Two's complement integer specifying the relative distance (in bytes) between the branch instruction and the next instruction to be executed if the condition is met.

16-bit Displacement field — Allows a larger displacement than 8 bits. Used only if the 8-bit displacement is equal to zero.

BCHG **Test a Bit and Change** BCHG

Operation: ~(<bit number> OF Destination) → Z;
~(<bit number> OF Destination) → <bit number > OF Destination
BCHG Dn OF <ea>
BCHG #<data> OF <ea>

Assembler Syntax: BCHG Dn,<ea>
BCHG #<data>,<ea>

Attributes: Size = (Word, Long)

Description: A bit in the destination operand is tested and the state of the specified bit is reflected in the Z condition code. After the test, the state of the specified bit is changed in the destination. If a data register is the destination, then the bit numbering is modulo 32 allowing bit manipulation on all bits in a data register. If a memory location is the destination, a byte is read from that location, the bit operation performed using the bit number modulo 8, and the byte written back to the location. The bit number for this operation may be specified in two different ways:

1. Immediate — the bit number is specified in a second word of the instruction.
2. Register — the bit number is contained in a data register specified in the instruction.

Condition Codes:

X	N	Z	V	C
—	—	*	—	—

N — Not affected.
Z — Set if the bit tested is zero. Cleared otherwise.
V — Not affected.
C — Not affected.
X — Not affected.

Instruction Format (Bit Number Dynamic):

15	14	13	12	11	10	9	8	7	6	5	4	3	2	1	0
0	0	0	0	Register			1	0	1	Effective Address					

Instruction Fields (Bit Number Dynamic):

Register field — Specifies the data register whose content is the bit number.
Effective Address field — Specifies the destination location. Only data alterable addressing modes are allowed.

Instruction Format (Bit Number Static):

15	14	13	12	11	10	9	8	7	6	5	4	3	2	1	0
0	0	0	0	1	0	0	0	0	1	Effective Address					
0	0	0	0	0	0	0	0	bit number							

Instruction Fields (Bit Number Static):

Effective Address field — Specifies the destination location. Only data alterable addressing modes are allowed.
bit number field — Specifies the bit numbers.

BCLR — Test a Bit and Clear — BCLR

Operation: ~(<bit number> OF Destination) → Z;
0 → <bit number> → OF Destination
BCLR Dn OF <ea>
BCLR #<data> OF <ea>

Assembler Syntax: BCLR Dn,<ea>
BCLR #<data>,<ea>

Attributes: Size = (Word, Long)

Description: A bit in the destination operand is tested and the state of the specified bit is reflected in the Z condition code. After the test, the specified bit is cleared in the destination. If a data register is the destination, then the bit numbering is modulo 32 allowing bit manipulation on all bits in a data register. If a memory location is the destination, a byte is read from that location, the bit operation performed using the bit number modulo 8, and the byte written back to the location. The bit number for this operation may be specified in two different ways:

1. Immediate — the bit number is specified in a second word of the instruction.
2. Register — the bit number is contained in a data register specified in the instruction.

Condition Codes:

X	N	Z	V	C
—	—	*	—	—

N — Not affected.
Z — Set if the bit tested is zero. Cleared otherwise.
V — Not affected.
C — Not affected.
X — Not affected.

Instruction Format (Bit Number Dynamic):

15	14	13	12	11	10	9	8	7	6	5	4	3	2	1	0
0	0	0	0	Register			1	1	0	Effective Address					

Instruction Fields (Bit Number Dynamic):

Register field — Specifies the data register whose content is the bit number.
Effective Address field — Specifies the destination location. Only data alterable addressing modes are allowed.

Instruction Format (Bit Number Static):

15	14	13	12	11	10	9	8	7	6	5	4	3	2	1	0
0	0	0	0	1	0	0	0	1	0	Effective Address					
bit number															

Instruction Fields (Bit Number Static):

Effective Address field — Specifies the destination location. Only data alterable addressing modes are allowed.
bit number field — Specifies the bit number.

BRA — Branch Always — BRA

Operation: PC + d → PC
BRA <label>

Assembler Syntax: BRA <label>

Attributes: Size = (Byte, Word)

Description: Program execution continues at location (PC) + displacement. Displacement is a two's complement integer which counts the relative distance in bytes. The value in PC is the current (instruction) location plus two. If the 8-bit displacement in the instruction word is zero, then the 16-bit displacement (word immediately following the instruction) is used.

Condition Codes:

X	N	Z	V	C
—	—	—	—	—

N — Not affected.
Z — Not affected.
V — Not affected.
C — Not affected.
X — Not affected.

Instruction Format:

15	14	13	12	11	10	9	8	7	6	5	4	3	2	1	0
0	1	1	0	0	0	0	0	8-bit Displacement							
16-bit Displacement if 8-bit Displacement = 0															

Instruction Fields:

8-bit Displacement field — Two's complement integer specifying the relative distance (in bytes) between the branch instruction and the next instruction to be executed if the condition is met.

16-bit Displacement field — Allows a larger displacement than 8 bits. Used only if the 8-bit displacement is equal to zero.

BSET Test a Bit and Set BSET

Operation: ~(<bit number>) OF Destination → Z
1 → <bit number> OF Destination
BSET Dn, OF <ea>
BSET #<data> OF <ea>

Assembler Syntax: BSET Dn, <ea>
BSET #<data>,<ea>

Attributes: Size = (Word, Long)

Description: A bit in the destination operand is tested and the state of the specified bit is reflected in the Z condition code. After the test, the specified bit is set in the destination. If a data register is the destination, then the bit numbering is modulo 32, allowing bit manipulation on all bits in a data register. If a memory location is the destination, a byte is read from that location, the bit operation performed using the bit number modulo 8, and the byte written back to the location. The bit number for this operation may be specified in two different ways:

1. Immediate — the bit number is specified in a second word of the instruction.
2. Register — the bit number is contained in a data register specified in the instruction.

Condition Codes:

X	N	Z	V	C
—	—	*	—	—

N — Not affected.
Z — Set if the bit tested is zero. Cleared otherwise.
V — Not affected.
C — Not affected.
X — Not affected.

Instruction Format (Bit Number Dynamic):

15	14	13	12	11	10	9	8	7	6	5	4	3	2	1	0
0	0	0	0	Register			1	1	1	Effective Address					

Instruction Fields (Bit Number Dynamic):

Register field — Specifies the data register whose content is the bit number.
Effective Address field — Specifies the destination location. Only data alterable addressing modes are allowed.

Instruction Format (Bit Number Static):

15	14	13	12	11	10	9	8	7	6	5	4	3	2	1	0
0	0	0	0	1	0	0	0	1	1	Effective Address					
bit number															

Instruction Fields (Bit Number Static):

Effective Address field — Specifies the destination location. Only data alterable addressing modes are allowed.
bit number field — Specifies the bit number.

BSR Branch to Subroutine BSR

Operation: PC → SP@-; PC + d → PC
BSR <label>

Assembler Syntax: BSR <label>

Attributes: Size = (Byte, Word)

Description: The address of the instruction immediately following the BSR instruction is pushed onto the system stack. Program execution then continues at location (PC) + displacement. Displacement is a two's complement integer which counts the relative distance in bytes. The value in PC is the current (instruction) location plus two. If the 8-bit displacement in the instruction word is zero, then the 16-bit displacement (word immediately following the instruction) is used.

Condition Codes:

X	N	Z	V	C
—	—	—	—	—

N — Not affected.
Z — Not affected.
V — Not affected.
C — Not affected.
X — Not affected.

Instruction Format:

15	14	13	12	11	10	9	8	7	6	5	4	3	2	1	0
0	1	1	0	0	0	0	1	8-bit Displacement							
16-bit Displacement if 8-bit Displacement = 0															

Instruction Fields:

8-bit Displacement field — Two's complement integer specifying the relative distance (in bytes) between the branch instruction and the next instruction to be executed if the condition is met.

16-bit Displacement field — Allows a larger displacement than 8 bits. Used only if the 8-bit displacement is equal to zero.

BTST Test a Bit BTST

Operation: ~(<bit number> OF Destination) → Z
BTST Dn OF <ea>
BTST #<data> OF <ea>

Assembler Syntax: BTST Dn,<ea>
BTST #<data>,<ea>

Attributes: Size = (Word, Long)

Description: A bit in the destination operand is tested and the state of the specified bit is reflected in the Z condition code. If a data register is the destination, then the bit numbering is modulo 32, allowing bit manipulation on all bits in a data register. If a memory location is the destination, a byte is read from that location, and the bit operation performed using the bit number modulo 8. The bit number for this operation may be specified in two different ways:

1. Immediate — the bit number is specified in a second word of the instruction.
2. Register — the bit number is contained in a data register specified in the instruction.

Condition Codes:

X	N	Z	V	C
—	—	*	—	—

N — Not affected.
Z — Set if the bit tested is zero. Cleared otherwise.
V — Not affected.
C — Not affected.
X — Not affected.

Instruction Format (Bit Number Dynamic):

15	14	13	12	11	10	9	8	7	6	5	4	3	2	1	0
0	0	0	0	Register			1	0	0	Effective Address					

Instruction Fields (Bit Number Dynamic):

Register field — Specifies the data register whose content is the bit number.
Effective Address field — Specifies the destination location. Only data addressing modes are allowed.

Instruction Format (Bit Number Static):

15	14	13	12	11	10	9	8	7	6	5	4	3	2	1	0
0	0	0	0	1	0	0	0	0	0	Effective Address					
bit number															

Instruction Fields (Bit Number Static):

Effective Address field — Specifies the destination location. Only data addressing modes are allowed, except the immediate addressing mode is not allowed.
bit number field — Specifies the bit number.

CHK — Check Register against Bounds — CHK

Operation: If Dn <0 or Dn> (<ea>) then TRAP
CHK Dn WITH <ea>

Assembler Syntax: CHK <ea>,Dn

Attributes: Size = (Word)

Description: The content of the low order word in the data register specified in the instruction is examined, and compared to the upper bound. The upper bound is a two's complement integer. If the register value is less than zero or greater than the upper bound contained in the operand word, then the processor initiates exception processing. The vector number is generated to reference the CHK instruction exception vector.

Condition Codes:

X	N	Z	V	C
—	*	U	U	U

N — Set if Dn <0; cleared if Dn> (<ea>). Undefined otherwise.
Z — Undefined.
V — Undefined.
C — Undefined.
X — Not affected.

Instruction Format:

15	14	13	12	11	10	9	8	7	6	5	4	3	2	1	0
0	1	0	0	Register			1	1	0	Effective Address					

Instruction Fields:

Register field — Specifies the data register whose content is checked.
Effective Address field — Specifies the upper bound operand word. Only data addressing modes are allowed.

CLR — Clear an Operand — CLR

Operation: 0 → Destination
CLR <ea>

Assembler Syntax: CLR <ea>

Attributes: Size = (Byte, Word, Long)

Description: The destination is cleared to all zero bits. The size of the operation may be specified to be byte, word or long.

Condition Codes:

X	N	Z	V	C
—	0	1	0	0

N — Always cleared.
Z — Always set.
V — Always cleared.
C — Always cleared.
X — Not affected.

Instruction Format:

15	14	13	12	11	10	9	8	7	6	5	4	3	2	1	0
0	1	0	0	0	0	1	0	Size		Effective Address					

Instruction Fields:

Size field — Specifies the size of the operation:
- 00 — byte operation.
- 01 — word operation.
- 10 — long operation.

Effective Address field — Specifies the destination location. Only data alterable addresses are allowed.

CMP Compare CMP

Operation: (Destination) - (Source)
CMP <ea> TO Dn

Assembler Syntax: CMP <ea>,Dn

Attributes: Size = (Byte, Word, Long)

Description: Subtract the source operand from the destination operand, and set the condition codes according to the result; the destination location is not changed. The size of the operation may be specified to be byte, word or long.

Condition Codes:

X	N	Z	V	C
—	*	*	*	*

N — Set if the result is negative. Cleared otherwise.
Z — Set if the result is zero. Cleared otherwise.
V — Set if an overflow is generated. Cleared otherwise.
C — Set if a borrow is generated. Cleared otherwise.
X — Not affected.

Instruction Format:

15	14	13	12	11	10	9	8	7	6	5	4	3	2	1	0
1	0	1	1	Register			Op-Mode			Effective Address					

Instruction Fields:

Register field — Specifies the destination data register.

Op-Mode field —

Byte	Word	Long	Operation
000	001	010	(<Dn>) - (<ea>)

Effective Address field — Specifies the source operand. All addressing modes are allowed. If the operation size is byte, then the address register direct addressing mode is not allowed.

CMPA Compare Address CMPA

Operation: (Destination) - (Source)
CMP <ea> TO An

Assembler Syntax: CMPA <ea>,An

Attributes: Size = (Word, Long)

Description: Subtract the source operand from the destination address register, and set the condition codes according to the result; the address register is not changed. The size of the operation may be specified to be word or long.

Condition Codes:

X	N	Z	V	C
—	*	*	*	*

N — Set if the result is negative. Cleared otherwise.
Z — Set if the result is zero. Cleared otherwise.
V — Set if an overflow is generated. Cleared otherwise.
C — Set if a borrow is generated. Cleared otherwise.
X — Not affected.

Instruction Format:

15	14	13	12	11	10	9	8	7	6	5	4	3	2	1	0
1	0	1	1	Register			Op-Mode			Effective Address					

Instruction Fields:

Register field — Specifies the destination address register.

Op-Mode field — Specifies the size of the operation:

011 — word operation. The source operand is sign-extended to a long operand and the operation is performed on the address register using all 32 bits.

111 — long operation.

Effective Address field — Specifies the source operand. All addressing modes are allowed.

CMPI — Compare Immediate — CMPI

Operation: (Destination) - Immediate Data
CMP #<data> TO <ea>

Assembler Syntax: CMPI #<data>,<ea>

Attributes: Size = (Byte, Word, Long)

Description: Subtract the immediate data from the destination operand, and set the condition codes according to the result; the destination location is not changed. The size of the operation may be specified to be byte, word or long. The size of the immediate data matches the operation size.

Condition Codes:

X	N	Z	V	C
—	*	*	*	*

N — Set if the result is negative. Cleared otherwise.
Z — Set if the result is zero. Cleared otherwise.
V — Set if an overflow is generated. Cleared otherwise.
C — Set if a borrow is generated. Cleared otherwise.
X — Not affected.

Instruction Format:

15	14	13	12	11	10	9	8	7	6	5	4	3	2	1	0
0	0	0	0	1	1	0	0	Size		Effective Address					
Word Data (16 bits)								Byte Data (8 bits)							
Long Data (32 bits, including previous word)															

Instruction Fields:

Size field — Specifies the size of the operation:
- 00 — byte operation.
- 01 — word operation.
- 10 — long operation.

Effective Address field — Specifies the destination operand. Only data alterable addressing modes are allowed.

Immediate field — (Data immediately following the instruction):
- If size = 00, then the data is the low order byte of the immediate word.
- If size = 01, then the data is the entire immediate word.
- If size = 10, then the data is the next two immediate words.

CMPM Compare Memory CMPM

Operation: (Destination) - (Source)
CMP Ay@+ TO Ax@+

Assembler Syntax: CMPM (Ay)+,(Ax)+

Attributes: Size = (Byte, Word, Long)

Description: Subtract the source operand from the destination operand, and set the condition codes according to the results; the destination location is not changed. The operands are always addressed with the postincrement addressing mode using the address registers specified in the instruction. The size of the operation may be specified to be byte, word or long.

Condition Codes:

X	N	Z	V	C
—	*	*	*	*

N — Set if the result is negative. Cleared otherwise.
Z — Set if the result is zero. Cleared otherwise.
V — Set if an overflow is generated. Cleared otherwise.
C — Set if a borrow is generated. Cleared otherwise.
X — Not affected.

Instruction Format:

15	14	13	12	11 10 9	8	7 6	5	4	3	2 1 0
1	0	1	1	Register Rx	1	Size	0	0	1	Register Ry

Instruction Fields:

Register Rx field — (always the destination) Specifies an address register for the postincrement addressing mode.

Size field — Specifies the size of the operation:
- 00 — byte operation.
- 01 — word operation.
- 10 — long operation.

Register Ry field — (always the source) Specifies an address register for the postincrement addressing mode.

DBcc — Test Condition, Decrement and Branch — DBcc

Operation: If ~cc then Dn - 1 → Dn; if Dn ≠ -1 then PC + d → PC
DBcc Dn, <label>

Assembler Syntax: DBcc Dn, <label>

Description: This instruction is a looping primitive of three parameters: a condition, a data register, and a displacement. The instruction first tests the condition to determine if the termination condition for the loop has been met, and if so, no operation is performed. If the termination condition is not true, the counter data register is decremented by one. If the result is -1, the counter is exhausted, and execution continues with the next instruction. If the result is not equal to -1, execution continues at the location indicated by the current value of PC plus the sign-extended 16-bit displacement. The value in PC is the address of the displacement word. "cc" may specify the following conditions:

CC	0100 — carry clear	LS	0011 — low or same
CS	0101 — carry set	LT	1101 — less
EQ	0111 — equal	MI	1011 — minus
F*	0001 — never true	NE	0110 — not equal
GE	1100 — greater or equal	PL	1010 — plus
GT	1110 — greater	T	0000 — always true
HI	0010 — high	VC	1000 — no overflow
LE	1111 — less or equal	VS	1001 — overflow

Condition Codes:

X	N	Z	V	C
—	—	—	—	—

N — Not affected.
Z — Not affected.
V — Not affected.
C — Not affected.
X — Not affected.

Instruction Format:

15	14	13	12	11	10	9	8	7	6	5	4	3	2	1	0
0	1	0	1	Condition				1	1	0	0	1	Register		
Displacement															

Instruction Fields:

Condition field — One of the sixteen conditions discussed in description.
Register field — Specifies the data register which is the counter.
Displacement field — Specifies the distance of the branch (in bytes).

* assembler accepts DBRA for this condition

DIVS Signed Divide DIVS

Operation: (Destination)/(Source) → Destination
DIVS Dn BY <ea>

Assembler Syntax: DIVS <ea>,Dn

Attributes: Size = (Word)

Description: Divide the destination operand by the source operand and store the result in the destination. The destination operand is a long operand (32-bits) and the source operand is a word operand (16-bits). The operation is performed using signed arithmetic. The result is a 32-bit result such that:

1. The quotient is in the lower word (least signifcant 16-bits).
2. The remainder is in the upper word (most significant 16-bits).

The sign of the remainder is always the same as the dividend unless the remainder is equal to zero. Two special conditions may arise:

1. Division by zero causes a trap.
2. Overflow may be detected and set before completion of the instruction. If overflow is detected, the condition is flagged but the operands are unaffected.

Condition Codes:

X	N	Z	V	C
—	*	*	*	0

N — Set if the quotient is negative. Cleared otherwise. Undefined if overflow.
Z — Set if the quotient is zero. Cleared otherwise. Undefined if overflow.
V — Set if division overflow is detected. Cleared otherwise.
C — Always cleared.
X — Not affected.

Instruction Format:

15	14	13	12	11	10	9	8	7	6	5	4	3	2	1	0
1	0	0	0	Register			1	1	1	Effective Address					

Instruction Fields:

Register field — Specifies any of the eight data registers. This field always specifies the destination operand.

Effective Address field — Specifies the source operand. Only data addressing modes are allowed.

DIVU Unsigned Divide DIVU

Operation: (Destination)/(Source) →Destination
DIVU Dn BY <ea>

Assembler Syntax: DIVU <ea>,Dn

Attributes: Size = (Word)

Description: Divide the destination operand by the source operand and store the result in the destination. The destination operand is a long operand (32-bits) and the source operand is a word (16-bit) operand. The operation is performed using unsigned arithmetic. The result is a 32-bit result such that:

1. The quotient is in the lower word (least significant 16-bits).
2. The remainder is in the upper word (most significant 16-bits)

Two special conditions may arise:

1. Division by zero causes a trap.
2. Overflow may be detected and set before completion of the instruction. If overflow is detected, the condition is flagged but the operands are unaffected.

Condition Codes:

X	N	Z	V	C
—	*	*	*	0

N — Set if the most significant bit of the quotient is set. Cleared otherwise. Undefined if overflow.
Z — Set if the quotient is zero. Cleared otherwise. Undefined if overflow.
V — Set if division overflow is detected. Cleared otherwise.
C — Always cleared.
X — Not affected.

Instruction Format:

15	14	13	12	11	10	9	8	7	6	5	4	3	2	1	0
1	0	0	0	Register			0	1	1	Effective Address					

Instruction Fields:

Register field — Specifies any of the eight data registers. This field always specifies the destination operand.

Effective Address field — Specifies the source operand. Only data addressing modes are allowed.

EOR — Exclusive OR Logical — EOR

Operation: (Destination) ⊕ (Source) → Destination
EOR Dn TO <ea>

Assembler Syntax: EOR Dn,<ea>

Attributes: Size = (Byte, Word, Long)

Description: Exclusive OR the source operand to the destination operand, and store the result in the destination location. The size of the operation may be specified to be byte, word or long. This operation is restricted to data registers as the source operand. The destination operand is specified in the effective address field.

Condition Codes:

X	N	Z	V	C
—	*	*	0	0

N — Set if the most significant bit of the result is set. Cleared otherwise.
Z — Set if the result is zero. Cleared otherwise.
V — Always cleared.
C — Always cleared.
X — Not affected.

Instruction Format:

15	14	13	12	11	10	9	8	7	6	5	4	3	2	1	0
1	0	1	1	Register			Op-Mode			Effective Address					

Instruction Fields:

Register field — Specifies any of the eight data registers.

Op-Mode field —

Byte	**Word**	**Long**	**Operation**
100	101	110	(<ea>) ⊕ (<Dx>) → <ea>

Effective Address field — Specifies the destination operand. Only data alterable addressing modes are allowed.

EORI — Exclusive OR Immediate — EORI

Operation: (Destination) ⊕ Immediate Data → Destination
EORI #<data> TO <ea>

Assembler Syntax: EORI #<data>,<ea>

Attributes: Size = (Byte, Word, Long)

Description: Exclusive OR the immediate data to the destination operand, and store the result in the destination location. The size of the operation may be specified to be byte, word or long. The immediate data matches the operation size. Access to the status register is available in two modes:

1. If the operation size is byte, the operation affects only the low order byte of the status register which contains the condition codes.
2. If the operation size is word, the operation is performed on the whole status register. This is a privileged operation.

Condition Codes:

X	N	Z	V	C
—	*	*	0	0

N — Set if the most significant bit of the result is set. Cleared otherwise.
Z — Set if the result is zero. Cleared otherwise.
V — Always cleared.
C — Always cleared.
X — Not affected.

When accessing the status register, the condition codes are affected according to the operation.

Instruction Format:

15	14	13	12	11	10	9	8	7	6	5	4	3	2	1	0
0	0	0	0	1	0	1	0	Size		Effective Address					
Word Data (16 bits)								Byte Data (8 bits)							
Long Data (32 bits, including previous word)															

Instruction Fields:

Size field — Specifies the size of the operation:
- 00 — byte operation.
- 01 — word operation.
- 10 — long operation.

Effective Address field — Specifies the destination operand. Only data alterable or the status register addressing modes are allowed.

Immediate field — (Data immediately following the instruction):
- If size = 00, then the data is the low order byte of the immediate word.
- If size = 01, then the data is the entire immediate word.
- If size = 10, then the data is the next two immediate words.

EXG — Exchange Registers — EXG

Operation: Rx↔Ry
EXG Rx WITH Ry

Assembler Syntax: EXG Rx,Ry

Attributes: Size = (Long)

Description: Exchange the contents of two registers. This exchange is always a long (32-bit) operation. Exchange works in three modes:

1. exchange data registers.
2. exchange address registers.
3. exchange a data register and an address register

Condition Codes:

X	N	Z	V	C
—	—	—	—	—

N — Not affected.
Z — Not affected.
V — Not affected.
C — Not affected.
X — Not affected.

Instruction Format:

15	14	13	12	11	10	9	8	7	6	5	4	3	2	1	0
1	1	0	0	Register Rx			1	Op-Mode					Register Ry		

Instruction Fields:

Register Rx field — Specifies either a data register or an address register depending on the mode. If the exchange is between data and address registers, this field always specifies the data register.

Op-Mode field — Specifies whether exchanging:
01000 — data registers.
01001 — address registers.
10001 — data register and address register.

Register Ry field — Specifies either a data register or an address register depending on the mode. If the exchange is between data and address registers, this field always specifies the address register.

EXT Sign Extend EXT

Operation: (Destination) Sign-extended → Destination
EXT Dn

Assembler Syntax: EXT Dn

Attributes: Size = (Word, Long)

Description: Extend the sign bit of a data register from a byte to a word or from a word to a long operand depending on the size selected. If the operation is word sized, bit [7] of the designated data register is copied to bits [15:8] of that data register. If the operation is long sized, bit [15] of the designated data register is copied to bits [31:16] of that data register.

Condition Codes:

X	N	Z	V	C
—	*	*	0	0

N — Set if the result is negative. Cleared otherwise.
Z — Set if the result is zero. Cleared otherwise.
V — Always cleared.
C — Always cleared.
X — Not affected.

Instruction Format:

15	14	13	12	11	10	9	8 7 6	5	4	3	2 1 0
0	1	0	0	1	0	0	Op-Mode	0	0	0	Register

Instruction Fields:

Op-Mode Field — Specifies the size of the sign-extension operation:
  010 — Sign-extend low order byte of data register to word.
  011 — Sign-extend low order word of data register to long.
Register field — Specifies the data register whose content is to be sign-extended.

JMP — Jump — JMP

Operation: Destination → PC
JMP <ea>

Assembler Syntax: JMP <ea>

Attributes: Unsized

Description: Program execution continues at the address specified by the instruction. The address is specified by the control addressing modes.

Condition Codes:

X	N	Z	V	C
—	—	—	—	—

N — Not affected.
Z — Not affected.
V — Not affected.
C — Not affected.
X — Not affected.

Instruction Format:

15	14	13	12	11	10	9	8	7	6	5	4	3	2	1	0
0	1	0	0	1	1	1	0	1	1	Effective Address					

Instruction Fields:

Effective Address field — Specifies the address of the next instruction. Only control addressing modes are allowed.

JSR — Jump to Subroutine — JSR

Operation: PC →SP@–; Destination →PC
JSR <ea>

Assembler Syntax: JSR <ea>

Attributes: Unsized

Description: The address of the instruction immediately following the JSR instruction is pushed onto the system stack. Program execution then continues at the address specified in the instruction.

Condition Codes:

X	N	Z	V	C
—	—	—	—	—

N — Not affected.
Z — Not affected.
V — Not affected.
C — Not affected.
X — Not affected.

Instruction Format:

15	14	13	12	11	10	9	8	7	6	5	4	3	2	1	0
0	1	0	0	1	1	1	0	1	0	Effective Address					

Instruction Fields:

Effective Address field — Specifies the address of the next instruction. Only control addressing modes are allowed.

LEA Load Effective Address LEA

Operation: Destination → An
LEA <ea> INTO An

Assembler Syntax: LEA <ea>,An

Attributes: Size = (Long)

Description: The effective address is loaded into the specified address register. All 32 bits of the address register are affected by this instruction.

Condition Codes:

X	N	Z	V	C
—	—	—	—	—

N — Not affected.
Z — Not affected.
V — Not affected.
C — Not affected.
X — Not affected.

Instruction Format:

15	14	13	12	11	10	9	8	7	6	5	4	3	2	1	0
0	1	0	0	Register			1	1	1	Effective Address					

Instruction Fields:

Register field — Specifies the address register which is to be loaded with the effective address.

Effective Address field — Specifies the address to be loaded into the address register. Only control addressing modes are allowed.

LINK — Link and Allocate — LINK

Operation: An → SP@–; SP → An; SP + d → SP
LINK An, #<displacement>

Assembler Syntax: LINK An,#<displacement>

Attributes: Unsized

Description: The current content of the specified address register is pushed onto the stack. After the push, the address register is loaded from the updated stack pointer. Finally, the sign-extended displacement is added to the stack pointer. The content of the address register occupies two words on the stack.
Note: LINK and UNLK can be used to maintain a linked list of local data and parameter areas on the stack for nested subroutine calls.

Condition Codes:

X	N	Z	V	C
—	—	—	—	—

N — Not affected.
Z — Not affected.
V — Not affected.
C — Not affected.
X — Not affected.

Instruction Format:

15	14	13	12	11	10	9	8	7	6	5	4	3	2	1	0
0	1	0	0	1	1	1	0	0	1	0	1	0	Register		
Displacement															

Instruction Fields:

Register field — Specifies the address register through which the link is to be constructed.

Displacement field — Specifies the two's complement integer which is to be added to the stack pointer.

LSL, LSR — Logical Shift — LSL, LSR

Operation: (Destination) Shifted by <count> → Destination
LSd Dy BY Dx
LSd Dy BY #<data>
LSd <ea>

Assembler Syntax: LSd Dx,Dy
LSd #<data>,Dy
LSd <ea>

Attributes: Size = (Byte, Word, Long)

Description: Shift the bits of the operand in the direction specified. The carry bit receives the last bit shifted out of the operand. The shift count for the shifting of a register may be specified in two different ways:

1. Immediate — the shift count is specified in the instruction (shift range, 1-8).
2. Register — the shift count is contained in a data register specified in the instruction.

The size of the operation may be specified to be byte, word or long. The content of memory may be shifted one bit only where the operand size is restricted to a word.

For LSL, the operand is shifted left; the number of positions shifted is the shift count. Bits shifted out of the high order bit go to both the carry and the extend bits; zeroes are shifted into the low order bit.

LSL:

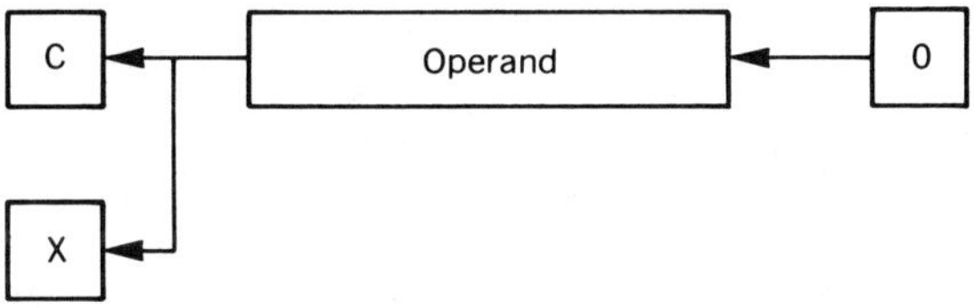

For LSR, the operand is shifted right; the number of positions shifted is the shift count. Bits shifted out of the low order bit go to both the carry and the extend bits; zeroes are shifted into the high order bit.

LSR:

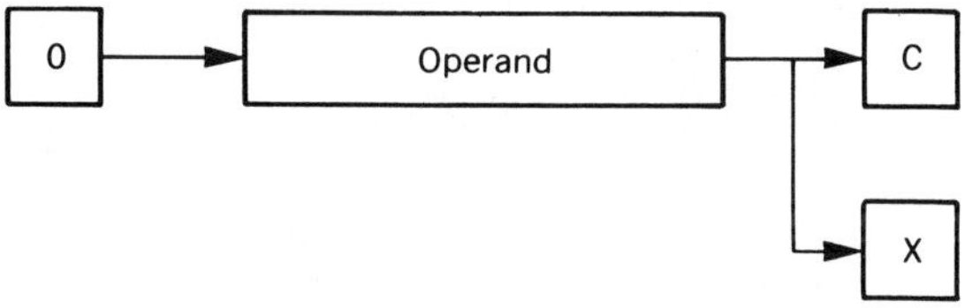

LSL, LSR — Logical Shift — LSL, LSR

Condition Codes:

X	N	Z	V	C
*	*	*	0	*

N — Set if the result is negative. Cleared otherwise.
Z — Set if the result is zero. Cleared otherwise.
V — Always cleared.
C — Set according to the last bit shifted out of the operand. Cleared for a shift count of zero.
X — Set according to the last bit shifted out of the operand. Unaffected for a shift count of zero.

Instruction Format (Register Shifts):

15	14	13	12	11 10 9	8	7 6	5	4	3	2 1 0
1	1	1	0	Count/ Register	dr	Size	i/r	0	1	Register

Instruction Fields (Register Shifts):

Count/Register field —
 If i/r = 0, the shift count is specified in this field. The values 0, 1-7 represent a range of 8, 1 to 7 respectively.
 If i/r = 1, the shift count (modulo 64) is contained in the data register specified in this field.

dr field — Specifies the direction of the shift:
 0 — shift right.
 1 — shift left.

Size field — Specifies the size of the operation:
 00 — byte operation.
 01 — word operation.
 10 — long operation.

i/r field —
 If i/r = 0, specifies immediate shift count.
 If i/r = 1, specifies register shift count.

Register field — Specifies a data register whose content is to be shifted.

Instruction Format (Memory Shifts):

15	14	13	12	11	10	9	8	7	6	5 4 3 2 1 0
1	1	1	0	0	0	1	dr	1	1	Effective Address

Instruction Fields (Memory Shifts):

dr field — Specifies the direction of the shift:
 0 — shift right.
 1 — shift left.

Effective Address field — Specifies the operand to be shifted. Only memory alterable addressing modes are allowed.

MOVE Move Data from Source to Destination MOVE

Operation: (Source) → Destination
MOVE <ea> TO <ea>

Assembler Syntax: MOVE <ea>,<ea>

Attributes: Size = (Byte, Word, Long)

Description: Move the content of the source to the destination location. The data is examined as it is moved, and the condition codes set accordingly. The size of the operation may be specified to be byte, word or long.

Condition Codes:

X	N	Z	V	C
—	*	*	0	0

N — Set if the result is negative. Cleared otherwise.
Z — Set if the result is zero. Cleared otherwise.
V — Always cleared.
C — Always cleared.
X — Not affected.

Instruction Format:

15	14	13	12	11	10	9	8	7	6	5	4	3	2	1	0
				Destination						Source					
0	0	Size		Register			Mode			Mode			Register		

Instruction Fields:

Size field — Specifies the size of the operand to be moved:
- 01 — byte operation.
- 11 — word operation.
- 10 — long operation.

Destination Effective Address field — Specifies the destination location. Only data alterable addressing modes are allowed.

Source Effective Address field — Specifies the source operand. All addressing modes are allowed. If the operation size is byte, the address register direct addressing mode is not allowed.

MOVE to CCR — Move to Condition Codes — MOVE to CCR

Operation: (Source) → CCR
MOVE <ea> TO CCR

Assembler Syntax: MOVE <ea>,CCR

Attributes: Size = (Word)

Description: The content of the source operand is moved to the condition codes. The source operand is a word, but only the low order byte is used to update the condition codes.

Condition Codes:

X	N	Z	V	C
*	*	*	*	*

N — Set according to the source operand.
Z — Set according to the source operand.
V — Set according to the source operand.
C — Set according to the source operand.
X — Set according to the source operand.

Instruction Format:

15	14	13	12	11	10	9	8	7	6	5	4	3	2	1	0
0	1	0	0	0	1	0	0	1	1	Effective Address					

Instruction Fields:

Effective Address field — Specifies the location of the source operand. Only data addressing modes are allowed.

MOVE to SR

Move to the Status Register

MOVE to SR

Operation: (Source) → SR
MOVE <ea> TO SR

Assembler Syntax: MOVE <ea>,SR

Attributes: Size = (Word)

Description: The content of the source operand is moved to the status register. The source operand is a word, and all bits of the status register are affected.
Note: This is a privileged instruction.

Condition Codes:

X	N	Z	V	C
*	*	*	*	*

N — Set according to the source operand.
Z — Set according to the source operand.
V — Set according to the source operand.
C — Set according to the source operand.
X — Set according to the source operand.

Instruction Format:

15	14	13	12	11	10	9	8	7	6	5	4	3	2	1	0
0	1	0	0	0	1	1	0	1	1	Effective Address					

Instruction Fields:

Effective Address field — Specifies the location of the source operand. Only data addressing modes are allowed.

MOVE from SR — Move from the Status Register — MOVE from SR

Operation: SR → Destination
MOVE SR TO <ea>

Assembler Syntax: MOVE SR,<ea>

Attributes: Size = (Word)

Description: The content of the status register is moved to the destination location. The operand size is a word.

Condition Codes:

X	N	Z	V	C
—	—	—	—	—

N — Not affected.
Z — Not affected.
V — Not affected.
C — Not affected.
X — Not affected.

Instruction Format:

15	14	13	12	11	10	9	8	7	6	5	4	3	2	1	0
0	1	0	0	0	0	0	0	1	1	Effective Address					

Instruction Fields:

Effective Address field — Specifies the destination location. Only data alterable addressing modes are allowed.

MOVE USP — Move User Stack Pointer — MOVE USP

Operation: USP → An;
An → USP
MOVE USP TO An
MOVE An TO USP

Assembler Syntax: MOVE USP,An
MOVE An,USP

Attributes: Size = (Long)

Description: The contents of the user stack pointer are transferred to or from the specified address register. This instruction is useful for supervisor state programs. **Note:** This is a privileged instruction.

Condition Codes:

X	N	Z	V	C
—	—	—	—	—

N — Not affected.
Z — Not affected.
V — Not affected.
C — Not affected.
X — Not affected.

Instruction Format:

15	14	13	12	11	10	9	8	7	6	5	4	3	2	1	0
0	1	0	0	1	1	1	0	0	1	1	0	dr	Register		

Instruction Fields:

dr field — Specifies the direction of transfer:
- 0 — transfer the address register to the USP.
- 1 — transfer the USP to the address register.

Register field — Specifies the address register to or from which the user stack Pointer is to be transferred.

MOVEA **Move Address** MOVEA

Operation: (Source) → Destination
MOVE <ea> TO An

Assembler Syntax: MOVEA <ea>,An

Attributes: Size = (Word, Long)

Description: Move the content of the source to the destination address register. The size of the operation may be specified to be word or long.

Condition Codes:

X	N	Z	V	C
—	—	—	—	—

N — Not affected.
Z — Not affected.
V — Not affected.
C — Not affected.
X — Not affected.

Instruction Format:

15	14	13	12	11	10	9	8	7	6	5	4	3	2	1	0
				Destination						Source					
0	0	Size		Register			0	0	1	Mode			Register		

Instruction Fields:

Size field — Specifies the size of the operand to be moved:
 11 — Word operation. The source operand is sign-extended to a long operand and all 32 bits are loaded into the address register.
 10 — Long operation.

Destination Register field — Specifies the destination address register.

Source Effective Address field — Specifies the location of the source operand. All addressing modes are allowed.

MOVEM Move Multiple Registers MOVEM

Operation: Registers → Destination
(Source) → Registers
MOVEM <register list> TO <ea>
MOVEM <ea> TO <register list>

Assembler Syntax: MOVEM <register list>,<ea>
MOVEM <ea>,<register list>

Attributes: Size = (Word, Long)

Description: Selected registers are transferred to or from consecutive memory locations starting at the location specified by the effective address. A register is transferred if the bit corresponding to that register is set in the mask field. The instruction selects how much of each register is transferred; either the entire long word can be moved, or just the low order word. In the case of a word transfer to the registers, each word is sign-extended to 32 bits and the resulting long word loaded into the associated register.

MOVEM allows three forms of address modes: the control modes, the predecrement mode, or the postincrement mode. If the effective address is in one of the control modes, the registers are transferred starting at the specified address and up through higher addresses. The order of transfer is from data register 0 to data register 7, then from address register 0 to address register 7.

If the effective address is in the predecrement mode, only a register to memory operation is allowed. The registers are stored starting at the specified address minus two and down through lower addresses. The order of storing is from address register 7 to address register 0, then from data register 7 to data register 0. The decremented address register is updated to contain the address of the last word stored.

If the effective address is in the postincrement mode, only a memory to register operation is allowed. The registers are loaded starting at the specified address and up through higher addresses. The order of loading is the same as for the control mode addressing. The incremented address register is updated to contain the address of the last word loaded plus two.

Condition Codes:

X	N	Z	V	C
—	—	—	—	—

N — Not affected.
Z — Not affected.
V — Not affected.
C — Not affected.
X — Not affected.

MOVEM Move Multiple Registers MOVEM

Instruction Format:

15	14	13	12	11	10	9	8	7	6	5	4	3	2	1	0
0	1	0	0	1	dr	0	0	1	Sz	Effective Address					
Register List Mask															

Instruction Fields:

dr field:

Specifies the direction of the transfer:

0 — register to memory.

1 — memory to register.

Sz field — Specifies the size of the registers being transferred:

0 — word transfer.

1 — long transfer.

Effective Address field — Specifies the memory address to or from which the registers are to be moved.

For register to memory transfer, only control alterable addressing modes, or the predecrement addressing mode are allowed.

For memory to register transfer, only control addressing modes, or the postincrement addressing mode are allowed.

Register List Mask field — Specifies which registers are to be transferred. The low order bit corresponds to the first register to be transferred; the high bit corresponds to the last register to be transferred. Thus, both for control modes and for the postincrement mode addresses, the mask correspondence is

15	14	13	12	11	10	9	8	7	6	5	4	3	2	1	0
A7	A6	A5	A4	A3	A2	A1	A0	D7	D6	D5	D4	D3	D2	D1	D0

while for the predecrement mode addresses, the mask correspondence is

15	14	13	12	11	10	9	8	7	6	5	4	3	2	1	0
D0	D1	D2	D3	D4	D5	D6	D7	A0	A1	A2	A3	A4	A5	A6	A7

MOVEP Move Peripheral Data MOVEP

Operation: (Source) → Destination
MOVEP Dx TO Ay@(d)
MOVEP Ay@(d) TO Dx

Assembler Syntax: MOVE Dx,d(Ay)
MOVEP d(Ay),Dx

Attributes: Size = (Word, Long)

Description: Data is transferred between a data register and alternate bytes of memory, starting at the location specified, and incrementing by two. The high order byte of the data register is transferred first, and the low order byte is transferred last. The memory address is specified using the address register indirect plus displacement addressing mode. If the address is even, all the transfers are made on the high order half of the data bus; if the address is odd, all the transfers are made on the low order half of the data bus.

Example: Long transfer to/from an even address.

Byte organization in register

31 – 24	23 – 16	15 – 8	7 – 0
hi-order	mid-upper	mid-lower	low-order

Byte organization in memory (low address at top)

15 14 13 12 11 10 9 8	7 6 5 4 3 2 1 0
hi-order	
mid-upper	
mid-lower	
low-order	

Example: Word transfer to/from an odd address.

Byte organization in register

31 – 24	23 – 16	15 – 8	7 – 0
		hi-order	low-order

Byte organization in memory (low address at top)

15 14 13 12 11 10 9 8	7 6 5 4 3 2 1 0
	hi-order
	low-order

MOVEP Move Peripheral Data MOVEP

Condition Codes:

X	N	Z	V	C
—	—	—	—	—

N — Not affected.
Z — Not affected.
V — Not affected.
C — Not affected.
X — Not affected.

Instruction Format:

15	14	13	12	11 10 9	8 7 6	5	4	3	2 1 0
0	0	0	0	Data Register	Op-Mode	0	0	1	Address Register
Displacement									

Instruction Fields:

Data Register field — Specifies the data register to or from which the data is to be transferred.

Op-Mode field — Specifies the direction and size of the operation:
- 100 — transfer word from memory to register.
- 101 — transfer long from memory to register.
- 110 — transfer word from register to memory.
- 111 — transfer long from register to memory.

Address Register field — Specifies the address register which is used in the address register indirect plus displacement addressing mode.

Displacement field — Specifies the displacement which is used in calculating the operand address.

MOVEQ — Move Quick — MOVEQ

Operation: Immediate Data → Destination
MOVEQ #<data> TO Dn

Assembler Syntax: MOVEQ #<data>,Dn

Attributes: Size = (Long)

Description: Move immediate data to a data register. The data is contained in an 8-bit field within the operation word. The data is sign-extended to a long operand, and all 32 bits are transferred to the data register.

Condition Codes:

X	N	Z	V	C
—	*	*	0	0

N — Set if the result is negative. Cleared otherwise.
Z — Set if the result is zero. Cleared otherwise.
V — Always cleared.
C — Always cleared.
X — Not affected.

Instruction Format:

15	14	13	12	11	10	9	8	7	6	5	4	3	2	1	0
0	1	1	1	Register			0	Data							

Instruction Fields:

Register field — Specifies the data register to be loaded.
Data field — 8 bits of data which are sign extended to a long operand.

MULS Signed Multiply MULS

Operation: (Destination) * (Source) → Destination
MULS Dn By <ea>

Assembler Syntax: MULS <ea>,Dn

Attributes: Size = (Word)

Description: Multiply two signed 16-bit operands yielding a 32-bit signed result. The operation is performed using signed arithmetic. A register operand is taken from the low order word, the upper word is unused. All 32 bits of the product are saved in the destination data register.

Condition Codes:

X	N	Z	V	C
—	*	*	0	0

N — Set if the result is negative. Cleared otherwise.
Z — Set if the result is zero. Cleared otherwise.
V — Always cleared.
C — Always cleared.
X — Not affected.

Instruction Format:

15	14	13	12	11	10	9	8	7	6	5	4	3	2	1	0
1	1	0	0	Register			1	1	1	Effective Address					

Instruction Fields:

Register field — Specifies one of the data registers. This field always specifies the destination.

Effective Address field — Specifies the source operand. Only data addressing modes are allowed.

MULU Unsigned Multiply MULU

Operation: (Destination) * (Source) → Destination
MULU Dn BY <ea>

Assembler Syntax: MULU <ea>,Dn

Attributes: Size = (Word)

Description: Multiply two unsigned 16-bit operands yielding a 32-bit unsigned result. The operation is performed using unsigned arithmetic. A register operand is taken from low order word; the upper word is unused. All 32 bits of the product are saved in the destination data register.

Condition Codes:

X	N	Z	V	C
—	*	*	0	0

N — Set if the most significant bit of the result is set. Cleared otherwise.
Z — Set if the result is zero. Cleared otherwise.
V — Always cleared.
C — Always cleared.
X — Not affected.

Instruction Format:

15	14	13	12	11	10	9	8	7	6	5	4	3	2	1	0
1	1	0	0	Register			0	1	1	Effective Address					

Instruction Fields:

Register field — Specifies one of the data registers. This field always specifies the destination.

Effective Address field — Specifies the source operand. Only data addressing modes are allowed.

NBCD — Negate Decimal with Extend — NBCD

Operation: $0 - (\text{Destination})_{10} - X \rightarrow \text{Destination}$
NBCD <ea>

Assembler Syntax: NBCD <ea>

Attributes: Size = (Byte)

Description: The operand addressed as the destination and the extend bit are subtracted from zero. The operation is performed using decimal arithmetic. The result is saved in the destination location. This instruction produces the ten's complement of the destination if the extend bit is clear, the nine's complement if the extend bit is set. This is a byte operation only.

Condition Codes:

X	N	Z	V	C
*	U	*	U	*

N — Undefined.
Z — Cleared if the result is non-zero. Unchanged otherwise.
V — Undefined.
C — Set if a borrow (decimal) was generated. Cleared otherwise.
X — Set the same as the carry bit.

Instruction Format:

15	14	13	12	11	10	9	8	7	6	5	4	3	2	1	0
0	1	0	0	1	0	0	0	0	0	Effective Address					

Instruction Fields:

Effective Address field — Specifies the destination operand. Only data alterable addressing modes are allowed.

NEG Negate NEG

Operation: 0 - (Destination) → Destination
NEG <ea>

Assembler Syntax: NEG <ea>

Attributes: Size = (Byte, Word, Long)

Description: The operand addressed as the destination is subtracted from zero. The result is stored in the destination location. The size of the operation may be specified to be byte, word, or long.

Condition Codes:

X	N	Z	V	C
*	*	*	*	*

N — Set if the result is negative. Cleared otherwise.
Z — Set if the result is zero. Cleared otherwise.
V — Set if an overflow is generated. Cleared otherwise.
C — Set if a borrow is generated. Cleared otherwise.
X — Set the same as the carry bit.

Instruction Format:

15	14	13	12	11	10	9	8	7	6	5	4	3	2	1	0
0	1	0	0	0	1	0	0	Size		Effective Address					

Instruction Fields:

Size field — Specifies the size of the operation:
- 00 — byte operation.
- 01 — word operation.
- 10 — long operation.

Effective Address field — Specifies the destination operand. Only data alterable addressing modes are allowed.

NEGX Negate with Extend NEGX

Operation: 0 - (Destination) - X → Destination
NEGX <ea>

Assembler Syntax: NEGX <ea>

Attributes: Size = (Byte, Word, Long)

Description: The operand addressed as the destination and the extend bit are subtracted from zero. The result is stored in the destination location. The size of the operation may be specified to be byte, word, or long.

Condition Codes:

X	N	Z	V	C
*	*	*	*	*

N — Set if the result is negative. Cleared otherwise.
Z — Cleared if the result is non-zero. Unchanged otherwise.
V — Set if an overflow is generated. Cleared otherwise.
C — Set if a borrow is generated. Cleared otherwise.
X — Set the same as the carry bit.

Instruction Format:

15	14	13	12	11	10	9	8	7	6	5	4	3	2	1	0
0	1	0	0	0	0	0	0	Size		Effective Address					

Instruction Fields:

Size field — Specifies the size of the operation:
- 00 — byte operation.
- 01 — word operation.
- 10 — long operation.

Effective Address field — Specifies the destination operand. Only data alterable addressing modes are allowed.

NOP — No Operation — NOP

Operation:

Assembler Syntax: NOP

Attributes: Unsized

Description: No operation occurs. The processor state, other than the program counter, is unaffected. Execution continues with the instruction following the NOP instruction.

Condition Codes:

X	N	Z	V	C
—	—	—	—	—

N — Not affected.
Z — Not affected.
V — Not affected.
C — Not affected.
X — Not affected.

Instruction Format:

15	14	13	12	11	10	9	8	7	6	5	4	3	2	1	0
0	1	0	0	1	1	1	0	0	1	1	1	0	0	0	1

NOT Logical Complement NOT

Operation: ~(Destination) → Destination
NOT <ea>

Assembler Syntax: NOT <ea>

Attributes: Size = (Byte, Word, Long)

Description: The one's complement of the destination operand is taken and the result stored in the destination location. The size of the operation may be specified to be byte, word, or long.

Condition Codes:

X	N	Z	V	C
—	*	*	0	0

N — Set if the result is negative. Cleared otherwise.
Z — Set if the result is zero. Cleared otherwise.
V — Always cleared.
C — Always cleared.
X — Not affected.

Instruction Format:

15	14	13	12	11	10	9	8	7	6	5	4	3	2	1	0
0	1	0	0	0	1	1	0	Size		Effective Address					

Instruction Fields:

Size field — Specifies the size of the operation:
- 00 — byte operation.
- 01 — word operation.
- 10 — long operation.

Effective Address field — Specifies the destination operand. Only data alterable addressing modes are allowed.

OR Inclusive OR Logical OR

Operation: (Destination) v (Source) → Destination
OR <ea> TO Dn
OR Dn TO <ea>

Assembler Syntax: OR <ea>,Dn
OR Dn,<ea>

Attributes: Size = (Byte, Word, Long)

Description: Inclusive OR the source operand to the destination operand, and store the result in the destination location. The size of the operation may be specified to be byte, word or long. The contents of an addresss register may not be used as an operand.

Condition Codes:

X	N	Z	V	C
—	*	*	0	0

N — Set if the most significant bit of the result is set. Cleared otherwise.
Z — Set if the result is zero. Cleared otherwise.
V — Always cleared.
C — Always cleared.
X — Not affected.

Instruction Format:

15	14	13	12	11 10 9	8 7 6	5 4 3 2 1 0
1	0	0	0	Register	Op-Mode	Effective Address

Instruction Fields:

Register field — Specifies any of the eight data registers.

Op-Mode field —

Byte	Word	Long	Operation
000	001	010	(<Dn>) v (<ea>) → <Dn>
100	101	110	(<ea>) v (<Dn>) → <ea>

Effective Address field —

If the location specified is a source operand then only data addressing modes are allowed.

If the location specified is a destination operand then only alterable memory addressing modes are allowed.

ORI — Inclusive OR Immediate — ORI

Operation: (Destination) v Immediate Data → Destination
OR #<data> TO <ea>

Assembler Syntax: ORI #<data>,<ea>

Attributes: Size = (Byte, Word, Long)

Description: Inclusive OR the immediate data to the destination operand, and store the result in the destination location. The size of the operation may be specified to be byte, word or long. The size of the immediate data matches the operation size. Access to the status register is available in two modes:

1. If the operation size is byte, the operation affects only the low order byte of the status register, which contains the condition codes.
2. If the operation size is word, the operation is performed on the whole status register. This is a privileged operation.

Condition Codes:

X	N	Z	V	C
—	*	*	0	0

N — Set if the most significant bit of the result is set. Cleared otherwise.
Z — Set if the result is zero. Cleared otherwise.
V — Always cleared.
C — Always cleared.
X — Not affected.

When accessing the status register, the condition codes are affected according to the operation.

Instruction Format:

15	14	13	12	11	10	9	8	7	6	5	4	3	2	1	0
0	0	0	0	0	0	0	0	Size		Effective Address					
Word Data (16 bits)								Byte Data (8 bits)							
Long Data (32 bits, including previous word)															

Instruction Fields:

Size field — Specifies the size of the operation:
- 00 — byte operation.
- 01 — word operation.
- 10 — long operation.

Effective Address field — Specifies the destination operand. Only data alterable or the status register addressing modes are allowed.

Immediate field — (Data immediately following the instruction):
- If size = 00, then the data is the low order byte of the immediate word.
- If size = 01, then the data is the entire immediate word
- If size = 10, then the data is the next two immediate words.

PEA — Push Effective Address — PEA

Operation: Destination →SP@-
PEA <ea>

Assembler Syntax: PEA <ea>

Attributes: Size = (Long)

Description: The effective address is computed and pushed onto the stack. A long word address is pushed onto the stack.

Condition Codes:

X	N	Z	V	C
—	—	—	—	—

N — Not affected.
Z — Not affected.
V — Not affected.
C — Not affected.
X — Not affected.

Instruction Format:

15	14	13	12	11	10	9	8	7	6	5	4	3	2	1	0
0	1	0	0	1	0	0	0	0	1	Effective Address					

Instruction Fields:

Effective Address field — Specifies the address to be pushed onto the stack. Only control addressing modes are allowed.

RESET Reset External Devices RESET

Operation:

Assembler Syntax: RESET

Attributes: Unsized

Description: The reset line is asserted causing all external devices to be reset. The processor state, other than the program counter, is unaffected and execution continues with the next instruction.

Note: This is a privileged instruction.

Condition Codes:

X	N	Z	V	C
—	—	—	—	—

N — Not affected.
Z — Not affected.
V — Not affected.
C — Not affected.
X — Not affected.

Instruction Format:

15	14	13	12	11	10	9	8	7	6	5	4	3	2	1	0
0	1	0	0	1	1	1	0	0	1	1	1	0	0	0	0

ROL ROR — Rotate (without Extend) — ROL ROR

Operation: (Destination) Rotated by <count> → Destination
ROd Dy BY Dx
ROd Dy #<data>
ROd <ea>

Assembler Syntax:
ROd Dx, Dy
ROd #<data>,Dy
ROd <ea>

Attributes: Size = (Byte, Word, Long)

Description: Rotate the bits of the operand in the direction specified. The extend bit is not included in the rotation. The shift count for the rotation of a register may be specified in two different ways:

1. Immediate — the shift count is specified in the instruction (shift range, 1-8).
2. Register — the shift count is contained in a data register specified in the instruction.

The size of the operation may be specified to be byte, word or long. The content of memory may be rotated one bit only where the operand size is restricted to a word.

For ROL, the operand is rotated left; the number of positions shifted is the shift count. Bits shifted out of the high order bit go both to the carry bit and back into the low order bit. The extend bit is not modified or used.

ROL:

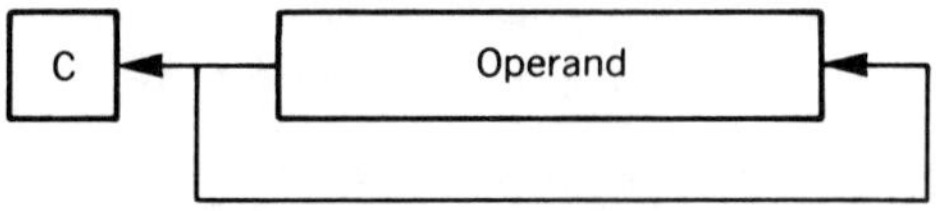

For ROR, the operand is rotated right; the number of positions shifted is the shift count. Bits shifted out of the low order bit go both to the carry bit and back into the high order bit. The extend bit is not modified or used.

ROR:

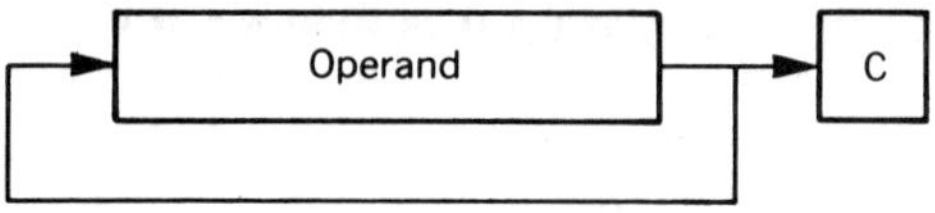

Condition Codes:

X	N	Z	V	C
—	*	*	0	*

N — Set if the most significant bit of the result is set. Cleared otherwise.
Z — Set if the result is zero. Cleared otherwise.
V — Always cleared.
C — Set according to the last bit shifted out of the operand. Cleared for a shift count of zero.
X — Not affected.

ROL ROR — Rotate (without Extend) — ROL ROR

Instruction Format (Register Rotate):

15	14	13	12	11	10	9	8	7	6	5	4	3	2	1	0
1	1	1	0	Count/ Register			dr	Size		i/r	1	1	Register		

Instruction Fields (Register Rotate):

Count/Register field —

If i/r = 0, the rotate count is specified in this field. The values 0, 1-7 represent a range of 8, 1 to 7 respectively.

If i/r = 1, the rotate count (modulo 64) is contained in the data register specified in this field.

dr field — Specifies the direction of the rotate:

0 — rotate right.

1 — rotate left.

Size field — Specifies the size of the operation:

00 — byte operation.

01 — word operation.

10 — long operation.

i/r field —

If i/r = 0, specifies immediate rotate count.

If i/r = 1, specifies register rotate count.

Register field — Specifies a data register whose content is to be rotated.

Instruction Format (Memory Rotate):

15	14	13	12	11	10	9	8	7	6	5	4	3	2	1	0
1	1	1	0	0	1	1	dr	1	1	Effective Address					

Instruction Fields (Memory Rotate):

dr field — Specifies the direction of the rotate:

0 — rotate right.

1 — rotate left.

Effective Address field — Specifies the operand to be rotated. Only memory alterable addressing modes are allowed.

ROXL ROXR — Rotate with Extend — ROXL ROXR

Operation: (Destination) Rotated by <count> → Destination
ROXd Dy BY Dx
ROXd Dy BY #<data>
ROXd <ea>

Assembler Syntax: ROXd Dx,Dy
ROXd #<data>,Dy
ROXd <ea>

Attributes: Size = (Byte, Word, Long)

Description: Rotate the bits of the destination operand in the direction specified. The extend bit is included in the rotation. The shift count for the rotation of a register may be specified in two different ways:

1. Immediate — the shift count is specified in the instruction (shift range, 1-8).
2. Register — the shift count is contained in a data register specified in the instruction.

The size of the operation may be specified to be byte, word or long. The content of memory may be rotated one bit only where the operand size is restricted to a word.

For ROXL, the operand is rotated left; the number of positions shifted is the shift count. Bits shifted out of the high order bit go to both the carry and extend bits; the previous value of the extend bit is shifted into the low order bit.

ROXL:

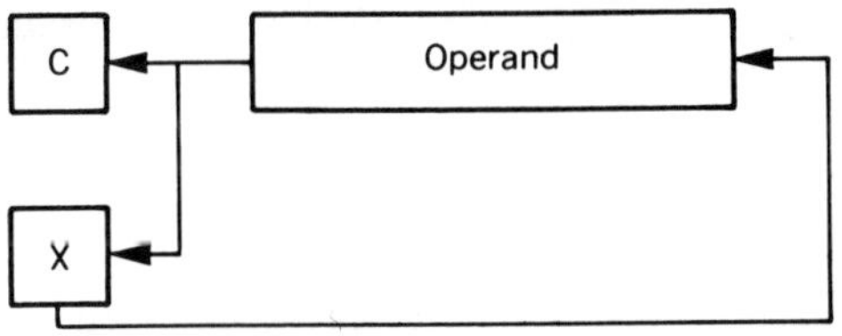

For ROXR, the operand is rotated right; the number of positions shifted is the shift count. Bits shifted out of the low order bit go to both the carry and extend bits; the previous value of the extend bit is shifted into the high order bit.

ROXR:

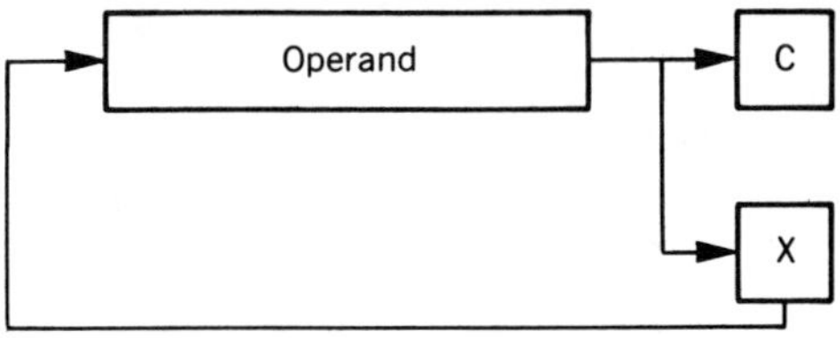

ROXL ROXR — Rotate with Extend — ROXL ROXR

Condition Codes:

X	N	Z	V	C
*	*	*	0	*

N — Set if the most significant bit of the result is set. Cleared otherwise.
Z — Set if the result is zero. Cleared otherwise.
V — Always cleared.
C — Set according to the last bit shifted out of the operand. Set to the value of the extend bit for a shift count of zero.
X — Set according to the last bit shifted out of the operand. Unaffected for a shift count of zero.

Instruction Format (Register Rotate):

15	14	13	12	11	10	9	8	7	6	5	4	3	2	1	0
1	1	1	0	Count/ Register			dr	Size		i/r	1	0	Register		

Instruction Fields (Register Rotate):

Count/Register field:
If i/r = 0, the rotate count is specified in this field. The values 0, 1-7 represent range of 8, 1 to 7 respectively.
If i/r = 1, the rotate count (modulo 64) is contained in the data register specified in this field.
dr field — Specifies the direction of the rotate:
0 — rotate right.
1 — rotate left.
Size field — Specifies the size of the operation:
00 — byte operation.
01 — word operation.
10 — long operation.
i/r field —
If i/r = 0, specifies immediate rotate count.
If i/r = 1, specifies register rotate count.
Register field — Specifies a data register whose content is to be rotated.

Instruction Format (Memory Rotate):

15	14	13	12	11	10	9	8	7	6	5	4	3	2	1	0
1	1	1	0	0	1	0	dr	1	1	Effective Address					

Instruction Fields (Memory Rotate):

dr field — Specifies the direction of the rotate:
0 — rotate right.
1 — rotate left.
Effective Address field — Specifies the operand to be rotated. Only memory alterable addressing modes are allowed.

RTE — Return from Exception — RTE

Operation: SP@+ → SR; SP@+ → PC
RTE

Assembler Syntax: RTE

Attributes: Unsized

Description: The status register and program counter are pulled from the system stack. The previous status register and program counter are lost. All bits in the status register are affected.
Note: This is a privileged instruction.

Condition Codes:

X	N	Z	V	C
*	*	*	*	*

N — Set according to the content of the word on the stack.
Z — Set according to the content of the word on the stack.
V — Set according to the content of the word on the stack.
C — Set according to the content of the word on the stack.
X — Set according to the content of the word on the stack.

Instruction Format:

15	14	13	12	11	10	9	8	7	6	5	4	3	2	1	0
0	1	0	0	1	1	1	0	0	1	1	1	0	0	1	1

RTR Return and Restore Condition Codes RTR

Operation: SP@+ → CC; SP@+ → PC
RTR

Assembler Syntax: RTR

Attributes: Unsized

Description: The condition codes and program counter are pulled from the stack. The previous condition codes and program counter are lost. The supervisor portion of the status register is unaffected.

Condition Codes:

X	N	Z	V	C
*	*	*	*	*

N — Set according to the content of the word on the stack.
Z — Set according to the content of the word on the stack.
V — Set according to the content of the word on the stack.
C — Set according to the content of the word on the stack.
X — Set according to the content of the word on the stack.

Instruction Format:

15	14	13	12	11	10	9	8	7	6	5	4	3	2	1	0
0	1	0	0	1	1	1	0	0	1	1	1	0	1	1	1

RTS Return from Subroutine RTS

Operation: SP@+ → PC
RTS

Assembler Syntax: RTS

Attributes: Unsized

Description: The program counter is pulled from the stack. The previous program counter is lost.

Condition Codes:

X	N	Z	V	C
—	—	—	—	—

N — Not affected.
Z — Not affected.
V — Not affected.
C — Not affected.
X — Not affected.

Instruction Format:

15	14	13	12	11	10	9	8	7	6	5	4	3	2	1	0
0	1	0	0	1	1	1	0	0	1	1	1	0	1	0	1

SBCD — Subtract Decimal with Extend — SBCD

Operation: $(Destination)_{10} - (Source)_{10} - X \rightarrow$ Destination
SBCD Dy FROM Dx
SBCD Ay@- FROM Ax@-

Assembler Syntax:
SBCD Dy,Dx
SBCD -(Ay),-(Ax)

Attributes: Size = (Byte)

Description: Subtract the source operand from the destination operand along with the extend bit, and store the result in the destination location. The subtraction is performed using binary coded decimal arithmetic. The operands may be addressed in two different ways:

1. Data register to data register: The operands are contained in the data registers specified in the instruction.
2. Memory to memory: The operands are addressed with the predecrement addressing mode using the address registers specified in the instruction.

This operation is a byte operation only.

Condition Codes:

X	N	Z	V	C
*	U	*	U	*

N — Undefined
Z — Cleared if the result is non-zero. Unchanged otherwise.
V — Undefined.
C — Set if a borrow (decimal) is generated. Cleared otherwise.
X — Set the same as the carry bit.

Instruction Format:

15	14	13	12	11 10 9	8	7	6	5	4	3	2 1 0
1	0	0	0	Register Rx	1	0	0	0	0	R/M	Register Ry

Instruction Fields:

Register Rx field — Specifies the destination register:
If R/M = 0, specifies a data register.
If R/M = 1, specifies an address register for the predecrement addressing mode.

R/M field — Specifies the operand addressing mode:
0 — The operation is data register to data register.
1 — The operation is memory to memory.

Register Ry field — Specifies the source register:
If R/M = 0, specifies a data register.
If R/M = 1, specifies an address register for the predecrement addressing mode.

Scc — Set According to Condition — Scc

Operation: If cc then 1's → Destination else 0's → Destination
Scc <ea>

Assembler Syntax: Scc <ea>

Attributes: Size = (Byte)

Description: The specified condition code is tested; if the condition is true, the byte specified by the effective address is set to TRUE (all ones), otherwise that byte is set to FALSE (all zeroes). "cc" may specify the following conditions:

CC	— carry clear	LS	— low or same
CS	— carry set	LT	— less
EQ	— equal	MI	— minus
F	— never true	NE	— not equal
GE	— greater or equal	PL	— plus
GT	— greater	T	— always true
HI	— high	VC	— no overflow
LE	— less or equal	VS	— overflow

Condition Codes:

X	N	Z	V	C
—	—	—	—	—

N — Not affected.
Z — Not affected.
V — Not affected.
C — Not affected.
X — Not affected.

Instruction Format:

15	14	13	12	11	10	9	8	7	6	5	4	3	2	1	0
0	1	0	1	Condition				1	1	Effective Address					

Instruction Fields:

Condition field — One of sixteen conditions:

CC	— 0100	LS	— 0011
CS	— 0101	LT	— 1101
EQ	— 0111	MI	— 1011
F	— 0001	NE	— 0110
GE	— 1100	PL	— 1010
GT	— 1110	T	— 0000
HI	— 0010	VC	— 1000
LE	— 1111	VS	— 1001

Effective Address field — Specifies the location in which the true/false byte is to be stored. Only data alterable addressing modes are allowed.

STOP Load Status Register and Stop STOP

Operation: Immediate Data → SR; STOP
STOP #xxx

Assembler Syntax: STOP #xxx

Attributes: Unsized

Description: The immediate operand is moved into the entire status register; the program counter is advanced to point to the next instruction, and the processor stops fetching and executing instructions. Execution of instructions resumes when a trace, interrupt, or reset exception occurs. A trace exception will occur if the trace state is on when the STOP instruction is executed. If an interrupt request arrives whose priority is higher than the current processor priority, an interrupt exception occurs, otherwise the interrupt request has no effect. If the bit of the immediate data corresponding the the S-bit is off, execution of the instruction will cause a privilege violation. External reset will always initiate reset exception processing.
Note: This is a privilege instruction.

Condition Codes:

X	N	Z	V	C
*	*	*	*	*

N — Set according to the immediate operand.
Z — Set according to the immediate operand.
V — Set according to the immediate operand.
C — Set according to the immediate operand.
X — Set according to the immediate operand.

Instruction Format:

15	14	13	12	11	10	9	8	7	6	5	4	3	2	1	0
0	1	0	0	1	1	1	0	0	1	1	1	0	0	1	0
Immediate Data															

Instruction Fields:
Immediate field — Specifies the data to be loaded into the status register.

SUB — Subtract Binary — SUB

Operation: (Destination) – (Source) → Destination
SUB <ea> FROM Dn
SUB Dn FROM <ea>

Assembler Syntax: SUB <ea>,Dn
SUB Dn,<ea>

Attributes: Size = (Byte, Word, Long)

Description: Subtract the source operand from the destination operand and store the result in the destination. The size of the operation may be specified to be byte, word or long. The mode of the instruction indicates which operand is the source and which is the destination as well as the operand size.

Condition Codes:

X	N	Z	V	C
*	*	*	*	*

N — Set if the result is negative. Cleared otherwise.
Z — Set if the result is zero. Cleared otherwise.
V — Set if an overflow is generated. Cleared otherwise.
C — Set if a borrow is generated. Cleared otherwise.
X — Set the same as the carry bit.

Instruction Format:

15	14	13	12	11	10	9	8	7	6	5	4	3	2	1	0
1	0	0	1	Register			Op-Mode			Effective Address					

Instruction Fields:

Register field — Specifies any of the eight data registers.

Op-Mode field —

Byte	Word	Long	Operation
000	001	010	(<Dn>) - (<ea> → <Dn>
100	101	110	(<ea>) - (<Dn>) → <ea>

Effective Address field — Determines addressing mode:

If the location specified is a source operand, then all addressing modes are allowed. If the operation size is byte, then the address register direct addressing mode is not allowed.

If the location specified is a destination operand, then only alterable memory addressing modes are allowed.

SUBA — Subtract Address — SUBA

Operation: (Destination) – (Source) → Destination
SUB <ea> FROM An

Assembler Syntax: SUBA <ea>,An

Attributes: Size = (Word, Long)

Description: Subtract the source operand from the destination address register, and store the result in the address register. The size of the operation may be specified to be word or long.

Condition Codes:

X	N	Z	V	C
—	—	—	—	—

N — Not affected.
Z — Not affected.
V — Not affected.
C — Not affected.
X — Not affected.

Instruction Format:

15	14	13	12	11 10 9	8 7 6	5 4 3 2 1 0
1	0	0	1	Register	Op-Mode	Effective Address

Instruction Fields:

Register field — Specifies any of the eight address registers. This is always the destination.

Op-Mode field — Specifies the size of the operation:

011 — Word operation. The source operand is sign-extended to a long operand and the operation is performed on the address register using all 32 bits.

111 — Long operations.

Effective Address field — Specifies the source operand. All addressing modes are allowed.

SUBI Subtract Immediate SUBI

Operation: (Destination) - Immediate Data → Destination
SUB #<data> FROM <ea>

Assembler Syntax: SUBI #<data>,<ea>

Attributes: Size = (Byte, Word, Long)

Description: Subtract the immediate data from the destination operand, and store the result in the destination location. The size of the operation may be specified to be byte, word or long. The size of the immediate data matches the operation size.

Condition Codes:

X	N	Z	V	C
*	*	*	*	*

N — Set if the result is negative. Cleared otherwise.
Z — Set if the result is zero. Cleared otherwise.
V — Set if an overflow is generated. Cleared otherwise.
C — Set if a borrow is generated. Cleared otherwise.
X — Set the same as the carry bit.

Instruction Format:

<table>
<tr><td>15</td><td>14</td><td>13</td><td>12</td><td>11</td><td>10</td><td>9</td><td>8</td><td>7</td><td>6</td><td>5</td><td>4</td><td>3</td><td>2</td><td>1</td><td>0</td></tr>
<tr><td>0</td><td>0</td><td>0</td><td>0</td><td>0</td><td>1</td><td>0</td><td>0</td><td colspan="2">Size</td><td colspan="6">Effective Address</td></tr>
<tr><td colspan="8">Word Data (16 bits)</td><td colspan="8">Byte Data (8 bits)</td></tr>
<tr><td colspan="16">Long Data (32 bits, including previous word)</td></tr>
</table>

Instruction Fields:

Size field — Specifies the size of the operation.
- 00 — byte operation.
- 01 — word operation.
- 10 — long operation.

Effective Address field — Specifies the destination operand. Only data alterable addressing modes are allowed.

Immediate field — (Data immediately following the instruction)
- If size = 00, then the data is the low order byte of the immediate word.
- If size = 01, then the data is the entire immediate word.
- If size = 10, then the data is the next two immediate words.

SUBQ Subtract Quick SUBQ

Operation: (Destination) - Immediate Data → Destination
SUBQ #<data> FROM <ea>

Assembler Syntax: SUBQ #<data>,<ea>

Attributes: Size = (Byte, Word, Long)

Description: Subtract the immediate data from the destination operand. The data range is from 1-8. The size of the operation may be specified to be byte, word, or long. Word and long operations are also allowed on the address registers.

Condition Codes:

X	N	Z	V	C
*	*	*	*	*

N — Set if the result is negative. Cleared otherwise.
Z — Set if the result is zero. Cleared otherwise.
V — Set if an overflow is generated. Cleared otherwise.
C — Set if a borrow is generated. Cleared otherwise.
X — Set the same as the carry bit.

The condition codes are not affected if a subtraction from an address register is made.

Instruction Format:

15	14	13	12	11	10	9	8	7	6	5	4	3	2	1	0
0	1	0	1	Data			1	Size		Effective Address					

Instruction Fields:

Data field — Three bits of immediate data, 0, 1-7 representing a range of 8, 1 to 7 respectively.

Size field — Specifies the size of the operation:
- 00 — byte operation.
- 01 — word operation.
- 10 — long operation.

Effective Address field — Specifies the destination location. Only alterable addressing modes are allowed. If the operation size is byte, the address register direct addressing mode is not allowed.

SUBX — Subtract with Extend — SUBX

Operation: (Destination) - (Source) - X → Destination
SUBX Dy FROM Dx
SUBX Ay@- FROM Ax@-

Assembler Syntax: SUBX Dy,Dx
SUBX -(Ay),-(Ax)

Attributes: Size = (Byte, Word, Long)

Description: Subtract the source operand from the destination operand along with the extend bit, and store the result in the destination location. The operands may be addressed in two different ways:

1. Data register to data register: The operands are contained in data registers specified in the instruction.
2. Memory to memory. The operands are contained in memory and addressed with the predecrement addressing mode using the address registers specified in the instruction.

The size of the operation may be specified to be byte, word or long.

Condition Codes:

X	N	Z	V	C
*	*	*	*	*

N — Set if the result is negative. Cleared otherwise.
Z — Cleared if the result is non-zero. Unchanged otherwise.
V — Set if an overflow is generated. Cleared otherwise.
C — Set if a carry is generated. Cleared otherwise.
X — Set the same as the carry bit.

Instruction Format:

15	14	13	12	11	10	9	8	7	6	5	4	3	2	1	0
1	0	0	1	Register Rx			1	Size		0	0	R/M	Register Ry		

Instruction Fields:

Register Rx field — Specifies the destination register:
If R/M = 0, specifies a data register.
If R/M = 1, specifies an address register for the predecrement addressing mode.

Size field — Specifies the size of the operation:
00 — byte operation.
01 — word operation.
10 — long operation.

R/M field — Specifies the operand addressing mode:
0 — The operation is data register to data register.
1 — The operation is memory to memory.

Register Ry field — Specifies the source register:
If R/M = 0, specifies a data register.
If R/M = 1, specifies an address register for the predecrement addressing mode.

SWAP Swap Register Halves SWAP

Operation: Register [31:16]↔Register [15:0]
SWAP Dn

Assembler Syntax: SWAP Dn

Attributes: Size = (Word)

Description: Exchange the 16-bit halves of a data register.

Condition Codes:

X	N	Z	V	C
—	*	*	0	0

N — Set if the most significant bit of the 32-bit result is set. Cleared otherwise.
Z — Set if the 32-bit result is zero. Cleared otherwise.
V — Always cleared.
C — Always cleared.
X — Not affected.

Instruction Format:

15	14	13	12	11	10	9	8	7	6	5	4	3	2	1	0
0	1	0	0	1	0	0	0	0	1	0	0	0	Register		

Instruction Fields:

Register field — Specifies the data register to swap.

TAS — Test and Set an Operand — TAS

Operation: (Destination) Tested → CC; 1 → # 7 OF Destination
TAS <ea>

Assembler Syntax: TAS <ea>

Attributes: Size = (Byte)

Description: Test and set the byte operand addressed by the effective address field. The current value of the operand is tested and N and Z are set accordingly. The high order bit of the operand is set. The operation is indivisible (using a read-modify-write memory cycle) to allow synchronization of several processors.

Condition Codes:

X	N	Z	V	C
—	*	*	0	0

N — Set if the most significant bit of the operand is set. Cleared otherwise.
Z — Set if the operand is zero. Cleared otherwise.
V — Always cleared.
C — Always cleared.
X — Not affected.

Instruction Format:

15	14	13	12	11	10	9	8	7	6	5	4	3	2	1	0
0	1	0	0	1	0	1	0	1	1	Effective Address					

Instruction Fields:

Effective Address field — Specifies the location of the tested operand. Only data alterable addressing modes are allowed.

TRAP — Trap — TRAP

Operation: PC →SSP@-; SR →SSP@-; (Vector) →PC
TRAP #<vector>

Assembler Syntax: TRAP #<vector>

Attributes: Unsized

Description: The processor initiates exception processing. The vector number is generated to reference the TRAP instruction exception vector specified by the low order four bits of the instruction. Sixteen TRAP instruction vectors are available.

Condition Codes:

X	N	Z	V	C
—	—	—	—	—

N — Not affected.
Z — Not affected.
V — Not affected.
C — Not affected.
X — Not affected.

Instruction Format:

15	14	13	12	11	10	9	8	7	6	5	4	3	2	1	0
0	1	0	0	1	1	1	0	0	1	0	0	Vector			

Instruction Fields:

Vector field — Specifies which trap vector contains the new program counter to be loaded.

TRAPV — Trap on Overflow — TRAPV

Operation: If V then TRAP
TRAPV

Assembler Syntax: TRAPV

Attributes: Unsized

Description: If the overflow condition is on, the processor initiates exception processing. The vector number is generated to reference the TRAPV exception vector. If the overflow condition is off, no operation is performed, and execution continues with the next instruction in sequence.

Condition Codes:

X	N	Z	V	C
—	—	—	—	—

N — Not affected.
Z — Not affected.
V — Not affected.
C — Not affected.
X — Not affected.

Instruction Format:

15	14	13	12	11	10	9	8	7	6	5	4	3	2	1	0
0	1	0	0	1	1	1	0	0	1	1	1	0	1	1	0

TST Test an Operand TST

Operation: (Destination) Tested →CC
TST <ea>

Assembler Syntax: TST <ea>

Attributes: Size = (Byte, Word, Long)

Description: Compare the operand with zero. No results are saved, however, the condition codes are set according to results of the test. The size of the operation may be specified to be byte, word or long.

Condition Codes:

X	N	Z	V	C
—	*	*	0	0

N — Set if the operand is negative. Cleared otherwise.
Z — Set if the operand is zero. Cleared otherwise.
V — Always cleared.
C — Always cleared.
X — Not affected.

Instruction Format:

15	14	13	12	11	10	9	8	7	6	5	4	3	2	1	0
0	1	0	0	1	0	1	0	Size		Effective Address					

Instruction Fields:

Size field — Specifies the size of the operation:
- 00 — byte operation.
- 01 — word operation.
- 10 — long operation.

Effective Address field — Specifies the destination operand. Only data alterable addressing modes are allowed.

UNLK Unlink UNLK

Operation: An → SP; SP@+ → An
UNLK An

Assembler Syntax: UNLK An

Attributes: Unsized

Description: The stack pointer is loaded from the specified address register. The address register is then loaded with the long word pulled from the top of the stack.

Condition Codes:

X	N	Z	V	C
—	—	—	—	—

N — Not affected.
Z — Not affected.
V — Not affected.
C — Not affected.
X — Not affected.

Instruction Format:

15	14	13	12	11	10	9	8	7	6	5	4	3	2 1 0
0	1	0	0	1	1	1	0	0	1	0	1	1	Register

Instruction Fields:

Register field — Specifies the address register through which the unlinking is to be done.

PROGRAM TITLE:

PAGE OF		PROGRAMMER:							
PC	MACHINE CODE	LABEL	MNEM	OPERAND	COMMENTS	N	Z	V	C

BIBLIOGRAPHY

DATA SHEETS

Fairchild F6800 Microprocessing Unit, January 1978

Motorola Semiconductors MC6800 Microprocessing Unit

Motorola Semiconductors MC6801 Microcomputer Unit, 1980

Fairchild F6802 Microprocessor with Clock & RAM, April 1980

Motorola Semiconductors MC6802 Microprocessor with Clock & RAM

Fairchild F6810 128 × 8-bit Static Random Access Memory, November 1981

Motorola Semiconductors MC6810 128 × 8-bit Static Random Access Memory

Fairchild F6820/6821 Peripheral Interface Adapter (PIA), November 1981

Motorola Semiconductors MC6820/6821 Peripheral Interface Adapter (PIA)

Fairchild F6840 Programmable Timer (PTM), November 1981

Motorola Semiconductors Programmable Timer (PTM)

Fairchild F6846 ROM-I/O-Timer, November 1981

Motorola Semiconductors MC6846 ROM-I/O-Timer

Fairchild F6850 Asynchronous Communication Interface Adapter (ACIA), November 1981

Motorola Semiconductors MC6850 Asynchronous Communication Interface Adapter (ACIA)

Fairchild F3846/6856 Synchronous Protocol Communication Controller (SPCC), November 1981

Fairchild F3870 Single-chip Microcomputer, May 1980

Mostek MK3870 Single-chip Micro Family

Motorola Semiconductors MC6809 8-bit Microprocessing Unit, 1980

Motorola Semiconductors MC68000 16-bit Microprocessor Unit, 1981

REFERENCE MANUALS

Fairchild F6800 Programming Reference Manual, 1977

Motorola Semiconductors 6800 Programming Reference Manual

Motorola Semiconductors MC6809—MC6809 Microprocessor Programming Manual Original Issue dated March 1, 1981—#M6809PM(AD)

Motorola Semiconductors MC68000—16-bit Microprocessor USER's Manual Second Edition dated January, 1980—#MC68000UM(AD2)

Motorola Semiconductors MEK6800DZ Evaluation Kit II Manual Second Edition dated 1977

Fairchild F6800 Training Manual

Motorola Semiconductors MC6800 Training Manual

Portions of actual documents were reproduced herein by permission of Fairchild Camera & Instrument Corp., Motorola, Inc. and Mostek Inc.

Index